The Letters and Journals of Robert Baillie ...
M.DC.XXXVII.-M.DC.LXII Volume 3

You are holding a reproduction of an original work that is in the public domain in the United States of America, and possibly other countries.You may freely copy and distribute this work as no entity (individual or corporate) has a copyright on the body of the work.This book may contain prior copyright references, and library stamps (as most of these works were scanned from library copies).These have been scanned and retained as part of the historical artifact.

This book may have occasional imperfections such as missing or blurred pages, poor pictures, errant marks, etc. that were either part of the original artifact, or were introduced by the scanning process. We believe this work is culturally important, and despite the imperfections, have elected to bring it back into print as part of our continuing commitment to the preservation of printed works worldwide. We appreciate your understanding of the imperfections in the preservation process, and hope you enjoy this valuable book.

THE
LETTERS AND JOURNALS
OF
ROBERT BAILLIE, A. M.
PRINCIPAL OF THE UNIVERSITY OF GLASGOW.

M.DC.XXXVII.—M.DC.LXII.

IN THREE VOLUMES.

VOLUME THIRD.

EDINBURGH: M.DCCC.XLII.

EDINBURGH ALEX. LAURIE & CO PRINTERS TO HER MAJESTY

TABLE OF CONTENTS.

LETTERS AND JOURNALS OF MR. ROBERT BAILLIE.

1647

	Page
Letter to Mr. William Spang, 26th January,	1
—— to the fame, (Poftfcript), 2d June,	5
—— to Sir Archibald Johnftone of Wariſton, 2d June,	6
—— from Theodore Haak, Eſq. (without date,)	7
—— to Mr. William Spang, 13th July,	9
His Speech in the Generall Aſſembly, Edinburgh, 6th Auguſt,	10
Letter to a Friend in Kilwinning, 20th Auguſt,	14
—— to Mr. William Spang, 1ſt September,	16
—— to his Noble and good Friend Poloni Alman, (the Earl of Lauderdaill), 13th October,	22
—— to Mr. William Spang, 13th October,	23

1648

Letter to a Worſhipfull Knight [Sir Daniel Carmichael,] 8th March,	24
—— to Mr. William Spang, 27th March,	31
—— to Mr Zachary Boyd, (without date,)	42
—— to Mr. Matthew Briſbane, (without date,)	43
—— to Mr. William Spang, 26th June,	43
—— to the fame, 23d Auguſt,	50

TABLE OF CONTENTS.

1649.

	Page
Letter to Mr. William Spang, 7th February,	66
——— from the fame, 7th March,	67
——— from the fame, 9-19th March,	71
——— from the fame, 19th March,	80
Baillie's Speech to King Charles the Second, at the Hague, 27th March,	84
The Commiffioners Letter to the Commiffion of the Affembly, 3d April,	86
Letter to Mr. Robert Douglas, 3d April,	88
——— to the fame, 17th April,	89
——— to Mr. William Spang, 14th September,	90
——— to Captain Titus, 7th September,	102
——— to George Wynrame, Lord Libberton, 7th September,	102
——— to Gisbertus Voetius, Idibus Septembris,	103

1650.

Letter from Mr Robert Blair, 29th July,	105
——— to [Mr. Chriftopher Love?] 20th December,	105
——— to Mr. David Dickfon, 18th November,	108
——— to Mr. Robert Douglas, 18th November,	109
——— to Scoutmaifter Buchan, (without date,)	110

1651.

Letter to Mr. David Dickfon and Mr. William Spang, 2d January,	110
The Commiffion's confolatory Letter to Edinburgh, 7th January,	130
Letter to Mr. David Dickfon, 8th March,	131
——— to Mr. Robert Douglas, 10th March,	134
——— to the King and the Eftates of Parliament, 10th March,	135
——— to the Earl of Balcarras, (without date),	136
——— to Mr. John Smith, &c 21ft March,	137
——— to the Earl of Lauderdaill, 11th March,	138
——— to Mr. James Blair, 11th March,	140
——— to Mr Robert Douglas, (without date,)	141
——— to the fame, 4th April,	142
——— to Mr. Andrew Ker, 4th April,	146

TABLE OF CONTENTS.

	Page
Letter to John Reid (the Earl of Lauderdaill), 4th April,	147
——— from Mr. James Durhame to George Lockhart, Rector of the Univerſity of Glaſgow, 31ſt March,	148
——— to Mr James Durhame, (without date,)	149
——— to Mr. Andrew Ker, (without date,)	153
——— to the Earl of Balcarras, (without date,)	154
——— to Mr. Robert Douglas, (without date,)	155
His Supplication to George Lockhart, Rector of the Univerſity,	156
His Proteſtation againſt Mr James Durhame's intruſion, 7th April,	158
Letter to the Earl of Balcarras, 17th April,	160
Information of the Cauſes of the Tumult at Glaſgow, &c. 30th April,	161
Information to Mr. George Young, (in May,)	163
Letter to Mr. Robert Douglas, 22d April,	165
——— to John or William Reid, (the Earls of Lauderdaill and Balcarras,) 3d May,	166
——— to Mr Andrew Ker, 2d May,	167
——— to Mr Robert Douglas, 6th May,	169
——— to the Earl of Lauderdaill, 6th May,	170
——— to the ſame, 12th May,	172

1652

Letter to Mr. David Dickſon, 24th February,	173
——— from Mr. Robert Blair, 23d March,	174
——— to the ſame, 1ſt April,	175
——— to Mr. James Wood, 1ſt April,	176
——— to the ſame, 1ſt April,	177
——— to Mr. Robert Douglas and Mr. John Smith, 8th April,	179
——— to Mr. James Wood, 8th April,	181
——— to Mr. Robert Ker, 8th April,	182
——— to the ſame, 25th April,	182
Mr. James Durhame's Overtures for Union, (without date,)	185
Letter to Mr. James Wood, 4th June,	186
——— to Mr. Robert Ker, 4th June,	188
——— to Mr. David Dickſon, 4th June,	189

TABLE OF CONTENTS.

	Page
Letter to Mr. Robert Ker, 7th June,	189
——— to Mr. James Durhame, 8th July,	190
——— to Mr. David Dickfon, 8th July,	193
Reafons of Proteft at the Prefbytery of Glafgow, 7th July,	194
Letter to Mr James Durhame, 11th July,	195
——— from Baillie, Young, and Blair, to the fame, 11th July,	195
——— to Mr. Rous, 20th Auguft,	197
——— to Mr. James Wood, 10th December,	199

1653.

Letter to Correfpondents with the Prefbytery of Glafgow, 3d January,	202
——— to Mr. Patrick Gillefpie, January,	203
——— to Mr. James Durhame, (without date,)	203
——— to Mr. Calamy and others at London, 21ft January,	204
——— from the Prefbytery of Glafgow to the Englifh Commiffioners for Vifiting the Univerfities, 8th February,	205
——— from the Englifh Commiffioners, 1ft February,	206
——— to the fame, 10th February,	207
——— to the fame, 10th February,	208
——— from the fame, 10th February,	209
——— to Mr. David Dickfon, 10th February,	209
——— to Mr. Robert Ker, 10th February,	211
——— to Mr James Wood, 10th February,	212
——— to the fame, 14th February,	212
Inftructions to Mr George Young, 8th April,	214
Letter to Mr Robert Douglas, 8th April,	218
——— to Mr. David Dickfon, 28th April,	219
——— to Mr. Mungo Law, (without date,)	220
——— to Mr. Rodgers's Mother in-law, 2d May,	221
——— to Mr. David Dickfon, 21ft May,	222
——— to Mr. Richard Robertfon, 26th July,	223
——— from the fame, (without date,)	223
——— to Mr. Edmund Calamy, 27th July,	224
——— to Mr. Samuel Clarke, 27th July,	226

	Page
Letter to Dr. Lazarus Seaman, 8th October,	227
——— from Mr. John Vauch, 11th November,	228
——— from the Earl of Lauderdaill, 17th December,	230
Letter to Mr. William Taylor, 19th December,	231
The Materials for a Prefbyteriall Warning,	232

1654.

Letter to the Earl of Lauderdaill, 10th February,	234
——— to Mr. Jeremiah Whittaker, 10th February,	235
——— to Mr. James Ferguffon, 8th March,	236
——— to Mr. William Spang, 19th July,	237
——— to the fame, (Poftfcript), 21ft July,	253
——— to Mr. John Young, (without date,)	259
——— from the Earl of Lauderdaill, 14th March,	265
——— to Mr Thomas Fuller, 22d Auguft,	265
——— to Gifbertus Voetius, Idibus Septembris,	267

1655.

Letter from Gifbertus Voetius, Eid. Aprilis,	270
——— to Mr. James Hamilton, 8th October,	275
——— to Mr. William Spang, (without date),	277
——— to the fame, (Poftfcript), 1ft–31ft December,	294
——— to Mr. Simeon Afhe, 31ft December,	302

1656.

Letter from Mr. Simeon Afhe, (without date),	306
——— from Mr. Edmund Calamy, (without date,)	307
——— to Mr. James Hamilton, 21ft January,	308
——— to Mr. James Cranford, 27th Auguft,	309
——— to Mr. William Spang, 1ft September,	311
——— to Mr. Francis Rous, 6th September,	325
——— to Mr. James Wood, 8th December,	326

TABLE OF CONTENTS.

1657.

	Page
Letter to Mr Afhe or Mr Calamy, 12th January,	328
———— to Mr. Francis Rous, 16th January,	332
———— to Mr. Robert Douglas, 18th January,	334
———— to Mr James Sharp, 18th January,	334
———— from Mr. Patrick Colvill, 5th March,	335
———— to Mr. James Sharp, 9th March,	336
———— from the fame, 21ft March,	338
———— to Mr. James Hamilton, 30th March,	340
———— from Mr James Sharp, 28th July,	341
———— to the fame, (without date),	343
———— to Mr. Francis Rous, 23d September,	344
———— from the fame, 10th October,	345
———— from Mr James Sharp, 13th October,	346
———— from the fame, 21ft November,	349

1658.

Letter from Mr. James Sharp, 25th February,	349
———— to the fame, 3d May,	350
———— to Sir George Maxwell, 3d May,	351
———— to Mr. John Young, 3d May,	351
———— to Mr. William Spang, (without date),	352
———— to Mr. Robert Douglas, 31ft July,	375
———— to Mr William Spang, 11th November,	382
———— to Mr. Simeon Afhe, 29th November,	391

1659.

Letter to Sir James Dundas, 11th April,	391
———— to Mr. Robert Douglas, 11th April,	392
———— to the fame, 18th May,	395
———— to Mr. James Sharp, 18th May,	396

1660.

Letter to Mr. James Sharp, 10th March,	398
———— to the fame, 16th April,	400

TABLE OF CONTENTS

	Page
Letter to Mr William Douglas, 23d May,	402
―――― to Mr. David Dickfon, 27th May,	404
―――― to the Earl of Lauderdaill, 16th June,	405
―――― to the fame, 2d July,	407
―――― to Mr. George Hutchefon, 13th Auguft,	408
―――― from Mr. James Sharp, 5th September,	409
―――― from the Earl of Lauderdaill, 22d Auguft,	411
―――― to the fame, 12th October,	412
―――― to Mr. George Hutchefon, 5th November,	414
―――― to Mr. David Dickfon, 3d December,	415
―――― from Mr. James Sharp, 13th December,	415
―――― to the fame, 17th December,	417

1661.

Letter to Mr. James Sharp, 1ft January,	418
―――― from the fame, (without date,)	420
―――― from the Earl of Lauderdaill, 24th January,	421
Warrant of the King's Prefentation to Mr Robert Baillie, as Principal of the Univerfity of Glafgow, 23d January,	422
Letter to Mr. William Spang, 31ft January,	423
―――― to Gifbertus Voetius, 1ft February,	451
―――― to the Earl of Glencairn, 4th February,	452
―――― to Mr. James Sharp, February,	453
Supplication of the Univerfity of Glafgow to the Eftates of Parliament,	454
Addrefs by Principal Baillie to the Lord High Commiffioner,	455
Letter to Mr James Robertfon of Bedlay, March,	455
―――― to the Earl of Lauderdaill, 10th April,	457
―――― to Mr. James Sharp, 13th April,	458
―――― to the Earl of Lauderdaill, 18th April,	458
―――― from Mr. James Sharp, end of April,	460
―――― to Mr George Hutchefon, 24th June,	461
―――― to the Prefbytery of Kirkcudbright, 15th July,	462
―――― to Mr. William Spang, (without date),	462
―――― to Mr. James Sharp, 29th Auguft,	473

TABLE OF CONTENTS.

	Page
Letter to the Earl of Glencairn, Lord Chancellor, (without date),	474
———— to the Earl of Lauderdaill, (without date),	476
———— to the fame, 9th September,	478
———— to the fame, 1ft October,	479
———— to Mr. James Sharp, 1ft October,	481
———— to the Duchefs of Hamilton, 1ft October,	482

1662.

Letter to Mr. William Spang, 12th May, ... 483

APPENDIX.

No I.—LIST OF PAPERS INSERTED IN VOLUME THIRD OF THE MANUSCRIPT COLLECTION OF BAILLIE'S LETTERS AND JOURNALS, 1648 TO 1661. . . . . . (485) 441

No. II.—ORIGINAL LETTERS AND PAPERS, CHIEFLY RELATING TO ECCLESIASTICAL AFFAIRS IN SCOTLAND, 1647 TO 1662

(Continued from Vol II. page 516.)

1647.

72 Mr George Gillefpie's Speech in the General Affembly, (489) 449

1648.

73. Atteftation in favour of Lieutenant-General Baillie, (495) 455

1649.

74. Letter from the Commiffioners of the General Affembly to King Charles the Second, 7th February, . . (498) 458
75. Inftructions for the Commiffioners of the Church fent to the King's Majeftie, in March, ... (500) 460

TABLE OF CONTENTS.

	Page
76. Letter from the Commiffion of the General Affembly to Dr. Frederick Spanheim, 27th February, . (501)	461
77. Letter from the fame, to Dr Andrew Rivet, fame date, (502)	462
78 Dr A Rivet's Letter to Baillie, 26th May, . . (503)	463
79. Memorandum from a Friend to reprefent to the Queen, (504)	464
80. A Note intended for Myn Here Willems, . .	507
81. The Commiffion from the Eftates of Parliament, .	507
82. Inftructions for the Commiffioners of Parliament fent to the King at the Hague, ...	508
83 The Report of the Commiffioners of the Church, of their proceedings with his Majefty at the Hague, made in the General Affembly, 10th July, . . .	510
84 Letters from George Wynrame of Libberton,	
1. To Mr. Robert Douglas, 31ft October 1649, .	522
2. To the fame, 18th November, . . .	522
3 To the fame, 30th April 1650, . .	523

1650.

85. Letter from King Charles the Second to Mr. Robert Douglas, 15th February 1649-[50.] . .	524
86. Notices regarding the Metrical Verfions of the Pfalms received by the Church of Scotland, . . .	525

1651.

87. Letters from Mr. Robert Blair, Minifter of St. Andrews,	
1. To Mr. Robert Douglas, ...	556
2 To the fame, 16th March, . . .	557
3. To the fame, 27th April, .	558
4. To the fame, end of July, .	558
5. To Mr. David Dickfon, 20th October, .	559
88. Letter from Mr. James Durham to Mr. Robert Douglas, 14th July,	560

1652.

89. Proteftation againft the Provincial Synod at Glafgow, 8th October.	561

TABLE OF CONTENTS.

		Page
90	Advices and Anſwers, from Douglas and others in the Tower of London, to Baillie's Queſtions, 29th June,	563

1654.

| 91. | Letter from Sir Archibald Johnſtone of Warriſton to Mr. James Guthrie, 29th March, | 566 |

1656.

92	Inſtructions from the Reſolutioners, to Mr. James Sharp, for London, 23d Auguſt,	568
93	Propoſals by the Pioteſters, to be fought from the Lord Protector,	573
94.	Letter from Lord Broghill to Mr. Robert Douglas, 10th Auguſt,	573
95	Articles exhibited againſt Mr Patrick Gilleſpie wherefore he ought not to be Principall of the Colledge of Glaſgow,	573

1657.

| 96. | Letter from Mr. Patrick Gilleſpie to Mr. David Dickson, 2d July, | 578 |

1658

| 97. | Letter from Mr. James Sharp to Mr Robert Baillie, and Baillie's Anſwer, in Auguſt, | 578 |
| 98. | Baillie's Commendatory Letter prefixed to Durham's Commentary on the Book of the Revelation, | 583 |

1660.

| 99. | Letter from General Monck to Mr. Robert Dowglas, 14th March, | 585 |

1661.

| 100. | Letter from the Earl of Middleton to the Lord Clerk Regiſter, 27th March, | 586 |

A GLOSSARY OF OBSOLETE WORDS, . . . 587

INDEX OF THE NAMES OF PERSONS MENTIONED IN BAILLIE'S LETTERS AND JOURNALS, ... 593

LETTERS AND JOURNALS

OF

MR. ROBERT BAILLIE.

To Mr. WILLIAM SPANG   JANUARY 26TH 1647.

DEAR COUSIGNE,

I WROTE to yow at length before I came from London; I have had a long and tedious, but, thanks to God, profperous journey. I am now here weell. I have made my report in the Commiffion of the Church to all their contentment; our errand in England being brought near a happie period, fo farr as concerned us the Commiffioners of the Church; for, by God's bleffing, the four points of Uniformitie, which wes all our Church gave us in commiffion to agent in the Affemblie at Weftminfter, were alfe good as obtained. The Directorie I brought down before. The modell of Government we have gotten it through the Affemblie according to our mind: it yet fticks in the hands of the Houfes. They have paft four ordinances at leaft about it, all prettie right, fo farr as concerns the conftitution and erection of Generall Affemblies, Provinciall Synods, Prefbyteries, and Seffions, and the power of ordination. In the province of London and Lancafhyre the bodies are fett up   That the like diligence is not ufed long agoe in all other places, it's the fottifh negligence of the minifters and gentrie in the fhyres more than the Parliament. That the power of jurifdiction in all things we require, excepting appealls from the Generall Affemblie to the Parliament, is not put in ordinances long agoe, it's by the [cunning] of the Independents and Eraftians in the Houfe of Commons; which obftacle we truft will now be removed by the zeale of the city of London; fo much the more, as [from] our nation are taken away, fooner and more eafily than any did expect, all grounds of jealoufie of our joyning with the King, the greateft prop of the Sectaries power in the Houfe. However, in the *Jus Divinum* of Prefbytery,[1] printed by the minifterie of London, yow may fee that burthen taken off our fhoulders; the body of the minifterie of England, not the Affemblie and Londoners only, being fully leavened with our fenfe in all the point of government, and become willing, and able abundantly, to manage that caufe, without us, againft all oppofites.

The third point [of Uniformity], the Confeffion of Faith, I brought it with me, now in print, as it wes offered to the Houfes by the Affemblie, without confiderable diffent of any. It's much cryed up by all, even many of our greateft oppofites, as the beft Confeffion yet extant; it's expected the Houfes fhall pafs it, as they did the Directorie, without much debate. Howbeit the retarding partie hes put the Affemblie to add Scriptures to it, which they omitted only to efchew the offence of the Houfe, whofe practife hitherto hes been, to enact nothing of religion on divine right or fcripturall grounds, but upon their owne authoritie alone. This innovation of our oppofites may weell coft the Affemblie fome time, who cannot doe the moft eafie things with any expedition; but it will be for the advantage and ftrength of the work. The fourth part of our defyred and covenanted Uniformitie is the Catechifme. A committee hes drawne and reported the whole: the Affemblie ere I came away had voted more than the halfe; a fhort time will end the reft; for they ftudie brevitie, and have voted to have no other head of divinitie into it than is fett doune in the Confeffion. This ended, we have no more adoe in the Affemblie, neither know we any more work the Affemblie hes in hand, but ane anfwer to the nine Queries of the Houfe of Commons about the *jus divinum* of diverfe parts of the government. The Minifters of London's late *Jus Divinum* of Prefbytery does this abundantly; alfo a committee of the Affemblie hes a full anfwer to all thefe Queries ready. The authors repents much of that motion: their aime wes, to have confounded and divided the Affemblie by their infnaring queftions,

---

[1] "*Jus Divinum Regiminis Ecclesiastici*: or, The Divine Right of Church-Government, afferted and evidenced by the Holy Scriptures, &c. By sundry Ministers within the City of London" Lond. 1646, 4to.

but finding the Affemblie's unanimitie in them, the Independents principles forceing them to joyne with the reft, in affertmg the divine right of thefe points of government whereupon the Parliament does moft fticke, the movers of thefe queftions wifhes they had been filent. There is no more work before the Affemblie. The tranflation of the Pfalms is paft long agoe in the Affemblie; yet it ftickes in the Houfes. The Commons paft their order long agoe; but the Lords joyned not, being folicited by divers of the Affemblie, and of the minifters of London, who loves better the more poetical paraphrafe of their colleague Mr Barton.[2] The too great accuracie of fome in the Affemblie, fticking too hard to the originall text, made the laft edition more concife and obfcure than the former. With this the Commiffion of our Church wes not fo weell pleafed; but we have gotten all thefe obfcurities helped; fo I think it fhall pafs. Our good friend Mr. Zacharie Boyd hes putt himfelf to a great deale of paines and charges to make a Pfalter, but I ever warned him his hopes were groundlefs to get it receaved in our Churches; yet the flatteries of his unadvyfed neighbours makes him infift in his fruitlefs defigne.

When I took my leave of the Affemblie I fpoke a little to them. The Proloquitor, in the name of the Affemblie, gave me ane honourable teftimonie,[3] and many thanks for my labours I had been ever filent in all their debates; and however this filence fometimes weighted my mind, yet I found it the beft and wifeft courfe. No man there is defyred to fpeake: four parts of five does not fpeak at all; and among thefe are many moft able men, and known by their wrytes and fermons to be much abler than fundrie of the fpeakers; and of thefe few that ufe to fpeak, fundry are fo tedious, and thrufts themfelves in with fuch mifregard of others, that it were better for them to be filent. Alfo there are fome eight or nyne fo able, and ready at all times, that hardly a man can fay any thing, but what others, without his labour, are fure to fay alfe weell or better. Finding, therefore, that filence wes a matter of no reproache, and of great eafe, and brought no hurt to the work, I wes content to ufe it, as Mr. Henderfon alfo did for the fair moft

[2] In the MS "Burton" The verfion alluded to is that by "William Barton, Mafter of Arts," which was printed in the year 1644, and paffed through several editions

[3] Probably the Silver Cup prefented to Baillie about this time, which remained in his family till a recent period, if it be not ftill preferved by one of his defcendents, who refides abroad

part of the laſt two years My wrytes did conciliate to me credite enough, and my fenſe of inabilitie to debate with the beſt, made me content to abſtain; whereof I did never as yet repent

We ſtayed eight or nine dayes at Newcaſtle. The King took very weell with me. I might have had occaſion to have ſaid to him what I pleaſed; but knowing his fixed reſolutions, I would not meddle at all neither to preach nor pray before him. His unhappie wilfulneſs does ſtill continue; and to this day he getts ſome miſchievous inſtruments to feed his madneſs Sundrie made us believe the Queen was content he ſhould do any thing, finding her diſappointment in France from all hands. There wes ſome whiſpering of the ſectaries plotting with him; but this I ſcarce believe; for each of them does reallie labour the others overthrow; the French Ambaſſador, for all his fair proteſtations, hes been no good inſtrument But that which hes undone him, hes been his hopes for Scotland, to gett them, by one means or other, to eſpouſe his quarrell: much dealings, ſome think, hes been both with the Army and Parliament for that end. It's very like, if he had done any dutie, though he had never taken the Covenant, but permitted it to be put in ane Act of Parliament in both Kingdomes, and given ſo ſatiſfactorie ane anſwer to the reſt of the Propoſitions, as eaſily he might. and ſometimes I know he was willing, certainly Scotland had been for him as one man; and the bodie of England, upon many grounds, wes upon a diſpoſition to have ſo cordiallie embraced him, that no man, for his life, durſt have muttered againſt his preſent reſtitution. But remaining what he wes in all his maxims, a full Canterburian, both in matters of religion and ſtate, he ſtill inclined to a new warre; and for that end reſolved to goe to Scotland. Some great men there preſſed the equitie of Scotland's protecting of him on any tearmes. This untymous exceſs of friendſhip hes ruined that unhappie Prince; for the better partie, finding the concluſion of the King's comeing to Scotland, and thereby their own preſent ruin, and ruin of the whole cauſe, the makeing the Malignants maſters of Church and State, the drawing the whole force of England upon Scotland for their perjurious violation of their Covenant, they reſolved by all means to croſſe that deſigne. So when others propoſed to the Parliament the aſſiſtance of the King to recover his government in England, notwithſtanding of any anſwer he might give to the Propoſitions, the better ſort, before they ſhould give anſwer to ſo high a queftion, defired a publick faft in the Parliament, and the advyce alfo of the Commiffion of the Church. Both with fome difficultie were obtained. But after that faft, and the diftinct anfwer of the Church, that it wes unlawfull for Scotland to affift the King for his recoverie of the Government in England if he approved not the Covenant, the Parliament wes peremptor to refufe the King free acceffe to Scotland, unlefs he fatiffied the propofitions. This much they fignified to him by their commiffioners, which we mett at Newcaftle. It wes eafy to be grieved, and to find what to reprehend in this refolution; for indeed it wes cloathed with many dangers and grievances; bot to fall at that nicke of time, on any conclufion, free of more dangers and grievances, feemed impoffible. Notwithftanding of the great foumes of money, yet the difbanding of our armie in peace will be a great tafke: to fett on foot fix thoufand foot and twelve hundred horfe, to the contentment of all, will be hard; and the intertaining of them will be harder What the King or his Englifh parliament will do next, there is no certaintie.

The peft increafes in Glafgow: my heart pities that much mifguided place; all that may, are fled out of it. The Lord be with yow. Forraigne intelligence to me muft now be the larger; for all here lives in great ignorance, and neglect of things abroad. So I reft,

Your Coufigne,

Edinburgh, January 26th 1647   R. BAYLIE.

A Postscript to Mr. Spang. June 2d 1647

What Dr. Strang writes to yow in the inclofed,[1] I pray yow fatiffie him therein with all diligence. I do not like his withdrawing from the Divine Decree the act and entitie of any finne, much leffe of free and indifferent actions: In this I think he fways too much to the one hand. But I fear thofe he refutes fhall be found in alfe dangerous errors. He indeed handles thefe Queftions in fuch a way that I doe pryze the man's ingyne and learn-

---

[1] A paper by Dr John Strang, Principal of the College of Glafgow, on the Divine Decrees and God's permiffion of the existence of Sin, is included in Baillie's MS It is entitled "Dr Strang's Stateing his Owne Question, 1647," but "such subtile questions," as Baillie calls them in this Postscript, are not suited for publication in the present work

ing much more than before, and thinks him now among the beft fchollars of the Reformed Church. It will be my endeavour that our Affemblie medle not with fuch fubtile queftions, but leave them to the fchools. Alwayes how fome men may labour to carie it I cannot fay.

After this letter lay a while befide me, I adde now, bleffed be God, good newes. David Lefley and Argyle raife from Dumblaine, the 17th of May, with a very fmall and ill-provided army. He made very long marches over the mountains, in ftormy weather, without houfes or tents Againft the 23d he come to Kintyre upon the enemie, fought and diffipate them, took in all Kintyre; hes fent a partie after Allafter, who, with a few, is fled to the Ifles. This quick and happie expedition, by God's mercy, may be to us of great advantage. If the Prince and Montrofe fhould come over to raife new broiles amongft us, as fome furmifes they intend, or if the King fhould put himfelfe in the head of the Sectarian army, which is not yet difbanded nor quiet, David Lefley being free of the Highlanders, by God's help, will keep Scotland quiet for this fummer with the little army he hes on foot. The peft hes diffipate the Colledges of St. Andrews, and kills many in the north. We had not fo ftormie a May thefe many years. Let me hear of your receipt of this letter. My fervice to your wife. I remaine

Your Coufine,

R. BAYLIE.

For [SIR ARCHIBALD JOHNSTONE OF] WARISTON.

MY LORD,

THESE are to congratulate your health, which I hope is now firm and good. I hear Dr Bruce, Principall of Leonard's Colledge of St. Andrews, is dead of the peft; if it be fo, I wifh yow to confider if it were not good to endeavour a call for Mr. Morus of Geneva to that place. I know it wes expected he would have been weell content to have accepted a call to the French Church at London the man would be an ornament and good inftrument in our land. If yow approve the motion, yow would fee who prefents, whether the Colledge itfelfe, or the Univerfity, or the King, or Southefk, or the Generall Affemblie. It were good ye fpoke with Mr. Robert Dowglafs about this purpofe: no others comes in my mind meet for that place except Dr. Stewart of Leyden. Be doeing good while yow have time. when yow are more ſtates-man than before, be no lefs than yow wont God's-man. No man I know hes all they have ſo evidently from God as yow: learn witt from your predeceſſor.[5] I hear he pretended to conſcience and walking with God, when the moſt judicious did behold him in a corrupt way; that ſuch a deluſion ſhould befall yow, what would be my ſorrow! Beware of Traquaire: let not the deſire of riches break in upon yow: leave not Church affaires; the Church wes the beginning and ground of all your advancement: ſet on foot again the commiſſion for the Church: diviſion of great paroches, and ſetleing of ſtipends wes a good worke, which will fall if yow mind it not in earneſt. As yow love the Chancelour's credite and reſpect in the countrie, keep him from medling more with the Annuitie; and make him ſhort in his diſcourſe at meetings; but I almoſt forgett myſelfe. Farewell

Your Mr. and Servant,

R BAYLIE

Kilwinning, June 2d 1647.
My ſervice to your Ladie.

MR. HAAK'S LETTER TO ME: [IN 1647?]

THE buſineſs of the Dutch Bible Notes ſtands thus. T. H.[6] haveing received in May laſt the two hundred pounds (which indeed came very ſeaſonablie to ſatiſſie his creditors,) being it wes the firſt and all the reall encouragement he had ſince the work wes firſt recommended unto him (in Auguſt 1644); to improve the ſame to the reall proſecution and perfecting of that work, he addreſt himſelfe again to the friends and favourers thereof here, and by name to Mr. [Corbet?]; who took the opportunitie ſoon after to make a motion in the Houſe that ſomething might be done for his further encouragement and ſupport; which it ſeems wes very weell reliſhed, and

[5] Shortly before this, Johnstone had been appointed Lord Advocate.

[6] "Theodore Haak, Esq" a native of the Palatinate, and one of the earliest members of the Royal Society, London, was the Translator of "The Dutch Annotations upon the whole Bible" This work, owing to want of encouragement, was not completed till the year 1657, in 2 vols. folio, when it was dedicated to his Highness the Lord Protector of the Commonwealth.

fomething ordered likewife; but through the multiplicitie of affaires, and the faid gentleman's frequent abfence for his health's fake, there is nothing yet effected, though I am ftill put in hopes I fhall not be neglected. In the mean tyme, I find myfelfe inthralled in very great ftraites. I [loft] a world of time, and many excellent opportunities, both here and abroad, to live comfortablie by honeft imployment, ftanding engaged for this, and finding of fmall encouragement here to fecond yeares [yours?], whereby I might be enabled to goe through with what I begane. Befides, I find whatever the ground may be, our minifters feem not to care to have the work advanced, and from the bookfellers I can promife myfelfe nothing at all Moreover, fome defireing to have only the bare Notes without the text, others the Notes and text together, feeing they comment upon their own reading, and the fame much differing from the Englifh, and much quotted throughout the Notes, and much clearing both text and notes; and I know not which fort I fhould moft labour to fatiffie, the former being loath there fhould be a new Englifh text publifhed:—And Mr. Blair indeed advyfed me to publifh the Pfalmes by themfelves for ane effay, and I have made them ready, the whole reading and text together interwoven. But there is ane great fcruple (though I might find one to undertake the printing) why that alfo is deferred, namely, that a great number of notes throughout the Pfalmes relate to other parts and notes, without which the reader muft needs remaine unfatiffied :—And the mifery is, there is none here with whom I might confult about thefe matters; and thefe [who,] one would think, fhould mind and further it moft, remove it furtheft from them: that, indeed, what to doe or refolve I know not, haveing adventured further in readinefs to ferve the publick in this kind than I am able to bear. Neverthelefs, if that I fhall be any wayes enabled to goe through with the worke, I hope I fhall give teftimony that my defires and endeavours are ftill the fame, and not to give it over, if, and alfe long as I can maintain it, without apparent hazard of my undoeing. I have enough to fhew that I meant fincerelie, and endeavoured reall performance. Had I mett more readie help the bufinefs had been accomplifhed by this time; now both it and myfelfe are out behind-hand, nothing troubling me more than that thereby fo many expectations are fruftrated, or at leaft fo long delayed. Alfe foon as any better hopes appears I fhall not faill to give further account.

To Mr. WILLIAM SPANG.   EDINBURGH, JULY 13TH 1647.

DEAR COUSINE,

I receaved yours, the 6th of July, this day, and another of yours, Aprile 9th, within thefe two or three weeks, together with your Honorius Reggius,[7] for which we are all much obliedged to your great paines in. That bufinefs which yow fo earneftlie recommended to Mr. David Dickfone and me, was not feafible, had we ufed all poffible diligence ; but the truth is, although I believe ye know my willingnefs to doe to my power in things that concerns yow, lefs than you wrote that matter did, yet it fell fo out, that I could ufe little diligence to fpeak of ; for your letter about that purpofe came not to my hand till near three monethts after it was written ; and when it came, our whole towne of Kilwinning were keeped up upon fome fufpition of the plague ; fo I could have no effectuall communication, neither by word nor wryte, with any ; and therefore I came to Edinburgh. That matter was fettled on Mr. Arnott, who had diverfe of the chiefe Lords of the Seffion to folift for him. For the great ficknefs of your good honeft wife I am forrie ; but glad for her grace and patience.

Thefe matters of England are fo extremely defperate, that now twyfe they have made me fick : except God arife, all is gone there. The imprudence and cowardice of the better part of the City and Parliament, which was triple or fextuple the greater, has permitted a company of filly rafcalles, which calls themfelves yet no more than fourteen thoufand, horfe and foot, to make themfelves mafters of the King, and Parliament, and City, and by them of all England ; fo that now that difgraced Parliament is but a committee to act all at their pleafure, and the City is ready to fright the Parliament, at every firft or fecond boaft from the army. No humane hope remaines but in the King's unparalleled willfulnefs, and the armie's unmeafurable pride. As yet they are not agreed, and fome writes they are not like to agree : for in our particular I expect certainly they will agree

---

[7] " Commentarius de Statu Ecclefiæ Britannicæ hodierno," a tract publifhed at Dantzick, 1647, under the name of ' Honorius Reggius,' the anagram of ' Georgius Hornius,' a learned writer who was a Profeffor fucceffively at Harderwyk and Leyd

VOL. III.

weel enough, at what diftance foever their affections and principles ftand. Allwayes if the finger of God in their fpirits fhould fo farr dement them as to difagree, I would think there were yet fome life in the play; for I know the body of England are overwearie long agoe of the Parliament, and ever hated the fectaries, but much more now for this their unexpected treacherie and oppreffion. On the other part, the King is much pitied and defyred; fo if they give him not contentment, he will overthrow them. If he and they agree, our hands are bound : we will be able, in our prefent pofture and humour of our highly diftracted people, to doe nothing; and whom fhall we goe to help, when none calls but the King? Parliament and City, as their mafters command, are ready to declare againft us if we fhould offer to arme : But if the King would call, I doubt not of rifeing of the beft armie ever we had, for the crufhing of thefe ferpents, enemies to God and man. David Lefley has gotten all Ifla, and old Collkitto, without quarters. He is now over to Mull, and purpofes within a fortnight to returne, having no more to doe in thefe bounds. That things goe weell abroad, it is comfort to us. That Leopold layes a little the French pride; that all the Dutch Princes, even Bavier, and the Ecclefiaftick Electour, have left the Emperor, I am glad; but counts it a ftrange prank of ingratitude in Bavier, and of unkyndnefs in the Swedes toward the poor Palatine, at whofe charge moft that neutralitie, I fear, be concluded. I think your States wife in taking peace with Spaine.

My Speech in the Generall Assembly [at Edinburgh,] Giving Account of our Labours at London. August 6th 1647

It is one of the Lord's promifes to us, that they who fow in teares fhall reap in joy; that they who goe out weeping and carry precious feed, fhall returne with rejoyceing and bring their fheaves. It was the Generall Affemblie's pleafure fome four yeares agoe, to fend fome of us, their weak brethren and fervants, to that very venerable and worthie Synod at Weftminfter, to fow in that famous place fome of the precious feed, not of our Church, as enemies do flander, but of God, the Father of all Light and Truth. Our poor labours in that fervice were fo bleffed by the good hand of our God, that although the fowing of the feed was often accompanied with much folicitude and perplexitie of mind, yea fometimes with great griefe of heart, and tears in a good meafure, yet the vifible appearance of a fair harveft, did bring a fenfible joy not only to ourfelves, but to many thoufands more on both fide the feas. The laft Affemblie wherein my prefent Colleague and I did appear in this place, we brought with us a bundle of fo goodlie fheaves, as did revive the hearts of many in that very fad time. This day the Lord has fent us againe to the fame place, loadened with more of thefe precious fruites, which we truft fhall help to refrefhe all honeft fpirits, though otherwife exceedinglie fadded with the late unhappie and much unexpected occurrences.

Right Honourable and Reverend, yow remember, that all your ecclefiaftick defyres from your brethren of England, that all the commiffions and inftructions laid upon us your fervants, were only for the obtaining of Uniformitie in four particulars,—in the Worfhip of God, in the Government of the Church, in a Confeffion of Faith, and Catechifme. For the firft, the Directorie we prefented in the forenamed Affemblie gave good and ample fatiffaction. It was then your pleafure to caufe both of us returne, for the affiftance of our other colleagues, in preffing your three remanent defyres. As for the Government of the Church, the goodnefs of our God gave us to obtaine, not only thefe initiall Propofitions, whereof at our laft appearance we gave ane account to the good likeing of all then prefent, but alfo a full and perfect modell of Difcipline, which, by the bleffing of God, may make in a fhort time the Churches in the three Kingdomes, in all confiderable parts of government, not only uniforme, but weell near one; as yow may fee, when you fhall think it convenient to take that modell of Difcipline into confideration.

In your third defyre, the Lord made our fucceffe no lefs profperous; a large Confeffion of Faith is perfyted with farr greater unanimitie than any living could have hoped for, among fo many learned divines, in fo diftempered a place and diftracted a feafon. I am confident, if the judgment of many my wifer do not deceave, this piece of work is fo fine and excellent, that whenever yow fhall be pleafed to look upon it, the fight of it fhall draw from the moft cenforious eye, a good acceptation.

For your fourth and laft defyre, the Catechifme, my Reverend Colleague, I know, is inftructed to give fatiffaction therein. I ftayed till fome good progreffe was made into it; but long three years and fundry odd monethis peregrination from my countrie, and abfence from my particular charge, wakened, I confefs, in me, a great langour to returne; yea, all of us fell very defireous to be at home, and joyntly did preffe the Commiffion of the Kirk for a libertie. At laft, it wes their favour to permitt to ourfelves the permiffion of fome one: by the providence of God, and equitie of the brethren there, the lott fell upon me. I was glad to be a carrier of a Confeffion of Faith; alfo of a Pfalter, which to my knowledge had coft the Affembly fome confiderable paines, and is like to be one neceffar part of the three Kingdoms uniformitie. I brought likewife a good affurance of a perfect Catechifme to follow with all convenient diligence. This meffage made me, in January laft, to obtain from the Commiffion of the Kirk that welcome which is my earneft defire may in due time be ratified and approven by this Venerable Affembly; for after the approbation of God and teftimony of confcience, their allowance of my meane endeavours is that which I wifh; not as a reward for fome labours and dangers I know I have undergone in your fervice, but as ane encouragement to returne with cheerfullnefs to my private charge, after fo long a diverfion. This is all I defyre for myfelfe, which, if I may obtaine, I fhall be defyreous to be thankfull to God and your reverences.

For my Colleagues, may I make bold, with permiffion, to offer fome few of my thoughts. That glorious Soule of bleffed memory,[8] who now is crowned with the reward of all his labours for God and for us, I wifh his remembrance may be fragrant among us, fo long as free and pure Affemblies remaine in this land, which we hope fhall be to the coming of our Lord. Yow know he fpent his ftrength, and wore out his dayes; he breathed out his life in the fervice of God, and of this Church: This binds it on our back, as we would not prove ungrate, to pay him his due. If the thoughts of others be conforme to my inmoft fence, in duety and reafon he ought to be accounted by us, and the pofteritie, the faireft ornament, after John Knox of incompareable memory, that ever the Church of Scotland did enjoy.

For my other Colleague,[9] who yet remains in the place of our long toyle, my defire is that this Reverend meeting may not forgett him, but, according to his very great worth and defervings, may take him to their wife confideration

For my prefent moft dear Brother,[1] all I now intreat is, that he may find

---

[8] Mr Alexander Henderson   [9] Mr. Samuel Rutherford.
[1] Mr George Gillespie His speech to the Assembly at this time, will be given in the Appendix.

in this place fuch an open eare and ready attention as ordinarly, I know, he had in the Englifh Affembly, where, indeed, no man was wont to find a greater attention and audience.

I hope the Lord fhall enable him to give yow fo clear an account of the true eftate of affaires, whereof, fince my departure, he hath been an eye and ear witnefs, as fhall make it vifible and palpable to all, that we have no reafon to repent of any of the labors of our love towards our neighbour Church and Kingdome; that the great work we doe intend there is fo well grounded, and fo farr advanced among them, that the ports of hell, and the greateft power of man, fhall never be able to overturne it; yea, that the prefent ftorme, how terrible foever, which the prime inftruments of Satan, this day on earth, and our greateft adverfaries, the Sectaries, have raifed, fhall, by the goodnefs, wifdome, and power of God, be turned over as the unreafonable rage and follie of the Prelates lately wes, to be a happy mean of haftening the accomplifhment of all our defires. I am very hopefull that the prefent earthquake, though it fhake the foundation, and threaten the fwallowing up of both Church and State, yet it fhall prove ane near antecedent to the fettling of all the three Kingdomes, and the Churches in them, in that peace and happinefs which fome cannot believe till they fee and feell it.

It is my heart's wifh, with which now I clofe, that the hands of our Church and State, which God hath made very inftrumentall in the laying the ground, and helping up every part of the wall of this exceeding great and glorious work, may not now be deficient in the end, when the top-ftone alone is to be laid: and deficient we muft needs be if ever we open a doore to the devill, of divifion to enter in, efpeciallie among us of the miniftrie This evill is fo great and deftructive, that the fears of it in zealous brethren, though never fo caufelefs, are very pardonable It has often been my great comfort fince my returne, that, when I have fearched fo farr as my mean knowledge can reach, I could find no reall ground at all for divifion in our Church as yet. It ought to be all our prayers that long it may fo continue, for the old ferpent is lying at all our doors; but the man with whom he fhall firft prevaill to make himfelf a ringleader, upon whatfoever caufe, to divide and trouble the Kirk of Scotland, let me fpeak prophecie unto him: Were he this day of never fo high a price, and great fragrancie among us, yet he fhall become a curfed foule, and his memory fhall ftinck to all generations. But trufting that our God will avert this, and all other mifchieves from us, I give place to that large and comfortable accompt which we expect from my Reverend Brother   FINIS

I did not truely intend to give offence to any, and leaft of all to one whom I purpofe, while I live, as hitherto himfelfe knows I have done, to reverence as a Father[*] of high worth and deferving. I have caufed write out the notes I fcribled that morning and the night before, that he may confider at leafure if any thing I faid was juftly offenfive. For the two paffages I heard was excepted againft, I make this Apologie :—

For the firft, I conceave it is the priviledge of every member of the Affemblie to fpeak out, upon a fair occafion, that which he is perfuaded to be a feafonable and ufefull truth: this truely wes my cafe in that particular: If I be deceaved, ignorance and charitie, not prefumption, are ingredients in my fault. For the fecond paffage, I intended, in truth, to give a caveat, not to our Father, but to thefe only with whom he ufes to be offended: however, the thing is a truth undenyable, which Scripture, and all reafon, will make good, and which, I am perfuaded, no member of the Affemblie will deny.

If any other paffage of my Speech wes excepted againft, I doe not know.

To a Friend in Kilwinning.

LONDON and the affaires of England lye fore on the breaft of many honeft men; yet the profperitie of our own affaires here, both of Church and State, gives us fome relief. Mr. Cheiflie fent us word that he wes detained at Newcaftle; which did much perplex us; for our State meeting did depend upon his meffage. It pleafed God to make his detainers let him goe before the meffenger of our State come to demand him. When he came, he gave us a full information how all affaires in England ftood   The inclofed papers will fhew the incredible change that a few dayes wrought. The City's declaration and diurnal declares in what a brave pofture both the City and Parliament once wes in: the other papers fhew how foon all wes overturned.

[*] Baillie here alludes to David Calderwood, who had taken some exceptions at the conclution of his speech: *Vide infra* page 20

The armie marched through the whole city by way of triumph; but ſtayed not in it, did no violence to any; only three or four regiments keeps the forts about Weſtminſter, and guards the Parliament ſtill. For all that, the Houſe of Commons votes ſundrie things contrare to the mind of the armie how long that courage will remaine I cannot ſay. It's thought that people, when it hes felt a little the burthen of the armie, will break that yoke by one mean or other. The armie's mind, much of it, may be ſeen in their propoſitions, a paper which I purpoſed to ſend, but now it's fallen by: By it they are cleare enough for a full libertie of conſcience, a deſtroying of our Covenant, a ſetting up of Biſhops, of inthralling the King ſo far, as in my judgement, he and they will not agree, albeit many thinks they are agreed allready. If this were, our caſe were very haid. Never more appearance ot a great diſcord, both in our Church and State ſome few dayes agoe; but, bleſſed be God, the appearances are now much changed Never Aſſemblie more harmonious than this yet hes been. Our declaration to England, a very good piece, is paſt without a contrare voice. An act againſt vagers from their own miniſters, and a large direction for private worſhip, drawn by Mr. Robert Blair, for the correcting of all the faults in worſhip, which offended many here, is paſt the Committee without a contrare voice; and, I think, ſhall paſſe the Aſſemblie alſo, no leſs unanimouſly; which demonſtrates the trueth of what I ſaid in my Aſſemblie-ſpeech, That for all the noiſe ſome made, yet truly there wes no diviſion as yet in our Church. Yeſterday, and this night, our State, after much irreconcileable difference, as appeared, are at laſt unanimouſlie agreed to ſend the Chancellor and Lanerick to the King and Parliament of England, to comfort and encourage both to keep our Covenant, and not to agree to the propoſitions of the army. No appearance, as yet, of any ſturreing in haſte in this Kingdome.

I think our Aſſemblie may ſitt all the next week. Mr. James Fergulhill may thank God, and his friends here, that he wes not ſent to winter in Ireland, in the Derrie. My ſervice to all my friends. I am ſure the prayers of pious people, for the Aſſemblie, are anſuered; which ſhould encourage them to continue to poure out their hearts unto God, in ſo ſad a time, for the Church and State, and men imployed therein. The Lord, we hope, will aryſe and blow away the preſent miſt.

Edinburgh, Auguſt 20th. Friday at night

[To Mr. William Spang.] September 1st 1647

Cousine,

Your fad letters of your dear Wyfe's death, I receaved I pray God comfort yow Publict forrow does not permitt us to be fo affected with any private grief, either of our owne or friends, as otherwife we would. London hes lyen like a mylneftone on my breaft now of a long time. The firft week, we came to this towne, my heart wes a little relieved. I thought the Lord had anfwered our prayers much fooner than I expected, and had put London in fo good a pofture for averting all our feares as I could have wifhed; but that joy lafted not full eight dayes. Stapleton and Hollis, and fome others of the eleven members, had been the maine perfuaders of us to remove out of England, and leave the King to them, upon aflurance, which wes moft lykelie, that this wes the only means to gett that evill army difbanded, the King and peace fettled according to our minds; but their bent execution of this reall intention hes undone them, and all, till God provyde a remeed. We were glad when Lifle wes recalled from his Lieutenantrie of Ireland, a creature of Cromwell's, who gott that great truft for no vertue at all but his ferviceablenefs to that faction. This wes the firft fenfible grievance to that army. The fecond was the employing of Skippon and Maffie, in the Irifh command, and giving to Fairfaxe fuch a command in England as made him not very formideable. But when the third ftroke came, of difbanding the moft of the fectaries, and cafhiering of their officers, this put them on that high and bold defigne, which as yet they follow, as, I think, not fo much on great preconception, as drawne on by the courfe of affaires, and light heads of their leaders. Vaine and Cromwell as I take it, are of nimble hot fancies for to put all in confufion, but not of any deep reach. St. John and Pierpoint are more ftayed, but not great heads; Say and his fon, not [James?], albeit wifer, yet of fo dull, and foure, and fearfull a temperament, that no great atchievement, in reafon, could be expected from them The reft, either in the armie or Parliament, of their partie, are not on their myfteries, and of no great parts either for counfell or action, fo farr as I could ever obferve. The follie of our friends wes apparent, when at the armie's firft back-march, and refufall to difband, they recalled their declaration againſt their mutinous petitions. Eafily might all their defignes have been crufhed at that nick of tyme, with one ſtout look more ; but it was a dementation to fitt ſtill amazed at the taking of the King, the accufation of the eleven members, the armie's approaching to the city. Here, had the City agreed, and our friends in Parliament ſhewed any refolution, their oppofites councell might even then have been eafily overturned, for all this while, the armie wes not much above ten thoufand ill-armed fojors. But the irrecoverable lofs of all, wes the ill manageing of the City's brave engagement Had they then made faſt the chief of the Sectarian partie in both Houfes, and ſtopped their flight to the armie; had Maffie and Waller, with any kind of mafculous activity, made ufe of that new truſt committed to them ; Mr. Marſhall, and his feventeen fervants of the Synod, for all Fowke's and Gibbs's fubornation, ſhould never have been bold to offer that deſtructive petition to the Houfes and Common Counfell, which, without any capitulation, put prefently in the armie's power, both Parliament, City, and all England, without the leaſt contradiction : ane example rarely paralelled, if not of treachery, yet at leaſt of childifh improvidence and bafe cowardice. Since that time they have been abfolute maſters of all. Which way they will ufe this unexpected foveraignitie, it will quickly appear As yet they are fetling themfelves in their new fadle Before they got up, they gave the King and his partie fair words ; but now, when all is their owne, they may put him in a harder condition than yet he has taſted of. Their propofalls, a part of their mind, gives to the King much of his defyre in bringing back Biſhops and Books, in putting down our Covenant and Prefbytery, in giving eafe to Malignants and Papiſts ; but fpoills him of his temporall power fo much, as many thinks, he will never acquiefce to, albeit it's fpoken loud, that he and they alreadie are fully agreed.

Our State here, after long expectation to have heard fomething of the King's own mind and defyres, as yet have heard nothing from him to count of. Although he ſhould employ their help againſt his oppreffors, yet he being ſtill altogether unwilling to give us any fatiffaction in the matter of our Covenant, we are uncertain what courfe to take ; only we doe refent to our Commiffioners to oppofe the propofalls, and to require a fafe-conduct to the Chancellour and Lanerick to come up to the King and Parliament. It coſt many debates before it came to this conclufion. Our great men are not like to

VOL

pack up their differences. . The Duke and his friends would have been thought men compofed of peace in any tearmes, and to have caft on others defignes of imbroiling Scotland in a new warre. But when all were weary of jangling debates, the conclufion whereto the Committee wes brought, wes fo farr to efpoufe the King's quarrell in anie tearmes, that Argyle and Warriftone behooved to proteft againft our engadgement in fuch tearmes. To avoid invidious proteftations, both parties agreed to paffe ane act of not ingadgement. The proceedings of fome are not only double and triple, but fo manifold, that as no other, fo, in my mind, themfelves know not what they finally intend. They who made themfelves gracious and ftrong, by making the world believe that it was their oppofites who had brought the country in all the former trouble, and would yet againe bring it into a new dangerous warre, when it came to the poynt, were found to precipitate us into dangers, and that in fuch tearmes as few with comfort could have undertaken. We have it from diverfe good hands at London, that fome here keep correfpondence with Sir Thomas Fairfaxe, which to me is an intollerable abhomination. The prefent fenfe of many is this : If the King and the armie agree, we muft be quiet and look to God : if they agree not, and the King be willing to ratifie our Covenant, we are all as one man to reftore him to all his rights, or die by the way : if he continue refolute to reject our Covenant, and only to give us fome parts of the matter of it, many here will be for him, even in thefe tearmes, but diverfe of the beft and wifeft are irrefolute, and waits till God give more light.

However, David Lefley, with a great deale of fidelitie, activitie, and fucceffe, hes quieted all our Highlands and Ifles, and brought back our little armie ; which, we think, fhall be quartered here and there, without difbanding, till we fee more of the Englifh affaires. The peft for the time, vexes us. In great mercie Edinburgh and Leith, and all about, which lately were afflicted with more of this evill than ever wes heard of in Scotland, are free . fome few infections now and then, but they fpread not. Aberdeen, Brechin, and other parts of the north, are miferablie wafted. St. Andrews and Glafgow, without great mortalitie, are fo threatened, that the fchooles and colledges now in all Scotland, bot Edinburgh, are fcattered. By this means my ftudies and domeftick affaires are clean difordered, and like fo to be ftill, if the Lord be not mercifull.

While I had written this farr, by the packett this day from London I learn that the armie daily goes higher and higher, which to me is a hopefull prefage of their quicker ruine. The chief fix of the eleven members, were coming to you: Stapleton, after[3] Hollis the fecond gentleman for all gallantrie in England, died at Calice. I think it will be hard to the Parliament and City to bear thefe men long; and I hope, if all men were dead, God will arife againft them. Munfter is not like to be a fchoole to them long. Cromwell and Vaine are like to run on to the end of Becold and Knipperdolling's race. Northumberland hes feafted the King at Sion-houfe, hence he went to Hampton-court. They fpeak of his coming to Whitehall. If he agree no better with the Sectaries than yet he does, that journey may prove fatall. He is not likely to come out of London willingly; and if the army fhould draw him, that violence may waken fleeping hounds. If they let him come to London, without affureance of his accord with them, they are more bold and ventorious than wife; and if the King agree to their ftate-defignes, I think he is not fo confonant to all his former principles and practifes as I took him.

I know you expect fome account of our Affemblie. Take it, if yow have patience to read what I have fcribled in hafte, on a very ill fheet of paper. I have no leafure to double, for our Commiffioners enters every day at feven, and we are about public bufinefs dayly till late at night. At our firft meeting, there wes clear appearance of formed parties for divifion; but God hes turned it fo about, that never Affemblie wes more harmonious and peaceable to the very end. The laft year, a minifter in the Merfe, one Mr. James Simpfone, whofe grandfire wes, as I take it, ane uncle or brother to famous Mr. Patrick of Stirling, a forward, pious, young man, being in fuite of a religious damfell, fifter to Mr. James Guthrie's wife, had kept with Mr. James Guthrie, and others, fome private meetings and exercifes, which gave great offence to many. When they came before the laft Generall Affemblie and Commiffion of the Kirk, Mr. David Calderwood and fundrie other very honeft men, oppofite to Malignants, were much grieved, and by that grief moved to joyne with Mr. William Colville, Mr. Andrew

---

[3] Baillie's amanuensis had miftaken this word, and makes it "Stapleton, Esler, Hollis,' &c. But the meaning is obvious, as on the 24th August 1647, Whitelocke informs us, there came "News of the fudden death of Sir Philip Stapleton at Calais of the plague."

Fairfoule, and fuch whom fome took to be more favorable to Malignants than need were. Thir two joyned together, made a great partie, efpeciallie when our Statefmen did make ufe of them to bear down thofe who had fwayed our former Affemblies. The conteft wes at the choyfeing of the Moderator. The forementioned partie were earneft for Mr. William Colville.[4] Many were for me; but I wes utterly unwilling for any fuch unfitt charge, and refolved to abfent myfelfe from the firft meeting, if by no other mean I could be fhifted the leett. At laft, with very much adoe, I gott myfelf off, and Mr. Robert Dowglafs on the leetts; who carried it from Mr. William Colville only by four votes. God's bleffing on this man's great wifdome and moderatione hes carried all our affaires right to the end, but Mr David Calderwood having miffed his purpofe, hes preffed foe a new way of leetting the moderator for time to come, that puts in the hand of bafe men to get one whom they pleafe, to our great danger. We fpent a number of dayes on fecklefle particulars. Mr. Gillefpie came home at our firft downfitting: he and I made our report to the great fatiffaction of all. Yow have here what I fpoke.[5] Mr. Calderwood was very offended with what I fpoke in the end; but my apologie in private fatiffied him[6] He, and others of his acquaintance, came with refolution to make great dinne about privie meetings and novations, being perfuaded, and willing to perfuade others, that our Church wes allready much peftered with fchifme. My mind wes cleane contrare; and now, when we have tryed all to the bottome, they are found to be much more miftaken than I; for they have obtained, with the hearty confent of thefe men whom they counted greateft patrons of fchifme, all the acts they pleafed againft that evill, wherein the wifdome and authoritie of Mr. Blair hes been exceeding ferviceable. This yielding on our fide, to their defyres, drew from them a quiet confent to thefe things we intended, from which at firft they feemed much averfe We agreed, *nemine contradicente*, to that declaration, which wes committed to Mr. Gillefpie and me, but wes drawne by him alone; alfo, after much debate in the Committee, to the Confeffion of Faith; and to the printing of the Directorie for government, for the examination of the next Generall Affemblie; of the Catechife alfo, when the little that remains fhall come downe; likewife for printing, to that fame end, two or three

---

[4] In the MS. the name " Coline,' uniformly occurs for Colvin, or Colville
[5] *Vide supra*, page 10   [6] *Vide supra*, page 14

sheet of Thefes againſt Eraſtianifme, committed to Mr. Gillefpie and me, bot done by him at London, at Voetius's motion; which we mind, when approven here, to fend to him; who is hopefull to get the confent of your Univerfities, and of the Generall Affemblie of France to them, which may ferve for good purpofe. We have put the new Pfalter alfo in a good way. In our Univerfitie correfpondence, we have made more progrefs in good defignes than I expected. With much adoe, at laſt, I have gotten Doctor Strang's bufinefs to a good and a fair end, according to his mind. In all thefe things Mr Blair wes my great affiſtant. If the Lord would be pleafed to give us peace, our Generall Affemblies would be channells of great bleffings to this Ifle.

We have this day very happily ended our Affemblie with good concord; albeit Mr. David Calderwood, ferving his owne very unrulie humor, did very much oft provoke. He hes been fo untollerable through our forbearance, that it's like he fhall never have fo much refpect among us. His impoitunitie forced us, not only to a new ridiculous way of choifeing the Moderator, but, on a conceit he hes, that a minifter depofed fhould not againe be repofed almoſt in no cafe, he hes fafhed us exceedingly about the power of the commiffion of the Kirk to depofe a minifter in any cafe; yet we carried it over him We have obtained leave to print all our Englifh papers, Catechife, Confeffion, Propofitions and Directorie for government and ordination, our debates for accommodation againſt tolleration, our papers to the grand Committee. The Propofitions for government, albeit paſt both in our Affemblie and Parliament 1643, Mr. David oppofed vehemently the printing, and his grand followers, Mr. John Smith and Mr. William Colville with him, becaufe they held forth a feffion of a particular congregation to have a ground in fcripture, which he, contrare to his Altar of Damafcus, believes to have no divine right, but to be only a commiffion, with a delegate power from the Prefbyterie, tollerat in our Church for a time. With great difficultie could we gett the printing of that paper paſt for his importunitie; bot at laſt we gott all, bleffed be God

An exprefs from London this day tells us, that the armie's parliament preffes the concurrence of our Commiffioners to fend to Hampton-court the propofitions to the King This feems to import the King's refufall of the propofalls, and difagreeing yet with the army. And what they will doe with the King, if he refuife the propofitions alfo, we know not; only their laſt remonſtrance ſhews their reſolution to caſt out of the Parliament many more members, and to take the lives of ſome for example. The ſpirit that leads them, and the mercy of God to that oppreſſed people, will not permitt theſe tyrannous hypocrites to reſt, till, by their own hands, they have pulled doune their Babell. The Lord be with yow. Let me hear of the receipt of this; and help us with forraigne newes more liberally.

Your Couſigne,
R. BAYLIE.

Edinburgh, September 1ſt 1647.

For his Noble and Good Friend Poloni Alman,[7] at Dulopolis in Slaveland. October 13th 1647.

I HOPE ſome man, for all his tranſgreſſions againſt my ſqueamiſh ſtomack, is at laſt weell payed, whom the old neat-driver hes lafcht foe grievouſlie in print, with your patience may weell be called a loger, a bull, or neats-head: heirafter yow know who hes the gift of a fair neats-tongue; but medle not with drivers ſo long as yow are near the Thames, leaſt they make yow ſwime, which my friend could never doe without bladders. Alwayes forget not that your one verie large man is not now at your back, therefore be verie toſt I have ſent yow with this bearer, what I promiſed long agoe, my little Bible, without points, of Plantin's Antwerpen edition. I will not permitt yow to forgett your bargane for my Chryſoſtome. I truſt neither God nor man will long permitt evill men to triumphe: in this confidence I reſt,

Yours, &c.

We have at this time a good and full Commiſſion of the Church: we have been unanimous in our Remonſtrance, the Committee of Estates gave us thanks (but by the wiſdome of their chieff who wes galled therewith) for our vigilance and care We hope at preſent to carry our poynt bot with ſuch difficultie, that now I conclude, (in which judgment I find the wiſeſt I ſpeak with concurr,) Scotland ſhall be unable for any reall ſervice, without cureing of

---

[7] This somewhat enigmatical epistle was most likely addressed to the Earl of Lauderdale: He was then in London, and had probably been abused in some of the Diurnals.

our divifions. We are very near to tuo or three equall parts. It's my heartie advice to you who ftill, I hope, may be a happie inftrument as yow defire your one man to be able to doe anie fervice at all at this time, either for God or the poore and ftill (alas!) deluded King, or for our lamentable perfecuted brethren and caufe there, or for the defence of the religion, liberties, lives, of us here againft a partie, who, I doubt not, at their firft leafure, will ftretch out their foot on our necks. Yet once againe doe your uttermoft endeavours to unite your three friends, who latelie have vifite yow from this. No means here are poffible for that end: if God give not yow a mind and abilitie to doe it, that reconciliation is defperat, and we muft give over to think of doeing any good abroad; and all our thoughts fhall be how we may cut off one another at home, to the loud laughter of fectaries and malignants farr and near. I obteft yow in name of God and the poor King, and enflaved England, and Scotland readie to be wracked, fetting afide all foolifh injuries yow have gotten, either from one or other, yow will ftirre up yourfelffe to make two or three men one. If God help yow to doe this, when I come to paint yow the third time, I fhall put a ray on your brow longer than any of Moyfes hornes.

For Mr. William Spang: From Edinburgh, October 13th 1647.

We gave in this day to the States a remonftrance of the hazard of Religion and Covenant, if our armie fhould difband. We hope that plott, long hatched, and with too great eagernefs driven on, fhall this day or to-morrow be broken. Our dangers of farder confufion are great, if God be not mercifull. The perfecution at London is untollerable. I am very confident that partie, fo much oppofite to God and man, cannot long ftand. Ere long, I may give yow, at my leafure, ane particular accompt of all our affaires.

What yow have of forraigne affaires, let me know fully and frequently. Gett to me, by Mr. Walter Bowie, Voetius's Thefes, all collected and bound in one. If the auctions of fchollars books there, be, as I hear, I think yow might provide, not only yourfelffe, but your friends, with ftore of good and cheap books. I think, fo foon as God frees us of the fear of the fword, and peſt, yow would doe weell to make a viſite of your friends for mutuall refreſhment. The Lord be with yow.

I ſee the little Hebrew Bible, with points, is printed at Amſterdam in Manaſſes Ben-Iſrael's houſe: it ſells here very weell. By ſome of your acquaintance yow could perſuade him or ſome other to print the Targum, one book, with the points and the Latine verſion; alſo the Maſora, which Buckſtorph's Bible hes on the margine, the ſame way; and ſome chief parts of the Talmud or the Rabbins wrytes, with the points and Latine expoſition. they would ſell weell, and doe much good. Send me Voetius's [Voſſius's?] Bibliothecas; and let me hear what yow know of good Chronologers old or late. I wiſh that the Arabick Bible and other books, which are come out in the late Paris Bible, were printed ſeverallie; for who will give a thouſand merks for a Bible of ten volumes. There is diverſe manuſcripts in England of Erpenius's Arabick Dictionary: I think Mr. Cheeſlie hes one of them. If L'Emperour will not move ſome there to print ane Arabick little handſome dictionary, (for who will be faſcht with theſe four volumes of that Italian,) I wiſh that of Erpenius were printed, till a better come. Our poor printers of old, the Stephens, etc. gave many a fair volume of new brave books, in all languages: ſhall we now gett no new printed books of any note, but from the Popiſh preſſes at Paris only.

MISTAKES RECTIFIED, IN A LETTER TO A WORSHIPFULL KNIGHT, S. D. C.[8]
FROM A MINISTER IN THE WEST. EDINBURGH, MARCH 8TH 1648.

RIGHT WORSHIPFULL,

FINDING your ingenuous profeſſion to be fully ſatiſfied with what I offered, the other night, for the clearing of the groſſe miſtakes which yow aſſured me were fleeing abroad of many the beſt men of my coate, that yow may be confirmed in that opinion of good men, which their preſent innocence and former great deſerving doth in juſtice call for, I ſend yow now in wryte, with ſome

[8] This letter was apparently addressed by Baillie to Sir Daniel Carmichael. He was nominated by Parliament to be Treasurer Depute, 10th March 1649. A copy of it, in a contemporary hand, with some slight corrections, (but not in Baillie's own hand,) is contained in Wodrow MSS Folio, Vol xxix No 33

little enlargement, the heads, which then I proponed, for taking off what yow told me, was the too common objection of men, otherwife not of the worft affections, either towards us or the caufe.

I gave yow affureance that my Brethren of the miniftrie were fo farr from that alleadged averfnefs from all Warre againft the Sectaries in England in any tearms, that I knew thefe of them that were moft afperfed with that flander, to be readie to goe alongft with ane army, and venture their perfons againft that enemie, if fo be they might obtaine the queftion of the Warre to be ftated, as, yourfelfe did acknowledge, everie pious, wife, and unbyaffed fpirit would gladly admit of as moft reafonable and neceffarie

We judge it indeed convenient, that minifters be verie warie of what they fpeak of any matter of ftate, and moft of all, what encouragement they give to the raifing of a Warre; yet everie fubject of a kingdome hes fo much to doe and fuffer in his perfone, eftate, and friends, when a warre comes on, and warre is fo great and weightie a cafe of confcience, that minifters, both as men and according to their calling in the Church, may well be admitted to delyver their fenfe of that which fo much concerns the confcience, both of themfelves and every foule of their flocke.

In the prefent cafe, three things are moft confiderable. 1. A conclufion. 2 The grounds thereof. 3 The impediments that lye in the way of its practice. Upon the firft two, which are the maine, I conceave no difference at all · the debates on the third may be fo eafily accomodat, that if there fhould remaine any fenfible difcrepance amongft us about them, that very unhappie and moft needlefs miffortoun muft be imputed to many other things rather than to any defigne of ours to impoffibilitat that undertaking, which we profefs ourfelves moft willing to further, with the hazard of all thefe things which on the earth are deareft unto us

The conclufion, that Scotland at this time hes a juft caufe of Warre againft the Sectarian army in England, and their adherents, none of us doth queftion; nor do we controvert the common and obvious grounds of this conclufion, whether yow fpeak of them in the Thefe, or of their application in the Hypothefe. We grant the notorious violation of a National League in the moft fub ftantial parts, where there is no appearance of fatiffaction for paft breaches, or of fecuritie for keeping in the future, except only by deluforie words, gives a juft right and call to the injured nation of vindicating their league by the fword.

We admit likewife the affumption, that while the Parliament and bodie of the Kingdome of England were upon very hopefull and promifing endeavours to keep every part of their league with us, there is arifen a faction of fectaries and hereticks, now prevalent in the Army and Parliament, who openly and obftinately doe tread under foote the whole and every part of our Covenant, without any hope of redreffe in any peaceable way; fo farr are they from having it impofed upon any by a law, that no entreatie could obtaine of them to let it ftand in the propofitions to the King, where the hand of the Parliaments of both Kingdomes had fixed it, as the maine and greateft demand: their carriage towards the Covenant in words and deeds, thefe yeais paft, in the fence of all, makes them moft manifeft deftroyers of it.

This we take to be true of every part, as weell as of the whole: the firft two articles are about religion and uniformity; this faction reformes religion by their advancing, to their power, and moft induftrioufly fpreading abroad, of more errors and herefies than did ever in any one age lodge in any one place of the world. Their uniformitie is to guard, both by law and force, every man who pleafes, in his maintainance, and practife for church difcipline, of that which is moft oppofite to prefbyteriall government.

For the third article, the defence of the priviledges of Parliament, and liberties of the Kingdomes, of the King's perfon and authoritie, they have turned their armes upon the Parliament, the City of London, and whole Kingdome of England, who oppofed their wayes; all thofe they keep ftill under foote, groaning and trembling under the fhaking of their fword · contrary to the declared will of both Kingdomes, they feafed upon the perfon of the King, and carying him about at their pleafure, have at laft clapt him up a cloffe and perpetuall prifoner, for his denyall of fuch bills, which gave the armie a power to be mafters for ever of all the force, treafure, and lawes of the kingdome of England; neither have we any fecuritie but that their way is pofting to the depryving of the King's pofteritie, of their birthright, and changing the government of the State in the whole Ifle.

For the fourth article, their punifhing of evill inftruments, for hindering the Reformation, for dividing one Kingdome from another, for making factions among the people contrare to the League and Covenant, is no other bot the fetting of the moft eminent of this kind in the higheft places of honor, profite, and power in the Parliament, in the armie, in the navie, in the city, in all the fhyres, for that very end, that thefe their inftruments may be encouraged to goe on in fuch evill fervices to both Kingdomes, againft their fworn league.

For the fifth, all their keeping the two Kingdomes in union is manifeftlie to breake and fcorne the greateft bonds of conjunction and common intereft of thefe two realmes.

For the laft article, their protection of all who enters in the League, is openly to banifhe, imprifon, affright, keep under, and perfecute the moft eminent both of the parliament, city, and fhyres, for nothing elfe but their fincere and cordiall endeavours to adhere to, and profecute the exprefle ends of the Covenant.

That the Sectarian faction is notorioufly guilty of fuch atrocious breaches of every article of the League, we doe not doubt ; nor doe we pretend to the fmalleft hope of recovering them by words, meffages, or any peaceable means from their paths of deftruction ; neither doe we contradict what is fpoken of the evident and imminent hazard of Scotland to have their church and kingdome embroyled in all the miferies of England, the religion and liberties of both kingdomes being laid up together in the fame veffell ; and the fpirit, the way, the intereft, the fafetie of the faction, dryving them on to the maftering of the utmoft corners of all the three Kingdomes ; yea, if the winds doe favour, to farr larger defigns and higher interprifes, for who can forget Cromwell's threatning with his army, in the face of Parliament, the very walls of Conftantinople.

If thus farr we be agreed, what hinders us from getting prefently up, hand in hand, to the way ? Certainly the retardments come from ane other fide of the Houfe than that which is called ours ; even from them who fo willfully, and, as I am bold to terme it, imprudently, have refufed all this while to give us fatisfaction in three things which we efteeme moft neceffare for us to have, and eafie for others to grant, without all prejudice to any of their avowed ends.

We defire that our Covenant, Religion, and Liberties, purchafed of old and maintained of late at very high rates, may not by this new Warre be putt in a condition every way as hazardous as they ftand in this day, which we think will be the cafe, if it be not provided for, after all the blood, loffes, hazards, labours of the nixt warre, even when we have obtained our end, the totall overthrow of the Sectarian faction, for then the King, though nothing changed in his mind, muſt be ſet up, and enabled with his former partie of malignants to act more vigorouſly than ever in all the three Kingdomes. The yoke of tyrannie in the ſtate, of poperie and prelacie in the Church, is lyklie to be put upon our neck, with alſe violent a hand as ever.

That we may be guarded againſt this apparent miſchief, we require bot two things; and a third for ſecuritie of theſe two when granted. Firſt, That the King be not entruſted with the full exerciſe of his Royall power, till he have given all aſſurance, that is poſſible for him in his preſent condition, of his own conſent and concurrence to ſettle the ſolemne League, and Religion according unto it, in all the three Kingdomes. We require not this as a previous condition to the King's reſcue, or to the putting of him in as good a condition as he was in before the faction ſeaſed on his perſon. We are not againſt any honor, freedome, or ſafetie which the Parliaments of both Kingdomes ſhall think meet to grant him for a treatie, before a full ſettlement; nor doe we ſpeake of capitulations for keeping of Monarchick government in the King's poſteritie; only we require the foreſaid condition to be previous to his Majeſtie's exerciſe of Royaltie, who hes declared his willingneſs to putt upon himſelf a harder condition than this in hand, the renouncing of all power in the militia, and nomination of officers of ſtate in England and Ireland, with diverſe other things of great importance dureing his whole life.

This our firſt Demand is no other than that which both our Kirk and State hes oft craved before in expreſſe tearms; and, that which ſome men compted the great rock of this demand, we are content to remove for a demonſtratione of our earneſtneſs to comply: we are willing to change the negative expreſſions of our Kirk and State into affirmatives; we inſiſt only upon the thing it ſelf, a real ſecuritie for our Covenant and Religion. This we truſt will not be ſo much ſtuck at by the King himſelfe, for readilie his Majeſtie is not ſo much here pinched with conſcience as ſome talks of: We know what laws he hes been content to paſſe in Scotland for the Covenant and Preſbytery, alſo what was promiſed to Ireland for Popery, and what in England for libertie to Sects and Errours We are very hopefull that all we preſſe for the Covenant and Preſbytery ſhall be obtained, if our State can be but conſtant to crave what all reaſon urges to be granted.

Our ſecond Demand is, that the Malignant partie of papiſts, prelates, and others oppoſite to our Covenant, may not be permitted to riſe to ſuch a strength as may enable them to give us the law; for this end we crave that all of them who are willing to joyne in armes with us, doe joyne likewife in the Covenant. We are perfuaded that many of them are not impeded fo much by fcruple of confcience, as reafons of ftate and oppofition of humour to take that oath; and we verily hope the moft of them (if dealt with in earneft) would readily joyne with us in our way for the love of our common end, to doe right to the King, and pull down the oppreffing faction of Sectaries. Thefe of the Malignants, who will not joyne with us, let them fit ftill and wait on till God change their minds. In this their quietnefs we are not to trouble them.

We truft the unanimitie of Scotland, and the concurrence of the Prefbyterian partie in England, by God's bleffing, will be abundantly able to doe the fervice; only we defire not to be impeded by the rifing of malignants in diftinct armies of their owne, for if armies aryfe to purfue ends contrary to our Covenant, and deftructive to our maine defigne, though in fome things they goe along with us, how can we take them for friends, and not be juftly affrayed that fo foon as they find it time, they will turne as bitter enemies to us as fometime we have felt them, fince their principles remaine unchanged.

In the matter of thefe two Demands, all I meet with profeffe a great deale of reafon; if there be any fcruple in the third and laft, let us fhortly confider :—Here we doe only require a fecuritie for keeping what fhall be promifed in the two former; we have been fo foully deceaved by many men who of late did make us very folemne promifes of conftant friendfhip, that our fcrupulofity in any new undertaking might juftly be excufed, yet all the fecurity here we crave, is but a verie fimple one as the affaires of the world now goe. What lefs can we require of men who avow their full refolution to performe all we crave, than their oath to be conftant When we have agreed on all the reft, fhall we differ in this? What is it that ftumbles in our third demand? Is it the matter of the oath? There fhall be nothing here bot what themfelves doe grant, and ufe to profeffe to be reafonable. Is it the forme of the oath? What needs any fcruple to fwear what they profeffe to be juft for the matter, and themfelves firmely refolved to performe. If this be ftood upon, will it not give us juft caufe to fear that all which is now promifed, is bot for ane allurement once to ingadge, and then to difappoint us of all our expectation? Is there not a militarie oath required of all armies? What prejudice were it if to the ordinary articles of the warre, fome few more were added for our fecuritie in our two demands, at leaft for the officers and committees, with a declaration of Parliament and Generall Affembly, injoyning fo much

I remitt it to your ingenuity if our fticking upon thefe fo few, fimple, moft neceffarie Demands, deferve the feveritie of that cenfure, which the unadvifednefle of fome is pleafed to put upon us; alfo whether it be not a great temerity in them, who rather than to give us fatiffaction, choofe to goe on without us to prefent action, though they know that without our affiftance, a great part of the people will neither have heart nor hand to concurre with them. We are extreame forry for this precipitation, and affrayed of its iffue. Where are either their men, money, or ammunition, requifite for fuch ane undertaking? Is not the enemie ready to receave them, and wayting on upon their firft too well known defigne? If they fhould be repulfed at firft, would it not extreamlie difcourage their friends in England, and hazard the ruin of all the remainder of the King's hopes? Were it not good to ftay but a little, till a more wife and patient dealing did unite us at home, and we had fome time to forme and furnifhe ane armie with things neceffare, and to ftrengthen our correfpondences abroad, in England, and elfewhere. The advantages of a little delay feem to preponder all we can expect by too fudden a motion; the breaking of that handfull, which for the time we can fend into England, may make the Prefbyterian partie there to faint, and give over all acting more for themfelves; may draw in upon Scotland fo much of the Sectarian armie as will overrun all our plaine countrey, and in a fhort time infect our Church with the leaven of their doctrine, and change the government of our eftate. When wife men will not be pleafed to goe on in a way of reafon, to avoid apparent dangers, occafion is given to fear their defignes, and of driveing them on for fome purpofes of their owne. Certainly the picking of quarrells with minifters, and moveing of controverfies betwixt the Parliament and Commiffion of the Church, at this nick of time, to the eyes of the moft beholders, proceeds either from little wifdome, or leffe fincerity to promote really the intended defigne of reftoring the King. Shall it be thought that wife men can intend to make warre abroad for any good purpofe, when, in the beginning of their enterprize, they keep up and increafe old divifions, and make more new quarrells at home. Men of judgment ufe to be perfuaded of reall intentions, not by great words and deep oathes, but by confonancy of actions.

It were all the pities of the world, that, when we are fo near to a full unanimitie for a cheerfull atchieving of fo brave an enterprize as is now in hand, we fhould by the malignant influence of any evill counfellors, moft need lefflie fall a-pieces, and lay, by our owne hands, in the ruins of our Church, State, neighbours, King, and pofteritie; the advancement of the Sectarian army to a higher pitch of power than yet they have attained, or fcarcely dare expect. Wayes of faction, of proud and haughty difdaine, mindfullnefs of wrongs, refolution to have all at under who ftand in the way of our overruleing, are unfitt medicines for our fore-fick and dying patients, whether the King and Royall Family, or our brethren of England, or our own much weakened and exceedinglie endangered Countrey.—So much of our other day's difcourfe have I drawn up for your memorie, that ye may know how ready I am to ferve yow upon all occafions.

Edinburgh, March 8th 1648.

For Mr. William Spang. March 27th [1648]

Reverend and Dear Cousine,

It's now long fince I heard from yow: in my laft by the London poft, I defyred yow to write allwayes what of mine yow receave, that I may know what mifcarries; alfo to try, with all the diligence yow can, who that Jean Dalyell, fpoufe to James Reid, can be, who gott a teftimoniall from the minifters of Gorcome of the birth of her fon. I deadly fufpect fhe is a whore who is retired to bear her child to fome man of quality near us: it were good to find it out. That book you wrote of, *Res Gestæ Marchionis Montis Rosini*,[9] let us have it. It's a mervaill to me that any there fhould be taken with De Cartes's way: Revius demonftrates him a very ignorant atheift. I have diverfe of his former pieces; fend to me what he has writ-

[9] The well known work by Dr. George Wishart, afterwards Bishop of Edinburgh containing a History of the War in Scotland under the conduct of the Marquis of Montrose, which was publifhed in 1647, under the title of "*De Rebus &c. sub imperio illustriss Jacobi Montisrosarum Marchionis, &c. præclare gestis, Commentarius*"

ten this laft yeare; alfo the laft decade of Strada; with the foume of all my compt I am in your debt: though I oft offered, yet did your Mother never call for a pennie from me. She and all friends are well. Your Nephew, I hope, fhall prove a gelly ladd; but how all is in Glafgow, I doe not know, for thefe fix weeks I have been in Edinburgh. I thank God I have gotten the differences betwixt the Principall and Mr. David, reafonable well compofed; this halfe year no difpleafure betwixt them.

In our great perplexities at home, it's fome comfort to us when we look abroad, that your churches, and thefe of France and Suits [Switzerland], enjoyes a happie quietnefs, both ecclefiafticall and civill. I am glad there is fo little dinn of Ameraut's new queftions. Alfo we bleffe God that the Swedes yet can keep the fields in Germanie, and that cruell perfecutor and oppreffer of Bavier is yet likely to be taken order with by the Swedes and French; and that the old cruelties of Spayne are now come to remembrance; that Portugall with all its appurtenances, that Catalonia and Naples doe ftill preferve themfelves: It muft be the juftice of the great revenger upon that proud and unjuft croune. If Modena could bring Millaine lykewife to revolt, Italy would be quite of all forraigne yocks; but I fear the fall of Spayne fhall lay open thefe parts of Chriftendome to the Ottoman invafion; yet that the Venetian alone for fo long a tyme hes been able to fuftaine the warre in Creta, againft the whole ftrength of that enemie, puts me in hope that the danger of them is not fo great as fometimes it hes been. The fpoill of Heffen and continuance of the Palatine's miferies, afflict us. We have no more of thefe forraigne affaires, than what yow and the London moderate intelligence furnifh us.

He is wyfer than a man who can informe what courfe our affaires here will take. This is the feventh week that I have been forced to attend in Edinburgh; and yet we fee fmall appearance of any good conclufion; but as they are I make yow the accompt of them. After that the King found himfelf difappointed of all the fair hopes made to him by Cromwell and his partie, whether on their repentance, or their feare from Lilburne, Rainborough, and their levelling friends, our Commiffioners made more ferious applications, and were more acceptable than before. At the Ifle of Wight, his Majeftie did live with them very lovinglie; and upon great hopes on all hands, Traquair, Sir John Cheefly, Callander, and all that came home before them, gave it out confidently, in the generall, that the King had given to our Commiſſioners full ſatiſfaction. This cauſed great joy, and a readineſs in all to riſe in arms quickly for his deliverance. But when I found all bound up by oath, [not] to reveale any of the particular conceſſions till the Commiſſioners returned, I feared the ſatiſfaction ſhould not be found ſo ſatiſfactory as wes ſpoken. The too long and ſtrict ſecreſie bred prejudice in the minds of the wifeſt: and when we heard the report from the Chancellour and Lauderdale at their returne, our ſuſpicions were turned into griefe. for we found the conceſſions no ways ſatiſfactory, and the engagement of ſome to the King upon them ſo great, as did much blemiſh their reputation with many of their moſt intime friends. Our debates more than a fortnight were to come to the bottom of theſe offers, and to find way how we might be free of them. We were malcontent with our Commiſſioners: their ſcurvy uſage by the Parliament of England, their compaſſion of the King's condition, Lanerick's power with Lauderdale, and both their workings on the Chancellour, made them to accept of leſſe, and promiſe more to the King, than we would ſtand to. They were content we ſhould declare our unſatiſfaction with the King's offers as we thought fitt, both by the Church and State, on condition we would conſent to a leavie againſt the faction of Sectaries. To this we were not unwilling, provyding we might be ſatiſfied in the ſtate of the queſtion, and might be aſſured, that the armie ſhould be putt in ſuch hands as we might confide in. Both theſe were promiſed to us in private; but while we found no performance, the buſſineſs is retarded to this day. Betwixt the Chancellour, Duke, Argyle, Treaſurer, Lauderdale, Lanerick, Balmerino, Warriſtone, Mr. Robert Dowglaſs, Mr. George Gilleſpie, Mr. David Calderwood, Mr. Robert Blair, Mr. David Dickſone, Mr. Samuell Rutherfoord, many meetings have been had, night and day, private and publick; but as yet our diſcords increaſe, and are ready to breake out in a fearfull rupture both of Church and State. Our meetings were long in private for a ſtate of a queſtion; we required peremptorily to ſtand to our former principles and Covenant; "To have religion ſettled firſt; and the King not reſtored till he had given ſecurity, by his oath, to conſent to ane Act of Parliament for injoyning the Covenant in all his dominions, and ſettling religion according to the Covenant." We ſtuck many days on that negative expreſſion, "The King not to be reſtored till he had ſworn the Covenant." Thus much had both our Parliament and Affemblie preffed upon him at Newcaftle; yet at laft we were content of affirmitive expreffions: "Religion and the Covenant to be fettled, and thereupon the King to be reftored." The next difficultie in the queftion was about the Malignants: we were peremptore to have none of them in our armie who fhould not take the Covenant, and to have all of them declared enemies who fhould aryfe in armies by themfelves for any end contrare to our caufe. Here we had great ftrugleing: In the wryte, which we called ane Agreement and Engagement, they the King's Offers, too great favour, was fhewed to Malignants: we refolved to beware of them fo much the more. The greateft ftick of all was on the oath· we refolved to have thefe things put in a formall oath, to be taken folemnlie by all the members of Parliament and officers of our armie; they declined ane oath by all means While we are like to come to no agreement about thefe things, the pulpits found loud againft the dangers from Malignants, but more fofthe againft Sectaries We prepare alfo a Declaration of dangeis and duties, wherein we expreffe to the full our difatiffaction with the King's conceffions in matters of religion This gave a great offence to our Commiffioners We had put them to it to give us in wryte the report of what paft between them and the King concerning religion; for his Majeftie in his letter to us had faid, he had offered to them what he was confident would give us fatiffaction. While they are neceffitate to give us in wryte thefe private conceffions, and be content to have them, and our reafons againft them, publifhed to the world; they were not a little offended: but there was no remeed To our fence, they had paft the bounds of their dutie, though both the Committee of Eftates, and Parliament itfelfe, had, in a faire generall, without examination, approved all they had done. We thought it deftructive to our caufe and Covenant, and ourfelves abfolutelie impeded from all motion for the King till thefe grounds of motion were publicklie difclaimed. It increafed our offence, that fo many noblemen did vex us with debates and votes openlie in face of the Commiffion, after we had changed, in private, for the fatiffaction of the Chancellour and Lauderdaill, many paffages of our wryte; alfo that they had laboured to their power to make a partie among the minifters to oppofe us, Mr. Andrew Ramfay, Mr. Andrew Fairfoule, Mr. Robert Laurie, Mr. Andrew Affleck, and diverfe others; but efpeciallie Mr William Colville, who had in private objected againft one paffage, inferring the neceffitie upon confcience to reftore the King prefentlie to the exercife of his full regall power in all his dominions, notwithftanding of all he had done, without any condition, either of Covenant, Religion, or Propofitions; that we were obliged to doe this duetie unto him, and never more to oppofe till we found him abufe this power; and then we might refift, albeit no more but the abufe of this power. I did think it enough in our fub-committee to bring him to acknowledge fo fhamefull a tenet, all of us thinking he would not have the boldnefs any more in publick to fpeak to fuch a purpofe, yet in the face of the Commiffion, in a very jeering infolent way, being a little provoked by the indifcreet challenge of Mr. Rutherfoord, he did offer to reafon for fuch a conclufion. We had not failled to have called him to ane accompt for his malapertnefs, had not the intervention of other greater affairs diverted us.

By this time the Parliament was fett. Never fo many noblemen prefent in any of our Parliaments; near fyftie Earls and Lords. Among whom were found but eight or nyne for our way; Argyle, Eglintone, Caffillis, Louthian, Arbuthnot, Torphichen, Roffe, Balmerino, Cowper, Burleigh, and fometimes the Chancellour and Balcarras. All the reft, with more than the halfe of the barrons, and almoft the halfe of the burgeffes, efpeciallie the greater tounes, Edinburgh, Perth, Dundee, Aberdeen, St. Andrews, Linlithgow, ran in a ftring after Duke Hamilton's vote. That partie, befides the advantage of the number of two at leaft to one, had lykewife the moft of the ableft fpeakers. For us none did fpeak but Argyle and Warrifton, and fometymes Caffillis and Balmerinoch; but they had the Duke, the Thefaurer, Lanerick, Lauderdale, Traquair, Glencarne, Cochrane, Lee, all able fpokesmen; yet the other partie had the advantage of reputation, having from the beginning been conftant in our caufe. alfo all the affiftance the Church could make was for them. The firft bickering was for our Declaration: when, contrare to their minds, we had paft it, they were earneft it might not be publifhed; but we had given order, as ever had been our cuftome, to print it, even before we had communicate it to the Parliament. They had diverfe purpofes, either by perfwafion or violence, to have keept it in; but we let it goe out on Monday, and ordained it to be read on Sunday thereafter in all the Kirks of Edinburgh, and about. That which haftened it out was our irritation by the Thefaurer's challenge of Argyle on the Monday morning; ane unhappie accident, that was ready to have kindled the fire amongft us all, had not the Lord prevented it. Argyle's enemies had of a long tyme burdened him, among many flanders, with that of cowardice and cullionrie. On the Fryday afternoon in Parliament, difcourfing merrilie with the Thefaurer, he faid, He heard of a meeting whereat the Theafurer had been the other night. Speaking a little of this purpofe, he apprehended, that the Thefaurer had faid, not only that the beft men of the kingdome had been at that meeting, but alfo that himfelfe was a better man than he. Upon this, Argyle goes out of the Houfe in anger, and calls for Major Innes, who had fitten at both their feet, and heard their difcourfe, to know if he had heard the Thefaurer fay, that himfelfe was a better man than Argyle. Innes did not avow the words; but being fent to the Thefaurer from Argyle, to try if he had fpoken fo, he faid, He would not make accompt to Argyle what he faid; but whatever it was, he would make it good with his fword. Upon this, Argyle defired him to appoint tyme and place, and on the Sunday, a publick faft-day, the Thefaurer fent back word, after both fermons, that on Mufleburgh Links, at feven o'clock to-morrow morning, he fhould meet him, and bring a nobleman for a fecond. Innes, albeit no great friend to Argyle, not only offered himfelfe to Argyle for a fecond, but told him he would refent it as a wrong if he were not admitted; fo Argyle with no flefh but Innes, the Thefaurer and Lanerick his fecond, did meet. Incontinent all were miffed, and many rann out to all quarters to fearch them, and, by God's providence, before they began their pley, fome fell on them, and made them part without a ftrocke. The counfell that night, with much adoe, gott them to a profeffed coldryfe friendfhip. We had refolved in the Commiffion of the Church, to have made both before the congregation acknowledge their fault; fo much the more, as Sinclare and David Lefley, Eghntone and Glencarne, fome dayes before, and fome dayes after, Kenmure and Cranftone, had been on the like engagements: but other matters put that out of our heads.

The publifhing of our printed Declaration put fome of the Parliament on many hard thoughts of us, but the refult of all was, the calling of fix of us to conferr with fix of their great committee upon a ftate of a queftion. For them were, Lauderdale, Lanerick, Humbie, Lee, Archibald Sidferfe, and Sir Alexander Wedderburn, with the Chancellour, for us, Mr. David Calderwood, Mr David Dickſone, Mr George Gilleſpie, Craighall, Libbertone, I, with the Moderator Mr. Robert Dowglaſs. They produced to us a draught of a declaration, penned with a great deall of deliberation, by the counſell of many, but ſpecially by Lanerick's pen. They had ſlandered us exceedinglie, as oppoſite to all warre with the Engliſh Sectaries in any termes. To clear that miſtake, I wrote, and put in diverſe hands, Lanerick's among others, the paper which herewith I ſend yow. Their draught did endeavour to give pretty good ſatiſfaction to moſt of our doubts; yet, after one day's advyſement, we found it ſo unſatiſſactorie, that themſelves were content we ſhould take it to our conſideration to be corrected as we found expedient. Mr. Gilleſpie and my Lord Warriſtone had drawne ane oath of aſſociation, which pleaſed themſelves well, but their oppoſites extreamly ill, and their beſt frends but ſo and ſo, when beſt corrected. In our draught we took ſo much of their declaration, and our frends oath of aſſociation, as we thought made a ſtate of a queſtion which ſhould be ſatiſfactorie to all; and here, to my great joy, were we on the very nick of a cordiall agreeance · but behold ane moſt unhappie accident, which did put us to, and yet hes keeped us in, a diſcord almoſt irreconcileable. There was a great deſyre in the cheife that were for ane engagment, to ſeaſe on Berwick and Carliſle, both for the extreame great advantage of theſe places, and alſo to beginne the warre, for the encourageing of our frends abroad, and wakening our people at home. This they counted no wrong, nor invaſion of England; their quarrell being only againſt the Sectaries and their adherents, for vindicating of our Covenant, for the reſcue of the King, and Parliament, and oppreſſed Covenanters. Ane indiction needed not againſt this enemie: the tounes of England, for our paſſing and ſafe retreat in the proſecution of the common cauſe, ought to be patent; yet the moſt of us were averſe from this deſigne, and had long kept it off. In a few dayes we found the Parliament, two parts for one, otherwiſe affected than we wiſhed. So ſoon as it was conſtitute, there was ane inclination to make a cloſe committee for the greateſt affaires: ſix of every ſtate were named. So long as their power was not determined, we were not ſtartled, but ſo ſoone as they gott ane abſolute power to doe what was fitting for the ſafetie of the Kingdome, in relation to Berwick and Carliſle, incontinent all was alarmed. Forty-ſeven of the truſtieſt members of Parliament did proteſt againſt that vote. The proteſtation was not admitted:

you have the copy here, but the protefters thereafter did keep themfelves together, and albeit the leaft, yet they keeped the reputation of the beft part of the Parliament Privately and publickly we gave warning, that the paffing of fuch a vote would break us irrecovereably ; but we were beleeved too late. My Lord Callander's partie were fo furiouflie earneft to poffeffe Berwick, and to begin action, that they threatened to defert Hamilton and his friends if they did delay that vote any longer . fo it paffed, notwithftanding our earneft intreatings, and our friends proteftations to the contrare. The iffue was, we refufed to conferr any more on the ftate of ane queftion. The protefters confirmed their union. Many of the fhires fent in to fupphcat againft all engagement, unlefs the Kirk were fatiffied in the ftate of a queftion. David Lefley, and Holborne, with the reft of the officers, declared their refolution, not to move without our fatiffaction After fome dayes conteft, we found a great change. The Chancellour, that had hitherto been too farr for the engagers, offended with their unreafonable proceedings, came almoft wholly off them to us his old friends and beft. The chieff of the Duke's friends came to entreat us to accept all we could defyre, to ftate the queftion according to our mind, to be affured to have fuch in our armies and committees as we lyked, to give over the furprife of Berwick, and all acting by the clofe committee. Thefe things, by the Thefaurer and others, were offered to us, with many faire and earneft expreffions. As yet we are not fatiffied by words, and fome of our leaders are likely never to be fatiffied, and refolves to truft to nothing which their oppofits can doe or fay, fo long as this Parliament, which they pronounce unfound, is in being. The danger of this rigiditie is lyke to be fatall to the King, to the whole Ifle, both Churches and States : we mourne for it to God Though it proceed from two or three men at moft, yet it feems remedielefs · if we be keeped from a prefent civill warre, it's God, and not the wifdome of our moft wife and beft men, which will fave us I am more and more in the mind, that it were for the good of the world, that Churchmen did meddle with Ecclefiaftick affaires only ; that were they never fo able otherwife, they are unhappie ftatefmen ; that as Erafliane Cæfaro-Papifme is hurtfull to the Church, fo ane Epifcopall Papa-Cæfarifme is unfortunate for the State. If no man were wifer than I am, we fhould not make fo many fcruples to fettle the throne, and pull down the fectaries. Never more high and more dangerous queſtions in Scotts hand: what the concluſion ſhall be, a few days will declare.

While we are ſticking in theſe labyrinths, one of our number, not of the moſt rigid, falls on the overture to propone the Commiſſion of the Generall Aſſemblie's deſires altogether immediately to the Parliament, wherein, if we gott ſatiſfaction, we were to goe on as they deſyred us, to ſtate a queſtion. The motion was approved. His draught of eight articles, after ſome changes of it to the worſe, was paſt, and preſented, in name of the Commiſſion of the Church, by Mr. Robert Blair, Mr. Robert Ramſay, and I. For anſwer, the eighteen of their firſt great committee, with the addition of ſix more, twenty-four in all, the prime members of Parliament, were appointed to conferr with us on theſe our deſyres. The Commiſſion, to theſe ſeven who had mett before with the ſub-Committee of Parliament upon their Declaration, added Mr. Robert Blair and Mr. Andrew Cant. On the Thurſday, before noon, they went through the firſt five of our deſyres. All the ſticking was on the fyfth, wherein we preſſed to have the Malignants who ſhould ryſe in armes by themſelves declared enemies, as well as Sectaries. This was contrare to the King's agreement with ſome, and their intentions, who, without the help of Malignants, made the worke impoſſible. At laſt we carried the article. In the afternoone we had almoſt differed on the ſixth, the King's oath to conſent to ane Act of Parliament for enjoyning the Solemn League before his reſtitution to the exerciſe of the royall power. We preſſed him not to take the Covenant; but whatever his conſcience was, we conceaved him bound to conſent to the neceſſare lawes of the Kingdome. Thus his good-dame Queen Mary aſſented to the Acts of Parliament for the Reformed Religion This alſo did paſſe for the ſubſtance; only a committee was appointed to ſmooth ſome expreſſions about the King's reſtitution. We had no power to recede from any word, and ſo would not be at any committee for changing any expreſſion, but believed the Commiſſion of the Kirk would not ſtick at words, if the matter were well ſecured. On the ſeventh article, for manageing the war by confident hands, there was not much debate. We could here fall on no words which might not be granted, and yet little for our advantage; albeit on this was the greateſt of all our difficulties. Upon the conſtitution of the army depended all our human ſafety, hope, and ſecuritie of whatever elſe was granted It goes now fo, that no truſt remaines to any words or oathes; except therefore force were in the hands of our friends, we refolved not to fturr; and yet we could not crave any fuch particulare, but had neceſſitie to have it done one way or other. Some underhand did move to have the Duke Generall. Callander and his friends were carefull to free us of this feare; for generally all but the Duke's owne followers doubted much the finceritie of his intentions, either for Religion or for the King; albeit I confeſſe, when ever I heard him or his Brother fpeake in earneſt, they feemed to me to give ample fatiſſaction; but as yet they have not the fortune to be much believed by many. Ochiltrie's bufinefs fticks ftill in the throats of fome. Upon too great probabilitie, Callander, by his owne partie, which is great, is wiſhed Generall: but his inflexibilitie to ferve againſt Montrofe, upon the fenfe of private injuries, whereby indelible marks of difgrace were printed on the face of Scotland, and his very ambiguous proceedings in England at Hereford and elfewhere, make us that we dare not put our lives and religion in his hand. David Lefley and Holborne are more beloved by us. The old Generall, for all his infirmitie, is acceptable; alfo Middleton, and the Generall of the artillery, will not be refufed. In private we were aſſured thefe fhould be the Generall Officers, but we will not be aſſured without fight, and our maine difficultie will be upon the committees to govern the State and Army in the intervalls of the feſſions of Parliament. If herein they permitt them whom we count truftie, to have full power, when they can carry what they will in Parliament, it's a great wonder, yet if in this we gett no fatiffaction, nothing elfe will fatiffie: we expect little debate on the eighth article, to have ane oath for all this; but herein we were peremptor, and hopes to obtaine. It was my wifh, that only the Parliament and officers of the army fhould fweare, and that the body of the land fhould be put to no more oaths; but it feems this aſſociation muſt be no leſſe fworne than our two former Covenants.

While thus farr we had proceeded on Thurfday, I thought we were as good as agreed, fo I refolved to go home to-morrow; for the opening of our provinciall Synod lay on me as the laft Moderator; alfo a new very dangerous infection was broken up in Glafgow, and come to my very gates. Upon thefe reafons, after eight weeks ftay, I gott leave from the Commiſſion to returne, albeit very hardly, for our bufinefs wes not fully clofed, and I had immediate acceſſe and truſt with fundry of the moſt leading men, with whom

I was efteemed to do no evill fervice; while others, by their way, did irritate more: Alfo we had refolved to have reafon of Mr William Colvill and his followers for their great and dangerous infolency, not fo much in their open contempt neglecting to read our Declaration, as in their fermons and private negotiations, both with noblemen and minifters, to frame a faction for dividing of our Church, wherein the peremptor rigidity of fome, the too great fimplicity of others, and the evill talents of more, gave them occafion to make too great progreffe; but having ftayed till I declared myfelfe abundantlie againft thefe men, and helped to bring them low, and put them in a way either to recant or be cenfured, I came away on the Fryday morning, and to my owne houfe at night, with one fhower from Falkirk, a wearie Monficur The Colledge was almoft totally diffolved for fear of the plague. My little daty was extreamely ficke, of a fudden, fo I found great appearance of the peft in my houfe; yet againft the morrow, the Lord, on as great a fudden, reftored my child to her full health. Since, we are waiting on the Lord's pleafure, what he will doe with Glafgow, whether yet it may be fpared from the plague, whereof I am not defperat; and what fhall be the next act of the long tragedie among us. Much fpeech of the Prince's coming · as yet our affaires are not in a condition to receave him as I could wifh, but ere long he may be welcome. I cannot, of certaine knowledge, hear any thing of that youth, whereby I can conjecture. on any hand, what to hope or feare His Mother's unkindnefs to the Queen of Boheme and her fones is vifibly retaliate in the eyes of all Europe. My beft wifhes are for the reftitution of King James's family · before this, I fee no appearance of any folid peace, either to Germany or Brittaine. This long letter fhall be a ground of a challenge, if yow wryte fo rare and fo fhort as this while bygone. Farewell.

Glafgow, this 28th of March 1648.

I have oft propofed to yow, which yet I repeat, that it would be a good fervice to fchollars, and profitable for printers, if yow could, by yourfelfe and friends there, ftur up fome of your Amfterdam and Leiden ftationers to print by the alone, the Chaldee Bible with a Latine verfion interlinear, or otherwife, in one or two volumes; Buxftorph's Bible, and the new Paris one would furnifh good helpe for the right printing; alfo ane Arabick Bible and

VOL. III

a Syriack Bible interlinear, and well printed, would not faill to fell; and the Paris Bible, which few doe or may buy, would furnifh a good prototype. It would likewife doe much good if young Buxftorph would print over his Father's Mafora and Rabbin commentares, in one book, in common Hebrew letters, with the points and Latine expofition. Give me ane account if any thing may be gotten done of this kind.

For Mr Z[achary] B[oyd.]

We are to intimate that this prefent Engagement, as it is ftated in the Parliament's Declaration, is holden by the Kirk to be unlawfull upon thefe three grounds efpecially :—

1. That the end of it is to bring the King to London with honour, freedome, and fafety, without fo much as craveing from him any fecurity for Religion, though he ftill declares himfelfe as much for Epifcopacie, and averfe from our Covenant, as ever

2. Becaufe all the Malignants in England and Ireland are permitted to rife in alfo many armies as they can, and we refufe to take them as before for enemies, except they profefs to oppofe us or the Covenant; this quicklie makes our former enemies our mafters.

3. The manageing of this Warre is putt in the hands principallie of thefe men, whofe bygone life and known profeffions declare they mind not religion; and they who have hitherto, in our bygone troubles, been moft eminent inftruments of God and the countrey, for the advancement of the worke of religion, and the liberty of the land, are fhuffled by, and all power plucked out of their hands.

Thefe and many more reafons make us, (who were moft cordiall for a Warre, againft the Sectaries of England and their adherents, for the vindication of our Covenant, for the delyverance of our oppreffed brethren in England, for the refcuing of our King from his unjuft imprifonment, and reftoreing of him to the exercife of his royall power, upon his performance of thefe neceffare duties which the Parliaments of both Kingdomes did require from him; and for the prefervation of our Church and State from the violence of that evill faction of fectaries, whofe principles drive at the everting of the foundations of all government, both of Church and State of the whole Ifle : We are hindered notwithftanding,) that we cannot joyne in the prefent Engagement, which is faid to be againft them, fince it's evident that the courfe now taken is either not truely againft them, but will tend to their eftablifhment, as many fear, or elfe for fetting up in their place our former enemies, for the overthrow of all we have been doing thefe eleven years. So in our judgement, none who will ferioufly mind religion and a good confcience, will joyne either in perfone, goods, or counfell, in this undertaking, and if by violence they be drawne to give any affiftance, they muft be content prefently to fuffer what may be put upon them, rather than to act any thing that may promove that which they efteem unlawfull.

For Mr. M[atthew] B[risbane.]

If the difcord goe on, it's humanlie impoffible to efchew either a grievous perfecution, or a civill warre at home, and a totall neglect of the pretended welfare of the King. For a remeed, I wifh the Parliament gave a good anfwer to our fupplications, and fufpended the leavy for a fortnight, and appointed a conference betwixt a doflan of the wifeft of both fides. I think we muft have fatiffaction in four things, in ane explanatorie Declaration. 1. That the State will not take from the Church the antecedent judgement in any matter of religion 2. That before the King's full freedome, they will crave of him fecurity for Religion. 3 That we declare, as before, againft Malignants in armes, without If's or And's 4 That in the Armie and Committees, men of conftant integritie may have much more power Some things of this kind, I wifh were offered, and that fo foon as may be.

For Mr William Spang. June 26th [1648.]

Reverend and Dear Cousin,

Since my laft, March 28th, I have heard nothing from yow, nor long before Our affaires fince have had a great progrefs, but no inch to the better; all appearance of any poffibilitie to agree, daylie does more and more evanifh A fpirit of bitternefs, jealoufie, and mutuall contempt, grows on all hands, and the ftronger partie is begun to perfecute the weaker; and that evill is lyke much to increafe quickhe. The courfe of affaires may draw both, befide any intention, to doe the worft of that which has been objected to either as their defigne. The fectaries and malignants may fhorthe divide the whole Ifle, to the great danger and hurt of the King and the honeft Prefbyterians in both kingdomes Our ftorm is yet but waxing; we can make but fmall judgement of its end.

When I clofed my laft to yow, as then I wrote, there was fome good hope of concord, a pretty good anfwer was expected to our eight defyres, but fome unhappie men made all thefe hopes to flee away. The Committee of twenty-four framed their anfwer, and gott it paft in ane Act of Parliament, before it came to the Commiffion of the Kirk. They to whom the confideration of it was committed, looked fo narrowly into every word of it, that they found fnares in every other line, and not one of our eight defyres fatiffied This much the Commiffion reprefented in a new paper, [and] added a new defyre, to declare againft the negative voice of the King, which the Commiffioners papers in England had fo much preffed. This draught of Mr. Ja[mes] G[uthrie's,] in the abfence of Mr. George G[illefpie,] was as ill taken when it came to the Parliament as any other, and fo was as good as laid afide, till in the large Declaration they gave it ane anfwer. In the mean time, they putt out the act of pofture for fetting all the Kingdome in a defence againft invafion; but in few dayes comes out the act of leavy, which, incontinent, allarumed all. The firft narrative was ill taken, a danger from the Malignants that had taken Berwick and Carlifle The world knew there was no danger to us from them, for they had been with us in Edinburgh, and their enterprize upon Berwick and Carlifle was generally beleaved not to have been undertaken without fome of our privities The act therefore, before publifhing, was helped, grounding our leavy on the danger from the army of fectaries, which thefe furprifes would draw downe on our Borders; and in this there is lyke to be no falfe prophecy

Here it was where our difference began firft to be irreconcilable We ftood on the managers of the warre as much as any one thing. The committees of fhyres, and crowners for the pofture, were indifferent; but when it came to the leavy, generally all the crowners of horfe and foot were chofen as my Lords Hammilton and Callander lyked. Our friends here gott very little of their will; but the cope-ftone was putt upon our defpaire, when we found Hammilton and Callander, how much contrare foever one to another, yet at laft, after there had been much fpeech and dealing of either to joyne with Argyle, and that, through whofe fault I know not, had mifcaryed; at laft I fay, Hammilton and Callander did joyne too friendly to our prejudice, and that in thefe termes, befides other, that the Duke fhould be Generall, and the Earle his Lieutenant Both of them to that time had been oppofed to the employment of either; and fo long as they had any hope of our complyance, both profeffed a great deale of willingnefs to continew the old generall officers, without any change, and each offered to marre the employment of the other; but when they could not draw our friends to ingage in any termes lyking them, then peremptorilie they ftrooke hands, and went on without much more notice of us

With threats and promifes they moved old Lefley to lay downe his place. For a long time we had hopes the army, which wee had keeped from diffolving, fhould have been firme to us; but Middleton fpoiled that our hope. All the officers had joyned in a fupplication to the Parliament backing the defyres of the Kirk. Had this been ftood to, the defignes of others had foon been broken; bot Middleton, who long had fhifted fubfcription, at laft was willing to joyne, with ane addition of a fhort poftfcript of the fubfcribers willingnefs notwithftanding to obey all the Parliament's directions. This commentare did fo enervate the text, that our friends perfuaded the officers to lay afide their petition, as that which was profitable for nothing, being clearlie emafculat by the poftfcript. From that day we loft the Army David Lefley, by much dealling of many, was made willing to keep his place, yet afterward he repented, and gave it over; and fo did Holborne, and diverfe more of the moft gallant of their officers, when they faw the Church's advyce totally neglected.

Thefe things did grieve much the fpirits of many, and I believe few more deeply than my owne, fo that my health by griefe for many dayes was impaired; yet, by the importunitie of many, I was (before fully recovered) drawn back againe to Edinburgh. Then I found that matters totally were defperate. Lauderdaill with greif, the Thefaurer with many tears, told me, how fore againft their heart they went the way now they were in, cafting the wyte on others; who yet aſſured me, for their parts, that they found never any truth in the faire generall offers was made them, when it came to any particular. However, then the dyce was caſt, every ſide were ingaged to go on in their own way

The Declaration, long and well ſtudied, and penned moſt by Lanerick, in very plauſible termes, was offered to us. We appointed a committee for it. It was my advice to be ſhort in obſerving, and to pitch but on the maine exceptions On ſundry we agreed, and what ſome offered of their own concepts I gott out; yet falling to take phyſick, I was forced to keep my chamber ten days with a dangerous ſuperpurgation. In this intervall Mr. Gillefpie, without much contradiction, gott in[to] his repreſentation whatever either himſelfe or W[arriſtone] or G[uthrie] had collected, which made it tedriouſhe long, and in ſundry things needleſhe quarrelſome, and to come ſo late, that the Parliament, after ten days waiting for it, at Lauderdaill's cankered motion, commanded their Declaration to goe out without any more notice of what we had to ſay againſt it

At this time a meſſenger went to the Parliament of England with fyve demands, craveing an anſwer peremptorilie in fifteen dayes. That which they feared moſt was to ingage in any treaty. This we ever preſſed, but they thought it needleſs, ſince they quarrelled not with the Parliament, but with the army and their adherents, with whom they were not oblidged to treat, and loſſe the ſeaſon of the Engliſh motions at home. The rumour of our warre made great ſturrs in many parts both of England and Ireland, and put the Parliament to alter much of their former way, to grant London their militia, the Tower, the guard of the Parliament as before, the freedome of their impriſoned Aldermen, the recalling of the eleven members to their places, the reſtoreing the impeached Lords, the making Warwick Admirall of the Navy: the Army alſo was forced to divide; Cromwell to Wales, where yet he ſticks; Fairfaxe to the north, but in his march he was recalled to ſuppreſſe the Kentiſh: The moſt of the ſhires were on their feet. Had not our unhappie diſcords marred our expedition; had we with a ſmall army, with any unanimitie, but appeared on the Border in time, appearandly, without ſtrokes, we might have gotten for the King, for our friends, for ourſelves, what we pleaſed; but our fatall diſcords were as well known at London as at Edinburgh, ſo leaſure is taken by Fairfaxe to quiet Kent and Eſſex, and by Cromwell to hold down Wales, and by others to keep in Cornewall. Lambert in Yorkſhire had time to keep back Langdale from York and Lancaſhire; and great pains are taken to joine the Preſbyterians and the Independents againſt all the ryſers in the ſhires, and our army, as againſt Malignants If this conjunction goe on, both the King and our Nation is in a hard taking.

In the mean time the Parliament and Commiſſion proceed in their paper-differences. Their Declaration and our Repreſentation are both printed They goe on to act, we to preach, againſt the lawfullneſs of the Engagement as it was ſtated The randeſvouſes are appointed for the ſhires againſt the 21ſt of May. Many preſbyteries, ſynods, burghs, ſhires, gave in ſupplications the firſt of June, to delay the leavy till the Church gott fatiſfaction Our poor towne, ſtill ſingular in that unhappineſs, is made the firſt example of ſuffering. All of us, the towne-miniſters, went up to ſupplicat the Duke in Hammilton, in the name of the Preſbyterie, to delay the lifting of our people till our ſupplications were anſwered by the Parliament I ſpoke oft, and at length, to his Grace and Excellency, as Moderator of the Preſbyterie. We gott courteous and civill words enough; but deeds very bitter. Incontinent all our magiſtrates and toune-counſell, that ſame night, were ſummoned to anſwer to the Parliament, for not keeping with their men the randeſvous; a fault common to them with all their neighbour townes and ſhires, yea with the whole kingdome well near; yet they were all caſt in the tolbooth, and kept there diverſe dayes; and becauſe they profeſſed ſcruple of conſcience to further the leavy, they were all deprived of their places, and a commiſſion ſent to the old counſell that before was removed, to elect new magiſtrates; who made leſſe ſcruple, than I wiſh, to ſitt downe and name Colline Campbell Provoſt, John Anderſone, James Tran, William Neilſon, Baillies, and theſe, for a counſell, took the old caſheered men with a very little change: ſo great greefe is amongſt the new faction in our toune, and too great contentment in the old, to ſee themſelves reſtored to their places by the ſame men and means they were caſheered, the Parliament putting them in, and others out, only for following the advyce of their miniſters and Commiſſion of the Church.

But this is not all our miſery. Before this change, ſome regiments of horſe and foot were ſent to our towne, with orders to quarter on no other but the magiftrates, counfell, and feffion, and their lovers. Thefe orders were exerced with rigour · on the moft religious people of our towne, hudge burdens did fall; on fome ten, on fome twenty, on fome thirty fojours, and more, did quarter; who, befide their meat and drink, wine and good cheer, and whatever they called for, did exact cruelie their daylie pay, and much more. In ten dayes they coft a few honeft, but mean people, above forty thoufand pounds [Scotifh money], befides plundering of thefe whom neceffity forced to flee from their houfes. Our loffe and danger was not fo great by James Grahame.

No relief gott we, but by a greater mifchief. Many yeomen in Clydefdaill, upon fear to be leavied by force, had fled from their houfes to Loudoun hill, and their had mett in a body of fome hundred horfe and foot. Sundry of the fojours who had left the army, joyned with them. Much fpeech began of a refiftance in the Weft. Too many minifters, both eaft and weft, were faid to be for it, if there fhould appear a lykeliehood of a party. For myfelfe, I was cleare againft all fuch thing: I thought we had neither a juft caufe nor a good authority for any fuch matter, and the furtheft we might goe was no more than fuffering. While we are on thefe debates, Callander and Middleton comes weft on the Saturday 10th of June. About a fortnight before, Argyle had mett with Eglintoun and Caffilhs at Irwin : this meeting gave a fhew to the talke of a refiftance in the Weft ; Fyfe alfo feemed to look that way. but it appears now well, that the named noblemen, whatever they mett for, did conclude of no fuch thing; for Argyle prefently went home to Inverary, and Eglintoun declared himfelfe willing to let his men be leavied. However, Callander made hafte to make the Weft fecure. The Clydefdaill men came, on the Saturday, to Mauchline to communicate: that night Callander lay at Pafley. On Monday he made a randefvous at Stewarton, of one thoufand fix hundred good horfe, and above two thoufand foot, at ten houres; from thence he marched to Mauchline, fending Middleton before him with three hundred horfe. The noblemen and gentlemen of the fheriffdom of Aire had fitten late on the Saturday at a committee in Riccartoun finding that Fyfe had yielded, that Argyle was farr off and quiet, and Callander with ane army in their bofome, they refolved to lay afide all thoughts of refiftance, and of this advertifed the people at Mauchline. They notwithftanding would not diffolve, but after the fermon in the morning of Monday, fome twelve hundred horfe and eight hundred foot, with eight minifters, goes out to Mauchline-moore ; gentlemen or officers very few was among them. While they are about to choyfe fome, Middleton appears they expected no enemy in hafte, fo they were amazed at the fight. The minifters went to Middleton, and capitulated for the fafety of all, except the fojours who had left their colours, whereof were one hundred or two. This written capitulation the minifters did carry to the people, and perfuaded to their power their difbanding. The moft of the men of Kyle and Cunninghame were content to goe, but the fojours and Clydefdaill men would needs fight While they are more than an houre in this confufed uncertainty, and fundry crying to fight, Middleton makes a few of his horfe to charge; but the people prefently fled. His fojours abftained from killing, only fell a taking horfe, armes, and purfes. A troup of the people fleeing to a bridge, and miffing the way, were forced to ftand; they turned on the fojours and fought very ftoutly. Here was the moft of the flaughter; near fourty here fell: fome fay as many of the troupers as of the people. Middleton himfelf wes fore put to it by a fmith : he gott fome wounds ; and confeffes, had he not ftabbed the fmith, (though not deadly,) while he was bringing on him too great a ftroke, he had undoubtedly killed him. Many of the people were wounded By the time Callander and the army came up, the people were difperfed. They fpeake as if the Clydefdaill horfe were gone to Galloway, with a mind yet to fight; but I believe it not. There is indeed in our people a great animofitie put in them, both by our preaching and difcourfe; alfo by the extream great oppreffion of the fojours; fo that, it fears me, if Lambert be come to Carlifle with frefh men, and have put Langdale into the town, as they fay, fo foon as our army fhall be intangled with the Englifh, many of our people rife on their backs To prevent this, they have paft a fevere, and, as I think, ane unjuft and tyrannous Act of Parliament, to put all the fubjects of the Kingdom to fubfcribe their readinefs with life and eftate, to further the execution of the acts of this Parliament, meaning above all, the act of the leavy, which the Church hes fo much contradicted as unlawfull ; alfo to declare that the execution of the acts of this Parliament, are the moft neceffare and fitteft means to remeed our troubles, and preferve religion : and that all who fhall not fubfcribe this much, without delay, are juftly to be holden enemies to the common caufe, religion, and countrey We think the beft part of the land will never fubfcribe this, and fo that all of us who fhall refufe fhall be at their mercy. If I be put to this fubfcription, as readily I may fhortly, I think I may once more come to yow, and that to remaine longer. A fervice to any of your regiments, or any company of Englifh merchants, will be very welcome to me; which yow will be thinking of; for however yet they let minifters alone, and I have as much favour as any other, yet I think our troubles may fo increafe, that I may be glad to be out of Scotland It feems many of our people may incline to venture their lives, either alone or with the Englifh army, if it come near, againft them who now are employed, I am not for any fuch matter For feare of Sectaries, we have not joyned with Malignants; if for feare of Malignants, we fhould joine with Sectaries, it would be to me abominable: we who refolve neither to joine with malignants nor fectaries, may fall into great inconvenients, but the Lord's will be done.

Our approaching Generall Affemblie is like to be a dangerous one. The Moderator's tafk will be hard: I am in doubt if I fhall be at his election; the laft time I was neare it; I am feared more for it now; I incline by abfence to efchew it. Yow have here the pofture of our affaires as now they ftand I think they fhall be much worfe before they amend. It's fome refrefhment to us to look a little abroad. If Melander's death, and the worfting of the Bavarian army, near Augfburg, be true, I will be glad: no prince in the world I wifh more to be humbled than that wicked fox of Bavaria. I pity the great and unexpected miffortune of Guife in Naples What means your Zealanders to diffent from the peace with Spaine? Dreame they that the French would be a better or fo good a neighbour? Yow never wrote to me fo rarely as thefe twelve moneths. help this fault

FOR MR WILLIAM SPANG.   AUGUST 23D 1648

REVEREND AND DEAR COUSIN,

WHAT is become of yow fince your journey to Dantzick? I long much to hear, defyreing earneftlie to know your fafe return, and underftand how affaires goe in thefe bounds How things goe here fince my laft, I give yow this account. So foon as the motion in the Weft was crufhed, which now I find had proven a very high and dangerous commotion, had Callander delayed but two or three days to fee to it, the Duke with diligence did draw his forces together to the Border, both to eafe the poor country of their free quarter and grievous oppreffion, as alfo to put Lambert from hazarding the regaining of Berwick and Carlifle. The leaguer lay long about Penrith and Appleby before the Irifh troops, and foot-regiments from the north, came to him At laft they became a very confiderable force; the greateft that came from Scotland fince the beginning of thefe troubles, though far from the number, as I conceave, of twenty-two thoufand foot, and eight thoufand horfe, which common report made them. Never ane army was fo great a charge to the countrey; the foot-fojour for leavy-money, cloathes, and armes, cofting generally one hundred pounds, the horfemen three hundred merks, and their free quarter, being ane unlimited plundering of many very good and pious people. Our State hes now found, which fcarcely could have been believed, that, contrare to the outmoft endeavours of the Church, and all their friends, they can raife and maintain ane army, and doe what they will at home and abroad The wifdome of fome of us has made that practick to paffe, and the myftery of our weaknefs to be divulged much fooner than needed All wayes what the end will be, a little time will try. They are now in Lancafhire; Lambert hes no force to look upon them; the trained bands of the fhyres joyne not with him. Cromwell, with the few he could bring from Pembroke Caftle, having marched mid-way, is forced to returne to Wales, where the Lord Biron did raife a party fo foone as he had left it. Fairfax is yet at Colchefter. It feems the Houfes, and City, and Committee of the fhyres, have of purpofe withdrawne affiftance, that Fairfax at Colchefter, and Cromwell at Pembroke, fhould lye till their forces might melt away, and become contemptible. If London permitt the Prince to lye ftill in the Downes, and be mafter of their trade, it cannot but breed great alterations quickly. That the curfed army of Sectaries fhould evanifh in fmoke, and their friends in the Houfes, City, and Countrey, be brought to their well-deferved ruine; that the King and his family fhould be at laft in fome neernefs to be reftored to their dignity and former condition, I am very glad but my fear is great, that his reftitution fhall come by thefe hands, and be fo ill prepared, that the glorious reformation we have fuffered fo much for, fhall be much endangered, and the moft that fhall be obtained be but ane Eraftian weak Prefbyterie, with a tolleration of Poperie and Epifcopacie at Court, and of diverfe fects elfe-where. We, who might have been the cheefe inftruments to have ftopped this evill, are for the time fo farr at odds with our State, Army, and King, that the defpight which I feare all three hes at us, is lyke to further much that evill in England, and draw it ere long on Scotland alfo; but the Lord can eafily difappoint our fears. Our State, on pretence to attend to the Prince, whom, by my Lord Lauderdaill, according to the agreement at the Ifle of Wight, they are inviting hither, but really to keep downe infurrections of people in the Weft, are leavying one thoufand five hundred horfe more. They fufpect deadly, that the diffenters in Parliament, with the help of the Church, may raife the countrey, if their army were once deeply engaged or worfted in England. Of this I know no ground; bot men who are confcious of occafioning much griefe to many, falls in needleffe feare, and by the means of preventing, draws on their defervings. Our condition for the time is fadd: The peftilence in Glafgow, Aberdeen, and Edinburgh alfo; the continuance of very intemperate rain upon the cornes; the irreconcileable differences of Church and State, looking towards a very great perfecution of them who have been the beft inftruments both of Church and State, are great figns of the wrath of God; efpecially the hearts of the body of people being evidently hardened, and the minds lykewayes of the minifterie diverted from preffing that humiliation and mourning, which the times call for above all things elfe.

But leaving the State, our Generall Affemblie fat doun on Wednefday July 12th. On the Saturday before, I had been tormented with a paine in my tooth, more vehemently than ever with any other paine: this put me from preaching on Sunday, and ryding on the Monday This farr I was glad that I had a true excufe for my not appearing the firft day in the Affemblie, whence I had refolved, however, to have been abfent. Mr. Robert Dowglafs and Mr. Robert Blair preached well at the faft. The Affemblie fat till near eight at night choifing their Moderator. Every man's addition of three to the Moderator's lift, albeit a equall and fatiffactory way, yet it proves very longfome. Mr Robert Dowglafs named for his two, Mr. Andrew Cant, and Mr. George Gillefpie; the Affemblie added Mr. David Dickfon, and Mr. Robert Blair, and Mr. John Smith. Many named me; but I was well away. Mr. Robert Blair was doubtlefs the meeteft man;

but becaufe lately he had moderate, he gott few votes; Mr. Andrew Cant gott two; Mr. David Dickfon none: it went betwixt Mr. George Gillefpie and Mr Smith. Mr George did much deprecate the burden, as he had great reafon, both for his health's fake, and other great caufes, yet he did carry it.

The Seffion on Thurfday was fpent on the nomination of the Committees In all prior Affemblies, fome few of us mett the night before the Affemblie in Warriftone's chamber, with Argyle, the Chancellour, and fome others of our wifeft friends, to confider about the choifing of the moderator, committees, and chiefe points of the Affemblie. This preparation was now to our hurt neceffarily omitted: Argyle and the Chancellour were both abfent in their owne houfes, to efchew the fubfcription of the bond of maintainance; Warriftone did not appeare, not only for that caufe, but alfo left he fhould have been preffed to have pleaded againft the minifters —for the eight [feven] minifters prefent at Mauchline-moore were fummoned to anfwer as raifers of that tumult: Mr. William Guthrie, Mr. Matthew Mowat, and Mr. Thomas Wylie, were diffuaded to appear; Mr. Gabriell Maxwell, Mr. John Nevay, Mr. William Adair, Mr. Alexander Blair, did appear, and under their hand protefted, that, directly nor indirectly, they had not perfuaded the people to meet there that day. When for diverfe weeks they had been putt off from day to day, they were at laft difmiffed to a new citation. Allwayes the good Advocate, being refolved in his mind, if he had been put to it, to have pleaded for the minifters, and not againft them, was, with much adoe, moved by his friends to lurk for fome time till the ftorme went over.

The want of thefe private preparatory meetings, which the Moderator's health permitted him not to attend, did make our Affemblie needleffly long, and very tedious; for befydes that the Moderator's way of enquireing at fo many before every voice, was not for difpatch, his unacquaintance with the affaires of the committees before they came to the face of the Affemblie, made the reports unrype and unadvyfed, and fo oft needfull, after much debate in the Affemblie, to be recommitted. The committee of prime importance was that of publick affaires. Upon this the prime men were putt; but fo mixed, that the farr moft part was of the moft rigid difpofition When Mr. Robert Ramfay, and fome others, were moved to be added to the Moderator's lift of this committee, it was peremptorly refufed, upon this pretence, that he was upon another committee. By this means, were got out of that meeting whomever the Moderator pleafed, and on it whom he would

For examination of the proceedings of the late commiffion, Mr. John Moncrieffe, and Mr. John Row, and fome who had not before been commiffioners, were named Upon the feare, that they who had corrupted the Parliament, fhould have been alyke active to have procured commiffioners to our Affemblie conforme to their mind, it was carefully provided, that in all Prefbyteries they fhould be chofen who were moft zealous for the Covenant, and for the proceedings of the Commiffion of the Kirk, and for the maintainance thereof: fo this Affemblie did confift of fuch whofe mind carried them moft againft the prefent Engagement, which was the great and only queftion for the tyme. The ruling elders were, Caffilis, Louthian, Balmerinoch, Cowper, Torphichen, Kirkcudbright, Angus, Creigh, Moncreife, Nether-Pollock, &c. Southefke and Loure were alfo commiffioners ; but Loure appeared not, and Southefke finding himfelf putt on a mean committee, appeared no more. The chief conteft betwixt us and the Committee of Eftate, was lyke to be about the work of this committee for the Commiffion-book. They fent in Glencairne to defyre us delay to approve the proceedings thereof, till they had prepared their confiderations againft them The cuftome of the Affemblie, according to prior acts, was to examine with the firft the Acts of the Commiffion of the preceding Affemblie. The exceptions the State took at their proceedings were fuch as made their perfons uncapable to voice in the Affemblie till they were cleared : now the men were a great and chief part of this Affemblie, alfo the matter in queftion, the Engagement, was of a great concernment, and had for many moneths been in agitation betwixt the Church and State ; fo that long time needed not to fett down any thing concerning it So foon, therefore, as the report of that committee was ready, it was thought meet, without longer delay than ane night or two, to receave and vote it : All without a contrary vote was approven. This angered our Statefmen, and made them fee, that all hope to make the Affemblie divert from the way of the former commiffion, was defperate.

The firft ten or twelve days we had but one feffion in the day, the afternoone being given to the committees to prepare work for the Affemblie. In our committee for publick affaires, at our firft meeting, I found more work cutted out, and putt in other hands, than I well lyked. I did agree, that we fhould goe on as far as the Commiffion of the Church had done againft the Engagement; but I wifhed no further progreffe; yet it was proponed, and carried, to make a new publick declaration againft it; yea, to have a declaration to England for the fame effect. The drawing of thefe was committed to a fub-committee of fix, whereof I was glad to be none, but I was not content, when, to Mr. David Catherwood, Mr. Robert Kerr, and Mr John Smith, were joined Mr James Guthrie, Mr. John Livingftone, and Mr. John Macklelland; Mr. Robert Blair, and Mr. David Dickfon, were afterward added; and I was required to be added, but peremptorly refufed; for my mind was not very forward for the wrytes they were to draw

Fryday and Saturday were fpent on trying the commiffions Thefe of the Prefbyteries of Dunfe and Chirnfyde were rejected; the one had chofen Mr. Samuell Dowglafs, modeiator, the fame day that a complaint of him had come to them from the Commiffion of the Church, for his never appearing there but once, and that to diffent from the Church's declaration againft the Engagement. The other Prefbyterie's commiffion was rejected, becaufe they had putt in a ruling elder, who had entered a wrytten proteftation in the Prefbyterie againft the caufes of the late faft, relating to the Engagement The difaffection of thefe two Prefbyteries was much fpoken of; therefore it was thought fitt to appoint a vifitation, confifting of the moft zealous brethren of Edinburgh, Lothian, and Merfe, to cognofce and cenfure their carriage as they found caufe. The lyke courfe was taken with the Prefbyteries of Stirling and Dunkell they had not been exact enough in trying the alleadged malignancy of one of their number. This occafioned a vifitation of them lykewife. Mr. Harie Guthrie, a very bold man, but in this and the late Affemblies very quiet, gave in a petition againft this courfe; but rather than to make dinn in vaine, took it up againe In our committee we had, thefe dayes, fome reafonings about the commiffions from Burrows. none of us was much for the thing, but all for tollerating of them, for fear of offending the Burrows at this time; only the commiffion of Edinburgh was thought to be wrong; but none offered themfelves from that towne. The difcord betwixt their Magiftrates and Minifters was much more than I defired to fee: their fpleen againft one or two of their minifters was great. The wilfullnefs of fome rafh men to have Sir John Smith out of his place hes coft us deare.

Since they have gotten the Magiftracy of that Towne, who, to their power, hes carried all things there to the mind of them whom we little affected, one of their great cares hes been, to keep their kirks rather vaiking, than to plant them with any whom they lyked not. In choifing of minifters and commiffioners they took a new way. their commiffioners for the Affemblie they named in their Towne-Councell; their minifters alfo, as patrons, they elected there: they were content to propone the men elected, to the Seffion of that church where they were to ferve, but to no other. Much debate there was with them in a committee appointed for that end; but the refult was, that the commiffioners elected in their Councell fhould have the confent of their great Seffion, which is their fix Seffions joined; alfo the minifters whom they name in Councell, as patrons, fhall have the confent of the fix Seffions before they be prefented to the Prefbyterie. And in regard of their neglect to fupply their vacant places, now of a long time, the Affemblie did vote fix, whom they recommended to the great Seffion to choife four of them, and to obtaine their orderly tranfportations from the Commiffion of the Church. The men were, Mr. John Macklelland, Mr. George Hutchefone, Mr. Hugh Mackell, Mr. James Ferguffon, Mr James Naefmith, and Mr Robert Traile. All this hes added to the towne of Edinburgh's offence, and is thought will not further the plantation of their vacand places.

One of the Affemblie's committees I have ever been againft, though yet without fruit The towne of Edinburgh is fupplyed with the ableft men of the kingdom; their chiefe fervice fhould be in Affemblie-time The cuftome ever has been, that fo long as the Affemblie fitts, all thefe men are idle, and all their kirks muft be provided by members of the Affemblie. This makes many weake and ill-accommodate countrey preachers to fill thefe eminent roomes, at moft confiderable times This made the pulpits of Edinburgh be provided for on the Sundays, and week thereafter, worfe than needed.

On Monday allwayes we have the forenoon free, becaufe many goes out on the Sunday to the churches about. That tyme I fpent in a meeting with the Univerfities, and gott them to meet twice or thrice more, where we debated, and concluded the moft part of the overtures, whereof yow have here a double I intreate yow read the preface of Burgerfdick to his Logicks I find, that twenty yeares agoe, the profeffors of Leyden, with the confent of the fynods of Holland, have agreed on a courfe, to be taught, both in grammar-fchools and colledges, which the magiftrate hes commanded to be every where but one. I pray yow try at Apollonius, or the fchoolmafter of Middleburgh, or fome other, if it be fo, and what that courfe is, which yow will fet downe, and fend over here to me in your firft letter

The three or four next feffions were fpent much of them in votes and debates upon papers betwixt us and the States. Glencairne and others prefented to us a petition from the Duke and the army for minifters, which they feconded, lykewife they offered all fecurity for religion they were able; and for removeing the prefent differences, they required a conference with us. To all this they required a prefent anfwer, at leaft before we paft on the tryell, in order to approbation of the Commiffion-book, againft which they profeffed they had diverfe new exceptions. To all thefe we gave anfwers in wryte. The proceedings of the commiffioners were unanimoufly approven; a conference was appointed; eight minifters named, and fome elders; the army's letter referred to our committee. The State neglected the conference, fince we had approven the proceedings of the Commiffion, and had refolved, that no fecurity to religion was poffible fo long as the Engagement did ftand; only they mett once for a fafhion, and gave in a paper craving feripture from us for the unlawfulnefs of the Engagement, and our meddleing with matters of warre and peace. This paper was referred to our committee. In ane afternoone fome few of us mett, and lett downe our fcripturall grounds for both thefe points; but thought fitt to put them in the Declaration rather than in a feverall paper.

Mr. Robert Blair and Mr John Smith were willing to draw the declaration, leift it fhould fall in Mr James Guthrie's brifk hand. I obtefted Mr Blair, that he would be carefull of two things; one, to be full againft the fectaries; another, to beware that his draught carried any thing which, directly or indirectly, might carry us to a refiftance of the State. I knew, that the moft of the leading men thought a refiftance by armes to the ways in hand lawfull enough, if the diffenters in Parliament, or any confiderable part of the Kingdome, had courage and probable force to act; but it was my greateft care, that nothing fhould be done or faid by the Affembly which might bear any fuch thing; and this I obtained to my great contentment. There were two points fomewhat fibb to this that I obtained alfo, but with much difficulty.

1. Sundry at diverfe times moved to have it determined, if it was lawfull to

pay any monethly maintainance, fince avowedly it was preffed for the ufe of the army, which was unlawfull. I avowed the lawfullnefs of it, as of a tribute agreed upon by the State before this army was in being; and that Cæfar in confcience muft have his tribute, let him employ it to what ufes he thinks fitt. Alfo, if this were refufed, the excife, the portion of annuelrents, and all other dues, which were employed for the fervice of the army, behooved to be denyed, which could not but make the State to take it by force, and the people to fight againft their fpoilers At laft we agreed to lay this queftion afyde It was lykewife much preffed, that fuch as had been active for the Engagement fhould be kept from the holy table; and, as I did think, the defigne of fome was to have our Statefmen put under Church cenfures for their diligence in this Engagement My mind in this yow have in a paper here by itfelfe. I gott it, by much fpeech and private dealing, carried according to my mind.

But other things were carried over my head. It was moved, for the further clearing of the wickednefs of the warre, to make a collection from the Commiffioners of all the Prefbyteries of the chief infolencies committed by the fojours before they went from among us, and to put thefe in our declaration I was willing they fhould be collected to be complained of both to Church and State, and cenfured by both fo feverely as poffible; but was averfe to have them regiftrate, for the infamy of the very nation, into our publick declaration. In this I was not heard Alfo, when it was preffed that minifters filent, who did not preach againft the Engagement, fhould for this be depofed, I wifhed, if men were modeft, and otherwife offended not, that this fault might carrie no more but ane rebuke; but not only it was made depofition, but, by the motion of two or three men at moft, it was carried againft my mind, and of diverfe others, that the prior acts againft depofed minifters for Malignancy fhould be made more ftrait. 1. That none of them fhould be ever admitted to any Church whence a man for Malignancy was depofed; but alfo, that they fhould be keept from preaching till a Generall Affemblie did open their mouth, and out of the minifterie, while ane other Generall Affemblie did find them fitt for a Church; alfo, if after their depofition they meddled with any part of the ftipend or glebe, it fhould be excommunication to them. It was preffed by fome, that the not paying of the ftipend to the next intrant, fhould be excommunication to the patrons or tennants, who, upon the Act of Parliament, paid it to him who was depofed for adhereing to the State. This hardly was gotten avoided.

It was againft the minds of fundrie to make a declaration to England at all; but this behooved to be. I was feared for Mr. James Guthrie his hand, and fo I found I had reafon. His draught was wanting of that which I thought was the chief thing it became us to fay to them, if fo we faid any thing, a fharp complaint againft the Sectarian army, and the Parliament's negligence to performe their part of the Covenant, which had brought on us all our prefent troubles. alfo it had fome dangerous expreffions, which I thought imported the rock I defyred to evite, calling our State, "A faction; yea, the mixed multitude that came out of Egypt; but the diffenters from the Engagement, the nation, and the Ifrael of God." With very much adoe I gott thefe helped, fome in the committee, and others in the face of the Affemblie.

I found the bent-faile of the fpirits of fome fo much on the Engagement, that all things elfe were lyke to be neglected; therefore I preffed, that the Doctrinalls, as moft proper for us, which the laft Generall Affemblie had recommended to all the Prefbyteries, might be taken to confideration. I gott in the Catechife; but no more · we paffed this, both the Larger and Shorter, as a part of uniformitie; but we thought the Shorter too long, and too high for our common people and children, and fo put it in Mr D. Dickfon's hand, to draw it fhorter and clearer. Of this he was carefull, and prefented us with a draught before the end of the Affemblie, which truely was very good and exact; but yet fo high and long, that it was recommitted to Mr John Levingftone: he was purpofed to remitt it to the minifters of Edinburgh.

We had three things more of great concernment to have paft, and might eafily have concluded them all, had not our time been worfe fpent, the Directorie of Government, the Theorems againft Eraftians, and the Pfalmes. The firft, a very excellent and profitable piece, the fourth part of our uniformitie, was fhuffled by through the pertinacious oppofition of Mr. David Caldeiwood, and two or three with him. Four or five things we all agreed in to except, in that wryte, from our confent; but that which grieved Mr David was the matter of Church feffions, which he maintains to have no divine right in particular, but to be only as a committee from the Prefbyterie, to execute thefe acts of jurifdiction which the Prefbyterie thinks fitt to committ thereto.

Leaft in the end of the Affemblie, when many were gone, we fhould come to fo grave a debait, or rather, leaft at a time of our fo great ftrife with the State, we fhould fall a jarring among ourfelves, it was thought beft to refer the whole wryte to the next Affemblie. Upon the fame ground, the Theorems were alfo remitted The Pfalmes were often revifed, and fent to Prefbyteries: had it not been for fome who had more regard than needed to Mr Zacharie [Boyd]'s Pfalter, I think they had paffed through in the end of the Affemblie; but thefe alfo, with almoft all the references from the former Affemblies, were remitted to the next.

One feffion was fpent on encouraging Mr David Calderwood to perfyte his Church ftory,[1] and to confider Mr. Andrew Kerr[2] for his good and great fervice to them. Both gott a teftimonie of our favour:[3] eight hundred pounds yearly for Mr. David Calderwood, and one thoufand yearly to Mr Andrew Kerr, with a gratuity of five thoufand merks for bygones, were appointed by the Affemblie to be payed to them out of the Church's five hundred pounds penfion; but we cannot, for any requeft, gett one penny payed by the Thefaurer, and have little hopes to gett any more in hafte Much fpeech we had of a [Hi]ftory of the late troubles. In every province fome were named to gather materials to be fent in to Mr. John Smith. The publick papers, in wryte or print, were defired to be all put together; but I expect no good from all thefe motions. If you would goe on with your Hiftory, I fhould be very glad of it

We were fafhed with the opening of the mouths of depofed minifters. Poor Mr Patrick Hamiltone, in the very nick when the Affemblie was to grant all his defire, was rejected by his oune unhappinefs He had let fall out of his pocket a poem too invective againft the Church's proceedings

[1] His History of the Church of Scotland *Vide* vol. ii p 374

[2] Mr. Andrew Ker, Advocate, son of John Ker, Minister of Prestonpans, was for some time Warriston's depute, and then his successor, as Clerk to the General Assembly. There was another person of the same name, also an Advocate, who was appointed one of the Commissioners for the Administration of Justice in Scotland, under the Protectorate of Cromwell

[3] " This modification (as it is called in the Index of the printed Acts of Assembly) to Mr David Calderwood for his publick employments;" and to " the Clerk of the Assembly for his services," was of course in Scotish money, or equivalent to £66 13 4 Sterling for Calderwood, and £83 6s for Ker: the 5000 merks amounted to £277 15 6½ additional, but in all probability these sums were never paid.

This, by mere accident, had come in the hands of Mr. Mungo Law, who gave it to Mr. James Guthrie, and he did read it in the face of the Affemblie, to Mr. Patrick's confufion. Alfo when the Affemblie was to have at laft, after three or four years refufall, fhewen favour to your old colleague Mr James Row, Mr Patrick Gillefpie, and his own coufins, did fo farr marre him, upon tacit furmifes, as I fufpect of fmall importance, that it's lyke he fhall never be permitted to preach : yet honeft John Gillon gott permiffion to preach, and for this I confeffe I was forward ; for the man, though he want letters, is very pious and well-gifted, and ftrong againft all fectaries. The preparative is not dangerous, for I believe few in ane age will fall to be in his cafe ; and if many fhould, I would grant them the like favour, though fome mifinterpret it.

The Affemblie fpent diverfe feffions, for fmall purpofe, upon tranfportations Thefe I love dayly worfe and worfe ; the moft are evidently packed bufineffes, little for the credit either of the tranfporters or tranfported. Mr. John Livingftone, refufed to Glafgow, and defigned for Ireland by the laft Affemblie, though earneftly futed by my Lord of Airds, and much ftucken to by my Lord Caffilhs, who, for his refpect, had made a conftant ftipend for his church, moft out of his owne rent, though his parifhioners had not been cited, yet was, at my Lord Louthian's fute, tranfported to Ancrum, where the benefice was great, and the way to Edinburgh fhort Dr Colvine, called by Edinburgh to the divinity profeffion, fo willing to come as it became a wife and modeft man, his colleagues willing to difmiffe him , yet the private refpects of a very few, made him to be fixed to his ftation, which I regretted. Mr. George Hutchefon, orderly appointed by his Prefbyterie to goe to Ayr, yet he, lykeing better to goe to Bruntifland or Edinburgh than to joine with Mr. William Adair, and Mr. William abfenting himfelfe when the action came in, was appointed to byde in his place. I think the miforder of tranfportations will not be gotten helped, till fome honeft men doe peremptorlie refufe to obey, which, I think, fome at laft will doe ; efpecially fince the filling of fo many places is referred to the Commiffion of the Kirk, with a power almoft arbitrary, to neglect all the rules before appointed by Generall Affemblies for tranfportation.

We were fafhed with Patrick Lefley of Aberdeen : his intemperate zeale for the leavie had made him overhaile. Mr. Andrew Cant gave in againft him a foule libell · he gave in another againſt the miniſters. It coſt a committee very much diligence to gett this matter accommodate; for it was manifeſt that Mr Andrew Cant could hardly live in Aberdeen, if that man were enraged; ſo for the miniſters cauſe he was much ſpared, and that matter packed up as it might be. ſome men are borne, if not to raiſe, yet continuallie to live in a fire We had in our committee ſome debate about conventicles: ſome of them we had heard of in Edinburgh, in the characters of ſectaries. Mr Robert Knox gott them in, to my great contentment, for I found ſome too ſpareing of them, and yet I feare how farr in their own time they may extend their duety of mutuall edification

The whole two weeks following were ſpent on theſe things. The moſt were faſhed for the Moderator's want of diſpatch, and too much ſticking wilfullie to his owne ſenſe. Mr. Robert Blair in the moſt, Mr. Robert Ramſay in all, was of my mind, Mr. Robert Douglaſs miſlyked ſome mens carriage. The Aſſembly of Divines wrote to us a generall letter. to this, Mr. Robert Blair his anſwer was good and uncontroverted. The ſubſcryving of the Bond was much againſt all our minds; but ane Act was drawn up againſt it in my abſence, which I much miſlyked; for it carried cenſure againſt the preſſers of it. This directly aimed at our ſtateſmen, the contrivers of it; but, in the face of the Aſſemblie, I gott it to be exponed only *ad futura*. Some of my neighbors before the Aſſemblie were ſo farr in love with this ſubſcription, that I was forced to wryte to them arguments againſt it, as yow may ſee herewith. Though in ſome parts of the countrey the ſubſcription goe on, yet in the chiefe and moſt parts it is not required of any

At this time I was greeved for the ſtate of Glaſgow. The peſt did increaſe My brother ſon's houſe was infected; my brother's houſe incloſed many in danger: one night near a doſſen dyed of the ſickneſs. Some good, but unadviſed people, were not much greeved for the calamity of that Towne; and if it had fallen only upon their oppoſites, their inſulting had been grievous, yet the Lord hes been marvellouſly gracious to my brother and his ſon: no harme at all hes come to them, and the danger of the Towne, bleſſed be God, is much diminiſhed. The long great raines for many weeks did prognoſticate famine, but theſe three dayes bypaſt there is alſo a great change of weather; the Lord continue it

Our Aſſemblie drave over to the end of the fifth week: many, dwelling farr off and fuperexpended, flaid away. I fufpected the Moderator drew long of purpofe, waiting for a letter from the Parliament of England, which came not. We hear now the Houfe of Commons paft a declaration to us, but the Lords confented not to it. I did not love to have any correfpondence with them now, but others loved it too well. Ane other motion in our committee I loved not, a letter to be written to the King: the motion was fathered on Mr James Hamiltone; and the drawing of it put on him, though no Commiffioner I knew there would a heavier load be laid by us on his Majeftie than was expedient to be meddled with; alfo that we fhould not expreffe fuch a fenfe of his unjuft fufferings as the world would expect, and fo I was earneft to let all alone; but the Moderator carried it: and though the draught of that letter came never to our committee, but at the firft was taken in to the Affemblie, and fome hours fpent in the Moderator's publick correcting of it, yet the thing behooved to paffe, and the wording of it to go to the Commiffion Many good overtures againft the fins of the time did lykewife paffe. One of them I was feared for; it was firft, that all Minifters converfing with Malignants fhould be cenfured by Prefbyteries This would have fnared many; for the notion of the Malignants now by the Engagement, is extended to very many: I gott it fome way qualified, but not fo as it will be found needfull.

That which fome dayes in the end of the Affemblie troubled us, was Mr Andrew Ramfay and Mr. William Colvill's proceffe. Mr Andrew had, in preaching, oft fallen out into diverfe impertinencies, and contradictions to his brethren; he had been oft admonifhed; but the man's weaknefs and age, and diverfe who reforted to him, permitted him not much to amend. Not only he had fpoken for the Engagement; but in prejudice of our proceedings, and Prefbyterial government itfelfe. Much he denied which was proven: he untimeoufly had fallen on an unhappie queftion, the Magiftrate's power to remitt blood. The generall Thefe which he profeffed to maintaine, "That the fupreame magiftrate, when the fafety of the commonwealth does require, may difpenfe with the execution of juftice againft fhedders of blood," many of us declined to meddle with; but the Moderator gladly would have had the Affemblie determining the negative expreffilie, which was efchewed; only the man for his doctrine and carriage was fufpended to the next Affemblie. Mr William Colvill was referred to us only for his filence about the Engagement

The man was generallie reputed too bufie to countenance and encourage our ftatefmen in their way, and the chiefe mover of Mr. Andrew to his courfe; however, he himfelfe walked very cannily I was indeed offended at his malapert carriage in the commiffion of the Church, and for it, albeit it was not libelled, I confented to his fufpenfion; but it was againft my mind that Doctor Barron fhould have been cenfured for mere filence, yet it was carried One or two of your friends in our Prefbyterie had been, for their filence and ambiguity about the Engagement, refeired to the Affemblie, had I not diverted and gotten that evill keept off them, for had they come before us, readily they had never come off.

We appointed vifitations for Univerfities and hofpitalls, and put on them the fharpeft men we had. Lykely Edinburgh will not fubmitt to have either Univerfitie or hofpitalls vifited, though they have moft need; and I preffed their vifitation before any other; fince, as yet, they have ever declined it

The Commiffioners for uniformitie with England were continued without change; only Lauderdaill, to my greefe, was juftly omitted. I was fcarce refolved to have feen him; yet my Lady Warriftone fent me to him, as trufting in his friendfhip for her hufband's buffinefs He told me, that, however, to his beft knowledge, there was no defigne either on his place or perfon for the time; yet that he could not anfwer what might be fhortly, efpecially when in debate and difcourfe thefe things might efcape him which might irritat Upon this good Warriftone, leaft by his unfriends he might be brought in by violence, thought meet to retire to Cantyre, where, for the prefent, he paffes time with Argyle Lauderdaill continues kind to me, and regrates much the difference betwixt us; fears it become a fountaine of great evills, either the overthrow of the defigne for the King againft the Sectarifts, or the putting up of the Malignant partie fo high, that they will hardly be gotten ruled; at beft, the making of the government of our Church, as we exercife it, to be abhorred by all in England and abroad, and intollerable to our owne State at home. I find the Thefaurer in the fame mind, but both of them faft enough, for ought I can fee, to our Covenant and perfons, except to one or two whom they efteem the prime caufes of the difference. In Mr William Colvill's cenfure, Mr. David Calderwood rafhly had faid, " He was the painfulleft minifter of Edinburgh:" this the Moderator exaggerat fo farr, as fome did fpeak of his removeall for cenfure The

Moderator before had taken him up for his impertinencies indeed : yet too roughly, and more, as I thought, than became   After this rancounter, Mr David went home, and came no more to the Affemblie. At this I grieved, it may doe harme.

The State, on the Fryday before we rofe, gave in a large paper of Obfervations on our Declaration   I take them to be Primrofe their clerk's draught. We appointed the Commiffion to fitt and anfwer them · they are but poor ones. That fame day we renewed the Commiffion of the Church   There is too great a change of the perfons, and too great addition of men who never have been members of any Affemblie; alfo their power is too much enlarged, even to proceffe all who oppofe their orders, as well as of the Generall Affemblie. I find diverfe in the mind, that if once our army in England had gotten any fenfible fucceffe, our State are refolved totally to fuppreffe the Commiffion of the Church, as a judicatorie not yet eftablifhed by law; and it's feared they will trouble the perfons of fome of us · but the Lord's will be done   I think indeed the cariage of fome is too high and peremptor, but if the State begin to trouble any of us with imprifonment, it will be a great ill of long and dangerous confequence.

On Saturday Auguft the 12th we arofe. In the morning I went away, defireous, after much toile, to be at home that night, unwilling to wait on the Commiffion, to jangle more with the Moderator   I was glad we had all ended in peace. The matter of this unhappie Engagement I hope will not laft, and fo the ground of our difference with the State fhall be removed: but new grounds of divifion may poffibly aryfe, which may make our contentions greater   This much I have written to yow, to obliedge yow to wryte ofter and larger; fo much the more as our intercourfe with London is ftopped, and we know not what is doeing either there or abroad. What yow learn weekly by your Gazetts, I pray, once in the moneth at leaft, let us have it's fumm, as yow fhall have occafion to fend it. So I reft,

Your Coufine, to ferve yow,

Auguft 23d [1648]   ROBERT BAILLIE.[1]

[1] " The confequences of the Engagement were fatal   The army was totally routed in Lancaster by Cromwell, the Duke [of Hamilton] taken prisoner, carried to London, and there executed '   In the printed copy 1775, this passage, which occurs as a postscript to the above letter, is evidently an explanation added by the Editor

VOL

For Mr Spang. February 7th 1649.

Cousine,

Your bygone letter, 12th, I receaved, and thanks yow for it. Yow complaine of my long filence; but gives no fatiffaction for your longer. In my nixt I fhall give yow contentment about all your inquirie this is upon a particular and great occafion. One Act of our lamentable Tragedy being ended, we are entering again upon the fcene. O! if it might be the Lord's pleafure to performe more happy and comfortable actions than have appeared thefe years bygone. To the great joy of all, in the midft of a very great and univerfall forrow, we proclaimed, on Monday laft, the Prince, King of Brittaine, France, and Ireland. We have fent the bearer,[5] a worthy gentleman, to fignifie fo much to his Majeftie at the Hague. We purpofe fpeedily to fend a honorable Commiffion from all Eftates. The dangers and difficulties wherewith both his Majeftie and all his Kingdomes at this time are involved, are exceeding great and many. The firft neceffare and prime one (as all here, without exception, conceave) doth put his Majeftie and his people both in a hopefull proceeding; and his Majeftie's joyning with us in the Nationall Covenant, fubfcribed by his grandfather King James, and the Solemne League and Covenant, wherein all the well-affected of the three Kingdomes are entered, and muft live and die in, upon all hazards.—If his Majeftie may be moved to joyne with us in this one point, he will have all Scotland readie to facrifice their lives for his fervice.—If he refufe, or fhift this duety, his beft and moft ufefull friends, both here and elfewhere, will be caft into inextricable labyrinths, we fear, for the ruine of us all. We know Satan will not want ill inftruments to keep him off from a tymeous yielding to this our moft earneft and neceffare defyre; bot as it is, and will be, one of all Scotland's ftrong petitions to God, to difpofe his heart to doe his duty without delay; fo we will acknowledge ourfelves much oblidged to any, whom the Lord may honor, to be the happie inftruments of his perfuafion. Many here remember, and are fenfible of your great

---

[5] Sir Jofeph Douglas, who carried a letter of the fame date to the King, from the Commiffion of the General Affembly. *Vide infra*, p 71; alfo the Appendix to this Volume.

and happie labours, for the clearing of our proceedings, from the very firft commotions among us: We truft ye will not refufe to be at any needfull paines, at this fo hard a tyme, for the fervice of God, your King, and Countrey, and all the Churches here, in their great diftrefs. I wifh yow made a voyadge to Hague, and dealt with our good friends, Dr. Rivet and Dr. Spanheim, to infinuate to the King their wholefome advyces. I know Somais [Salmafius], Voffius, Apollonius, and others there, underftand fo much of our proceedings, that a fmall defyre from any interefts would move them to contribute their beft helps for his Majeftie's information.

I recommend it therefore moft earneftlie to yow, to beftirre yourfelfe in a private clanculary way to further this work. If yours, or any other men's labours be bleffed of God to work the prefent, you will find all here (I fhall anfwer for it) reache to acknowledge, as becomes your pains, by fuch teftimonies, in due time, as fhall give yow fatiffaction. What yow doe muft be done quicklie; for every hour's delay prejudgeth (we know not how much) his Majeftie and all his dominions.

Your Coufine,

Edinburgh, February 7th 1649.   ROBERT BAILLIE.

MR. WILLIAM SPANG TO MR ROBERT BAILLIE.[6]

REVEREND COUSIN,

SINCE May laft, the firft letter I have feen of yours was of the 4th December, very concife, and moft of it in complaint of my long filence; of which ye fould have had no reafon, if thefe to whom I entrufted my letters for yow have been honeft; for I never let any occafion flip with which I have not written, and that at large. I am affrayed leaft the freedom I have ufed in them may beget truble to me, if they have fallen into any invyous hand; and yet what I writ was but a rehearfel of the judgement, which the godly

---

[6] This and the two following letters are printed from the originals contained in Wodrow MSS. Folio, Vol LXVII. Nos 83, 84, and 85. Spang, it will be obferved, writes in the name of Anderfon, and refers to Baillie, as Jamefon. The orthography of the originals is ufually retained, but the final *e* has been added to fuch words as *Prince, large, place, thefe, &c* to make them intelligible. Spang's long refidence abroad, offers fome excufe for fuch peculiarities.

and wyfe, who ever affected our caufe, did profefs to me both by word and letters Moft of my letters to yow wer inclofed in pakkets to Mr. George Gillefpie, of quhoes death, to my great grief, I have latly heard. Certanly he was as able a man as our Kirk had ; of a clear judgement :—that which fome miflyked in him, wald eafely have been bettered by experience and years. I fee he hes had a better opinion of thefe Sectaries than he wald have had, if he had lived till now, and had heard their vile perjured treacheries againft al bands · Alace ! for that reproach caft upon our relligion, and the treuth of God, by thefe mens unparalelled proceedings, and for the prefent danger of relligion in al the thrie Kingdoms ; yea, and the civil liberties of al who will not rune to the fame exces of madnes with them.

Let Scotland chuis what fyde they pleas, that poor land fal be the feat of war, by al appearance, this fummer, for a confiderable army is marching northward againft yow ; and Cromwel affurs his brethren in evil, of a more eafy conqueft of that Kingdom than al the Englifh Kings ever had His ground is, as I have heard from one who is of their councel, that the bitternefs betwixt thefe who wer for the laft engadgement into England, and thefe who wer againft it, is fo great, that ther is no means left to reconcile parties, and he is able to crufhe thefe who hes authority now in their hand, if they be alone ; fo that our domeftik divifions is the cheif ftay of that party, and which will mak us either fal into their hands as a conqueft, or hinder us from being able to doe any thing to purpofe They encurradge themfelfs in thefe their hopes, by ane alledget diffent entred by fom of the eminenteft of our nobility againft the proclaming of our new King, which, though it be moft fals, yet it is enough to flander thefe noblemen ; and becaus their authority is fo great in our Kingdome, to mak many fufpect al runs not fo fmooth and fair as is given out by us, fo much the more, fince no publik Declaration is emitted by our cleargie, to vindicat themfelfs from having given a precedent quhilk thefe perjured Independents have folloued.

I am fure it hes bein a matter of unconceavable grief to yow all, when ye heard of that bloody murthering the late King ; and it is reafon, that following the example of the zealous preachers in London, ye teftifie your utter abhorring of it, that ther may be extant a teftimony to the world of the loyaltie of your hearts, whereby the foul mouths of Papifts and Malignants may be ftopped, as Jacob did, Genefis xlix. 6 ; and David, 2 Samuel iii. 35, 36, 37.

All the miniſters in this province doe publickly declar their abhorring of it, and many has chofen feleᶜt texts for that purpofe, and ever with that tender refpeᶜt to our countrey and their proceedings, as was matter of joy for us to hear. Now ye have proclaimed the Prince to be King; and bliſſed be God, who hath put it in your hearts fo to doe! this maks your names like a fragrant fmel, and if ye be put to any hazard for the maintenance of that aᶜt, if ye will manadge your credit weel abroad, ye will find real friends. But firſt, all wiſhe that cair were taken to cement at home with you, and for that purpofe to remit of that rigour, in the which, if ye continew, no man fees how ye can fubfiſt, for, be aſſured, the party that now is under will rake hell to vindicat themfelfs, and put yow to that neceſſity, that ye muſt joine your forces with thefe murtherers, and bring them again into the bouels of our kingdom, yea, and to be fubfervient to them, and to recal what has been done with fuch abfolute agreement It wer to be wiſhed that men of all fydes wald now learne to deny themfelfs, if they wald approve their former profeſſions for Religion, King, Countrey.

There is arryved at Rotterdam fome Commiſſioneris from Scotland to the Prince, upon the 2d March, new ſtyle, amongſt whom there is one Sir Jofeph Douglafs, who entreated Mr. Alexander Petrie to writ to me in all haiſt, that I fould com thither, or to the Hague unto him; for what errand I know not; yet I mynd to-morrow, God willing, to goe thither, fo much the more, becaus I hear my Lord Chancellor is upon his way thither in a ſhip, quhair, if I can ferve them for any ufe, I fal not be fayling

We have no news more than what your Engliſh moderat Intelligencer printeth. Germany is in *ſtatu dubio*, al hankering for the effeᶜt of that Munſter treaty, yet not willing to quyt their poſts till they fee performance. France is in a fyre for that unhappy Mazarin : both parties ar refolut, and they have met feveral tyms in parties, fomtyms with lofs of the one, fomtyms of the uther. Spain, whatfoever he mynd, yet he is arming a grit Armado, of which we can fee little ufe, except it be for Irland. If peace be made in France, England will feel the fmart of it ; and when parties fal be then engaged, uthers ar lying in wait alfo

I do fend yow, for the Colledge, al of Amiraut's that I could get, his Apologie in 4to, et Specimen Animadverfionum contra Spanhemium, bound, his treatife De Abfoluto Reprobationis Decreto, in 4to unbound, his uther final treatifes bound together in 8vo : Item, Ludovic de Dieu Animadverfiones in omnes Libros Veteris Teftamenti, bound in 4to., Rivetorum Fratrum Apologia contra Calumnias Amirautij ; Cocceius de Fœdere et Teftamento Dei, Linfchotani Itinerarium Indiæ Orientalis, in folio, Amftelodamenfium Hiftoria, Pontani, both rare books, fit for Biblıotheks.

I fal be looking out for what our freind did writ of his removal. Alace! that matters fould be brought thus far ; but a wyfe man feeth the evil day, and fleeth from it. When I return out of the Hague, I fal give Mr Jamefon ane account of it I am glad my nephew pleafeth yow fo weel ; keep him in a modeft opinion of himfelf I fee he is hinkering after his old conceit, and fhaues more inclination to uther ftudies than Divinity, by reffon of the little hopes of preferment for one who will not eafily enflave his judgement to uther δοκουντες. Ye know what is the beft way to put that out of his head. Grit will the account be of thefe who, by fuch imperious and partial courfes, goe about to fmother the graces God puts in fuch young fprouts

I fend yow a new peece of that Craftianifme againft the worthy fervant of God, Jodocus Larenus, minifter of Flufhing ; who hes ane anfuer to it under the pres, whilk ye fal have when it comes furth Marezius at Groning hes begun his virulency again againft honeft Voetius, whom he accufeth of poprie, focinianifme, and what not. The divel is not idle, and the Kirk is like to receive, as in former tymes, mor damadge by fuch than by publick enemies. My wyf hopes, if ye wer acquaint with her, that ye fould tak revendge upon yourfelf for having fuch a opinion of her, as if by her my deuty to my freinds fould be neglected ; of this I may purge her, becaus I have, as I have writen, left no occafion unpaft And I am fure ye will find my letters, if ye have not got them alreddy, in Mr. George Gillefpie's chalmer : His feiknefs and death hes bein the hinderence I wifh, if ye have not got them unopened, that they had perifhed ; for we live in dangerous tyms, wherein a man is made a tranfgreffor for a word, and whatfoever freedom I ufe with my freinds muft not be mifinterpretate. Let your bedfellow, children, freinds, be faluted in my name, efpecially your brother-in-law, Dr. Strang. When I returne out of Holland, ye may exfpect, God willing, a large letter, and that with the firft. The good God comfort yow, and direct yow in the right way, that ye may enjoy the fruit of your labours in peace. If our King will not tak the Covenant, and feparat himfelf from the counfels of thefe who hes driven his Father to that mifery, I forfee he and we al fal be miferable. Let our eyes be toward God; he rulis al· To his mercy ye ar recommended by

Your Coufine,

At my Duelling place, 7th March 1649.   ANDERSON.

I have no leifure to writ to any elfe at this tym. Commend me to my mother and my freinds.—Let my coufine have ufe of fuch books in your Bibliothek, as he has need of. Sie how familiar I am with yow.—I fal anfuer Mr. David Dickfon's letter, when I gett ane anfuer out of Amfterdam.

(*Addreffed*) For the Reverend and much honored Mr. Robert Baillie, Profeffor of Divinity in the Univerfity of Glafgow
M
With ane bundel of books, marked R B
By ane noble freind, who will direct them to William Cunyngham, merchant at the Cuftome-hous in Edinburgh

MR WILLIAM SPANG TO MR. ROBERT BAILLIE.[7]

Tibi foli

REVEREND AND DEAR COUSIN,

AFTER the clofing of my laft letters, which goe alongs with the fame bearer, my Lord Confervatour, I receaved ane letter from Mr. Alexander Petrie, requiring me, in all haift, to com to the Hague: and that in the name of Sir Jofeph Douglas, a commiffioner then aryved from Scotland, with letters to the King's Majeftie; but about what errand he did not writ, neither could he. Though the weather was very unfeafonable and ftormie, and my health not the beft, as ufually it falls out with me in March, yet I chufed rather to rune thefe hazards then to be wanting to that gentleman's defyre. When I come to the Hague, I enquyred for him, and afked what was the errand for which he had fent for me. He told me, that he had brought over letters from the Commiffion of the Kirk, and delyvered them to Mr. Alexander

[7] The envelopes or addreffes of this and the next letter are not preferved.

Petrie, to be fent to me; fo I fent a expres to Rotterdam for thefe letters, which, when they come to my hand, I fand them a pakket from yow of the 7th February, wherby ye defyre me to haften to the Hague, and deal with fuch who are lykly to have credite with the King's Majefty, for perfuading him to doe what ye require of him, viz. to joyne with Scotland in both the Covenants. The perfons whom ye defigned were ether abfent out of Holland, as Dr Rivet, Apollonius, or fuch who are not of credite with courtiers, or fuch who are knouen to make only ufe of the Court favour for their privat ends; and therfor I did bethink my felf of another mean to effectuat that end, which was by addreffing my felf to the Prince of Orange his Highnes

For this purpofe I took pains to informe my felf, the beft I could, of the prefent pofture of counfels fuggefted to the King's Majefty, and the reafons for them; and I fand, that all thefe defigned by our late Soverainge to be his Son's counfellours, while he was Prince of Walis, viz. Cottington, Andover, Culpeper, Hyde, advyfed, that he fould goe directly for Ireland; this did James Grame [Marquis of Montrofe] urge alfo in gritteft vehemency; and if that could not prevail, uthers wer of advyfe that the King was to com to Scotland *armata manu*, becaus no truft could be given to fuch who were leading men in our Parliament, partly becaus they thought ther was reafon to fufpect the fincerity and reality of fom who ufed fuch a fair invitation, only to get the King in their pouer, whoes advancement they never thought more to procure then they did his Father's, partly becaus they thought that though thefe who invite him do really intend, yet they are not able to mantein him againft the Englifh ufurpers, if they doe not recal their late acts againft fuch who has had a hand in the engadgment, and joine al their pouers together : " But (this fay they) they will never doe, and fo they fal not be able to protect the King; but being ftrained by the Englifh, will be content to buy their peace with quyting the King." And heir, to mak this probable, pregnant inftances are brought in of my Lord Chancelours papers againft the delyvery of the King to the Parliament, preffed by unanfuerable reafons which yet was neglected altogether, by delyvery of the King within few monteths therefter. The uther inftance was of the treating of our Commiffioners with the late King at the Iland of Wight, and our not performing our promife accordingly But ther was a thrid party, who, though they be not of the King's counfel, yet, out of love to him and their countrey, rejected the two former projects as bloody, tending to the utter ruining of the King and all Proteftants, and did by all means labour to perfuade his Majefty to go to Scotland upon the very fame terms they did require That if he did not goe, and that haftely, with a refolution to feal the Covenants, he wald alienat the hearts of all the Proteftants in al his kingdoms from him: and this was preffed by the Erls Lauderdail, Calender, Lanrick, with fuch evident felf denyal of ther oune interefts, as being grievoufly cenfured by this prefent Parliament, that had the King bein left to himfelf, it was thought he could not but follow their advyfe. This honeft carriadge of thefe thrie Noblemen I can bear witnes unto, as having heard them proteft it in privat, and underftanding from uthers alfo, who are our enemies, and do curfe the hour that they have bein caft hein to fpoyle the game they thought fure. Beleive me, I doe acknowledge the good providence of God in cafting them heir at this tyme: they have done more good for the countrey than if they had bein fitting in Parlament

My next was to find out wherto the Prince of Orange was inclined. For this purpofe, I went to tuo of the States General, of whofe intimacy with the Prince's counfels all men did fpeak I fand them not only declaring their aune judgement for the King's going to Scotland, and embracing the Covenant; but that that alfo was the Prince's mynd. From thence I went to fundry uthers, but from none did I get furer information then from the Lord of Beverwerd, governour of Bergen, natural fon to Prince Maurice, a nobleman treuly pious, and of a publick fpirit, refolute to imploy his credite for relligion, and of high account with the Prince, in whofe counfels he hes chief influence; as in fpeaking to fome of the Eftates and uthers, the Confervatour joyned himfelf with me, fo heir alfo, for which it will be weell done to thank him, for ye may be affured he was both faithful and diligent even at that nik of tyme, when the buffines was in a crifis Now having found whereto the Prince inclined, my nixt thoughts wer to underftand fo much out of his oune mouth, and to confirme him in what good refolution I fould find in him, efpecially to remove fome fcruples and objections wherwith many told he was dayly affaulted. For this end, a contreyman of ours promifed to bring me to the Prince; bot performed it not, or at leaft wald have me to wait fo long upon it, that I fould be made to think it fome gritt favour. For this court policy I learned, which made me refolve to goe in my old way, and by the mediation of one of his Highnes counfellers, I was brought in to him, and had the freedom of a long hour's fpeech, where I fand God's affiftance and blefling; his affiftance, in inabling me both with words and matter, for it was in Dutch, and his bliffing, in making the Prince fo attentive to what I faid, fo defirous to know the trew grounds of things, fo apprehenfive, and fo fully refolved with us for his Majefty going to Scotland upon the conditions proponed. I fal give yow a fhort and compendious account of what paffed then.

After I had thanked his Highnefs for his favour in granting me fo reddy audience, and defyred to know if I might, with his good lyking, propone what I intended in Latin or Englifh, rather than Dutch, and he defyring me to doe it in Dutch Then I firft condoled the parricid of our late King his Father[8] fhow how it was abhorred by the Eftaits of our Kingdom, how contrar to our Covenant, whofe end, among uther things, was the faifty of the King's perfon; how not only the State had proclaimed his Son to be their King, bot the miniftery of the kingdom alfo according to their places, had done their deuty, and had given affurance of their loyal affection to our prefent King, by their letters to him, and by their cair that he may be perfwaded in tyme to fhun that wicked counfel, whilk drove his late Father to fuch courfes, that they had given me ordour to deal with al who could contribute any thing to the advancement of this good work; and that I could look upon none from whom I had reafon to exfpect more good than his High nes, who, by being inftrumental heirin, wald gaine gritter honour then by gayning of touns, &c. He anfuered, "That ther was nothing more acceptable to him, than that he was looked upon as one who fould employ himfelf for the advancement of relligion, and that now, if ever, the Reformed Relligion was in danger; that ther was no probable means to prevem the utter extirpation of it, but by efpoufing the young King's quarrell; and that he, for his part, could not but pitty the young King, torne as it were betuixt fuch contrary counfels; that reafons produced by all parties feemed to be fpecious, yet how fair foever men did fpeak, he thought it madnes for a Proteftant to chuis rather to truft to a Papift, than a Proteftant who mynded truely" "And if ever (fayd I) any State mynded treuly, it is our prefent State, their

[8] William of Nassau, Prince of Orange married Mary, eldest daughter of King Charles the First He died 6th of November 1650, aged 24

haftines in proclayming, that cheerfulnes of all joining togethei, doe witnes this; and now their reddines to efpoufe the King's caufs, if he firft will efpoufe God's caufs, though they know any undertakings of that kynd to be joyned with grit dangers." "But what (fayd he) may be exfpected of the minifters? And heir he fpok much of the grit influence their advyfe hes in the Eftait. To this I anfwered, that whatfoever any Prince can exfpect of good fubjects, that may our King look for at the hands of the Minifters, if he imploy his pouer for the honouring of C[hrift]; and that al the pouer they have in the hearts of the people will be for the King's advantage. Hen he fpok fomthing of the grit piecifnes of our minifters, who could not be content with that about relligion, whilk our late King had granted, and wherewith the Parlament of England itfelf was weel neigh fatiffied. Heir I was reddy to have anfuered; but he paffed this, and fpoke of the conditions we require of the King, viz. his accepting and entering into the Covenants. And I, at his defyre, having explaned what thefe Covenants were, and how diftinguifhed: "Then (fayed he) he will be eafely brought to fubfcribe the Covenant, whilk concerns Scotland alone; (he meant our Nationall Covenant;) but that uther Covenant betuixt Scotland and England, he feared fould find gritter difficulty. 1. Becaufe al the King's counfellers, to wit, thefe four Englifh wald be againft it: 2 Becaufe it requyred a delyvering up to juftice thefe who are called malignants 3 Becaufe, as by fubfcribing it the King wald pleafe us, fo he wald difpleafs the Papifts in Ireland, and all foiraine Popifh princes, who will not be fo foolifh as to favour him whoes advancement is the ruine of ther relligion in his dominions. Uther reffons (fayd he) are urged, and I fal propone them ere ye goe" So I began to anfuer, and, firft, I fhow that the firft Covenant of Scotland only provyds as grit fecurity for relligion as the fecond doth, and therfor the King's counfellers who advyfe him to fubfcrib the one, and not the uther, for fear of difpleafing Papifts, fpeaks they know not of what, for ther is not a Papift who is not more difpleafed with the firft than the fecond." And he afking me, Why ar the King's counfellors fo much againft it? I anfuered, "That they durft not doe utherwayes than diffuade our yong King from the Solem League, fince they had ever diffuaded his Father from it; if they wald now chainge, the yong King, and your Highnes, who is fo gritly intereffed, fould have reafon to look upon them as men whofe confcience did condem them for the abufing the father " Heir I took occafion to reprefent to his Highnes the grit inconvenience of the aboad of fuch counfellers about the King's perfon ; that if a courfe were not taken to banifhe them from his prefence, they wald reddely prove as unhappy inftruments to the Son as they have been to the Father ; and that they are they who advyfe the King to flight the prefentation of Scotland, and to go to Irland, chuifing rather he fould not reigne then that they fould not reigne alfo with him ; men, of whofe religion the world, to this hour, was never fatiffied. So far as I could mark, his Highnes feemed not to be difpleafed with this. " As for the King's delyvering up of all malignants to juftice, (I anfuered,) the Covenant doth not requyr that all malignants fal be punifhed, but only tryed, and left to the judgement of the Parlament " " But (fayed he) ye cal any man a malignant whom ye pleas, though he profes he adhers to the Covenant, and all his aims are for the ends of it." Heir he brought in, for inftance, the Acts of our prefent Parlament, declaring all who had ane hand for the engadgement uncapable of any place of truft ther whole lyf: And yet, fayed he, " The world did read their declaration, quhilk fpak very fair, and the Parlament did all that work : I wald therfor gladly know who are the Malignants, for I find that ther is no argument that fo works upon his Majeftie as that " Heir, I profes, I was at a ftrait · for to have given him fuch a character of a Malignant as the Commiffioners of the Generall Affemblie did give fome two yeers fince, wald not have ferved the turne, the cafe being now altogether altered, in fo far, that he is to be thought more a malignant who doth approve the bloody acts of that treacherous crew, now ufurping the name of a Parlament in England, then any who did ever fight againft them , and therfor I came to the diftinguifhing of malignants, fome whofe aimes appeared evidently to be for their aune felfs, either that they might abyd in a capacity to tyrannize over their fellow-fubjects, or to raife their fortuns, alreddy difperat by the publik trubles. Such malignants were juftly unpardonable, and they had none to blame for the ruine of themfelfs and their families, but their aune obftinacie. As for uthers, in whom it doth appear that privat and by-ends hes not fet them a work, their cafe is pitied , and it hes ever bein the cuftom of the Parlaments of Scotland, to fail rather in too grit clemency then cruelty "Weil, (fays the Prince,) if ye that are minifters will not imploy your utmoft credite for uniting of all your contrey (I mean not, fays he, of fuch who have bein bloody obftinat enemies to yow,) ye may lofs both yourfelfs and the caule, and I know ther is nothing that fould more confound the counfels of al your enemies than to fee yow forget quarrells amongft yourfelfs; for this, they always fay, How can Scotland, thus divided, be able to doe any thing of moment, fince the forces of the party who now rules, is but waik enough to fupprefs their enemies? I therfor doe as earneftly recommend this to yow, that ye wald acquaint your minifters with it, as they by yow do recommend their buffines · If I did not think it tending to the inabling of yow to make your party good, I fould not open my mouth about it." Heir he enlarged himfelf very pertinently, and fel upon the project of ane act of oblivion, and told me " That the party who now rules, will not be fo evil advyfed as to reject this motion, if they but wald confider how fuddenly things may be changed " I affure yow he could tell me faults committed in our prefent governement, whereof I was wholly ignorant; which he fayeth he learned from the King's Englifh counfel, when they were debatting the very laufulnes of our Scottifh Parlament, whither laufully indyted, mantening ftrongly that that Committee quhilk called it, had no pouer becaufe they had not fubfcryved the acts of the former Parlament; " but (fayed he) I quikly crufhed fuch a motion in the very fhell."

" But (fayes he) the King by fubfcryving that Covenant will difengadge al Papifts from his fervice, both in Irland and elfwher, and al but Prefbyterians; for it obleidges the King to root out Papiftry every wher in his dominions, quhilk he is not able to doe in the condition wherein he is." I anfuered, " That fame argument our late Soveraingne ufed; but how dommadgful his going about to pleafour papifts was, doolful experience hes taught, for Irland fpecially · it lies bein that quhilk hes withdrauen the hearts of the Proteftants from him, more than any thing elfe. And what advantadge took thefe Irifch papifts at the King's weaknes? When they capitulated with him, what little performance did the King find of their big promifes, and fince ever he began to meddle with them, did not his condition decay dayly? That the condition of Proteftants called Prefbyterians, in Grit Britan and Irland is not fo mean, but if the King wald chearfully joine himfelf to them, as *Caput et Vindex Fœderis*, ther wald be no doubt of grit and good fucces. As for the particulers, how much they could doe, I durft not take it upon me to fpeak · only I was fure that in al Scotland ther was not a man who wald not be for the King; and in England, for one Independant, ther wald be found thrie Prefbyterians; and the reft, being either Hieraichical men or Papifts, if they wald not affift the King, they wald far les affift the traiterous fectaries." " I perceive (fayed his Highnes) what ye mean, but how many Prefbyterians fo ever ye be, if ye live at a diftance, as I hear ye doe now in Scotland, ye will be able to doe nothing at all. It is a work fitting your callings to unite the hearts of all your grit men, whom ye know to be Proteftants." And heir, I fufpecting that it might his Highnes did mean Montrofe, as they call him, who is frequently at Court, and more hemly with many than welcome, I fayed, " I hoped his Highnes did not mean of that man, whom apoftacie, perjurie, and unheard cruelty had made fo odious to all in our contrey, that they could not hear of his name." He prefently gave me to underftand that he meant not him, or any fuch; for by the comportment of our Scottifh noblemen at Court now, he perceives how odious James Grame moft be at home; for they will not falute or fpeik to him; nay, not look where they think he is, and this I have obferved with my auine eyes.

At laft, having anfuered al his queftions, I repeited my defire, and humbly prayed his Highnes to continew in that holy and wholfome refolution; and to improve his credite with our King, that a fatiffactory anfuer may be given with all haift, fhauing the danger of delay "But (fays he) when will your Commiffioners come to his Majeftie? I anfuered, " I thought not until the gentleman returned with ane anfuer to Scotland" He afked me If I knew who they fould be? I anfuered, that I knew not. " Will any minifters come?" fayed he. I anfuered, " That I queftioned not but fome fould come, who fould be able to fatiffy al his Highnes's fcruples better then I poffibly could" " I wifhe (fayes he) fome minifters fould come for fundry reffons." I replyed, " That they fal come the more cheerfully when they fal underftand how much your Highnes doth engadge yourfelf for perfuading the King's Majeftie to go to Scotland, with a refolution to fubfcrive both the Covenants." " Then (fayed the Prince) ye may confidently affure them that I fal doe my utmoft endeavour; and come ye to me to-morrow, and I fal tel yow what ye may exfpect"

So away went I, and to-morrow, being admitted to his prefence, he told me, " He had made it his work yefternight to perfuade the King's Majefty; that the refolution was taken to fatiffie the defires of the Parlament of Scotland,

and that in al haift letters were to be written of, in anfuer to what the King received." And heir againe he recommended the cair of uniting all our noblemen in one, in paffing by what faults hes bein the laft yeer; and told me, it fould be moft welcom news to him, if I fould let him know that any thing were done in reference to this. And

Thus, Coufine, ye have the fubftance of that difcourfe, by which ye may fie I have obtained the end of your letter, and that in a fitter way then ye prefcribed. I moft earneftly entreat yow, that ye would reprefent to the Reverend Brethren of the Commiffion how much the fame of rigidity, ufed by them againft the laft yeer's engadgers, is lyke to endanger the reputation of our Kirk abroad, and lyke alfo to make prefbyterial governement hatefull. My heart trembles when I think of this; for I am certanly enformed, by a printer, that that infamous perfon who goes under the name of Grallator,[9] hes a big volume reddy, of the late practifes of the Scottifh Kirk in the exercife of difciphne, which ye may think are willingly furnifhed to him by fome banifhed Scotfmen. Secondly, That all lovers of our caus and nation do unanimoufly judge that ther is no probable means of our faifty if we unite not and pack not up all quarrels amongft our felfs; if ther be not ane *amneftia* for the laft yeer's engadgement; for that fuch had reafon to challenge the Englifh army overpouring the Parliament, for breach of Covenant; and that their feares of mifcheif againft the King were not caufles, he is blind who fees not. If their were faults in the compaffing that work, as I doubt not but ther lies bein very grit ones, yet let not defyre of juftice againft thefe circumftantial faylings, lead us to feek the ruine of thefe men; or by excluding them from governement, deprive the kingdom of their abilities, and waiken our felfs fo, that we fall not be able to oppofe thefe treacherous and bloody Sectaries to purpofe. If any of our Reverend Brethren had been heir to have been ear-witneffes what three of the Lords now put in your firft claffis, did heir, in oppofition to the Englifh counfel and Montrofe, and all uthers who were for Irland, fure I am they wald have bleffed God who brought them hither in this nick of tyme.

If any Commiffioners fal come, I intreat yow, fie that fome of the ableft of our miniftery come alfo, who may be able to ftand againft Dr. Steuart and fuch lyke, if occafion fould ferve, and may ferve for the honour of our Kirk

---

[1] *Grallator*, one who walks on stilts or crutches.—Spang here alludes to Dr Bramhall's publication, *vide infra*, note page 87

with the Dutches alfo. If the lot fal on yow that ye moft come, ye will let me know fo much, that I may attend yow Ye may be fure I fal moft willingly contribute my little myte for the advancing of this fo good a work Oh ! if the Lord wald blifs it, fo might we yet hope for light in the midft of this darknes wherewith we are threatened. Ye writ to me that Mr. James Hamiltoune hes ordour to keep correfpondence with me He hes begun, I hear, with Mr Alexander Petrie, but forgotten me; yet falute him, together wit hall the reverend brethren of the miniftery of my acquaintance; efpecially Mr. David, Mr. Robert Douglas, and our freinds in the Weft.

The $\frac{9}{19}$th March 1649,   Your Coufine,
In my Chalmer at Hague   W ANDERSON

MR. WILLIAM SPANG TO MR. ROBERT BAILLIE.

Tibi foli.
COUSIN,

THE inclofed will acquaint yow with my diligence in what ye recommended to me. I have reafon to be glad that the honeft party at home with yow have fuch a good opinion of me, as of one whom they conceive willing to imploy himfelf for the publict Let me never live longer than whilft I have a defire to improve what is in me that way, which makes me more curious in afking for the grounds of your actions then utherwayes I wald be; and my doubts are meerly propofed that I, getting fatiffaction, may be able to fatiffy uthers. With all whom I have conferred with about the buffines for which I went to Holland, I fand none complayning lefs of the rigid feverity of the Kirk and Parlament's proceidings with yow than thefe thrie Noblemen, whom it moft concerned, as being thefe who are made to leave their countrey, and to fuffer the plundering of their goods by thefe fevere acts. I will not queftion what equity is in your dealing fo with them, but ye will find it had conduced more for the publick to have ufed gritter lenity. Neither (fo far as wyfer men then I am doe fee,) fal ye ever have any fure peace without refcinding this laft act, of your ranking, whom ye have pleafed to call Malignants, into four claffes. paffion hes bein too grit in that act; for it is judged a gritter fin not to proteft againft that late Engadgment than to be a ordinary drunkard, fince it is declared punifhable with a more fevere punifhment. Both freinds and enemies told me, that that favoured much of the Romifh feverity, where eating of flefh being a breach of man's law, is more heavely punifhed then notorious tranfgreffions of God's; and be affured that our enemies will proclame quickly this, with much more to the world, by print. Yet, as I have written, thefe three Noblemen digeft patiently all what is done againft them, and are moft vigilant and active for promoving of your ends Ye are not difappointed in your hopes of noble Lauderdail and Lanrick, and, I affure yow, of the Earl of Calender, who told me, in plaine terms, that the King may with gritter affurance confide in thefe who now rule with yow then in uthers · ye know whom I mean. If ye come hither, and do not bring a full refcinding of what the Parlament hes decreed againft them, ye will be looked upon as moft ingrate men; and none fhall be gladder of their mifery than the Englifh malignants and James Grame, becaufe they doe and have fo oppofed their plots Lykwife, it wald be needfull that ye remitted much of that rigour quhilk, in your Church Affemblies, ye ufe againft minifters who have proven your grit freinds ever before. It will be better to let the fails fal fomquhat laigher in tyme, befor a ftorme compel yow, or thefe who think God fo highly glorified by cafting out their brethren, and putting fo many to beggerie, making roume through fuch depofitiones to yong youths, who are oft mifcaried with ignorant zeal, may be made, through their aune experience, to feel what it is, which now, without pitty, is executed upon uthers. Generally, the grit pouer quhilk the Commiffion of the Kirk exerceth difpleafeth all: It is but a extraordinary meeting, and yet fits conftantly and more ordinarly than any Synod; yea and without the knouledge of provincial Synods and Prefbyteries, depofes minifters, injoyns, *pro authoritate*, what writs they pleafe to be read, inflicts cenfures on thefe who will not read them. If the Kirk of Scotland look not to this in tyme, we will lament it when we can not mend it. They fay four or fyve rule that meeting; and is not the liberty of the Kirk come to a fair market therby? We have an act that nothing fal be brought to a gritter meeting quhilk hes not firft bein treated of in a fmaller; but now your compend of the Generall Affemblie, or rather deputies of it, at the firft inftance, judge of matters, which might be better handled in leffer meetings For God's faik, look this courfe in tyme be ftopped, elfe the Commiffion of the Kirk will fwallow up all uther ecclefiaftick judicatories; and fuch miniſters who refide in and about Edinburgh, fall at laſt ingrofs all church pouer in their hands. I know ther is a peece of prudence herby ufed, to get the pouer in the hands of thefe who are good; but what affurance have we but they may change, or uthers, following this courfe, creep into their places? We meet with dayly regraits that the antient miniſters are contemned, and the infolency of yong ones foftered, the very forrunner of Jerufalem's deſtruction. The Lord mak us wyfe in tyme

Mr Samuel Rutherford is called to be Profeffor of Divinity and the Hebrew tonge in the new Univerfity of Harderwick I have prefently received a letter from Dr Valkemer, Profeffor of Divinity there, with one inclofed to Mr. Samuel; he writes to me that the States of Gelder, to whom that Univerfity doth belong, hes fent him his letters of call fome moneths fince, and defirs me to write alfo to him to haften his coming: This is by Dr Voetius and Steuart's ftirring. Ye moft be weil advyfed at home what to doe, if our Kirk can want fuch a man, in the grit fcarfnefs of fuch. It is not his Englifh writs that commendeth him fo much, as his Latin treatife againft the Jefuites and Arminians. If ye had publifhed any thing in Latin ye wald not be fuffred to ſtay where ye are, but then ye fould have loft your place in yeerly Provincial Synods Scottiſh miniſters are generally looked upon by the Englifh to be fo rigid in difciplme that there is no hope for any of our nation to have a place among them. Befides, the diffention of the nations, what a fearfull judgment of God is this upon us, that what we thought fould have joyned the nations unfeparably, is lyk to be the great feparator of them. it fears me many of our hearts in the perfute of it have not been upright I know not how this my freenefs may be taken by fome; but it comforts me that I am affured ye know it comes from a heart addicted to the weelfair of our Kirk, no wayes difcontented, that the godly party have fuch a fuey; only I wifhe we ufed prudence, leift we open a door to tyrannie, whilft we think to fhut out tyrants out of the Kirk The Divel hes many wyles to miflead men That monfter of Papacy walked modeftly at firft, and it was good but imprudent men that led the way to it

Ye will not doe weil to refuis coming hither when our Commiffioners come I wifhe both wyfe and moderat godly men come with you: all the countrey's eyes will be upon yow more than upon thefe whom the State fends. I hear much of Mr. Robert Douglas's moderation, (Oh! we mifs now that precious fervant of Chrift, Mr. Alexander Henderfon) · he wald be a man fitt for this purpofe whofoever comes, fee that ye come, and byde not behind. If ye think I can be ufeful for yow, let me be informed at your firft arryval to Holland. Ye will find our yong Prince of Orange, one of the hopfulleft youths that ever Europe brought forth, and willing to doe al good offices for the caufe; but more of this if God bring yow hither, and I be alive. My wyfe hopes to fee yow heir, and to clear your mynd from thefe doubts ye conceive that fhe is the caufe of my filence. Salute yours with your hopefull family, and all our freinds, both your colleagues in the Colledge and Miniftry, and our blood freinds the Lord direct yow al by his Holy Spirit.

When ye fend Commiffioners of State, let them be fuch as fpeak good French, if not Latine. It will be no great wifdom that who are fent muft be directed or made to depend upon any but ther auine prudence. Ye will doe weil to confider weel of the letter, quhilk *anno* 1646, the Affemblie writ to our late King; for the Independents makes it a part of the rule they walked by. And, 2dly, they fay, that in your laft Affembly ye have declared that thefe words of the Covenant wher ye fpeak of defending the King's perfon and authority, in the defence of religion and liberties, are explayned to be a limitation and excluding your obedience to him and defence of him, except in fuch acts: And then fays the bloody Independant, "Their putting the King to a violent death is not againft the Covenant; for they have put him to death not for his defending religion and the Parlament's liberties, but for going about the overthrow of both." Think of this. 3dly, Be ready to clear your late practifes againft the refolution of a lauful Parlament, and that by fome few, from being a ground of the army as privat men doing the lyk in England.

I mervel where Sir Jofeph Douglas ftayed fo long, that we doe not hear from him thefe eight dayes. The fhip of war quhilk our Confervatour got for himfelf, he procured a letter from the Prince to caufe it ftay for Sir Jofeph; and when it comes to Scotland it muft ftay the Parlament or my Lord Chancellor's ordour. it is reddy, and the winds fair, but Sir Jofeph is yet at the Hague. Certanly our countrey is much oblidged to our prefent Lord Confervatour, Thomas Cunyngham. It is a pity they let him be fo great a lofer for his grit reddines to furnifhe them in their need

That wretched committee of your former Parlament, by the Lord Cochran's malice, were going about to wrong him gritly; if he get not contentment now when honeſt men rule, ye will find leſs credite heirafter. Let him know how reall I am for him, as ye know I am to all to whom I profeſs friendſhip.

Since the wryting of this, and the uther letter of this fame dait, I bethought myſelf to write another letter, quhilk, if ye think fit, ye may communicat it to uthers, yea to the Commiſſion, but upon condition that no man miſconſtrue my meaning I know how reddy men will be in thir ticklefom tyms to intertane jealouſies of their brethren, and to make men offenders for a word; and therfor I remit the publiſhing of it to uthers to your prudence I only relate what I have from uthers, and theſe not malignants, but freinds. Moderat counfells uſed to be of account, and *feſtina lente* was a advyſe never a man repented of

I write this thrid letter ſince Sir Joſeph his coming hither, and that I heard fuch a change in the King I entreat yow not to ſpair any occaſion in wryting to me · with our Conſervatour, or the ſhip of war, ye will have a fit opportunity Tymous and ful information how matters ſtand with yow in good earneſt, may do much good, and ſince our Prince of Orange is fo earneſt, from tyme to tyme, to know the eſtait of our effairs, that he may be able to help us wherein he can, it is reaſon we fatiſſie him I have promiſed to give him notice of what I ſal know.

Your Couſin,
W. ANDERSON.

19th March 1649

For your felf only.

MR ROBERT BAILLIE'S SPEECH TO KING CHARLES THE SECOND, MARCH 27TH 1649: SPOKEN AT THE HAGUE IN THE KING'S BED-CHAMBER, TUESDAY, THREE O'CLOCK IN THE AFTERNOON.

MOST GRACIOUS SOVERAIGNE,

IN this very ſad and calamitous time, THE CHURCH OF SCOTLAND hath ſent ſome of us, who are here, Miniſters and Ruleing Elders, and others who are yet behind, in Commiſſion to your Majeſtie, to declare, in their name, not only the fincere and deep griefe of that whole Church for your Majeftie's moft lamentable afflictions, but alfo their reall and great joy for your Majeftie's fucceffion to the Throne, and their confident hopes, by the bleffing of the Moft High on your royall perfon and government, now at laft to come up out of that pitt of grievous confufions, calamities, fears, and dangers, wherein long they have been finking

According therefore to this our truft, we doe declare, what in our owne breaft often we have felt, and generally in the people among whom we live, have feen with our eyes, ane mournfull forrow for that execrable and tragick parricide; which, though all men on earth fhould paffe over unqueftioned, yet we nothing doubt but the great Judge of the world will arife, and plead againft every one, of what condition foever, who have been either authors, or actors, or confenters, or approvers, of that hardly expreffible crime, which ftamps and ftigmatifes, with a new and before unfeen character of infamy, the face of the whole generation of Sectaries and their adherents, from whofe hearts and hands that vileft villany did proceed

We doe alfo profeffe, in name of them who have fent us hither, the great joy of all forts of men in our land for the immediate filling of the vacant Throne with your Majeftie's moft gracious and hopefull perfon; earneftly praying, that the light of the Lord's countenance may fhyne fo bright upon your Majeftie's reign, that the very thick clouds of our prefent dangers and fears may flie away, and a new morning may fpring up, to all your three Kingdomes, of greater peace and profperitie, of more righteoufnefs and virtue, efpeciallie of more religion and piety, than hath been feen in the days of any, the moft pious, the moft juft, the moft profperous, of all your numerous Anceftors.

For the prefent, we are loath to take up more of your Majeftie's precious time, only we prefent the Letter[1] of our Church; and what furthr moft loyall defyres we have in commiffion, we fhall, God willing, be ready, in all humility, to offer fo foone as we fhall know of a fitt opportunity, to ftand againe in your Majeftie's moft gracious prefence.

[1] The letter from the Commiffion of the Church is dated the 7th February 1649 It will be given in the Appendix, along with a copy of 'The Report of the Commiffioners of the Church of their Proceedings with his Majesty at the Hague, made in the General Assembly, July 10, 1649."

Our Letter to the Commission. April 3d [1649.]

REVEREND AND BELOVED BRETHREN,

This is the firſt opportunity we have had of making to you any accompt of our proceedings. On Thurſday, at night, March 22d, the Lord brought us all ſafe to Rotterdame ; on the Fryday we went to Delph. There we thought meet to reſt till the Monday, both becauſe of our own reſolution to keep one day of humiliation in our familie for making our firſt addreſſes to God, as alſo becauſe of our information, by ſome of our friends who mett us at the Delph, that his Majeſtie would be taken up with his Eaſter devotions till Tueſday following We therefore, on the Sabbath, did preach and pray in our familie, and found the goodneſs of the Lord with us ; and on the Monday did put our papers and affaires in order At night we came to the Hague, and ſpake with ſome friends, who were not many here. On the Tueſday, the ſecond afternoon, we went to the Court, and had a favourable reception. My Lord Caſſillis did ſpeak to his Majeſtie in name of the Parliament and Kingdome, and Mr. Robert Baillie in name of the Church So farr as we could learn, what was ſpoken was taken in good part by all who heard We then delyvered our letters to his Majeſtie The reſt of that day, and the following, was ſpent in viſiting the Queen of Boheme, the Princeſs Royall. the Prince of Orange, the Princeſs Dowager, and the Eſtates Generall.

The Commiſſioners of Parliament found it neceſſary to give in, as previous to their deſyres, a paper, for removeing of James Grahame from Court. His Majeſtie's anſwer, under his owne hand, was, "That he deſyred and expected all our propoſitions together; to which he hoped to give a ſatiſfactorie anſwer. With this we were not content; bot preſſed againe our deſyre, the Commiſſioners of Parliament by ane other paper; and we alſo by one, ſecond theirs, a copie whereof we ſend yow herewith The King's ſecond anſwer was an abyding in the firſt We had all of us ſome diſcourſe with his Majeſtie about the equity and neceſſity of that our deſyre ; bot James Grahame hath ſo many and ſo powerfull friends in the Engliſh Councill, that as yet we cannot gett the King to diſcountenance him.

On the Saturday morning we delyvered to his Majeſtie the Nationall

Covenant, the Solemne League and Covenant, the Directory, the Confeſſion of Faith, the Catechiſe, the Propoſitions of Government, bound together in a booke ſo handſome as we could gett them. We ſpoke ſomething on the matter, and deſyred of his Majeſtie more frequent and private conferences, who ſhew his willingneſſe, and promiſed to ſend to us to advertiſe of his fitteſt opportunities. On the Sunday we preached in our own houſe. We thought not meet to go to the Engliſh congregation; their diſtractions amongſt themſelves for the preſent being ſo great, that our goeing there, we conceave, ſhould have given offence, and prejudged our affaires.

On the Monday we purpoſed to have given in our deſyres, in the paper which herewith alſo we ſend, bot his Majeſtie was abroad in the afternoon, ſo we delayed till this day. We cannot yet make any judgement of the ſucceſſe. The moſt part of the Councill are averſe from our deſyres; yet we have our friends. His Majeſtie is of a very ſweet and courteous diſpoſition: it were all the pities in the world bot he were in good company. We hope he is not ſo far rooted in any principles contrarie to us, bot that, by God's bleſſing on our friends labours, he may be gotten to doe us reaſone, whatſoever our fears be for the preſent. There is a very evill generation both of Engliſh and Scotts here, who vomite out all their evill humour againſt all our proceedings. The peace of France, and ane unhappie book, Εἰκὼν Βασιλική, does us much prejudice. Alſo the ſuppoſed death of Huntlye[2] is wreſted to our diſadvantage. Doctor Bramble[3] of Derne hes printed the other day at Delph a wicked pamphlet againſt our Church. We have no time, nor doe we think it fitt, to print ane Anſwer; bot by the grace of God, ſhall indeavour, with all faithfullneſs and diligence, to goe about our inſtructions. We had much need of your prayers. The grace of the Lord Jeſus Chriſt be with yow, and protect that Church and Kingdome from all the miſchiefs that the inſtruments of Satan on all hands are prepareing to

---

[2] George ſecond Marquis of Huntly, one of the Royaliſts who ſuffered at this time, was beheaded at the Croſs of Edinburgh, 22d March 1649.

[3] Dr John Bramhall, Biſhop of Derry, and afterwards Archbiſhop of Armagh. His tract here mentioned, bears the title of "A Fair Warning to take heed of the Scotiſh Diſcipline, &c." 1649, 4to. Baillie, notwithſtanding the remark that follows, publiſhed a reply to it, under this title, "A Review of Doctor Bramble, late Biſhop of Londonderry, his Faire Warning against the Scotes Diſciplin. By R. B. G. Printed at Delf, 1649," 4to.

bring upon us; bot our hope is in the name of the Lord, to whofe protection we committ yow, and refts,

     Your Brethren and Servants in the Lord,
       CASSILLIS.   ROBERT BAILLIE
       GEO. WINRAHAM. JAMES WOOD.

Hague, April 3d 1649.

MY FIRST LETTER TO MR ROBERT DOUGLASS. APRIL 3D [1649]

REVEREND AND DEAR BROTHER,

By the inclofed to the Commiffion of the Church, yow fee the ftate of our affaires here. I wrote to Warriftone fiom Rotterdam what was the pofture of our affaires, as then we were informed. As yet our fears are great of a fore ftorme to Scotland; yet yefternight I learned from a great perfon here, that our affaires, bleffed be God, are not defperate There is no Scotfman that is on the King's councill · the five or fix Englifh that are, Cottington, Culpepper, Hyde, Long, and fome more, are divided. The moft are of Prince Rupert's faction, who careffes Montrofe, and preffe mightily to have the King to Ireland Culpepper and fome bed-chalmer-men, as Willmot, Byron, Gerard, and the mafter of the horfe, Peircie, are of the Queen's faction, and thefe are for the King's joyning with us; bot all of them are much averfe from the League and Covenant The Prince of Orange, and by him all the Nobles here, are for the laft; and by their means we are fomewhat hopefull yet to cary his Majeftie to our Covenant, and the moft of our defyres for Religion; bot I dare not promife fo much: yet the greateft ftick, I fufpect, fhall be our fevere Acts of Parliament It feems all here, even our beft friends, will be peremptor for a greater mitigation than, I fear, fhall be granted by yow here. It were verily a great pitty of the King: he is one of the moft gentle, innocent, well-inclyned Princes, fo far as yet appears, that lives in the world; a trimme perfon, and of a manlie carriage; underftands prettie well; fpeaks not much: Would God he were amongft us. I fend yow herewith a copie of what I faid to him. Becaufe it was bot a tranfient fpeech, I give out no copies of it here at all; yet that we fpoke fo, it did us much good; for heavy flanders lay upon us here, which the report of our fpeeches helped to mitigate. Our enemies have great confidence, by the French peace, to gett powerfull affiftance from France. I verily think, if the King and we fhall agree, affiftance fhall be gotten from this State, and the Marquefs of Brandeburg, and fome others, for good purpofe. I pray God guide yow there to put no more impediments to our agreeance than are neceffary. My heart bleeds to think of a neceffitie for Scotland to have any friendfhip with the Englifh fectaries, the worft of men, and a warre with our King and countreymen in our own bowels. What relaxation yow may grant with confcience, and fafelie, let it be done freely and publicklie with this expreffe: It will admit upon no longer delay. Ye will communicat this to my Lord Warriftone.

Your Brother,

Hague, April 3d 1649. R. BAYLIE.

MY SECOND LETTER TO MR. ROBERT DOUGLASS APRIL 17TH [1649].[1]

REVEREND AND DEAR BROTHER,

THOUGH I have nothing at this time for the Commiffion of the Church, yet to yow I give this account of our further proceedings After we had given in our chiefe paper, a double whereof yow had in my laft, it was thought meet we fhould fpeake with the King feverally and privately. I went to him firft. He gave me a long and very favourable audience, from ten at night till near eleven The contents of our free conference poffibly I may fend yow on a fure occafion : at this time it is fcarce fafe, for there is ane Englifh man-of-warre near the Brile that fearches all letters comes from this : as yet we cannot gett it helped. In this conference I found the King, in my judgement, of a very meeke and equitable difpofition, under-ftanding, and judicious enough, though firme to the tenets his education and companie hes planted in him If God would fend him among us, with-out fome of his prefent counfellers, I think he might make, by God's bleff-ing, as good a King as Brittaine faw thefe hundred yeares. Finding the great fticke to be upon the League and Covenant, his own taking it, and affureing to paffe it for England and Ireland ; of his perfuafion that his paff-

---

[1] In Bailhe's MS. this letter is repeated but the second copy only has the postscript

VOL I

ing all the Acts of Parliament, paſſed or to be paſſed in Scotland, for taking of it there, would be fatiſfactory, I ſtrove by many reaſons to ſhew the unſatiſfactorineſs of ſuch a conceſſion; and the day thereafter, putt in wryte, the chiefe of theſe my reaſons, which I gave in wryte to the Prince of Orange, whom, after two long private conferences, I left, as it ſeemed to me, fatiſfied with every one of them, and promiſing to preſs them as hard as he could on the King. I fand he had cauſed tranſlate them in French, and had the fubſtance of them by heart. I found a way to acquaint his Mother with them, who is a wiſe and religious lady, and promiſes to hold her Son right. The moſt of the counſellors are for Ireland, and all, both they and the bed-chalmer men, even they who are very great and reall friends, are yet againſt our deſyre of the Covenant in England; yet I am not deſperate to get ſome fatiſfaction therein. We are looking daylie for ane anſwer. I feare I muſt engage with Doctor Bramble; for his Warning, it does ſo much ill to the King and all about him. We marvell ye write nothing to us. We have been vexed theſe eight days with conſtant reports here of the North's ryſeing, and David Lefley's retireing. However it be, ye ſhould not leave us ſo long without all information. No ſcrape hes any of us gotten, ſince we ſaw yow, from any man. In haſte, I reſt,

Your Brother,

Hague, April 17th 1649. R. BAYLIE.

By a good friend of myne, a Dutch Stateſman, I gott this double of the two papers the King gave in to the States-Generall, as yet he hes gotten no anſwer. The particular Provinces are acquainted therewith, but hes not yet returned their mind. Surely, if his Majeſtie and we agree not, I ſee no human way either of his or our preſervation; but God is great and good. It were a thouſand pities that ſo ſweet a man ſhould not be at one with all his people.

For MR. WILLIAM SPANG. SEPTEMBER 14TH 1649.

REVEREND AND BELOVED BROTHER,

YOUR letters are much rarer than they wont to be. Except that with Captain Gorcum, I ſaw none of yours ſince I was with yow; only I have heard thefe yow fent with the young man Thomfon of Edinburgh were taken with his trunk by ane Irifh fuggat I hope yow gott my old long ones, which my nephew David Donald delivered to my Lord Lauderdaill to be fent to yow; let me know if you have them, and thefe I gave to the Confervator, to be fent back with Gorcum, wherein was my letter to Mr. Nivein of Dort, to deliver yow fourtie crofs-dollers. For his negligence to fend them, as he promifed when I was there, I have payed to their owner thirty Scotts pounds When yow have gotten thefe fourty dollers, and the twelve rex-dollers I gave to your mother, let me know what yow want of three hundreth merks in crofs-dollers which I gott from the Colledge. In your firft letters to the Colledge, tell them yow have that much of me, for which yow fhall compt. Shew me what I am refting, and if I fhall fend it in crofs-dollers to yow with the firft occafion, or what other way yow will Caffillis and Warriftone lykes weell of your intelligence let it be continued

I thought to have fent yow a particular accompt of this Generall Affemblie as I had done of fome others; bot the diary I wrote in the time, I loft, fo I cannot now doe it; neither were there much in it worth the remembrance The hteing of two for the moderation fell to Mr. Robert Douglafs, the antepenult moderator: Mr. Gillefpie, the laft, was departed, and Mr. Blaire, the penult, never thorough weell fince his Englifh journey, was not able to come to Edinburgh, whereof I was very forry. The two Mr. Robert lited were, Mr. Andrew Cant in earneft, and Mr Mungo Law for a fafhion. The three the Affembly added were, Mr Robert Douglafs, Mr. John Livingfton, and, by equall voyces, Mr David Dickfone and me, but neither of us two would remove upon equall voyces, fo, without queftion, the voyces for moderation, fell on Mr. Robert Douglafs, whereof my heart was exceeding glad; for I was very feared for it, and it had done me great hurt The committees were framed according to the cuftom by the Moderator and Clerk in private, and read at the next feffion, without any change confiderable. We fpent very much time; whole five weeks. I thought a fortnight lefs might weell have done our turne Tranfportations took up much tyme, and depofitions of minifters. There had been diverfe commiffions, eaft, weft, fouth, and north, who had depofed many minifters, to the pitie and griefe of my heart, for fundry of them I thought might have been, for more advantage every way, with a rebuke, keeped in their places, but there was few durft profeffe fo much; and I, for my ingenuous freedom, loft much of my reputation, as one who was inclyning to malignancie

My Speech to the King, fpeaking fo fharphe of his Father's death, and the commendations I gave to himfelfe in the preface of my book, but efpecially a paffage of a letter I wrote from Holland, wherein, to a familiar friend, I fpeak of the act of Claffes as fo fevere, that it will be needfull to difpenfe with fome part of it for the peace of the countrey · for thefe things, before the Affemblie, fundry fpake of me all their pleafure, yet I conforted myfelf in this, that I knew I was farr from the calumnie impofed, and that all the wyfe men I knew profeffed their agreeance with me in the three things named. My unacquaintance with obloquie made my fkin, at this firft affay, more tender than needed; for I had fo oft in print declared my fenfe againft, not Sectaries alone, bot Malignants alfo, and that fo liberally, in my laft book, that I thought in reafon I fhould have been reputed above all fufpicion of that crime; yet I was neceffitate to drink more of that cup than I did truly deferve; for whoever in my Sermon to the Parliament, I was as clear as needed, and in my Report of our treatie did obtaine the unanimous approbation and thanks of the whole Affemblie, now in print; yet I behoved, in fundry voices of the Affemblie, either [to] quitt the libertie of my mind, or endure the whifperings of my malignancie to continue. This laft, though to my great grief, I behoved to choyce. I could not vote to depofe Mr. William Colvill upon his libell: The man indeed had, in my judgment, been ane evill inftrument in tyme of the Engagement, yet all was libelled againft him was mere filence in that Engagement. For that alone I could depofe no man, for the reafons I gave in the committee of the former Affemblie, when that act did pafs to depofe for filence alone, if continued in. My mind did never goe along with that act; though therefore I knew the whole Affembhe almoft was otherways minded, and forefaw the miftake of my voyce by fome, yet I behoved to voyce his fufpenfion to continue, and no farder. As for Mr. Andrew Ramfay, more was libelled and proven againft him, and all this year he carried himfelf in a cankerd untoward way; yet I told, I could not voyce to depofe a man of fuch age and parts: fo in that vote I was filent, to the peace of my own mind, though fome of my friends wrote fharp letters to me for it. I had alfo fome conteft with my neighbours in Mr. William Wilkie's procefs, whom I judged more hotly perfued than there was caufe. But my fharpeft conteft was for the

Principall, whom I fand fome men to perfew ſtill without any ground at all confiderable : contrare to their defigne, I gott him reafonably faire off Thefe contefts, and wrak of my friends were very bitter to my mind, and, joyning with the obloquie in the ear againſt me by fome, did faſch my fpirit fometyme, till I gott my grief and wrong vented and poured out to God; for there was no other whom I fand able and willing to help me It was a piece of confort to me, that I knew the beſt of the land were more (and on more probable grounds,) taxed for compliance with Sectaries, than I with Malignants, whom yet I knew to be innocent ; and that I remembered the cloud of infamie under which fuper-excellent Mr Henderſon lay, to my knowledge, till God and tyme blew it away I have been ofter and forer feared for the woe of Chriſt to them whom all the world love and fpeak good of, than I was grieved for any reproachfull fpeeches which fome were begun to mutter againſt me ; bot this now is our condition, that the cheife men both in Church, State, and Army, how innocent foever, are whifperit to favour either fectaries or malignants.

In our Report, when I had ended what yow read in print,[5] my colleague Mr. Wood, of his own motion, truelie gave a very ample teſtimonie to my Lord Lauderdaill and yow, for your fervice. What was fpoken of yow, all did take weell; but fundry were pleafed to miſtake what was fpoken of Lauderdaill, albeit my Lord Caffillis, in his report to the Parliament, had faid as much of him ; bot fome men fearing a defigne to bring Lauderdaill in imployment at this very tyme, was not pleaſed with any motions in that kind, otherwayes I had debaited in the grand committee much to have the fatiſfaction of the Engagers much fairer than it ſtands ; and once I had gotten Mr. Livingſtone, with the good lyking of the committee, to a draught near to Lauderdaill's mind ; yet thereafter that was cancelled, and the act framed as [it] ſtands, to my grief I wiſhed earneſthe, and fo did the Chancellor intreat Mr. Robert Douglafs, but out of tyme, that the frameing of the declaration ſhould have been committed to ane other hand than that it fell in ; who, how able foever, yet was generallie thought to be among the moſt fevere of the company to the King but this could not be helped Only many clauſes we gott altered in the committee ; yet, as it ſtands, I much fear it ſhall prove a diviſion wall betwixt the King and us for ever.

[5] " The Report of the Commiſſioners of the Church," &c 1649 *Vide supra*, p. 85.

We were alwayes expecting the promifed expreffes from him, and for that end, fome of us held off all we could, determinations of every thing concerned him; bot while none did appear, and when at laft Will Murray had come, but without any letter or inftruction, either private or publick, then there was no remedie, but the declaration and letter, in the ftyle yow fee it, and the Act about the Engagers, went out without contradiction; which, as I forefaw and foretold in the Hague, puts harder and more peremptor conditions on the King than there would have given fatiffaction.

We had greateft debate for ane act of election of minifters. Mr. David Calderwood was peremptor, that according to the Second Book of Difcipline, the election fhould be given to the Prefbyterie with power to the major part of the people to diffent, upon reafon to be judged of by the Prefbyterie Mr. Rutherfoord and Mr. Wood were as peremptor to put the power and voyces of election in the body of the people, contradiftinct from their elderfhip; but the moft of us was in Mr. Gillefpie's mind, in his Mifcellanies, that the direction was the Prefbyteries, the election the Seffions, and the confent the peoples Sundry draughts were offered · Mr Wood's, moft ftudied, was refufed, Mr. Calderwood's alfo, Mr. Livingftone's came near our mind, yet was laid afyde; mine came nearer the mind of all, and almoft had paft; but for avoyding debate, a generall confufed draught (avoyding indeed the prefent queftion, bot leading us into fo many queftions thereafter as any pleafed to make) did pafs with my confent. But Mr David Calderwood and Mr John Smith did reafon much againft it in face of the Affemblie, where, againft my mind, the Book of Difcipline was preffed againft them, and a double election made, one before tryall, and another after, as if the election before, and the tryall, by the Second Book of Difcipline, were given to the people, and that after-tryall, before ordination, to the Prefbyterie. This I thought was nothing fo, but was filent, being in my mind contrare to Mr David in the maine, though, in this incident debate of the fenfe of the Book of Difciphne, I was for him. However, allready we find the defect of our act; for, as I conceave, and expreffed it, fo in my draught, fo much direction in this act is due to Prefbyteries, that they ought to recommend to the Seffion men to be elected, without prejudice of their libertie to add whom they think fitt but I find it the defigne now of leading brethren, that the Prefbyteries fhall not meddle at all with any recommendations, but leave that whollie to any particular buffie man of the Prefbyterie, to whifper in the ear fome leading perfon of the parifh, to gett voices to any young man, though never heard in privie exercife, that he, by defyre of the people to the Prefbyterie, may be put on tryalls for fuch a church. This I find will be the way of our elections, which I think unorderly However, Mr. David Calderwood entered a very fharp proteftatione againft our act, which he required to be regiftrate. This is the firft proteftation we heard of in our time; and had it come from any other, he had not efcaped cenfure.

There was a defigne, at the laft Affemblie, to have gotten the hands of many minifters to a fupplication for moderating, in fome things, the power of the Commiffion of the Church ; which was expounded by this Affemblie truely to have been ane overthrowing, in favour of the malignant partie, the power of the Kirk. Great dinn was made for this Supplication, to try what was the bottome of it, and a very fevere act was made againft the thing; yet Mr Douglafs caried it fo, that no man at all, even the chief contryvers, did fuffer any thing for it, upon what ground I could never learn to my fatilfaction; whether, becaufe to Mr. Robert Laurie, the confeffed penner of the principall Supplication, impunitie was promifed for his ingenuous and early confeffion, and he being fecure, others lefs guiltie could not be gotten punifhed ; or becaufe others, forefeeing what neceffitie there might be for themfelves to doe more than fupplicate a Generall Affemblie, had no will that any fupplication whatfoever, efpeciallie being only intended, and never offered, fhould be a ground of Church-cenfure However, albeit a terrible act was made againft the thing, contrare to my mind, yet no man was to this day called to any account for it, nor, as I hear, ever fhall be

I was much afraid that the fubfcription requyred of the Engagers fould have made many prime men in our land defperate, but I am now very glad that fo many offers themfelves to doe all that is requyred · as I expect there fhall be very few who fhall ftick upon it, fo I wifh from my heart that Lauderdaill may be moved to doe what I fand Callander and Dumfermling ready for, when I was there with yow ; and what I faw in the Affemblie, Middleton very near, and others, as Galloway, Lithgow, Ogilvie, Bayhe, Innes, Cochran, Kenmur, Fleeming, &c. actuallie to offer I doe not expect now above three or four perfons in Scotland who fhall make fcruple of that fubfcription, which, I hope, may be a means to teach that man (for whom alone my love makes me afraid,) fome more wifdome. Mr. Harie Guthrie, in his appeall to the Affemblie, had ufed fome fharp and reflecting reafons, for which they fummoned him to appear, refolveing to have excommunicate him, if they did not find fubmiffion. bot quickly his fpirit was daunted; in all humilitie he appeared, and paffed from his appeall, which obtained him favour not to be farder proceeded againft. Mr. William Colvill took his fentence of depofition fubmiffively; Mr. Andrew Ramfay profeffed his fuffering: fome would have been at the prefent proceffing of both, as guilty of all the blood, and all the confequents of the Engagement; but Mr. Robert Douglafs did quafs thefe motions, which otherwayes eafily had been carried on.

It was all our minds to have had tranfportations better regulate than they had been; for indeed their needlefs frequencie was intollerable, yet Mr. Robert Douglafs gott all that fhifted till Edinburgh once againe be provided both of minifters and profeffours. For their Univerfity they moved for Mr Rutherfoord, but that was thought abfurd It feems they would be at Dr. Colvin, but he will not be given them, as a man demi-malignant. They who judges fo of that man, would give them Mr. James Wood, or Mr. David Dickfone, but in my mind, neither of thefe may be tranfported without greater hurt to the places they are in than benefit to Edinburgh, if they could get them. But as yet Edinburgh defyres neither, and on whom they will fall yet, it does not appear: we fear they trouble us one way or other.

One day I efcaped, to my fenfe, one of the greateft burdens ever was laid on me. Our committee, after many motions, had refolved for drawing up of the Storie of the tymes, to propone to the Affemblie a lite of three or four; Mr James Wood, Mr. John Livingftone, Mr James Guthrie, and me. My profeffion made me fecure of all danger, as I thought; and I minded it no more: but in the end of the Affemblie, when it came to be voyced, it ran wholly betwixt Mr. John Livingftone and me; and had not the opinion of my malignacie diverted fome voyces, I had undoubtedly been oppreffed with that charge As it was, I efchewed it bot by two three voyces; but I bleffed the Lord moft heartily for it; for to me it had all the days of my life been a burthen intollerable, for many caufes.

The Affemblie, for the full purgation of the Church, as in former years, fo in this alfo, hes appointed diverfe committees; one in Angus, one in Stirlingshyre, one in the Merse, one in Rofs, one in Argyle, with moft ample power On thefe committees the moft zealous men are put, that fome few can choyce, even of very young men lately admitted minifters, for depofing of fuch as Prefbyteries and Synods does fpare I acknowledge the difinclination of my mind to fo frequent depofitions of minifters, and to all courfes that furthers that, to me fo fevere ane action; but this is a great part of my malignacie.

I think at laft we fhall gett a new Pfalter I have furthered that work ever with my beft wifhes; but the fcruple now aryfes of it in my mind, the firft author of the tranflation, Mr. Rous, my good friend, hes complyed with the Sectaries, and is a member of their republick how a Pfalter of his framing, albeit with much variation, fhall be receaved by our Church, I doe not weell know; yet it is needfull we fhould have one, and a better in hafte we cannot have. The Affemblie hes referred it to the Commiffion[6] to caufe print it after the laft revifion, and put it in practife.

Thefe were the chiefe things of our long and tedious fyve weeks labour; only we appointed a letter to be drawne for our brethren of England for their encouragement The draught was Mr James Durham's: it was his firft; it did not fo fully pleafe as to pafs, but was referred to the commiffion to perfyte Our brethren of Ireland had fent Mr. John Greig to us, to have our advyce about their carriage in my Lord of Aird's defection. No publick advice was given, but Mr. Livingftone, and Mr Macklellan were appointed to conferr with him on all his propofitions.

All this while the Parliament did fitt, though ready to ryfe at our firft down-fitting, more than at our ryfing Their main caufe of fitting was to fee what we brought from the King. Thereafter, being to ryfe, conftant reports, week after week, of Cromwell's purpofe, to bring down the armie on us before it went to Ireland, made them fitt ftill to fee to the defence of the countrey. To encreafe the leavies, was to put the countrey to a farther burthen, while the prefent was fo great as could be borne, and caufed dan-

---

[6] This version of the Psalms, by an Act of the Commission of the Assembly 23d November 1649, confirmed by an order of the Committee of Estates 8th January 1650, was accordingly authorised for public use throughout this Kingdom after the 1st May 1650, and the same version still continues in use by the Established Church, and the great body of Dissenters in Scotland Some further particulars respecting its history will be given in the Appendix

gerous grumbling every where; alfo, if ane greater army had been on foot, the world would not keep them out of England, which we did not intend, being farr from any agreeance with the King; fo nothing confiderable was done or could be done, though the Englifh had come on us. They had written a letter, with a meffenger, to defire a Treaty with us. Our anfwer was, if they returned to their duty according to the Covenant, we were readie to treat with both the Houfes of Parliament; bot could not acknowledge the prefent authoritie. This drew from them a printed paper, in reafonable foft words; bot clearly enough renounceing all former Treaties and Covenants, as broken by our Parliament's invafion, ane advantage which they would openly make that ufe of, as to have it a breach of all their obligations to us. To this we made no reply; for what needs paper-debates at fuch a tyme?

While there is nothing to doe in our Parliament, they make themfelves buffinefs enough Our Weftland fhyres had, in the rates of monthly maintenance in bygane tymes, been burthened above other fhyres. Oft they had complained; bot no redrefs; they refolved therefore, now or never, to have it helped Caffillis, Ceffnock, Sir John Cheiflie, and others, got it fo contryved, that ane act paffed for their eafe, with the burthening of the Eaftern fhyres Againft this they entered a proteftation, efpecially the Commiffioners of Lothian and Fyfe, and well near the half of the Parliament, having Burleigh, Balcarras, Libberton, Louthian, to countenance them with their proteftation they arofe and left the Houfe. This divifion was very fafchious and fcandalous: it continued near a fortnight; bot was at laft accommodat, yet fo that the Weftland-men had their defyre This was not well fettled till the Burrowes fell out amongft themfelves in a great heat. Sundry of the burrowes had been long grudging that Edinburgh fhould bear fo fmall a proportion of the common burden, judging that for their trade and their wealth, the one-half of the whole burrowes burden might be laid on them, fifty of a hundreth, whileas they payed but a twenty-feventh part, or thereaway; fo in their Convention, at the Queen's ferrie, they advanced them towards a thirty-fixth part, and diminifhed Glafgow, St. Andrews, Irvine, and fome others, a part of their proportion This the Provoft and Counfell of Edinburgh took in ane exceeding evill part, and ftormed much at it, yet could not remeed it. But the moft bitter difference was the laft day of their fitting. Caſſillis and others, of a long tyme, had a great deſyre to have the annualrent ſo low as might be. Many wayes had been projected for the payment of your Lamſons; bot all had failed. The money had payed to the publict of the eighth that was due in the hundreth, one and a half; it was moved to put it to ſix in the hundreth, for the time to come, bot during the troubles to keep it at eight, whereof one and a half to be payed as of before, and the other half-merk to go to the Lamſons. When this was going, the whole Burrowes, except two or three obſcure ones, proteſted, with a high paſſion, and went out; the reſt ſatt ſtill, and for no dealling of Warriſtone and Mr. Robert Douglaſs, would ſo much as delay the cloſeing of the Parliament that night, for they feared, if they had delayed till the morrow, that the people ſhould have been ſett on them with tumultuarie ſupplications; ſo the Parliament cloſed without the Burrowes; yea, the Committee of Eſtates was made of a quorum, which ſhould ſubſiſt without them, if they ſhould perſiſt to abſent themſelves, as they threatened they would. Much high language paſſed on both ſydes; yet ſome days thereafter, the Burrowes were made content to ſitt in the Committee of Eſtates: But all theſe grudges ſticks in the ſtomacks of many, waiting but ane opportunitie to diſgorge them.

By William Murray's private dealing, it ſeemes Louthian was made willing, with Argyle's conſent, to have been ſent to the King, bot alone. Argyle therefore, off hand, moved in Parliament, in the abſence of Warriſtone, and without the privitie of the Chancellor, or any other of his friends of the Church, to have ane new Addreſs to the King, and carried it without any oppoſition. Bot incontinent many thoughts began to aryſe about the matter: ſome began to be jealous of Argyle, that he was inclyning to a new trinketting with the King by himſelfe; others, that the manner of his proceeding was to marr the matter of purpoſe. However, the raſhneſs of that unrype motion did no good: Louthian's employment was ſhifted. All it ended in, was a new letter to be carried by a gentleman; and, in the laſt day, he was voyced to be Libbertoun[7]; who finding the letter, drawne by Sir John Cheiſlie, though much ſmoother than the Church's drawn by Mr James Wood, yet to be ſo haſk, and the inſtructions ſo ſcabrous, that there was no

[7] The "Act appointing Mr. George Winrame of Libbertoun one of the Senators of the Colledge of Juſtice to repaire to the King's Majeſtie," &c. was paſſed on the 7th Auguſt 1649. The letter of the Committee of Eſtates, is dated 12th September, and with his Inſtructions, will be found in the Acts of Parl. vol. vi. p 506.

hope of doeing any good with the King thereby, has to this day shifted to goe for all his call. Yet I think it not unlyke he may be moved to goe now on the great change of the Irish affaires. His Majestie's chiefe hope was Ireland; and indeed it looked once prettie fair for him. Ormond had taken in all the South but Dublin, which he had straitly besieged. Cromwell, for all his diligence, had delayed very long to come over. My Lord of Airds, in a very subtill false way, had put himselfe in the government of Ulster. Sir Robert Stewart and George Monroe had joyned with him, and laid siedge to the Derrie. If Derrie and Dublin had been gott, there was no more adoe, bot to have sent for the King, and come over with him, first to Scotland, and then to England: This was the King's great snare all this yeare, to keep him off ane agreeance with us. But behold how soon all this hope evanished; Jones, having gotten some supply of men from England, makes an eruption on Ormond's camp so prosperously, that he well neer raised the siege. However, he encourages Cromwell, without more delay, to come over, shewing Ormond, for all his great force, so easie to be dealt with. Mackart, in the meantyme, joyned with Sir Charles Cutts [Coote], and coming towards the Derrie, made all our besiegers gett away, becaufe the ministers before had preached so much against Aird's treacherie, that few of the people had heart or hand to serve him, but generally all deserted him; wherefore he and his party, as it were by Ormond's command, began to threaten the ministers, which made them altogether leave the countrey, and come over to us. In the meantyme, Cromwell, in the South, hes put Ormond, without stroke of sword, to his garifons, and keeps Prince Rupert with his ships in Kinsail. Mackart, with his army, plunders at his pleafure in the North, and shortly it is expected Cromwell shall be clear master of all Ireland, as he is of England, and then have at the third poor broken Kingdome, more easy than any of the other to be swallowed down.

This being our case, lyklie our Committee of Estates may haste Libbertoun to the King, to see if, when the rotten reed of Ireland is broken, he will think better of our propositions than he did before; so much the more as the Presbyterians in England, by a very pithie supplication, which they sent to me, and I to our State, doe prefs the fame point. If either we neglect to feek him, or he continue to refufe our conditions, the ruine of both feems to be near; and though he were joyned with us in our terms, yet he hes delayed fo long, that our difficulties and his would be infuperable bot by the hand of God. Allwayes, we would fuffer all hardfhips with the greater comfort, that he and we were conjoyned in God againft the common enemie of God, of his houfe, and our countrey. If we make ane new application, who ever hinders the King to condefcend to any terms we fhall or can propone, I fhall conclude them in my heart, moft unhappie, and either very malicious or very foolifh men. My laft to Libbertoun, yow have here the double of it; and to my friend at London. In your next, let me know where the Duke, Callander, Seaforth, Sinclair, James Grahame are; but above all, what Lauderdaill minds [to do.] What is become of Willoughby, Maffey, Bunch? Alfo try to your power if there be any fufpicion of Captaine Titus's complyance, either with Sectaries or Malignants: it concerns me to know his quickly, if yow can learn. If your intelligence to Caffillis and our State be fo rare as it is to me, it will be little worth.

In my laft, I wrote for Bochartus, and Petavius's two volumes De Doctrina Temporum, fail not to fend them; alfo all Voetius and Marefius's late things. I pray yow fend what can be had of Chronologie that is worth; Apollonius or Morus will informe: we have Scaliger, Calvitius, Lanfbergius. Hafte to us Petavius. I purpofe to teach fome of it this year; and to affift me, write to me what yow know of Morus, and what is become of Spanheim and Salmafius's pieces for the King. When ye write to me ye ufe not to look on my letters, fo yow forgett to anfwer fundry things I require. help this: fhould ye not alwayes fend to us Mercurius Gallo-Belgicus. Try, by Mynheer William, (to whom recommend me heartily,) the ftate of the peace of Germanie, and of Spain with France; and if any hopes from Denmark or Swedden for our King. I wifh we had fome treatifes of the lawfullnefs of confederations, as of yours with the French and Swedifh, for it's lyke we muft preach againft the King's taking any help, either of Papifts or Lutherans, or any Malignants: if there be any Latine or French books of that fubject, let me have them. My beft affections to your every way good wyfe. I hope my next may be to your nurfe and fon. Read and clofe what I write to Voetius and Mr. Walter. If there be no danger in Morus for Ameraut's tenets, if he and Apollonius, by your means, can be made to agree weell on it, I hope he may doe much good: while I know by yow the man's temper, I wald not know him.

For Captaine Titus.[8]

Sir,

Master Trotter sent to me what ye wrote to him Auguſt 28th, September 3d. It came this afternoon to my hands · I was glad of it. I think we will now quickly ſend our letters with ane honeſt bearer All with us is in a deep quietneſs and ſilence. It ſeems Ireland is loſt; I think we ſhall be next tryed. James Grahame cannot come hither for the King's good: If he think to have any ſervice of us without If's and And's, he muſt come up, and that ſhortly, to our demands; which if he doe, he may have us yet to be his ſervants againſt all his enemies, without exception, whatever it ſhall coſt us. Whatever ye ſend to John Trotter it will come ſafe, though ſometimes late to me. The Lord be with yow, and all your friends there.

September 7th [1649.]   Yours.

For My Lord Libbertoun [9]

My Lord,

What yow and my Lord Warriſtone ſent to me, on Monday the 3d, came not to me till Fryday the 7th in the afternoon, becauſe given to a cadger; but if it had been to a barker, or any merchant, it might have come farr ſooner. What I anſwer ye will read and cloſe. I marvell ye are ſo long in ſending your letters It ſeems ye will ſtay till Cromwell perfyte his Iriſh conqueſt; which I think will not take long tyme, and then I expect him or his deputes in the heart of Scotland. Who thinks not ſo, or is not feared for this, I muſt have leave to ſuſpect much either his prudencie or his

---

[8] Captain afterwards Colonel Silas Titus, well known as the author, under the assumed name of William Allen, in 1657, of the celebrated tract, " Killing noe Murder, briefly discourst in three Questions," which is said to have occasioned so much alarm to Cromwell during the later period of his life

[9] George Winrame of Libberton, one of the Commissioners sent by the Estates of Scotland to Charles the Second, at the Hague. After his return from Holland, he had been appointed a Senator of the College of Justice, and was admitted 22d June 1649 He was employed on a similar mission to the King, in September, (vide p 99,) and again at Breda, in March 1650 He was present at the battle of Dunbar, 3d September, 1650, where he was so severely wounded that he died within a few days.

honeſtie. In our preſent condition of heart diviſion, for all our quietneſs, and ſubſcriptions to any thing ye will, I think him blind and fooliſh who ſees not our defence againſt the pooreſt invader is inconſiderable. I would bleſs the man that could ſhew the poſſibilitie of any reall reunion of our nation, for their own defence againſt any common enemie · bot the grounds of union, as matters now ſtands, are to me maine dreams. My hopes are in God only; bot for any help in man, not only our King and royaltie, bot religion, libertie, and all that's dear, ſeem to me weell near loſt, without recoverie, for a long tyme. O, if my fears were vain!

Yours,

September 7th [1649]   [R. BAILLIE.]

POSTSCRIPT.

If yow have any thing to ſay to Inchequin or Ormond, I think Sir Patrick Weems, who is in Edinburgh, could agent it better than any I know. I think both would [ſhould] be tryed, if they would renounce their Popiſh aſſociations, and be inſtrumentall to bring in all their Proteſtant friends to our Covenant Why doe yow ſend none to lye[1] for yow at the Court of Sweden ? Haſte ſome away to the King, if it were bot to underſtand what he is doeing Yow our watchmen ſhould not ſleep, though all the land be in a deep ſlumber, when a fearfull ſtorme, as I take it, is ſo imminent from the Sectaries to our Church and Kingdome and lives of ſome who mind to be honeſt againſt them, which I believe all mind not to be.

CLARISSIMO ET DOCTISSIMO VIRO D. GISBERTO VOETIO, SACRÆ THEOLOGIÆ IN ACADEMIA ULTRAJECTINA PROFESSORI

REVERENDISSIME VIR,

Ex literis dilecti fratris Walteri Bovii noſtratis, vicini tui, nuper cognovi ſtudium curamque tuam ut meus contra Doctorem Bramblium jam Belgice loquentem libellus tranſferretur etiam Belgice, et de novo apud vos typis mandaretur Agnoſco fraternum officium, et multum hoc etiam nomine me tibi debere profiteor, nec leviter devinctum probis illis piiſque viris qui te auctore

---

[1] Here *to lye* evidently ſignifies *to reſide*

id fibi oneris imponere voluerunt, ut opufculi mei cum tranflationem tum editionem, haud parva fua nullus dubito cum moleftia, procurarent. Quam vellem mihi daretur aliquando occafio exprimendi vel tibi vel ipfis partem faltem aliquam gratiarum quas in præfentia multas animo meo vobis conceptas fentio. Docebit, fi voles, D. Bovius ex meis ad D. Spangium literis quis fit rerum hodie noftrarum ftatus, et quam ingens nobis imminere videatur tempeftas, qua a Malignantibus quos vocamus, fi pergat Rex peffimis ipforum confiliis utramque fuam prout hactenus aurem præbere, qua a Sectariis, quorum res mutabili adhuc etiam in Hibernia, non Anglia tantum, fucceffu fluunt. Utraque hæc factio pari in nos odio æftuat, et ab utraque extrema omnia metuimus. Unica nobis in Jehova fpes eft. Ut multum egemus, ita valde defideramus tranfmarinorum fratrum in feriis ad Deum pro nobis precibus perfeverentiam. Ab initio ufque noftrorum motuum tot in nos noftramque caufam a tua pietate finceriffimæ charitatis fpecimina comperimus, ut fideliorem nobis in rebus quantumlibet arctis operam ab exterorum Theologorum ullo non polliceamur. Quare unice nobis in votis eft ut velit Dominus ad extremam feneétam te incolumem fervare, ut in domo Dei infignis illa tua lux diu fulgeat ad multos, quod facis quotidie, illuftrandos, et ad diffipandos non eos tantum errorum fumos quibus Pontificii, Arminiani et Sociniani veftias pro viribus ecclefias offufcare conantur, fed illas etiam tenebras quibus Independentes, Anabaptiftæ, Chiliaftæ, Antinomiani, cæteraque Sectariorum turba noftræ Britanniæ coelum maximo jam nifu obfcurare moliuntur. Hoc voto fupplex tuo nomine Deum veneratur

Addictiffimus tibi Frater,

ROBERTUS BALÆUS.

Plurimum falvere cupio doctiffimum collegam tuum D. Dematium, cujus magnam erga me humanitatem licet, in acuti morbi fervore, non fas eft oblivifci me. Salvere quoque peropto heroinam illam veftram Annam Mariam,[2] quam quod non falutaverim dum tecum effem perfæpe dolui.

Glafguæ, idibus Septemb ciɔ iɔc xlix.

[2] Anna Maria a Schurmann. This learned lady, whom Baillie regrets not having visited when in Holland, had obtained very high reputation by the publication in 1648 of a volume of Letters and Poems "Opuscula Hebræa, Græca, Latina, Gallica; prosaica et metrica," edited by Frederick Spanheim, and republished in 1650, and again in 1652. She was a native of Cologne, but was then residing at Utrecht. She died in the year 1678.

Mr Robert Blair to Mr. Robert Baillie.

Reverend and Dear Brother,

If it had been the Lord's will, I wish we had mett for many caufes. I hardly think that Dr. Strang can be in any hazard for what was before tofled and fettled by the authoritie of the Aflemblie, except there be fome new matter; and if foe, let him anfwer for it, and doe not ye, by intermedling in that kind, defyle your confcience and deftroy your name, which already fuffers not a little. Your folitarie vote concerning the two mifleaders[2] of that finfull Engagement, with wings flees abroad, to my no fmall grief: I think Lauderdaill and Middletone, and many of that rank, nothing fo culpable; and I affure yow, had I been there, I would have cordiallie caften them out. They have been more inftrumentall to advance that wicked work, both by their filence and fpeaking, than fuch as I have now mentioned. Get yow to your book and your work, and meddle not unhappilie to your prejudice. The Spirit of truth and grace reft upon yow. So heartily prays,

         Your loving Brother,

St. Andrewes, 29th July 1650   R Blair.

Letter from Mr Robert Baillie, under his assumed name.[3]

Reverend and Beloved Brother,

The letters of our friends, thir to Mr Douglafs and to Mr Jamifone, alfo

---

[2] Colvill and Ramsay. *Vide supra* p 92.—As Baillie, in his MS has inferted scarcely any letters addressed to himself, it is singular he should have made this one, containing some sharp but not unfriendly advice, an exception It is to be regretted that his own letters for twelve months at this period should not be preferved

[3] This letter has no address The Editor in 1775 supposed it "to be wrote to Mr. Chriftopher Love, beheaded on Tower-hill for corresponding with Argyle and Mr Baillie" Love was an eminent Presbyterian divine, and was one of the London Minifters who signed the Declaration against the execution of Charles the First It appears from Love's Trial, that a material part of the evidence rested upon a letter he was said to have received from Col Bamfield, which enclosed others from the Earls of Argyle Loudoun, &c and one from 'Mr Bailey,

two to the Generall Affemblie, the one of ane old date, the other fince the defeat at Dunbar,[4] came but latche to our hands. For feare of your hazard then, we thought it expedient to communicat them but to a few. At firft were called together, the Lord Chancellour, the Marquis of Argyle, the Earles of Caffillis and Louthian, with Mr. Douglafs, Mr. Blair, Mr. Jamifone, and Mr Wood. One and all were very much refrefhed and encouraged by the two publick moft gracious and moft feafonable letters. The anfwer to them was remitted to the nixt meeting of the Commiffion of the Church the laft of this moneth, where we purpofe to make more publick ufe of thefe, if we fhall then find [it] ftand with your fafety. In the mean time, Mr. Jamifone [*i. e* Mr. Baillie] was appoynted to give yow fome fhort accompt of affaires here; which be pleafed to receave.

This whole eight days before the defeat at Dunbar, the Lord had foe difpofed, that, to the apprehenfion of moft in both armies, a victorie feemed to inclyne to our fide. When, contrary to all appearance, the Lord, by our owne negligence, had overthrown us, we have ftill lyen under that ftroke, not fo much by any active profecution of the enemie, as by the Lord's hand now upon us, our divifions. A ftrong partie in the North, whom we have excluded from our armie for the late Engageing, did putt theirfelves in armes without publick order: It coft us fome time before we could quyet them. That danger was fcarce over, when ane other partie in the Weft, whom we have permitted to ryfe, and from whom we expected readie and happie fervice againft the enemie, fell in wayes of their owne, to our great and long difturbance; which we fuppofe Cromwell long before this has caufed print there. Unto it very myld anfwers were given, both by Church and State, as yow will read here in the copies fubjoyned: A while, notwithftanding, they perfued in their diverfe way; the enemie fell on, and putt them to a totall routt, whereby he inlarged his quarters now where he pleafes

in Scotland;" but these letters had no other address than a large L on the back, and when brought to him by one of the witnesses for perusal, they had been opened. Love, moreover, most solemnly denied, both at his Trial and Execution, his having had any correspondence whatever, either " with the King, the Church, or State, or any particular person in Scotland," since the War began between the two nations. But for such alleged conspiracy to assist the Scotish army in advancing Charles the Second to the Throne of England Love was condemned, and beheaded on Tower-hill, 22d August 1651.

[4] On the 3d of September 1650.

be-south Forth. However our griefe and shame for this defeat be great, yet the loss of men was much withm a hundied, and the prisoners are not foe many; and among neither, any man of note, but (who is now prisoner) Collonell Keri. Strachan indeed, the chief author of all this mischieffe, had before foullie betrayed his trust, and since is gone unto the enemie.

These mischieffes have laid us now lower in the dust before the Lord On Sunday nixt, the 22d of December, we have a generall humiliation, most for contempt of the gospell, the fountaine of all our plagues. On Thuisday theicafter, the 26th, we have another, for the sinnes of the King's familie, old and late, which we feare may have influence in the Lord's controverſie with us, yet for all this, we have not casten away our hope and confidence in the Lord; but with more vigour than ever we purpose, with all possible speed, to make use of all the remainder of our forces. The Parliament the other week did call together the Commission of the Church, to be resolved, how farre it was lawfull to imploy, in this case of extreme necessitie, these who, for sometime, and while we had choise of men, were excluded from the service The unanimous answer be them present yow have here subjoyned. By the blessing of God this may be a greater beginning of union among ourselves, and of a more happie acting against the enemie, than formerlie There is indeed some among us against the imploying of these who before were excluded; but we hope that in a little tyme this shall change, so much the more, as in very few, in whom it is greatest, there yet appears the least inclination to comply with the enemie And to guard the better against this evill, the Church, the other day, did passe the subsequent Act, which the Parliament is about to confirme, with a severe civill censure against all transgressors.

After our foresaid applications to God on the 22d and 26th of this instant, we have appointed to Crowne our King, the 1st of January, at Scoone, the ordinarie place of our old Coronations; and thereafter, so soon as we are able, to march, with the strength we can make, under the conduct of our King, with all our nobilitie and gentrie to Stirling, where it will be resolved, whether to goe with the body of our army to England, leaving such a partie here as to keep and guard the passes of Forth against the enemie; or, with the bodie [of our army], to attend Cromwell here, and to send Massey to England with some thousands of horse and dragoons. To the former the moſt part inclynes; but yow, with the next, ſhall be acquainted with our concluſions But, in the mean time, the neceſſitie is apparent for the extraordinarie diligence of our friends there to procure to us their poſſible aſſiſtance in this our ſoe neceſſare undertaking for the common ſafetie The particular way we are thinking on, I leave to ane other letter, ſent herewith, and to the inſtructions given to the bearer, C. B.,[5] whom we have found a faithfull, wiſe, and diligent agent for your deſyres to us, and whom we hope ſhall be no leſs ſuch for our deſyres to yow We have great need of your earneſt interceſſion with the Lord of Hoſts for his powerfull concurrence with us in this our great extreamitie Expecting this duetie of love from yow and our dear Brethren, I add but this one word, that the brethren there would be carefull, as we have been, and purpoſe ſtill to be, to lay, at this their new beginning, ſuch foundations for their Armie and Parliament, that the leading men in both may be firme and zealous to preſerve the Covenant, and our former principles, entire without violation Alſo, if it ſhall ſeem good in the Lord's eyes to bleſſe our mutuall endeavours, that our friends there may be zealouſlie conſcientious, that what progreſs was made in the Aſſemblie of Divines for the reformation of religion be not loſt, bot procured untill a finall concluſion and all be ratified by King and Parliament. I reſt,

Your Brother and Servant in the Lord,

JAMISONE.

Perth, Fryday, December 20th 1650.

For Mr. DAVID DICKSONE.

I SENT to my Lord Argyle and yow the two Remonſtrances, in my judgement very inſolent and ſcandalous pieces. If yow connive with them, and permitt two or three bold men to carry the Commiſſion of the Church to allow any ſuch wryte, I think yow conſent to put upon our Church the fouleſt blot that ever yet it got. This will be a fore tryall to yow: if either yow ſide with, or be a conniver at the wayes of the Remonſtranters, it will be to me a great griefe, a great diſappointment had I either been on the Commiſſion of

---

[5] Probably Col Bamfield, who appears from Mr Chriſtopher Love's Trial, to have been employed at this time in such negociations

the Church, or been written for by any at Stirling, or, on the Commiſſioners generall letter to our Preſbyterie, I had been defyred by our Preſbyterie to ryde, and not through Mr. Patrick's comeing been expreſslie ſhifted, I would have certainly come to the Commiſſion of the Church, and told freely my mind of theſe injurious invectives, invented only for diviſion, and increaſing of our preſent miſeries. I hope the Lord will aſſiſt yow to help our Church, our King, and State, when, by the deſignes of the Devill, and, at beſt, the imprudence of ſome men and ſimplicitie of others, all are lyke to be overthrowne with our owne hands: The hands of lurking Joabs will in time be diſcovered. This much to yow to whom I uſe to open my moſt ſecret thoughts.

A Postscript to Mr. D. D.'s Letter.

If my Lord Argyle at this ſtrait ſhould deſert the King, and verifie the too common ſurmiſes of many, which I truſt ſhall be found moſt falſe, and ſhortly ſhall be refuted by his deeds, I think, and many more with me of the beſt I ſpeak with, that it would be a fearfull ſinne in him, which God will revenge. We are not without our fears that the King's flight has been procured by Hamiltone's greateſt friends, expreſslie for the King's ruyne. But if Argyle ſhould have any hand with the Remonſtrants for the ſame end, his ſinne would be no leſs. That man my heart has loved till now; I hope he ſhall give me cauſe to continue.⁶

Your Brother,

Glaſgow, November 18th [1650.]   R B.

For Mr. Robert Douglass.

Howsoever the want of a call, either from the Commiſſion or our Preſbyterie, keeps me from the Commiſſion at this tyme, yet I am bold to tell yow my mind of the Weſtern Remonſtrance, that in my ſenſe it is a very ſcandalous piece, and exceedingly injurious both to the King and State, which, if our Kirk ſhould countenance, would bring exceeding great griefe to the hearts of many, I am ſure to the heart of one. I have knowne yow keep the

---

⁶ Baillie's fears were unfounded, as the Marquis of Argyle was the person who crowned Charles the Second at Scone.

Commiſſion from going the way of fome peremptorie men, howſoever I have been grieved, at other times, to fee yow let things goe with them which I fuppofed was contrare to your mind. If at this time yow fuffer yourfelf to be drawne over or to connive at fuch an infolent paſſage, I think you will contribute to give our Kirk and State a wound which in hafte will not be gotten remedied. It is an eafe to me to have fignified fo much of my mind to yow, whom I know by God's help to be able enough to doe good yet in this matter. If it goe further I will prepare myfelfe, as God pleafes, for fuffering, but withall to give the world ane accompt of my diſſent from the Remonſtrants wrytes and wayes. The Lord be with yow.

Glaſgow, November 18th [1650.]

For Scout, Mr. Buchan. [1650.]

If great words would putt our State from crowning the King at this time and make them fubmitt to the commands of our Remonſtranters, they may: If they will keep promife to the King, and tell us our duety, with any vigorous authoritie, I doubt not of our fubmitting in a ſhort time to all their juſt commands.

For Mr. D. Dickson, and Mr. W Spang.[7]

Reverend and Dear Brother,

I sent the inclofed to yow by Mr Robert Ramfay, thinking yow fhould have been at the meetings of Stirling and Perth, whither I was refolved not to goe, notwithſtanding of many earneſt intreaties to the contrare; yet, after the diſſolving of the meeting at Stirling, I followed to Perth, upon fundry letters from Stirling to me for that effect. Your abfence wes not weell taken by many; though I verily think your prefence would not have had more influence on the Remonſtrants than that of Mr Douglaſs, Blair, Cant, Rutherfoord, Durham, Wood, and others, who could in nothing prevaill

---

[7] This letter was at first defigned for Mr. David Dickson, but, as we learn from the letter itfelf, it was enlarged and sent to Spang.

with them. Of the whole matter, as it comes in my mind, I will give you a fimple accompt, but to yourfelf alone, and after to the fyre; for, as in all the meetings I was filent, and a meer fpectator, except one forenoon, wherein in fome things I declared my mind, fo I would defire to medle als little as may be with this unhappie ftrife.

After the woefull rout at Dunbar, in the firft meeting at Stirling, it wes openly and vehemently preffed to have David Leflie laid afide, as long before wes defigned, but covertly, by the chiefe purgers of the tymes. The man himfelfe did als much preffe as any to have libertie to demitt his charge, being covered with fhame and difcouragement for his late unhappinefs, and irritate with Mr. James Guthrie's publict invectives againft him from the pulpit. The moft of the Committee of Eftates, and Commiffion of the Kirk, would have been content to let him goe; but finding no man tolerablie able to fupply his place, and the greateft part of the remaining officers of horfe and foot peremptor to lay downe, if he continued not; and after all tryalls finding no mal-adminiftration on him to count of, but the removeall of the Armie from the hill the night before the rowt, which yet wes a confequence of the Committee's order, contrare to his mind, to ftop the enemies retreat, and for that end to ftorme Brockfmouth Houfe fo foone as poffible, on thefe confiderations, the State, unanimoufly, did with all earneftnefs intreat him to keep ftill his charge. Againft this order, my Lord Warriftone, and as I fuppofe, Sir John Cheiflie, did enter their diffent; I am fure Mr. James Guthrie did his, at which, as a great impertinencie, many [were] offended. Colonell Strachan did offer to lay downe his charge, being unwilling more to be commanded be David Leflie. Some more inclyned to doe foe; but all were quieted by this expedient.

Mr Patrick Gillefpie, by his diligence with fome Brethren of the Weft, had procured a meeting, at Kilmarnock, of fome chiefe gentlemen and minifters of the fheriffdomes of Ayr, Clydefdale, Barenfrew, and Galloway, where he perfuaded them, for the prefent neceffitie, to raife a ftrength of horfe and dragoones, as they had defigned in their Affociation, but farr above the proportion of any bygane leavie. This conclufion obtained, he perfuaded next to put them all under the command of four colonells, the lyklieft men to act fpeedilie againft the enemie, Ker, Strachan, Robin Hacket, and Sir Robert Adaire. They made their account to make up the old broken regiments of thefe four to the number of near four thoufand, befyde volunteers. With this voluntarie offer, Mr. Patrick Gillefpie, Sir George Maxwell, and Glanderftone, rode to Stirling However many did fmell, and feare the defigne of a divifione, yet the offer wes fo fair, and promifes of prefent acting fo great, that eafily, even by the Chancellor and Mr. Robert Douglafs's procurement, they obtained ane Act of State for all their defyres. By this they ftopped all mens mouths, and forced them of Barenfrew and Carrick to joyne with them. The committee of Barenfrew feeing the vaft expence of the enterpryfe, (for the very firft outreek would amount to five hundred thoufand pounds,[8] and the daily charge to four or five thoufand pounds,[9] upon the fhyres forefaid,) were generally averfe from the motion. My Lord Caffillis keeped off Carrick; Galloway alfo did difrelifh the matter; but the committee of Clydefdale, confifting of a few mean perfones, who were totallie led by Mr. Patrick and Sir John Cheiflie, being very forward, the committee of Kyle and Cunynghame being perfuaded by Mr. John Nevay, Mr. Gabriell Maxwell, and a few more minifters, the Act of State fuperveening, did quafhe all farder oppofition. All of us in pulpit, myfelf alfmuch as others, did promove the work. In a very fhort tyme three thoufand five hundred horfe are gotten together, with hopes, by volunteers, to make them above five thoufand. We were all in expectation of ready and happy acting, by infalls on the enemies quarters, but behold how all our hopes were foone moft miferablie blafted! Colonell Strachan his fcruples were not only about David Leflie's command; for in this his friends had procured him ample enough fatiffaction, getting affurance, from the Committee of State, that David Leflie fhould gladly permitt the forces of the Weft to act apart, and never trouble them with any of his orders, but Strachan's fcruples went much higher. Since the amendment of his once very leud life, he inclyned much in opinion towards the Sectaries; and having joyned with Cromwell at Prefton againft the Engagers, had continued with them to the King's death. At that tyme, by Mr Blair and our Commiffioners at London, he was fomewhat altered, yet not fo farre as to joyne with us in Covenant, till, by the great labours of Mr James Guthrie and Mr. Patrick Gillefpie, his doubts were fo farr fatiffied or fmothered, that he was brought to content the Com-

[8] £41,666 13 4 Sterling.   [9] £1000 Scots, was equal to £83 6 8, Sterling money.

miſſion of the Church for that, and diverſe other ſcandals againſt him: yet it ſeems that importunitie hes made him profeſſe large als much complyance with us as his heart did yield to. His eminent ſervice, firſt againſt Pluſcardie, and then againſt James Grahame, got him the Church's extraordinarie favour, to be helped with one hundred thouſand merks out of their purſes, for the mounting him a regiment, the greateſt offering which ever our churchmen made at one tyme. This did not a little lift his ſpirit, and gett him the farr beſt regiment in the armie · with the Weſtern recruite, it became ſtronger than any two regiments in the kingdome. At this tyme many of his old doubts revives upon him, which, by the knaverie of his Capt.-Lieutenant Govane, and frequent meſſages of his late friends, Cromwell and theſe about him, became ſo high, that though extraordinarie paines were taken upon him, yet he would receave no ſatiſfaction, ſo fair as to act any thing againſt the enemie, except there might be a treatie. And it did appear therein, that Cromwell wes not willing to retire, upon our aſſureance not to moleſt England on the King's quarrell, whom he profeſſed to be ſo farr fallen from all his right to England, that, for his wrongs to Scotland, he aught at leaſt to be baniſhed the land, or made ane perpetuall priſoner.

Strachan's axiome and debates did put the whole armie and committee of the Weſt in ſuch confuſion and diſcouragement that all acting againſt the enemie was made impoſſible. Bot the matter ſtood not at this poynt. In our debates, at the time of the Engagement, our publick profeſſions were, of our clearneſs to fight againſt the Engliſh ſectaries, for vindication of the Covenant, and the King's juſt rights, on the Parliament's grant to us of ſome few deſyres. Meſſrs. James Guthrie and John Livingſtone their whiſperings a little in the eare to the contrare, were not then audible · It wes ſtrange to me thereafter, when I heard Wariſtone and Mr. Guthrie ſpeak it out, that it would take a long debate to cleare from the Covenant the lawfullneſs of ane offenſive warre againſt Cromwell and his partie, yet in a ſhort tyme it appeared, that the quarrell of the King or Covenant or any quarrell tending to warre with the Engliſh, became to diverſe more queſtionable than it wont to be. Whether a fear of the troubles of warre, or deſpaire of conqueiſing the King to the publict or their owne perſonall intereſts, or a deſyre to keep the government not only in the forme but in the hands it wes in, or truely judgement of mind, did draw men to thoſe changes of former profeſt principles, I cannot fay, only a great deale of zeale wes begun to be practifed againft all who did fmell in any excefse of favour towards the King What ftrict acts of Kirk and State were made againft malignancie? What numbers were caft out of their charges both in the church, ftate, and armie? What barrs were putt to their readmitting? Yow know too much pleading wes for the juftice of beheading the King; what ever fault was in the actors Mr. Guthrie and Mr. Gillefpie's debates were paffionate againft the proclaiming of the King, till his qualification for government had firft been tryed and allowed You may remember the labour wes taken to hinder the addreffes to the King, and how lyke it was to have prevailed, had not the reafon, authoritie, and diligence of Argyle, overfwayed it; and, for all that could be faid, the voteing of Meffrs. Guthrie, Gillefpie, Hutchefone, and Durham that no commiffioner fhould be fent till a change in the King fhould appeare: and when it was carried to fend commiffioners, I will not forget the great ftudie of fome to make their inftructions fo rigid, that few had any hope the King would ever affent to them; and when (above hope) the King had yielded to all the Commiffioners had requyred, the induftrie of thefe fame men to gett new inftructions pofted away to Holland, which, if they had come thither before the King's imbarking, were expected by all fhould have ruyned the Treatie Yet when, by the extraordinare favour of God, the King wes brought in Scotland, to doe what either Kirk or State had requyred, and, upon this agreeance, the noyfe of Cromwell's march towards us wes growne loud, Sir John Cheiflie, Hoptone, and Swintone, keeped off, by their debates in Parliament, the raifeing of our armie fo long, that we were near furpryfed, and when our armie wes gotten together at Leith, the fame men helped, by their continuall croffe debates, to keep all in confufion; their ftrange affronting of the King at Leith; the putting of him to a new declaration; and, when he ftucke but at fome hard expreffions concerning the perfons of his Father and Mother, their procuring from the Kirk and State that terrible Act of difclaiming his intereft, of the 13th of Auguft; that fame night, without the Kirk's knowledge, printed it, and fent to Cromwell with a trumpet· All thefe things bred jealoufies in the obfervers, what the intentions of fome men might be, yet all wes diffembled, till after the defeat at Dunbar thefe intentions brack out in their actions.

Soe foone as they faw it probable that they were to have a force to be ruled by themfelves alone, it became their work to have that armie fo great, and the other at Stirling fo fmall, as they were able. Then, in thefe meetings with Mr. Patrick Gillefpie, where Sir John Cheiflie and fome three of our burgeffes did meet oft and long, propofitions of a ftrange and high nature were in hand, as Robert Lockhart, who fometymes wes prefent, did fhow to Argyle and others. The firft vent of their motions wes at the Provinciall [Synod] in Glafgow, where Mr. Patrick, Mr G., Mr. Hutchefone, Ker, Strachan and others, with much night-wakeing, did bring forth that ftrange Remonftrance of the fynod, where Mr. Patrick obtaining a Committee to confider the finnes procuring the wrath of God on the land, did put fuch men on it as he lyked beft, and by them the frameing of the draught was put upon himfelfe, who quickly begatt that prettie piece which I fent you It doubtlefs had been the fubject of more difcourfe, had it not been drowned in the fubfequent more abfurd one [by] the fame hand, in name of the Armie; for at the very firft, it fell on the face of the Generall Affemblie and Parliament, and condemns both for their firft treating with the King, and for the renewing of it in a fecond addreffe, but moft for clofeing of it without evidence of his reall change. Then thefe moft bitter invectives againft the State, for which Mr. Patrick had ufed foe high language with yow and Mr. Douglafs, in face of the commiffion, at Leith, are all brought in, with large additions to any thing was then heard. I have oft regrated of late to fee the Judicatories of the Church foe eafily ledd to whatever fome few of our bufie men defigned, but never more than in the particular in hand I am fure the moft of that wryte wes without the knowledge of the moft, and againft the fence of many, of the Brethren; yet all wes voted, *nemine contradicente*, except honeft Mr William Ruffell, Mr Robert Ramfay, and Mr. John Bell, fpoke a little to fome words, but on the matter let all goe. Fearing what was in hand, I could fpeak little The night before I expected nothing more fhould have been preffed but a keeping out Engagers from the armie · I loved not to appear in contradiction to fome violent men; yet my heart being againft their conclufion, I wes, after much foliciting and prayer, brought to a neceffitie of contradicting, and had thought on fome reafons for that poynt to have been mainly proponed for my diffent, although I doubt not but my impatience and canker had broken out, if I had heard, which I never dreamed of, their invectives againft the Treaties; but the Lord, in a very fenfible way to me, caryed it foe, that neither the Synod wes troubled with me, nor the peace of my mind by them. I once inclyned to abfent myfelfe, and had indeed gone out, but behooved to return, not daring to take that courfe. But behold, when I was ready to goe to the Synod at that dyett when the Remonftrance came in, my Lord Caffillis fent his man to call me to fpeake with him at his lodgeing. While we are a little ferious about fundry of the publick affaires, I found that more tyme had gone than either of us had obferved, and telling him that my abfence from the Synod might be miftaken, I took my leave, and with all the hafte I could make I gott up to the Church; where I found, at my entrie, that all the debates on that paper were clofed, and after thrice reading, it wes goeing to the vote. I adored Divine providence, who truely befyde my purpofe, but much to my content, had given me a faire occafion to fay nothing of a wryte, whereof I never heard lyne read. This, for the time, and fince, wes a fatiffactorie ground for my filence, to my owne mind, in that Remonftrance, which brought to the confenters, let be contryvers, but fmall credit; the commiffion of the Church having fo farr difavowed it, as for no requeft they could be induced to countenance it towards the Committee of Eftates; but Mr Patrick behooved to prefent it himfelf, without the companie of any from that meeting, which would have occafioned a noyfe, had not the fecond Remonftrance filled the eares of the whole kingdom with a louder found.

Mr Robert Ramfay and others had preffed in the Synod that for removeing of jealoufies from many who were then fpeaking their doubts of fome men's intentions, the officers of the Armie fhould putt forth a declaration of their defignes. To me the motion favoured not; fince the raifeing of thefe forces wes allowed by the State, all declarations from particular officers feemed needlefs. yet, on the Synod's motion to Colonell Ker, a declaration by him and his fellows wes promifed, and prefently gone about by Mr. Patrick and the chieffe affociates then prefent. But, as Mr. Patrick told us, it wes laid afide by the advyce fent them by Wariftone from Stirling and Mr James Guthrie, (betwixt whom and them the pofts then and thereafter runne very thick night and day,) not fo much on that ground he told us, that they thought it illegall for fuch private perfons to make publick manifeftoes, as for that, as I fufpect, which he told us not.

About this tyme the King's head was filled by fome unhappie men about him, efpeciallie Doctor Frafer and Henry [Jermyn,] with many extreame fears After the affront at Leith, they had raifed fufpicions in his mind, whilk, upon the defeat at Dunbar were increafed, but by the feparate ryfeing in the Weft brought near to the head of a defigne to break the treatie with him, and agree upon his expenfes with Cromwell. Upon thefe motions the Malignants in the North ftept in, and by the forenamed perfons began a correfpondence for the raifing of the North, under the conduct of Middletone, for his prefent fervice. So many Noblemen were on this unhappie enterprife · Craufurd wes given out for its head and contryver, albeit he profeffed to me his oppofition to it : Lauderdaill knew of it ; but he hes laid fo farre to me, that I believe him, he oppofed it to his power However, the thing was fo foolifhlie laid, and the King, by the counfells of thefe about him, wes foe various in giving order for that ryfeing, fometymes commanding and then countermanding to ryfe, that all the party wes put in a confufion ; yet, by the information of thefe forefaid fooles, the King being put in fear, that Lorne, goeing timelie to bury a fojour, wes drawing together his regiment to lay hands on him, contrare to his former refolutions, he took horfe with fome two or three, as if he had been for to goe for a haulking, but croffed Tay, and ftayed not till he came to Cloue [Clova] in Angus By the way be repented of the journey, and meeting with Lauderdaill at Dudhope, and Balcarras coming from Dundee by accident, wes almoft perfuaded by them to returne , yet by Dudhope and Buchan he was keeped into Cloue But when he came to that miferablie accommodate houfe, and in place of the great promifed forces, he faw nothing but a fmall companie of Highlanders , he prefently fent for Robert Montgomerie, who wes near with his regiment, and without more adoe, did willinglie returne, exceedinglie confounded and dejected for that ill-advyfed ftart When it was firft blazed abroad, it filled all good men with great griefe, and to my owne heart it brought one of the moft fenfible forrowes that in all my life I had felt. Yet his quick returne of his owne accord, and his readinefs to give all fatiffaction for that failzie, and his kind receaveing by the Committee of Eftates, among whom he ever fatt after his returne, (though never before,) did turne our griefe fuddenlie into joy, his abfence not lafting above two full dayes. Yet all men were not fo foone fatiffied. Sundry of them who had been on the plott, fearing a difcoverie and punifhment, lappe to armes ; Lewis Gordon, Ogilvie, Athole, and others, under Middletone's command, putting out a number of faire pretexts for their ryfeing This might have deftroyed all, yet, by God's mercie, all wes quicklie quyeted. David Leflie, with all his horfe, marched towards them; the King wrote earneftly to them to lay downe. The Committee of Eftates fent a faire act of indemnitie, and foe without more adoe they went home. Mr. James Guthrie had weell near marred this peace: he moved Middletone's fummar excommunication. Mr Robert Douglafs, and moft number prefent, were againft it, yet Mr. James and Mr. Patrick, by two or three votes of elders, did obtain it; and though the Committee of Eftates, by ane earneft letter, intreated Mr James to delay a little the execution, yet on the next Sabbath he did execute the fentence, to the regrate of many

When the Northern ftorme wes ended, the Weftern winds began to blow the louder I told their declaration wes keept in by advice from Stirling, as many thought, to make vantage of the new failings at Court; for thefe wes looked on with a greedy eye, and exaggerate to the height of trueth. When, with a great deall of expenfes and trouble, our forces in the Weft were levied, and prefent action againft Cromwell promifed and expected, the very firft march is to Dumfreifs, the fardeft place they were able to choife from the enemies quarters. The pretence was, to attend the motion of the enemie comeing from Carlile; but when the partie who went from Edinburgh to fetch them, neither in the goeing nor comeing, wes looked upon, nor any good at all done by that long march, but the hazarding of the countrey, and the fpoyling of a number of noblemen and gentlemen of their fadle-horfes, and lying ftill at Dumfreifs, while Cromwell took up Glafgow; this made it vifible they had fomething other in hand than to mind the enemie By their earneft miffives they had brought Wariftone from Stirling to Dumfreifs. There, after fome debate, the draught of the Remonftrance is brought to fome perfection, you fee. It feems one maine end of both Remonftrances wes to fatiffie Strachan, and for that end they did come up weell near to his full length both about the King and the State, the Malignants and England For in this laft paper they are cleare in condemning the Treatie as finfull, and notwithftanding of it, to fufpend the King's government till he fhould give fatiffactory evidence of his reall change, whereof they were to be judges, who were never like to be fatiffied, although they were not like to be troubled with the judgeing of thefe fignes, for the King, who had ftarted away upon the fufpition of thefe things, upon the fight of them in ane Army-Remonftrance, wes not like to ftay; foe on this efcape the government of the Kingdome, and the diftribution of the Royall rent in new penfions, all the former being voyd, fell in our own hand; and if the King fhould have ventured to ftay, then ane effectuall courfe wes moved to be taken with him to keep him from joyning with Malignants, which could not be but by a ftrong guard or imprifonment; albeit this was needleffe, if the courfe againft Malignants had been taken to putt them out of all capacitie to hurt the people and caufe of God, for this could not be but by executing, forfaulting, and impriffoning of the chiefe of them, as we thought fitt.

As for our prefent ftate, fo many and groffe faults wes preffed againft Argyle, the Chancellour, Louthian, Balcarras, and others, that in all reafon, they behooved to be laid afide, and our State modelled of new; foe that no active nobleman fhould have had any hand therein; and as for England, they might reft fecure of our Armies, not only till Church and State fhould agree on the lawfullnefs and expediency of that warre wes found, but alfo a cleare call from England fhould appeare, and if we could not marre the one, and Cromwell the other, yet we behooved to move nothing of bringing this King to England, whom we had found unmeett to governe Scotland, and though thereafter he fhould change never foe much to the better, yet it wes injuftice for us to medle with a Kingdome not fubordinate to us. Thus farr the Remonftrance went on, and clofed with a folemne ingadgement on all their hearts, (if God bleffed their armies,) to fee all thefe things performed. I have oft marvelled that Strachan remained diffatiffied for all this, for I verily think, whatever he or Cromwell could have defyred in Scotland, would eafily have followed upon the former premifes.

While thefe things are a-doeing at Dumfreifs, Cromwell, with the whole body of his army and canon, comes peaceably by the way of Kilfyth to Glafgow. The minifters and magiftrates flee all away. I got to the Ifle of Connay, with my Lady Montgomerie, bot left all my family and goods to Cromwell's courtefie, which indeed was great, for he took fuch a courfe with his fojours that they did leffe difpleafure at Glafgow nor if they had been at London, though Mr. Zacharie Boyd railled on them all to their very face in the High

Church. I took this extraordinarie favour from their coming alone to gaine the people, and to pleafe Strachan, with whom he was then keeping correfpondence, and by whom he had great hopes to draw over the Weſtern army, at leaſt to a ceffation with him; as indeed he brought them by his means to be altogether ufelefs; though on a report of their marching towards Edinburgh, he left the weſt in a great fuddentie and demi-diforder.

So foone as the Remonſtrance was perfected, and all prefent at Dumfreifs profeſſed their aſſent to it, except Strachan, conceaving it to be too low for his meridian, Mr. Patrick and Mr. John Stirling, with fome of the gentlemen, went along with it to Stirling, and Wariſtone in their companie. The Commiſſion of the Kirk refuifes to medle with it, only Mr Robert Douglaſs writes to the Preſbyteries to fend to the next meeting at Stirling, with their commiſſioners of the Church, fome more of their number, of greateſt experience and wifdome, to advyfe in matters of great importance. The Committee of Eſtates, by Wariſtone's means, at their firſt prefenting, put no affront on it; but what wes a verie dangerous errour, gave too good words to the carriers; and, to allure them to action againſt the enemie, increafes their forces, by joyning with them the dragoons of Niddefdale and the Lennox; and overfeeing alfo the feathers which they had drawne out of the Stirling's wing, the putting them in hope to gett the Stirling's neſt, which made them march quicklie weſt to Partick, in order to Stirling, thinking that Leſlie and Middletone ſhould have been in others fleſh in the north. But to their open difcontent, the northern ſtorme being compofed, and David Leſlie returned to Stirling, they turned their head ane other way.

When, after my return to Glafgow, I did fee their Remonſtrance, and Cromwell's letter thereupon, on the occafion of Strachan's Quæries, requyring a treatie, which at that fame time he fent his prifoners Mr Jaffray and Mr. Carſtairs to agent, I wes fore grieved, but knew not how to help it; only I fent the copies of all, with expreſſe bearers to Argyle and yow at Innerary, and to the Chancellour at Perth, and Mr. James Fergufone at Kilwinning, with my beſt advyce to yow all, and refolved myfelfe to keep the next meeting of the Commiſſion, on the call of their letter, to declare my diſſent, if I could doe no more. But behold, the next Preſbyterie day, when I am abfent, Mr. Patrick [Gilleſpie] caufes read again the Commiſſion's letter, and had led it foe, that by the elders votes, [the] men of greateſt experience and wifdome of our Prefbyterie were the two youngeft we had, Mr Hew Binning and Mr Andrew Morton Then when it was preffed that I might be but added to them, it wes, by a vote, refufed upon fuppofition it wes needlefs, being clear I would doubtlefs goe howfoever. Thefe defpytefull votes wrought foe on my mind when I heard of them, that I refolved not to goe, for all that could be faid to me by many of the brethren, yet the clerk of the Commiffion, at the Moderator's direction, writing to me from Stirling a preffing letter, I went along to Perth; where, by God's good providence, I have ftayed fince for many good purpofes

At the meeting of Sterling, there was a conference appointed of the chief members of the Committee of Eftate and Commiffion of the Church, on the Remonftrance; wherein there were many high words about it betwixt Wariftone and Mr. Robert Douglas, Mr Robert Ramfay and Mr. Patrick Gillefpie, Mr. James Wood and Mr James Guthrie, and others · no appearance there was of any iffue The time of Parliament at Perth drawing near, the King, by his letter, invited the meeting of Church and State to Perth. The defyre of many wes but to have fome agreeance before; if no other way were poffible, as none appeared, that the Remonftrance might be laid afide, and much of the matter of it be preffed in ane orderly way by the Commiffion of the Kirk, and the forces of the Weft be joyned with thefe at Stirling; fince for fo long a time, they had acted nothing apart, and never like to act nothing for any purpofe alone The Remonftrants were averfe from thefe motions; fo all wes laid afide till they came to Perth; at which time a new conference wes appointed, and four whole dayes kept in Argyle's chamber. I then, and thereafter, wes witnefs to all, and little more than a witnefs; for not being a commiffioner, I thought meet to be filent. For the one fide, Mr Patrick and Wariftone fpoke moft; for the other, Argyle, the Chancellour, the Advocate, and Mr. Robert Douglafs; but Mr Wood fpake moft, and to beft purpofe. Mr. Rutherfoord and Mr. Durham faid fome little for fundrie points of the Remonftrance Mr James Guthrie moft ingenuouflie and freely, did vent his mind, for the principal point, (as he avowed he had oft before maintained,) " That the clofe of our treatie wes a finne, to promife any power to the King before he had evidenced the change of his principles; and the continuing of that power in his hand wes finfull till that change did appear." Though it wes vifible, that every day the kingdome languifhes, under thefe debates, which impeded that action, there was no remead: by no perfuafion the Remonftrance could be taken up, yea, the gentlemen gave in a petition to the Eftates at Perth, in the prefence of the King, urgeing the anfwer thereof, from which petition they would not paffe yea, when they were moft earneftly dealt with to conjoyne their forces, all that could be obtained, both by publict and diverfe private intreaties, both of their beft friends, Argyle, and others, there wes a willingnefs to joyne on two conditions The firft wes, ane expreffe laying afide of the King's quarrell in the ftate of the queftion; the other, to keep none in the armie of Stirling but according to the qualifications in the act of Parliament. When in thefe two all of the gentlemen and officers were found peremptor, the conference on the Fryday, the fourth day of it, wes broken off as fruitlefs, though, for their fatiffaction, the Parliament had been fhifted from the Wednefday to the Fryday, and from the Fryday to the Tuefday againe, for all the iffue of blood, and ftarveing, that wes every day over the Kingdome.

Before the meeting at Stirling, the Remonftrants had a folemne meeting at Glafgow, by Mr. Patrick [Gillefpie s] call, where, the fubfcryving of the Remonftrance was much preffed on the great committee of gentlemen and officers, by the minifters, who did fitt apart in the Tolbuith, and called themfelves the Prefbyterie of the Weftern Armie That fubfcription was generally declyned, and by no perfuafion any more could be obtained nor a warrant, fubfcryved by Crofbie the prefident of the committee, to fome few commiffioners, to prefent the Remonftrance to the State Mr. Robert Ramfay, fore againft my mind, did offer, in his owne and my name, once and againe, to come and debate, in their prefence, with the brethren, the injuftice of that Remonftrance This offer was told in the committee: all the anfwer it gott was, that no man wes excluded to come and propone what they pleafed. Upon fuch intertainment we let them alone Here it wes where Strachan, before having laid downe his charge, wes commanded to goe no more to the regiment; bot he told them expreffie, he could not obey. Some would have been at laying him faft, for feare of his goeing to the enemie; but leaft that Ker and many more fhould thereby have been provocked, they let him alone Govane, for his known correfpondence with the enemie, wes cafheired, and their fhout-mafter Dundafs alfo. Sundry of the officers were fufpected to be of Strachan's principles, albeit the moft went not beyond the Remonftrance.

When the conference wes broken off, the Committee of State went about their anfwer to the petitioners; and there began debate; the moft found the matter high treafon: the divefting the King of his authoritie; the breaking of the Treatie clofed and approven by Kirk and State; the felandering highly of the Judicatories; and ingadgeing of private men to change the government: the deepnefs of thefe crymes did trouble the judges; the refpect the moft of them had to the perfons guilty, moveing them to goe farr lower than the wryte's deferving; and all of them being refolved to make no more of it than was in the Committee's power to pardon, they went therefore no higher in the cenfure than you have in the fentence; from which yet near fyfteen diffented for one or other word, though all profeffed their difallowance of the wryte. This diffent wes in the King's prefence If he had been abfent, as fome would have perfuaded him, the diffent might have been greater; for Wariftone wes very long and paffionate in his exhortation to wave it fimply, which had been very unhandfome, fince the parties peremptorlie refufed to take it up. At the fentence, the gentlemen did ftorme, but the minifters much more. It came next to the Commiffion of the Church, the States had given in their fenfe to them, and requyred the Kirk's judgement. Here came the vehement oppofition: The Remonftrants petitioned to have the prefent confideration thereof laid afide, leift the parties fhould be difcouraged to act againft the enemie: Mr. Rutherfoord preft this with much more paffion than reafon, and Mr. James Guthrie alfo. Here it wes where I fpoke but fo much as declared my fenfe againft the thing. Much dealing wes ftill to take it up: Meffrs. Cant, Blair, Rutherfoord, Durham, were fent to perfwade them; but Mr Patrick wes peremptor to fhew their willingnefs to quit their life rather than their teftimonie. So when there wes no remeed, at laft, by Mr. Robert Douglafs and Mr. James Wood's induftrie moft, it came to that mild fentence which yow fee here fubfcryvit. With it the parties were highly offended, and entered their loud proteftation. Mr. Robert Blair came in the hinder-end. He and yow, by your letters, had fignified your judgement much averfe from the Remonftrance; which in a fcolding way wes cryed out by Mr. John Nevay in Mr. Blair's face: to which he replyed nothing. Mr. David Bennet and Mr. Hugh Peebles expreft themfelves bitterlie, and were anfuered accordingly by others. Our Provoft, George [Porterfield,] fpoke in his proteftation of fomething like fealing the Remonftrance with his blood. All of them went out of town highlie mifcontent; though als little occafion was given them as poffible could be, either by Church, or State, or any perfone I thought the fepaiation exceeding unhappie, both to oui Weft countrey and to the whole Kingdome, but remeedilefs, God giving over the chiefe mifleaders, who had oppreft, to my griefe, many others, to follow their owne fenfe in that which the reft of us thought a high and dangerous finne. Mr. Patrick [Gillefpie] and Mr James Guthrie, wheie ever they came, uttered their paffion. I heard one who had mairied Mr. Patrick's fifter's daughter, report to Mr Robert Douglafs, that Mr. Hew Binny [Binning], with Mr. Patrick, in Kirkaldie, had fpoken like a diftracted man, faying to Mr. Robert Douglafs's owne wife, and the young man himfelfe, and his mother-in-law, Mr. Patrick's fifter, "That the Commiffion of the Kirk would approve nothing that wes right; that a hypocrite ought not to reigne over us; that we ought to treat with Cromwell, and give him fecuritie not to trouble England with a King; and who marred this tieatie, the blood of the flaine in this quarrell fhould be on their head!" Strange words, if true Allwayes behold the fearfull confequence of that pride of ftomacke.

The State fent Colonell Robert Montgomerie weft, to joyne the beft part of the horfe they had with the Weftern forces, or any pait of them that would joyne with him. For this end, he fpoke with the commiffioners of the Weft, at Stirling, who had been at Perth; but they fhew great averfnefs from any fuch junction He wrote alfo to Ker for this effect, and marched towards Glafgow. On the Sunday at night he came to Campfie; but on the Saturday, Ker, with all his foices, lying at Curmunnock, refolves to prevent Colonell Robert's approach, and by themfelves to make ane infall on the Englifh before day. Our intelligence wes, that the Englifh at Hamiltone were but twelve hundred; though Lambert lay there with above three thoufand of their beft horfe They called ours fifteen hundied; but fome doubles the number: for of all their forces, there wes not above four or fyve of Strachan's troups away Some fpeak of treacherie; for Govane, for all his cafheiring, wes re-admitted by Ker on fair promifes: Strachan was not farr off It is certain when, at four o'clock in the morning, December 1ft, our men came to fett on, the enemie wes ready to receave them, having founded to horfe halfe ane hour before, as it were for a march to

Glasgow All speak of a great rashness, as in ane anger, or what else, to cast away these forces Lieutenant-Colonell Ralstone, with a small partie of a hundred horse, entered Hamiltone, and most gallantlie carried all before him, killed sundrie; some spoke of hundreds, others are within scores; however, he cleared the towne of the enemie Colonell Ker, with fewer than two hundred, seconded him weell, but at the end of the towne, where the body of the English drew up againe in the field at the back of a ditch, when Ker saw it not easy to passe, he reteared a little, which they behind took for a flight, and all turned their backs; yea, the whole rest fled apart; not one would stay. The English persued als farr as Paisley and Kilmarnock that day; yet very few were killed, some say, scarce twenty; not above eighty prisoners, whereof Colonell Ker made one; as some say, deadly, as others, slightly wounded : Argyle said to me, he heard he might have scaped if he would. The next day, two or three hundred, who did rally in Kyle, by Strachan's persuasion disbanded, and himselfe, as fearing to be taken by us, went in to Cromwell, with Swintone, whose first work wes, to agent the randering of the Castle of Edinburgh, with their dear comerad young Dundass, who most basely, and, as yet it is taken, treacherouslie gave over that most considerable strength of our kingdome. But of this more certainlie afterwards.

The miscarriage of affaires in the West by a few unhappie men, put us all under the foot of the enemie They presently ran over all the countrey, without any stop, destroying cattell and cornes, putting Glasgow and all others under grievous contributions. This makes me yet to sticke at Perth, not dareing to goe where the enemie is master, as now he is of all Scotland beyond Forth, not so much by his owne vertue as our vices The loss of the West, the magazine of our best forces, put the State presently to new thoughts. We had long much debates about imploying malignants in our armies some were of opinion that the Acts of Church and State wes unjust, and for particular ends, from the beginning All agreed, that common sojours, after satisffaction to the Church, might be taken in, but as for officers, noblemen, and gentlemen volunteers, that we were not to take them in at all, at least not without ane eminent degree of evident repentance. The most thought they might be imployed as sojours, on their admittance by the Church to the Sacrament and Covenant As for places of counsell and trust, that this was to be left to the State's difcretion. However, when the cafe wes clearlie altered, and now there wes no choife of men, the Parliament wrote to Mr. Robert Douglafs to call the Commiffion extraordinarlie · A quorum wes gott, moft of thefe of Fyfe. The queftion wes proponed, of the lawfullnefs of employing fuch who before were excluded. The queftion wes alleadged to be altered from that which Mr. Gillefpie wrytes of, and that whereto Mr Guthrie had folemnlie ingadged, a defence of our life and countrey, in extreame neceffitie, againft fectarians and ftrangers, who had twyce been victors My heart was in great perplexitie for this queftion. I wes much in prayer to God, and in fome action with men, for a concord in it The Parliament were neceffitate to employ more than before, or give over their defence Mr. Samuel Rutherfoord and Mr. James Guthrie wrote peremptor letters to the old way, on all hazards Mr. Robert Douglafs and Mr. David Dick had of a long time been in my fenfe, that in the warre againft invadeing ftrangers, our former ftricknefs had been unadvyfed and unjuft. Mr Blair and Mr Durham were a little ambiguous, which I much feared fhould have devided the Commiffion; and likelie had done foe, if with the loffe of the Weft, the abfence of all the brethren of the Weft had not concurred. However, we carried unanimouflie at laft the anfwer heirwith fent to yow. My joy for this was foon tempered when I faw the confequence, the ugging of fundrie good people to fee numbers of grievous bloodfhedders ready to come in, and fo many malignant noblemen as were not lyke to lay downe armes till they were put into fome places of truft, and reftored to their vote in Parliament : Againft this, neceffitie for our very being, and hope that the guides of our State would, by their wifdome and vertue, and adherence of the Church and good men, get keepit what they had of authoritie; the Chancellour oft remembering us, that in this there wes ane fearfull alteration of the cafe, that the King being now in Covenant, the moft, whofe malignancie ftood in following the King againft the Covenant, were no more to be counted Malignants, the fountaine of that evill being ftopped in them, there was juft ground why that blot and name of diftinction in that refpect fhould be now abolifhed Ane other inconvenient wes like to trouble us, a feed of Hyper-Brownifme, which had been fecreitly fowen in the minds of fundry of the fojours, that it wes unlawfull to joyne in armes with fuch and fuch men, and foe that they were neceffitate to make a civill feparation from fuch, for fear of finne and curfeing of their interprizes. The maine fomenters of thefe doubts feemed not at all to be led by confcience, but by intereft; for the officers of our ftanding armie, fince the defeat at Dunbar, being fent to recruite the regiments to the northern fhyres, did little increafe that number, but takeing large money for men, and yet exacted quarters for men which were not; this vexed the countrey, and difappointed the fervice. The officers, by the new leavies, thought it eafy to be recruited at their pleafure; but ane Act paffing, that the new leavies fhould not recruite the old regiments, they ftormed, and gladly would have blafted the new way for their owne ends Under thefe evills we wreftle as yet, but hopes for a good end of thefe divifions alfo; in the meane tyme Cromwell is daylie expected to march towards Stirling to marre the Coronation, which, fore againft my heart, was delayed to the firft of January, on pretence of keeping a faft for the finnes of the King's family on Thurfday next. We mourned on Sunday laft for the contempt of the Gofpell, according to Mr. Dickfon's motion, branched out by Mr. Wood Alfo yow fee in the printed papers, upon other particulars the Commiffion at Stirling, which appointed thefe fafts, could not agree The Remonftrants preffed to have fundry finnes acknowledged which others denyed, and would not now permitt them to fett down as they would what caufes of faft they liked Surely we had never more caufe of mourning, be the caufes, what God knowes, vifible or invifible, confeft or denyed, unfeen or feen, by all but the moft guiltie. It cannot be denyed but our miferies and dangers of ruine are greater nor for many ages have been; a potent victorious enemy mafter of our feas, and for fome good time of the beft part of our land; our ftanding forces againft this his imminent invafion, few, weak, inconfiderable; our Kirk, State, Armie, full of divifions and jealoufies; the body of our people be-fouth Forth fpoyled, and near ftarveing; they be-north Forth extreamlie ill ufed by a handfull of our owne; many inclyning to treat and agree with Cromwell, without care either of King or Covenant; none of our neighbours called upon by us, or willing to give us any help, though called What the end of all fhall be, the Lord knowes. Many are ready to faint with difcouragement and defpaire: yet diverfe are waiting on the Lord, expecting he will help us in our great extreamitie againft our moft unjuft oppreffors.

I hope you received my laft inclofed in Callander's packett. You have here a large narration of many of our proceedings. When I began to write it, my intention was for Mr David Dick; but a little after I had begun, finding this bearer going towards you, I enlarged my letter for your [information] : hafte and want of good inftruments for the tyme, makes the write, I fear, illegible; but guefs it as you may. You have with it a copy of a letter of mine to our friends in England, which for a tyme keep fecret to yourfelf alone. I fend you alfo a copy of diverfe other wrytes, which I think you may defyre to fee

This day we have done that what I earneftly defyred, and long expected, Crowned our noble King with all the folemnities at Scoone, fo peaceablie and magnificentlie as if no enemy had been among us. This is of God for it was Cromwell's purpofe, which I thought eafily he might have performed, to have marred by armes that action, at leaft the folemnitie of it. The Remonftrants, with all their power, would have oppofed it; others prolonged it fo long as they were able : allwayes, bleffed be God ! it is this day celebrate with great joy and contentment to all honeft-hearted men here.[1] Mr. Douglafs, from 2 Kings xi., Joafh's coronation, had a very pertinent, wife, and good fermon. The King fware the Covenant, the League and Covenant, the Coronation Oath : when Argyle put on the Crown, Mr Robert Douglafs prayed weell, when the Chancellour fet him in the throne, he exhorted weell; when all were ended, he, with great earneftnefs, preffed finceritie and conftancie in the Covenant on the King, delateing at length King James's breach of the Covenant, perfewed yet againft the family, from Nehemiah v. 13 God's cafting the King out of his lap, and the 34th of Jeremiah, many plagues on him if he doe not fincerely keep the oathes now taken : He clofed all with a prayer, and the 20th Pfalm

Dundas and Major Abernethie hes moft bafely delyvered the Caftle to Cromwell. All the minifters faw the treacherie, and protefted againft it. Warnftone, Sir John Cheiflie, and the Provoft of Edinburgh, who put them in that truft, contrare to the minds of others, have little credit by it.

Now the Parliament having, by the needlefs length of fome, fitten fo long, and ended their feffion on Mononday after twelve at night; none of the

---

[1] There was published at the time " The Form and Order of the Coronation of Charles the Second, King of Scotland, England, France, and Ireland. as it was acted and done at Scoone. the first day of Januarie 1651. Aberdene, Imprinted by James Brown, 1651," 4to This tract, which includes the Sermon by Douglas has been several times reprinted

Remonstrants are on the Committee of Estates: Wariston, with great difficulty, was gotten on; all diligence will now be used to get up ane armie. The Lord be with us. Our greater danger will be from famine now; [and to] get victualls to starving Ireland. It were ane happy benefite if your Hollanders would bring us in victuall for money; the Spaniard, nor any other, could never, by their persuasion nor force, hinder them to trade wherever they find gain. Is not this a strange slaverie, [through] love to the Englsh murtherers, that they, for their pleasure, should give over all trade with us their brethren and weell-deserving friends? Though we should never be able to revenge their ingratitude; yet there is a God who will see to it. Our case will be exceeding hard if, before the summer, your Zealanders, on piety and pity, be not moved to bring us victualls for all the money we have resting, though it may be the Lord may be pleased to open some other door which yet is not visible to us.

Perth, January 2d 1651.

Postscript.

I think to-morrow we shall give order to excommunicate Strachan, and relax Middleton the next Sabbath. By the cunning of some, all ingadging officers and noblemen were all purged out of our armies; but now I think all of them, without any considerable exception, are received. On this necessare conclusion, some turbulent men are like to be factious, but to-morrow a Warning[1] is to be putt out for their reclaiming if possible. By God's blessing, our affairs shortly may be in a better posture: our great troublers, both in Church and State, have sett themselves aside. If God give us over to Cromwell, we expect little good from these men but a violent executing of all in their Remonstrance; but otherwayes I think they may be brought quicklie to repent their needless quarrelling. However, the Lord's will be done, who has begunne to comfort us, with the smallest appearance of better hopes.

[1] ' A Solemn Warning to all the Members of this Kirk, from the Commission of the Generall Assemblie: With an Act, for censuring such as act, or comply with the Sectarian Armie, now infesting this Kingdom. Aberdene, Imprinted by James Brown, Anno 1651. 4to pp. 19. The Warning is dated at Perth, 7th January 1651.

The Commission's Consolatory Letter to Edinburgh.[3]

Dearly Beloved in the Lord,

As the fad fufferings of the reft of the land doe much afflict us, fo your more eminent afflictions, by the continuall oppreffions of the incumbent enemie, doe more deeplie peirce our hearts. Our prayers to God in your behalf are for the abundance of his moft tender confolations, whereby your fpirits may be upholden from fainting in this day of your very fore tryall. We have been comforted to hear of your conftancie in adhereing to the truth and caufe of God, notwithstanding of all the indeavours which thefe inftruments of Sathan, who night and day are among you, have ufed, whether by terror or allurements againft your ftabilitie. We truft the Lord, who yet has made you to ftand, fhall confirme you and make you perfevere to the end, keeping your garments clean and your confciences pure of all the abominations which are either openly avowed or more fecretly harboured by that evill generation. For this end we earneftlie exhort yow, and, by the power we have over you in the Lord, require you, to avoid all familiar converfing with thefe feducers; but above all, that you beware to joyne with them in publick worfhip, or in any private exercife of religion: Who ventures to touch pitch will be defyled before they be aware; who will take fire in their bofome cannot but be fcorched therewith; who will not abftaine from the harlot's houfe fhall not be innocent: beware of the wyles and fubtile deeps of the Devill; and, among all his inftruments, we intreat yow to avoid none more than thefe miferable apoftates of our own nation; for we conceave none to be more fitted of the Devill, and given over of God to work milchiefe among yow than thefe. Encourage one another in the Lord; and now, while publick ordinances may be wanting, let every one apart, and every man in his own familie, be carefull of holy exercifes to keep in and encreafe the fpunk of grace and zeal before attained; labouring with all care to obtaine from the Lord that foftnefs and melting of heart, that earneftnefs and pouring out of a praying fpirit, that firme adherance

---

[3] To the title of this paper, (the date of which was 7th January 1651,) Baillie adds, " By my hand," that is, Written by him, whilft at Perth.

unto and continuall dependance upon God, which may fitt yow to hold out in bearing your croffes, to that day of deliverance which fhall be fent from the Lord, and which we believe he is haftening to yow and the reft of your fellow-fufferers over the land with all convenient fpeed · as for us, be affured we fhall not be inlacking in our addreffes both to God and men in your behalfe. Our Remonftrance to the Committee of Eftates, our Letter to the Prefbyteries, our Warning to the whole land, and our Anfwer to the exceptions of fome men againft fome of our proceedings, we have fent to you, whereof we know ye will make good ufe So commending you unto the mercifull upholding and direction of the Comforter, till thir times of thick darknefs be over, and for ever We reft.

For Mr. David Dickson, at Inneraray. March 8th [1651.]

As yet I could not get Mr Patrick [Gillefpie]'s papers fo as to write animadverfions on them. He has (which yow defyre) goeing athort a long paper of feven or nyne fheets, and a compend of it of three or four fheets, alfo ane anfwer to yow of four fheets, and Mr. James Guthrie's anfwer to yow of four fheets, and Mr. James Guthrie's reply to the Commiffion's anfwer to his letter. I have no time for this, for on Monday I dyte Thefes of the Errors of the Time ; on Thurfday and Fryday I dyte long leffons in Chronologie ; on Thurfday I have a long Hebrew leffon ; Thurfday, before noone, I wait on the Homilies, and will goe through the Directorie for preaching, prayer, facraments, &c. ; Saturday is for Sunday I have many letters for the publick to write every other day. I hardly enough hold up with all thir in fo calamitous a time, fo albeit I was minded to tell my mind of thefe papers, I muft let it alone ; only of the light view I took of fome of them I had thefe thoughts :—They are a heap of clatters, mere teftimonies of late papers (which Mr. James Guthrie and two or three with him put on the Church) which touch not the prefent cafe ; without fcripture, reafon, or any light, or any life of difcourfe ; they goe in a way of confufion and will not ftate a queftion ; never tells pofitivelie and clearlie what they call a Malignant, and what a Malignant partie, and what places of truft, and what convincing figns of repentance It feems to me their way is directlie for deftroying both our Church and Kingdome, if God help not you, and the like of you, to croffe them. The prefent queftion about the more generall junction, is but a mere pretext. Before any fuch queftion was moved, they were peremptor to doe as now they are doeing. After all poffible intreaties of the Church and State, they would not confent to joyne their forces of the Weft to this of Stirling, as being truelie then Malignant and not to be joyned with; from which they had withdrawne all they were able, both officers and fojours, after Dunbar, to bring them to nothing, and to make the Weftern armie the only armie of the Kingdome, to be difpofed on abfolutelie at their owne pleafure. They gave, in my hearing, at St. Johnftone, a kind of unwilling promife of endeavour to joyne the Weft forces with the North, bot with two expreffe conditions, which they knew would never be granted: The one, of purgeing the North forces according to the Act of State, which was to lay David Leflie afide, and who elfe, officers and fojours, they liked, that Strachan, and who they liked, might rule the new-modelled armie als abfolutelie as Cromwell did the Englifh 2*dly*, That the King's intereft might formallie and pofitivelie be laid afide out of our quarrell with Cromwell; and that not only his Englifh intereft, which yet they ftand to, bot alfo his Scottifh intereft, as it ftands in the Remonftrance, from which to this day they have not paft, but by their appeale adheres to. The queftion, as they make it, is high enough: a formall rebellion againft both Church and State; a publick contradiction to both; yea, while they call for the nation's help in a vifible extreame danger, our brethren, by daylie publick preaching, and prayer, and writes, openlie doe hinder all they can to ryfe, and perfuades all they are able to fitt ftill, till the King, Kingdome, and Church be devoured by Cromwell. The finne, fhame, and hurt of this their clear and avowed deed, is nothing helped by their excufes and intentions; albeit, if they will fpeak out their clear mind, I doubt their intentions are farr higher than to fitt ftill and let Cromwell deftroy their brethren. I feare their principles give them clear libertie, yea, will putt them to act againft them they cannot joyne with; and they will give no fecuritie I fuppone that they will, with force of armes, with the bloodfhed of all who ftand in their way, when they fee it time, fuppreffe the prefent Armie, Parliament, and Commiffion of Church, and frame both Church and Kingdome according to their owne modell. Grounds for this will be found in their papers and daylie practifes. I fear, however, for the Church · they are goeing clearlie enough to rent it. The moft eminent perfons and higheft judicatories thereof, that are againft them only in this State and Militarie queftion, they totallie mifregard, as the language of thefe papers bears. They defend a libertie for a part of the congregation to feparate from the reft, where the difcipline alone is not execute according to their mind. The feparating part, before any fentence obtained or fought, may not always want ordinances, fo muft put themfelves in a church ftate by themfelves, and that independent from any of thefe judicatories with which they are at odds. This one principle Mr. Patrick is now preaching, and others defending in difcourfe, if ftood to, will force them to all the reft Befide ane other queftion, they will find it out of queftion that Church fellowfhip is ftraiter and more tender than any State focietie, and moft of all than Militarie ; and where a State and Militarie feparation is neceffarie, there a Church feparation is much more neceffarie. I think you will make this fo cleare that they will not gett it denyed The affumption of the neceffitie of a Militarie feparation, the naturall and judiciall ftiffnefs of fome men, I fear, will not fuffer them to quate, and fo the conclufion will inevitablie follow, the neceffitie of a Church feparation. God grant my logick here may be wrong ; but of a long time I have feared fome mens way tended to this end on diverfe prefumptions

I think God in his goodnefs to this land has engaged you, Mr Robert Blair, Mr. James Wood, and Mr. Douglafs, and my Lord Argyle in this quarrell. It's no time now to dallie, where is the boldnefs and diligence of thefe men : have you your anfwers fo full and ftrong as yow may expect no favour from them here after. I think yow would [fhould] not follow their roving wrytes; fay to the purpofe, and fpeak out before God to their confcience, though fome of their writers will not hear yow, yet I believe God will make yow inftrumentall to many of our good people, whom for the time they have deeply enfnared, and will carie any where, if God remeed it not, to the huge fcandall of all the churches abroad, and the indangering of the ftanding of our Church and Kingdome, and the loffe of many precious foules : Ane unexpected moft dangerous ftratagem of Satan againft poor Scotland, yea Britaine, as any yet we have feen on a very fimple and caufelefs occafion. Up, and the Lord affift yow in this fpeciall battell of his Son.

For Mr Robert Dowglass at Kirkaldie.
March 10th 1651.

Whether yow receaved a packett of myne fome twentie dayes agoe, I fhould be glad by a lyne from yow to know. In it wes one to Generall Major Maffie, and one to Balcarras, both open for your reading; alfo three or four fheets, called Mr. Patrick Gillefpie's, againft the refolutions of the Church and State, a compend of a larger paper of feven or eight fheets, which now I fend yow, together with Mr. Patrick's anfwer to Mr. David Dickfon's letter in four fheets, alfo Mr. James Guthrie's anfwer to the fame letter. there is two fheets of it more, which I know not yet if now can be readie. My owne opinion of thefe papers, I fent to Mr. David; a copie whereof ye have alfo here. God hes oft made your wifdome and ftoutnefs happie for our poor Church; never more need of it than now If ye think it expedient to let fo many fcurvie lybells, be openly fent abroad againft the King, Kirk, State, and moft eminent of the brethren, I fubmitt to your wifdome, which I have found allwayes greater than my owne, only I affure yow the boldnefs of fome men in daily preaching, writing, and I fear too pragmatick confultations, is haidly tollerable. Yow fee in Mr. David's letter to me his mind that the Commiffion fhould yet once againe warne and declare. I wifh withall that Mr James Wood would once more take to confideration fome of the matters of all thefe papers together; indeed thereafter the Kirk fhould take courfe to ftop contradictions. Our Synods now are comeing on, I wifh the Commiffion might take courfe they be not corrupted fhould writers, preachers, and bold debaters againft the Commiffion, have votes in Synods and Prefbyteries, efpeciallie in election of commiffioners to a Generall Affemblie. It wont not to be fo. Yow will not forget a Faft for the Armie. Your Warning is not yet come to our Prefbyterie: that is a monftrous neglect. If Duncan Munne had keeped his gift of printing, we had gotten a preffe long ere now; it's a very great pitie that a preffe in any terms fhould be wanting. I have fent yow herewith a paper, called Mr. James Fergufon's, which hes done good here. In Mr. Alexander Nifbett's laft letter to me yow will fee the condition of Cunynghame, and in Mr. Robert Wallace's the condition of Kyle and Carrick: make what ufe of all thefe papers yow lyke, bot mifken my name. Though yow have all, yet I thought fitt to be fure of it. I did fee juft now two proteftations of Mr Guthrie's againft King and State, goeing among our people. I think they force the Commiffion to doe what fundry of the wifeft here thought they fhould have done before, to take that matter to confideration, and pronounce a fentence upon it clearly and plainly, without Iffs or Ands. If the State be right, yow are obliedged in confcience to affift them, and goe before them in judging men of your coat, who, with fo high a hand, every way oppofes them under pretext of ecclefiaftick liberties; and your not judging any their contradictions to be againft your acts, I think they have left you no more place of conniving. You fee what Mr. Alexander Nifbett writes to me; I underftand it not, but feares there is fome practice with England to hinder all rifeing for us and the King, as being all malignants together James Grahame, the other night, fatt up all night with fome taylors for a new fute, and the morning after, well armed and horfed, rode eaft, I fufpect to England, whether his mafter may follow. Were it not good to iffue a declaration to England, both by the King and Kirk to prevent men's malice? When they hinder Scotland to rife againft Cromwell, how much more will they and muft they doe foe in England; and what can be more malicious and dangerous if not feen to?

UNTO THE KING'S MOST EXCELLENT MAJESTIE, AND HIS HONOURABLE ESTATES CONVEENED IN PARLIAMENT.

HUMBLY MEANS AND SHEWS,

WHEREAS in bygane Parliaments it hath been ane ordinane favour granted to all the Univerfities in the Kingdome to appoint Vifitors for them, it is the Supplicant's humble defyre, that his Majeftie and prefent Parliament would be pleafed to name fuch as they fhall think fitting to fitt at Glafgow, or any where they fhall think it expedient, for the vifitation of the Univerfitie of Glafgow, with fuch power as his Majeftie and former Parliaments have ordinarlie granted to Vifitors in fuch cafes.

And your Majeftie's and Honours Anfwer, humbly I expect,

Martii 10, 1651.   M. R. BAYLIE.

For My Lord Balcarras

My Lord,

As I wrote to you twyce before, I now intreat againe, if there be any fitting of Parliament, you will gett the enclofed defyre paft, if it can be without prefenting of my bill, or my name heard. When I wes laft with yow, the Rector and Dean of Facultie fubfcryved a defyre unto me for this end, by the advyce of the reft of the Moderators, I fent lately that letter to you, which poffibhe with others is mifcarried. Mr. Patrick Gillefpie, without the knowledge, and contrare to the mind of all our Moderators except one, by whifpering Wariftone in the eare, paft our laft Vifitation in the laft Parliament 1649, without all dinne or obfervation, in the termes you have here inclofed, to a lift of names he prefented, without the alteration of one, to fitt where they liked, and till they were difcharged, as I think. the quorum, as I think, was feven, or at moft nine: That yet ftands above our head; they may meet any morning when Mr. Patrick pleafes, and doe with us all what they like beft. The handfomeft way to be quite of them is to appoint a new one I wifh the quorum be fyve or feven at moft. For feare of tyning I have putt the lift on the back of this letter;[1] change whom you will, but not yourfelf: if Lauderdaill be gotten in the Parliament, let him be one. have a care of this I command and charge. I think yow fhould prefs the Kirk by all means to take Mr James Guthrie off your hand· if they doe it not, they putt yow on a needlefs rocke. I feare, but cannot make it out, that befyde other refults of many meetings here, one be to deall with the Prefbyterians in England, not to joyne more with the King and this Armie than they did before with the Engagers. The mifchiefe of this malice cannot

---

[1] My Lord Chancellour, my Lord Argyle, my Lord Eglintoun, my Lord Angus, my Lord Balcarras, the Laird of Houstone, the Laird of Bishoptoune, the Laird of Lusse, the Laird of Blair, my Lord Broomhall, Mr David Buchanan The Laird of Cunynghame, Mr James Robertsone of Bedlaw, Adam Blair of Bogtoune, Mr Robert Barclay, Hew Kennedie, Mr. John Dunlop of Garnkirk: Mr Robert Dowglass, Mr. John Smith, Mungo Law, Mr. Robert Kerr, Mr Robert Blair, Mr James Bonnar, Mr John Bell, Mr Patrick Colvill, Mr William Russell, Mr Richard English, Mr. Patrick Scharpe, Mr David Elphingstone, Mr Robert Wallace, Mr Gabriel Cunynghame, elder

be prevented but by the King and Church's fair declaration to England and Maffie's meffengers. I confeffe, if yow could gett your armie any way maintained without diffolution, I inclyne to a waiting on without any needlefs hafte. Time may doe us good. Yours,

S Jamisone

The King's goodnefs will daylie gaine our hearts, and Cromwell's armie, I hope, will faill more and more I have written my mind freelie and fullie to Mr Robert Dowglafs.

For Mr John Smyth, Mr. Robert Kerr, or James Schairpe, March 21st [1651.]

I have written fundry long fcrolles to Mr. Robert Dowglafs fince I faw yow, but he hes never been pleafed to let me know whether he hes receaved any of them. I take it in good part, for I know the multitude of his weightie affairs: The Lord help him with them: only I pray yow, if ye have any time, call for a fight of my letters, and for him write me fome lynes of ane anfwer. We know not what yow are doing Our neighbours hes dayly large informations, I fufpect to your prejudice, and of the publict, which we are not inftructed to refute. I have fent this expreffe to yow, to learne how all goes, fo farr as may be communicat. By the inclofed yow may fee part of our condition. Ayr is prettie right, not feven minifters of the twenty-fix wrong; Galloway alfo is almoft whollie right; foe Dumbartan; Hamiltone is waltering. If yow take not fome courfe, our ftryving is in vaine, and what by our labour we have gained, your negligence will loffe it to us. By Mr. David Dick's letter, I fee he is bufie on a reply to Mr. Gillefpie and Mr. Guthrie he would be incouraged. We are extreamlie evill ferved with correfpondence from yow there If we heard more, we might be more ufefull My fervice to Mr. Andrew [Ker] · he hes no time nor leifure for the likes of me. I need feek no more extracts from him, fince he hes fent all our Regifters back againe to Leith

Your Brother,

Glafgow, March 20th 1651

Rob Baylii

Our Synod is comeing on. I have done my beft to have none, or to have it right if poffible; bot I am almoft defperate of this. The diligence of fome men is too great to gett their partie to keep, and the negligence of the other to gather their friends no lefs. Did not the Commiffion fie that no man accefforie to the divifive fupplication fhould fit in ane Affemblie till cleared? If fome fuch courfe be not taken with adherers to the Remonftrance, protefters, preachers, writers againft King, Kirk, and Commiffion, not only fundry Synods, bot our Generall Affemblie, is like in evident hazard to be overthrowne. I pray fee we gett intelligence what ye are doing. I advyfe to fend a letter to our Prefbyteries, with the former Warning: fend but one copie in write to our Prefbyterie. I fhall be anfwerable for copies to all the Prefbyteries in the weft, or what other papers yow will be pleafed to fend: I fhall be at the charge and paynes of fpreading them for one moneth at leaft. If Mr. Andrew [Ker] have the Minutes of the laft Affemblie befide him, I pray yow take out what concerns our Colledge, and putt in any hand to write, that Mr Andrew may fubfcryve it only, and yow fend it to me with this boy, who fhall wait on yow for it fo long as yow think fit. It concerns us much to have thefe extracts, if poffible to be had. I have written to Balcarras for ane extract of our Vifitation, paft the other day in the Parliament: I pray fo quietly and quickly let that extract be gotten, and fent with this boy als foon as may be.

To [THE EARL OF] LAUDERDAILL. MARCH 11TH 1651.

LOVING FRIEND,

I have now oft fent to fundry of yow there, and fometimes exprefs bearers, who have brought me back no anfwers at all. I am almoft angrie; did I not hold in a time, when I fee the anger of impotent men is neglected. I have once more refolved to try your difcretions, and fent that exprefs to your felfe and your coufigne William to crave two or three lynes under one of your hands, had yow never fo much adoe, or elfe to give up gofsoprie. Anfwer fo much of my laft as yow think fitt, in fuch termes as yow care not who may fee it. We are altogether ignorant here what yow are doing, and are abufed by a number, I am fure, of falfe reports. Refolves the Commiffion to mifken Mr. James Guthrie, and let the Parliament take minifters to tafk, that the King, in his firft entry, fhall have that load on his fhoulders? Will the Act of claffes make a new divifion, even among the Anti Remonftrants? Shall no ufe be made of Cromwell's yet fuppofed death? againft which yet we have nothing Eglintone writes to William Home, his fervant, our baillie, that he hes throught our Vifitation: I wifh he had rather written it to myfelfe, for the quieter that matter be it's the better. I fhall write thanks to my Lord for his care; but I know your coufigne William Reid[5] is the man. The chief errand of the bearer is to gett a formal extract of that Vifitation, therefore, William muft perfect what he hes begunne, and fee yow put him to it, to command the clerk to provyde with all poffible fpeed ane extract to him, according to this inclofed forme, or any other that fhall be better, which he will give to my bearer, who waits for it. I lay the charge on yow and another, and I have done for this time

We fent to the Chancellor the laft week for ane very ordinarie favour, a difpenfation, which any Lord of the Seffion ufes to give to any private gentleman, for the Commiffioners of Glafgow and Hamiltone to fitt to perfect our decreits of the Univerfitie of Glafgow, for our teynds and ftipends the laft year, that wes near a poynt. The Chancellor advyfed, fince he had no power during the fitting of Parliament, to give in our petition to the Parliament itfelf; we did foe, our bill wes read and remitted to the Committee of Bills; there, for want of agenting, it wes flighted and refufed on two falfe narratives. One, that the people we had to doe with, lay under the feet of the enemie, and could not appear in Glafgow: This is falfe, for all we have to doe with, are in four paroches, Kilbride, Govane, Glafgow, and Renfrew, who comes alfe freely hither as in greateft peace; neither needs any of them be here to anfwer, for the decreit we crave is only for forme, wherein is no matter of contraverfie, but for our ordinarie unqueftioned rents, wherein we are in long ufe of payment The other information wes, that a partie of the Englifh wes to lye at Glafgow This is one, I hope, of the many falfe proffers of the time. I have knowne when yow have had fkill to help a friend in need, and in his juft caufe. Try yet if Wilham and my Lord Eglintoune can make a difpenfation to us, according to our laft week's bill, pafs after our Vifitation Yow are ane old mafon, and may be one againe I take it yow are a good-enough agent

[5] The Earl of Balcarras, in like manner he often addreffed Lord Lauderdale as John Reid. *I a*

and pockbearer at the Parliament doore, when I have to doe. Send home the bearer to me with the extract of the Visitation, and the dispensation, and I shall say yow are a good fellow, worthy to be advanced one classe were it *per saltum*, only be warre of Mr. James Guthrie's loope By all means eschew new divisions, keep Argyle by any means possible; bot for no cause losse the Kirk, if yow resolve not to losse yourselffe: be content to take what they will give, if yow be not mad

For Mr. James Blair   March 11th 1651.

James,

Your kind letter to me wes very welcome, and allwayes what comes from yow shall be welcome to me, read and close the inclosed. Mr. James Guthrie and Mr. Patrick Gillespie are goeing on with their work to destroy our State and rent our Kirk, but we hope it shall not lye in their power Mr. Robert Dowglass, Mr Robert Blair, and Mr. David Dick, stand very right and zealous against their evill way. The most of the brethren of the West are fallen off them, and more daily will, for their pryde and schisme will appear daily more and more intollerable: their only confidence is in Cromwell's victorie, which God avert; or, if it should be God's pleasure to try us yet further, honest men will get from their good God patience and courage, to be readie to suffer the most which tyrants malice can impose.—these things to yourselfe. Use all diligence by yourselfe, or any of the gentrie and ministrie yow know faithfull and active, to hold your countrey right, and above all, to get the ministrie of Ireland well informed Try if James Wallace, younger Achans, be to Ireland; he hes left the King, I fear, for no good offices, he is poysoned. For our new schisme, Mr John Park lay it on him to gett all papers · these that are good, are Mr. James Wood's, Mr. David Dick's, Mr James Fergusone's; have yow the care to gett them copied and sent to Ireland Be not slack as yow love God, the King, the poor Kirks, and Kingdomes of the three dominions which are lyke to be cast in a new danger by our brethren, the imprudence of some, and malicioussness of others. Send me ane accompt both of your diligence in Galloway and Ireland, and the condition of both countreys Your knowledge of the truth hereof may doe good

For Mr. Robert Dowglass

Reverend and Beloved Brother,

I hope yow have received the packett I fent yow with James Campbell. On Saturday at even laft, there came a poft to Glafgow from Mr. James Guthrie to Mr. Patrick, fhewing, that he was to appear before the King and State on Monday laft, the 10th of this inftant, and for that end defyred the prayers of the people of God here Upon this alarum, Mr. Patrick and Mr. John Carftairs on the Sunday, caft their doctrine on the fuffering of faithfull minifters, and the great defection of Church and State. On the Monday, Mr John Carftairs choifed expreflly the 4th of the Coloffians, the Apoftle in bonds his defyre of the people's prayers ; and did exhort the godly to be much in prayer for help to them who were now on the ftage, that they might carie themfelves honourable, and perfect their teftimonie ; or to this purpofe : accordingly the moft of that day wes fpent in fafting and prayer by fundry of our beft people, in Mr. Patrick's houfe and other places On Tuefday, much confultation wes in Mr. Patrick's houfe how to gett our Prefbyterie ingadged in a letter to the Commiffion for Mr. James Guthrie. When we come there, Mr Patrick preffed a letter exhortatorie of the Commiffion to fee the Committee of Eftates incroached not on the liberties of the Church For a while I intreated fuch motions might be lett alone , when intreaties prevailed not, we came to debate it, and after long pleading that all fuch letters, how fpareing foever, were ane imputation on the King and State of a high cryme, which were rafhnefs in us to fuppone, not having heard them firft fpeak for themfelves ; and that it were to give the Commiffion a needlefs admonition, while our Prefbyterie had given them no fatiffaction yet for our laft open difobedience to their injunction, which many of us judged very juft and neceffare ; that our writing wes preffed only to be a leading cafe to other Prefbyteries to give fome incouragement and countenance to Mr. James Guthrie in his contradictions to Church and State, which we judged very finfull, fcandalous, and dangerous ; which we would not now debate, bot on a juft occafion were refolved to witnefs againft Debates to this purpofe could not obtain a delay to the next meeting, bot it behooved to goe to a prefent vote. We knew Mr Patrick, by the multitude of his yeomen elders, could carie what he pleafed; we could doe no more but enter our diffent, which I did in my owne and for eight more, Mafters Ramfay, Hew Blair, Zacharie Boyd, George Young, Gabriell Cunynghame, Archibald Denneftone, Robert Young, William Hoome I fhall doe what I can to keep other Prefbyteries off yow, but if the Commiffion will not in time look to fome men's ways and reftleffnefs, the fchifme will get fuch ftrength that the end may be doolefull. All this to yourfelfe, and to fuch few friends yow pleafe. The Lord help and direct yow

I defyre not to put yow to any writing but one two lynes, if yow receaved this and my two former packetts. What ftrange work we had for the intimation of Strachan's excommunication, I fpeak not till ane other occafion Your Warning will never, it feems, come to us, and when it comes, it will be refuifed, except by diffenters

For Mr. Robert Douglass.   April 4th 1651.

Sir,

I wes refrefhed with your kind and large letter, and made the beft ufe I could of the many feafonable inftructions therein However, we expected not a Synod in tymes and places fo full of danger; yet I fand our brethren here had made it foe to have a Synod kept, and by many letters and great induftrie had conveened from all the Prefbyteries the brethren of their mind with multitudes of yeomen elders. At the very firft blenk it was apparent there wes fome defigne in hand. Fearing it before, I had written it before to fome in all the Prefbyteries, to caufe brethren of their mind keep fo weell as might be; but parthe the ftorme of the weather, and partlie the moving of the enemie, made few from Aire and Dumbartane, whence I expected moft help, to come in We purpofed to make Mr. James Fergufone, Moderator, but they carried Mr. Matthew Mowat, and by this I perceived clearlie they had gotten fo many fillie yeomen prefently chofen for the purpofe, that they could carie in the Synod whatever they pleafed They moved a committee for publict affaires; fearing the end of it, I oppofed it as needlefs; but it wes voted, and a dozen of their ftrongeft men put on it. I only could gett three of my mind on it; Masters Robert Ramsay, James Fergusone, Patrick Colville. The first thing there Mr. Patrick Gillespie pressed, wes the danger from junction with the Malignants, and our deutie about it Three or four votes past directlie, running towards a new Remonstrance. This long I keept up the Commission's letters, staying till I fand their designe, and then seeing it clearlie, I delyvered the letters whereby I put them off their purpose for one night. Mr. James Guthrie wes then lodged with Mr. Patrick, and Mr James Durhame also, for his familie for the time dwelt with Mr. Patrick, and Mr. James Naefmith's with Mr. John Carstairs. The Synod wes putting off the time with ordinarie forms; but the hearts and eyes of all wes on the bussinefs of our Committee, for which the Synod at this unseasonable time wes conveened. At our next meeting in the Committee, they pretending a rage at the Commission's letters, Mr. Patrick, as a moderating man, proposed from his cabbin-counsell to send commissioners from the assemblie, onlie with some few instructions, to crave satisfaction from the Commission in the doubts of the brethren who were dissatisfied. Fearing the designe after all the nixt days tough debates, we desyred to see the letter and instructions put in forme, that we might judge on them. At last they were brought forth · We fand them very high and injurious to the Commission and State; yet for peace cause, and preventing of a rupture, we were content to adjourne the Synod, to permitt the brethren yet dissatisfied, to send whom they pleased to the Commission for conferrence on their doubts; in the meantime to delay the fast, and reading of the papers, only we required that the Synod should not be ingadged in the dissatisfaction of the brethren. Thus farre we came with some reluctancie of our owne mind, and thereby gained almost the Committee to our desyre; but Mr. Patrick, knowing his advantage, wes peremptor to have the Synod involved in the dissatisfaction, and us in the dissent; we, after much toyle, gave over. In the Synod we had long fruitlefs debates on the overture of laying aside the reading of the Warnings, and delaying the Fast, adjourning the Synod till the commissioners returne from the Commission On the letter, and strange instructions, our reasons were long and tough enough, but calme and without irritation on either hand. At last I gave in this dissent, to which diverse in every Presbyterie did adhere Eight commissioners, the rigidest opposers of the union of the forces, were voted to goe to yow, viz: Masters Patrick Gillespie, James Naefmith, John Knave [Nevay], Gabriell

Maxwell, Alexander Dunlop, Matthew Mowatt, John Carftairs. Their hope is to gaine yow particularlie, and a pluralitie of the Commiffion; when yow for this conference have appointed it at Stirling, or any near place, and they brought hither by their follicitation all the members affected to them. If they faill in this, at the nixt feffion of the adjourned [Synod], expect ftrange work from them: yow had great need to deal prudently in this bufinefs. I find very many of the minifters of the Synod, who joyned not in our diffent, to be in their heart for joyning with the armie, notwithftanding of all their diffatiffaction otherways I find the body of our people in all our fhyres to be heartily for the fame conclufion But Mr. Patrick and two or three other by their cunning and extreame diligence, are like to involve the body of the minifters, and, by a little time, of the people, into a remedilefs diffatiffaction.

Having mett after the Synod with fome of the wifeft of our mind in all our Prefbyteries, I was defyred to have your opinion in fundrie things. 1 If yow have no power to difcharge this noveltie amongft us, ane adjourned Synod, or yow think it not expedient to ufe your power to difcharge it, as being keept of a clear defigne to croffe the publick judicatories, whether in that cafe yow think it expedient that we, the diffenters, fhall all be abfent, or fhall endeavour to be fo frequent at it as we are able? for yet we are hopefull, upon diligence, if not to carry the Synod, yet to make our diffent ftronger. 2ly, If this Synod fhall medle to cenfure Prefbyteries for their obedience to the Generall Affemblie, or Commiffion of the Church, if it fhall not be declyned as ane uncompetent judge? 3ly, If it fhall not be expedient, till that conference end, or till we receave directions from yow, to let alone reading of your papers, and keeping of the Faft? We think if yow write feverallie to Prefbyteries to crave an anfwer from them of the willingnefs of every minifter to further the leavies and junction of them with the prefent army, without any more, would draw a good anfwer from the moft to this maine and principall queftion, wherein whoever were not truelie ingadged, and openlie, would fhortlie come to all elfe required, and prefenthe would fall off the oppofite party. We think a privat kind of letter from your felfe to Mafters Thomas Kirkaldie, William Cockburne, and to Francis Aird, for the ingadgeing of thefe three (who, as we are informed, and I am fure of Mr. Francis, are in their mind for joyning in the leavies,) would much help to gett their three Prefbyteries with us, Lanerk, Ayr, and Hamiltone. Thefe parts of your papers and letters which threatened cenfure to our brethren were taken by them in high difdaine; and by diverfe others wondered at, that yow would recommend to Prefbytries and Synods to cenfure any whom the Commiffion wes farr from beginning a procefs with, the prime delinquents in this kind. We are all farr from defyreing the leaft trouble to any; but we think if the Commiffion on this occafion declare not their approbation of our diffent, and whatever fatiffaction they may give to our Synod's commiffioners, (which from our hearts we defyre may be fo great as to gaine them all,) yet if by them the Commiffion be drawne from any of their juft refolutions, that we who have been following their directions fo really and prudently as we could, are fcarce well ufed; and the body of the countrey which yet are for the way of State and Kirk, will quickly be in danger to fall off to ane other way. We fear our brethren have als high thoughts to gett the Kirk and State brought about to the modell of their Remonftrance as ever, coft what it may to themfelves, or to whomfoever who ftands in their way. See weell to it at this very time: yow had never more need. If we have any fkill to difcerne, take heed what yow grant in changing of the place of the Commiffion; and in your meeting of the commiffioners from the Weft, there is hopes of turning the Commiffion on your owne head. The taking of Eglintone confirmes us of the great treacherie of thefe about the King. Alace¹ that fo good a King fhould have come among us to be deftroyed by our owne hands, moft by traitors and dividers. What Mr. Durhame minds we know not; in the Synod, and the Committee, wherein his name wes allwayes called, and fometimes he fatt, he wes not againft us; but if he had been pleafed to have fyded any wayes with us who were for the Publict Refolutions, it might have done us much good. We wifh all our fears of his way may be found vaine. Faill not to fee Mr Andrew [Ker] anfwer what I wrote to him in Mr. James Durhame's matters. I made good ufe of all the papers he fent me in the time of the Synod: the anfwer to Ayr is excellent. Mr. David Dick his vindication is very good. Mr. Robert Ramfay hes put out a long, and as I conceave, a ftrong paper. But I hear our brethren puffes at all, and minds to write no more, thinking their partie faft enough; but refolves to act, and let us be talking.

I have fent this bearer expreſſlie to yow and Mr. Andrew [Ker], to wait on yow, if need be, for two or three dayes As yet Mr. Guthrie and Mr. Bennet hes been quiet among us; we know not how long it will be foe. I held up in my hand, in the Synod, the Commiſſion's fupplication to the Parliament, defyring to read it; and aſſuring it would take off much of the burthen that is caufeleſſlie laid on the Commiſſion; but this wes refuifed. Remember, if the brethren in the Weſt, (for all their appealls from the Commiſſion, and carying of the Synod againſt it, and difobedience to it,) ſhall yet be permitted to fitt and vote in thefe things they have preached againſt, their multitude will put yow hard to it. The Lord, who oft hes given yow wifdome and courage, defert yow not now. Your Brother,

R. BAILLIE.

[TO MR. ANDREW KER, CLERK OF THE GENERAL ASSEMBLY.]

ANDREW,

THESE are thanks for your laſt kind long letter. I delivered all the papers, and followed all the directions ye fent me I pray yow let me know who drew the Anfwer to the Prefbyterie at Ayr: I like the hand, be who he will, exceedingly weell. How all goes here my long letter to Mr. Robert Dowglafs will ſhow yow. I have oft defyred, and now againe hes fent this expreſſe, to wait on yow, if yow appoint, for two or three dayes; and if now yow cannot, to intreat yow fo foone as yow can, to fend me the full and fubfcryveit extracts of what paſſed concerning our Colledge and its Vifitation in the laſt Aſſemblie, efpecially the Vifitors act about our ſtipends and filling our vacant places; alfo two acts about Mr. Durhame. I pray yow for your owne advyce, and the brethren's about yow. Mr James Durhame is preſſing himfelfe in a fair way, directlie and at once, I fear many ſhall preſſe it for him in a boiſterous way, to be admitted to actuale fervice in the Colledge prefently. We are here in a great ſtraite: I pray yow faill not with the bearer, to fend us full and free advyce. We conceave Mr. Durhame's fettling in the Colledge is fo paſſionately craved, whileas peaceably he might have a good place in the towne, for this end chiefly, that by him the mind of our youth may be framed to the temper fome would be at. We fear his deferting of the King hurt his Majeſtie; and his coming hither increafe our divifions, and comforts and ſtrengthens much the faction that profeſſe difference from the Public Reſolutions, though he as yet profeſſe none. We believe, and ſtill muſt doe, till your extracts or advyce putt us off it, that the General Aſſemblie did truely tranſport him from Glaſgow to be the Miniſter of the King's familie; and that the place in the Colledge, to which he wes only deſigned, bot never entered, wes truely vaikeing, to which we did elect Mr. Robert Ramſay; and in many ſharp debates with the Magiſtrates and Mr. Patrick Gilleſpie, have hitherto ſtood to this election. But now, when Mr. James himſelfe is come to plead, that he was not fully tranſported, bot by a poſterior act of the Aſſemblie, wes to have his place recognoſced in the next Aſſemblie; and in the meane time defyres us to admitt him according to his election, we know not what to doe. To wrong Mr. Ramſay, ourſelves, and the King, and the public, and, as we conceave and fear, the peace of theſe parts, we are loath to refiſt Mr. James Durhame's own defyres and his powerfull follicitors: we will find it hard enough. But if they would have patience till the Aſſemblie, or be content to be directed by the Commiſſion, all might be ſatiſfied; but we fear the precipitancie of ſome will not let us reſt ſoe long. We begg your advyce.

April 4th 1651.

For JOHN REID; My L. L. [THE EARL OF LAUDERDALE.]

LOVING FRIEND,

Your kindneſs to the bearer on my token to yow, drawes this from me now, both for thanks, and renewing of my defyre to yow and your couſine William, to hear and aſſiſt him againe in his honeſt affaires. Yow ſhall have eight commiſſioners from our Synod, the ſtrongeſt Remonſtrants we have, to give the Commiſſion ane aſſault more, if it be poſſible, to winne it from the Malignant partie that now does poſſeſs it. I have written my mind fully about it to Mr. Robert Dowglaſs. I have done here, to prevent miſchiefe at our Synod, what lay in my power, though to ſmall purpoſe, if my advyces to Mr. Robert Dowglaſs be ſlighted. My Lord Eglintone's lamentable ſurpriſe confirmes us all in our long fuſpitions, that the King, Armie, and State, if not Church, is in greater hazard to be quickly deſtroyed, by villanous traitors among yow beyond Forth, than either by the Engliſh or Scots be-fouth Forth. God help us, all of yow are fufpected by diverfe; treacherie and divifion is feared will deftroy all. I thought yow had taken fome courfe to have keept Mr Durhame there, but I fee that matter hes been neglected, for he is here this fortnight, requiring to be admitted to fervice in the Colledge, wherein he never entered, and, however, wes tranfported from Glafgow to the King's familie. His comeing hither at this time, by his flighting there, I think, will prejudge both the King, us, and himfelffe, as long agoe I wrote fully to your Coufigne. It had been good to have made no noyfe at all for any caufe now, till God had given us a day of Cromwell. Without this all prefent toyle is vaine; with this no prefent reft or filence prejudges any man's affaires, except impatient, rafhe-headie fooles, or falfe traitors.

Aprile 4th 1651. R. B.

To the Rector [of the Univerſity of Glasgow,] G. Lockart.

Honoured Sir,

Seeing Providence hes fo difpofed, that according to the meaning of the Generall Affemblie, I have gotten fome time's retirement, and thinking it my duty to fpend that time in the place I ftand in relation unto amongft yow, till the Generall Affemblie determine in the ultimate judgement of that they referved to themfelves; and not having had opportunitie of addreffing myfelfe to the Moderators, I have thought fitt to communicate my intention to yow as Rector, that fo by yow it being made knowne to them, I may be exonored, either by undertaking fomething, or abftaining, as fhall be beft for the good of the Colledge. My purpofe in this is only to teftifie my willingnefs to doe what lyes in me as duty on the one fide, and to doe it foe as may prevent any offence which appearing miftakes amongft us at fuch a time might give. I have chofen writeing therefore, the rather that I might not appear in this; and I hope ye will foe do in it as may attaine one, if not both thefe ends, which is all the defire of,

Your loving friend to ferve yow,

March laft 1651. Mr Ja. Durhame

For Mr James Durhame.[7]

Reverend and Beloved Brother,

I have thought meet to give yow ane accompt of what latelie hes past amongst us, being willing to lye under the hazard of your sharpest censure, upon my experience of your equitie and wisdome, rather than of the more rash judgement of some in whom I have not found any such vertue. Some dayes after my comeing home, the great necessitie of planting our vacant places in the Colledge being represented to me, by diverse who understand our affaires best, a Rector's meeting wes called, and there I shew, that the fault of not filling our places had not been in us hitherto; for, by the last Generall Assemblie, we were referred, as St. Andrewes and Aberdeen, to the Commission of the Church, whom I knew and had seen in the case of Aberdeen, peremptor not to meddle at all in such matters, for want of the papers which bare the reference, lying for the time in the besiedged Castle of Edinburgh; but now the Commission being masters of these papers, I knew no impediment why we might not proceed to a planting of our vacant places. I was, for my part, the more willing to make no more delay, being very uncertaine of more free and full meetings; the motion of the enemy, with his head-quarter toward us, being, upon too great probabilitie, daylie expected, which was like to scatter us asunder we knew not how long. Hereupon we agreed on the expediencie to fill presentlie our places, if possible. Our next debate was upon the places to be filled: One moved that the Professor's place seemed not to be vaiking, you being like to returne to it in a short time. The Commissioners of the Universitie to the last Assemblie being required to declare how ye were transported, affirmed your transportation (as the act about it will shew) was absolute, and whatever might be said for Mr. Blair and Mr Hutchesou, yet your submitting to that act as it was, and according to it having constantly attended the King's service, there could be no doubt of the vacancie of the Professor's place, to which you had never entered. Also that your tye

[7] A "double" of this letter (Wodrow MSS. Folio Vol XXV, No 122,) has furnished some corrections. A few words at the end of it are deleted, and it wants the Postscript.

to your prefent miniftrie was fuch as the Commiffion of the Church had declared to my hearing diverfe times, they were neither willing nor able to unloofe. As for any willingnefs in yow to returne to Glafgow, I did believe yow were very defirous to be freed of that grievous burthen of the King's miniftrie, and that your inclination was, I conceived, more towards Glafgow, where God had evidently bleffed your labours, than towards any place elfe. Yet that yow had any inclination to a profeffion in the College, I knew not at all, and though both yow and we were never fo willing to any fuch thing, yet I had no hopes that the Generall Affemblie would ever confent to tranfport yow back again to Glafgow without his Majeftie's confent, whofe minifter now yow are; and that ever he would confent to any fuch thing, I did not think. Upon difcourfes of this kind we concluded the true vacancie of the Profeffor's place. Of the vacancie of the Principall his place, we did not much debate. Our next queftion was about the prefent election to both thofe charges. We all agreed that the greateft neceffitie for the time was, to plant the Principall's place; yet the man whom the moft of us inclyned to name for Principall not being poffible in our apprehenfion to be gotten before the Generall Affemblie; and he whom the moft of us inclyned to name for the Profeffion, being like to be obtained at the firft quarterly meeting of the Commiffion, we agreed to name him prefenthe, and the other thereafter; foe much the more, that if we purfued for two at once, we were almoft fure to lofe the one. In our nomination, upon the fuppofition that your place was truely vacant, the Rector, the Vice-chancellor, myfelfe, Mr. George Young, Mr. Hew Blair, Mr. John Young, Mr William Strang, named Mr. Robert Ramfay, as the farr fitteft we knew for that charge; Mr Richard Robertfone named Mr. Patrick Gillefpie; Mr. James Vetch was not ripe to voice any. It was appointed that we fhould goe up together to Mr Robert Ramfay his houfe, and give him the call; and it was laid on me, with one of the Regents, to profecute the call before the Commiffion of the Church. All this was done at leafure in three or four hours calme debate, without the leaft heat or noife, or any offer of a diffent from any. All went up together to Mr. Robert Ramfay's, except two of the Regents, who could not in tyme gett their cloaks and fhoes, and by the heartie invitation of all, Mr Robert Ramfay was called. So we went all home, thinking that matter to be als good as ended.

Early the next morning, I went to the Provoft's houfe, and acquainted him with all our proceedings, telling him that our not confulting before hand the Towne-Counfell in matters of our election, did proceed from tendernefs of our priviledges, which I knew fome, on their great miftakes of our acts of courtefie fometimes before, were inclyning to encroach upon. But before I could come home, I fand our brother Mr. Patrick, who (yow know) refuifes to countenance our Univerfitie meetings, who had given to the Rector and fent to the Dean of Facultie a proteftation againft all we had done, telling withall that the Generall Affemblie had not made your place vacant, and that this was your owne mind, and that ye were refolved fhortlie to come and take up your place in the Colledge. For the proteftation, I fand nothing in it confiderable; however, we fhall anfwer it as we may, in time and place convenient; for his alleadgeance of the act or mind of the Generall Affemblie, if there be any truth in it, we are all miftaken, bot the act will fpeak its owne mind. The only thing that fticks with me is, what I heare alleadged of your owne mind. I heard, indeed, that thefe two moneths bygone, fome in a way fo clancularie, that no fyllable of it was ever communicate to any member of the Colledge, was earneftlie dealing to draw yow from the King back to Glafgow. This dealing, I confeffe, I underftood not, nor yet doeth, for however, in my heart's finceritie, I think I am behind few in the Kingdome in my high eftimation of the grace and gifts of God beftowed on yow, and of the fweet fruits are likelie to be reaped of your miniftrie, wherefoever God fhall caft it, and of the eminent bleffing I would expect to Glafgow, (which I love above all places,) and to my owne familie, and my owne foule, if God were pleafed to fix your miniftrie among us; yet I do really judge that your leaving of your prefent charge were a more eminent hurt to the Churches in all the three Kingdomes, by the clear and certain hurt and griefe it would bring to the King and Court; alfo the great difreputation and fore reflection would by it fall on the King in this time when he has no fuch need, and great ftrengthening of their injurious miftakes, who long have been holding out the hypocrifie and mifdemeanours of the King. I think alfo, in my heart, if yow were now amongft us, you would be in great hazard to be drawne the way wherein many who love yow, and yow love, are deeplie plunged, which I apprehend were a great hurt both to yow and them, and a great furtherance of a way which I count finfull and exceeding dangerous, and your living in the Univerfitie in that way, I apprehend, would waken and greatlie encreafe our now quyet and dung-out divifions If notwithftanding, in your owne wifdome, yow think fitt to come here, there is a fair doore opened for your miniftrie in Mr Robert Ramfay his place; wherein yow will have thefe hearty imbracements of us all, even of thofe who are oblidged now to ftand to the late election of Mr. Robert Ramfay, wherein they will be exceiding loath and forrowfull to have the leift juftling with yow, whom they doe profeffe highlie to efteem and love, and are not to profeffe any thing but what truelie they find in their mind. Thefe are the moft fecret and true thoughts I have for the time of this whole bufinefs. I befeech yow, after prayer to God and matuie confideration, to fend me your thoughts lykeways with this bearer, whom I have fent exprefhe to attend your leafure. I hope God may help yow to fall upon expedience which fhall extricate us from thefe troubles

Postscript

After all this is written a common feffion was defyred by the Piovoft, wherein he was hot enough; as in the Toune Counfell before, great difatiffaction was uttered againft us, as wrongers of yow, as putters of yow from your place, and clofers of the doore of all hopes of your returne to Glafgow. The conclufion was a craveing of a conference with the Colledge, where betwixt him and us was changed much too high and free language; efpeciallie I confefs myfelfe, being tempted by the needlefs expreffions of fome. The refult of all wes, we promifed, upon their defire, to furceafe a profecution of the act of our late election till the firft of March, againft which time both they and we might, we hoped, fullie underftand your mind in the poynts controverted, and we might gett ane extract of the acts of the late Affemblie which concerned us. I did oft proteft that thefe might not be counted to efteem and love yow or the Towne of Glafgow lefs, who thought in their heart a greater good to yow and Glafgow and all the Churches in the three Kingdomes, that, while yow lived, yow were fixed to the King's fide as the Affemblie had appointed, than thefe who pleaded loudeft for your returne to Glafgow. However, I was thought by fome to fpeak ftrange language, yet I fpoke not fo much as I have written to yourfelfe, which I believe and know does weell ftand with eftimation and affection enough towards your perfone.

For Mr. Andrew Kir

Right Worshipfull,

What your man promifed me, at St. Johnftone, I wrote for fince to your felfe, bot yet have gotten no anfwer; fo I have now fent expreflie to yow this bearer to wait upon yow ever till he gett thefe papers with which we have fo much adoe. The extract of all concerns our Univerfitie in the laft Affemblie, I fhould be very glad of; but if your man have no leafure in two or three days to write all thefe things, I befeech yow fend me fubfcribed thefe papers following. the reference of our vacant places to the Commiffion of the Church; the act of Mr. James Durhame's tranfportation to the King's familie; the act of Vifitation of the Colledge of Glafgow; that part of the report of the Vifitors whilk concernes our ftipends. Faill not to fend thefe with the bearer, whom I have directed to wait on yow als long as yow will. There is great diligence ufed to caufe every one of our Prefbyteries in the Weft fend in their diffents to the Commiffion after the example of Stirling However, the bodie of our people and gentrie, and I hope minifterie alfo, be for the State and Church's way. The confultation of the chiefe Remonftrants here are frequent and long: I doubt there is fomewhat among them which time will bring out; their bitterneffe againft the publick way is great: the fermons and prayers of fome are ftrange Communicat the inclofed to Mr. Robert Douglafs. I pray yow let me have both your opinions and advyces if we will not be able to carrie our point at the Commiffion of the Church: I pray yow tell us if ye think our cafe cleare · I pray yow fend me with the bearer fummonds for Mr. Robert Ramfay and his parochiners, and all others who has intereft to appear at the next dyett of the Commiffion, or blank dayes thereafter If God give us Mr Ramfay, I hope we have peace in our Colledge, and be anfwerable for our fchollers: If Mr. Patrick get his will of us in this our Univerfitie, he will be their owne to fow what feed in it they like. I hope ye will informe friends, Meffrs John Smith, Mungo Law, James Sharpe, your brother, etc to help us in our juft caufe Keep the copie of my letter to Mr. James Durhame quiet among friends: Let me know the event of the conference

I would think it expedient, if fo yow think fitt, to communicat this whole matter to my Lord Balcarras, with Mr Robert Douglafs opinion upon it; for I verily think, as I have written to Mr. James Durhame himfelf, if Mr. Patrick prevaile to draw away Mr. James Durhame, it fhall hurt much the King in his reputation; it fhall ftrengthen much the dangerous faction here, it fhall weaken and divide us here in our Colledge and toune: for to help this I wifhe my Lord did ufe the expedient I propone to him. Read his letter, clofe it and fend it away, with this bearer, to my Lord wherever he be. I have directed the boy when he has gotten Mr James Durhame's anfwer to come back by yow and Mr Robert Dowglafs, and to offer yow what letters he carries to me, or Mr. Robert Ramfay, or the Colledge, that yow may break all up and confider all So foone as the boy comes firft to yow, difpatch him quicklie, that he may goe to Lauderdaill, whom I ufe to call John Reid, or Balcarras, whom I call Wilham Reid, yow will tell him where they and Mr. James Durhame will be found, and where he will finde yow at his returne from them; at which time I hope yow will be ready to difpatch him hither. Mr. Patrick Gillefpie in publick did avow ye would not fend us the extract of the act of Mr. James Durhame's tranfportation I hope neither he nor any other has fo much power with yow as to caufe yow deny us this duety and juftice

To [My Lord] Balcarras

My Lord,

I have thought fitt to acquaint yow with a new fafherie Mr Patrick Gillefpie is putting us to in our election of a fucceffor to Mr. James Durhame. You will confider the whole matter[5] in the copie of my letter to Mr James Durhame and Mr Andrew Ker, which I hope is communicate to

[5] The 'whole matter' referred to in these letters, may be briefly stated Durham, in July 1650, had been appointed by the Assembly to attend Charles the Second, as his domestic chaplain He was then minister of the Blackfriars Church, Glasgow About the same time, when Dickson was translated from the College of Glasgow to Edinburgh, as Professor of Divinity, Durham was chosen in his stead to be Baillie's colleague, but he was never inducted Having at length relinquished this charge, in September 1651, on the death of Mr. Robert Ramsay, (who had shortly before been successively elected Professor of Divinity, and Principal of the University of Glasgow, but who appears never to have officiated in either capacity,) Durham became his successor as one of the ministers of the Inner High Church.

yow. If Mr. Patrick prevaill with Mr. James, I fear it fhall be very prejudiciall to the King's reputation, and publict affaires. I fufpect, indeed, ane of the grounds on which Mr James hes reafone of malcontentment, is the neglect of his maintainance. I think he hes his owne burthens on his lands, befyde that the quarterings this yeare, and fome yeares bygone, hath made his rent fmall in itfelf, neare to nothing ; he hes a numerous familie, he hes no ftipend from Glafgow : I fee not how he muft not be ftraitned. Therefore, in the midft of all the fcarcitie that can be among yow, I advyfe, that without more delay, in the firft day of Exchequer, yow appoint him a ftipend at leaft of two hundred pounds, and that Sir Daniel Carmichael be commanded to furnifhe the firft year of it prefenthe : I believe he will not be flow to obey that commandment If this be neglected I think you are unadvifed and unreafonable, and yow will repent that neglect. If yow have leafure, write to me how all goes, for I have fent this exprefs to wait on yow. I find a great enough readinefs in the body of our Toune, and I hope, of all the Weft, to ryfe for the King, if they might fafely doe it, notwithftanding of the great labour and diligence of fome to the contrare Mind Maffie and England principally. I cannot hear bot your old lethargie lyeth yet upon yow all, and little of your readynefs for any action comes to our eares. We cannot heare of any fturring in the King.

For Mr Robert Dowglass

Reverend and Beloved Brother,

From our letters and papers to Mr. Andrew Ker, which I pray yow read and confider, yow will fee our prefent condition here. I humblie intreat yow, either by your owne letter, or by Mr. Andrew Ker, to give us your particular advyce and opinion In our judgment our caufe is clear ; if yow think it will not paffe the Commiffion, as I marvell if it fhould not, on your advyce we fhall defift I have directed the bearer, when he returns frae Mr. James Durhame to come by yow . yow fhall break up and confider what Mr James writes to me, to the Colledge, or Mr Robert Ramfay ; foe we entreat yow to doe, that accordinghe yow may frame your advice to us If my heart deceave me not, as many men are deceaved by their owne heart, my intentions in all this bufineſſe are to prevent hurt to the publict, to the King, to our Colledge, to Mr. James Durhame, and to Mr. Robert Ramfay his perfone, which I conceave Mr Gillefpie's practices, whatever be his intentions, will draw one quickly by this his polypragmofine. The Lord keep yow at thir times to be conftant and couragious at thir times for God, and for the diftreſſed lands.

UNTO THE RIGHT WORSHIPFULL GEORGE LOCKART, COMISSARY OF GLASGOW, AND RECTOR OF THE UNIVERSITY, THE HUMBLE SUPPLICATION OF MR ROBERT BAYLIE.

MY LORD,

BEING called by the bedell this morning, at your Lordſhip's command, to be prefent at ane meeting of the Univerfitie this afternoone, wherein I underftand the only or chiefe purpofe to be handled is a defyre of the Town's common feſſion, of our concurrence in a letter of invitation to Mr. James Durhame to returne to his charge here for the time of his permiſſion to vaike from his Majeſtie's attendance; I thought meet to fignifie to your Lordſhip my thoughts of this meeting. Your Lordſhip is fully acquaint with my mind in this whole bufineſs. Of my refpects to Mr James Durhame's perfone, to his grace and eminent gifts, I hope himfelf doubts not, for he has thefe very amplie under my hand latelie. My earneſt defyre to efchew every word and deed that may hurt or offend, not only the Toune of Glafgow, and every man in charge therein, but the meaneft perfone of the burgh, I doe profeſſe it to all the world, and I know my heart and intentions ufes not to contrare my profeſſions. I thought we had been agreed, on your Lordſhip's overture, of letting our late election lye over intire for the Generall Aſſembhe, without touching it, to make it better or worfe, directly or indirectly, which yow conceaved was all the Town had craved, and would give them in all reafon, full fatiſfaction. But fince now your Lordſhip is preſſed by them to call a meeting for our concurrence in ane invitation to Mr. James unto his charge here, I am forced earneſthe to fupplicat the declyning of any fuch meeting, for thefe reafons following:—1. Any meeting for this end is like to produce fuch debates among us, as in our laft meeting for that fame purpofe were vifible. I passe needlefs and very untymeous heats occafioned through our information, of exceeding injurious and opprobrious language in the common feffion, againft the members of our meeting, for doeing that which we conceave duty, without any cenfure, at the time or fince, by that venerable meeting upon any of their members for thefe fpeeches againft us. I remember only the long earneft reafonings there we had from diverfe againft our moft materiall and fundamentall privileges of paffing elections to our vaikeing profeffions, by ourfelves, without the concurrence of the Toune of Glafgow. 2ly, Any concurrence of ours in the invitation defired, everts our former maturelie deliberat conclufion of the true vacancie and neceffitie to provide our Divinitie profeffion, which rubbs on the Univerfitie no fmall difgrace. 3ly, Our required concurrence makes us inftrumentall to draw Mr. James Durhame from the King, which I conceave at this time would be a hurt, and a caufe of true grief to his Majeftie, and a ground to fruftrate the defire and conclufion of the Generall Affemblie; in which evills I wifh none of us fhould have any hand. 4ly, This meeting, I conceave, will make new and farder divifions, both betwixt the Colledge and Towne, and in the Colledge among ourfelves, which moft gladly I defyre to have efchewed, if poffible. 5ly, This meeting, I think, will produce that which fhall grieve our Reverend Brother, and, I fear, may hinder him either now or hereafter among us, as is defired; whileas your overture makes a fair way for a prefent invitation of him to the towne miniftrie; and after the Affemblie, if it be found expedient, to fome place alfo in the Univerfitie, upon a new call, which the precipitancie of fome men, in my judgement, goes on to croffe fo farr as lyes in them. 6ly, This meeting feems to be contrare to the declared mind of your chiefe affeffors, without whofe confent yow are obliedged, in your Rector's oath, not to proceed in any matter of confequence, as the prefent is one of the higheft.

For thefe and other reafons we have oft fpoken off, I earneftly fupplicat your Lordfhip would be pleafed to forbear all meeting on this purpofe, and if, notwithftanding of all my earneft and humble defyres, your Lordfhip fhall think meet to proceed, I fhall be forced to proteft in my owne name, and of all who hes intereft, and are willing to joyne in this or the like proteftation, which Supplication and Proteftation your Lordfhip will be pleafed to command the clerk to enter in the Univerfitie regifter, that it may be forthcoming in time and place convenient.

Protestation against Mr. James Durhame's Intrusion.

My Lord,

Being called be the beddell to a meeting, wherein I underftand not only an anfwer is to be given to a letter of our reverend brother Mr. James Durhame unto your Lordfhip, bot alfo our former acts of filling that place to which he was defigned, are to be reallie revocked; I have thought meet to fignifie, that as I conceave your Lordfhip may not call a meeting for any fuch purpofe, for when we mett laft, it wes debated, and, as I remember, acknowledged, without the contradiction of any, that the Rector in his inauguration oath ftands oblidged to call no meeting for any matter of weight, without the confent of his affeffors, and all your Lordfhip's affeffors, as I fuppone, diffenting from the calling of this meeting, according to their agreement in our laft federunt, after too much debate, in ane act, written with your Lordfhip's hand, not to meet more upon that fubject till the matter in controverfie were cleared by thofe who had power This being the cafe, it feems that this meeting and your Lordfhip's calling of it fhall not be found juft, nor at all neceffarie; if fo be, the overture that I made the other day to your Lordfhip, which all then prefent did thinke could not faill to fatiffie our Reverend Brother, if not diverted be other counfell nor his owne, muft yet be thought upon, which here I repeat, that it may be knowne how farr it is frae my mind to oppofe any right, yea, any defire of my much beloved and highly reverenced Brother

I am firmly enough perfuaded of the Generall Affemblie's tranflating of him from any charge he had here to his Majeftie's fervice, and whatever hearing of his grievances at the next Generall Affemblie wes promifed, if he fhould find that fervice too burthenfome, it did not at all import the continuance of any relation he had to his former miniftrie and charge here, fo as to hinder the true vacancie of that place in the Colledge; to which he wes chofen, now about a yeai fince, bot never admitted, as all amongft us ever are before they can claime to any right, or any benefite of the place they have been defigned unto I am alfo firmly enough perfuaded that our filling of that place by a new election fhall be found right and legall, and all fruftrating of that election, direct or indirect, fhall be found wrong and contrare to order.

Notwithstanding, for our Reverend Brother's satisfaction, albeit to the Universitie's and our own suffering, in the meantime, we were content not only to supersede all proceeding upon our act till it might be recognosced by those our superiours whom it concerned; bot also we did assure we were most willing, if by them we should be found to have mistaken, presentlie to rectifie, at our Brother's owne sight, that our error. And though we were, as indeed we are, very hopefull to be justified by them in this action, yet if our Brother could not be persuaded to remaine with his Majestie, which we think the greater and more generall good, neither to stay in the ministrie of the burgh, bot should be determined to accept a school-charge, so soon as we could be gotten cleared by any judicatorie of our right and power, we promised to give him a fair call, so farre as lay in us who spoke to your Lordship, to a Divinitie profession among us; and that to be reckoned not only from the day of his entrance thereto, bot from any day he thought fitt, were it from his first nomination to any chaige here. This loving and respectfull offer we all conceaved would have satiffied our Brother fullie. Bot if nothing else can give content except a reall and present revocation of our former acts, and that without the judgement or advyce of any of the judicatories, to which in such cafes we are referred, bot only be your Lordship, who is a sworne patrone of our priviledges, and that in a meeting from whilk the major part of the members of the Universitie, and these the most considerable, (except your Lordship's selffe,) and who are nearheft intereft[ed] in a bufiness of this nature, doth absent themselves, and diffents from it, and what may follow on it, as contrare to their former acts, and the refolutions of the Colledge in diverfe full meetings of all its members: also of the very few who I think shall be present the greater part being these who are lesse considerable, and whose charge is yet controverted, as standing under a formall appeall, in the hands of the last Assemblie, yet undifcuffed So that their meeting, if any should, would be illegall, and what it could doe upon this ground alone, would be of no effect as being done, *a non habentibus potestatem* in this cafe. I therefore doe deprecate such a proceeding; and if no intreaties can be beard, I protest against it, upon the alleadged reasons, and what farder are in my former proteftation This write I hope your Lordship will be pleafed to keep in *retentis*, that it may be forthcoming before competent judges, in time and place convenient

 April 7th 1651.   R. B.

For My Lord Balcarras. Aprile 17th 1651.

My Lord,

My advyces to John and William Reid, in my two or three laft letters, whether they were received or not, I know not. This is for a particular which your Lordfhip will anfwer with this bearer, or when it's ready, by Mr. Robert Young. Yow gott us a Vifitation of our Colledge, as I defyred; but one claufe in it made it improfitable, which now yow muft help, it lafted bot to the nixt feffion of Parliament, fo it's expired this day You muft obtain the renewing of the former Commiffion of vifitation of the Colledge of Glafgow, to continue till it be recalled, or at leaft till the next trienniall Parliament, or fome longer than to the next feffion, which may be too fhort a time; and fo much for this. What wifdome is it in yow to put the Church to a prefent declaration of their mind in the Act of Claffes? Are our friends fo foolifhly impatient as not to wait fome little time? Why reft they not content with what they have gotten, above their expectation, till they have made fome ufe of it? If they beat Cromwell, doubt they to obtaine all their defyre? If they be beat of him, whatever they gett, can it any wayes profite them? By their rafhnefs they have made fuch a committee for the armie, which they muft either correct, to the fmall reputation of their wifdome, or loffe the Church Are they fo wife alfo as to force the Church, either to eftablifh the Act of Claffes by a favourable declaration for it, or by a diffavourable declaration on it, fuch as I think it weell deferves, to hazard a new ftrengthening of the Remonftrants, by adding to them the late diffenters in Parliament, and a good part of the armie, and to raife fuch new confufions as, at this nick of time, may deftroy all our affaires. When wife men act fuch things as evidently are productive of fuch effects, let them be content to be efteemed, by all beholders, reall plotters and defigners of fuch ends, deny and men fwear them as they will. Union at this time, by all means, is needfull. Keep the Kirk and Argyle, on any condition, or elfe fpeak it out, that yow refolve and have plotted to ruine the King and your Countrey, for bad ends

Aprile 17th 1651.   R. B.

ANE INFORMATION OF THE TRUE GROUNDS AND CAUSES OF THE LATE TUMULT IN GLASGOW, WEDNESDAY APRILE 30TH, AT THE VERIE TIME OF CROMWELL'S REMOVEALL. 1651.

1. IMMEDIATELIE after the defeate at Hamiltone, the Garrison there fent to the Magiftrates of Glafgow to pay a Ceffe, under the paine of prefent plundering and facking.

2. The Magiftrates did all leave the Towne, without any care of their charge, or of the wellfare of the people, in that extreame danger.

3. The bodie of the people in that neceffitie did meet and appoint a Committee of a few of thefe they conceaved wifeft and free of all blemifhe for Malignancie; for of them all, they were only two that ever had been queftioned for that fault, both whereof had given all fatiffaction, and the one at the tyme of the Tumult wes out of the towne.

4 That Committee, by the means of the ordinarie Excyfe and a fmall contribution, by the knowledge and tollerance both of Kirk and State, did weeklie pay the Ceffe, with the good likeing of all the Towne, and allowance of the Magiftrates themfelves, from December to the end of Aprile.

5 All the moneys they intromitted with, were regiftrate and diftribute by a prefident chofen every fortnight for that effect; and fo clear ane accompt wes ready allwayes to be made, without one penny taken by any of them for their paines in collecting or diftributing or attending that fervice, that the bodie of the people were exceedingly fatiffied with their labours.

6. But thefe who wont to manage the Excife in fome part, as wes thought, for their owne and their friends advantage, grudged to fee that mean of profite in any other hand than their owne, and were preffing the Magiftrates to put the manageing of the Excife in the former hands, who had never made fo cleare ane accompt of their diftributions as the Commonalitie did wifh.

7 The Committee, finding themfelves in poffeffion, not only by the earneft defyre of the people, and avowed allowance of the Magiftrates, but by the approbation, as they conceaved, of King and Parliament, were not willing to be put by violence from that charge, which neceffitie and love to their poor neighbours had put upon them

8. At laft on Tuefday morning laft, Aprile 29, before fermon, the Provoft

John Grahame, and Clerk Mr. John Spreule, fent for John Wyllie, the Prefident of the Committee; and when he came, defired, he and the Committee might defift from medleing further with that Excife, as belonging now no wayes to them but to him and the Magiftrates, to be difpofed on as they thought expedient. The other refufeing on diverfe reafons, it went to hot words; and when the Provoft publictly at the crofs, under Cromwell's guard in the Tolbooth, wes pleafed to call the Prefident of the Committee a knave and villaine, and command him to ward, and laid himfelff hands on him to take him to ward without all order or procefs of law; he lykewayes laid his hand on the Provoft's cloake, and faid, he charged him to ward for wronging the Committee of the commonalitie. In all this William Wodrow, late prefes of the Committee, did countenance John Wyllie

9. Immediately after fermon, the Provoft and Clerk calls the Minifters together, declares the great affront they had gotten, crave their advyce in the matter. Mr. James Durhame, Mr John Carftairs, Mr George [Young] and Mr Hugh Blair's unanimous opinion wes, that it wes beft, while the enemie wes in the place, to lay afide the whole matter, to be cognofced upon in a more fitt time. Mr. Robert Ramfay and Mr. Robert Baillie were abfent. But Mr. Patrick Gillefpie did fay,³ this wes according to his former difcourfe very publict, wherein he had faid By thefe incentives, and other confultations that day keeped betwixt the Provoft, Mr Patrick and the Clerk, John Wyllie and John Wodrow were fummoned to appear before the Towne-Councell the day following, Wednefday before noon

10. At that time the Englifh were removeing, and the towne in a ftirre. Yet they appeared before eleven at the place appointed; and attending long, at laft they fend in word by officers, once and againe, that they were prefent ready to anfwer In the meane while the Provoft comes out, and walking a while befide them, goes in againe.

11. The Councell, fo foone as they fat downe, finding the parties fummoned not to appear; without any delay, or calling of them when they were advertifed of their prefence, inflicts on them the moft rigid fentence they were able, deceines their freedome and burgefship to be cried downe, as of men unworthie to live in the towne, having affronted the Magiftrates contraie to their oath; alfo decernes them to be commanded to ward.

³ In this place there must have been some words omitted by Baillie's amanuensis

12. The Magiftrates and Counfell comeing out of the Church finds the parties, with other three of the Committee with them, walking in the Church-yard, and without any intimation of their fentence, paffes by them downe the ftreets towards the Tolbooth, backed not only with all the Counfellors, bot alfo the moft of all the five Seffions who were of their mind, and the moft of the affociat troupe, who it feems upon [fore-warned] defigne were waiting on, and came out, in fours and fives, out of diverfe clofes to attend the purpofe in hand.

13 The five young men went downe the way peaceablie at their back without one word, till the Clerk, feeing his back[ing] gieat, cryed out, to lay hold on thefe men and carie them to ward; at the hearing whereof they, lifting their hats, went by the company foftlie towards the Tolbooth When they were come there the Provoft and Clerk commanded the officers to carie them to prifone, they alleadged the Provoft had no power to put any burgefs in prifone, who wes willing to anfwer to their court according to law, while they are not heard. But the Provoft and Clerk continues verie paffionathe [for] the officers to lay hands on them. The people flockt about, and a noife begins.

14. The officers not dareing to obey the magiftrates, Matthew Wilfon laid hands on William Wodrow. Upon this, his brother Adam Wilfon, towks him, calling him a foole, and bidding him defift, wherefore Matthew falls a ftriking his brother Adam, and a number falls by the eares, ftriking one at ane other with their hands, without any weapons; but no man offered a ftroke either to the Provoft or any of the Baillies In the meane time the Englifh comes in with their fwords and piftolls, and fcatters them all.

15. The chiefe caufe of all what hes paft, and yet is like to paffe on this fubject, many lays it on Mr. Patrick Gillefpie and Mr. John Spreull.

16. All the premifes are offered to be verified by fufficient witneffes.

Information to Mr G[eorge] Young. [Mai] 1651

THAT this unhappie rupture grow no worfe, my opinion is, yow caufe your Committee meet, if it may be, at feven hours: have a letter and a boy ready, that their firft action may be to fend for John Bell peremptorilie to be at them on the fight thereof If the letter be to be framed, and the boy to be fought, till the committee meet and ryfe, he cannot be here this night See prefently Wyllie be not away Let them appoint two of their beft fpokefmen to goe to all the minifters with a true, fhort, clear information. They muft informe the States in wryte. See if they can now prepare a wryte which all of them can approve as true, which neither by witneffes nor their owne contradictions can be oppugned. See if, before meeting, yow and ane other can frame a draught If yow decline, or complaine of any, fee yow can prove alleadgeances. In your fupplication to the Minifters fpeak with all reverence and humilitie; cleare the queftion to be meerly civile, depending before the State; intreat they would not predetermine ; That the violence wes ufed is much to their griefe ; That the clerk and others were the occafioners, beginners, and authors of it; That they are not for contemning of magiftrates, either their perfones or places, but when violence is offered to their perfones publicthe, contrare to the lawes and cuftomes of the burgh, if the perfones of magiftrates in the others juft defence fuffer any affront, it's no more than themfelffes profefs to be juft in the higheft magiftrates, the King and Parliament themfelffes , That they are farr from defireing the magiftrates to lay down their place : this is ane unjuft fclander ; they defyre no more, bot as they are moft willing and ready, in a clear accompt, to fhew not only to them who have intereft to crave ane accompt, bot to all the world, that all the moneys they have receaved are truely deburfed for the relief of the Burgh, and no fexpence of them is taken to their owne ufe nor the ufe of any of their friends ; fo it might be the Magiftrates pleafure to fhew to thefe who are intereft, that the very great foumes of moneys which have been this while bygane taken up, are truely deburfed for the reliefe of the Burgh, and no confiderable part of them intervertit to private ufes . Alfo to fett doune a cleare way for time to come, how it may be feen that all publict moneys may be beftowed on publict ufes alone ; and no part, or no more than needs muft, on collectors or any others, at leaft not without the knowledge and confent of the Deane of Guild, and Deacon Conveener's courts ; That the Commonalties proceedings wes, on meer neceffitie, for the faving of the Burgh's deftruction, on the Magiftrates deferting of their charge without any neceffitie ; That in their proceedings they were weell allowed, firft by the Magiftrates themfelves ; then, as they conceave, by the King and Parliament; alfo by the body of all the people, whom they ferved with great toyle to themfelffes, and no gaine at all Why, while Cromwell is in towne, a quarrell fhould be pickit, and fo eagerlie preffit, they marvell, fince they were allwayes willing that any who had intereft, efpeciallie the King and State, which then wes very near, fhould, by the leift fignification of their pleafure, have them moft readie to give over their bypaft very troublefome imployment; albeit they were not willing to be commanded and threatened by them, whom they conceived to be direct parties in this caufe, and that for fomething elfe than what looked towards the publict good, either of the Kingdome or of the Town of Glafgow, at this time groaning under the feet of a publict enemy, when they conceived it very unfeafonable to trouble the Town with needlefs quarrells.

While they are gathering, be yow and fome one or two thinking of fome fuch paper. As yow would not wrong me, let no flefh fee this paper, or know of my name Have one readie in the afternoone to carry all paffes this day to Robert Marfchell Bring or fend this to me foe foon as yow can. Yow had need be wife and diligent. Let their Commiffioners, if they can be readie, goe to Mr. Robert Ramfay and Mr James Durhame before nyne: neither of thefe will be in Church

For Mr. Robert Dowglass.   Apryle 1651

Reverend and Beloved Brother,

For preventing of miftakes, we have thought meet to advertife yow, that Cromwell, haveing come to Hamiltone on Fryday late, and to Glafgow on Saturday, with a body of his armie, fooner than with fafety we could weell have retired ourfelves; on Sunday before noone, he came unexpectedlie to the High Inner Church, where quietlie he heard Mr Robert Ramfay preach a very good honeft fermon, pertinent for his cafe. In the afternoon, he come als unexpectedlie to the High Outer Kirk, where he heard Mr. John Carftairs lecture, and Mr James Durhame preach, gracioullie and weell to the times as could have been defyred. Generallie all who preached that day in the Towne gave a fair enough teftimonie againft the Sectaries That night, fome of the armie wes trying if the minifters would be pleafed, of their own accord, to conferr with their Generall When none had shewed any willingnefs, on Monday, a gentleman from Cromwell come to the moft of the Brethren, feverallie defyring, yea, requyring them, and the reft of the minifters in towne, to come and fpeak with their Generall. All of us did meet to advyfe; and, after fome debate, we were all content to goe and hear what would be faid When we come, he fpoke long and fmoothlie, fhewing the fcandale himfelffe and others had taken at the doctrine they had heard preached; efpeciallie that they were condemned, 1ft, As unjuft invaders: 2 As contemners and tramplers under foot of the ordinances· 3. As perfecutors of the minifters of Ireland: That as they were unwilling to offend us by a publict contradicting of us in the Church, fo they expected we would be willing to give them a reafon when they craved it in private. We fhew our willingnefs to give a reafon either for thefe three, or what elfe was excepted againft in any of our fermons. The time appointed for this was this day, at two o'clock, at Cromwell s lodgeing. But this morning he fent us word, it would be to-morrow, at that fame time and place, he would attend us. We truft, by the grace of God, to fpeak nothing for the difadvantage of the truth and caufe in hand. Let the Lord make of this what he will: we had no mind to beginne, and have no pleafure to continue, any conference with any of thefe men; but all of us conceave it was unavoidable, without a greater fcandale, to do what we have done. The Lord be with yow.

Your Brethren, the Minifters on the place.

[Glafgow,] Aprile 22d 1651.

For John or William Reid.[9] May 3d, Saturnday, 1651.

Sir,

The enemie's motion from us was on no want; for, contrarie to all expectation, they fand provifions hereabout both for foot and horfe, which we and they conceaved might have lafted them longer It was packetts from Edinburgh, or England, the day before that put them to this haftie departure We think, by weekly printed invitations, yow would [fhould] be drawing the

[9] That is, for the Earl of Lauderdale or Lord Balcarras· Vide p. 155

Englifh over: many of them incline to the King I affure yow Take heed to Tuefday's conference of the commiffioners of our Synod with the Commiffion: I am feared for its iffue, and expects no good from it. The King and all his friends has need to look to it, that the Commiffion be not, by fome men's legerdemain, drawne to alter former conclufions, and put all to a new confufion, both in State, Kirk, and Armie If yow neglect this warning now, blame not me hereafter.

The other day, betwixt our Towne-Counfell and Committee of Commonalitie, there fell out a very foule toyllie [tuilyie]. yow had need to take heed to it. By him I recommendit to yow before, or fome other, yow will get full information of it. See that they gett no wrong by the too great diligence and mifinformation of fome who moft cordiallie mind the King and weell of the publict I hope Argyle, and the Chancellor, and fome others, are fo wife and juft as not to be over-fweyed with any man's report, till all be tryed to the bottom I am not fo feared for Mr. Patrick Gillefpie's diligence as Mr. James Durhame's recommendation If yow look not carefullie to this buffinefs alfo, yow defert your friends in the time of their need, for your own hurt Give a fair hearing, and judge rightlie, and we crave no more.

Your Servant,

JAMISONE

The King and Balcarras would be ferious with Mr. Robert Dowglafs and Mr. James Wood, and Mr. Robert Blair if prefent, that they may be fixed. See for no caufe yow lofe the Kirk nor Argyle. I hope David Leflie be very fure for King and countrey. fee it be fo, whatever the world fpeak of him and others.

FOR MR. ANDREW KERR

ANDREW,

Your packett of Aprile 25th came to my hand this morning, being delyvered yefterday afternoone, in Stirling, to one of our common carriers Immediatelie I fent up to Mr. Patrick Gillefpie your anfuer to the Moderator of our Synod, and your's to Lanark I fhall fend with the firft occafion For all the letters and expreffe meffengers I have oft fent to yow for the extracts, yow fend me nothing bot falfe promifes; therefore, once againe, I earneftlie entreat yow will be at the paines to fend me thefe extracts fubfcryved. both I myfelfe, and our Colledge, and fome more of our dear friends, have very much need of them. At leaft, let me have the extracts of what concerns the provifion of our vacant places, our ftipends in the report of the two Vifitations, and the Affemblie's acts concerning Mr. James Durhame. If at laft yow will not beftow foe much time on your too good friends, I will fay yow have little regard to them, and yow are looking over the dyke to follow the Remonftrants; for that's the way to thrive; and better for yow to thrive late than never. I am fure our Synod has gotten a fyne beginning of their defyres the place and perfons of a committee as they would have wifhed. I wifh a good agreeance; but I hope the Commiffion will be loath, for their fatiffaction, to put the State and Armie in a new confufion, by altering of their former grounds: we repent, if this advyce was not good. I fent to yow and Mr. Robert Dowglafs, by Mr. James Hamiltone, Mr. Robert Ramfay's large treatife · of the receipt of it, our brethren's like or diflike, yow write nothing. How our conference with Cromwell was contryved, or for what ends, I may weell guefs fomething, bot can affirm nothing: it was foe put on us, that we could not decline it. Yow will fee the fumme of it, drawne by Mr. James Guthrie and Mr. Patrick Gillefpie, the maine fpeakers: We had no difadvantage in the thing. The tumult of Glafgow, procured by the rafh and headie counfell of fome, might have drawne to great ill, had not the Englifh been very feafonable redders. Matters will not reft here if the infolencie of fome be not compefced: believe not all you hear till both parties be heard. I purpofe not to meddle with that matter, bot I doubt not yow will hear too much of it. Yow tell not what the Commiffion did at Falkland: let me hear from yow. Your prefs is exceeding flow. I think, before this, the Commiffion's anfwer to Stirling and Ayre, Mr. David Dick's, Mr Robert Ramfay's, and Mr James Fergufone's papers might have been printed; and fome invitation to the Englifh to leave Cromwell, whither many of them doe incline: mend this.

Your Brother,

R. B.

Fryday, May 2d 1651.

For Mr. [Robert] Dowglass.

Sir,

I hope yow faw what I wrote the other day to Mr Andrew Ker. I have now little to adde, bot that the courteflie of your letter to Mr Patrick Gillefpie has made him fpeak fince to his friends with great chearfulnefs and confidence, and this day and yefterday to preach als largelie and boldlie againft the Publick Refolutions as ever. Whereupon I conclude, that his and the reft of their refolutions who are comeing along with him, is to be firme to their principles, and that their endeavours will be to gaine the conference to them, either all or fome. I hear they have adjourned againe our Synod, of purpofe that themfelves, and all more of the Weft they can make, may attend the quarterlie meeting, and either mifcarrie it, or if a pluralitie of others, (diverfe whereof they fpeak of as they pleafe,) fhould carry it againft them, yet they may make fo loud and confiderable a partie as may give life to their defignes, that we believe be als high and dangerous as ever. We marvell ye have put not one man of all the Weft on the conference, bot we know your wifdome, and therefore moft fecurelie we acquiefce in it; only all here in your mind defires me to tell yow their opinion, with fubmiffion, that they conceave it very unexpedient to tranflate the conference to St. Andrewes. We who know them better than yow, think none of them is to be gained one hair-bread; bot we fear if they gett yow to St Andrewes, they will gaine on diverfe men more than fhall be convenient. If yow keep ftill at Stirling, our Synod may be keeped; yow may be quate of them at your quarterlie meeting, or we at our Synod: doe what yow think expedient. We know other men's obftinacie will make none of yow unconftant; and if all your courtefie will draw none of them to their duetie, that yow will not faill from your quarterlie meeting to write to our Synod or feverall Prefbyteries to doe our dueties, in keeping at leaft the Faft, and reading your Warnings; and if it be your will to let our pulpits beat [on] one another, and moft boldly the Kirk and States juft proceedings to be preached and prayed againft, and doe nothing at all but bid Prefbytries cenfure thefe great men, we will not now fpeak out what the world about us muft think of fuch a proceeding. We are for the time a little feared for the iffue of this conference, but our truft is in God, and in your oft-tryed wifdome.

Your Brother,

Tuefday, May 6th 1651

R. B.

This bearer will wait on till yow caufe fome about yow wryte fomething to me how to guard, the beft I can, againft the evill of our Synod, according to the inftructions I expect from yow.

For [the Earl of] Lauderdaill.

My Lord,

I hope yow read what twyce or thryce I wrote lately to John and William Reid; yow have here the double of my laft to Mr. Robert Dowglafs, and of my former to Mr. Andrew Ker. I advertife yow this once more, as yow mind the King, or the Armie, or the Kirk, look to this conference; it's a mafter piece of your bufinefs, as I conceave The prefaces to it, the perfons of the committee, and privat letters, makes Mr. Patrick very high . if it lye in your power let not the meeting be tranfferred to St. Andrews. Doe not dreame by your conference to gain any of them, only guarde yow lofe none of your friends, and fee that they who refolve to differ gett no more by their journey to joyne with them. Succeffe is from God, wife going-about a buffinefs is from the parts God hes given, but if I find yow carelefs to ufe diligentlie all poffible endeavours, be content to have me one witnefs of this fault in yow; which fome will fwear can be no lefs than deep treacherie and high treafon, which if yow and your Coufigne, my friend, will wittinghe be guilty of, pardon me no more to truft men on earth. I advyfe yow to fee it gone reallie about, that your fojours be more civill; their open prophanitie and cruell oppreffion among our people, makes the Englifh more lowlie [lovehe]. Alfo do not provoke nor make defperate the Remonftrants; guard againft their defignes with all care, but wrong and hurt no flefh without clear caufe.

Your Friend,

May 6th 1651.

R. B.

[POSTSCRIPT.]

Our Provoſt's[1] letter to the King, which we doubt not was penned in Mr Patrick's houſe, I wiſh yow ſent a copie of it. See if a committee of two or three might be ſent here to try that whole buſineſs, bot ſee well to their choiſe. Let them have power to take ane accompt not only of the exciſe, but all taxations and publick moneys for two or three years, to try the receipts and diſburſements, alſo complyance with the enemie. Let Mr. John Smith, and ane other miniſter, come along to try Mr. Patrick's part; there will be many witneſſes in that buſineſs that cannot come along; or if this way ſhall not be found fitt, but yow think fitt the principall parties be ſummoned before yourſelf, give power to the miniſters here to examine witneſſes. If yow lay this matter altogether aſide, I fear they ſhall make a clamour of it againſt the King, as unjuſt and unwilling to protect magiſtrates when oppreſt by malignants, a falſe calumnie in this caſe. If your committee for this be no better than that of our conference, I am glad I have nothing to doe with them. Farewell. Doe me the favour to putt all my letters in Vulcan or honeſt Jacchæus's cuſtodie.

Why hes not every regiment a miniſter? Why is there no Preſbyterie in your armie? Had you ever ſo many miniſters out of charge? I like weel your delay of fighting, if yow could keep up your armie, but beware it melt not, and the countrey faint not under its oppreſſion Why train yow not your fojours, and daylie exerciſe them? Upon the hudge large quarters of the enemie will yow make no infall? I think Mr James Durhame will come along to the conference, contrare to my advyſe, and without, (as he ſayes to me) any invitation from any there I feare his accommodations more than all the eight commiſſioners violence. I doubt not bot Robert Marſchell has informed yow of Lambert's ſecret letters to ſome here, and of our fears for Dumbartane. If yow be not aſſured of the honeſtie and watchfullneſs of the men (for courage they need none,) who are intruſted with that place, ſome of yow are unworthie the truſt the King and State have given yow. My laſt word to yow is, loſe not the King nor Argyle in any termes

[1] John Graham, Provoſt of Glasgow

For [the Earl of] Lauderdaill   May 12th 1651.

My Lord,

The honeft man John Reid's canker at me, and his coufignes William alfo, I take in good pait; for my jealoufie of them, and theirs of me, comeing all out of mutuall love to a third, whom all three minds truely to ferve; and Jamefon, the third, als much in his ftation as either of the former two, or any who goes on Scots ground, to his underftanding and pith this being, we will pack up all our pleas till Cromwell be difpatched, and then have with yow both. However, I befeek yow look well to this conference, whether they goe to St. Andrewes or Perth. For the quarterly meeting I am much afrayed for the event of it, that if fome of yow there with all your witts watch not over it, it produce great harme both in Church, State, and Armie; I fhould be glad herein to be miftaken. For our Glafgow bufinefs, I thank yow heartily for the favor thefe I recommended to yow has gotten; I muft ftill intreat yow to favour them fo farr as yow find equitie on their fide. If my mind had been followed, yow at fuch a time fhould not have been troubled with that buffinefs; and fo foon as reafon can be gotten, if my opinion be followed, yow fhall be no more fafhed with us. Fear from fome of yow, and counfell from fome of us, hes made our Magiftrates inclineable to give to your fupplicants much of their defyres, and all I fufpect they fhall obtaine from yow, after much toyle both to yow and themfelves: If they truely can gett this, I think, after their agents hes fpoken with yow, and approven to yow their proceedings, they are unwife to refufe it. Without all prejudice to the King and State, at a much more convenient time, they may call any here they think fitt to ane accompt, either for publick moneys, or complyance with the enemy, or whatfoever fault elfe can be made good againft them.

While I had written this farr I find that fome incouragement, as it feemes, from your act, hes made our Magiftrates fo high that accommodation here is impoffible, bot when they come among yow I hope it fhall be more feafible. If I come to fee yow I hope to be welcome, were it to fpue all my gall in your bofome, for [comifits] yow will have none; however, wherever I be, I pray yow, firft and laft, mind the Church conference and Commiffion

Your's.   S. J.

For Mr D Dicksone.   February 24th 1652.

Reverend and Dear Brother,
The moſt of theſe we expected mett in Edinburgh, Maſters James Wood, David Forreſt, Robert Kerr, etc. After prayer and deliberation, we reſolved on the neceſſitie of a Warning and Teſtimonie, defections being ſo ryfe, and dangers ſo evident; but to make it more effectuall, we thought fitt to invite our diſſenting brethren to joyne with us in it, the duetie being uncontroverted, and confeſſed to be neceſſar If we joyned in this, it was a ſtep to further [union]; if this wes refuſed, we had little hope to joyne in haſte in any thing elſe. We fand the chiefe of them in toune, at a ſerious meeting among themſelves, Maſters John Livingſtone, Patrick Gilleſpie, James Guthrie, Wariſtone, Sir John Cheiſlie, Brodie, etc.: they had made animadverſions on the Engliſh papers, which were communicat to Finnik [Col Fenwick]; bot we could not ſee them They profeſſed all to be als much againſt the Engliſh as we could be, yet they were not pleaſed one of them to open their mouth to any of us; bot we behooved to ſeek to them, which we did without any grudge. Mr. George Hamiltone and I were ſent to Mr. Hew M'Kell and Mr. George Hutcheſone, to defyre them to propone our motion to Warriſtone, or to whom elſe he or they pleaſed: they undertook this very cheerfully, and defyred me to ſpeak to Brodie, whom they had oft found on the ſame thing. I did ſo, and he promiſed to joyne in dealing effectualhe for it. The iſſue wes, Warriſtone, Mr. Gilleſpie, and Mr. Guthrie, mett with them, and after a long debate, gave them a ſhifting anſwer; that their meeting wes diſſolved, and the brethren gone home, and they could ſay nothing, though none of note wes gone but Mr. John Livingſtone, and their chieff men were all preſent This dealling did grieve us all, and made us ſee more of the progreſs and incurableneſs of the ſchiſme For all this we would not give over; we agreed to the materialls of a Warning which we ſent to Mr. Blair, to be put in forme, and to go alongs the Preſbytries ſo ſoon as may be. I drew them ſo that no word of them ſhould be offenſive; ſo our brethren and we defired Mr Blair to be carefull that in his draught there ſhould be no word to irritate, hopeing, when it comes to the brethren in Preſbytries, they will be loath to diſſent and oppoſe alone,

for our defect, that we cannot confeffe fuch guilt as they will have to be on us without conviction. We eftablifhed a correfpondence betwixt the Prefbytries of Edinburgh and St. Andrewes, and, in the mean tyme, drew a fhort direction for brethren's carriage, and advice to people, efpeciallie commiffioners of fhyres and burghs. I have no time to get thefe things doubled for yow now. All the minifters of Edinburgh prays ftill for the King, and preaches very freely and zealouflie againft the way of the Englifh: this they are very angry at, and threatens to remeed it. They impute much of this to Wariftone, who, on the advyce of fiiends, is gone out of the toune. Good Sir John Seaton wes the firft that fubfcribed his free and willing acceptance of the incorporation for Eaft Louthian. The two Swintons followed for the Merfe, Stobs for Tiviotdale, Dundas for Weft Louthian, William Thomfon and Fairbairne, I think, have done the like for Edinburgh, and it's like almoft all burghs and fhyres will, under their hand, renounce their Covenant. Glafgow and the Weft purpofes to refufe, for which we are like deeply to fuffer; but the will of the Lord be done Yow fhall hereafter hear what I know. I expect no fatiffaction to your defyre from Edinburgh It were good ye were at a poynt what ye will doe for us The Lord direct yow. My fervice to Margaret

Your Brother,
R. BAILLIE

Mr Robert Dowglafs and all our brethren are in health and courage. God is with them. They affure us the King goes to Charrantone to fermon, and hes put forth a declaration for the Covenant.

FOR MR. BAYLIE.   MARCH 23D 1652.

MY REVEREND AND WELL BELOVED BROTHER,

THE longer brethren live at diftance, they will fee the greater neceffitie to unite in the Lord. Ye fee what a wicked complyance is made with our oppreffours, and how our Solemn League and Covenant is groffly violated by this fubfcription. In the defection of fo many, the ftanding out of your Commiffioners wes fingular. Ours began well; a great part of the inhabitants had fubfcribed a letter to their Commiffioner, forbidding him to fubfcribe that tender as they call it; but danger being reprefented, they fainted. We hear that with yow there is a partie of them that never was gracie, and I think never will be, who inclyne ftrongly to goe on in the common byaffe; I fear they were too much countenanced the laft year. Oh! the nakednefs of our land is fearfully difcovered: we are generallie a very rotten and hollow-hearted people. Upon this, and many other confiderations, the fervants of our Lord Chrift ought to haften their union; without this extreamities will be followed, fome in flacknefs, others in rigorous ftricknefs of difcipline, whereby matters will be put clofe out of fiame

I know needlefs it is to exhort yow, to incline to and follow after peace and union: ye would rather expect of me overtures. I have been defyrous, for fome fpace, that not only debates about former refolutions, but determinations, acts, cenfures, all be quite laid afide; all authoritative acting either by Commiffion 1650 or 1651 laid afide; correfpondence entertained by all Synodals in the kingdome, that by confent we may fall upon a publict way againe; in the mean time, about planting of kirks, neither fatiffaction nor diffatiffaction to be taken notice of If uniting on fuch termes may be had, they are accurfed that would hinder the fame, by feeking fatiffaction for what is paffed: for my owne part, I think I fee evidentlie enough fome things amiffe *utrinque;* bot I would preferr one act of oblivion herein, leaft new debating exulcerate our fores I remember my love to Mr. James Fergufone, and communicate my mind herein to him. Grace be with yow

Your loving Brother,

R. BLAIR.

ANSWER TO MR. BLAIR. APRIL 1ST 1652.

REVEREND AND DEAR BROTHER,

YOUR's of March 23d, I receaved this night. The fubfcription of the Englifh tender is againft no man's mind more than mine; a partie of our Toune hes now done it publickly and privately: I have declared myfelfe againft it more than any other have; but the refufeall of thefe who make no fcruple to lay afide the King, and to make the third article of our Covenant ftand well enough with a freedome to change Monarchie with a Scottifh Republic, this to me is a high-enough crime. Our commonalitie wes never countenanced by me the laft year, in any thing I knew, either then or now, to have been wrong. How gladlie I would be at union in any tollerable termes many know, but for the quite laying afide all the acts of the laft Affemblie, and that men cenfured fhall not make fo much as the leaft acknowledgement for all their erroneous and very evill Remonftrances, Proteftations, and other mifcarriages, whereby they have directly ruined the Commiffion and the Generall Affemblie, and hes been very inftrumentall in the publict calamitie, and to this day goes on with a high hand in deftructive wayes to their power; to clap their heads in all this, I doubt it be acceptable to God, or the men's good, or can ftand with the being of our difcipline in any time to come; but that you pronounce all thefe men accurfed that are not for thefe termes of Union, when I read it, I was amazed. Yow may know how much the hearts of our dear Prifoners,[2] and many more gracious fervants of Chrift, are againft fuch termes of peace, albeit it be faid to us, in the face of Prefbytries, that we, or who ever are not for fuch a union, are unworthie either to fitt in Prefbytries or Synods. All this I take, albeit with grief, yet in patience and filence, bot fo as I count fuch writes and fpeeches, no lenitives at all for healling. The God of truth and peace fend fuch overtures of peace, as may be imbraced without a greater mifchieffe than is that of our prefent rupture, though it be one great enough. The Lord be with yow. I fhall be loath to deferve the eftimation of accurfed man by any, bot leaft of all from yow, whom hitherto I have profeffed a Father in Chrift.

Your Son in Chrift,

R. B.

For Mr. James Wood. April 1st 1652

Reverend and Dear Brother,

Read the inclofed, yow and Mr. Andrew Honyman, clofe and caufe de-

[2] On being informed of a meeting of the Committee of Estates holding at Alyth, and said "to be cairless, wanting a guard" &c General Monk "raid up fra Dundie quyethe in the nycht, upon Thursday the 28th of August, came upone the Committee quyethe in the morning, tuik thame prissoneris, and robbit thame of all that thai had, and schippit thame toward England quhair thai war committit" to the Tower of London and they remained prisoners till Sep

liver it I write it with a foic heart I fear Mr. Blair and Mr. Durhame be on ways to increafe our mifchieves: I fee the Synod of Glafgow and Fyfe are prefently to be affaulted in their new way for Union, to burie the Affemblie indeed, and to put tyrranous men's feet againe on the neck of our Church. If yow there will contribute to thefe courfes, anfwer to God and men for it. Is this the fruit of our Edinburgh meeting, and all the promifes wes made to us of a teftimonie and a commiffion? I fee our prifoners at London's letters, which I faw, have not been fo groundlefs as I took them. I would defyre ane account of your Synod's proceedings, and what ye have been doing fince we parted. The Lord direct yow; yow to whom the managing of the Church affaires wes chiefly committed: If for the name of a peace (worfe I fear than all our difference yet hes been) with your own hands yow will overthrow all, I fhall be, by God's grace, a mournfull witnefs thereof, bot not a confenter thereto; though over againe, bot for one fober word to this purpofe, I fhould be openly avowed unworthie to fitt in a Prefbyterie; yea, though I fhould be counted worfe than all that, and worfe hardly can be than ane accurfed man: I groan at fuch [horrible] termes for no caufe at all, bot fober dutie in the fear of God. The Lord be mercifull. If yow pleafe, yow will write with the firft occafion.

Your Brother,
R. BAYLIE

For Mr Wood. April 1st 1652.

Our Ufurping Brethren, (as Mr. Blair wont to terme them,) fo farr as I fee or can learn, minds no Union with us bot in their own termes, to be fet up againe, to goe on where they left, to make havock among poor brethren, from which all your caveats and other promifes will not guard. They here, who may and fhould know, fay, that Mr. Lockier at Aberdeen gott a paper from Mr. James Simpfone of Airth, defyreing a conference for union betwixt ours and fome of their divines. This paper wes fent from Aberdeen to the Commiffioners at Dalkeith, by Lockier,[5] who did difrelifh the motion and

---

[5] Nicholas Lockyer, an English Independent minister, who was in Scotland at this time with the English forces. *Vide infra* p. 213.

discharged it. There is strong hopes that Cromwell, on sundry obligations, will send with Sir Henrie Vane back to our brethren, either a Scottish Republict or such conditions as will satiffie them : Will yow not have patience to look on a little ? before the time of the Generall Affembly, we will fee much more Why should our precipitation contribute to further evill designes of dangerous men ? Alfo that Mr. Lockier wes fent for by fome of the Scots to overfee the erecting of new congregations in the North : what is doeing there, and what fpeed Gairdner, in his rebaptizings, hes come, yow will know better than I. We expect shortlie Lockier and Oxenbridge here. All that fears me not, fo much as the counfells and actings of mild and moderate brethren · Marfhall alone, in fome of our judgments, deftroyed more the Kirk, Kingdome, and Covenant, in England, than all the feven diffenting brethren. Had the half of fome men's zeale and authoritie been fpent againft the fhamefull prefumption of a few turbulent men, which hes been to fhew faults *utrinque*, and to put the whole Affembly juft in their condition, it had been better this day than it is with our Church. Nothing hes more encouraged, and does daylie more, thefe men in their hardnefs, than their declining Mr. Dickfon and Mr. Dowglafs are farr from fuch thoughts ; they will be, when they hear them, ane addition to their griefe, and the fruit, I fear, the lengthening of their imprifonments. This work I fear make but a third faction, whofe violence may prove alfe great as any of the two former in the end ; when, at the very beginning of their overtuie, they are fo modeft as to pronounce all who will not follow their propofition to be unworthie to fitt in a Prefbyterie, yea, in termes, to be accurfed. I fear when yow and I both, and all who will follow Mr. Blair's advyce, hes done our beft, very many brethren and their flocks will beg the Englifh protection, that in no termes they may ever come under fome men's government, either ecclefiafticall or civill; though no man hes been, and no man, I fear, fhall be readier than my foolifh felfe ; yet I thank God, Mr. Blair, and his great counfellor Mr Durhame, hes wakened me at this time to give both him and yow this watch-word in the beginning of this your dangerous Synod I hope yow will mifken to Mr. Blair, and all others, except thefe who are intime friends to the Affembly and Commiffion, all this my freedome, which for the time great both grief and feare hes expreffed. Faill not to communicate this to Mr. Andrew Honyman and Mr. David Forreft, that I may have yow three witnesses of my heart's temper, which I submitt humbly to your censure.

The act about expectants came first from your Presbytrie and Synod; how just soever and expedient it be, yet I never practised it, and assure yow it wes never practised to this day in the West. No example can be given bot of one in Dumbartane; and I find that is false. Bot I am sure our brethren are carefull, one way or another, to plant all vacant kirks I know only with men of their owne stamp, and to marre all others; neither hope I they will change this dealing The fardest, I think, yow can goe, is to appoint some two or three of your Synod to joyne with some of other Synods, men all clearly for the Assembly, without If's or And's, to conferr first with themselves and then with oppofite brethren; that betwixt thefe some mid-men, as Mr. Blair, etc. deall; the tyme to be May; the place to be Edinburgh, or St. Andrewes, or Kirkcaldie: only medle not in your Synod with the matters themfelves I wifh our prifoners minds at London were founder. I would be loath to compone without them. A fhort paper from yow will be gotten eafily conveyed to them, and fafe enough, weekly by Mr Robert Lowrie.

For ROBERT DOWGLASS, AND JOHN SMITH [6] APRIL 8TH 1652.

BRETHREN,

THE compaffion of our heart, and our prayers to God for yow, and thanks for his prefence with yow in all your fad fufferings, have been continuall. Though fear of mifcarriadges and miftakes have hindered our writing to yow, our earneft defyre and very great need of your counfell hes made us venture at this time. Our ufurping brethren, through their unnaturall divifions have added much to our calamities: the lamentable evills of that breach increafe dayly. To expect union on the fmalleft fubmiffion of thefe men, it is in vain, though the little remainder of our Church and State fhould perifh before their eyes. The crying neceffitie of fome healing of that breach makes the moft of thefe who have been, and are oppofite to them, defyreous to have it in any tollerable termes, and for that end hes had many thoughts and fundry meetings, but as yet all in vaine. At laft Mr. Blair and Mr. Durhame, men of

[6] They were at this time prifoners at London, and this letter, as appears from the MS was addr...ed to them under th... a... ur... 1 n...m... o --B'a.k an...t R...ert ...tr

the greateſt authoritie and parts among us, have taken ſuch a dealling in it, that it is like either to agree the parties or work them to more ſubdiviſion. It wes intended, and ſtrongly preſſed, to have carried our Synod of Glaſgow yeſterday to the termes of agreement yow may read in the incloſed. By our prayers to God, and all the diligence we were able to uſe, though the minor and weaker part, yet we keept them off at this time from all, ſo much as ingadgeing in the matter, till we had leaſure to advertiſe and take counſell with all our friends, we pleaſed, far and near. We had a very ſore labour to gett it to this. What is done in the Synod of Fyfe, where the like aſſault, I ſuppoſe, hes been made, I doe not know; bot am ſure I ſent to ſome of them tymeous warning of all this defigne. We purpoſe to ſeek the Lord, and advyſe among ourſelves what is to be done; but it is my very earneſt defyre to have your mind of the whole matter ſo particularlie, and ſo ſoon as is poſſible, yow being thoſe whoſe mind in theſe things I defyre moſt to follow. Upon the one hand I ſee, for all the ſafeguards expreſſed, the acts and proceedings of the Aſſemblie are alſe good as buried; the authoritie of all poſterior Aſſemblies is fearfullie ſhaken, and putt in hazard to be trod underfoot, by the error and willfullneſs of any the like partie, theſe brethren who hes been, in our judgement, the greateſt troublers of our Church and State, are put againe in a preſent capacitie to goe on, by their purgeing, to create great moleſtations to many. But, on the other hand, the miſerable daylie fruits of our diviſion are hardly tollerable; they who now preſſe the Union are like to carry to it many of our chieff and beſt men, ſo that the refuiſers will be exceedinglie weakened by this abſtraction, and become both odious and contemptible. What to doe I am in a ſtraite: faill not, if poſſible, to give your advyce, for it will be to me of great weight. The great and kind Lord uphold your hearts, and furniſh yow with all comforts needfull, both in the inward and outward man, to the honourable diſcharge of that great and high taſk of ſore ſuffering for himſelffe and us, and haſte your bringing out of that furnace as gold purified ſeven times.

Your Brother,

Glaſgow, April 8th 1652. R. B.

Your free anſwer to this harmleſs and innocent caſe of conſcience, in a matter meerly eccleſiaſticall, though found, ſhall offend no juſt man; though fundrie of good note be for this paper, yet the moſt [of] our mind in the Synod are againſt it, and I love it not. It will be needfull to fett downe, befydes the faults yow find in it, your pofitive mind of the termes yow wiſh us to agree; or otherwayes, to goe on as we may in our differences.

For Mr. Wood.   April 8th [1652]

Reverend and Dear Brother,

We have had great and fore labour thefe dayes bygone; before, and in our Synod, fundrie of our brethren were inclyned to break off prefently from the declyners of the Affemblie. When, with enough adoe, I had gotten thefe quieted, others of our brethren, as James Ferguffon and Patrick Colvin, etc., were clear for agreement to this paper, which Mr. James Durhame, as from Mr. Blair, alfo Mr. Patrick Gillefpie, etc. did prefs with all their power, great vehemencie, and fubtilitie. By the help of God, we gott all held off, and the Synod not at all ingaged fo much as in hearing one lyne of the paper till we had tyme fufficient to advyfe with all our friends. We have adjourned to the firſt Tuefday of June, at which tyme doubtlefs the agreement will paffe in our Synod in thefe very termes, and the chiefe of thefe who have adheared to the Affemblie will joyne in it, and the refufers will bear great odium to proteſt againſt it. It is exceeding neceflare we had frequent letters about it, and a meeting, even a commiffion, if yow think fitt. I wiſh we had the mind of our Brethren in bonds: it would be a great encouragement to me, on either hand, as they inclyned I have written to them for it; and if you think fitt, I wiſhe yow, or Mr. Blair, did the like, with all poffible fpeed. My mind I have written to yow at fuch length latelie twyce, that I need not now repeat Your mind on the whole matter fend over, with the firſt occafion, to Mr. Robert Lowrie, that I may make the beſt ufe of it I can.

Your Brother,

R. Baylie.

Our brethren hes difpatched correfpondents to Galloway, Argyle, and Drumfreifs to endeavour the fynodick paffing of this agreement there prefentlie, but I fhall doe my beft to keep it off at this tyme. I think yow would write to Mr. Robert Young, Mr. William Rait, and Mr. William Strachan, to be thinking, feverallie with the brethren of our mind in Perth, Angus, and Aberdeen fhyres, on the paper which yow would fend them there, they may be readier to give their opinion when yow call them to meet. Though fome of our friends, as Mr. James Ferguffon, etc, be almoft for all the paper, yet the moft of our brethren, as Mr. David Elphingftone, Mr. John Bell, Mr. George Young, are paffionatelie againft it.

For Mr. Robert Ker. April 8th 1652.

Reverend Brother,

I THOUGHT before this to have had your mind in thefe things I fent to Mr. James Wood; I marvell it came not, being fo earneftly preffed. Mr. Robert Lowrie will fend yow a double of what I wrote to Mr. Robert Dowglafs and Mr. James Wood. I wifh yow meet with fome about yourfelfe, and call Mr. William Jamefone and Mr. Knox to yow, to fee what yow diflike in this paper, and to fet downe pofitively yow will[7] agree; elfe they will, ere we be aware, have the moft of all our confiderable brethren ingaged in thefe termes. Ufe all poffible means to have your mind at me if yow can before a fourtnight. I wifh alfo yow write to your brethren and others at London, and to others, with all fpeed.

Your Brother,

Glafgow, April 8th 1652. R B

For Mr. Robert Ker. April 25th 1652.

Reverend and Dear Brother,

I WAS very glad of your laft letter, for by it I wes confirmed in that which ever had been my fenfe of this laft motion for Union; only yow miftake that yow apprehend I wes ever for thefe Overtures, and for your clearing take

[7] The word *not* seems to have been here omitted, judging from Baillie's explanation at the commencement of the following letter

the hiftorie · When, after waiting long for our teftimonie from St Andrewes, agreed on in our laft meeting at Edinburgh, and my fharpe craveing of it from Mr. Wood, in that letter yow faw, at laft I got a long letter from Mr. Robert Blair, the purpofe whereof wes thefe Overtures in effect, which difpleafes yow, and with that certification, " That he accounteth them accurfed who would hinder fuch an Union.' [8] Being fore greeved with this expreffion, I wrote fharpe back to him, and to Mr. Wood, a long bitter letter, all which yow fhall fee at meeting. Finding at the fame time, as I conceaved, Mr Durhame the author of thofe termes of Union, and fetter of Mr. Blair a-worke for them, I was a little perplexed for the iffue, efpeciallie being told, in face of Prefbyterie, diftinctlie by Mr. Durhame, " That who would be againft fuch an Union were not worthie to fitt either in Prefbyterie or Synods." I gott only this for declining, and that modeftlie, to be on a committee of our Prefbyterie to draw fuch Overtures to be a reference from us to our approaching Synod. To this terrible reflection, I faid no more but fimplie, " Brother, this requires no an anfwer." Conjecturing by all this the defigne with all earneftnefs, to engadge the Synods of Fife and Glafgow in thefe dangerous Overtures, and being a little wakened by Mr Blair's wryte and Mr. Durhame's words, I difpatched prefently ane other letter to Mr. Wood, to be communicat to Mr. Andrew Honyman and Mr. David Forreft, obteftıng them to guard againft this affault, and to do their utmoft to fave their Synod from meddling with the matter of thefe Overtures, and go no farther than a conference on the general, without prelimitation When we come to the Synod, we had a fore labour. A committee they carried by their number, whether we would or not; the Overtures were the draught of Mr. Durhame alone, prefented to the committee, which we carried, much contrare to their mind, that they fhould not be fo much as prefented to the Synod; and to keep the Synod from ingadgeing, we were peremptor, and carried it, that they fhould not be fo much as read or fpoken of, under whatfoever notion, in the Synod; only we confented to the adjournment of the Synod to June 2d; againft which time, in the Committee, we promifed to propone thefe Overtures to our friends far and near for their advyce, and to be readie then to fpeak our mind on them, which now we would not; though the moft

[8] These Overtures, by Durham, were presented to the Synod at Glasgow, in April 1652 A copy of them is given in Baillie's MS and will be added to this letter.

of us fhew our averfenefs from the matter of them, and moft for the forme, that any Synod fhould take upon them to meddle with what concerned the Generall Affemblie. My great fear was, farther drawing off us, by this motion, fome of our chiefe friends; yet God guided it fo that it was prevented. Mr. James Ferguffon, and Mr. Patrick Colvin, were at firft inclineable to much of the matter in the Overtures; yet, ere we parted, I fand both faft enough to oppofe them as they ftood, and in the way they were defyred, whereof I was glad. What fince I wrote about this matter to London, and Fife, and elfewhere, I defyred Mr. Robert Lowrie to fhew yow. This is the whole matter, whereby I hope yow fee my forwardnefs for thefe Overtures wes not fo great as yow fuppofe. Write once more to our brethren at London, that, if poffiblie, I much defyre we may have their mind at our meeting in Edinburgh. Mr Dickfon, in both his fermons here, and oft in his private difcourfe, declares himfelfe clear for the Affemblie *in omnibus*, without If's and And's, and contrare to thefe Overtures, and all thefe men's wrong ways. It were good yow, Mr. James Fleeming, and Mr John Ofwald, come in and confirmed him, as I have done with all my power. he will have great affaults from Warriftone, Mr. Hew M'Kell, Mr. Blair and others.

I purpofe to enquire for yow, as I wrote laft, at Mr. Robert Lowrie's houfe, on Monday at night May 10th, or Tuefday at noon the 11th, God willing, except yow have taken courfe with thefe of St. Andrewes to fhift the meeting, whereof I could be glad. Yow will be doubtlefs, as I have been, much refrefhed with Mr. Dickfon's zeal and wifdome in this bufinefs, whereof I wifh our brethren at London and elfewhere were advertifed. Caufe fend to Glafgow, to Mr. George Young's houfe, fo foone as yow can, twenty or thirty of Trochrig's books[9] to begin with: let me hear from yow of the receipt of this, with the prices. The great and good Lord be with yow, and direct us in the manifold fnares which Sathan, by diverfe hands, better and worfe, now dayly fetts for our feet.

Your Brother,

Glafgow, April 25th 1652 R. BAYLIE.

[9] The posthumous work of Robert Boyd of Trochrigg, *In Epiftolam Pauli Apoftoli ad Ephesios Prælectiones*, which was publifhed, with a preface by Baillie, at London, 1652, folio.

[Mr James] Durhame's Overtures for Union

Being ſtill more and more convinced of the neceſſitie of Union among the Miniſters of this Church, be the many evills that accompanie theſe differences, [the Synod] doe therefore think it expedient, to endeavour ſome way of healing, at leaſt of preventing the growing, of the fame. And though they neither intend hereby judiciallie to condemne or reflect on any acts or proceedings of any of them, either on the one ſide or the other, preceding this time, (bot to leave both ſides without prejudice by this agreement,) yet for the ends foreſaid, they doe voluntarlie condeſcend mutuallie in the things controverted, in als farr as concerns their practice for the interim, as followes:

1. That they ſhall eſchew all publick wakening or lengthening theſe debates by preaching or ſpreading papers, either in favours of the one ſide or the other

2. That they ſhall forbear the practiſing, executing or preſſing of all acts concluded in the laſt Aſſemblie at St. Andrewes and Dundee, and alſo the preſſing or ſpreading appeals, declinators or proteſtations againſt the fame; and that both theſe forſaids, together with any ſentence intended or followed thereupon, ſhall be for the time, (as to practiſe and our uſe-making of them in any thing) as though they had not been; this being allwayes ſo underſtood as inferring no actuall condemning of either of them, as is ſaid.

3. That none of thoſe be to any, whatſoever rank, miniſter or elder or expectant, a ground or aggravation of challenge or cenſure, or of exception againſt their being admitted to office, they being in other things found qualified.

4 That ſome be named as correſpondents who may carry theſe Overtures to be conferred of with and recommended unto brethren of other Synods; who are to be written unto to ſend ſome of their number to meet at ane convenient time and place for that end.

5 Likeas it is their purpoſe, if God ſhall give ane free Generall Aſſemblie, to indeavour for a full and judiciall ſettleing and oblivion of the foreſaid differences, and all conſequences that hes followed on them; and, in the meantime, to proceed in all affaires according to the uncontroverted rules and acts of our Church

This Agreeance may be drawne to the laying afide of all the prefent controverfie, the matter being, for the particulars, removed but by the Affemblie itfelfe and fubmiffion of men cenfured; elfe no Affemblie firme hereafter: And with cautions againft feared domination, and a due proceffing of novelties tending to feparate congregations, Why fhould not ane oblivion of Malignants, the King and they having fatiffied, be granted alfo? Why not depofed minifters and elders, for no other fcandall, on fubmiffion, made capable? What Union elfe firme?

For Mr. James Wood. June 4th 1652

Reverend and Beloved Brother,

What yow have done in your Synod of Fife, it were good we knew. In our Synod we had thefe two dayes fell bickering Brethren of our judgement were rarely conveened; the other very frequently. We thought we had nothing at all to doe, but they fand us unexpected work. The Prefbyterie of Dumbartane had found the tryall of Mr. Robert Law, for one of their kirks, unfatiffactorie, the people appealled to the Synod; after much loud and clamorous debate, Sir John Cheiflie and Mr Patrick Gillefpie gott a committee, allmoft all of men of their own judgement, to put the young man to fome new tryall, and, if they thought fitt, to ordaine him without the Prefbyterie; alfo another Committee to try and cenfure fundrie members of that Prefbyterie, being joined with fome of the Prefbyterie itfelf. *Vis et modis* they have drawne fome of the Prefbyterie to their fide, whereby that Prefbyterie, that had hereto been very unanimous and diligent to doe their dutie, is put in a pitifull confufion, and difabled wholly for doeing any more good for the time, againft this moft tyrannous courfe. When no intreaties, nor fair overtures for peace could be heard, the whole party of the Prefbyterie protefted, that no declyner of the Generall Affemblie fhould be a judge to them, to which they of our mind adhered; for which Mr. Patrick Gillefpie and Sir John Cheiflie did preffe vehementlie that all of us fhould be removed for cenfure. We were willing to remove, on condition that they againft whom we protefted fhould be removed with us as our partie, who could not fitt to judge us for protefting againft themfelves on fo great a ground ; on their refufall to remove we likewife refufed. The next caufe was Mr Robert Hume, where they proceeded the clean contrare way, though the people were unanimous and conftant in their call: the whole Prefbyterie had unanimouflie approven him in his tryalls as ane expectant, and the moft minifters were fullie fatiffied with all his tryalls ; yet on a parties diffatiffaction, for no confiderable reafon, they could not be brought to determine any admiffion, fo the people appealed from their clearlie partiall judgement The letters of the Commiffion they will not have read without a proteftation, and no election will they permitt where they are able. It is in vain to dream of peace with thefe men ' they mind nought bot to fett themfelves up, and to caft out and hold out all they can, and fill all places with their profelytes , to frame people to ane new devotion in *materia proxima* to a feparation. However Charteris be inbodying in a church fo faft as he can, and celebrating the communion to his profelytes, yet, for all our dinne about him in our laft Synod, he was not fo much as cited for the beginning of a proceffe either before Synod or Prefbyterie; all their fire for cenfureing their other brether, yet (as they mutter for fear to provocke the Englifh) is turned to cold water, and a great deall of tendernefs, when they have adoe with Sectaries. We befeek yow ingadge us no more in enfnaring conferences. Goe on in the high clear pathway of our Generall Affemblies without all prelimitations : Lead us no more into temptation Alfo our brethren in Glafgow, Lanerk, Dumbartan, Irvine, and Ayr inclines ftronghe to elect by themfelves , when others (though the major part by one or two led declineing elders) refufe at all to elect, I hope yow will not be againft it, that in this act we make ufe of our right I defyre your judgement of this quicklie, after yow have communicate with Mr. David Forreft and Mr Andrew Honyman. I have moved the brethren not to move any thing till I hear from yow. All my arguments prevailes little with diverfe. Beware of neuters their counfells ; no man ferves the diffenters fo ftrongly as they : A great deal better for the trueth that they did declare themfelffes oppofite wholly Send your returne to Laurence fo foon as yow can.

Your loveing Brother,

R. B.

In the end of our Synod, Mr Patrick with Sir John, with confent of our

Moderator, obtained ane act for keeping our Synod book from going back to the next Affemblie; againft which we protefted. This is a clear evidence of their purpofe towards the Affemblie following.

For Mr. Robert Ker.   June 4th 1652.

REVEREND AND BELOVED BROTHER,

By the inclofed ye fee the condition of our affaires. I pray yow fend me your own fenfe of my queftion about elections. Sundrie of us purpofes to be in Edinburgh a little before the Affemblie, whether commiffioners or no, to guard the beft we can againft previous undermyning. I hear Mr Blair has joyned in the diffent from the act of the Synod approving the conftitution of the Affemblie. I hope this muft be a miftake, he having fo oft fpoken for the conftitution of the Affemblie. So great and caufelefs a change cannot, I am fure, befall him. However, I would think it expedient, if fo it feem good to yow, to write to the Towre, that our confeffors there would be pleafed to write ferioufie to Mr Dickfone, Mr. Wood, and above all to Mr. Blair, to doe their duetie in the Affemblie, and to oppofe as it becomes them, not only manifeft oppofition to the Affemblie, bot that which is more dangerous, all tampering by enfnaring and betraying conferences; and to turn the edge of their zeal, and pen, not to flatter and ftrengthen, but to rebuke and gainfay them who truely deferve it. As their letters broke our laft fnare, fo I think a wife and plaine admonition at this time, would doe much good. I wifh yow write for it, bot withall give them a caveat to provide, that farr lefs noife be made of letters either to them or from them than lately hes been; for I am much afrayed that fome malicious men, finding their crooked defignes crufhed als much by their letters as any other mean, procure them fhrewd offices. Try where the Synod of Glafgow's book is, and how we may gett it. Your Brother[1] had it to write on it the Minutes of the laft Affemblie.

Your Brother,
R. B.

---

[1] Robert Ker, to whom this and many other letters are addreffed, was Minifter of Haddington, and brother of Andrew Ker. Clerk of the General Affembly.

For Mr. David Dickson.   June 4th 1652.

Reverend and Beloved Brother,

I have defyred Mr. Robert Lowrie to communicate to yow my letter to Mr James Wood and Mr. Robert Kerr. I pray yow fend me your advyce on the whole matter, efpecially on the point of election The boldnefs and violence of our brethren growes. accommodation with the fpirit that leads them is defperate. If Mr. Blair and Mr Durhame will ftill go on to draw us by [out of] our right ftraight way, we muft befeek them to fpeak plainly their mind, and not to halt betwixt two, but at laft to fide Or, if they will make a third partie, we muft tell them they lay but ftepping ftones to lead over our friends from us to our oppofites, which is the worft office they can performe, and farr more evill than any thing they can doe now who ftand in the extreameft oppofition. The Lord help yow to doe what yow may for God and his caufe in this fo pitifull a time.

Your Brother,

R. B

For Mr. Robert Ker.   June 7th 1652.

I expect with the firft your anfwer to my laft; alfo I add this, that I would think it very expedient yow had the advyce of Mr. Robert Dowglafs, your Brother, and Mr. John Smith, of our whole proceedings, in the next Affemblie; both in generall, concerning all comes in their owne thought for our direction, alfo, in all comes in your mind to propone to them, efpecially what we fhall doe with the men cenfured, when they add their proteftation againft the nixt Affemblie to their former contempt 2 What fhall we doe for a Teftimony againft the Englifh, if we may fpare it; and if not, how farr fhall we goe in declaring againft their tyrannie, and their adherents, efpeciallie the Commiffioners for Union? The giving of it is apparentlie our ruine and of our Generall Affemblie, and the great defire of brethren who are waiting for this occafion to gett us removed, and the Kirk put in their hands · The fparing of it for any danger, will, I fear. be fcandalous I earneftlie defyre your and their mind concerning this our greateſt point 3 Alſo, what advyce they will give us anent our other brethren If we receive them, we will ſtumble the other; If we keep them ſtill out, who, for little faults, were depoſed, or are willing to doe all for ſatiſfaction we ought to require, we are injurious, and puts them to deſperat courſes. Beware of prelimiting conferences: beſide your giving a juſt exception againſt the Aſſemblie, they are exceeding dangerous, and only to enſnare us: conſent not to countenance them. The Aſſemblie may not be ſo ſhort as only to adjourn with doing nothing at all: this will not be yielded to by many who finds the oppoſite brethren ſo active and ſucceſſfull in evill, that, if a ſtoppe be not putt to their ruſheing into all vacant places wiſer modeſt men only of their cavell, they will not find the Church out of danger, before ane other Aſſemblie, to be overwhelmed by them. The counſell of neuters muſt not be regarded; it is they, above all, who increaſe that partie, and weakens us moſt by all their counſells and proceedings Write to me before yow go out of Edinburgh.

Your Brother,

Rob. Baillie.

For Mr. James Durhame. July 8th 1652.

Reverend and Dear Brother,

Haveing looked upon together the Cauſes of the Faſt communicat to us, we have thought meet to acquaint yow with theſe our thoughts thereof, in private, to receave your brotherlie advyce and direction thereupon, as God ſhall put it in your mind.

We have been earneſt of a long time to have had publict and ſolemne Faſtings, for many moſt important Cauſes, both to the land and this place; bot have alwayes been peremptorly refuiſed all concurrence therein, unleſs we would make our duties ſins, and other men's ſins our duties. When the Lord's ſtrange judgements on us hath put us now once againe to Faſt together, upon Cauſes uncontroverted, we are very willing and deſyreous to continue this gracious and very neceſſare exerciſe upon any Cauſes we know, or which, beſyde our preſent knowledge, we ſhall be inſtructed in, by yow or any.

As for the paper preſented to us; in the Firſt Cauſe, we deſire to be informed what be the reproaches in this place against the ordinances. 2 We defyre the unfrequenting of the ordinances, beside others, to be specified in this most eminent particular, which for some time hes appeared to us, and to many more, a very grievous scandall, and a clear beginning of a schifme, that the ordinances out of the mouths of these of us who have been for the publict, have been alse good as deserted, and that without any resentment or reall endeavour we know of in our brethren to help it, since the beginning and continuance of this open scandale, hath been in the persons with whom their power and interest is manifest.

Concerning the Second Cause, we defyre to be informed what constant tract of opposition to Christ hes been in this place, more than in others; and that the principles of enmitie to Christ, wherein many are said to be rooted, were clearlie and positivelie sett downe. Also, what are the kythings that never here have been missed to obstruct the thryvings of the gospell; and what ventings of hatred at the power of godlinefs; what bitternefs and mockings of pietie is understood: these most heavy crymes would not be charged without clear and convincing evidences. We think the madnefs of a few rascall persones is not here pointed at, neither the speeches against the true misbehaviour of pious people can be taken for any wronging of pietie; and what there hes been more here, we defyred to be informed of it; and when we know it, we shall (God willing) heartily concurre in mourning for bygones, and amending in time coming We think also, that what is said of the affrontings with a high hand of the ordinances of Christ, would be made particular if the late protestation against the common session be here understood, it would first be shewed to be guiltie of such a high challenge.

And why here is the unparallelled affronting of the Generall Affemblie and the Commission of the Kirk, which in the prime men of this place, hes been, and is greater than in any towne in the kingdome, altogether buried in silence? Also the manifest contempt of the messengers of the gospell, and the spurnings against faithfull warnings would be sett doune in particular We fear that to our brethren's knowledge and small resentment, some of our persones and ministrie be in too great contempt with their chieffe familiars; and though many be discontent with the personall misbehaviors of some of us against the supreame authoritie of Church and State, what concerns that the message of the gospell?

That the late conjunction of these now in place, should be alse farr aggravate as possible, we heartilie consent, and have many witnesses of our diligence herein at diverse occasions. But we think it a sinfull partiality to be silent, and whollie to connive at the scandalls of others who gave great occasion to this sinne Who were the men who went first to procure the sharpe orders of strangers against their neighbours? By whom and where wes the unhappie Remonstrance contryved? Who avowes every line of it to this day? Who were the authors and persevering fomenters of these fatall divisions that visiblie hes ruinated the land, both Kirk and Kingdome? Who, in contempt of uncontroverted Generall Assemblies and Parliaments, pressed to their power the laying aside of the King, and to this day putts him out of their prayers? Who have given great occasion to think that no conscience needs be made of the Third Article of our Solemne League, and by this means were the first removers of the great barre against the now prevalent temptation? Can all this be dallied with and connived at with the Lord's good liking?

In the Third, we acquiesce.

In the Fourth, we think what is spoken of malice, invyings, and variances in families, would be much more particularlie aggravate as one of the most visible sinnes of the place; which, if the root of it were truely searched, we take it for a sinfull fomenting of this grievous ill to make the fountaine of it enmitie at the power of godlinefs, and to esteem the one pairtie to be the people of God, (as the dialect of some is,) that so the other may be counted the people of the Devill; we are willing heartilie to goe along in chargeing the one partie deeplie with every particular offence we know them to be guilty of; bot not to charge the other side alfo, with that which visiblie lyes on them, in our judgement, it is but to perpetuate divifions among this people, to the reall hurt of pietie, and the continuall miserie of this poor place.

As for the Fifth, we acquiesce in it.

The last part of the Sixth, we underftand not We think there hes been alfe great cheerfullnefs in this people to contribute for the diftreffed, as ordinarilie any where elfe, except at sometimes when through miftakes they have been hindered, and with the glorylngs of the richer we are not acquainted

In the seventh, we acquiesce

Thefe are our thoughts of that Paper. If the Lord fhall be pleafed to help yow to clear us in the things named; and if ye hope there may be any tollerable agreement in them, we shall be glad not only to joyne in the Humiliation itselff, but in all the Caufes yow bring, for all that we queftion is bot fome parts of a few. Before that this matter be precipitat, either in a committee or feffion, we wifh yow delayed it for fome time. But herein let the Lord direct. We reft,

> Your loveing Brethren, for the time much grieved in fpirit, and abafed before the Lord, for many things we cannot mend neither in ourfelves nor others.

For Mr. David Dickson

REVEREND AND DEAR BROTHER,

I WROTE to yow this week with James Hamiltone: I add now this one word farther. On Wednefday, in our Prefbyterie, Mr Patrick caried it to make no election; we did give in, without dinne, the inclofed Proteftation. The churches of Leinzie, Cathcart, and Kilbride, they will plant only with the moft violent young men of their owne fide, and are fure, by one mean or other, to marre all others to the utmoft of their power; they mind nought bot to compafle their defigne, and for that end to tread downe all in their way. Some in Finnick have declared for feparation, againft whom M. W.[2] preaches with tears, bot in vaine. I find they will have one more onfett on yow and the minifters of Edinburgh, this next week, to tempt yow to paffe from the laft Affemblie, and their cenfures, as if they had never been, and all the reft of the acts, controverted. God, we doubt not, will affift yow to doe your duetie. But take good heed, I pray yow, to your colleagues, that they be not entangled; for if all of them, and many more with them, would betray the liberties of our church in the day of her diftrefle, I truft there fhall be witneffes for her without all fuch, be they who they will. The fruite of this labour will be but a new fchifme to ftrengthen the former, a renting of the next Affemblie, als dangeroufly, as wes the laft; and whoever will be a leader to this work they will fucceed to Mr. James Guthrie and Mr. Patrick Gillefpie. Our eyes are on God; but under him on yow, as a good inftrument to prevent this new evill defigne. Look well to fome of Fife, and to Mr. George Hutchefone and Mr. Hew [Mackaill.] Beware of my Lord Wariftone's importunitie. The Lord help yow. Mr. John Livingftone is very buflie.

Your Brother,

Glafgow, July 8th 1652. R. B.

[REASONS OF PROTEST.] WEDNESDAY, JULY 7TH 1652.

The Moderator having put the queftion, What anfwer fhould be given to the Letter of the Commiffion of the late Generall Affemblie; and the pluralitie of the Prefbyterie having voted, that, contrarie to the defire of that Letter, no Commiffioners fhould be choifen to the Affemblie to be holden in Edinburgh the third Wednefday of July; We under-fubfcryvers did diffent from that vote, and entered our proteftation againft it; protefting lykewife, that it fhould be free for us, for the preferving of the libertie of the Prefbyterie and doing of our duetie, to choife Commiffioners as we fhall find convenient for the next enfueing Generall Affemblie, which is to fitt doune the 21ft of July inftant. The Reafons of our Proteftation are thefe following, and fuch others as we fhall give in in time and place convenient :—

1 That vote did reflect upon, and reallie nullifie not only the acts, but the verie conftitution and authoritie of the laft Affemblie and Commiffion thereof.

2 It does marre the next and all fubfequent Generall Affembhes, ever till the protefters againft the laft Affemblie fhall obtaine affureance that the fubfequent Affemblies fhall be willing to paffe from, and lay afide that of St. Andrewes and Dundee as a null Affemblie. Which affureance were a moft unjuft and unreafonable prelimitation of the Affemblie following

3. Becaufe not only the chiefe leader in that vote wes Mr. Patrick Gilleſpie, who, according to our former proteftation, oft renewed, ought not to have had voice at all, nor to have fitten in the Prefbyterie, being depofed from his miniftric by that late Generall Affemblie; bot alfo more nor a triple number of minifters were againft that vote, only two being for it, to witt : Mr. James Hamiltone and Mr William Young, other feven having voted pofitively for a prefent election, to witt. Mafters Zacharie Boyd, George Young, Hew Blair, Robert Young, Robert Baylie, Gabriel Cunynghame, Archibald Den-

neſtone ; whiles Mr. John Carſtaires voiced *non liquet*, and Mr James Durhame did refuſe to declare his mind *pro* or *contra* ; Mr. Andrew Morton and Mr. Thomas Melvill being abſent, and Mr. Hew Binning not preſent at the voyceing. The ruling elders alſo who caried the vote ſhould not have voiced in that particulare; becauſe they all ſtood in actuale oppoſition to the laſt Generall Aſſemblie, being either actuall proteſters againſt it, or being ſent by theſe who were ſuch.

For Mr. James Durhame. July 11th 1652

Reverend and Dear Brother,

That any thing which came from me ſhould have grieved yow, eſpeciallie in ſuch a degree, I am ſorrie; for wittingly I would not grieve yow, from whoſe word my heart hes been ſo oft refieſhed. Your anſwer, I confeſs, hes grieved me to purpoſe; but that all farther provocation may be broken off, we have written once more, I hope without all gall, though the tenth part of your anſwer might have wakened better hung ſplenes than are the beſt of yours. But we deſire to fear God, and to love and honour yow, doc and ſay what yow pleaſe. Your loveing Brother,

R. B.

For Mr. James Durhame. July 11th 1652.

Reverend and Dear Brother,

Yow have been pleaſed to give us ſuch ane ſtrange anſwer to our humble and modeſt letter, as truely we intended it, that we purpoſe not to faſche yow with more of that kind We ſhew yow what we miſliked in your paper; that without all dinne and debate it might have been helped by yow in private. We went alongſt with yow in all the Cauſes of the Faſt : the moſt of them abſolutely. The exceptions we took at ſome parts of a few, concerned one exceſs, and ane other defect, as we conceaved. The great diviſions of this place are knowne. About the authors and fomenters of them, we ſaid, we ſay nothing; only we wiſhed that what oft we heard from pulpits, this paper, which wes to conclude us, might not bear, as if the one fide of the divided were the people of God, and the other God's enemies. We think fuch ane application of this diftinction injurious, and many wayes very hurtfull. What fins were in this place in James Grahame's dayes, and in the time of the Engadgement, and now, in this late conjunction, we have witneffed too much and too fharply againft them, privately and publictly, that now we fhould excufe any of them: We are not fo blind as not to fee much ignorance, profanitie, and enmitie to God and his gofpell, into many among whom we converfe: Yet to apply all this to the one fide of our divided people, as we apprehend fome men's fermons ordinarily doe, and this paper imported, this was it that we defyred to be clear ere we had joyned in it Chrift's mercies to us have been fo many, and our hopes of falvation by his bleffed blood fo great, that we would be loath, upon knowledge, to excufe a thought that reflected on him; bot the bickerings of neighbours among themfelves, merely for the things of this world, to put all thofe on Chrift, and what the humours of provoked people does caft out one upon another for mifcariages, whether true or but apprehended, to father all this on enmitie to Chrift and religion, to us is not juftice This wes all we purpofed, and all the matter, we think, wes written by us. What high and deep cenfures ye are pleafed to put upon us for this, and that without all paffion, if we fhould fett them doune before yow together, we hope ye would not like them fo weell at the fecond fight as at the firft We truft ye would change thefe your thoughts of us, when yow fee they want all foundation. We tell yow, in paffing, but this one word. Upon our converfing with this people, more than feven times longer than yet yow have done, that, in our judgement, this way of preaching and writing is one of the chief ftumbling blocks and great marrs of the progrefs of pietie we know here: continue in it fo long as any think fitt.

What yow fpeak of reproaches of Mr. Dickfon's miniftrie, that they fhould be putt in the Caufes of a Faft, we doubt it fhall not be the feffion's mind. The late moft fhamefull reproaches of his preaching and perfone, too well knowne, were never fo much as cognofced upon, more than the publict revilings to his face of that other brother yow name, (now bleffed), yea, the bafe threatnings of him, and the reft of us, with ftroakes, and more, in the face of feffion, and in papers laid at our doors; yea, the preparing of cudgells by too many of that fide, to have fallen upon us in our very pulpits for no caufe at all. Doe not efteem thir things calumnies, for we know too well the truth of the facts, though we be altogether ignorant of any notice wes ever taken of any of them by thefe whom it concerned, when yet words againft the perfones of others have ufuallie been followed to the outmoft, and cenfured with all poffible rigour. Yow may remember when exceeding grofs calumnies, againft fome of us, judicialhe convicted of falfhood were notwithftanding totallie flighted. The defect we complained of wes the conniveing at the many moft fcandalous finnes of the other fide, as if no fuch thing ever had been. This ftill yow feem altogether to mifregard. We are not willing to apply to this your neglect, the terrible cenfures yow put upon us for no luch caufe. How great occafion foever yow give us, yet we forbear to provoke yow in the leaft, but committs this whole matter to your owne review, if yow continue in your firft fenfe, we muft lay it over on our common Mafter, and continue to mourne before him for that which oft hes been the burden of our fpirits, waiting for his help and remead in his owne time, fince to us the help of man is vaine. The effect of all our defires, firft and laft, is, That without noife, thefe parts of your paper we touched, may be put in fuch expreffions as fhall avoide that evill we fpoke of, and that ye would caufe add thefe other open fcandalls, a pairt whereof we have named, leaving many more which eafily may be remembered; for, in our judgement, in a day of folemne acknowledgement of the finnes of this place, fuch things cannot be omitted, without a great deal of undutifullnefs both to God and man. The Lord direct yow what to doe in this grave bufinefs, for with yow alone we have dealt in this matter, neither intend we, for our part, that it fhall come to any other hand nor yours.

Your loveing Brethren,

R B[aillie].
G Y[oung].
H B[lair].

For Mr Rous   August 20th 1652

Right Worshipfull,

Being intreated by the bearer Miftrefs Lamy, upon the remembrance of old friendfhip, I make bold to recommend her to your favour. I have been oft a folicitor to yow for her, and, as fhe tells me, never in vaine; for this I can give but hearty thanks, withall intreating for the continuance of your charitable indeavours for that her penfion and almes, which, I fuppofe, is all the fubfiftance fhe hes, after a long and faithfull fervice to thefe who now are removed I am hopefull, by your affiftance, fhe fhall obtaine fo much, if no juftice, yet charitie and mercy, that fhe fhall give thanks to God and yow fo long as fhe lives. She tells of a letter yow wrote to me without ane anfwer, be affured I never faw it, for if any thing from yow had come to my hand, I would not have been long in anfwering. I have been oft follicitous in this terrible tempeft for yow in particular, bot could learne nothing certainlie of your condition, before this bearer the other day did informe me of it I was very glad to hear yow wes alive, and, in the great change of many men's minds and eftates, that yow were the fame I left yow,[3] fincere in the Covenant, and ftill to your power furthering what concerned God and godly men; the continuance, for the little remainder of your life, in this gracious courfe, will crowne your (long agoe) very white hairs with a rare and almoft fingular garland of inward peace and outward honour, among the generation of the juft.

If I were befide yow, I would ufe my wonted freedome to poure out before yow many complaints, and much grief for what is paft, and no fmall fear for what I yet apprehend is imminent, but diftance of place, and iniquitie of time, makes me cutt off fuch purpofes · only I cannot fuppreffe one thought, that, in my judgement, the long and heavy fufferings of Mr Dowglafs and his fellows, on the part of the agents, will not be very acceptable to God, nor honourable before equitable men. Thefe men are eminent fervants of Jefus Chrift; they have done and fuffered much in the fervice of the Parliament of England; if they fhall be forgott thus, year after year, and permitted to languifhe in prifone, their Mafter will require it If yow were able to procure their freedome, it would be a favour which not only I, your faithfull friend, but the whole Church of Scotland, would highly efteem and blefs your memorie for it Wifhing the prolongation of your days yet for fome time, for this and fuch fervices to Chrift and his faints, I reft,

Your affectionat friend and humble Servant,

R B.

[3] *Supra* p. 97: Baillie speaks of Rous, with regret, as having complied with the Sectaries

A Postscript.

Your Judges are goeing the next week, as we hear, to vifite our Univerfities If they be inftructed to minifter the Tender to us, they muft purge out of St Andrewes Mr Blair, Mr. Rutherfoord, and Mr Wood; out of Edinburgh Mr Dickfon; and me out of Glafgow; and thereafter multitudes of our moft precious minifters. Whatever differences be among us, yet all of us of any good efteem, are refolved, by God's grace, to fuffer what fhall be impofed, rather than to quate any article of that Covenant, which, at the follicitation of the Parliament of England, we were brought into. For the tyme we are all very quiet and peaceable; but if, for confcience fake, we fhall be wracked, by thefe of whom we have deferved the beft things, our filent mourning will cry aloud in the eares of the Lord, to the fmall advantage of them who trouble us without all caufe. If yow be able to prevent this mifchiefe, it will be a good fervice, not only to God, and many of us his children, but alfo to thefe who, by troubling us, may procure to themfelves, from the hand of our Saviour, much more evill than they are aware of If Mr Tate be alive, and in his old credite, I hope he will gladly, after his ufe and wont, joyne with yow in fuch imployments. I wont to find bot a few there lyke-minded to yow two in the things of God and his Church.

For Mr James Wood. December 10th 1652 [1]

Reverend and Beloved Brother,

I have been expecting, as you promifed, a calling of our Commiffion. I wes hoping alfo for ane account of their conference at St. Andrewes, to have helped us in our conference here, but hearing nothing from yow of either purpofe, I have fent this expreffe to give yow ane account of our proceedings yefterday, the 9th of this inftant, as we were defired There mett in Mr. John Carftairs's chamber, of our mind, Mafters James Ferguffon,

[1] Although this letter bears the date of December 1652, and is entered among others of that period, there is some reason to believe that the date is wrong, and that it may have been written in December 1651.

Patrick Colvill, William Fullerton, John Gemmill, and myfelf; Mr. David Dickfon excufed himfelf, in a letter to his fonne, by the weaknefs of his body, and the length of the journey Of the other mind there came bot four · Mafters Patrick Gillefpie, John Carftairs, Alexander Dunlop, and Hugh Binning. We fhew ourfelves willing to hear whatever they had to fay to us for the agreeing of our prefent differences They propounded to fpeak our minds of the differences, if fo be we could be brought nearer to them, were it but to acknowledge fome defection and backfliding, hopeing, as we fand it thereafter, to have drawne out fome difference among ourfelves about this propofition, as it's faid it did among yow. The points they required our fenfe of wes: The treatie with the King, the Commiffion's anfwer to the Querie, and their anfwer about the Act of Claffes, the conftitution of the Generall Affemblie, and the controverted acts thereof. We were willing to declare our mind in all things; bot defyred alfo to know their fenfe of the feparation from the forces at Stirling, of the Weftern remonftrance, of their oppofeing ever fince the publict refolutions of Kirk and State, of 'their proteftation againft the Generall Affemblie, of their erecting of a Commiffion, of their giving out Caufes of publict fafts, wherein they determine all our controverfies, and layes the main caufes of the wrath of God on their oppofites proceedings. We did declare our mind unanimouflie enough in all the firft. They did declare their mind als unanimouflie in the rigour of all the other; fo any drawing near one to ane other, while we remained in our prefent judgements, appeared defperate to us all; yet, after much talking, and on their profeffions to be very defirous of peace, and of their willingnefs to have all differences laid afide for their part, we were not averfe from trying if any juft peace were poffible. And for this end did offer to propone to the brethren of our mind, to meet among ourfelves, fo foon as might be, to fee, 1ft, How farr they might be content, without all reflection on the Generall Affemblie, and former Commiffion, or any of their Acts, for peace caufe, to lay afide thefe debates which did caufe this prefent rupture, 2d, To agree what Teftimonie to give, fo far as concerned the minifters of Chrift, againft all falling away from the Covenant, which now is like to be the generall temptation of many. That from thefe meetings fome few, were it one from a Prefbyterie, might come to Edinburgh, or fome where elfe, to confer with thefe who fhall attend them from our differing brethren; who, if God may be pleafed to help them to come toward fome reall agreeance, may return with diligence to thefe who fent them, and report what they had found either in the two named particulars, or in what elfe yow pleafe to add I have fent this exprefs bearer to yow, to know how ye like of this motion; for howfoever all of us inclined towards it, yet we refolve to follow it no further, if ye be not alike well pleafed with it If, after confideration, yow think good it be followed, yow then will call to fpeak with yow, at St. Andrewes, fuch of the brethren of Fyfe, Perth, and Angus, as yow find expedient; and, on your advertifement, we fhall write to thefe we find moft fitt of Aire and Galloway to meet at Munyboill, of Clydefdale and Dumbartan to meet at Glafgow, of Louthian and the South to meet at Edinburgh. Mr Patrick Gillefpie will have fome of the other mind ready to wait upon thefe who fhall come from thefe meetings at what time and place we fhall appoint. If ye find not this courfe good or tymeous, advertife me with the boy, and there fhall be no more of it. I will write to none to keep this appointment, till I hear from yow, and yow have named both the time and the place, and the matter of the conference, both among ourfelves and our differing brethren. If yow name a time, let it be fuch wherein there may be fpace to advertife the forenamed parties, firft to meet among themfelves, and then to fend their commiffioners to the common meeting at the place yow fhall name If yow think fitt, yow may defire the brethren of the North of our mind to meet for the fame purpofe among themfelves at Aberdeen. Thefe things would be done with all diligence Expecting your anfwer, I remaine,

Your loveing Brother,

Glafgow, Wednefday, 10th December 1652   R. BAYLIE.

I receaved your letter, and followed all your advyce. Communicate this to Mr. Andrew Honyman, whofe letter alfo I receaved, and thanks him for it There is very great noife here of Mr Blair's letter to Mr. James Durhame, and of his fpeeches in your late conference, to the very great difadvantage of the late Generall Affemblie and Commiffion, contrare to his own former profeffions. If this could be gotten amended by yow there, we would be very glad of it, both for the publick caufe and for that reverend brother his owne reputation.

FOR THE CORRESPONDENTS WITH THE PRESBYTERIE OF GLASGOW IN THE PLANTING OF LEINZIE.[5]

REVEREND AND BELOVED BROTHER,

The Commiſſion of the Kirk, according to the act of the Generall Aſſemblie, having nominate a committee to joyne with the Preſbyterie of Glaſgow for the ſpeedie planting of the Kirk of Leinzie, and given power to any of the Preſbyterie to call that committee whenſoever they fand themſelff grieved by the Preſbyterie's delaying any longer to plant that kirk according to the acts of the late Generall Aſſemblie; We, underſubſcryvers, haveing with much patience waited on and uſed all means in our power to move the Preſbyterie at laſt to plant that exceeding long deſolate congregation, are now reallie grieved to ſee that plantation ſo much fruſtrated, that we have no hope at all to gett it done in any convenient time without the help of the appointed committee. This forces us at laſt, according to our expreſs commiſſion, to call it; and yow being one of the number, with your ruleing elder, are earneſthe intreated to keep with us at Glaſgow the ſecond Wedneſday of January the 12th day of this inſtant, whereby yow ſhall doe ane ſervice acceptable to God and very comfortable to us, and neceſſarie to that poor deſolate people who has wanted ane miniſter near three years; and without God's help and yours, is like to want one much longer Expecting that herein ye will not be inlacking, We reſt,

Your loveing Brethren in the Lord.

Glaſgow, January 3d 1653.

There joyne with us in this deſyre, albeit for the time abſent from toune, Maſters Robert Young, Gabriell Cunynghame, and Mr. Archibald Denneſtone.

---

[5] This circular letter, written by Bailhe, refers to a case which he frequently mentions in his letters at this time The barony and pariſh of Leinzie or Leinyie, in Dumbartonſhire, comprehending the two pariſhes of Kirkintilloch and Cumbernauld, originally belonged to Stirlingſhire The pariſh was ordered to be disjoined in 1649, into Eaſter Leinzie or Cumbernauld, and Weſter Leinzie or Kirkintilloch, but it was not till 1659, when a new church for the eaſtern pariſh was erected

For Mr Patrick Gillespie. January 1653.

RIGHT REVEREND,

Yow had no caufe to wonder for that which wes expreflie told yow, and neceffarlie did follow from the principles we walked upon. Thefe Brethren who arofe and left us were, yow know, not acknowledged by us as the Prefbyterie after our laft proteftation, but thefe who fatt ftill with the Commiffioners, to performe the duetie recommended to them by a fpeciall act of the Generall Affemblie and Commiffion of the Church, were taken by us for the only allowable Prefbyterie of Glafgow. Their delegation of minifters to preach in Leinzie to us was a lawfull and expedient prefbyteriall act That I was one of thefe who were fent, was burthenfome to me and truelie againft my heart; but being unanimouflie defired and voted to goe there the nixt Sunday, I thought it my duetie to obey. My purpofe is to give no offence to any, but fincerelie to preach the word of God, as the Lord gives me grace, for the beft advantage of the kingdome of Chrift in the hearts of my hearers, as I fhall be enabled. If in this purpofe any unadvyfed people fhall doe violence either to me or others, it fhall be my endeavour not to deferve any fuch affront; but if yow know tumults to be defigned, I fhall pray God to pardone the actors and fomentors thereof, and remaine,

Your Brother,

R. B.

For Mr. James Durhame.

As I thank yow heartilie for your kinde and brotherlie warning, fo fhall I intreat yow for that Chriftian duetie to imploy your power with thefe rafhe people that they finne not againft God, nor hurt the Lord's fervants who never wronged them, and are only going about that which they conceave a part of their calling, and the Lord's fervice for the good of people's foules. Herein if yow be deficient, yow cannot bot be grieved for it hereafter when yow fee ill done, which poffiblie if yow had pleafed yow might have prevented   However, I am in confcience obliedged to goe about that which I conceave my duety, let the Lord permitt what obftruction he pleafes to be putt in my way.

Your loveing Brother,
R. B.

Postscript

Truely if I did not think in my heart the bodie of that people to be the givers of the call, and the oppofers to be bot a fmall partie, in regard of the whole, who in reafon ought not to prejudge the right of the farr moft part, I fhould not at all have meddled in that matter. However fair and fober dealling will be found the beft of it, both before God and all men.

For his Reverend and Dear Brethren, Mr. Calamy, Mr. Whittaker, Mr Ash, Mr. Cranford, Mr Clerk, faithfull Ministers of Jesus Christ, within the City of London   January 21st 1653

Reverend and Dear Brethren,

Yow have been pleafed to accept fo kindly of my former letter, as the bearer, Mr Wilkie, made me to underftand, that I am emboldened to importune yow with this fecond. My long experience of your refpects to me, and more of your pious and compaffionate difpofition to all our fuffering Brethren, made me expect no lefs than what Mr Wilkie wrote of your kind acceptance of my recommendation, and your readinefs to endeavour by your beft advyce and affiftance, the relief of our numerous fupplicants, in their very fad condition reprefented to yow by that gentleman our agent there   We were once in good hopes, to the comfort of many here, of fome confiderable fupport from your Parliament   But the unexpected increafe of their weighty affaires which hes interveened, hes much blafted all our former expectation. The long and chargeable attendance of our agent, without appearance of any fruit, makes us inclyne to recall him   The difappointment of our fair hopes will add to the affliction of our wracked people, bot the will of the Lord be done.   Only before his departure I thought fitt to return to yow, my Dear Brethren, heartie thanks for all the kindnefs yow have fhewed to him, and to intreat yow for your beft counfell to him, if in fuch a juncture of your affaires, he may yet have hope, by fome further ftay, of any fucceffe in his negotiation, worthie of his charge and paines In the meantime our prayers to God fhall be for yow and the reft of our Brethren there, that in this day of darknefs the light which the Lord hes put in your veffels may continue to fhine for the comfort and direction of the Lord's people there and elfewhere. That the good hand of the Lord may be on all your fpirits for enabling of yow for every fervice his Majeftie calleth for at your hands, fo prayes

Your very loveing and much honouring Brother,

Glafgow, January 21ft 1653 R. BAYLIE

FOR THE RIGHT HONOURABLE THE COMMISSIONERS FOR THE VISITING THE UNIVERSITIES.

RIGHT HONOURABLE,

Your Honours letter of February 1ft, being this day communicate to us, according to your direction, we make unto it this humble returne; That we believe in our confciences the right of Ordination of minifters to vacant congregations belongs to the Church by divine right, and the gift of Jefus Chrift In this truth we conceave we have the full confent, not only of all the minifters of Scotland, whatever otherwife be their differences, bot of all Proteftant Churches, yea of thofe who are of the Congregationall way, and who refufe infant baptifme. We have feen many declarations of the Parliament of England for this truth, which, fo farr as we know, ftand unrepelled. In the late ordinations which have been in our owne Prefbyterie, or in the neighbour Prefbyteries of Hamilton, Lanerk, Dumbartan, Pafley, Lithgow, Biggart, or any where elfe in Scotland, we have not heard that your Honours hes quarrelled that right The planting of fome Kirks among us at this tyme lyes heavilie upon us, not only as upon the Prefbyterie of the bounds, bot by a fpeciall appointment of the Generall Affemblie, and a renewed ordinance from the Commiffion of the Church A very numerous, and now almoft three years defolate congregation, hes long been moft earneftlie preffing us for it All the tryells of the young man were clofed to the great fatiffaction of all who were prefent, and his edict wes ferved before your letter come to our hands. We therefore humbly intreat your Honours to take in good part that we goe about that which we believe in confcience to be our duetie in a matter meerly fpirituall, wherein we medle with nothing Civile, and wherein the Civile power, wherever it gives any tolleration at all, makes no queftion any where, to our beft knowledge We are fure in France the Prince, though Popifh, denyes not this libertie, and all the Eaftern world, where there are any Chriftians, the Magiftrate does not controvert it. We have very good hopes that as the Civile power in this land did never offer to take that libertie from the Church, fo your Honours will be loath to mind any fuch thing Praying yow may be pleafed to take this our humble and confcientious anfwer in good part, we reft,

     Your Honours, in all Chriftian duty, the Prefbyterie
     of Glafgow, and Committee joined to them by the
     Generall Affemblie and Commiffion of the Church,
     fubfcryved at our direction by our Moderator,
             MR. HEW BLAIR.

Glafgow, February 8th 1653.

FOR OUR WORTHIE FRIENDS, THE RECTOR, DEAN OF FACULTIE, AND THE REST OF THE MASTERS OF THE COLLEGE OF GLASGOW.

WE haveing formerly made knowne unto yow our defires of Mr. Gillefpie's being Principall of your Colledge; and hearing yow are not at all unanimous in your defyres of the fame; bot that fome doe either directly and expreffie or obliquely and fecretly oppofe it, which may adminifter fome ground of difcouragement to him to accept thereof, We doe therefore defire to hear from yow, and clearlie to receave it, under your owne hands, who are willing and approve of the fame, and who, and how many doe oppofe it, and their reafons for the fame. This we defyre may be fpeedily returned unto us under your owne hands, that fo this neceffary work may not be retarded and obftructed; but that we may have occafion to expreffe ourfelffes, as we defyre, to be your loveing Friends,

              GEO. SMITH
              EDW. MOYSLEY.
Edinburgh, February 1ft 1653   ROB. SALTONSTALL

My Letter to the Judges anent the Grounds of my Protestation against Mr. Patrick Gillespie's Entrie in the Place of Principall (⁶)

Right Honourable,

Being required by a letter from your Honours, February 1ſt, preſented in our meeting February 7th, to make clearlie known unto yow our minde concerning Mr Patrick Gilleſpie his being Principall of our Colledge, in all humility I doe offer theſe my thoughts on that matter. When your Honours order appointing Mr. Patrick Gilleſpie to be our Principall wes preſented unto us, I profeſt I ſhould make no oppoſition thereunto; and when ever Mr. Patrick Gilleſpie ſhould accept that charge, according to that order, my carriage in my ſtation ſhould be ſuch as ſhould miniſter to him no juſt cauſe of complaint; neither ſince that time, directly or indirectly, to my knowledge, have I oppoſed or made any impediment to him to obey that order But when, as I conceave befyde that order we were required to defire and invite him to accept of that place, the moſt part of the Facultie did ſhow that we could not in confcience doe it, for ſundrie reaſons that had weight with us. For myſelfe, at your Honours command I make mention now of theſe few following

1. I conceave it is one of the rights and priviledges of our Univerſitie, whereunto I am tyed by oath, to make choiſe by a free election, as of all the reſt of the Maſters, ſo of our Principall And when we have made choiſe to try his qualifications ſo farr as we finde it expedient; bot where neither a voice in election nor any place to try is left to us, though I will not oppoſe, yet I cannot defyre nor invite any man to accept ſuch a kind of call as infringes our priviledges.

(⁶) *Supra* p 154, it was noticed that Mr Robert Ramſay was elected Principal of the University of Glasgow, and a doubt was expreſſed of his ever having officiated in that capacity. I ſince find, from the College Records, that he was duly admitted and ſubſcribed the Oath as Principal, but the date is omitted. It muſt, however, have been in April or May 1651, and he ſurvived at moſt only a few months He ſigns a deed as Principal, 27th July 1651. After ſome interval Mr Patrick Gillespie was appointed his succeſſor, by the English Commiſſioners, and he was admitted 14th February (16th calends of March) 1653

2 Mr Patrick Gillefpie ftands a depofed minifter by a Generall Affemblie, which to me wes a very lawfull one, and which in my judgement, I am obliedged to obey. Wherefore till he have fatiffied the Generall Affemblie I cannot invite him to any charge, either in the Church or Schools, according to the order of our Church.

3 I conceave that Mr. Patrick Gillefpie is not furnifhed with that meafure of learning which the place of our Principall does necefsarily require.

<blockquote>Thefe things, at your Honours commands, I doe fubfcryve.</blockquote>

Glafgow. February 10th 1653   [ROBERT BAILLIE]

FOR THE RIGHT HONOURABLE THE COMMISSIONERS FOR VISITATION OF THE UNIVERSITIES.

RIGHT HONOURABLE,

Your Honours letter came to our hands on Saturday at night, the 5th of this inftant. According to your commands we did communicat it to the Prefbyterie, at their firft meeting, on Tuefday thereafter, whereunto they returned the inclofed anfuer, which now we fend unto yow with ane expreffe of our owne, humbly intreating that, in your accuftomed juftice and equitie in the like cafes, notwithftanding of any mifinformation from thefe who differ from us, yow would be pleafed to believe, that in this whole matter we have indeavoured to doe no more than what in confcience we did efteem ourfelves obliedged to doe, and without all purpofe to doe the leaft offence to any of your Honours. For what ever may be the difference of our judgments from yow in fome things, yet it hes been, is, and fhall be our refolution, fo farr as the Lord will give us wifdome, to walk fo humbly and circumfpectly therein, as to be loath to give any juft ground of exception againft us. Befeeking that we may finde this benigne and charitable interpretation with your Honours, we reft,

<blockquote>Your Honours, in all Chriftian duetie,
R BAYLIE
GEO. YOUNG.</blockquote>

Glafgow. Thurfday. February 10th 1653.

For our Honoured Friends Mr. Robert Baylie and Mr. George Young, at Glasgow.

Gentlemen,

Whereas power and authoritie is given to us, the Commiffioners for Vifiting the Univerfities, Colledges, and Schools of learning in Scotland, by the Parliament of England, to fee all vacant Churches in this land fupplied with godly and able minifters, according to our former declaration, we conceave it fitt, at this time alfo, by letter to give yow notice thereof, that fo ye may forbear to attempt to fettle any minifter in any church within your Prefbyterie, without our approbation, leaft ye contract a further trouble upon yourfelves, and the people whom ye thinke to pleafure therein. This is the defire of

Geo. Smyth.[6]
Edw. Moisley.
Edinburgh, February 10th 1653.   Rob. Saltonstall.

We defyre this may be communicat to the reft of the Miniftrie that are with yow

For his Reverend and Well-Beloved Brother, Mr. David Dickson, at Edinburgh.

Reverend Brother,

Yow will perceave by the inclofed what ftormes Mr Patrick Gillefpie hes been brewing againft us from the Englifh, and indeed, if God prevent it not, he is like to make them fall upon me the firft, of all the minifters of Scotland, but not the laft, that fo he may have, without any more impediment, the full rule of our Colledge and Prefbyterie, which long he hes been feeking, and is now on point of receaving it. I have great comfort and

[6] George Smyth, Esq. and Edward Mosely, Esq were two of the Englifh Judges or Commissioners appointed for the Administration of Justice in Civil Cases in Scotland, 18th May 1652.

peace of mind for the time, that, when the worſt comes, I have not drawn it on by any wrong done to any men. How innocent, and little reflecting on Mr. Patrick, my cariage hes been in the matter of the Colledge, you will fee in my anſwer to the Judge's letter to our Colledge; and what neceſſitie wes laid upon us, not to be hindered in doeing the dueties of our calling upon ane human unlawfull command, yow will fee in the Preſbyterie's letter to the fame Judges, wherein we were all fully unanimous, and none more nor our brethren Mr James Ferguſſon and Mr. Patrick Colvile, though, in fome circumſtances, they did modeſtlie differ that day from the reſt. We conceaved ourſelves neceſſitate to goe on, without delay, to the ordination, not only becauſe we fand no juſt nor legall cauſe of any delay, which all acknowledged; bot alſo, on the delay of never fo few dayes, we faw a great many more difficulties coming upon us than we durſt venture upon This cafe is a leading on to all Scotland, and will be a beginning of fore perfecution to many, if God prevent it not. I wiſh yow may doe your beſt endeavour to hold off us now, and yourſelff next, this ſtorme. The Judges hes their meeting on Monday upon thefe matters. I wiſh that yow, with Mr. H. M'Kell, and Mr G Hutchefone, did fpeak with the Judge Smyth together, at leaſt that yourfelff did fpeake with him to take our letter in good part; yow muſt doe it fome time on Sunday, or not at all. I have fent yow two doubles of all, the one, when yow there have confidered them, to be fent to Mr James Wood, with my letter to him, and the other to Mr Robert Ker, with the firſt fure hand Mr Alexander can find Yow had need to take courfe for a very frequent Commiſſion at your next quarterly meeting. It lyes on yow to give fair warning, and tymeous advertifement, that the ſpoiling of the liberties of the Kirk of the higheſt confequence, and the corrupting of our Univerſities, may not be done before our eyes, and we be altogether filent; fuch puſillanimitie and unfaithfullneſs will provocke the Lord, grieve and ſtumble many, incourage our adverſaries, and nothing prevent our perfecution The Lord help and direct yow in this buſineſs. Let me hear from yow with this my expreſs. The teſtimoniall yow defired, when I confidered it with your fonne, I thought not meet to crave it, for the reafons which will fatiſfie yow at meeting. The Lord be with yow.

                        Your Brother,

Glafgow, February 10th 1653   R. B

Mr. Patrick Gillefpie, after advyfement with thefe of his mind, both eaſt and weſt, it feemes is refolved, without more delay, to take from the Englifh our Principall's place, and to be a ſtirrer up of them to perfecute us all He invites carefully our new Divinitic Profeffor, Mr John Young, to be a member of his feparate Prefbyterie, though neither miniſter nor ruleing elder, which is likelie the other will accept of. He is likelie to fummond us before the Civile Judge for the delyverance of our Prefbyterie book to him, and fo to make the Englifh determine, which of us are the right Prefbyterie, Synod, and Generall Affemblie, to whom the rights of the Kirk, and ſtipends, etc., doe belong · The man is reſtlefs

After advyfement, we have thought fitt not to prefent our Prefbyterie's and Colledge letter to the Judges before Monday at night, only to make way by Mr. John Flefher to fpeak them according to the information, bot not to give it them in write, for they will but fend it to Mr. Patrick Gillefpie to make a needlefs noife on it, and to tell, that fatiffactory letters are comeing It is neceſſare to keep very fecret both the Englifh letter to us, and our anfwers to them, for if they goe abroad, it will irritat them alsmuch as any thing elfe : we are on a ticklifh buſſinefs ; we had need of much prayer to God. If the Lord be pleafed to keep my foul in the light and life I have this while enjoyed, I am fecure of the event; it muſt be good, bleffed be his holy name. In this point of tryell there feemes no darknefs to me at all.

For Mr. Robert Ker. February 10th 1653.

Reverend and Dear Brother,

Yow will fee, in my letter to Mr. Dickfon, and the papers I fent him to be communicat with yow, what is our condition. I wifh, on the fight hereof, yow came in and conferred with him ; he hes need to be ſtrengthened and directed. Let me hear from yow the firſt occafion. The Lord be with yow.

Your Brother,

R. B.

For Mr. James Wood.   February 10th 1653.

Reverend and Beloved Brother,

Yow have here bot a part of our long ftories, yow will confider them, and acquaint Mr. Andrew Honyman, Mr. David Forreft, and Mr. James Sharp with all. Mr. Robert Blair is not for reading of papers; acquaint him with what of the matter yow think fitt. Yow have here my Lord Wigton's information to a friend; the grievances wherefore we called the committee; our anfwer to the Englifh letter; my anfwer to their letter to the Colledge; my letter to Mr Dickfon. I hope yow will not condemne us of rafhnefs, who would not be ftopped by the Englifh letter to doe our duetie, and execute the commiffion laid on us by the Affemblie, the commiffion of the Church, and Prefbyterie. Our ftay had been very fcandalous and hurtfull, though our goeing on we forefaw it full of hazard; but after much feeking of God, and mutuale advyce, all of us thought it beft not to take that ftoppe The Lord his will be done I hope to fee yow at the Commiffion, I wifh it may be frequent. The Lord be with yow

Your Brother,

R. B

My heartie affections to your neighbour, my Lord Balcarras and his Ladie.

For Mr James Wood.   February 14th 1653

James,

Yours from St. Andrewes the fexth of this inftant I received this day. Yow complaine of my long filence; I have, I hope, anfwered abundantly by my large packett this laft week. I add now this paffage: This morning the Rector fummoned us to a meeting, to hear what Mr. Patrick Gillefpie would fay to the Facultie. The Vice-Chancellor, Mr. Zacharie Boyd, wes ficke; the Dean of Facultie, Mr. George Young, wes abfent, on what occafion I yet know not; the affeffors were not defired by the beddell to meet; the four

Regents and I keept with the Rector. Mr. Patrick Gillefpie told us, that though as yet he could not fullie nor finallie accept the Principall's charge he wes invited to, yet he would offer us this overture, That till the Generall Affemblie, which, rightlie conftitute, had ane great overfight of Univerfitie places, he would be content to accept fo much of that charge as might ftand with his miniftrie in the toune, to overfee the difcipline of the houfe, and to doe what elfe he wes able in that charge. When he wes removed, I defyred them to advyfe till to-morrow before we concluded anything in a matter of that confequence. Two of the principall members were abfent; none of the affeffors were fummonded. The matter wes totallie new, a Principall in part, not fullie for a time, not finallie, bot till a Generall Affemblie rightlie conftitute; a Principall with a full miniftrie in the towne; a Principall, upon no invitation from the Colledge, bot fome private men, after a Faculty had judiciallie refufed all invitation. Such things were great novelties, deferveing one night's advyfement; notwithftanding the Rector put it to a vote, and caried to accept Mr Patrick's offer, to admit him prefentlie Principall, and take his oath of doeing his duetie in that charge. Againft this I did proteft, as a violation of the rights of the Church of Scotland, and priviledge of our Univerfitie, and for diverfe other caufes, to be produced in time and place. When Mr Patrick is called in he is put to his oath. I at length debated with him upon the former and other reafones, calmely, without heat, yet fadly, but when I had faid all, without any fcruple he accept[ed the] charge, and gave his oath of faithfull adminiftration; and prefently moved, that our factor, a near allye of mine, might be removed, and Mr John Spreule choifen in his place, which accordingly wes done, and a new meeting appointed by our Principall to regulate all our Colledge affaires. Thus goes the game with us. This to me is a demonftration that there is more betwixt that partie and the Englifh than we yet know.

I have read more than the half of that good book,[7] much more Mr Guthrie's, as I take it, than my Lord Wariftone's. I thought it needfull

[7] The Nullity of the pretended Affemblie at Saint Andrewes and Dundee. Wherein are contained The Representation for Adjournment, The Protestation and Reasons thereof together with a Review and Examination of the Vindication of the said P[retended] Affembly, &c. Printed in the year 1652," 4to. The Vindication of the Assembly was written by James Wood, and the Review, probably by Guthrie from Warriston's notes.

to anfwer it prefentlie with five or fix fheets, or at moft within ten, of Animadverfions, fetting down the points whereto their controverfie is now drawne, efpecialhe the heads of the Weftern Remonftrance, which there, and the groffeft of their tenets, are all clearhe defended. I thought to have done it myfelf, bot feeing the vaine janglemgs of the body of the book are mere formalities of federunts of meetings and niggie-naggies, for no edification, I utterlie abhorred the labour, and caft by the book, fending my advyce to Mr. Ker that yow fhould not meddle with it, whofe way is infinite, bot fend fome few fhort notes, if yow can be fhort, to Mr. Robert Knox, or Mr John Smyth, or if he would think on it, Mr. Robert Ker himfelf, who for a folid, fuccinct, handfome, modeft taking anfwer, I conceave would doe it better than any other, and thefe ftill are my thoughts of that matter. Will yow let Lockier triumph whole yeares?[8] O lazinefs, lazinefs! To the anfwer of my Lord Warriftone, I would prefix the Weftern Remonftrance, and Mr Blair's cenfure on it. Muircraft's letter to Lancafhire was Mr. Rutherfoord's, as himfelf fayes. See the Commiffion may be frequent. The Lord help us, our ftorm is but growing

Your Brother,

Glafgow, Mononday, February 14th 1653. R B.

Instructions to Mr. George Young, for Edinburgh April 8th 1653.

Our Diffenting Brethren being extraordinarie diligent to fill all vacant places with no other but oppofers of the laft Generall Affemblie, for this end, ufing many both cunning and violent devices, and in the Weft coming too good fpeed; fome of us, who to our power have been watching againft their evill defignes, are now almoft fainting, and if not affifted at this time by our brethren, are almoft inclineing to fit ftill and give all over to their

---

[8] Lockyer (vide supra, p 177) preached at Edinburgh a lecture-sermon, "concerning the matter of a Visible Church,' which he published under this title,—" A Little Stone out of the Mountain Church-Order briefly opened, by Nicholas Lockyer, Minister of the Gospel Printed at Leith, by Evan Tyler, anno 1652" 18mo. It was refuted at great length by James Wood, Professor of Theology in St Andrews, in a volume printed at Edinburgh, 1654, 4to.

will, to make havock of all, with our diffent alone and fruitlefs proteftations.

1 What extraordinarie toyle we had in the planting of the two laft vacant places of Cathcart and Leinzie, the countrey knowes. The Baronie of Glafgow is now on the ftage; the Seffion and people are fullie in our mind, except a very few. Our diffenting brethren are labouring by thefe few to have a minifter oppofite to the Generall Affemblie, if they obtain this, our caufe will hereby receive a wound almoft incurable. To prevent this, the only remedie we can thinke on for the time, is to gett to that people fome eminent man, without all exception. Doubtlefs Mr. James Hamiltone is one fuch. We have fpoken of him, and all that people, as we think, without exception of one man, would embrace him moft gladlie: we know the Towne of Edinburgh is not able to pay all the minifters, and gladlie would be content to have fewer. We think Mr. James Hamiltone, (however alsweell beloved as any there,) yet if he could be difmiffed to this eafy and weell-provided charge, would have als fair ane occafion to ferve his mafter, and provyde for his family, as ever he had or can readilie have; his being here would ftrengthen and encourage us exceedinglie. If Mr Robert Dowglafs, and Mr. David Dickfon, and fome few more, would befriend us, we think the Prefbyterie of Edinburgh and Town-Counfell would pity us and him, and grant that paroche and our Prefbyterie's earneft fupplication for his tranfportation. To try if this favour may be obtained, we have fent Mr. George Young to the parties chiefly interefted. If this cannot be obtained, we truelie know not what to doe, but to give our oppofers that moft confiderable Church, and with it all other that fhall vaike among us hereafter. We will fitt downe and mourne, but we can ftryve no longer, if our brethren affift us not in this particular.

2 Farder, in our Synod the next week we will prefs, That men depofed and fufpended by the Generall Affemblie, and elders avowing their proteftation againft the Generall Affemblie, may not have voice among us. when they, contrare to expreffe Acts of Affemblies, will fitt and voice, and by their voice carrie the Synod to all they will, fhall not we, (when the more part,) when fuch voters are numbered, goe and keep the Synod by ourfelves? or fhall we goe and leave them? or fhall we fitt ftill with a proteftation, and let them goe on to appoint purging committees? We think it beft to keep a

Synod apart. If our brethren there will approve us herein, we entreat their counfell and direction.

3. When our Prefbyterie, with a Committee from the Generall Affemblie, have gone to try and admitt Mr. James Ramfay[9] to the Leinzie, according to the order of our Kirk, our diffenting brethren procured ane order from the Englifh, difcharging us to give any ordination in our bounds, without their approbation goeing before; and when, with modeft words and ftrong arguments as we could ufe, we had excufed ourfelves, and gone on to ordination, the fame brethren procured a charge to our brother Mr. James, not to preach in that church, and to the people not to hear him, under high paynes; and a few of them, not content to have procured thofe incroachments of the Englifh, are goeing on as a Prefbyterie, in a procefs againft our brother, on the pretext of fcandalls, which, when all diligence is ufed to try him to the uttermoft, nothing can be found but two vaine words, though all were true which malice alleadges What here fhall be done? Shall our brother preach, and fuffer fyning and imprifonment? or fhall he forbear?

4 When the Englifh hes put in a depofed minifter to be Principall of our Colledge, for the poifoning of the feminarie, is there no remeid after our Proteftation? fhall we fitt ftill in filence?

> Our meffenger, Mr. George [Young], having ftayed here a week longer than we intended, we crave your direction in thefe particulars farder.—
>
> 1. Though by our threats of ane Anti-Synod, we obtained the diffolution of our Synod before conftituton, yet our diffenters, by the cannie conveyance of fome, obtained a confultative committee for our differences; which we could not well get putt off, though we faw it would prove at length very factious to us. Yow will read the tennor of it. The firft work, and generallie intended, is to vifite the Prefbyterie of Glafgow What fhall we doe herein? We, with much adoe, have gotten our anfwer delayed for twenty dayes, till, in a fecret way, we might have your advyce. We purpofe to offer Union in the termes the Generall Aflemblie allowes, that is, the exclufion

---

[9] He was the fon of Mr Robert Ramsay. Baillie speaks of him in terms of high commendation; and in a letter addreffed to Spang, 1st September 1656, he notices his translation from Leinzie to Linlithgow

of depofed minifters and protefting ruling elders, but if this be refufed, as certainlie it will, we muft delay our joyning with them who, without caufe, feparate from us, till the Generall Affemblie or Commiffion of the Kirk fhall otherwife appoint. Our joyning with them in the termes which they alone will accept of, burying all publick differences, is but to give them the caufe to ftrengthen their fchifme, to make them to wrack whom they will, as we think they purpofe to doe diverfe.

2. We find more of their crueltie againft Mr. James Ramfay, to pronounce fome kind of new fentence againft him notwithftanding of his declyning of them as no judicatorie: yea, they purpofe to plant his church with fome other, over the head of all heritors feffion, and almoft all the people, and in this they doe free the paroche from the Englifh, who have appointed Mr. Beverlie to be minifter there, at the defire of twenty feven perfones, the chief of thefe whom our brethren ftirred up to oppofe Mr James Ramfay.

3. We underftand, by the direction of fome, thefe people of Leinzie now declared fectaries, are to petition the Englifh to inhibite the fitting of our Prefbyterie as a null Prefbyterie, under the paine of fequeftration to all minifters and elders who fhall fitt, and to all that fhall appear before us. Is there no remeid for this? Doe the Englifh at London allow Judge Movfley to execute all Mr. Patrick Gillefpie's devyces, to the utter overthrow of all our church liberties, and the cruell wracking of all who muft adhere to their duetie.

4 Yefterday there was delivered to us a letter, fubfcryved by Mr. Andrew Cant, directed to Mr Robert Baylie and Mr. James Ferguffon, to be communicat to the reft of our mind in the Weft, a large and injurious invective againft all who will not joyne with the protefters to ferve the enemie to continue the yocke of ftrangers for ever on their native countrie, and to lay a neceffitie on the confciences of people, to exclude, without all caufe, the King, the Nobilitie, and all who will not be profelytes to them, from poffeffing their civile rights It feems to us exceeding neceffare to caufe revife all the wrytes of thefe fchifmatique men, and draw their tenets together in their own words, that the world may fee their principles in a fhort mappe, whereby they overthrow not only the government of our Church and Kingdome, but the grounds of all Civile government any where in the world. This fhort

mappe we wifh backed with reafons againft their principall tenets, and anfwers to the chiefe objections: We think Mafters John Smith, Robert Hamilton, and Robert Ker, would be put to this tafke.

For Mr. Robert Dowglass. April 8th 1653.

Sir,

As our prayers to God were for your gracious upholding, dureing the time of your imprifonment, fo have we heartilie bleffed God for your happie delyverance and fafe return to your ftation, with the great joy of all in the Nation who love the welfare of it. Sundry of us here who defyre to be faithfull, have fent one of our number, Mr. George Young, to falute yow and your fellow prifoners, and rejoyce with yow in our name for all the kindnefs the Lord hath fhowen to yow and to us; yea, the whole land, in your perfones, dureing the time of your fuffering for the publick, and for us in your common caufe. The God of Heaven be bleffed who hath mercifullie preferved yow all, and returned yow free to us of all, and adorned with much praife to the grace of God, who, all the tyme of your tryell has enabled yow to walk exemplarly in faithfullnefs, courage, humilitie, patience, and wifdome, for the great comfort of many of both nations, though to the confufion and griefe of fome. We truft the fame grace of God fhall enable yow to the end to goe through what remains of farder tryell, and make others in thefe miferable times to undergoe, by your example, with the greater chearfullnefs and confidence, what piece of affliction the Lord fhall thinke fitt to meafure out unto them. It is no fmall joy and ftrength to us all, that we have gotten yow againe, to be advyfed and directed by yow, as we wont to be in all our perplexed caufes. For the time, there be fundry things we have directed the bearer to intreat your counfell and affiftance. If yow think it fitt, at the firft houre of your leafure, we wifh yow called to your chamber, Mafters David Dickfon, John Smith, James Hamilton, Mungo Law, or any yow think fitt to hear our brother, in what we have inftructed him to propone unto yow, that, after confultation, yow may fend us your advyce what to doe, for at this time we have great need. The Lord's beft bleffings be upon yow, and preferve yow long with us in thefe very miferable and dangerous times. So prayes to God many of your brethren here, who have directed me to write to this purpofe.

Your very loveing Brother, R. B

For Mr. David Dickson. April 28th 1653

Reverend and Dear Brother,

According to your defyre with Mr George Young, Mr. James Ferguffon, and Mr. Patrick Colville, are come in. Mr James hes aue anfwer to Mr. Andrew Cant's letter, which at the firft reading I liked fo weell, that with a fmall or no review, after it's gone to Mr. Andrew Cant firft, it may goe to the preffe, for good advantage to the truth, till our other wrytes may come forth My Wife and youngeft daughter are under a languifhing difeafe, both liker to die than live; alfo my charge and diftractions are fuch that I can doe nothing in the publict for the time. Mr Patrick Gillefpie and the reft of his minde, are become fo impudent as to fett themfelves with all their ftrength againft Mr. James Hamilton's coming among us But if they carie that point our caufe will be worfe than before The people in the Barronie are paffionatly for him, which they have putt under their hands, except a very few yeomen, whom our brethren diverts, and who are like, if not prevented, to make the Barronie in the cafe of Kilbryde and Leinzie. To prevent this, we have been content to take truce for a moneth till our next meeting, that, in the meantyme, we may have help from our brethren there to keep the Englifh off us, and to difpofe Mr. James's owne mind to mifregard the malice of that handfull, ftirred up only by unreafonable men, to further their error and deftructive defignes. Mr. James Ferguffon will informe yow of all Communicat this letter to Mr Mungo Law and Mr John Smith, from whom I expect all the help they are able, as they love either us or the publict Mr. Robert Dowglafs muft help us, or we muft faint, and give all over. So foon as my familie will permitt me, I purpofe to come in and fee yow After yow have fpoken together, faill not to wryte your advyce to me, befydes what you think fitt to fpeak by tongue, with Mr James [Ferguffon]: his pen, yow fee, is exceeding good: I wifh yow had from him fome obfervations on the Nullity. The Lord help yow.

Your Brother. R B.

For Mr. Mungo Law.

Mungo,

I have defyred Mr. David Dickfon to fhow yow and Mr. John Smith my letter to him, which I pray yow call for, and confider Mr. James Ferguffon will informe yow farder. Let me know, with Mr. James, what hopes and encouragements we may have from yow, whether compaffion, wifdome, and zeale, will caufe yow to let Mr. James Hamilton come to us, and confirme him againft thefe unreafonable creatures plotts; but above all, to tell us, if, by God's bleffing, yow can foe reprefent tiuth to Mr. Moyfley, as he, on the exceeding falfe informations of our oppofites, will not goe on to make havock of our churches with foe tyrannous and high oppreffion, that I perfuade myfelfe his mafters in England will have no caufe to give him thanks for Inftead of granting Mr James Ramfay the favour he expected from him in his laft letter to my Lord Wigton, he hath difcharged him to preach in the neighbour churches, which is to make his cafe worfe than it wes; and yet yefterday, at our meeting, when we put Mr Patrick Gillefpie to it, to read all thefe terrible fcandalls, for which he wont to fay, we would depofe his Father, there wes nothing but the two particulars ye heard, which not one of oui meeting, bot one wife man, did think deferved any farder than a Prefbyteriall rebuke: I hear fince that two other alfo wes [for] fome farder Let me know if yet yow can gett Judge Moyfley off him, and off my good neighbour, who will never ceafe to fyre all with new motions, week after week, according to his reftleffnefs. Communicat this to Mr. John Smith.

Yours, R. B.

They are moveing to celebrate a communion heie, which will fett all in flame: our Magiftrates and all their paitie, who hes advyfed to take places from the Englifh, muft be excluded, the Seffions protefting againft the Generall Affemblie we will hardly admit; they will exclude fuch multitudes for one caufe or for ane other, that the end will be the fetting up of a new refyned congregation of their owne adherents. We purpofe, by all the fair means we can, to keep off thefe very untimeous motions In the mean time, let us have your advyce in this alfo.

For Mr. Rodgers's Mother-in-Law, at Newcastle.

Mistres,

Yours of the 11th of March I receaved: but before this I could not give yow ane particular account of your defires, the liberall almes yow fent to me doubtlefs the Lord will accept and reward it; it refrefhed the bowells of one and twenty houfeholders, almoft all widowes, for to foe many did I give it: to nineteen ten fhillings to two fyve I fent to Mr Rodgers Mr Patrick Gillefpie's teftificate of this, as he required I held up your name as yow required, except in a generall. I doe compaffionate the afflicted condition both of your body, mind, and eftate, whereof yow write to me; bot the Father of Mercies, and God of all Confolation, is able to caufe your comforts fuperabound above all your fufferings Your experience, now of a long time, of the Lord's love, obliedges yow to have hope and confidence of ane happie iffue out of all temptations, only continue to feek, and yow fhall find more kindnefs in Chrift than yow can afk or think, for his mercies endureth for ever: however your daughter's error and fon's flight fpirit doe grieve your heart, yet give not over to pray, and wait for the Lord's returne: the feed of prayer for our children may have a plentifull harveft long after our death, though it appear not above ground fo long as we live: your fighs are regiftrate in the Lord's book, and your tears put up in his bottle, to come downe in a fhowre of healing grace; yow know not when, only be waiting and hopeing, were it in death, above hope, and all yow can fee, that your Covenant promifes are keept in the hand of Chrift, even for your children's children, reft upon the Lord for them without too much anxietie, he keeps tymes and feafons of working in his own hand, and let him injoy that his foveraigne prerogative.

Our woeful and very caufelefs divifions doe yet continue to fome of us very grievous, but as yet remedilefs, except we would forfake that which our confcience fayes to us is truely and right: for which our Mafter commands us to contend for bot with all the humilitie and charitie towards our fellow-fervants, which we, through the mercies of God, can attain to. Thefe moft unfeafonable queftions are a part of the Lord's hand on us, which we muſt bear till the Lord returne, and cauſe his owne face ſhyne clearer among us. The Lord's beſt bleſſings be with your ſpirit and familie I reſt,

     Your Brother and Servant in Chriſt,

Glaſgow, May 2d 1653.   R B

For Mr. David Dickson.

Reverend and Dear Brother,

That now I come not to the Commiſſion, and that long agoe I came not to ſee Mr. Dowglaſs and the brethren, it is ſore againſt my heart; bot my Wife hes, theſe ſix weeks and more, been in that condition that I could not be abſent from her, and yet I have bot ſmall hopes of her life. Upon your laſt letter with Mr. James Ferguſſon, I have done my beſt to have to yow my little *ſymbolum*. make what uſe of it yow find expedient; only let it be in private, and not come abroad, for it's of that ſtrain that might bring me to cumber. I think Mr. James Ferguſſon's letter may well goe abroad. Cauſe Mr. Dowglaſs joyne with yow to ſett on Mr. James Durhame effectualhe. he will be with yow the next week; he hes declared himſelff a little more againſt our brethren's way: yow may doe him good. Their way thryves no where in Scotland ſo much as here about, whereof I conceave Mr. Durhame the chiefe inſtrument, though oft beſide his purpoſe the man is of exceeding great weight deſervedly I have deſired him to write Caſe-Divinitie,[1] wherein he is excellent, and daylie growes. If yow further not Mr. James Hamilton's dimiſſion to us, yow loſe our Preſbyterie, and inbeares to the publict cauſe, for we will not be able to ſtrive more, bot give it over. Advyſe with the brethren what ſhall be done in Mr. James Ramſay's ſtrong caſe; if it be neglected, yow will have many more ſuch ſhorthe; and, however, even his caſe alone muſt not be forgotten by yow, to whom he and we, who have intereſt in it, are dear. The Lord be with yow So ſoone as I may, I ſhall, God willing, come in

       Your Brother,

May 21ſt Saturday 1653.   R. B

---

[1] That is, Casuistic Divinity, or Cases of Conscience

My papers, that have coſt me labour, keep them well, that I may get them againe, when I come or fend for them, for I have no other legible copy

[To Mr Richard Robertson. July 26th 1653.]

Mr. Richard,

That the other day, when yow did read your Notes in our meeting, my grieve and anger appeared more than ordinary ; fince yow crave of me the reafon, I give it to yow now as I promifed in write, that yow may lay the matter more to heart, and I may be exonered both towards you and others, efpeciallie, if (which the Lord forbid) yow fhould continue in your judgement, and refufe the wholfome counfell of all your brethren.[a]

. . . .

Thefe paſſages I have fhortly poynted at, wifhing yow not only to fcrape them out for our fatiffaction, as very fcandalous errors, which I fee yow are now willing enough to doe, bot really to mind their fin before God, and to mourne for your unhappinefs, that in thefe miferable tymes have been the firſt who have labored to corrupt our Univerfitie, with diverfe pernicious and foul deftroying errors, as fundry of the forenamed are, if I underſtand rightly the nature of error.

For Mr. Robert Bailie

Sir,

Whereas, in your paper, yow accufe me of Sabellianifme, in denying the Trinitie of Perfons. 2. Of Neftorianifme, in denying the Union of the Divine and Humane Nature in the one perfon of Chriſt. 3 Of Blafphemie,

[a] Robertson was admitted one of the Regents or Professors in the College of Glasgow, 29th July 1649 In this letter, Baillie, at great length, made remarks on thirty-one passages of his Latin Dictates or Lectures, which contained various points of unsound doctrine, quoted in the margin of Baillie's MS , but these remarks and extracts being obviously unsuited for a work like the present, are omitted. Soon after this Robertson resigned his Professorship on the plea of ill-health *Vide infra*, pp 239-240

in making God the author of finne. 4. Of other Blafphemies, in denying the Unitie of God, or the unfuccefive permanencie of that attribute of God's Eternitie: I deteft all thefe horrid things, in my judgement; and if, from any antecedents in my Notes, thefe confequents doe not neceffarly follow, I doe not owne my Notes in fo farre, bot deteft both the antecedents and confequents But to write of the particulars, and to examine them at length, my bodilie weaknefs will not permitt me now.

Whereas yow make me worfe than Vorftius, truely Sir, in the fection after that *de Subfiftentia*, I expreflie oppofe and refute Vorftius, who queftions God's fimplicitie, and I anfwer his arguments as I can. If I be not deceaved, when Vorftius calls Eternitie fucceffive, he makes it fome inward accident in God, (which is blafphemie I think,) but I mean no fuch thing, but only that *hodie et cras* coexift not; and, therefore, when God coexifts to this day, he doth not *fimul* coexift to the next day, becaufe the next day is not yet; but I mean no fucceffion at all in God, but only in the creature without him.

In the matter of the Holy Trinitie, I doe not deny any thing, (I mean now whatever unadvyfed expreffions be in the Notes), I think the myfterie moft evident from the Word; but for the way of it, I think it fafeft to keep our conceptions and expreffions within the fimplicitie of the Scripture, and to wait for the clear underftanding of the manner of it in Heaven. This is all that I have to fay, Sir The Lord lay not to your charge the heavie accufations yow lay on me.

RICH ROBERTSONE.

FOR HIS REVEREND AND DEAR BROTHER MR CALAMY, MINISTER AT LONDON.

REVEREND AND DEAR BROTHER,

This, my third to yow, is only to give thanks for your kind acceptance, and anfwering in deed, of my two former. Mr. Wilkie, our commiffioner, hes reported fo much of your care to us, to promove to the uttermoft of your power the charitable fupply of our diftreffed people, that all of us are much obliedged to blefs God in your behalfe, who hes made yow inftrumentall to procure a liberall fupport, both in your owne congregation, and over all the city, to the many families of this wracked people with that ftrangeft fire that ever was heard of in our land. I am confident enough of your readinefs to goe on for the perfyteing of what is fo weell begun, even to give your beft advyce and affiftance to this fame gentleman, whom we have fent againe, with fome others, to receave, in the city and countrey, what fhall be freely offered by the pious benevolence of thefe whofe hearts God fhall ftirr up, by yow and your brethren, to contribute to that work of compaffion and charitie.

At this time I have no more to adde, bot this one word, to let yow know, That on the 20th of July laft, when our Generall Affemblie wes fett in the ordinarie tyme and place, Lieutenant-Colonell Cotterall befett the Church with fome rattes of mufqueteirs and a troup of horfe, himfelf, (after our faft, wherein Mr. Dickfon and Mr. Dowglafs had two gracious fermons,) entered the Affemblie-houfe, and, immediately after Mr Dickfon the Moderator his prayer, required audience; wherein he inquired, If we did fitt there by the authority of the Parliament of the Commonwealth of England? or of the Commanders-in-Chiefe of the Englifh forces? or of the Englifh Judges in Scotland? The Moderator replyed, That we were ane Ecclefiafticall fynod, ane Spirituall court of Jefus Chrift, which medled not with any thing Civile; that our authoritie wes from God, and eftablifhed by the Lawes of the land yet ftanding unrepealed; that, by the Solemn League and Covenant, the moft of the Englifh army ftood obliedged to defend our Generall Affemblie. When fome fpeeches of this kind had paffed, the Lieutenant-Colonell told us, his order wes to diffolve us; whereupon he commanded all of us to follow him, elfe he would drag us out of the rowme. When we had entered a Proteftation of this unheard-of and unexampled violence, we did ryfe and follow him, he ledd us all through the whole ftreets a myle out of the towne, encompaffing us with foot-companies of mufqueteirs, and horfemen without; all the people gazing and mourning as at the faddeft fpectacle they had ever feen When he had ledd us a myle without the towne, he then declared what further he had in commiffion, That we fhould not dare to meet any more above three in number, and that againft eight o'clock to-morrow, we fhould depart the towne, under paine of being guiltie of breaking the publick peace: And the day following, by found of trumpet, we were commanded off towne under the paine of prefent imprifonment. Thus our Generall Affemblie, the glory and ftrength of our Chuich upon earth, is, by your fouldiarie, crufhed and trod under foot, without the leaft provocatione from us, at this time, either in word or deed For this our hearts are fadd, our eyes runn downe with water, we figh to God againft whom we have finned, and wait for the help of his hand ; bot from thofe who opprefled us we deferved no evill. We hear a noife of farder orders, to difcharge all our Synods and Prefbyteries, and all prayer for our King: many the moft moderate reckons fuch orders will make havock of our Church, and raife againft many the beft men we have, a fore perfecution which, God willing, we purpofe to endure all patience and faith, giving juft offence to none

I detame yow no more The Lord mind his Zion in thefe lands, and bleffe yow, who for the tyme ftand in the moft eminent pinacle thereof Thus refts,

Your Brother to ferve yow,

Glafgow, 27th July 1653. R. BAYLIE.

FOR HIS REVEREND AND DEAR BROTHER, MR. CLERK,[1] MINISTER AT LONDON

REVEREND AND DEAR BROTHER,

Your kind and refpectfull letter I receaved from Mr. Wilkie, our townes commiffioner. Your affiftance to him, in furthering the charitie of your neighbours to our diftreffed people, I affure [yow], wes a very good and pious work. I muft intreat yow to continue your beft advyce and help to him for the perfecting of what is begun, for I know there is great need of it. Your very precious work, of the Lives of late Divines, I have read much of it ; the defigne I like weell, and thinks yow can hardly fpend your tyme on a better fubject. I doe well approve your purpofe, to take in, among the reft, our Mr. Boyd, not Bodie, though, in Latin, we call our Boyds Bodij : that man, indeed, was one of the moft eminent divines of the Reformed Churches for all good qualities There is fo much, before his Commentarie on the Epiftle to the Ephefians,[2] as will be ground enough for a compleat narrative

---

[1] The Rev Samuel Clarke, " Pastor of Bennet Finck, London," the author of the " Marrow of Ecclesiastical History," " A Martyrologie" &c , and other biographical works

[2] *Vide supra* p 184 Clarke in one of his works inserts an account of Boyd of Trochrig

of his life. Neverthelefs I have communicate your letter to Mr. Douglafs, who, I fuppofe, againft the tyme yow fpeak of, may have a more perfect narration at yow. I wifh we had a narrative of ane other of ours alfo to fend to yow, I mean your fometime good friend Mr Henderfone, a truely heroick divine, for piety, learning, wifdome, eloquence, humilitie, fingle life, and every good part, for fome yeares the moft-eyed man of the three Kingdoms. Wifhing yow good fpeed in that and the reft of your labours, I reft.

Your Brother to ferve yow,

Glafgow, July 27th 1653. R. BAYLIE.

For Dr Lazarus Seaman.

REVEREND AND DEAR BROTHER,

UNDERSTANDING, by our towne's agent, Mr. Wilkie's letter, your kind remembrance of me, I thought fitt to let yow know that my remembrance of yow is very frefh, and oft fweet to my mind, in thefe moft lamentable tymes. It is one of the grounds of my hope, that the Lord will not be pleafed to permitt thefe confufions, and thefe oppreffions, to be perpetuall, when I fee yow and others preferved in a right mind in the midft of fo great apoftacie; for what elfe would the Lord preferve men of eminent parts and grace, bot to be not only prefent witneffes of truth and right, bot, in the Lord's approaching feafon, powerfull inftruments to profligate, by their light, the prefent eriors and confufions. I did write to fome of my dear brethren there, to affift the bearer heirof in that lamentable buffinefs he wes fent to agent. I wrote not to yow, thinking yow had lived at Cambridge,[5] and not at London; but feeing it is otherwife, I intreat yow alfo to confider the gentleman's informations, and further him in his work. I affure yow his papers and reports are true: I fhall need to fay no more to yow of this matter.

I have long continued in Mr Cotton and Mr. Tombes debt: I purpofed never to have payed thefe creditors, for thefe good reafons in my Preface; yet having this year a longer vacation from my charge than ordinar, I have taken

[5] Dr Seaman, Minifter of Allhallows, London, was conftituted Mafter of Peter-Houfe, Cambridge, 11th April 1644 He was ejected at the Reftoration on account of his Noncon_formity.

fome courfe with that debt [6] I purpofe with the next to fend my papers to Mr. Calamy. If yow be in towne, and have a little leafure, I wifh yow may revife them, and let them goe, or fuppreffe them, as yow and your orthodox brethren fhall think fitt. The Lord be mercifull to the diftreffed nations, and furnifhe yow, who there ftand on the pinacles of the ruined temple, with a large meafure of the Spirit of Chrift. We here oft defire to commend yow there to the Lord's grace.

This is one who, from my firft acquaintance, did ever highly reverence and dearly love yow,

Glafgow, October 8th 1653. R. BAYLIE.

From Mr. John Vauch,[7] in the Castle of Edinburgh

REVEREND BROTHER,

I have many times been mindfull of yow fince I came to this place, and wes refolved now and then to have written to yow oftner than once, were it not that two things hindered me, the one wes, my fear leaft ye might come to danger by my correfponding with yow at this time; the other wes, my very earneft defyre to lurk, even in this place, not thinking myfelfe worthie (the Lord knowes) to be taken notice of by any, bot rather to have my habitation amongft the owles of the defart, becaufe of my very great ufeleffnefs and fruitleffnefs amongft the fons of men. And though this my defire of lurking (truely not for any fear of danger in doeing of my duetie, but upon the fore-mentioned accompt) hes been much in my heart and amongft my wifhes. I have been fo farr from attaining it, that though the malice and envy of my evill neighbours, and other unnaturall countreymen, (the Lord in his wonderfull providence fo difpofing it,) I am brought to the top of this rock, where (I cannot bot acknowledge it to his praife) I find my God gracioufly prefent with me, furnifhing me with courage, joy peace, and content-

---

[6] In his anfwer entitled 'The Diffwafive from the Errors of the Time, Vindicated from the exceptions of Mr. Cotton and Mr. Tombes," which was printed at London, 1655, 4to

[7] Vauch or Waugh who addreffed this letter (under the affumed name of Jamieson,) to Baillie, was minifter of Borrowftonnefs He was for the time confined in Edinburgh Caftle, His offence was praying for the King; but he was releafed before the 20th July 1654: *Vide infra*, p 253

ment; so that whatever hes been in the mind, either of these who are in power and put me here, or of these, who being their favourites, hes their ear, and stirred them up to put me here, I dare say, as Joseph spoke to his brethren, Genesis, ult. The Lord's meaning therein is for good, and there is a full [Covenant-]blessing in my being here; than full fruit whereof, though I should never see myselfe, yet I believe that not only the truely gracious, honest, and loyall, in the land, shall gett good thereof hereafter; bot even these also, who in their hatred hes had a hand in my affliction, imprisonment, and persecution. And amongst other mercies, I cannot bot observe this for one; that though I want not my owne conflicts, privately in my mind, anent other things, even this long time, yet in this I have no scruple at all. The Lord in his goodness hes made the ground of my suffering very clear to me; honour be to His name for it; so that though others are ready to cry it downe and reproach me for it, yet through the Lord's strength, (he calling me to it,) I durst hazard to suffer whatever men shall be permitted to put me farther unto than this same ground. And it is my very earnest desyre, that privatelie and prudentlie, as ye may have opportunitie, ye may, in my name, exhort your honest brethren, and other gracious acquaintances, not to faint or shrink in the least measure because of my afflictions, bot rather to be resolute and bold in the Lord, in doeing of their duetie, and particularlie in adhereing to that poynt in hand, which by men is inhibited, omitted, and controverted; for certainlie, as the Lord shall gett glory, and trueth ane advantagious growth, so the faithfull servants of Christ shall have victorie, till they shall be more than conquerors by your patient suffering, even the very uttermost, for the truth, and for his name's sake. And for my owne part, although I wes made to tremble at the first alarum, and the matter lookt somewhat terrible while it wes afarr off, yet since I wes helped of the Lord to buckle with it, and by submission to his will, to lay it fully over upon himselff, I have found the burthen to be light and easie; yea, by the bearing of it, I am helped to bear other particular burthens, which before did trouble me not a little. And though of late I have gotten a new alarum, by threatning to banish me, yet neither that, nor the sequestration of my stipend, doeth trouble me in the least, for I have laid my compt for the worst they can doe. I know they are all in chains and can doe nothing, but as the Lord, for his own honour and my good, shall be pleased to permitt them to doe, and fo whatever he fends I fhall make it welcome : Lo! here am I, let his Majeftie doe with me what feems good in his eyes.

I fay no more, bot referring yow to the inclofed paper, I earneftly beg the help of your prayers, and remains,

Your loveing Brother,

November 11th 1653   J. JAMISONE.

THE EARL OF LAUDERDAILL TO MR. ROBERT BAILLIE.

REVEREND AND WORTHIE FREIND,

THESE fufferings which it hath pleaf'd God to call me to this long time paft, having difabled me from doing any fervice to my freinds, I have forborne to give them the unneceffarie trouble of letters ; yet feing I am informed yow doe often remember me, I could not but returne yow my acknowledgments for the continuation of your kindenes, and to intreat the help of your prayers, that the Lord wold fanctifie more and more this condition unto me, and afford me more and more teftimonies how good it is for me that I have been afflicted. All I fhall tell yow is, that I have a greater meafure of health then I could have expected in this cours, fo different from the life I formerly led. Althogh in that I finde great prejudice by my long reftraint ; yet it pleafes God to give me fome meafure of patience and of contentednes under the rod ; more then yow wold have looked for, who know my former temper.

I will not fay any thing of publick concern which I doe not at all medle with. All I fhall defire of yow is, that yow wold remember me to all thofe yow know to be my freinds, and to my fometimes fellow prifoners of your owne coate, when yow fee any of them. Be pleafed to continue your kindenes to, and your prayers for,

Your moft affectionat freind,

Tower, the 17th of December 1653.   LAUDERDAILL.

For my reverend and worthie freind, Mr. Robert Bailly,
    Profeffor of Divinity at Glafgow.[8]

[8] The original letter thus addressed, is preserved in Wodrow MSS Folio Vol. XLIX, No 27.

For Mr. William Taylor, Moderator of the Provinciall Synod at London.

Reverend and Dear Brother,

Understanding, by our commiffioner Mr Wilkie, your fingular care and affection to further that work of pietie and charitie towards my poor fuffering neighbours, not only in your owne congregation, bot among your neighbours, I give yow very heartie thanks in name of my brethren, and many honeft people here, affureing myfelff, that this pious charitie in yow and diverfe of your brethren, is a fweet favour both to God and men. Yow will be intreated to affift, both by your advyce and countenance, our Commiffioner, towards the perfyting of that worke, as he may have occafion to call on you, for which labour of love yow fhall have our hearty acknowledgement, and defires to God for your reward.

I have thought fitt to acquaint yow with ane other particular. When I was there, I and my brethren had acquaintance with Mr. Theodor Haak, a learned and gracious gentleman of the Palatinate; myfelf, above others, moved him to labour in the tranflating of the Dutch Notes.[9] Before I come away he had made good progrefs in the work. I had moved Mr. Rous, and others of my friends in the Houfe of Commons, to incourage him to that good work: I had fpoken fome of your ftationers for that end. When I come to Scotland, 1647, I moved the Generall Affemblie, with the affiftance of Mr Blair and Mr. Gillefpie, to appoint him, out of their not very great plenty, two hundred pounds fterling, for the perfecting of this work. This foume we caufed faithfully to delyver him there, the Affemblie, on our report, nothing doubting of the gentleman's German, and candid honeftie to performe his undertaking. When fome tyme had gone over, and the book did not appear, I wrote once and againe of his promife, and my undertaking for him: at laft he returned me fomewhat a bitter anfwer, refufeing to goe on in that work, unlefs your Parliament or Stationers would give him further confideration. For this I and my brethren were both greeved and afhamed. I think, for a leffe foume, I might have gotten that work done in

---

[9] *Vide supra*, Letter and Note, p 7

Holland. it's a pity that this piece of fervice fhould lye behind. I know your Synod hes no jurifdiction; yet, if the gentlemen be in London, I think if fome two or three, deputed from your Synod, would be pleafed to deal with him, he might be poffiblie moved to performe that fervice, or give back the money he got from us, as he wrote to me he would, that we might beftow it on fome other, who, we are perfuaded, on fuch a recompence, would gladly doe it for him. Yow will be pleafed to confider of this motion for the publick good. The tranflation of the whole Dutch Bible I think needlefs, bot only of the Notes, like that of Diodati's. If yow cannot make ufe of my evill hand, the bearer, Mr. Wilkie, will help yow. I reft,

Your loving Brother and Servant,

ROB. BAYLIE.

Glafgow, December 19th 1653

THE MATERIALLS OF A PRESBYTERIALL WARNING, TO BE DRAWN WITH ALL POSSIBLE EXPEDITION BY MR. BLAIR, AND, BY WAY OF CORRESPONDENCE, SENT FROM THE PRESBYTERY OF ST. ANDREWES AND EDINBURGH THROUGH THE WHOLE KINGDOM, SO SOON AS MAY BE; TO BE READ IN PULPITS WHERE SAIFELY IT MAY, AND WHERE NOT, TO BE PRESSED BY ALL MINISTERS, IN DOCTRINE AND OTHERWAYS.

Firft, To mention and lament the particular fteps of the fore judgments of God upon the land, which yet are going on, not only towards the utter ruin of many our greateft families, bot the totall everfion both of Church and Kingdome, yea of the very being of the Nation.

2. To give glory to God, in acknowledging our juft deferving from his hand, of all that is come or comeing, by the continuall tract of the uncontroverted finnes in all ranks and eftates, efpeciallie fince our late reformation 1638, notwithftanding of all God's warnings from his word, his mercies, and judgments upon us; above all, the finnes of our prefent unhappie divifions, ftupid fecuritie, and, through the incumbent terrour, the totall laying afide by many of the cleareft, oft-fworne, and covenanted dueties to God, Church, King, and Kingdome.

3 To waken, by pithie exhortations, unto a great mourning, privatelie and

pubhćtlie, together and apart, to crying and wreftling with the Lord for mercie, grace, and delyverance, from our great finnes and fore judgements.

4. To exhort unto the confcientious keeping of all the articles of our Covenant, in this houre of darknefs, wherein allurements, terrours, and evill examples brangle the ftabilitie of many. The fubftance of every article would be repeated, efpeciallie of thefe which, by the mift of new gloffes, are moft overclouded, and where weak ones had moft need to be confirmed

5. To preffe, after the ftudie of Scripture, the ferious reading of our precious Confeffion, Catechifme, and Directorie, for the eftablifhing of our heart againft the herefies of the Anabaptifts, Antinomians, Antitrinitarians, Familifts, Seekers, and Atheifts, alfo the diligent perufall of the Propofitions for government againft the fchifmatick errors of the Independents, Brownifts, Eraftians, and others; againft all which the Affemblies and Parliaments of Scotland has laboured to guard this Nation by oaths, covenants, acts, and other means, much more than any Nation this day under heaven ever attained. The Lord who knew our weaknefs, and forefaw this hour of ftrong temptation coming upon us, fo providing it of his great mercie

6. To fpeak, in the bowells of tender compaffion, and yet in the juft and neceffare zeall of holy indignation, to the confcience of the many apoftates of this Nation for their reclaiming, and of ftaggerers for their confirmation.

7 In the wifdome and fear of God, to fpeak a word, tentilie and cautioufhe, to our woefull divifions of Kirk and State, without all reflection or irritation; to put all to a perfeverance in prayer to God, for a remead of that judiciall evill, and to endeavour to keep all poffible charitie in their owne hearts towards them who differ; and to watch carefullie, leaft by the ftumbling-block of thefe divifions, they be tempted to fchifme or any error of the time, or to any other way, which they know their owne heart fometimes would much have miflyked

8 To endeavour the compofing of the hearts of people to hve quietlie and peaceablie under the yock of the prevalent power, and to fuffer patientlie what the Lord fhall permitt to be laid upon them in their eftate, libertie, or perfone, for their neceffare abftinence from all they know to be finne againft God.

9 Laftly, after a pithie exhortation to accurate walking in the practice of

repentance, faith, love, and hope, to end with fome grounds of comfort and expectation of deliverance, in the Lord's convenient feafon.

Thefe my Articles were agreed upon by the meeting in Edinburgh, and fent by Mr. George Hutchefone and Mr. Hugh M'Kell to the Remonftrators, particularlie to my Lord Warriftone, my Lord Brodie, Mr. James Guthrie, and Mr. Patrick Gillefpie; who refufed to accept of them.

For My Lord Lauderdaill.[1] Glasgow, February 10th 1654

Sir,

That your late fhort one, and your long one a year agoe, was not anfuered, and that yow had no frequent aneugh letters from my evill hand, came not from want of good-will; for except one whom I knew you would be content, [there is] none of my afflicted countreymen, whom I ufe to remember more either to God or man than yourfelf: my defire to be filent and keep no correfpondence in this evill time, was the only caufe of it. Bot underftanding your mifcontent with it, I thought fitt to tell yow that I was much refrefhed to fee under your hand the fubmiffion of your fpirit to the incumbent calamitie. It was often my fear it fhould have broken yow both in body and mind long before this; bot fince God has fpared your life, which to my apprehenfion was in great hazard, more wayes than one or two, and has given yow to put your mouth in the duft, and take your very heavie chaftifements out of the Lord's hands humblie and lovinglie, I am very hopefull your iffue fhall be good. Continue your ftudies to better your knowledge, whereof I have heard much by your late companions; bot above all, your religious exercifes of mortification of all known vanities. As it is often my prayer to God, fo for all is come and gone, it's my prettie confident hope, that thefe many and great endeuments which God has given to yow, and yow by his great mercie, I hear, have improven, fhall yet be imployed for the good and comfort of many.

[1] This letter seems from Baillie's MS to have been addressed "To John Langtoung," which may explain its commencing with 'Sir "—Lord Lauderdale was still a prisoner, and in fact he was detained in the Tower till the Restoration of Charles the Second.

I did fee a piece of a letter of your neighbour, my dear friend C. his gracious wife to her coufine Mrs. Kennedy, that did much refrefh me Such fweet fubmiffion and eminent grace cannot bot be looked on by God and bleft I muft break of. I am juft what I wont to be to all men and to yow.

Your's,
R. B

For Jeremie Whittaker, Minister at London.[2]

Reverend and Dear Brother,

Underftanding by Mr. Wilkie, our agent, your great care to further him in that his labour for that poor diftreffed people here, and withall your kind remembrance of me, I could not but give yow heartie thanks for both. I am glad to know yow are yet to the fore. I believe it goes the better with many for your interceffions to your Mafter, which, with delight, I remember wont to be very gracious and fingularlie melting. We here are groaning to God under many heavie preffours. The beauty, ftrength, and ordor of our ecclefiaftick meetings are well near gone, I grant much by our owne fault The abolition of almoft all our Church liberties, and putting the power of planting and difplanting of Minifters in the hand of ftrangers, to whom church difcipline does not belong, is heavy to us. The putting downe of our Generall Affemblies and Kirk Commiffion, and giving a liberty to any who will to profeffe many grievous errors, when we did expect, in performance of a very folemne fworn Covenant, a full and perfect reformation, does oft break our heart, and a flood of farder evills ready to break in on us does much perplex us; bot the confcience of our juft defervings, not at all from men, bot the Lord, makes us put our mouth in the duft, and acknowledge it for great mercy that we are not yet confumed, bot have yet any kind of fubfiftence. I fhall at this tyme fay no more to yow, bot earneftlie defyre yow would continue your prayers to the Lord Jefus for the defolate Church of Scotland, that the Lord would reftore us, as we were that day when love and compaffion drew us in a Covenant with yow. The Lord be with yow,

---

[2] Mr. Jeremiah Whittaker was minister of Mary Magdalene Bermondsey, in Southwark He died within four months from the date of this letter.

and continue yow, and other gracious brethren there, till, by your prayers at the throne of grace, yow have gotten that very thick cloud which now overfhaddows us all difpelled.

Your Brother in the Lord to bleffe God
and pray for yow.

February 10th 1654

For Mr. James Fergusson.[3]

James,

It's lyke yow and I fhall wear out of acquaintance. If your leafure ferved, I wifh yow took a ftart for a night that we might have one hour's clatter If this cannot conveniently be, as yow left laft with me, anent the Synod this is my purpofe: howfoever fundry of our Brether, and thefe alfo there Eaft, thinks our being together fo long hes been for our hurt, yet I am fo loath to break, that for this time it fhall be my earneft endeavour to keep together upon our ordinary proteftation, if fo our Brether be content on the nameing of the Moderator to adjourn till October. But if they will trouble us by their committees, or mint to medle with any thing controverted, they lay a neceffitie on us to fitt by ourfelves. However, all thinks it neceffary that we be fo frequent, minifters and elders, as we can Yow will not faill to be in tymeoufly on the Monday, for it muft be yow and Mr. Durhame who muft deall betwixt us to keep us together, and bear witnefs on whofe fault the breach comes It were a pitie if your mind fhould be content to defert us at fuch a tyme. I would think it very needfull that yow would, fome day or other of the next week, call together Mafters William Cobrun, William Fullarton, and Robert Wallace, to fpeak a little with yow, Mr. J Bell, M. P. C., M A. N.,[4] to refolve how, with the leaft dinn, yow may have in whom yow can againft that time, and to advyfe what elfe is needfull Shall others for evill be fo active, and keep fo frequent meetings farr and near, and we ftill fit looking one upon another while all be loft. The Lord be with yow

Your Brother.

Wednefday, March 8th [1654.]

[3] In the MS Baillie's amanuensis has written this name as Forgishall

[4] That is, Mr John Bell, Mr. Patrick Colvill, and Mr. Alexander Nisbet

For Mr. William Spang.   July 19th 1654

Cousigne,

I think yow marvell not at my long and unusuall silence. Warre being flameing betwixt the lands of our abode, though neither yow nor I have any interest therein, yet the passage being stopt, or difficult, and all corresponding betwixt any in these and thir parts being lyable to misconstruction, I choised rather to be silent than for that tyme to write any. But now, the Peace being subscryved and ready to be proclaimed, I resume my old way of letting yow know the true condition both of myself, and of our Colledge, Church, and Countrey, expecting the like from yow of your affaires there, and of the world abroad, at your first opportunitie.

I have had many a weary heart these tymes bygone, for many a crosse accident both private and publict. But still the goodness of God upheld me, and to this day hes protected and assisted me in every thing, and given to me a comfortable subsistence, rather more as lesse than any of my neighbours, blessed be his holy name. After a long decaying and sickness my most gracious and vertuous companion wes removed June 7th 1653. In the midst of a great and just griefe I had this mixture of comfort, that, to the full satisfaction of all, in her whole life, sickness and death, the grace and wisdome of God did shine forth in her, till all wes crowned with great applause, and regrate of all who knew her. Since, the Lord hes guided my family and fix children weell as I could have expected or wished. Besyde my ordinarie labours, I have gotten my Hebrew Praxis, with much fascherie, at last, from the presse; also, I expected to have had my Catechise, and Answer to Cotton and Tombes, printed before this: If in such miserable tymes I can gett out these testimonies of my faithfullness and diligence in my calling, I will be glad. My little Chronologie growes in my hand, and I hope it may doe good: it is my greatest taske for the tyme.

The case of our Colledge is thus: When by great studie and violence, Dr. Strang wes made to dimitt his place, I fand, by Mr. James Durhame, that the designe then wes to putt in Mr Patrick Gillespie for our Principall; but most of us esteeming that purpose exceeding absurd, we gave a call to Mr.

Blair, not much contrare to his owne mind, as I thought ; but when that did not fucceed, we gott Mr. Robert Ramfay fettled in it. Before his entry, death removed that gracious and able man, much for our hurt. I wes, both before and after, much dealt with by thefe whom it concerned, to accept that place ; but I ever peremptorilie refuifed : I knew it belonged to Dr. Strang, and in the manifold depofitions, and dimiffions of places, we have had thefe years bygone, in Church, State, and Schooles, I had feen few thryve, but exceeding many who fucceeded to fall in great hurts, if not fhame and death : I loved no changes, efpecially to a place of civile action ; however, God guided my mind to be refolute not to medle with it So foon as the Englifh come amongft us, one of their firft cares wes to plant our Univerfities with their owne. Mr Patrick Gillefpie and our Regent Mr. John Young, fell to be great among themfelffes and with the Englifh : both of them aimed at the place ; at laft they agreed, fo that Mr Patrick fhould be Principall, and Mr. John Divinitie Profeffor. Our Rector, Commiffar Lockhart, having joyned affectionately with the Englifh, concurred in the defigne. I wes much grieved with it, for I faw, befyde many other incongruities, it put our Colledge prefently in the hands of the Remonftrators, and fuch as joyned heartily enough with the Englifh. Mr. Zacharie Boyd, Vice-Chancellar, wes foolifhly peremptor to eftablifh Mr. John Young Profeffor · the Englifh were ready to have done it; but at Mr. John's defyre, permitted the Colledge to do it themfelves : his father, Mr. George, our Dean, dealt long effectuallie with his fonne, not to grieve me by accepting of that charge, but in vaine. When it come to the election, for refpect to Mr. George, I wes content to be abfent, with a declaration of my diffent and refolution, which yet I have keeped, in not countenancing him in the exercife of that charge , for to me it feemed hard, that a young man, a Regent in Philofophie, how able foever, fhould immediately turne Divinitie Profeffor without any call from the Church, efpecially being profeffedly oppofite to our Church and Generall Affemblie. At the election, the Rector moderating had no voice, but when the voters were equallie divided , his father and brother could have no voice, neither in reafon nor ordinarie practife ; the other two Regents were againft the thing at that tyme, intending Mr. James Durhame, who indeed had been our lawfullie elected Profeffor, whofe entrie, for good reafons, we had ftopped ; but thereafter I moft gladly would have had him in, when, by Mr. John

Young, for his owne defigne, I wes difabled to doe it. fo Mr. John's call refted only on the voice of Mr. Zacharie; yet he accepted, and thereafter, to his father's and my great griefe, hes ever gone on the wrong way, with all his ftrength.

After much whifpering with the Englifh, at laft ane order and command wes prefented to us by our Rector, from the Englifh Judges, to accept of Mr Patrick, whom they, according to their power, had appointed our Principall Mr. John Young, Mr James Veitch, and Mr Richard Robertfon, were willing to doe what wes defyred; but the moft part of the Facultie, Mr George Young, Dean, Mr. Zacharie Boyd, Vice-Chancellar, I, and Mr Patrick Young, diffented and protefted   The Rector, in this inequalitie, profeffed he had no voice, and acknowledged that the Facultie had refufed to choice Mr. Patrick; yet, as a private man, he would goe with the three diffenters, and encourage Mr. Patrick to obey the Englifh order · thereafter, the Englifh fent us a command to write our reafons why we refufed. This, the Dean of Facultie, Vice-Chancellar, and I, did feverallie under our hands. Notwithftanding, Mr. Patrick accepted the charge, and fince hes poffeffed it, albeit, in this the fecond year, he hes been pleafed to make not fo much as one leffon. I doe not abftain from the moft of Colledge meetings, with my proteftations, oft at the beginning repeated, of my not acknowledging by my prefence either of the two for Principall or Profeffor; and when we fubfcryve common writes, I ufually adde to my name P. S. S. *Proteftationibus Salvis.* In other things, we keep prettie faire; but I fear we cannot long agree. At Mr. Patrick's firft entrie, the eldeft Regent, Mr Richard Robertfon, (whom violently they had thruft in over all our priviledges, by a committee of their Vifitation,) had putt in his Dictats exceeding many open errors, herefies, and blafphemies. I mifkent the matter long, only I defyred Mr. Patrick, who had become fo intimate with him, as after that fcandale to boord him at his owne table, and Mr John Young who alfo boorded there, to fee to it   After the fcandale grew very flagrant, and no courfe at all wes like to be taken with it, at laft, I called for the Notes, and drew out that paper I heirwith fend to yow, and communicate it to the Facultie, in the young man's own prefence They appointed him with his owne hand to delete out of his Dictates, fundrie of the wicked errors. They all profeffed they miflyked the tenets alfmuch as I, yet they conceaved the young man to be boly, and would not difgrace him with any farder cenfure. I defyred Mr. Patrick to advyfe this matter with his friends, and told him plainly, if he keeped in the Colledge one who had taught fo blafphemous herefies, and who yet was not fenfible, for any purpofe, of his finne, I would let the world know it for my owne exoneration, and would charge this connivance on him, and the whole fide on which he wes. Finding me that clear, I think Warriftone and Mr. James Guthrie advyfed him not to be heard with me in this; fo, not before the very end of the year, he wes removed, but with no cenfure at all; only on a narrative of weaknefs of bodie, he dimitted his place, and contrare to my mind, his dimiffion wes accepted; yea, a penfion of twelve fcore merks during his life wes appointed to him. It grieved me to fee no zeale at all againft the moft grievous errors in the moft of my neighbours; yea, though I communicate that paper to Mr. James Durhame, I fand him nothing commoved thereat.

Our next bout wes for the planting of the vaiking places. The year before, Mr. John Young, to make way for his call, laid down his Regent's place in the midft of a terme, with profeffion not to be willing for any requeft to medle more with it. According to our order, a program wes affixt in all the four Univerfities, to invite at a day all who pleafed to compear. Two of our own, Mr Hew Smith and Mr. John Glen, did appear, very good youths and fchollars both: while we are goeing to prefcryve them their tryell, ane order from the Englifh is delyvered to us, by our Rector, difcharging us to admitt any to tryall for any place, without their appointment. Some nights before, Mr. John Young had come to me to enquire, If I could be content to admitt to the vacant place Mr. Sandilands, the Rector's brother, without competition? I told him I could not in confcience, for befide that I conceaved the young man unfitt, by our old priviledges, lately injoyned very ftrictlie by our Vifitors, we were obliedged to a competition, for which we had then affixt a program. Mr. John, finding me refolute, without dinne, at no man's defyre, continued in his Regent's place to the end of that year, though he had entered in the Divinitie profeffion; which he let lye for the exercife of it, but not for its ftipend. However, when the vacant places of Mr. John Young and Mr. Richard Robertfon came to be fupplied the nixt year, Mr Patrick Gillefpie defires to call to the firft Mr. R. M^cquard [McWard], without any competition: for this we have a new conteft. I told him of our lawes renewed in our laft Vifitation, wherein his owne hand wes chieff; alfo that two of our owne, invited by our Programme, wes waiting for their tryell; that the young man he named I knew to be nothing fitter than any of the two; and that the old Colledge of St. Andrewes, wherein he wes Regent of Humanitie, had refufed, that fame year, to admitt him to a vaiking place without competition. Notwithftanding, it wes carried in the Facultie, to call him without competition or any tryell. Our Facultie was now fully conforme; the Vice-Chancellar was dead; Mr George Young wes changed, and his fonne, the Profeffor, wes made Dean of Facultie in his father's place, contrare, as I conceaved, to his promife not to accept of that place; the Rector, in all they defyred, wes ever for them, for their common mafters fake the Englifh, Mr. James Veitch wes put in by them againft order, and wes made ever for them; Mr. Patrick Young wes winne, by his brother Mr John, to be quyet; Affeffors were declaired, by their laft Vifitation, to have no decifive voice: Soe I wes left alone; and then indeed, fpeaking fharphe for the evident overthrow of our priviledges, when my offer wes refufed that I would be filent if Mr. Robert Blair, Mr. Samuel Rutherfoord, and Mr. James Wood, who were the young man's beft friends, would declare they conceived him to be one of that qualification for whom our law of competition fhould be broken, Mr. Patrick Gillefpie did publictlie boaft that he would take a courfe with me. With indignation I bade him doe his worft quicklie. The firft night he come among us, he cairied the change of our factor, Mr. John Herbertfone, to Mr. John Spreule, his confident on the Englifh intereft; fo he gripped our purfe, that no man fhould gett any ftipend bot as he thought expedient; and this ever fince I have found. With all thefe injuries, I fatt ftill expecting worfe. At the Regent's entrie, I abfented myfelf; the young man incontinent fell fick, as before he had been fickhe: he is like not long to live⁵; fo, to all our fenfe, it had been his good never to have come hither. There was a competition for the other place,

⁵ Mr Robert M'Ward, however, survived Baillie many years. He was admitted a Regent in the College 4th Auguft 1653, and three years later became one of the Minifters in Glasgow, as noticed in Baillie's letter to Spang, 1ft September 1656 He was ejected at the Restoration, and was, moreover, tried for alleged sedition in one of his sermons, but his expected sentence of execution was changed to perpetual banishment He retired to Holland, from whence by his writings he greatly supported the fainting hearts of his suffering brethren in Scotland during " their fiery trials," in the time of persecution He died in exile in December 1681 —(Steven's History of the Scottish in Rotterdam, pp 25, &c 336)

becaufe Mr. Patrick knew of none to thruft in, only he wrote to Aberdeen, where almoft all in both Colledges, from Remonftrators, had avowedlie gone over to Independencie and Separation; from them he fetcht a young man, Mr. Andrew Burnet. In all the tryalls, to the fenfe of almoft all, Mr. John Glen clearlie warrit him, yet there wes no remeid, Mr. Burnet behooved to have the place. The young man, Mr. John Glen, had faid among his commerads, that he fear'd his favour was fo little as he fhould not carrie the place: of this mote fuch a mountain was made, that Mr. Patrick began a procefs againft him, to declare him uncapable to compete. With difficultie he was admitted to a hearing. In the time of our judging, I fand many fenfible of ane evident partialitie: I departed in filence; for this Mr. Patrick cryed after me, He would teach me better manners At this I fmiled, and went away. My chief exception was, that the young man, though he had the teftimonie of all the apoftates in the Colledge of Aberdeen, yet Mr. Andrew Cant's, though written to, was not gotten, and Mr. Patrick, with paffion, had refufed to put him to fubfcryve the Covenant, when I in his ear defyred it. At the beginning of the year he took all the keys of the little chambers from my fchollars, whereof they had long, by my allowance, been in poffeffion, and gave them to whom he liked better Dr. Strang had beftowed fix hundred merks on the building, for which the Facultie moft unanimouflie had affigned him a chamber for his ufe during his life time, in ane act fubfcryved with all our hands. Mr. Patrick will have him out of it; by reiterate order from the Englifh, he had made him flitt from his houfe; and when he was unwilling to give him the key of his chamber in the Colledge, till he had been heard in a Facultie to fpeak for his right, without more adoe, he caufes break up the doore, and put on a new lock, and fetts Mr. John Young in the chamber, which we thought he would not have accepted. And to fhew more of his good-will to his predeceffor, he quarrells his compts for his ftipend, and queftions two yeares as unjuftly intromitted with, though allowed and fubfcryved by all the auditors of the compts for more than twenty years, without queftion. Alfo, of my receipts he challenges fix hundred pounds, which I offered to be determined by the Colledge own lawyers, or other arbitrators; but without law there is no remeid; and to law I told him, I will not goe, though I fhould lofe the foume. This is but a little part of our vexation.

Lately Dr Strang had drawne up ane act, that the ftudents of Divinitie fhould fubfcryve their due obedience and attendance of the leffons of the Principall and Profeffors, under the paine of a mulct. This by many of the chief fchollars was never fubfcryved, and never preffed on any, and laid afide a little after the firft making, and out of mind and forgot. But behold, at the beginning of this year, Mr Patrick will have all the Divinitie ftudents to fubfcryve this, or elfe put them out of the Colledge. Some of them, efpeciallie your nephew and Mr Hew Blair's fonne, being in confcience bound up, declyned modefthe that fubfcription, thinking in their minds (as many more did) that Mr. Patrick was not lawfull Principall, nor Mr. John Young lawfull Profeffor; but withall gave him no offence· for this no fubfcryveing he put them publictlie out of the hall from the exercife. I did not know of this till Mr. Patrick wrote a very imperious letter to me, out of Edinburgh, not to admitt thefe two young men to any of my leffons. This infolence grieved me, yet I neglected it; only told him at meeting that I could concurre in no fuch violence. While we are vexed dayhe with new unexpected motions, there is affixed diverfe tymes on the Colledge gate, and fcattered in the Colledge Clofe, and put in the mouth of all the fchollars, a number of moft bafe and fcandalous Latine verfes, abufeing Mr. Patrick and Mr. John Young very vylelie, and fcoffing at all the Regents Before I had heard of it, they had put a number of boys to a tryall upon it, being unable to find the author. They fcourged fundrie publictlie and privatelie, and made fuch affrightment among the fchollars that fundrie got away: fome of the beft qualitie would no more returne. This remedie did no good, for every other day new papers, of many bafe villanies, were fpread and fent over all the countrie. This put Mr Patrick in a high humor to goe for Edinburgh, with ane Englifh troup, excommunicate Govan, in his armes, ryding before his wife through the ftreets openlie. While he is there ane order came to him fra the Protector, and other two to Mr. John Livingftone and Mr. John Menzies, to come to London againft the 10th of Aprile, to give their advyce in matters of high concernment. This has frayed us all, feaiing leaft the Protector purpofe to put our Church in a new mule, and beginne upon us a fore perfecution, which is like not foon to end. I parted fair with Mr. Patrick, for my own part, which I fcarce expected: for our Rector, falling in a foule fornication, behooved to be changed, and the designe being to have none of the Ministers or others, convenient on the list, but only the laird of Pollock and goodman of Glanderstone, and the Covenant being to be laid aside at that election, when usually it wont very solemnly to be taken, I would not countenance the action; also our Factor, Mr John Spreule, being now in the charge of clerk to the Lords of Session, and being to make his accompts, I could not subscryve without my prejudice, and the Colledge giving sundrie instructions to be agented by Mr. Patrick at London, with the Protector, I would subscryve none of them. I expected for all this a storme, yet God guided me so that we parted calmlie, for the which I was glad, and since his departure have lived in peace.

As for our Church affaires, thus they stand: The Parliament of England had given to the English Judges and Sequestrators a very ample commission to put out and in ministers as they saw cause, to plant and displant our Universities. According to this power, they put Mr John Row in Aberdeen, Mr. Robert Leighton in Edinburgh, Mr. Patrick Gillespie in Glasgow, and Mr. Samuell Colvile they offered to the Old Colledge of St Andrews; this last is yet holden off, but the other three acts as Principalls. All our Colledges are quicklie like to be undone. Our Churches are in great confusion; no intrant getts any stipend till he have petitioned and subscryved some acknowledgment to the English. When a very few of the Remonstrators or Independent partie will call a man, he gets a kirk and the stipend; but whom the Presbyterie, and well near the whole congregation, calls and admitts, he must preach in the fields, or in a barne, without stipend. So a sectarie is planted in Kilbryde, ane other in Leinzie, and this guyse will grow ryfe to the wrack of many a soull. We thought at the Generall Assemblie to have gotten some course for this; but Colonell Lilburne, the commander-in-chiefe, gave order to sojors to break our Assemblie before it wes constitute, to the exceeding great grief of all, except the Remonstrators, who insulted upon it, the English violence haveing trysted with their protestation against it. Since that tyme we have had no meeting for the whole Church, not so much as for counsell, though the Remonstrants have mett oft, and are like to sett up a Commission and Assemblie of their owne, for very ill purpose. They are most bitter against those who adhere to their Covenant in the matter of the King and Assemblies: they are alse bent as ever to purge the Church: to punish men truely deserveing censure, we are alse willing as they; but their purgeing is for common a very injurious oppreffion Sundry of them falls openly to the Englifh errors, both of Church and State, and many more are near to that evill; yet my Lord Warriftone, Mr. James Guthrie, and others, ftill profefs their great averfion to the Englifh way however, their great averfation of the King, and of the late Affemblies, and their zeal to make up the Kirk and armie, and places of truft, only of the godly partie, (that is their own confidents,) make them dear and precious men to the Englifh, doe or fay what they will, and their oppofites bot rafkalhe Malignants This makes them exceeding bold, knowing of their back; and were it not for a few more moderate men among them, they, before this, would have plaid ftrange pranks: however, they are goeing on prettie faft; their wracking of the congregation of Leinzie, and dividing of the Prefbyterie of Glafgow; their doeing the like in the congregation and Prefbyterie of Lithgow, yow heard long agoe; alfo what they have done in Bathgate, and fundry parts of the fouth. I will only give fome accompt of their laft dealings

From their meeting in Edinburgh, they were inftructed to have monethly fafts and communions as they could have them at their communions they excluded more than the halfe of thofe who were ordinarlie admitted: fex or feven minifters, leaveing their own congregations defolate, were about the action; numbers of ftrangers flocked to thefe meetings; at their fafts, four or five minifters of their beft preachers in the bounds, exercifed from morning to even The great defigne of all this wes evidently but to increafe their partie, whereof yet in moft places they miffed. Alwayes the word went, that they purpofed to put up committees for purging and planting every where as they thought fitt. I wes fo charitable as not to fufpect them of any fuch purpofe, when the land wes full of confufion and danger; yet I fand myfelf difappointed; for at our fynod, the Moderator's fermon ran on the neceffitie of taking up the too-long neglected work of purging. The man's vehemencie in this, and in his prayer, a ftrange kind of fighing, the like whereof I had never heard, as a pythonifing out of the bellie of a fecond perfon, made me amazed To prevent this foolifh and cruell enterprize, we preffed, in the entrie of the Synod, that in thefe tymes of confufion we might be affured of peace till the nixt Synod, as we had been in the three former Synods We intimate our great willingnefs to caft out of the miniftrie all whom we conceaved either unfitt for weaknefs, or fcandalous; but a Synod fo divided in judgement as we were, we conceaved very unfitt for any fuch work. When we found our defyre flatly refufed, and perceaved a clear defigne to fett up prefently their tyrannous committees, we, as we had refolved before hand, and were advyfed by the miniftrie ot Edinburgh, and others of our mind, required them, that our Synod might be rightly conftitute, That minifters cenfured by the Generall Affemblie, and elders notorioufly oppofite to the laft three Generall Affemblies, might have no voyce. When this wes flatly refuifed, we fhew we were neceffitate to fitt by our felves, and leave them in their feparation from the Generall Affemblie and Kirk of Scotland. When, by all we could fay, nothing could be obtained, all of us who adhered to the Generall Affemblie went to the Blackfriers, and there keeped the Synod, leaving our Proteftation with them (C.) Some brethren travelled all the next day betwixt us for a union; we offered it gladly, on condition, that they would be content for this tyme of the land's trouble and danger, to leave all medling with things controverted, or elfe to conftitute the Synod according to the Act of the Generall Affemblie. When neither could be obtained, (as yow may fee in the paper of mediation (D.), we did conftitute ourfelves in a Synod by ane act; whereof yow have the tennor fubjoyned (E); and when we had appointed a faft, the caufes whereof I likewife fubjoyne (F.), we clofed to meet at Irvine at the nixt dyet To our abfent brethren we fent the letter following (G), and ane information of our proceedings to the neighbouring Synods of Lothian, Galloway, Argyle; alfo Fyffe, Perth, and the Merfe.

The Remonftrators choifed Mr William Guthrie for their Moderator, and one James Porter, a devote fervant of their partie for clerk; named a Committee of their moft forward men to goe immediately to Lanark, to purge and plant as they found caufe; fent two of their gentlemen, Sir George Maxwell and Walkinfchaw, with the help of their good friends Bogs and Commiffar Lockhart; and when they prevailed not, two of their minifters, Mr. William Somervaill and Mr. William Jack, [went] to the Governor of Glafgow, Colonell Cooper, for a troup of horfe to guard them at Lanark and Douglafs[6] Some of them had to their power, fomented a very injurious fcandall

---

[6] There is inferted in the MS this marginal note, in Baillie's own hand "Mr Somervail and Mr. Jak cleirit themfelfes to me of this falt"

on Mr. R. Hoome, whom we had made minister at Crauford-Johne contrare to their mind: their committee laboured to their power to try that their owne invention; but failed therein. There is an old man, Mr. John Veitch, minister of Roberton, they sent ministers, two or three of their number to hear him preach; on their report, they pronounced a sentence of deposition on him as unsufficient. But their chief work was at Dowglafs. The noblemen, gentlemen, whole heritors and people, and session, unanimously had called Mr. Archibald Inglish, a verie good and able youth, to his father's place. They stirred up some of the elders, who subscryved a call to the young man, to defyre his tryells might be before the United Presbyterie, and not before our part of it, from which the Remonstrators had separate. This motion they so fomented, that these few elders, with a very few of the people, were moved by them, contrare to all the congregation, to give a call to a silly young man, a meer stranger, from Fife, one Mr Francis Kidd, who had never been heard nor seen in the bounds. This man they bring to the kirk on the Sunday when the people refused to let him or them enter, he preached on a brayside to some strangers and a few of the people of Dowglafs, and even these runne away from hearing of him, except a very few. Preaching ended, they sent one to read a edict at the church-door, who refused to give a copie of what he read: without more adoe, on Monday morning, they past all his tryells in one houre, and came to the church of Dowglafs in the afternoone to give him imposition of hands. The body of the people and heritors hindered their coming into the church and church-yard; whereupon they sent once and againe for their Englifh guard. By all their importunitie they could gett none of the troupe to countenance them, except twelve, with the Lieutenant: by the power of their sword, as wes avowed on all hands, on a bray-side, without preaching, they admitted him minister of Dowglafs · ane abominable example, generally much abhorred, which shews what we may expect from that partie. Our Synod appointed some to joyne with the true Presbyterie of Lanark; who mett the week thereafter; tryed with all accuracie possible what could be found in the scandale of Mr. Robert Hoome, fand nothing but malice of some parties, fomented by ministers; with the unanimous consent of the people of Roberton, strengthened the minister, and appointed a helper to be settled there in ane orderly way, admitted to the Church of Dowglafs Mr Archibald Inglish, after all tryells duely performed, with the bleſſings and tears of the congregation. Readily they will procure ane order from the Engliſh, that the ſtipend and church ſhall goe to Mr Kidd, and his twelve or ſixteen followers, and Mr. Archibald Ingliſh ſhall be tollerated, with much adoe to preach to the whole congregation, Marqueſs of Dowglaſs, Earle of Angus, whole heritors and people, in the fields, or a barne, without a ſexpence of ſtipend

In this glaſs ſee our condition. It is ſo in ſundrie congregations allreadie, and like to be ſoe in many more; not ſo much through the violence of the Engliſh, as the unreaſonable headineſs of the Remonſtrators, which for the tyme is remedileſs; and we, for fear of worſe from their very evill humour, give way to permitt them to plant diverſe churches as they like beſt This formed ſchiſme is very bitter to us, but remedileſs, except on intollerable conditions, which no wyfe orthodoxe divine will advyſe us to accept · We muſt imbrace without contradiction, and let grow, the principles of the Remonſtrants, which all reformed divines, and all ſtates in the whole world abhorres, we muſt permitt a few headie men to waſte our Church with our conſent or connivance; we muſt let them frame our people to the Sectarian modell; a few more forward ones joyned among themſelffes by privie meetings to be the godly partie, and the congregation, the reſt, to be the raſcallie malignant mulitude: So that the bodie of our people are to be caſt out of all churches; and the few who are countenanced, are fitted, as ſundry of them already hes done, to imbrace the errors of the tyme for their deſtruction. Againſt theſe abominations we ſtrive ſo much, and ſo wyſely, as we can Mr Robert Dowglaſs, Mr David Dickſon, and others, hes yet gotten Edinburgh right: The faction which Mr. Robert Traill and Mr John Stirling have there is unconſiderable. Mr. Robert Blair and Mr. James Wood keep St. Andrewes and Fyfe prettie right: Mr Rutherfoord, to the uttermoſt of his power, advances the other partie Mr. John Robertſon and Mr. William Rate gets Angus and Dundee right; but the naturally headie men of Aberdeen are come up to the full deſigne too ſoone; yet the bodie of the people and country are right In this Mr. James Guthrie in Stirling comes but ſmall ſpeed; albeit his confident Sir William Bruce of Stanhouſe be made the Engliſh ſherriff. In Lithgowſhire they have uſed great violence, impriſoned their chiefe oppoſite Mr. Jo. Vaugh, forced a ſillie man on the miniſtrie of Lithgow, and ane other on Bathgate, contrare to all the Synod of Lothian could doe, yet the bodie of the people is flat there againſt them. Their greateſt prevalence is with us in Glaſgow, which comes much more by Mr. James Durhame's neutralitie profeſſed, bot reall joyning with the moſt of the others deſignes, and Mr. John Carſtares's zeall, than any thing that Mr. Patrick Gilleſpie hes done, or could doe, by himſelff. This is the pitifull condition of our Church which is but goeing on from evill to worſe till the Lord remeed it

As for our State, this is its caſe : Our Nobilitie, weell near all are wracked; Dukes Hamilton, the one execute, the other flaine; their ſtate forfault; one part of it gifted to Engliſh ſojours; the reſt will not pay the debt, little left to the heretrix, almoſt the whole name undone with debt.—Huntlie execute; his ſonnes all dead bot the youngeſt; there is more debt on the Houſe nor the land can pay :—Lennox is living, as a man buried, in his houſe of Cobhame : Dowglaſs and his ſonne Angus are quyet men, of no reſpect.—Argyle almoſt drowned with debt, in friendſhip with the Engliſh, but in hatred with the countrey · he courts the Remonſtrators, who were and are averſe from him;— Chancellar Loudoun lives like ane outlaw about Athole, his lands compryſed for debt, under a generall very great diſgrace :—Marſchell, Rothes, Eglinton and his three ſonnes, Craufurd, Lauderdaill, and others, priſoners in England; and their lands all either ſequeſtrate or forfault, and gifted to Engliſh ſojours :— Balmerinoch ſuddenly dead, and his ſonne, for publict debt, compryſeings, and captions, keeps not the calſie :—Warriſton, haveing refounded much of what he got for places, lives privilie, in a hard enough condition, much hated by the moſt, and neglected by all, except the Remonſtrants, to whom he is guide. Our Criminall Judicatories are all in the hands of the Engliſh, our Civile Courts in their hands alſo, only ſome of the Remonſtrators are adjoyned with them : In the Seſſion[7] are Craighall, (now dead,) and his brother Hopetoun, Mr A. Perſon, Southhall, Colonell Lockhart, and Swinton The only clerks to the Seſſion are Mr. John Spreule and William Downie. The Commiſſariat and Sherriffs Courts are all in the hands of Engliſh ſojours, with the adjunction, in ſome places, of ſome few Remonſtrants Strong gariſones in Leith, Edinburgh towne and caſtell, Glaſgow, Ayr, Dumbartan, Stirling,

[7] The Judges here named were Sir John Hope of Craighall who died 24th April 1654. his brother Sir James Hope of Hopetoun, Alexander Pearson of Southhall, Colonell afterwards Sir William Lockhart, and John Swinton of Swinton

Lithgow, Perth, Dundee, Bruntifland, Dunnotter, Aberdeen, Innernefs, Inneraray, Dunftaffnage, etc

Of a long tyme no man in the whole Ifle did mute· all were lulled up in a lethargick fear and defpaire. Only the other year, Glencairne and Balcarras, underftanding of ane order to apprehend them as correfponding with the King, retired to the hills of Athole. Kenmure haveing efcaped from England, when his houfe wes burnt and his rents feafed upon, got to the Lennox with a few horfe. Lorne, being but coarfelie ufed by his father, joyned with Kenmure. To thefe fundrie did affociat, Glengarie, Athole, Seaforth, not fo much to doe any thing againft the Englifh, as to make fome noyfe of a partie, to encourage the King's friends abroad to fend him fupplies of men, armes, and money. At once a great animofitie did ryfe in every fhyre of the land; very many young gentlemen made bold with all the ferviceable horfe they could find about them; and notwithftanding of all the dihgence the Englifh could ufe to prevent, great numbers came fafe to the hills. The warre with Holland, and rumor of great help from over-feas, did increafe dayly both the number and courage of this partie.

But behold inward divifion doth hazard all at the very beginning. The irreconcileable difcords of Argyle and Hamilton had undone the Ifle, and almoft both the families. Glencairne, Hamilton's coufigne, did much miftruft and flight Lorne. Ralftone, and the Remonftrant gentlemen of Kintyre, feemed readie to arme for the Englifh, againft the King's partie. Lorne and Kenmure, with the men they had raifed, went to Kintyre to fuppreffe thefe They, on hope of the Englifh affiftance from Aire, fortified the caftle of Lochheid; but while neither Argyle nor the Englifh appear in their defence, they rander the houfe to Lorne's difcretion Kenmure thinking the befiedged better ufed by Lorne than they deferved, fell in a mifcontent, and went frome Lorne to Glencairne with many complaints Balcarras alfo unwilling to have Glencairne above him, and conceaveing that it wes beft for the advanceing of the King's affaires, that till the King himfelff, or one of authoritie from him, fhould come, the partie fhould be ruled by a committee, without any fupreame officer, and that all admitted to counfells and command in the armie fhould declare for the Solemne League and Covenant. For thefe ends he dealt with Lorne, Seaforth, and Athole, till Glencairne produced a commiffion under the King's hand to be Generall, till himfelff or fome from him, fhould come to take the command. This unexpected commiffion put all to a fubmiffive filence, but increafed heart-burnings Lorne, profeffing all firmnefs to the King and caufe, wes not willing to take orders from Glencairne, till he did know more particularlie the King's pleafure. For this end, he, Balcarras, and others, wrote to the King their difcontent with Glencairne's command. Thefe letters were intercepted and brought to Glencairne, whereupon he gave order to Glengarie to apprehend Lorne, to anfwer for his fedition. Lorne hardlie enough efcaped Glengarie's perfute; Balcarras retired, and, a little after, with his Lady, went difguifed through England to the King. Notwithftanding of all thefe pitiefull and fhamefull debates, Glencairne's partie ftill increafed, and his conduct became confiderable : the whole Highlands, Ifles, and much of the North, and numbers from the Lowlands, wes come unto him; fo it wes thought, at Midletone's coming, he had here and there eight or nine thoufand foot, and two or three thoufand horfe, of very ftout and refolute men as we ever had on the fields, the moft of them old fojours. But at Midletone's comeing, when neither the King, nor his brother, nor any foraigne force, did appear, the hearts of many began to doubt, and when, after his coming, fome months, notwithftanding of all the reiterat promifes, no foraigne affiftance at all did come, but on the contrare, the Holland peace was proclaimed; the treaty of the Protector with Swane [Sweden] went on; the French ambaffador at London wes folemnly receaved, as the Spanifh and Portugale had been; all humane hope began much to faill, efpeciallie after Monck's coming downe as Generall, the Proclamation of the Protector, the Act of Union, and the Ordinance of Grace, which forfaulted and deeply fyned fo many, and fubjected the whole priviledges of the Nation to the Protector and his Councill's pleafure, with the abolition of Royaltie, the whole branches of the Family-Royall, and all Scots Parliaments and Conventions of Eftates; the takeing of Kinnoule, Lieutenant-Colonells Herriot, Wifhart, Forfyth, and fundry more of our Scotfmen unhappily : All thefe things were fo hard prefages, that the moft gave all the King's affaires for gone; and many did think that the King, whether through perfonall weaknefs, or the treacherie of the few counfellors about him, or the crofs afpect of all Europe towards him, had fo far difappointed the expectation of his friends, that while he lived he was not like to get fuch a partie for his fervice in Scotland.

So for the time the cafe of our Land is moft fad: Monck, by fea and land, is to befett Glencairne and his partie, and with much feveritie to crufh them, and for their fakes to lye more heavily on the whole fubdued countrey, beginning with the beft of the minifters, who, after mutuall advyce, find themfelves in confcience neceffitate to keep the King ftill in their publict prayers. We have been very carefull to give the Englifh no other offence at all, for in all this Northland ryfeing, to my beft knowledge, there is no minifter in Scotland who has had the leift hand or any medling. However, for this our great treafon of naming the King in our publict prayers, (as we conceive our duety, Covenant, and Directorie for worfhip do require, as ye will fee in the papers herewith fent unto yow,) (H.), we are like to fuffer heavie things. For all this, our eyes are towards the Lord · we expect protection from him, and if fo he think meet, we are willing to feall our teftimonie, in faith and humble modeftie, with all the fufferings which the injuftice of men may be permitted of our Heavenlie Father to impofe upon us.

Being called the other week to confer with the Brethren of Edinburgh, I was comforted to find all that mett, fully in my fenfe both about prayer for the King, and affaires of our divided Synod, divided Prefbyterie, troubled Colledge, and all elfe we fpoke of. But it was a fad fight to fee the generall affliction at the Proclamation of the Protector, of the Act of Union, the Act of Forfaultrie and deep fyning of fo many, the preparation of Monck by fea and land prefentlie to fwallow up the Northern partie, deftitute of all hope of the oft-promifed foraigne fupplies, as common fame furmifed. As our miferies, (without a kingdome wholly, without any judicatories to count off of our owne, without a church well near,) are great; fo we expect they fhall increafe, and the next heavie dint fhall fall on the chief of the miniftrie At once it will not be fafe to have any audible complaints of thefe things, either to God or man.

I fhall clofe at this time, with a defire of your advyce, with the firft occafion, in a particular of my familie My fecond fonne, Henry, a prettie boy of feventeen years, among the beft fchollars of his claffe, very diligent and carefull of all duetie, and welbeloved of all as a gracious and vertuous youth, befyde my expectation, and contrare to my defyre, tells me, that of a long time he has been inclyned, and now is refolved, to be a merchant All I, or other friends, can fay, does not divert him from this refolution, which, he fayes, after frequent and earneft prayer, grows in him. This is his Batcheller year; with difficultie I can move him to ftay it out; he could be content to ferve as a prentice. I conceive it his beft, if his refolution continue, to fend him over in the hinder-end of harveft to yow, to fpend the winter, and what time more yow think fitt, to learn Dutch and French, to keep a merchant-book, or what elfe yow made my brother's fonne learn, and then to give him a little ftock to ware, at the direction, and with the overfight, of fome friends. Yow who underftand thefe things, give me your full and free advyce in this whole matter. I had purpofed him, as alfo my eldeft fonne, for the miniftrie, and I thought he had alfe faire beginnings as any of his age, towards that holy calling. But his peremptor refolution makes me, with grief, change that my defigne for him.

A Postscript. July 20th 1654.

While I waited long for a bearer, I add further: Our Triumvirn, Mafters Leviftone, Gillefpie, and Menzies, ftayed long at London without much accefs to the Protector: He thought it good to write for Meffrs. Dowglafs, Blair, and Guthrie. Mr Blair excufed his health; Mr. Guthrie, by a fair letter, declared his peremptorinefs not to goe, Mr. Dowglafs, by Monk's friendlie letter, gott himfelf alfo excufed. On their not comeing, Mr. Leviftone gott leave to returne, and is at home, Mr. G[illefpie] and M[enzies] are expected. The buffinefs of the plott gave not the Protector much leafure for auditing of them. Only we fear that our Church fhall be caft under fuch a Committee as now guides all ecclefiafticall affaires in England, abfolutelie as the Protector thinks fitt, the moft whereof are Anabaptifts and Independents, and gentlemen of no ecclefiafticall relation. We thank God that perfecution on the miniftrie is not yet begun, except what the Remonftrators drawes from the Englifh on fome few. Mr John Vaugh and Mr. Robert Knox were long prifoners for naming the King in their prayers; yet now they are at liberty, and at their charges, to our great joy.

Through Mr. Gillefpie's abfence, our Colledge has been long at peace, though thefe diverfe monetles all difciplne has been loofe among us; the boys, after the fray among them for the fcandalous verfes, never weell fettleing; no examination at the end of the year, no folemne laureation, nor much attendance on claffes I think Mr. P. G., if he were prefent, would fee better order. In my preface to my Praxis, I noted the fcurvy dictates of fome Regents, which all the Univerfities acknowledged, and were in a fair way to have helped. For this Mr. James Veitch, our eldeft regent, did dyte to his fchollers, in the midft of his Notes, a pitifull invective againft me, (I); a fowller injurie than I ever heard was done to any honeft man for fuch a caufe. The Lord armed my mind with Chriftian patience fo that I totallie mifkent it; only I wrote the inclofed paper and fent it to himfelf, whereupon he fcraped out of his fchollers bookes, after fome dayes, that evill leffon, and no more dinne was here of that matter.

My next vexation was with our Anti-Synod: after their pranckes in Lanark, they mett fynodicallie very frequent at Glafgow, fell on a committee for purging all the Prefbyteries; I alone went up to them, intreated them with many fair words to delay at leaft any fuch work, and for that end gave them in a large paper, which a very gracious and wife brother, fomewhat a mid-man betwixt us, had drawn for that end, (K)[8]; which I fend alfo to yow, that from it yow may more fullie leaine our prefent temper. All this labor produced little; for notwithftanding they proceeded in their work, and appointed their purging and planting committees; bot with this provifo, that they fhould have, at their next meeting, a conference with any I pleafed of my mind before they proceeded. Againft their day I had our part of the Synod mett, and full information of the brethren of Edinburgh and others for our proceeding. We prefentlie put up a purging and planting committee alfe well as they, and of thefe we appointed a number to conferr with them. With much adoe we gott them to ftay till the firft of Auguft, upon a new conference: againft that day Mr. James Fergufone drew up a paper of his Overtures for our reunion (L), and I drew up another (M.). yow have both here. What the iffue fhall be yow may hear afterward; only thefe things lye heavier on my heart nor on any man's elfe I know, for ufuallie at the tyme of thefe comfortlefs janglings, I am fick and diftempered with grieff and difcontent, though every one of them gives me more refpect than to any other; yet for the remedilefs breach I am heavilie oft troubled

[8] In Baillie's MS. the paper referred to, is entitled, "Mr. James Ferguson's letter, given to the Anti-Synod, by M R B Junii 12, 1654"

in my owne mind, which I ufe to powre out before God, and getts then courage and ftrength to goe on, and bear the burthen.

Generall Monck went to the fields in the beginning of June, thinking and profeffing that the difcuffing of the northern Tories would coft him bot a few weeks labour, and we indeed did expect no other, for the Englifh in men, horfe, money, and all things they could defyre, had the clear advantage. yet we cannot hear of any great progrefs he has made. So foone as Glencairne had rendered his commiffion to Midletone, on a jarre between Monroe and Glengarie, Glencairne, fpeaking for Glengarie, got a challenge from Monroe; which he anfwered, and beat Monroe, to his great commendation. This affront, not fo much refented by Midletoune as need had been, together with the King's too much neglect, as fome fay, in his late commiffions, of Glencairne's very great fervices, upon the information, as it's thought, of Lorne and Balcarras, he left Midletone, and came with a fmall partie to the Lennox. The noife of this malcontentment did exceedinglie difcourage many; bot at once Glencairne carried it foe, that all this difcouragement was quicklie changed; for with the fmall partie he had he defended the pafs of Aberfoyle fo well againft Monck's frequent affaults, and fent out, for good purpofe fo many fmall parties to Clydefdale, Barranthrow, Cunnynghame, Kyle, Carrick, and Galloway, as retarded a while Monck's march to the north, and when Monck went north, notwithftanding of all his garifones, and befide them one full regiment of foot and ane other of horfe, left at Glafgow and Kilfyth, the partie fent out from Glencarne did runne up and downe the whole countrie, and did what they liked, without great impediment. Monck fand his march to the north very troublefome: the people caried all out of his way; ftragglers were fnapped up; the hills made fundrie, both horfe and men, ficken and die. It was oft printed, that Morgan had Midletone fo inclofed in Sutherland that he could not efcape to the fouth; yet when Midletone thought it time, he divided his men in parties, and paffed by with eafe, both Morgan and Monck, coming to Perthfhyre and Argyle, notwithftanding all they could doe to impede him. Colonell Brian's regiment from Ireland, landing in Lochaber, was lighted on by the countriepeople, and near a hundred of them flaine. for this Monck did caufe burn all the lands of the Laird of Lochaber, Glengarie, and Seaforth he came through. Glenurchie had been too great a intelligencer to the Enghſh, and ſided with Argyle againſt Lorne his ſonne; ſo Midletoune cauſed burn much of his land. This burning, now begunne on both hands, may ruine the whole countrie. It's thought the Engliſh have their fill of the Highland Hunting, and that the flux is fallen among them, which makes them ſpeak alreadie of quartering It ſeems Midletone minds no fighting in any bodie, bot ſhiftes till he ſee what tyme may bring forth. The countrie every where ſuffers much; yet is patient, for they ſee no remead; alſo the victuall all this year is at four pound the boll, and great appearance of the continuance of this greater plenty than hes been ſeen in our days

What the world abroad is doeing we know noe more then the London Diurnall tells us. What the myſterie may be of the Queen of Swan's [Sweden's] dimiſſion, and why her laſt act ſhould have been (without all neceſſitie) a ſtrict friendſhip with the Protector, is much marvelled. Alſo, why for the Protector's friendſhip, contrare to the mind of the other Provinces, theſe of Holland ſhould have caſt off the Prince of Orange? And if Spayne be with the Protector upon a league offenſive and defenſive, how comes it that both France and Portugall ſhould, by their ambaſſadors, be begging his friendſhip? What all this may meane we underſtand not, nor what our King's journey to the Spa imports. Yow poſſiblie may make us underſtand theſe things. Is Salmaſius dead? What is become of Blondell? What new books are among yow? Try to me what of Chronologie is lately come out.

Dr Strang, your good friend, having to doe in Edinburgh with the lawyers anent the unjuſt trouble he wes put to for his ſtipend, after a few day's ſickneſs did die, ſo ſweetlie, and graciouſlie, as wes ſatiſfactorie to all, and much applauded over all the citie, his very perſecutors giving him an ample teſtimonie. His treatiſe, *De Providentia Dei circa Peccatum*, he has enlarged, and made it ready for the preſſe. Be carefull to get it well printed, according to the conſtant friendſhip that wes allwayes betwixt yow and him. They hope yow will get it printed freely, for the piece is likely to ſell; bot if yow muſt give any money for its printing, they will bear the charge. Let me know with the firſt, your anſwer herein; for they will ſend yow the copie ſo ſoone as your mind is knowne, and your advice given. How is your condition in Midleburgh?[9] The Engliſh congregations uſe to be very fickle, and hard to be keeped by their miniſters: if your lot be better with yours, I

---

[9] Spang was translated from Campvere to Middleburgh, 10th November 1652.

shall be glad This letter is after my old fashion it deserves a long answer. My love to your wife and children. I rest in the Lord,

Your Cousigne, R. B.

Glasgow, July 21st 1654

That yow may know the way of planting our Churches, have this late practife Mr John Galbraith of Bothkennar wes depofed for tippling and other faults, three or foure yeares agoe. When Mr James Guthrie continued to preach in Stirling, after his depofition by the Generall Affemblie, Mr. John Galbraith followed his example, and returned to his pulpit: his people did love him better than Stirling did the other. Of the Prefbyterie of Stirling, Mr. James Simpfone of Airth, likewife depofed, and Mr John Hog of Lairbare, adhered to Mr. James Guthrie, and thefe three made one prefbyterie Mr. Robert Wright, and other two or three, adhering to the Affemblie, made themfelffes another prefbyterie. Mr. George Bennet and other two were neutralls, and abftained from both Mr. James Guthrie began a procefs of excommunication againft Mr. John Galbraith, bot he boafted fo faft to excommunicate Mr. James, if he proceeded againft him, that this wes left off. Mr. James profeffes to have no medleing with the Englifh at all, and to be much averfe from all complyance with them, yea, to miflike Mr. Patrick Gillefpie's way; yet Sir William Bruce of Stanehoufe, his fpeciall and intime friend to this day, hes taken the fheriffhip of Stirling from the Englifh, and continues ruling elder in Mr. James Guthrie's prefbyterie By his means ane order is procured from the Englifh, that Mr. John Galbraith fhall give over preaching: this he is forced to obey. The whole paroch gives ane unanimous call to Mr. William Galbraith, a good young man; bot ane order comes from the Englifh to hinder his plantation; and the whole paroch fupplications, oft prefented to the Englifh, could not get it helped; for the Judges are fully for the Remonftrants, though Generall Monck feems to miflyke them Thereafter one Mr. John Blair, never heard nor feen by the paroch, is named by Mr. James Guthrie's prefbyterie to be minifter of that kirk; for that people haveing adhered to a depofed minifter, muft be counted malignant, and fo loffe their right to call, and their right of calling muft fall in the hand of the prefbyterie; fo ane order is procured by the prefbyterie's ruling elder, Sir William Bruce, from the Englifh, to admitt that Blair. Mr. James Guthrie caufes conveen a great number of his faction, from diverfe paroches about, and gets Mr Robert Traill from Edinburgh, and Mr. John Carftares from Glafgow, and others, to fpend a day in preaching and prayer at this admiffion. The whole people of the paroch meets, and keeps the other out of the kirk; the tumult begins; dry ftraikes are diftributed; fome fell upon the Sheriff's neck. The gentlemen-parifhioners, fo foon as the Sheriff produced his Englifh orders for the admiffion, did cede; but the people continued all day cafting ftones and crying: yet they went on with their work, and thruft in the man. For all this, Mr. James Guthrie hes no dealing with the Englifh, and does no wrong! Our oppreffion is great and crying

At Glafgow, Mr. Andrew Gray, a youth of twenty-two yeares at moft, lately laureat at St Andrewes, upon one preaching or two at Glafgow, Mr Patrick Gillefpie and his friends will have him admitted to his place.[1] I refufed to confent; the youth being fo young, and utterly a ftranger to us; his tryells of expectant being haftilie paft in the Prefbyterie of Hamilton; and none of the minifters either of Edinburgh or St. Andrewes, the places of his refidence, being acquainted with him, as he profeffed; alfo his voyce being fo weak, that the moft in our kirks heard him not The Magiftrates and Town-Counfell being utterly againft his admiffion, dealt with him earneftly not to trouble them: at firft, his modefty wes fo great, that a fmall impediment feemed enough to fkarre him from accepting of any charge, bot fo foone as our Seffion (which is bot the echo of what our brethren fpeaks) had given him a call, without hoaft he went on to his tryells, and, over the bellie of the towne's proteftation, wes admitted by their part of the Prefbyterie minifter of Glafgow. His voice is not yet fo good as to be heard by diverfe He hes the new guyfe of preaching, which Mr Hew Binning and Mr. Robert Leighton began, contemning the ordinarie way of exponing and dividing a text, of raifing doctrines and ufes; bot runs out in a difcourfe on fome common head, in a high, romancing, unfcripturall ftyle,[2] tickling the ear for the

[1] Mr Andrew Gray became Gillespie's successor, as minister of the Outer High Church, Glasgow, in 1653, but died of fever in 1656, as noticed by Baillie in a subsequent letter

[2] His Sermons and other practical writings, like those of Binning and Leighton, notwithstanding " the new guyse" which offended Baillie, have retained their popularity, and are still occasionally republished

prefent, and moving the affections in fome, bot leaving, as he confefies, little or nought to the memorie and underftanding. This we muft mifken, for we cannot help it.

This faction growes much among us: I fear the iffue The Covenant they mifregard; the King his reftitution, or his partie's thryving, they feem to fear; their pietie and zeal is very fufceptible of fchifme and error. I am oft feared for their apoftacie. Many conferences hes been among them, Argyle, and Colonell Lockhart, for takeing up armes againft the northern partie; yet nothing of this kind is done, though diverfe mints have been made: tyme will clear the honeftie and difhoneftie of many. Our life here is a warfare, yet God fupports us, and we faint not. Bleffed be our Father! who, through all thefe confufions, will bring his children to glory.

One of our friends wrote to us fome fcruples againft the conftitution of our feparate Synod; to which I returned the inclofed anfwer (N.) On the 1ft of Auguft, fome of both fides did meet, bot could come to no agreement: we gave them in our Overtures, caft in ane other mould, as yow may fee at (O.); and they theirs to us, at (P.). Our unabilitie to deal with the Englifh, and their continuall affiftance from that power, (fought or unfought, I cannot fay, while they deny and many affirme,) makes us daylie loffe, and them gaine, and many incline to their thryving fide

After fome refrefhment from a fruitlefs journey through the hills, Monck is againe to the field. He, Cooper, Twiflingtone, and Argyle, are at Dumbartone, advyfeing on a hard and forrowfull work, what houfes and what cornes to burne: this work is begun on both fides already: we know not where it will end.

For his Reverend and well-blloved Brother, Mr John Young.

Reverend and Beloved Brother,

The other day when yow told me that Mr James Veitch wes very angry with the Preface of my Praxis, as if a part of it had been defigned againft him, I defyred yow, of your certaine knowledge, to affure him of the contrare, and as I had told him before myfelff, foe I wes purpofed at my firft leafure againe to affure him of that great miftake for truely I would have been loath to have given him or any of my colleagues the leaft offence. If I had forefeen, or yow had told me, when yow did perufe it a year agoe, before it was printed, that yow had conceived either he or any in our Houfe, would have been grieved with any thing in that or any other of my wrytes, I would have willingly fcraped it out · bot neither yow nor I had any fuch thought. Yow know that Preface wes written fome yeares agoe, and, as I think, printed the laft year,³ before Mr James had begun his Logick notes, and fo could not fpeak of them Alfo all the faults I complean of, as my words expreflie bear, relate to thefe times when neither he nor any other now in our Houfe, except yow and I, were Regents or fcarce fchollers, and in that refpect could not concern any of them.

Befide the complaint which offends him, I made it bot of fome, and that *aliquando*, and for fuch things which in our meeting of the whole four Univerfities wes denyed by no one man, bot heartily condefcended by all to be remedied, as the book of our correfpondence makes clear. As for Mr. James he wes of thefe years that, when laureat, let be fince, he could not be called *Adolefcens*, and his way of teaching (as himfelf and others long agoe told me to my wonder, for to this day was I myfelfe never able to attaine it) wes by dyteing, without all books and all papers, whether of his owne or others I take it to be many wayes evident, that in my wryte there wes no word that concerned Mr. James his perfon at all, neither doe I know that I have ever given him any caufe of offence. At his tryells and admiffion I wes at Edinburgh, at my returne I confented indeed to the proteftation which the Rector, Dean of Facultie, yow, and others, had made concerning the Colledge priviledges, but without any reflection on Mr. James his perfon. Since that tyme he and I have keeped fo good correfpondence as he did defyre, nor by a look, to my knowledge, have I ever offended him.

Notwithftanding, he is pleafed to fall upon me perfonally, with the moft atrocious injuries that ever in my life have been offered to me by any. I have had much contention, private and publict, in write and print, with diverfe profeffed enemies of our Church. But put all in one, I have not receaved the fifth part of the ill ufage which Mr. James is pleafed to give me, in that invective which, the other morning, he dyted to his fchollers expreflie againft

³ Baillie's "Appendix Practica ad Joannis Buxtorfii Epitomen Grammaticæ Hebrææ," was printed at Edinburgh, in 1653, small 8vo.

me. It's not enough to make me a printer of contradictions, ("Sed quid multis? Hæc proprio gladio seipsa jugulant, aperta sunt contradictoria"); to make me so ridiculous a blatterer as I must be laughen at in the schollers books, with ane Ha, ha, hæ! ("Domino hæc blateranti imputanda sunt.—Ha, ha, hæ!") not only to declare me, from his owne sad experience, bot to make it good upon me in a single combate, and to demonstrate it in a publict tryell betwixt me and him, that I am ane more dull and ane more unfitt man for teaching than any the most dull and unfitt Regents in Scotland of whom I complaine, ("Sed vos estis obtusi, et ad docendum inepti,—quæ si alicui, imprimis domino hæc blateranti imputanda sunt; quod experientia nunquam satis dolenda demonstrare possumus :—age ineatur singulare certamen, agatur duello, in quo apparuerit quis ineptus, quis pinguis, quis crassus, quis obtusus, imo et quibus vel ob indolem, vel ob eruditionem, bellius convenit doctorum cathedra, et quibus melius discipulorum subsellia") : All this I could have born, for it is bot of my weaknefs, which I will not deny to be great, yea, in my solemne inauguration to the place I now stand in, when with much importunitie, and long dealing by all who had interest, I wes drawn unto it, I publickly professed myself to be much fitter to be a scholler to others than a master to any. For indeed, I am farr from these abilities which Mr. James professeth here to be in himselfe : I am none of these who are conscious of no infirmitie, ("Nec ullius infirmitatis confcii.") However, I take it no wayes well that he dytes me to his schollers to be guiltie of great wickednefs, whereof I think I am free · he proclaimes me a "Vitiligator," that is "Vitiosus litigator," a man like Theon, a poet, "rabiosæ loquacitatis et petulantissimæ maledicentiæ," gnawing with my teeth on the good name of my neighbours; yea, a very Momus, eating up my owne bowels with envie, and that for a poor cause, that my neighbours are pleased to make use of good books, ("Nos vindicemus a quibusdam vitilitigatoribus, Theonino dente aliorum famam rodere conantibus,—libris cum scriptis tum impressis usi sumus, utimur, et utemur, rodente interim sua interiora Momo"); all my writes, for diverse whereof I have receaved thanks from the most judicious divines, not only of Scotland, bot of the Churches abroad, must be pronounced not only void of all learning, bot a foolish spending of my time in writing nothing bot fables and toyes; ("Neque eruditionem esse existimo in congerendis et confarciendis nugis et fabulis ætatem terere"), yea, I am declared to be possessed with a bitter fpirit, with bitternefs itfelff, with a fpirit plainly malignant, which I take to be no other than the devill: I muft be a kaill-wyfe crying out with her ftinking breath, and openly rageing; I muft be a falfe man, and without reafon; I muft be a beaft, a horfe, and that a furious one, running on my neighbors, ("Quidam hodie—fpiritu acerbo, et plane malignante, inftar habitus vetulæ olera vendentis, fefe oftentante, falfo et fine ratione debacchati funt,—non audentes fuum amarorem depromere,—inftar equi ferocientis invehuntur.") But that which is worft of all, I muft be dyted to the fchollers, and for my fake the Brethren of my mind, which I think none will deny to be amongft the beft divynes of the kingdome, for all good qualities, fuch as Mr Robert Dowglafs, Mr. David Dickfone, Mr. Robert Blair, Mr. James Wood, etc, we muft altogether be dyted a faction, fo great enemies to grace and pietie, that by our impious attempts piety is deftroyed, ("Homines quidam quorum impio conatu corrupta jacet pietas"); that we are men who greedily feek after vaine glory and popular applaufe and worldly wealth, ("Umbratilem honorem, inanem gloriam, ventofam vulgi famam, et alia hujus vitæ commoda, unice venantur et aucupantur"); that we count it a peft and ane epidemick difeafe that God is filling the kirks and the fchooles with a generation of young men, whofe eminent pietie and great learning does good to foules, which we with our impietie would corrupt, ("Res quæ eos angit eft peftis et morbus epidemicus, qua laborat ecclefia et ferme opprimitur, in fcholam irrepfit; foboles adolefcentum exorta eft quos Deus replevit vera pietate et egregus in omni literarum genere dotibus, in quos homines quidam, quorum impio conatu corrupta jacet pietas, invehuntur"); and, as if all this had been bot little, he imports, that he hes much worfe than what is expreffed alreadie, ("Cætera prætereo," "cætera taceo," "at pluribus parco.")

I wifh yow may fpeak to him of this his ftrange fact If he will ftand to the defence of it, I pray yow tell him from me, that whatever fenfe I may have of his exceeding great wrong, yet my purpofe is to be as a deaf man that heard not, and as a dumb man that openeth not his mouth; to be as a man that heareth not, and in whofe mouth are no reproofes; that not only at this tyme, when the whole land, Kirk, and State, are full of the fury of the Lord, and of the rebuke of our God, drinking the cup of trembling, and the dregs of the cup of the Lord's fury, while they that afflict us fay to our foule, bow downe that we may goe over, I purpofe, at the Lord's command, to lay downe my body as the ground and as the ftreet to them that will goe over; and after Chrift his example, to give my back to the fmiters, and my checks to them that pluck off the hair, and not to hide my face from fhame and fpitting; yea, if he pleafe to dyte alfmuch againft me to-morrow, and once a-week to write invectives of me to the end of the year, I can take them on my fhoulder, and bind them as a crowne unto me, as a part of my fufferings for righteoufnefs. Thefe many years bygane it hes been my refolved practife, wherein I purpofe, by God's grace, to continue, in all my perfonall injuries, to doe good for ill, to pray for them that perfecute me; fo I mind not to revenge, I require no fatiffaction, but profefs my only mind is, even through this outragious injurie, be vertew of Chrift's command, to doe to Mr. James a good turne, if it lye in my way.

This much I thought fitt to communicate unto yow, to be told to Mr. James, who, I think, will take it better from yow, at this tyme of his caufelefs anger, than from me. Now, leaft yow fhould think I had put a worfe conftruction on his words than they may bear, take that whole paffage I complaine off, in the beft and moft correct write I could find, when I had compared three of the beft written books I could get There is, indeed, fundrie things in this leffon whilk I fuppofe will trouble both yow and me to fett well together, for any good fence; bot in what I have touched, I think I have gueffed right enough at his meaning.

"ETSI magna pars anni jam elapfa fit, et temporis anguftiæ quibus ftringimur nos moveant ut ad finem Moralis Difciplinæ, in cujus amœnis hortis diu fpatiati fimus, properemus, ne tamen inter moralitatem actuum humanorum et ipfam virtutem moralem, nullius difcriminis confcientia convicti, aut nullius infirmitatis confcii, togam deponamus, et ex Almæ Matris ædibus rei clamitantes fugiamus, coacti fumus hic unum vel alterum verbum apponere, ut nos vindicemus a quibufdam vitilitigatoribus, Theonino dente aliorum famam rodere conantibus. Res eft, afferere audemus, Difputationes hafce Ethicas, et iis præmiffas Logicas, etfi proprio Marte concinnatas, non tamen effe lafcinias ex libris qua fcriptis qua impreffis, (neque exiftimo cordatum aliquem fcholafticum vitio vertere alicui uti libris, cum fcriptis tum impreffis, quibus ufi fumus, utimur, et utemur, rodente interim fua interiora Momo,) imprimis ex penu recentiffimorum Jefuitarum furreptas, aut confutam mendici pallam, aut confarcinatum multarum nugarum magnum centonem; neque refertas effe erroribus et veris in philofophia hærefibus, ex Jefuitarum doleis hauftus, five vanitate animi, five indolis protervia, five incauta prudentia, quod quidam hodie in doctores philofophiæ hujus regni, (quia in eos exiftimant fefe poffe impune licere, prætermiffis aliis in quos non audent fuum amarorem depromere,) fpiritu acerbo et plane malignante, inftar halitus vetulæ olera vendentis, fefe oftentante, falfo et fine ratione debacchati funt Sed vos eftis adolefcentes Fateor, fed adolefcentia non eft vitium fi cætera recte procedant, imo et plures ecclefiæ paftores funt adolefcentes, in quos dudum plura hujus farinæ deblaterata effent, nifi timor notæ impietatis et infamiæ, ab iis inuftæ quorum animi eorum pietate, eruditione, et fedulitate aluntur, extrinfeco obftaculo fuiffet. Sed vos eftis obtufi et ad docendum inepti, (cætera prætereo, quæ fi alicui, imprimis domino hæc blateranti imputanda funt, quod experientia, nunquam fatis dolenda, edocti demonftrare poffumus.) Ha, ha, hæ! Forfan verum, fed male a te ferimus; quædam a quibufdam, fed non ab omnibus Age ineatur fingulare certamen, agatur duello, in quo apparuerit quis ineptus, quis pinguis, quis craffus, quis obtufus, imo et quibus vel ob indolem, vel ob eruditionem (neque eruditionem effe exiftimo in congerendis et confarciendis nugis et fabulis ætatem terere) quibus adjiciatur, fi fit animus, ætas, bellius convenit doctorum philofophiæ cathedra, et quibus melius difcipulorum fubfellia. Sed quid multis? Hæc proprio gladio feipfa jugulant, aperta funt contradictoria; ac penes obtufum aliquem eft tot plauftra metaphyficarum quæftionum congerere, quas non omnes capiunt, multo minus intelligunt · iniqui igitur Judices, at pluribus parco. Res uno verbo eft quæ vos angit, peftis et morbus epidemicus qua laborat ecclefia, et ferme opprimitur, in fcholam irrepfit; nimirum Dei providentia in commodum ecclefiæ et reipublicæ literariæ, foboles adolefcentum exorta eft quos Deus replevit vera et fincera pietate in Deum, et egregiis in omni literarum genere dotibus, in quos homines quidam, quorum impio conatu (cætera taceo) corrupta jacet pietas (quod quidem mea fententia pejus eft quam difciplinas alicujus magiftelli arbitrio corruptas effe, quod neque concedimus, cum contrarium fit in aperto) inftar equi ferocientis invehuntur, quia fplendor pietatis et eruditionis illorum his præripit umbratilem honorem, inanem gloriam, ventofam vulgi famam, et alia hujus vitæ commoda, quæ unice venantur et aucupantur ·

[THE EARL OF LAUDERDALE TO MR. ROBERT BAILLIE [5]]

KIND FRIEND,

THOUGH it be a great refreſhment to me to hear from my friends that they are well, (which is all the intelligence I covet, and which can prejudice no bodie,) yet I thought yow had known me better than to believe that I would miſunderſtand your ſilence, or intertaine the leaſt doubt of your friendſhip, of which I have ſo many teſtimonies   Therefore, they did no right who informed yow that I was malcontent with your not writing; though I did expreſs a defyre to hear from yow, yet I am not ſo eaſily ſubject to take the pett, eſpeciallie at a friend of whoſe kindneſs I am ſo confident   I ſhall labour to obey your counſell, and doe ſtill defyre the continuance of your prayers in my behalf, for more ſubmiſſion to the good will of God, and for patience in this my condition, which, for ought I can fee, is not intended here to be altered in haſte.   But I will labour, through the grace of God, to have patience and not to make haſte ; for He that made tymes and ſeaſons, knows what is fitteſt for me, and will, in His due time, turne all to the beſt.   This is the ſtay and comfort of Yours,

LAUDERDAILL

London, the 14th March 1654

FOR MR THOMAS FULLER [4]

REVEREND SIR,

HAVING latelie, and but latelie, gone through your Holy Warr, and Deſcription of Paleſtine, I am fallen ſo in love with your pen, that I am ſorry I was not before acquaint with it, and with yourſelf, when from the

[5] This letter is miſplaced in Baillie's MS , as it occurs among letters written in 1656. It is in reply to his communication on the 10th of February 1654, *supra,* page 235, which therefore it ought to have followed

[4] The well known and much admired author of " The Hiſtory of the Worthies of England.' In Baillie's MS the name is written ' Fowler " This eminent historian and divine was created D D after the Restoration : his death, on the 15th August 1661, prevented his preferment to a Biſhopr

1643 to 1647, I lived at Worcefter Houfe, and preached in the Savoy, that then, when I had fome credite there, I might have ufed my beft endeavours to have done yow pleafure Yow feem to promife ane Ecclefiaftick Storie · it were a pity but it fhould be haftened ³ However I am one of thofe who could gladlie confent to the burning of many thoufand volumes of improfitable wiiters, that burthens and harms the world; yet there are fome pens whom I wifh did write much, of which your's is one. Mr Purchafe in his Pilgrimes, from the intelligence he had by Englifh and Dutch travellers and merchants, together with the printed treatifes of fome late Italian, Spanifh, and French writeis, gave us a very good accompt of the World, the whole Univerfe, the prefent condition of it, as in his time. I conceave no man were fitter than yow to let us know, in a handfome, fyne, and wyfe way, the State of the World as now it ftands. If the Lord would put in your heart to mind it, and give yow encouragement for fuch a performance, if yow would put out one part of it, were it the prefent ftate of Afia, I truft it fhould be fo accepted by judicious men, that yow fhould have from many all defireable encouragements for the perfyting of the reft. Your cartes are very neatly and fingularly well done. yow would not be fpareing of them. I wifh, in your Paleftine, yow added fome more, as one or two of Chaldæa, becaufe of many Scriptures relating to Babylon, Nineve, Ur, &c.; the voyage of Paul; fome cartes of the prefent ftate, joyned with thefe of the old Scripturall ftate, as of Egypt, Jerufalem, &c. For thefe and the like happy labours, we, at fo great a diftance, can but encourage yow with praife, love, and prayers to God; which yow fhall have, I promife yow, from me, as one who very highly pryfes the two wrytes I have feen of your hand, and judges by thefe that the reft yow have done or fhall doe, will be of the fame excellencie. The Lord blefs yow and all your intentions; So prays

Your very loveing and much honouring Brother,

Glafgow in Scotland, Auguft 22d 1654. R B.

³ Fullers work, "The Church History of Britain, from the Birth of Jesus Christ until the year 1648," the publication of which Baillie was desirous might be hastened, appeared in 1656, folio The author, in his address to the Reader, in his usual quaint manner, thus mentions a similar wish expressed by another friend " An ingenious gentleman some months since, in jest-earnest, advised me to make haste with my History of the Church of England ; ' for fear (said he) lest the Church of England be ended before the History thereof' "

REVERENDISSIMO CLARISSIMOQUE VIRO D. GISBERTO VOETIO, S. LITER-
ARUM PROFESSORI IN ACADEMIA ULTRAJECTINA

REVERENDISSIME VIR,

SINGULARIS tua in me coram humanitas, et amica femel iterumque per literas falutatio, imprimis vero eximium illud et nunquam obliterandum officium, de quo interea temporis per epiftolam multas ferio gratias habui, Belgica meæ ad Bramblium replicæ editio Ultrajecti; ifta omnia faciunt ut jam aufus fim ad te tranfmittere binos hofce tractatulos, quos nuper in ftudiofæ noftræ juventutis gratiam publicavi : priorem grammaticum, cujus tria habes exemplaria; eorum unum tua cura deferri cupio Lugdunum D Golio, et alterum Bafileam Joanni Buxtorphio, eo fine quem in præfatione indigito. Utinam hac occafione a viris præftantiffimis, tibi, nullus dubito, amiciffimis et intus notis, tua auctoritate impetres meum multorumque defiderium; tres intelligo Praxes, Chaldaico-Syriacam, Rabbinico-Maforeticam, et Arabicam. Magna ifta beneficia non folum auctoribus, fed etiam tibi exoratori, Chriftianæ omnes fcholæ lubentes debebunt. Si vero contingat, quod nollem, ut uterque de quacunque feu caufa feu prætextu refugiat puerilem illum quidem, etfi viris, ut ego arbitror, fatis dignum laborem, et academiis omnibus, fat fcio, perutilem, habes, ni fallor, ex tuis difcipulis non paucos, qui tuo hortatu animati et confilio inftructi, omnes iftas Praxes, parvo tempore magna fua cum laude et aliorum commodo, poffunt edere. Egregius tuus in commoda fcholarum zelus longe lateque dudum innotuit; ut hoc etiam ipfis beneficium velis quam fieri poteft mature procurare, multorum eft defiderium, et mea magna fpes. Illic vos habetis, præter alia fupra nos, ingens commodum Latinorum, Græcorum, Hebraicorum, et Arabicorum typographos, qui meditata veftra omnia eleganter et emendate ftatim imprimunt. Quidni ex Parifienfibus et jam Londinenfibus Bibliis edant ilh, in ftudioforum et fuum etiam amplum commodum, feorfim Biblia Arabica et Syriaca, cum interlineari Latino; quotufquifque enim eft qui cæterorum omnium fumptui ferendo par eft?

Verum id quod animum meum magis folicitum habet, eft radicatum jam in omnibus Proteftantium fcholis cacoethes; artium et philofophiæ Encyclopædia nullibi, quantum intelligo, ea accuratia traditur, quam vel doctorum vel difciplinarum dignitas poftularet. In Jefuitarum, aliorumque monachorum Hifpanorum, Gallorum, Italorum, et Germanorum, curfibus verfandis noftri difcipuli omne fuum tempus propemodum conterunt: quantum hoc eft noftris Academiis cum dedecus tum detrimentum? Nulline in Ifraele fabri? Quamdiu nos ad Philiftæos ob exacuenda ferramenta defcendere cogemur? Præter alia multa hujufce pudendi mali incommoda, annon nimis quam multi noftrorum adolefcentum a teneris ipfis unguiculis ea hauriunt incauti principia, quorum odorem tetrum et venenatum non nifi fero et difficulter, fi modo unquam, eluunt? Præter ea quæ corruptarum mentium magiftri dedita opera infpergunt, ut inde retia et laquei difcipulis tendantur, quibus aliquando pertrahantur ad tranfubftantiationis, adorationis imaginum, liberi arbitrii, Trinitatis in unitate, duarum naturarum in una perfona inconfiftentiæ, et alia Pontificiorum, Arminianorum, Socinianorum praviffima dogmata; probe nofti quæ fatuus hæreticus Cartefius fub novæ fuæ et perfectioris philofophiæ velo molitus fit. Profecto non parum intereft Ecclefiis Reformatis, ut orthodoxum, folidum, et perfpicuum philofophiæ corpus, tam fyftematicum quam textuale et quæftionarium, exftet, in communem, fi fieri poffet, omnium Academiarum ufum. Erant apud nos non ita pridem multi egregii philofophi, qui, fi id agere voluiffent, curfus philofophicos non contemnendos publico dediffe poterant; fed ea hodie noftras Ecclefias et fcholas una cum regno calamitas premit, ut a nobis nihil ejufmodi jam fit expectandum Nefcio fi in Anglia aut Gallia fratres ullos in præfentiarum habeamus, quibus volentibus fimul et valentibus onus hoc poffet imponi. Quantum hactenus intelligere potui, ratio tradendæ philofophiæ locis iftis ad hunc diem apud noftros curta nimis fuit et fuperficiaria. Unica in vobis reftat fpes. Exiftimo in veftro Belgio, etiam in Helvetia, Haffia, ac Palatinatu reperiri viros, a quorum eruditione et induftria, modo huic operæ ferio incumbere a quoquam perfuaderentur, pulchra adeo liberarum omnium artium et philofophiæ Encyclopædia poffet exfpectari; ut eam omnes, certe permultæ Proteftantium fcholæ, magnis cum gratiis ambabus ulnis amplecterentur; quæ magno cum fructu, magnaque cum voluptate ftudiofis prælegeretur, qua dictatorum hodie a regentibus, ut nos folemus nuncupare, multi defectus fupplerentur, errata corrigerentur, plurimi abufus apud multos, alias incorrigibiles, profligarentur, et a Proteftanti nomine fœda dedecoris nota tandem aliquando ablueretur. cum non ultra neceffe haberemus ad Pontificiorum philofophorum infectiffimas lacunas tenellam nostram juventutem emandare, dicam an prutrudere? Systemata logica, ethica, physica, et metaphysica dudum accepimus a doctissimis et summe industriis viris Keckermanno, Burgersdicio, Scheiblero, et a Vossio rhetorica, sed quod ultra desideramus est, præter libros commode suis incipientibus fundamenta. Aristotelici etiam textus in logicis, ethicis, et metaphysicis, brevis ac perspicua explicatio, partibus quæ nostro sæculo non sunt accommodatæ omissis, et ad singula capita aut saltem libros subjecta quæstionum et locorum communium vulgarium paulo fusior enodatio, sed brevior, nervosior, et clarior quam suis hodie discipulis Jesuitæ tradunt. Mathematicorum etiam corpus plenum et ad juventutis usus accommodatum nolles negligi. Aliæden sceleta non satisfaciunt. Unam Academiarum curatores auctoritate, consilio, hortatibus, præmiis, aut etiam imperio, professores suos a lopus hocce perficiendum vellent impellere: præsens posteræque ætates, mihi persuadeo, gratissimam et utilissimam hujusce sementis metlem demeterent. Multoties hac de re anxie et majori cum dolore quam ipse meditanti, unus tu occurrebas, qui mihi videbare apud omnes nostrorum in Germania et Helvetia Academias, ea merito auctoritate pollere, eaque instrui prudentia, ac boni publici zelo flagrare, ut, si quis alius, posses, Deo tuis conatibus aspirante, vires huic cœpto perficiendo non ineptos reperire, repertosque illis a teipso et aliis incitamentis animare, ut non illubentes velint, Deo reformatis Ecclesiis, nostrae huic et sequentibus sæculis, laudatissimam hanc suam operam collocare. Meministi etiam quot et quam salebrosæ chronologorum quæstiones, eæque ad diserta Scripturæ verba elucidanda necessariæ, in tenebris adhuc jaceant. Quantopere nuper apud nostros fervere solebat hoc studium, Scaligeri, Funccii, Bucholceri, Calvisii, Capelli, Emmii, et aliorum laudatissimi labores demonstrant: hanc nobis gloriam Jesuitæ nunc ereptum eunt voluminosis Saliani, Petavii, Tornielli et aliorum scriptis. An nemo quisquam est vel in Belgio vel Helvetia, vel in superiori Germania, qui volens est et sciens huic vacare curæ?

Multi jam sunt anni ex quo Bibliothecam edidisti, valde desideratur editio ejus altera cum auctario; sed quod ante omnia studiosi hic omnes a te expetunt, est cæterarum tuarum Disputationum publicatio, cui dudum in primo volumine obstrinxisti tete occlamitant, et mirantur qui tam tardum nomen evaseris. Propinquum, nuperum, et dolendum nimis Spanhemii (heu qualis theologi!) exemplum docere te potest, quam maturanda, imo festinanda fint omnia quæ habes in fcriniis; nimis quam multorum pofthumi labores variis cafibus perierunt.

Vides quam familiariter in tuum finum effuderim animi mei fenfa, confidens fummum tuum candorem æqui bonique omnia confulturum.

Quod ad alterum meum tractatulum, adolefcentibus etiam noftris deftinatum, fi quid in eo veritati non confonet, oro doceas, ut quanto ocius corrigatur. Tandem finio, Dominum venerans, velit tibi largiri multos et felices dies, quo fuo honori, et Ecclefiarum emolumento ac folamini aliquandiu adhuc in terris alacer infervias. Votum hoc eft fratris tui obfervantiffimi,

R B.

Glafguæ, Idibus Septembris 1654.

Poft Syftemata, apud nos præleguntur a magiftris Ariftotelis Organon, Ethica ad Nicomachum, Phyfica Acroafis, de Generatione et Corruptione, de Cœlo, Meteoris, et Anima. Librorum illorum exemplaria pauca admodum fuperfunt vel Londini vel Amfterodami. Si tuo monitu veftri typographi vellent recudere Organon, cum verfione et notis Pacii, fimiliter Ethicam, cum notis Riccoboni, et Phyfica, cum verfione et notis editionum priorum, officium facerent nobis pergratum, et fibi ipfis, ut arbitror, perutile.

REVERENDO ET CLARISSIMO VIRO ROBERTO BALÆO, THEOLOGIÆ IN ACADEMIA GLASCUENSI PROFESSORI DIGNISSIMO.

REVERENDE et clariffime Vir, Frater in Chrifto obfervande, tuas Eid. Septembris fuperioris anni ad me fcriptas tandem accepi circa 13 aut 14 Martii conjunctas cum fcriptione communis amici noftri D. Gul Spangii, 8 Martii. Nunc tandem ad fingula literis tuis contenta, ordine refpondeo Quod ad exemplaria utrufque libelli a te in gratiam ftudioforum editi, pro dono et opera impenfa gratias tibi debeo et ago quas poffum maximas. Catechefin Elencticam, compendiofe ex Scripturarum fontibus propofitam, video imprimis Anglis et Scotis tuis effe neceffariam. Quod fi adverfarii eam admordere incipiant (de quo exulcerata hæc tempora vix dubitare me finunt) dabitur tibi infignis occafio objectionum et exceptionum folutionibus opufculum hoc tuum locupletandi. Manuductionem tuam Analyticam puto omnibus φιλεβραίοις abunde fatiffacturam. Nihil ergo in illo ftudii genere reftabit, quam ut textum Biblicum quotidie legant et relegant, eumque quam familiariffimum fibi reddant, confultis, ubi opus fuerit, Buxtorfii Epitome Radicum, et incomparabili Thefauro Grammatico Hanc matrem ubi quis fibi conciliarit, haud difficulter filiam quamvis exambiet Sunt illæ in univerfum fex, aut, fi mavis, feptem; Rabbinica, Talmudica, Chaldaica, Samaritana, Syriaca, Arabica, Æthiopica. 1 Manuductionem ad intelligentiam Rabbinifmi, quem ufurpant commentatores textuales feu grammatici (quorum lectio theologis utiliffima, pene neceffaria) propediem dabit clariff. collega nofter Joannes Leufden, in hac Academia Hebraicæ Linguæ profeffor: fudet enim fub prælo propheta Jonas, cum Rabbinorum commentariis, ut et utraque Mafora, punctatis et in Latinum tranflatis, cum fubjecta analyfi grammatica et notis. Iftius libelli folo ductu, abfque præceptore in legendis omnibus Rabbinicis commentariis, iftius fcilicet generis quos Peroufchin appellare folent, pro arbitrio σὺν θεῷ pergere poterunt vulgares quique ftudiofi Rabbinicos commentarios allegoricos, quos Derafchim appellant, fi quis iftarum rerum curiofus tanti faciat, illos proprio Marte fcrutari poterit, quifquis abbreviaturas Buxtorfii et Lexicon ejufdem Rabbinicum ad manum habuerit. 2. Talmudicæ cognitionem longe faciliorem nunc reddidit editio Mifchaniot, cum punctis Amftelodami adjectis; facillimam vero reddet interpretatio interlinearis aut marginalis Latina alicujus faltem tractatus cum aliquo capite τοῦ Gemara, adjecta analyfi grammatica et notis. Hanc operam non gravate in fe fufcipiet laudatus modo collega. Ita via patebit doctrinæ Talmudicæ ftudiofis ad totum Talmud, auxiliante Lexico Rabbinico Buxtorfii nunquam fatis laudando. 3 Chaldaicam dialectum jam fatis mihi vifus illuftraffe Buxtorfius in Grammatica Chaldaica et Syriaca, cui exercitatio fubjecta· plura fi quis forte defideret, is poterit uti Jonæ paraphrafi Chaldaica, cum verfione, analyfi grammatica, et notis, a collega noftro edendis. Adminicula perpetua hic erunt Lexicon Rabbinicum Buxtorfii (quod etiam Targumica omnia explicat) et Lexicon Syro-Chaldaicum Buxtorfii filii, in 4°. 4. Samaritana dialectus, quamvis ab Hebraica et Chaldaica parum differat, difficilis tamen prima fronte apparet, quod alio plane charactere utatur Cœpi agere et porro agam cum D. Niffelio, qui Lugduni Batavorum privatim vexillum linguarum orientalium effert, ut capita aliquot Pentateuchi Samaritani, ex magnis Bibliis Parifienfibus excerpta, cum notis et tranflatione excudi curet. 5. Syriacæ dialecti notitiam etiam complanavit Buxtorfius in Grammatica modo dicta, ubi etiam exercitatio comparet Unum folummodo deeft, quod charactere Syro deftitutus fuerit typographus; fed nuper defectum illum fupplevit Dilcherus, qui Grammaticam hujus linguæ, cum exercitatione, vocabulis Syris Syro charactere expreffis, publicavit tit Eclogarum Syriacarum. Lexicon Syriacum, fi quis requirat, indico illi Crinefii et Buxtorfii filii; fed utrumque ex folo Novo Teftamento et Rituali Severi collectum. Nunc, quia Parifiis etiam Vetus Teftamentum Syriace editum fuit, Lexica augenda erunt 6. Arabicæ dialecti Grammaticam et exercitationem dedit Erpenius, quæ fufficere videtur. Poftea legant ftudiofi D Niffehi epiftolas Jacobi, Johannis, Judæ, Arabice cum punctis et verfione Latina. Hoc labore peracto, inoffenfo pede pergant ad reliquos facros, aut alios libros quos nancifci poterunt, comitante ipfos Lexico Arabico D. Golii. 7. Æthiopica dialectus, ex Chaldaica et Arabica conflata, nullo fere labore addifci poterit, et quidem proprio Marte, ab iis qui Arabicæ et Chaldaicæ plane rudes non funt. Libri antehac difficulter haberi potuerunt. Ego folo Pialterio Æthiopico, una cum Gr. Heb. Lat., Coloniæ per Joh. Potkens emiffo, hucufque ufus fum, ut retinerem et augerem quæ, manu ducente ad pauculas horas amico iftius linguæ fatis gnaro, cœperam alphabetare. Sed nuper D. Niffelius Æthiopice Jacobi, Johannis, et Judæ Epiftolas, cum verfione Latina nobis impertivit, et fpem fecit epiftolas Petri propediem fecuturas. Hunc ergo libellum comparent fibi ftudiofi, et in eo ftudii hujus tyrocinia ponant. Extant Grammaticæ duæ Romæ excufæ, ideoque non ita parabiles. Ernefti Joh. Gerardi, filii celebris theologi Lutherani Joh. Gerardi, Grammatica Harmonica, Hebr. Chald. Syr. Arab. Æthiop. in 4°. ftudiofis ad alia properantibus abunde fufficiet Lexicon Æthiopicum Wenmeri in tranfalpinis bibliopoliis non extat, præterquam quod longe auctius defideretur; et multo magis fcriptores Æthiopici, qui an alicujus pretii illic extent, aut etiam integra Biblia, hactenus fciri non potuit. Feruntur effe miffalia feu liturgica fcripta; fed ut olim Græcorum, fic hodie Romanorum fidei parum aut nihil tribuendum eft. Fuerunt viri docti, qui alias quafdam linguas orientales Hebraicæ filias, aut propagines, aut dialectos ftatuerunt, fed imperite, cum omnes fint linguæ peculiares. Propter Hebraicam ergo, aut cum refpectu ad eam et ad philologiam facram, tales a theologis conferri haud opus. Inter eas tres funt, quæ charactere Arabico utuntur, Perfica, Turcica, Malacica; quod forte viros doctos in errorem duxit. Duæ, ut vocabulis, fic etiam charactere ab Hebraica reliquisque ejus dialectis distinctissimæ sunt, Armenica scilicet, et antiqua Coptica, seu Ægyptiaca Hodierna Ægyptiaca ante 400 annos introducta, aut potius facta vulgaris, est ipsissima Arabica Has quinque orientales si quis ex abundanti a limine salutaverit, operam non luserit, sed non puto operæ pretium facturum quenquam theologorum, si in penetralia earum se immiserit, antequam rariores et præstantiores scriptores viderit ad scopum suum aliqua ratione facientes. Multa de Coptica Athanasius Kircherus in Copto Prodromo, multa de Persica alii, plura de Armenica nonnulli buccinant; sed manus oculatæ sunt, credunt quod vident. Libelli parænetici seu morales, liturgici, rhythmico-poetici, catechismi papistici, mythologici, non tantum temporis merentur Satis mihi fuit acquisita facultate legendi, et perlustratis grammaticis, partem aliquam in scriptore delibasse, tum ut curiositati meæ satisfacerem, tum ut proprio judicio discernere, et propriis oculis videre possem, an linguæ illæ essent distinctæ ab Hebraica, cum dialectis seu filiabus, an vero ei propius aut remotius affines. Hactenus plus satis de linguis

De chronologia non ita solicitus sum, cum copia magis scriptorum hic laboremus quam inopia. Unum solum meo judicio restat, ut quis historiarum professor, aut potius minister, unus atque alter vicarius, (illi enim in minoribus ecclesiis mole negotiorum minus premuntur,) ex omnibus scriptoribus chronologicis, tam pontificiis quam nostris, magnam partem a me in Bibliotheca Theologica indicatis, methodum artis chronologicæ colligat, per definitiones et divisiones, ad exemplum Alstedii in Præcognitis Theologicis, et Scaligeri in Canonibus Isagogicis; additis ad singula capita quæstionibus et controversiis, cum rationibus in utramque partem adferri solitis, et indicatis quorumcunque auctorum libris ac nominibus. In secunda parte hujus artis, quam canonicam vocant, velim tantum annos ab initio mundi usque in hunc diem per ætates, intervalla, articulos, et secula, quasi in tabella distribui, et singulis quæstiones et controversias cum rationibus utrinque allatis subjici Videbo an uni atque alteri ex nostratibus ministris opus hoc commendari queat.

Accedamus nunc ad philosophiæ curium, de quo maxime laboratur Systemata, compendia, synopses tecum relinquo Certe in illis plus satis præstitum videtur Restat solummodo, ut controversiæ logicæ, physicæ, metaphysicæ, imprimis, deinde etiam ethicæ ac politicæ, (quæ tamen ad theologiam pleraque si rejiciantur, nihil absurdi committitur,) accurate, breviter, perspicue ventilentur, et rationes atque exceptiones utriusque partis examinentur; ac tandem pro veritate, hoc eft, pro philofophia, facris literis atque orthodoxiæ ancillante, determinetur, contra recentiores Suarezium, Conimbricenfes, Ruvium, Telefium, Baranzanum, Oviedo, Mendoza, Vafquez, imprimis protervum paradoxium et novaturientem fophiftem Ariaga, ad hæc, contra Taurellum, Gorlæum, Cartefium, et Cartefianos, Socinianos, Remonftrantes, Libertinos. Ariftotelis textum an feorfim cum brevibus et perfpicuis notis, et generali librorum ac capitum analyfi, feu hypothefi, per modum tabellæ excudi conveniat, an vero potius cum curfu quæftionum feu controverfiarum, nondum ftatuere poffum. Certe prolixi illi libri Metaphyficorum vix ullo ordine confcripti, et farraginem multarum rerum continentes, non videntur juventuti facro ftudio deftinatæ proponendi. Totius mathefeos concretæ, muficæ fcilicet, ftaticæ, opticæ, aftronomiæ, geographiæ, illuftriores quæftiones in fafciculum ex præftantioribus artificibus colligendæ, præmiffis folum elementis neceffariis, ex arithmetica, geometria, fpherica, mufica collectis Syftemata ipfa ftaticæ, aftronomiæ, geographiæ, opticæ, ftudiofi dictis elementis imbuti, abfque manuductione fuo tempore legerent. Hoc quidem confilium noftrum effet. Quibus autem hac tempeftate tam utile opus demandandum fit, et a quibus expectandum, fateor me nondum videre. Si enim veftrarum quatuor Academiarum tam præclarum inftitutum in fpongiam incubuit, quid de noftris Belgicis fperandum? Quædam ex illis per Cartefianam philofophiam graviter concuffæ funt; aliæ inteftinis fuper eadem philofophia diffidiis admodum adhuc vacillant et fluctuant, turbonibus nufquam figentibus, nufquam quiefcentibus; fobrie philofophantibus contra obnitentibus, et hoc unice agentibus ut clavum teneant, nec fluctibus opprimantur. Nifi Deus ex alto nos refpexiffet, jam præfentiffimum periculum alicubi imminebat, trahendum ad partes theologiæ; ita impletum fuiffet in nobis, quod Bernardus de ecclefia paulatim collapfa olim pronunciabat: "In pace mea amaritudo amariffima," etc. Quod fi hæc tempeftas aliquando defæviat, et non amplius protrudantur in cathedras philofophicas novi philofophaftri, et ftulti ac petulantes juvenculi, tum demum nobis de curfibus philofophicis conjuncta Academiarum opera adornandis cogitandum effet De Palatinatu, Haffia, aliifque Germaniæ partibus, fruftra verba facimus; quod fcholis nondum aut vix inftauratis, veterani et exercitati philofophi illic non fuppetant, quod fciam, qui fubtiliter et erudite graviffimis controverfiis ventilandis, et ad theologiæ ftabilimentum adaptandis fufficiant Celebris nunc apud Gallos et Helvetios est Derodo, professor philosophiæ Arausionensis, qui cursum logicum, physicum, metaphysicum, ethicum dicitur editurus. Admodum subtilis audit, et utriusque philosophiæ, tam pontificiæ quam nostræ, peritus. Amplius inquiram in Theses Academicas ipsius, et librum quendam Gallicum de Eucharistia, contra pseudo-philosophemata Papistica editum, ut ex ungue leonem cognoscam : ut quidem quasdam ipsius disputationes ann. 1648. editas cursim inspicio, deprehendo eum in tota physica satis esse paradoxum Atque hæc de instauranda in Academiis philosophia.

Exemplar libri tui D. Golio destinatum curavi, atque una literis meis ad ipsum consilium et votum tuum de adminiculis linguarum orientalium significavi ; sed nihil responsi hactenus recepi. Alterum exemplar D. Buxtorfio transmittam, simul ac studiosus quis eo peregrinaturus obtulerit De statu ecclesiæ vestræ in particulari parum aut nihil hic certo cognoscimus non definimus tamen eam precibus nostris Deo commendare Post tenebras lucem speramus. Hoc omnibus vobis agendum, ut ἀκρίβειαν doctrinæ reformatæ cum simplicitate rituum ac regiminis religiose custodiatis, atque una praxin pietatis qua publice qua privatim studiose promoveatis. Quod ut quisque nostrum in sua statione ex animo velit et agat, Deum nostrum in Christo supplex veneror.

Tui observantiss.

Ultrajecti, Eid. Ap. cɪɔ ɪɔc.lv   GISBERTUS VOETIUS.

For his Reverend and Weel-Belovit Brother Mr J Hamiltoun, Minister at Edinburgh.[6]

JAMES,

I HOPE you gott myn of October 1. Mr. George [Young] heirwith gives you ane account of our Sinod, and Mr Ja. F[ergusson], which I sent you on Friday,[7] ane account of their Comittee efter the Synod Mr. Ja. Fer hes ondertaken for some in Irwin, and I am doing heir for Mr. Melvill ; you shall get ane ac-

[6] From the original in Wodrow MSS Folio Vol. XXVI, No 16 It is entirely in Baillie's own hand, but his peculiar and scarcely intelligible orthography has not been closely followed Wodrow indorsed this letter as written in 1656, but it belongs to the previous year

[7] Fergusson's letter, dated "Glasgow, October 5th 1655," is preserved in the same Vol No 6.

count of it ere long. M. P. G[illefpie,] and S. G[eorge] Maxwell, and Mr. Alex. Dunlope, puipofes to be there on Tuyfday, with Broghil and Munk, to tak of their party all thefe calumnies which Mr. R. Trayl wreit you had laid on them. Be on your guard, for they ar to prefs you for a meeting for Union I fheu them a meeting was needlefs, till firft they gave their fence of our Overtur at our laft meeting; which, for that end, I gave them. I think you would ftand by our laft conclufion, that it is needlefs for us to meet who have deliverit our full mynd to them, except they can cum to it, or towards it If you agree with the Inglifh, you need feir them the lefs. It feems Mr P G as he hes crufhit Wariftoun and M. Guthry's motion of the Covenant, fo he is refolut to cary on the Union, contrary to their mynd, though they fould divid on it, if fo he be fure to be accomodat for himfelf. A paper is neceffar to aunfuer your former arg[uments] of piayer for the King, even in cafe of fuffering; (call no needlefs meeting of thefe who ar farr off; wher your letters may do as weell: faill no to let us knou all you ar doing;) I can not aunfuer, (nor can I find in my hert to affay it,) what was brought from the Covenant for that deuty. Let fome there be cairfull to fatiffie Mr. Thomas Boyd: M. R. Douglas knoues him, he is a zelous man for our caufe, to his pith, and, if onfatiffied, he may ftumble a multitude of good people he walkes among. My fervice to your kind D. [daughter?]

Yours,

October 8[th 1655] R B.

Nothing I faw from you the laft week.

They who have redd the New Covenant, fayes it's a very fhreud peice, of tuo fheet of paper. It would [fhould] be fearcht for[8] with all poffible cair. it declairs the mynd of thefe who are foi it, to ftate the fhifme of our Church for ever; it reveels more of their purpofes. They profefs this their motion for Union is their *ultimus conatus ;* and if it faill on our fyd, fome of them fpeeks of ane Eraftian Comittee from the Inglifh, of gentilmen and minifters, to purge and plant all the land. Albeit I tak this for a vain boaft, which

---

[8] This alludes to a paper on " Perſonal Covenanting," which was drawn up by some of the Protesters at this time, but with no intention on their part wholly to renounce the former Covenants. Baillie *infra* p 297, attributes it to Guthrie, but he evidently had not seen the paper itself, the copies of which, as never formally adopted, were not allowed to get into circulation.

fundry of themfelf ar againft, yit you had need to be very warry of Mr P G[illefpie] at this tyme, both of his dealing with you for Union, and with the Inglifh for pouer to their fyd. The Lord give you wifdom, courage, and diligence at this nick of tym. I wifh Mr. Wood and Mr. Kerr wer with you. I think if they agree, it's to fkrew themfelf in the reft of the Sinods and Prefbiteries, whence now they ar excludit, to act, with our confent, all the materialls of their New Covenant.

To Mr. WILLIAM SPANG.

Cousin,

I GOE on to give yow ane account of our affaires where I left, in my laft long letter. The Lord has given myfelf above this twelvemoneth much more peace than I had before, and than I expected upon this occafion Yow heard the overtures we proponed for the Union of our Synod, which were the leaft we could receave before we fhould joyne. Though among ourfelves unanimouflie we had agreed to keep up our part of the Synod, if the fubftance of all thefe were not granted, and the brether of Edinburgh, to whom I went for advyce, had approven that our refolution; and the chief of the prefbyteries of Aire and Irvine, with whom I had mett alfo at Irvine, had agreed to adhere to thefe overtures; and if they, being *minimum quod fic*, fhould be refufed, they concluded to fet up their two prefbyteries in a fynod by themfelves, according to their ancient priviledge acknowledged in all our late Generall Affemblies, alfo, when we mett at our fynod, thefe on our fide agreed agane to adhere to former refolutions: Notwithftanding, when the brethren of the other fide had peremptorilie refufed our overtures, and drawne on a new conference, to try if two of each fide, particularlie Mr. James Fergufone and Mr George Young for us, Mr. James Durhame and Mr Patrick Gillefpie for them, could fall on any other overtures which might unite us, thefe four among themfelves condefcended to the inclofed paper (A.), and ingaged themfelves to doe their beft to perfuade others thereto. When I did fee the paper, I fand clearlie, that the finall determination of all things was left in the fynod, whereof Remonftrants were the pluralitie; and that no remeid was left us againft the oppreffion, either in purging or planting, that was for any purpofe ; and that this agreement was a clear receding from our former determination   I did not yield to it : yet fear from the Remonftrants violence, and love of peace, and hope, by yielding, to make them more moderat, made the moft declare their contentment to accept of it, the neutrals of Aire, Mr. Cobroun and others, were fo much for it, that they threatened to joyne with the others if we refufed it; all they of Lanerik were willing to accept of it ; all of Glafgow, except one; and of Dumbartane except two, and of Irvine except two. Finding it fo, I was glad at my heart that a fair door to my private peace was opened ; for not being willing to accept of the termes of that agreement, I had a clear reafon to abfent myfelf from the fynod and prefbyterie, united on fo unjuft termes   The brethren of my former mind finding me refolute not to joyne with them, were defirous to keep with me, efpeciallie the authors of the late overture, Mr. Fergufone and Mr Young. Bot this by no means I would permitt ; for they having declared almoft all their willingnefs to unite on thefe mean termes, I would not have them diaw back, contrare to their minds, upon my diffent : fo with much adoe I got them to joyne, and let me, and a few more, ferve my owne mind of abftaining from their united meetings. This hitherto I have done, to the great quietnefs of my owne mind, and freedome of the very frequent and vexatious janglings, wherewith, in all meetings, I was wont exceedinglie to be troubled · only I am grieved to fee my predictions too truehe to come to pafs ; the Remonftrators, as unqueftionablie mafters, to doe within the bounds of the fynod whatever they think expedient. Mr. Archibald Denniftone, without any confiderable fault, they depofed   when he fled to the Englifh, Mr. Patrick Gillefpie, as I forefaw, by his greater credite, ftopped all hearing there. Mr David Adamfone, though of many libelled fcandalls they got not one proven, yet ftill they keep on the pannell, and our moft regular plantation of Mr James Ramfay, Mr. Archibald Inglifh, and one in Robertoun, they will have annulled, and the moft irregular plantations of their men to ftand. At their next dyett they will fall on whom they pleafe, without controll. However, being free of publict debates, without, as I think, my oune procurement, but the rafh imprudence (if not the too much wifdome) of others, I am glad.

I was like to have been more troubled by another defigne of a larger Union. Mr. Durhame goeing through Saint Andrewes to his houfe of Purie, he fell with Mr. Blair to refume his old counfells of a generall union with the Remonftrators, by ane overtuie of oblivion of bygones. For this end, Mr. Blair and he deall with Mr. Wood to be content of a conference at Edinburgh upon that fubject, together with the other purpofes we were much vexed with, prayer for the King, and admiffion of complyers to the communion, alfo they went on to defigne the conferrers. For us they named Mr. Robert Dowglafs, Mr David Dickfon, Mr Hew Mackell, Mr. W Raite, Mr William Dowglafs of Aberdeene, Mr. John Robifone of Dundee, Mr James Wood, Mr. James Fergufone and me. For the other, Mr. James Guthrie, Mr. Patrick Gillefpie, Mr. John Livingftone, Mr. Samuel Rutherfoord, Mr Robert Traile, Mr. John Carftares, Mr. Samuell Auften, and fome three more So foon as I heard of this motion fo farr advanced, I was much feared for the confequence of it, and therefore writ to Mr. David Dickfon to beware of the danger; and being Weft, called Mr. John Bell, Mr William Ruffell, and Mr Robert Wallace, to advyfe on it. All of them were afraid of the iffue; yet none would be at the paines of rideing to Edinburgh to confult about it. This I behooved to doe myfelfe. When I came there, I fand the brethren not at all minding the matter; but fetting the hazard before their eyes, I got them roufed up to look about them, and to commiffionat me to bring from the Weft whom I thought fitt for that conference, to write themfelves to Mr. Knox and Mr. Jamifone, with others in the South, and to Mr. Robert Young, Mr. James Sharpe, and others in the North, to be prefent. When we came to the meeting, I was glad the danger was not fo great as I apprehended. The Remonftrators had as little a mind to unite with us as we with them. Mr. Patrick Gillefpie indeed, and Mr. John Carftares, and a few others, were for capitulating; but Warnftone, Mr James Guthrie, and others, were as rigid as ever; yea, whether by their contriveing or otherwayes, it wes fo, that we could have no conference. We had drawne up ane overture, as we thought, very favourable, and fo far as we could goe (C.1.), according to the Affemblie's late overture for union (C 2.), and by the hands of the tryfters, Mr. Blair, and Mr. Durhame, fent it into their meeting: alfo the tryfters had given us both their overtures (D) to be thought upon; but the Remonftrators told us, in regard of Mr Rutherfoord's and Mr Livingftone's abfence, they could not at that time engage in a conference; and therefore defyred a new meeting We were not content that they had made us travell in vaine, and thought not fitt to appoint a meeting, till they mett among themfelves, and confidered the paper we had given to them, if they could acquiefce to it, or fend us any better whereto we could acquiefce : upon the advertifement of fome probabilitie of accommodation from Mr. Dickfon to us, and Mr. Traile to them, there might be a meeting fo foone as they thought fit Soe, after a little prefacing by delegates from both meetings, we parted before we entered in any conference We underftood, that our overture was laughen at by their high ftomacks ; and as for that of Mr. Blair's, we were offended all of us with it, as granting to the Remonftrators almoft all their unreafonable defyres. For this we expoftulated fharply enough with Mr. Blair, and he with us. But he was much more offended with the other ; and both he and Mr. Durhame faid, that fo long as Warıftone and Mr. James Guthrie did guide that partie, there could no peace be poffible.

Though the great and much talked-of errand of our meeting had evanıfhed, yet we conferred among ourfelves, and with Mr Blair, Mr. Durhame, Traile, Stirling, and Carftares, on other things for good purpofe. For a number of years, the communion had not been celebrate in Edinburgh, Glafgow, St. Andrewes, Dundee, etc moft becaufe all the Magiftrates were fo deep in complying with the Inglifh, that they wer excludit from the table by the Act of our Church, and long conftant practife, except they declared their repentance, which they would not doe, nor durft we crave it of them : alfo they were fo importunat to have the communion, and impatient to be longer excluded, that they were on headie and evill defignes againft us, if we gave them not fatiffaction herein. The Minifters of Edinburgh inclined to admitt them on very fmall acknowledgement We in Glafgow were all for that, except Mr Durhame and myfelfe, albeit we were both much modified at that time ; bot thefe of St. Andrewes were very averfe from their admiffion, except on conditions not to be expected from them. For this end, they had fent us a long paper (F); yet, after fome dayes conference, we came to agree to admitt them on a generall teftimonie in our doctrine againft their complyance, and private admonifhing of them to repent for it, laying it on their confcience to come or not as they thought good. We thought, indeed, time had much altered the cafe ; and I drew Mr. Blair by, and told him roundlie, it wes verie unconcordant, not to quarrell Mr. Livingftone's and Mr. Gillefpie's celebration, notwithftanding their voluntar moft groffe and avowed complyance, and to controvert the admiffion of Magiftrates for compelled complyance in a farre leffer degree This ftopped his mouth, and he contradicted no more. As for prayer for the King, we fpake not much of it in publict; bot in private I fand, that moft of the companie thought it might be forborne, were not for the proclamation to forbear it under the penaltie of lofing our ftipends; that leaving of it now would occafion a great fcandal While we were in private conferring on this, Mr. Wood overtured, that a way might be found to fatiffie the Englifh, and keep ftill our prayer for the King. I thought this impoffible; and before I could learne it from him, he wes neceffitate to goe home. Thereafter I found that Mr. James Sharp had perfuaded him and Mr. Robert Dowglafs to goe with Monk's recommendation to the Protector, to entreat for our fpareing in this confcientious practife, and for the freedome of our Affemblies, on promife of peaceable behaviour How farr the Remonftrators provocations put on fuch a refolution, I know not; but no fuch thing is yet done, and to me it's a matter of a very doubtfome nature It's true, all the eftates of the kingdome, yea, every particular perfone of note, have fubmitted, and on occafion of civile rights, have acknowledged the prefent power, except fome of us minifters; and that our protefting brethren, of their owne accord, ever fince Worcefter, having put the King out of their prayers, have provocked heirby the Englifh to perfecute us; yet if all be true what fome of us have written for this dutie, how we fhall for any trouble leave it, it's hard to fay. I fent you three papers from very good hands, for the continuance of this practife; and Mr. Hutchefon wrote a fourth, which I did not fee, better, as I heard, than all the former. For myfelfe, I never wrote a line on that queftion, bot adhered to the thing without queftion; albeit what ye wrote from Voetius ftumbled me, aud the generall practife of all our brethren of England and Ireland more What we fhall doe in the end we doe not know This is the greateft difficultie that fticks in our ftomacks; albeit in mine, Mr. Dickfon's, Mr. Durhame's, Mr Smith's, and others, more; in Mr. Dowglafs, Mr. Blair, Mr. Wood, and Mr Fergufone, and moft of others, leffe. It's our prefent deliberation: the Lord direct us in it. I hear the King himfelf would gladly permitt us to forbear it, and our flocks would earneftly requeft us to the fame; but for myfelf I know not yet how to doe it Mr. James Fergufone and Mr. Alexander Nifbet, by the malevolence of fome of their neighbours, were forely perfecute, and chafed some weeks from their flocks, and with very much adoe obtained some forbearance of the Generall How long we shall be spared, we cannot tell

I did write to some of the ministers at London (F.) to cause some friends represent our case to the Protector; but the answer (G.) I got did promise little · yet (by what means I know not,) to this day the storme is holden off; whether conscience, or pitie, or fear, or diversion by other affaires hes helped, it's uncertaine.

When Mr. Patrick Gillespie wes with Cromwell, he assisted and pleasured sundrie in the matter of their fines. All the three did preach once or twice in the chappell. Cromwell wes kinde enough to them all; but Mr. J. Livingstone came first away. Mr. P. G. and Mr. J. M. for the two Colledges of Glasgow and Aberdeene, obtained sundry favours; the superiorities of Galloway as the Bishop had them, and two thousand nine hundred merks a-year out of the customes of Glasgow, for maintainance of bursars at our own nomination, with the Toune's maintainance for the use of the poor who were hurt by the burning. For this service the Toune gave to Mr. Patrick a gratuitie of thirty pieces, which he took; and haveing regrated to us his great charge in that halfe-year, that it had exceeded two hundred and fifty pound sterling, and all that he had receaved of Cromwell was one hundred pound, I was content the Colledge should allow him ane hundred pound; but it wes caried by vote to three thousand merks. His stipend that yeare, I think, was two thousand merks, and his depursements for us about (one thing and another,) ane other thousand merks, beside one thousand merks for books to the Librarie. For all this I think he was no gainer. his journey and way of living at London was sumptuous. Yet all this would have been weell taken, had not the last halfe of his gift (H.) contained ane order to the Judges to allow no intrants any stipends but these who had the testimonie of so many of the Remonstrant faction, in every diocefs, as they set doune. There were only a few of our mind joyned, who could have carried nothing against the others, so the planting of all the churches was, in effect, devolved on that faction The clauses in the order appointed the judges to assist them in the ejection of all whom they should declare scandalous, as ye may read in the order itselfe printed by the councill So soone as this wes knowne, however, the Remonstrants in our bounds and in the south were glad, and begane to make use of it; yet generally it wes cryed out upon:

the minifters of Edinburgh preached much againft it; the Prefbyterie of Edinburgh and Synod of Lothian declared againft it (J.), the Synod of Fyfe and the Merfe did the like: yea, Mr. James Guthrie wrote fharphe againft it (K.); and the minifters of Edinburgh gave in to Monk a paper, to be communicat to the Protector, as both the Synod and Prefbyterie of Edinburgh had declared before againft it (K. 2.) And in a meeting of the Remonftrants, Wariftone carried a vote of a teftimonie againft it: but this wes fuppreft, for fear of dividing their partie, who in other things alfo did not weell agree; for fome of them were much more complying with the Englifh than Wariftone or Mr James Guthrie allowed. Yet Mr. Guthrie's way became doubtfull on this much talked of occafion:—

His colleague, Mr David Bennet, had under his hand engaged himfelf fome more to the Affemblie of Dundie, than did agree with his former rafhnefs, and Mr. James Guthrie's way; though after the breaking of the land Mr. David retracted fomewhat of this retractation, yet fo much ftuck of it as made him not fully of Mr James his judgment. The people did like neither weell, but Mr. David beft of the two. thence emulation and fome contefts in the feffion began to arife; but Mr David being on his death-bed, and advyfeing to plant his place with a man peaceable, not factious, Mr. James and the Toune fell in a ftrife about that matter immediately after his death. Mr. James had formed the feffion to his owne mind: who oppofed his way, were removed, on diverfe pretences; the remainder were but few, thefe were perfuaded to call to Mr. David Bennet's charge, one Mr. Rule from Angus. To this election the bodie of the toune wes oppofite; but when Mr. James, neglecting their oppofition, went on to admitt him, the people did tumultuoufly, with cryes, and fhouts, and ftrokes, oppofe it; yet Mr James admitted the man, and caufed fummond above threefcore of the chief burgeffes before the Englifh Criminal Court at Edinburgh for a ryot Being all put to ane affife, to the Judges open difatiffaction, they were all abfolved once and againe. Their advocate did publictlie ferve Mr. James with very coarfe language; but the Judges did favour him all in their power. This all did miflyke in Mr James as a dangerous preparative to the whole land: however, it made his people irreconcileable to him. The Synod of Perth mett at Dumblane: when they were about to declare againft the violent intrufion of Mr. Rule, Mr. Guthrie appeared with a declinature of their judicature

This did irritate them fo farr as they did appoint fome of their number to goe to Stirling, and intimat his fentence of depofition by the Generall Affemblie, the nullitie of Mr. Rule's admiffion to Stirling, and of Mr. Blair's to Bothkenner, to elect a new feffion for calling of minifters to Stirling, and to approve that as the Prefbyterie of Stirling from which Mr. James had feparat. This provocked the Remonftrant partie to meet at Edinburgh, where, what courfe of revenge they have refolved upon, I fear we fhall hear in tyme There is fpeaking of propofitions to be fent to Cromwell for invefting the Church-government in their parties hands. However, Mr. Rutherfoord wes fent to Stirling to preach againft the Synod's proceeding, though Mr. Rule wes a known fornicator. There wes ane other very enormous practife of our brethren· a good and able young man, Mr. John Jamefone, being planted, almoft unanimoufly, in the parifh of Eccles, by the whole Prefbyterie of Dunfe, fome few of the Remonftrator fide gives a call to Mr. Andrew Rutherfoord; Mr. John Livingftone, with two of the Prefbyterie of Chirnfide, admitts him to his tryell in reference to that church. The brethren of Edinburgh hearing of it, did earneftly write to Mr. John to beware of fuch a cleare overturning of our fundamentall difcipline (L.). you fee what an anfwer Mr. John returns (M.) However, they goe on with all fpeed with the tryell; and, with an Englifh order and guard, forces him on the people. When the Synod were about to declare againft this unheard-of intrufion, Mr. John and his friends give in a ftrong proteftation (N.). The Synod declared againft them (O), and they, be the Englifh force, keep out Jamefone, and put in Rutherfoord. The Prefbyterie of Edinburgh, and St Andrewes, and, as I think, the Synod of Fyfe and Lothian declared againft this fhamefull ufurpation(P); but our brethren regard little either Prefbyteries or Synods when oppofit to their defires. that fame Synod of Lothian [it was], which, in a well framed act (P 2.), opened Mr William Colvin's mouth. Thefe fatall divifions, which wracked England and our Kingdom firft and laft, which with our eyes we have feen the only confiderable means of the ruine of thefe who are down, and ryfeing of thefe who are up, are like to put in the hand of that unquiet faction of our brethren, or elfe into the hands of Eraftian ftatefmen, all church-jurifdiction, fo at once we fhall have no difcipline to look after, but to preach, pray, and celebrat the facraments, and be glad to be tollerat to goe about that without controll When Quakers falls a-raileing on all the miniftrie, in the face of our congregations, on the Sabbath-day, they are not punifhed at all, nor, for ought I know, is there any church difcipline at all to this day any where in England. The minifters there, are herein fo heartlefs and difcouraged, that they dare fpeak nothing which may be interpreted to give the leaft offence I marvelled, that when I fent my anfwer to Cotton and Tombes, to Mr Calamie for his *Imprimatur*, yea, a Dedicatorie epiftle (Q.),[7] he wes fo feeble-minded as to refufe both my Dedication, and his owne *Imprimatur*; yea, with difficultie could I gett his *Imprimatur* to my verie Catechife: A ftrange change of tymes, and great feeblenefs of men!

Concerning our Colledge-affaires, this year we had nothing but quietnefs; for I have given over to ftirr more in vaine, abfenting myfelf from what I lyke not, and the reft are all of one piece. At the beginning of the year, when Mr. Robert Makquard, being unable to deal more with his charge, had dimitted, I made the Toune-Councell deall yet againe for Mr. John Glen with Mr Patrick, but he would not hear of him, but brought one from St. Andrewes, a pedagogue, Mr. George Sinclaire,[8] and admitted him without all competition. The young man Mr. James Wood recommended to me as peaceable and well-conditioned, which I have found him, but inferior farr to Mr John Glen in all parts of fcholar-craft: through ficknefs the laft part of the year he could not wait on his claffe: our fchollars were few, the laureation private, and tryells fuperficiarie I got leave to bring all the fchollars twice a-week to my Hebrew leffons, and difcourfes on the Catechife; whereof I was very glad, for divinitie ftudents we have very few. To thefe I dyted, twyfe a-week all the year, my chronologick queftions Mr. John Young difcourfed and dyted enough after to them, in fundrie fubjects whereof I took no notice. Mr. Patrick, before the end of the year, dyted two or three hours fomething on the firft of Ezechiel; but his maine tafk was, that which he goes about very weell, the building of a very fair houfe, on Mr. Zacharie Boyd's legacie: this he does fo that no man can do it better; but the cheapnefs of victuall makes our rent fo fmall, and our prodigalitie is fo great, that we are like to fall in the common difeafe of great fcarcitie of

[7] The copy of this Epiftle, and moft of the articles mentioned in this letter, are not contained in the MS volume of Baillie's papers.

[8] The author of various works, but beft known by his "Satans Invisible World Discovered."

moneys I was lyke to have had a particular fafhrie, whereof yet I am not free: our Bibliothecarie's place was but ane honorarie attendance, without more charge; the benefite of it is, the dyet with the Regents, a good chamber, and fome twelve pieces a-year. This I had defigned for a fon of John Barnes, who lived with his brother a minifter of England: the Toune-Councell prefented to one part of the provifion, Mr. David Dick to ane other, and the Colledge to the reft, I thought the Proveft, (James Bell, the youth's uncle,) would carrie the Toune-Councell, and Mr. Patrick Gillefpie alfo, for the Colledge, the Proveft being very great with him; for Mr. David Dickfon I undertook for him. Of all this I fent word to the boy in England. While fecretly I had gone this farr, my fon, Mr Robert, falls in love with the place. I a while diffuaded him from all thoughts of it, yet at laft he perfuaded me to be of his mind, if fo I could be fairly difengaged with Mr. George Barnes: This Providence did for me, for the young man's friends fand it not expedient he fhould leave England, and fo thanked me for my kindnefs. Being freed of this voluntare impediment, I told Mr. Patrick Gillefpie the cafe, fhewing him, that though I wes fure to carry the Toune and Mr Dickfon's prefentation, yet I would neither feek, nor accept them, unlefs he were content of my boy to that charge. He defyred to fpeak with the boy, and finding him difcreet enough, and as fit as any other, he told me he would be for it. To ingage him farder, at his defyre, I left the fpeaking of the Toune and Regents to him, and did open my mouth to none of them; but behold, when I was fecure, and had no more doubt of the thing, after a moneth he calls me, and fhews me, that the Regents and others had been at him, heavilie regrating, and rebuking him for ingagement to my fon in that place; yea, that Mr. Robert Hodges had, befides his knowledge, obtained a prefentation from the Toune-Councell. This unexpected newes fafhed me; yet I told him the firft motion had come from the boy, and not myfelf; that if I had not left the management of it to him, I could eafilie have helped all, and yet I would affay it, if he knew no impediment in my boy himfelf. He affured, that none had made any exception againft him but that he needed it not I fhew him that exception was of ignorance, if not malice; for the place in queftion was not like thefe of Profeffours and Regents, which requried much abilitie of gifts; nor of our Burfars, either of Divinitie or Philofophie, whofe foundation required povertie;

but that was of a third nature. He acknowledged it was fo; yet he knew not what to fay to obloquie. I told him the juftice of our proceeding would quiet that quicklie; only I would try if I could reduce the prefentation, which was obtained by furprize from the Toune-Councell. This I quicklie and eafilie got done, and a prefentation from them, and Mr. D. D., to my fon with great cheerfullnefs. When I fpoke to the Rector, Dean of Facultie, and Regents, all affured me, at the firft word, of their great willingnefs to concurre with me. When I had brought the prefentation to Mr. Patrick, and the report of the favour of all who had intereft, he fhewed his good content; yet all this half-year has he fhifted to conclude it. If in the end he fhould elude me, I fhould take it for an egregious injurie; but would put it up with the reft in filence; but I doe not expect it. The great obloquie was all from my good friends, John Graham, and fpeciallie Mr. John Spreule, who ftirred up Mr. Hodges to feek that prefentation, when he did not mind of it, having ane other place of the Colledge that might ferve him. For my familie, the Lord keeps all my children in health and welfare as ever, and my mind at peace, bleffed be his name! and affifts me in all I have to doe, as I would wifh. For mariage, I dare not yet meddle with it, till I fee what the Lord will do, with my great hazard, about that which they may expone, if they pleafe, in me and others, high treafon, praying for the King. If in this I were fecure, it's like I would follow your example in a fecond mariage, albeit I know not yet the partie; but I truft in this the Lord will be mercifull to me.

Concerning our Commonwealth, how it is conceived here, I give yow this account. The rifeing of the Highlands has proven, as the moft of wife men ever expected, hurtfull to us. The countrey was much oppreffed by it; the King's partie much weakened, the Englifh embittered the more againft us; and their inward divifions and factions holden in fo long as that partie ftood confiderable. It did grow indeed to a greater height than any could have imagined; yet the Holland peace, and the King's full difappointment abroad, with their owne foolifh pride and divifions, brought them to nothing, and made them capitulate one after another, till at laft all are come in. John Grahame of Duchray is the laft, who indeed was among the moft honeft, ftout, and wife men of them all. The Englifh gave tolerable termes to them all, and by this wifdome has gotten them all quiet. Glencairne ledd the way to the reft, as of going out, fo of coming in; for which much blame lyes on him Athole's friends brought him off with the firft ; Seaforth alfo became wife in tyme. Lorne's difference with his Father keeped him longer out ; yet he alfo at laft was perfuaded to come in, albeit he and his father are not lyke to be good friends His Father, leaft he give any occafion to the Englifh to fufpect his collufion with his fon, keeps the greater diftance from him, albeit the moft think the domeftick divifions among them are fo real and true as makes both their lives bitter and uncomfortable to them ; and the great burthen of debt puts their verie houfe in a hazard to ruine, if the Englifh be no more kind to them than they have been, or it feems they will be The father fought a garifone to lye in Argyle, to keep it from his fon's violence , bot when it was on the way, he repented, and gott a new order for their returne : yet they would [goe] on ; yea, took up his owne beft houfe of Inneraray, made the kirk and fchooll their ftables, and hardlie at this very time have been gotten removed The people's great hatred lyes on him above any one man, and whatever befalls him, few does pitie it : at this very time his ftate is very ftaggering. The Chancellour gott better conditions in his capitulation than any did expect, albeit his debts and infamie lye very heavie upon him

For the tyme, all Scotland is exceeding quiet, but in a very uncomfortable condition , very many of the Noblemen and gentlemen, what with imprifonments, banifhments, forfaulters, fynes, as yet continueing without any releafement, and private debts from their former troubles, are wracked or going to wrack The commonalitie and others are oppreffed with maintainance to the Englifh armie. Strange want of money upon want of trade, for our towns have no confiderable trade ; and what is, the Englifh has poffeffed it. The victuall is extraordinarie cheap, in God's mercie, but judgment to many. Want of juftice, for we have no Barron-Courts , our fheriffs have little fkill, for common being Englifh fojours; our Lords of Seffion, a few Englifh, unexperienced with our law, and who, this twelve moneth, hes done little or nought : great is our fuffering through want of that Court After long neglect of us as no nation, at laft a fupreme Councell of State, with power in all things, is come doune, of fix or feven Englifh fojours and two of our complying gentlemen, Colonell Lockhart and Colonell Swinton We expect little good from them ; but if ane heavie excife, as is faid, be added to our maintainance, and the paying of all the garisons lye on us, our condition will be infupportable, yet be what it will, it muft be borne, we have deferved it. But we hope the Lord will look doune on the affliction of the unjuftlie afflicted by men.

The other year, when the good Parliament fatt doune, we were in great fear. Their firft declarations were fo pious, but to me fo full of the Anabaptiftick ftraine, that I was afraid of them. They were elected abfoluthe by the officers of the annie, and the minifters of their caball, fullie according to the mind of the Sectarian partie, but they were no fooner fet, than they flew fo high, as to mind nothing but a Fifth Monarchie on earth, to overthrow all magiftracie and miniftrie as it ftood, and put all in a new mule of their owne, wherein publicklie fome fomented them for their owne wifer defignes. However, they were far on in overturning all remaining foundations of Church and State. The Generall, with fome of his confident friends of the army, diffolved them by force, leaft they fhould have overwhelmed him, themfelffes, and all, in their new Babell, and took on himfelf the new office of Protectour, with a power, to him and his councell-fupreme, beyond, as it feemed to many, the regall line, yet neceffarie for the tyme, and quietlie acquiefced in without contradiction. To mollifie it a Parliament was called, after the old way, but of men ingadgeing to the new way of government: they went from Scotland threttie, and from Ireland alfe many. Ours and their choices were men who, for peace, were refolved to doe or fay any thing they fand tollerable to their owne large mind, and, I think, were all fo complying with the Protectour as he would have wifhed: yet many of the chiefe in this meeting were fo unfatiffied with one above a Parliament, (a true and high royaltie as they conceaved,) that at their very firft doun-fitting they fet themfelves to overturne this new building, for their love of their too much-fancied republick, in a free and abfolutely fupreame parliament: Ane unhappie dreame! unfitt for the government of the people of this ifle at any time, and moft as now difpofed. The Protectour finding it fo, made no fcruple to difcipline them, and, without more adoe, to purge the Houfe prefently of all who, under their hand, did not ingage againe to preferve the modell of government appointed by the Protectour and his friends. When many of the moft fturring heads, by the refuifeall of this engagement, were put out of the Houfe, it was expected, that the reft would have fo fully complyed as they had written with their hand; yet for what caufes we know not, the Protectour found them alfo fo undermining of his government, that he thought it fitt to diffolve them Hence all filled with new difcontents: but the Protectour had fo farr, with his witt and diligence, provided for all, that there was no confiderable fturr. Lambert and the chiefe of the army were, by hopes, made fo faft, that they concurred chearfully in all things. Lieut.-Colonell Lilburne, a moft turbulent man, whom I thought no force or fkill would ever have gotten quiet, was fo cunningly conveyed to Jerfey, and there fo ftrickly keeped, that there hes been nothing more heard of him than he had been dead Captain Joyce was put in the fame condition Generall-Majors Harrifons and Overtoun, with fundrie other officers of the armie, both in Scotland and England, are clofe prifoners, for defignes to turne the armie againft the Protectour. A number of the Royall partie arifeing, in a very confufed imprudent way, in many fhires, were all eafily fcattered, and the chiefe of them made faft, and fundry execute for their confpiring; albeit in what, and how farr, we know it not. We were glad that no Scotfman was found accefforie to any of thefe defignes: it feems our people were fo illburnt, that they had no ftomach for any farder medling; only Cranford, Lauderdaill, and David Leflie, when the Tower was filled with new prifoners, were fent to farder and worfe prifons, for no new fault that we hear tell of.

Thefe fturrs make the Protector more vigilant The fall out of his coach, and the attempts more than once for his life, by Gerard the taylor, and others, fhews the violence of fome fpirits. The raifeing of all the three laft Parliaments; the fpeaking of a Croune, and title of a King or Emperour, which fome thinks is not vaine; the putting of Ireland under the government of his fon Henrie; and Scotland under a Councell onlie of fome fix or feven officers of the armie, and chiefly of his neece's Robina Seufter's hufband,[9] the young Laird of Lee, made great malecontentment in the heart of the moft To help this, all poffible courfes are taken to fatiffie England; but Scotland is not worth the minding: in England, fixty thoufand pound fterling a moneth, the halfe of the maintainance is diminifhed; but we fear the new excife fhall double our maintainance. Albeit the rifeing in England

[9] Robina, daughter of one of Cromwell's aunts, whofe hufband's name was Sheufter, or Sewſter, was married, 20th February 1654, to Col afterwards Sir William Lockhart of Lee. —(*Analecta Scotica*, vol ii. p 203.)

feems to have been great, yet few have fuffered, and we hear of few forfaulters or fynes there; but many of our nation are fent to the plantations; our fynes are many and great, and our grievances much neglected.

For fatiffieing of the people of England, the two great navies, the one, on the coafts of Africk, Italie, and Spaine, under Blake; the other, in the Weft Indies, under Penn, did ferve much for a tyme: for it wes thought at firft, that the navie under Blake, for to affift the Spanifh againft the French, invading by fea, both Naples and Catalonia, befide the fecureing of the fhips and cannon, fhould have had affured from the Spanifh for pay two hundred thoufand pound fterling; and thereafter, that their defigne was to free all the Englifh captives at Tunes, Alger, and Saly, and to intercept the Spanifh plate at Cales. Alfo that Penn's great armie of twelve thoufand men had been, not only to have taken St. Domingo in Hifpaniola, but alfo Mexico in New Spaine. Thefe high and advantageous defignes did much pleafe the fpirits of the vulgare; but now mifcontentments are feared, even on that ground alfo, to arife, that fo hudge expence hes been laid on the people for fruitlefs defignes; and that in their farr voyages, many lives have been loft for no purpofe. Since this tyme Blake hes lived on the Englifh charge: the Spanifh hes born no expence The burning of the Turkifh fhips at Tunes is faid to have provocked the Turks at Conftantinople, and elfewhere, to robb many Englifh of life and goods; that none of the Spanifh fleet is yet gotten, and if medled with, it were a breach with Spaine, which were a beginning of a needlefs warr at ane unfeafonable tyme; that Penn's great navie and armie hes done no fervice at all, but in Hifpaniola hes gotten a great affront.—Thefe things from the Diurnals. the mifcontent Royalifts blaze farr, bot the Protectour is wife enough to fee to all thefe murmurings of fillie people: in quieting of malecontents he hes a ftrange both dexteritie and fkill.

For Church matters, there is no ecclefiaftick government at all we can hear of; yet the hand of power is not heavie on any for matters of religion, no not on Quakers, who are open raillers againft the Protectour's perfon; yea, we hear of little trouble of Papifts, who grow much in the North of Scotland, more than thefe eighty years, without any controll. We expect our Councell of State will fee to it

For things abroad, they are thus reprefented to us: that the French totallie neglect our King, the Cardinall being unwilling in the King's minoritie to undertake a warre with England, for the marring of the great advancement of the French interest against their cheef enemies, the Spanish and Austrian; that for this end they passe by the daily taking of numbers of their ships; the defeat of the royall navie in its way to Dunkirk, whereupon alone followed the losse of Dunkirk; the taking from them the plantations of Canada, and St. Christophers, and others, that all this, the French dissembles, and seeks the English friendship, till they have done their businefs elsewhere, as daily they make so good progresse; that Conty takes in towne after towne in Catalonia, which is interpret the great weaknefs of Spaine, that is not able in Spaine itselfe to crush a little French armie; in Italie also, the Spansh in Millaine is put hard to it, when the French, with all the power of Savoy and Modena, and the neutralitie of the Venetian, Pope, Florence, and Genoa, deals with him. Only it's marvelled what follie moved the French, in their passage through Savoy, to fall on the quiet Protestants of the vailhes. If this massacre be the half of the thing it's called, it were enough, not only before God, but with men, to marr the full carreer of the French victorie But many here do suspect the matter not to be so great; not so much becaufe the French King, and Pope, and Savoyart, disclaimes it as none of their deeds; but becaufe so manie diurnals does so much insist upon it, and so much noise is made of it here, the Royalists say, that of this blood of the faints this politick ufe is made, to make people fee the happinefs of our prefent government, wherein we live in peace, free from the crueltie of Papists, and if Charles Stuart came here, the people had caufe to fear, from him and his mother, thefe uncredible murders, which the Protestants of Savoy find from the Duke, the King's coufin-german, by the advyce of his mother, the Queen's true fifter. But we fear too much of this perfecution be true, let any exaggerate and abufe it to what end they think fitt But the terrible progresse of the French, and most to our prejudice, is in Flanders, where the English junction with Spaine, if in tyme, might easily have stopped them; but if to the conquiese of Loraine and Halfatia, they add Flanders, and get of the Spanish the Low Countreys, their neighbourhood, both to England and Holland, will be more formidable than ever Spain's was: and whatever progress the French make this year against the Spanish, many imputes it to the English, who have hindered the Spanish filver-fleet to come home, whereby the

Spanish hes been difabled to keep the fields againft the French any where, let be in Flanders againft the King in perfone, with the great royall armie.

We think here it's good for yow that the Swedes are gone to Pole; for had the vulgar reports and your late fears being grounded, that this hudge armie and their confederate Brandeburgh, with the confent of the French, been againft yow for your ufurpations on the Dutchy of Gulick Cleive, the oppreffion of the Orange familie, and what other quarrells willing men would not have wanted; we thought your States in as great hazard to have loft their verie libertie, notwithftanding of all the help the Englifh could have made them, as they had been under thefe fourty years. and whatever evill had come on them, their late carriages to all their neighbours would have made many not at all to have pitied them, but for myfelf, my prayers to God was, and fhall be, for the prefervation of fo noble a member of the Reformed Church, which feemed to be in a clear hazard of ruine If the Swedes be gone to Pole, in this height of the Polonian calamitie, when the Mufcovites and Cofacks and their own divifions have fo lamentablie wracked them, to accomplifh their miferie, and prey on that kingdome, without any new caufe fince their laft peace, they will not have the bleffing of many Chriftians to go along with them. For albeit that proud kingdome of Pole, for their groffe poperie and other foule herefies and fhamefull avowed inceftuous marriages of their two laft Kings agreed to by their States, be highly finfull, yet they were a good barr for Chriftendome on that fide againft the Turks and Tarters incroachments; and if they be ruined, a great gap will be opened for thefe Scythian barbarians to fall on us all. Many here did think the Swedifh defigne had been for Germanie, albeit we knew no particular quarrell; yet that which we fee this day, and know ever hes been the greateft quarrell among States and Princes, ambition and appearance of advantage was evident enough. The Swedes being mafter of fo great and well provided ane armie of their owne, both by fea and land, and having fo great alliances in Germanie, and intereft by their new conqueft; the Emperour being fo weak, ficklie, and near death; his fon fo young and unfitt for government; the Croune of Hungary being fo long denyed, the Hungarian divifions being fo great, and the Tranfylvanian fo powerfull, wife and famous a Prince; the Elector of Saxony being fo oft beat by the Swedes, and the Bavarian yet being little above a child; the houfe of Palatine, Brandeburgh,

Hesse, and Brunswick so nearly at this tyme related to the King of Sweden; Spaine and Pole utterlie unable for to assist the Emperour, and France so willing to joyne his forces for the ruine of the Austrian familie; these things made many here believe it was the Empire the Swedish did now aime at, only we think it a singular example of secrecie, that to this day, even after beginning to march, their counsells are so hid, that it is not knowne whither they are going.

We are glad the Lord hes so long enabled the Venetians, alone destitute of all help, to keep up the Turks from Crete. It seemes the inward diseases of that empire must be great, that disables them so as to be beat, year after year, both by sea and land, by the Venetian only. How comes it that we are so ignorant of the Turkish affaires, when the State of China, and the outmost Tartars, is so well known. I wish yow sent us that Atlas of China, which latche that Flemish priest did print at Amsterdam. The vanquishing of the great kingdome of China by the unhappie Tartarians, is a most great and remarkable occurrence as hes been in the world for many ages. O, that all these things of the Earth were for the advancement of Christ's Kingdome, and of making souls to be saved, which now so evidently perish! It is for this end chiefly that I ever took notice of the motions of States and Princes, to see if any beginning did appear of performing the Lord's great promises; the coming in of the Jewes, the abolishing of Antichrist, and reforming of the Roman church, the bringing of Mahometan and Pagane princes to the faith of Christ. While nothing of all this does yet appear, my heart is oft grieved, and prayes the Lord to arise to glorify his Sone, and comfort believers. The great declining of Spaine, without a sone, and but ane old daughter, and weaknefs of the Austrian family, made me once hope that the tyme wes near when these bloudie and great supporters of Antichrist should fall· but the Lord is wife, and knows what he is doing

Postscript. December 1st 1655.

While, for lack of a bearer, this lyes long beside me, my sone Harie, to my joy, comes safe home. Not only by your letters, but by himself more, I see the singular care ye have had of him as I could have expected or wished. I will not in words expref's the sense of this kindnefs, especially in that your wife and ferious dealing with him to returne to his book, it hes prevailed, and he is again as diligent a ftudent as ever, without any inclination to merchandife, for which I thank God and yow. I think his being with yow well worth all the tyme, labour, and charge he hes fpent on it. The fix pounds fterling he borrowed from Mr. Winch at London, I have caufed pay, and received Mr. Winch's difcharge of it. The reft of his account to yow fhall be anfuered with the firft opportunity. In your care of Dr Strang's book, yow fhew your friendfhip both to the dead and living: I am glad it is in Elzevir's hand; caufe hafte it fo much as may be. I find this fault in the fheet yow fent me, that the marginall index is confounded with all notes or citations which were any wayes on the margine, without any diftinction of place, character, or diftance It is not tyme now to get this helped I hope it is near ane end.

While Mr. Wood, Rector of the Univerfitie of St. Andrewes, had oft to doe with Generall Monk for the Univerfitie, and alwayes gotten civile hearing, it was thought fitt, that Mr. Dowglafs and he fhould reprefent to the Generall the manifold and increafing grievances of the Church; which they did in this paper, (R 1). The Generall profeffed himfelf willing, but unable to remeed them; only undertook to fend them to the Protector; with whom yet they fleep, together with their reprefentation againft Mr. Gillefpie's charter, as they call it. The Generall oft fpoke anent prayer for the King Mr. Dowglafs, and others, fhew their utter unwillingnefs to quite it fo long as the Proclamation ftood; and when the Sheriff was fet to trouble them, had he not given over his begun procefs, they had prepared proteftations The Generall declared his unabilitie to take off the Proclamation for the tyme, bot hoped the new Councell, when it came doune, fhould doe it. At their coming, the Prefident Broghill, having a good impreffion from his fifter-in-law, the Ladie Clotworthie, of Mr. Dowglafs and Mr. Dickfon, dealt kindlie with them; and underftanding their ftick at the Proclamation, albeit with fome difficultie, got the Councell to take it off, (R. 2.); fhewing withall to the minifters the ftrictnefs of his inftructions againft all who continued publickie naming of the King After much deliberation, they thought fitt to give it over They once purpofed a declaration, and a paper for removeall of objections; but forefeeing the offence from thefe writes would have been equall to the continuance of their practice, they abftained, and only drew this paper, which they fent to me, and no other, (S 1.): Mr. Wood's larger anfwer to objections I have not yet gotten, (S. 2.). The example of thefe in Edinburgh is like to be followed by all. fome yet ftick Our Remonftrants did grieve and mock at this change. Some of our people, from whom we did not expect it, were offended; bot above all, Generall Monk was irritat againft us, as if we had yielded to Bioghill what we denyed to him and from that day, in all occafions, befriended openlie the Remonftrants, to our prejudice, as men to be trufted beyond us, their principles being oppofite to the intereft of their enemie Charles Stewart, whom we did affect ftill, notwithftanding of our filence in our publict prayers. Mr. Traile, who converfed much with him, write in the time of our laft Synod a long letter to Mr. P. G[illefpie,] which he read publictlie to a grand committee of his mind, as if we had uttered to the Generall and Prefident very many calumnies againft them, efpeciallie their averfenefs fiom all peace with us their brethren. On occafion thereafter, both the Prefident and Generall, to their owne faces, witneffed our innocencie; affirming, that in all our fpeeches to them, we had never fpoken one word to their prejudice. However, the Remonftrators of our Synod, ftirred up by Mr Traile's calumnious letter, fent Mr. P. G[illefpie] and others to clear them of our imputations, and to defyre, that the minifters of Edinburgh might call a meeting for Union, if poffible; or, if no, that it might be feen by whofe fault the difcord continued The meeting was called, and keeped, November 8th, by a number of both fydes from all the parts of the Kingdome It was not long before it was clear who were the men who made the Union defperat, except on conditions intollerable. Our meetings appointed nine of every fyde to confeir. Theirs were Wariftoune, Sir John Cheiflie, Colonell Ker, Mr. S Rutherfoord, Mr James Guthrie, Mr P. G[illefpie,] Mr James Naefmith, Mr Robert Traile, Mr Gabriell Maxwell. Ours were Mr Robert Dowglafs, Mr. D Dickfon, Mr. James Wood, Mr. Robert Ker, Mr. James Fergufone, Mr. Robert Young, Mr. Hew Mackell, Mr John Smith, and I. Mr. Robert Blair and Mr. James Durhame appeared as mid-men; albeit of our judgement for the main, and in the whole debate, grieved with the other. Their papers were all framed by Mr James Guthrie's hand, of my Lord Wariftoune's materialls. The firft was this, (T): It to us was fo high and abfurd, that we could fcarcelie believe our own apprehenfions of it, and refolved, by queries, to try their pofitive mind anent it I drew this paraphrafe on it, (V.), and Mr. James Fergufone ane other; out of which Mr. Wood drew this third, which we gave them to anfwer, (X.) To be even with us, they, November 13th, gave us Querees on our overture, the firft of June, (Y.); and withall, ane anfwer to our Querees, (Z.). Having pondered thefe, we returned ane anfwer to their Querees, (A A.), and our fenfe of their overture, (B. B.) Our conceffions were fo many and great, that Mr. Patrick Gillefpie, Mr. John Carftares, and others of their meeting, not Mr. Durhame and Mr. Blair only, feemed fullie fatiffied therewith, and we began to hope for a concord. But Wariftoune and Mr. Guthrie did carrie it fo in their meeting over Mr. P G[illefpie,] that this verie captious paper was given in to us, (C. C.), which Mr. P. G[illefpie] denyed openlie to be the fenfe of their meeting, and Mr. G[uthrie] affirmed it was; and hardly by diftinctions could they be brought, even in our meeting, to agree among themfelves about that paper. However, we agreed to give it a foft unreflecting anfwer, though much provocked, (D. D.); yea, to gaine them, we gave in this reprefentation alfo. At laft they gave us their clear and finall fenfe, (E. E.); with which Mr. Gillefpie refuifed to joyne, but deferted their meeting Mr. Wood was here called from us to fee his father die, but we gave them this laft paper, of Mr. James Fergufone's hand, (F. F.); and foe, after twenty-three dayes ftay, we clofed the meeting. We heard in the midft of our conference, they had voted the fetting up of twenty-four minifters and fix elders, twenty-nine of all, even their part of the Commiffion of the Affemblie [16]50, with abfolute power of a full jurifdiction over the whole Kirk of Scotland, on fuppofition we fhould not agree to their defires; and had lykewayes agreed on ane fupplication to the Councell for affiftance to that their moft prefumptuous and unreafonable committee which ever our Church did fee

At our Synod of Glafgow, where this conference for union was hatched, there was other two dangerous motions. Wariftone and Mr James Guthrie had fallen on a new conceit, to put all the godly in the land, of their faction, under the band of a new Covenant, which Mr. Guthrie hae drawne in fome fheets of paper, from which he had cut off all the articles of our former Covenants which concerned the King, Parliament, or liberties of the land, or mutuall defence. At this motion the Councell was highlie offended, and fpoke threatening words of Wariftoune and Mr James Guthrie for this attempt: yet after their apologie, were fo well pleafed, that the Generall gave Wariftoune a vifit in his houfe, which I know not if he hath yet done to any other of the nation; and Mr. Guthrie has that familiaritie with him, that when both are in toune, he fends his mind to him in clofed epiftles, which I doubt if any other of the nation has yet made bold to doe. In their meeting at Edinburgh, January firft, they proponed this Covenant. The Englifh agents, Mr. Gillefpie, and Mr. Leviftoune, difputed againft it in vaine. Mr Gillefpie, fo foon as he went weft, called a meeting at Kilmarnock to crufh it if he could. Wariftoune hearing of his defigne, fent S[ir] J[ohn] Cheiflie to keep that meeting, where there were bitter and reflecting debates betwixt S[ir] J[ohn] and Mr. P[atrick]; yet Mr. P. carried it over S[ir] J[ohn,] that all fhould declare their mind anent the Covenant; where all, except four or five of little weight, diffented, yet fo that they fhould enquire the fenfe of the godly of the bounds anent it, and report at the next Synod S[ir] J[ohn,] in this toyled, prevailed againft Mr. P[atrick] in ane other vote of their mind, for erecting of the Commiffion [16]50 for purgeing the Kirk. Thefe interfeirings put us in hope that faction would divide among themfelves. At Glafgow, the report was, that all the godlie in thefe parts miflyked the motion of the Covenant; however, the godlie in Fyfe and Lothian were faid to lyke it; yet, on the Weft's miflyke, the motion for the tyme was laid afide. But behold, from fome of the feffions of Glafgow it was moved, that the oidinance for teftifieing, notwithftanding of all the contradiction had been made to it, feemed very innocent and exceeding good to be practifed. To this Sir John oppofed, and Mr Patrick avowed he knew nought of the motion; but fo foon as he went to Edinburgh to feek a conference for union, the Prefident and other counfellers, of their owne proper motion altogether, without his knowledge, as he affirmes, refolved to proclame his oidinance, and did it after his departure; but after his preaching to the Councell, and keeping of their kirk the whole Sabbath, and going with the Prefident in his coach to dinner, thefe things made us not at all to underftand Mr Gillefpie's meaning; yet this was vifible, as Mr Guthrie wrote fharpelie againft his ordinance, fo he oppofed his Covenant and commiffion, and looked towards an union with us; but for what end many did much doubt. A little more tyme will clear more myfteries Yow will perceave in the papers, as is evident in the conference, that our Remonftrants fixt refolution is, 1. Not to reft content with an oblivion of what is paft, of enjoying their own judgement in peace, and taking off their cenfures; but will have us confent to their libertie of profecuting their Proteftations in pofterior Generall Affemblies, not only for condemning of the Publick Refolutions, (which we in confcience judge neceffar truths, the grounds of our apologie to forraigne Churches, and the world, for our innocencie in all thefe fearfull fcandalls which our brethren's tenets and practifes hes occafioned to be caft upon the face of our Church and Nation), but alfo for condemning the laft two Generall Affemblies, as null in their very conftitution, which to us were in their grave to burie all Generall Affemblies for ever, which for conftitution cannot be more lawfull than thefe two. 2. That whatever neceffitie we may have of a Generall Affemblie, or whatever defyre we may have of one, or libertie from the Englifh to get it; yet we muft never have it till they be willing to joyne with us to feek it in their termes. 3. That as peace with them may not be had, except during the paucitie of their partie, compared with the multitude of their oppofites in the generalitie of the Prefbyteries and Synods, (for fundry whole Synods will not have anie one of them, as Angus, Murray, Argyle, and I think fundrie others, diverfe Synods hes bot very few of them; as Fife bot feven, whereof two only confiderable; Perth at moft fourteen, whereof bot one confiderable; Lothian, if ye except them of Lithgow and Biggar, but three), the whole Synods and Prefbyteries of the kingdome will be content to furceafe from their jurifdiction, and devolve it on a committee for the bounds of every Synod, of the number whereof they fhall make the equall half, to judge and determine all matters of planting and purgeing, and whatever falls to be controverted, whofe acts the Synods fhall have no power to ranverfe without the previous advyce of a generall confultatorie committee out of all the Synods, whereof alfo the equall half fhall be of their judgement, and nominat by them. When we in the Synod of Glafgow defyred fomething lyke this in a far other cafe, we being the right conftitute Synod, and they a fchifmatick faction, we, near the half, we juftly fearing their unjuft violence, and more diffimilitudes apparent in our cafe, from this of their demand for the whole land, yet they paffionately cryed downe our motion, and rather choiced to reject all peace with us than to hear of any fuch overture. 4. All plantations moft be taken from the congregations and feffions, to be put in the hand of a few whom they count the godlie partie; for they avow that the pluralitie of all congregations in the land are fo ignorant and fcandalous or ungracious, that they are to be excluded from the communion and voice in choifeing of a minifter. By this devyce they hope quickly to fill all vacant places with intrants of their faction, as they are carefull to doe wherever they have any power to doe it. 5 Though we fhould yield to them all their defyres, yet doe they expreflie deny to us that which we count the effence of Prefbyteriall fubordination, a fubmiffion to the fentence of our Judicatures for tyme to come. They feem to be for the thing in generall, but not for a fubmiffion to our Judicatures in their prefent corrupt conftitution of fo many unfitt members. In this cafe of the Church they plead for a libertie both of judgement and practife, both to diffent and contradict the fentences of the beft Synods of Scotland, fuch as Lothian and Fife, in any planting or purgeing that is contrare to their mind. And a fixth now they are come to, a few of them to name fome twenty-nine of their faction which were of the Commiffion [16]50, to be a fettled judicature, with abfolute jurifdiction over the whole Church, ever while they think tyme to call a Generall Affemblie. This to us is worfe than Mr. Gillefpie's ordinance, which they fo much cry doune, for it was alone for ftipends in order to planting; but this is ane ufurpation of the whole immediat jurifdiction; worfe than Independencie, that incroaches not on others, but exempts only their owne adherents from others jurifdiction; worfe than Epifcopacie, that never made fuch havock, and fo caufeleflie, of all Prefbyteries and Synods at once. The event, is feared, will be the forfaulter of all our ecclefiaftick liberties, in taking of them out of both our hands, to be depofited in an Eraftian State-committee, till our Remonftrators think fitt to joyne with us; whereof I have no hopes as things now goe in the land. Near two year agoe I drew up the ftate of the queftions they had then ftarted · from this and my former letter yow fee what they have added, and it's not unlyke, as error is very fertile, they will not ftand at all they have declared, but hes a farder race to runne; however, I fend yow herewith that paper alfo, (G G), as ane evidence of my care to difcharge that part of my fpeciall office, to attend to the doctrine, and obferve the corrupters of it, and their corruptions, the great caufe hes put me on moft of my labours thefe years bygone.

For matters of State, at home and abroad, we meddle not at all with them, only we obferve the footfteps of Divine Providence as they offer themfelves to the eyes of all beholders. Generall Blake's navie hes coft a vaft charge, without any profite. The expedition of Hifpaniola, as I read it in a London defcription, is full of fhame and loffe, both of charges and men, hes drawn on ane open warr with Spain, which will hurt our trade. Our emptie coffers will not be furnifhed with all the ordinarie incomes, though great, and much greater than before; nor by this new preffour of the cavileers, the feparating of them from others, even thefe againft whom no new tranfgreffion is alleadged, only for the holding doune, as is profeffed, the great and reftlefs faction of the Royalifts, we fear doe more harme than good, albeit Lilly's prognoftick we count meerly knavifh. We are grieved at the fearfull fcandale of that unhappie apoftate the Queen of Swan[1]: it's good fhe fignifies a meer cypher for civile power, and is of fo bad a reputation for her carriage thefe years bygone; it's lyke her maintainance will be more burdenfome than ufefull to the Popifh partie. The progreffe of the King of Swan is ftrange. Since the taking of Cracow, we know not what he wants of that great kingdome, I cannot think that Brandeburgh can be fo ill-advyfed as to draw the remainder of that ftorme on his own head, without all occafion. If the Lord will be pleafed to advance the gofpell by that prodigious change, we will quicklie fee: it feems he takes that kingdome by the right alone of arms, and makes it hereditarie to himfelf and the Croune of Swan, with the Poles univerfall confent.

Since I came from Edinburgh, there is two or three papers more paft betwixt us and the Remonftrators, which makes our wounds wyder, efpeciallie fince by violence they avow openly to oppiefs us; one pait of them under Wariftone and Mr. Guthrie's patronage, though diffallowed by others, puts into their hand the power of making all the churches voyd They look, by their fupplicating of the Englifh, for erecting of themfelves in a commiffion for purging, againft which the Prefbyterie of Edinburgh hes given ane honeft teftimonie, (II.). Ane other part, under the patrocinie of Mr. Patrick Gillefpie and Mr. J. L[ivingftone,] by the Englifh ordinance, takes the power

---

[1] Chriftina, Queen of Sweden. She fucceeded her father Guftavus Adolphus in 1632, when only five years of age; but refigned the crown in 1654, and soon after abjured the Lutheran religion She spent most of her subsequent life at Rome, where she died in 1689 She was interred in St Peter's, Rome, where there is a splendid monument to her memory, by Fontana, erected at the expenfe of Pope Alexander VIII

of planting all with their own friends, though paſſionately diſclaimed by the other. Againſt theſe fearfull oppreſſions we have no humane help We can not make ſuch cordiall application to the Engliſh as they doe; ſo we fear they ſhall lend their power to the other for our hurt; whereof, and other things, ye ſee how I expreſs my ſenſe to a friend at London, (K K.); the return to which yow have here alſo, (L L.). I break off here till the next occaſion. My ſervice to your kind wife.

Your Couſin,

December 31ſt 1655. R. B.

(K K.) For his Reverend and much-beloved Brother Mr Simeon Aſhe, Miniſter at London

Reverend and Dear Brother,

Your's of November 15th, was very refreſhfull, that the Lord is pleaſed yet to lend ſome of yow to his people there I have no yet ſeen your funerall [ſermon] on Mr. Whitaker: ſend me one of them; my intereſt in that precious ſaint was great, for eſtimation and love mutuall. I am ſorie Mr Marſhall is a-dying, he was ever in my heart a very eminent man. His many ſermons on that verſe of John viii, 36, "If the Son make yow free, ye ſhall be free indeed," I have oft preſſed him to make publict: he was the preacher now living who ordinarly moſt affected my heart; I wiſh yow preſſed him to let ſo many of his papers be publiſhed as may be. I hear Dr. Young hes a good treatiſe for the preſſe. I am ſure zealous Mr. Edwards had ſundrie: yow have been midwife to ſome already after their death, and I alſo. A pitie ſome men's labors ſhould periſh, and others ſhould not periſh. Mr Marſhall long ago loſt the hearts of our Nation. He was the main inſtrument of that Nationall Covenant with God, and among ourſelves, which wont to hing on the walls of your churches: it will hing ever before the eye of God, the prime Covenanter: never a league ſo openlie and univerſallie tread upon, and obliterate without all juſt cauſe I wiſh Mr. Marſhall, for ſaving of his own ſoule, before he appear at Chriſt's barr did exoner himſelf with the Protectour, if he come to viſit him, as I think he will, or otherwayes in write, about everie article of that Covenant. I think the Protectour will take it as weell to be freely and friendly dealt with by dying Mr. Marſhall as any man on earth; and I hope Mr. Marſhall will be loath to deny this very neceſſary and laſt ſervice to Chriſt and his owne ſoule, if yow there will require it of him. But as *ſilentium perdidit Amyclas*, ſo in theſe days gracious men's fear to offend their friends by their freedome, leaves them even in their death to the dangerous offence of God. I bleſs God yow have ſo much as the ſhew of a Preſbyterie and Synod. Why has not all England and Ireland ſo much? Why want yow a Generall Aſſemblie? Why have ye no power at all to execute eccleſiaſtick juriſdiction, not ſo much as Independents, Anabaptiſts, or Papiſts have among their owne. For all theſe, as we hear, are tollerate to exerciſe their diſcipline among themſelves; only yow Preſbyterians are either reſtrained or not carefull to uſe your libertie. Can it be any maxim of State to deny that libertie to Preſbyterians in England for the exerciſe of Proteſtant diſcipline, which the Popiſh Kings of France and Pole did never deny to our brethren, to whom they permitted the libertie of their religion? But ſo far as we know, yow have never fought this benefite. Whatever ye doe or leave undone, we here take all in the beſt part it may be taken; conſidering your difficulties yet, for myſelf, I loved ever ane ingenuous ſimplicitie and honeſt zeal more than too much cautious wiſdome. While yow are permitted to uſe the ſhaddow of your powerleſs Provinciall ſynod, were it not good to appoint a committee of a few the fitteſt to conſult, as on other things ſo, how to ſtirr up theſe whom they know fitteſt in all England for writing on every needfull ſubject. Yow have many moſt able pens as any Church this day; for want of upſtirring many of them are like to doe no ſervice. What yow commend to me, I have no leaſure for it, beſide all elſe, my weekly preaching and four publict leſſons in our Colledge take up all my time; and in our vacation, ſome other things which I have of my own, and of other men's, for the preſſe, take me up. Yow have a multitude there much fitter than I for that and all things elſe. Mr Rutherfoord tells me yow have his Anſwer to Hooker at laſt: let it be printed if yow there think fitt. Mr. Dickſon's Caſes of Conſcience will be abroad, I hope, before this come to yow. But ſome of yow there would be put on to proſecute that excellent ſubject. Will yow let Mr Cotton's oſtentative bragges, of the Independents appropriating to their faction this part of divinity, go as a ſenſible truth? Mr. Baxter's writs are read with a good eye by many; his laſt peice of Judgement, preached and printed in the mids of your citie, in the preface, commending yow citie miniſters, and your diſcipline, ſo highly offends and ſtumbles many: it ſeems to be ſtuffed with groſſe Arminianiſme: Why take yow no care either to gaine the man from his errors, or yoke with him ſome able divines to guard againſt his infection? Sundry here are thinking to take him to taſk; but I love and highly eſteeme the man, for much good I find in his writs: I think him ill loſt Noble Mr. Vynes or Mr. Burgeſs, if they were ſet to deale with him in a loving private way, might doe weell; mind this. I ſee Mr. Haak, at laſt, is printing there the Dordracen Notes in Engliſh; his longſomeneſs, for ſo many years, made me almoſt repent of getting him, of our penurie, two hundred pounds for that ſervice. The Polyglott Bible, now on your preſſe, is to me the moſt excellent book that ever any where was printed, if Dr. Waltham[2] perfyte his undertaking If either yow or any of your friends had faſhions of[3] that to me very commendable man, I wiſh yow made my addreſſe to him, that now and then I might write to him for the publict good let me know if this may be without your faſherie. Our arme here is broken for all diſcipline, moſt by our diſſenting brethren running to a ſchiſme. Poperie encreaſes more than theſe ſeventy years. We lately had a long twenty dayes conference at Edinburgh for union with our brethren; more than a dozen of papers paſt among us. I ſend yow here one to ſhew yow what we offered; but we find the true ſtick to be beyond their old errour, (which yet no Church, ſurely no ſettled State in the world, will approve) of the unlawfullneſs to joyne in defence of the nation againſt the invaſion of a forraigne enemie, if ſo the nation's armie have ſome officers otherwayes qualified than a few private perſons think fitt, though both the Kirk and State, (the Parliament and Generall Aſſembly,) declare their full ſatiſfaction with them. This unnatural principle, which as much as any one thing on earth, did openly and viſible procure our late ruine, our brethren are ſtill obſtinately for it, and will not be content we permitt them to enjoy their opinion, except we conſent to their impugning the verie conſtitution of that Generall Aſſemblie which allowed our judgement, which is doubtleſs the judgement of all Churches, and all nations which yet

[2] Dr Brian Walton, afterwards Biſhop of Cheſter. His noble edition of the Polyglott Bible was, after several years labour completed at London 1657, in six vo's folio

[3] By this phrase he no doubt means, " had acquaintance with "

hes lived on earth. But our brethren now are proceeded further to declare the body of our presbyteries, synods, and congregations, to consist of a pluralitie of corrupt members, so farr as they refuse openly submission to the sentences of any of our Kirk Judicatories. We deny not much humane frailtie; and we offer to goe on to purge out both of congregations, presbyteries, and synods, faithfullie in the sight of God, whomever the word of God, or any rule of our Church, or any just reason requires to be purged out, albeit we think the pluralitie of our Church judicatories and congregations was never better than this day, or ever, in their eye, shall be better in any Nationall Church. However, because we are not so rash as they to condemne so many unheard, they have flowne out to a strange devise, to set up a few of themselves as a Committee of the Generall Assemblie, with full jurisdiction over all our land, to put in and out of the ministrie whom they think fitt. Against this horrible usurpation, the Presbyterie of Edinburgh hes given this inclosed Testimonie, wherein almost all the presbyteries and synods of this land will joyn. Our fear is not so much that the Councell of State, whom they have supplicat, will authorize them in so unexampled ane tyrannie, as that our division be used for ane occasion by the State to take in their owne hands, from us both, all ecclesiastick jurisdiction, which will be to us a great increase of our miseries. When we had satisfied the proclamation against publict prayer for the King, we expected more equitie and favour than before: we wish we find no much lesse. The Supplication which our Dissenters gave in to the Councell for power, under the name of purging, to make havock of our Church, hes yet gott no answer. we suspect it is sent up to the Protectour to have his mind of it, and there we have no friends to represent the truth. The grievances we gave to the Generall, anent many grievous abuses in our Church, which we believe was sent up by him, according to his promise, doe lye there, without any returne we know. But the Ordinance, which some of our brethren did obtaine of the Protectour, that no stipend should be given to any intrant but such as in effect they lyke, though not only we did demonstrate its mischief, but the chief of the Dissenters themselves disclaimed it, in this paper of Waristoune's and Mr. Guthrie's; yet it firmlie continues, to our great grief and hurt. In all these, and many more grievances, we mourne to God; and upon this occasion I let yow know our condition, that yow may mourne with us, for more can no be expected from yow at fuch a tyme. It's ane eafe to a burdened fpirit to difcharge itfelfe in the bofome of a compaffionate friend, fuch as long yow have been to the Church of Scotland, and myfelf in particular The Lord uphold your fpirits in his wayes in thefe very defective tymes. My prayer and bleffing be on the conftant brethren there, and all their labours. My fpeciall love to yourfelf.

Your Brother,

December 31ft 1655 R B

(L. L.). [To Mr. Robert Baillie.]

Sir,

By reafon of a weak head and a goutie hand, I cannot poffiblie write fo largelie as yow may expect, and as your letter doth require. This is the firft writing which I have undertaken for the fpace of a fourtnight, and now I put pen unto paper with difficultie, that I may not feem regardlefs of, nor unthankfull for your intelligence.

Mr. Marfhall[1] was dead before I received your letter, and I cannot give yow intelligence of any conferrence with the Protector, either in reference to the Covenant, or any other concernment. He was more fatiffied with the change of government, both civill and ecclefiafticall, than many of his brethren. Dr Young[2] is dead alfo; and his papers about Difcipline are fo voluminous, that no ftationer will undertake to print them, becaufe that controverfie lyeth dead among us, and few inquire for any books of that fubject: Hence it is that Mr. Crooke is fo backward in putting to preffe that Anfwer to Mr. Hooker, which Mr. Rutherfoord hath made and fent hither. We have latelie loft worthie Mr. Vines.[6] thus God increafeth our breaches His Majeftie teach us favinglie the meaning of thefe very fad providences The lame courfe (whereof yow juftly complained) is taken in England, to over-

[1] Stephen Marfhall B D died in November 1655, and was interred in Westminster Abbey

[2] Thomas Young D D Vicar of Stow-market, in Suffolk, and Master of Jesus College, Cambridge Vide vol 1 p 366; and Appendix to the present Volume.

[6] In the MS "Wines"—Richard Vines, A M Minister of Weddington, and Master of Pembroke Hall Cambridge, died in February 1655

throw the power and practife of Prefbyteriall government, and to advance Independencie, as alfo to indulge Anabaptifts, and other erroneous perfons. As for Mr Baxter, he is doubtlefs a godly man, though tenacious in his miftakes Mr. Burgefs and Mr Vines dealt with him to reduce him, but could not convince him to fatiffaction There are many good treatifes publifhed by able men among us, though diverfe others are fo much in the pulpit, that they cannot appear in the preffe. Through God's mercy, many act prefbyterialhe in London, and in many counties, both in reference to ordination and admiffion to the facrament, notwithftanding of difcouragements.

Sir, I hope yow will accept thefe lines, and pardon my brevitie upon the account forementioned. I have fent the fermon which you defyre. I pray yow prefent my refpects to all my friends, as yow have occafion. We mind yow in our prayers heartilie. The Lord help yow and us to wait by faith with patience for his falvation through Chrift, in whom I am

Your loving friend and brother,

S. Ashe.

[To Mr Robert Baillie]

Sir,

I must crave pardon for my long filence: it is not out of difrefpectfullnefs, or forgetfullnefs of yow, or of the fad condition yow and the reft of our dear Brethren with yow are in, but out of the multitude of bufineffes that have hitherto hindered me. Truely, Sir, yow are in my heart, and my prayers are not wanting for yow, that the Lord would teach yow the meaning of his fevere difpenfations towards your Nation, and that yow may learn righteoufnefs by them, and that the Lord would heall the fad divifions that are between yow and your godlie brethren I fhall fhorthe find a fpare tyme to wryte to yow more largelie, but being now at Mr Afhe's, while he was wryting his letter, I took the opportunitie to prefent my dear refpects to yow, and Mr. Douglafs, Mr. Hamilton, Mr Smith, and the reft of our godlie brethren, whofe daylie prayers I heartilie implore, and fhall ever remaine.

Your true friend and brother in the work of the Lord,

Edm Calamy.

For Mr. James Hammiltoun

James,

The cafe yow propone to me is very fad and dangerous My firft thoughts are thefe; that yow guefſe right, the authors and on-putters of it hes, and will be, thefe unhappie foxes who, haveing caft of their owne tailes, cannot reft till they force all their neighbours to caft of theirs alfo: your dilemm is hard. If yow refufe, it's very lyke they will employ the Remonftrators, diverfe of whom will follow their leader, and will put themfelfes in power, both for ftipends and all things elfe belonging to Eraftian jurifdiction, for making havock of our Church, againſt whom all our complaints will be flighted, and yow and all of our mind muft fuffer what the Remonftrators pleafe to procure. If yow embrace the reft, yow fhall feem to your people and all the countrie fo farr to comply that your perfons and miniftrie will become unfavorie; and for our fake, the little remainder of love that remains to the Covenant and work of God in the land will totallie evanifh, and many hearts will be caft fully open to returne where they were, or runn out to any bye-way they like, with a high mifregard and difdaine of all we can fay or doe to the contrare 2. Our fellows in thefe labours, and moft be loved, fhall be our Remonftrating brethren, yea, our northern feparatifts, the flock will be our excommunicat, etc. with whom we muft joyne in filence. 3 We muft ferve in our turns as chaplaines at their call who will not be of our Church, but diverfe may be known Independents, Anabaptifts, Eraftians, apoftates from our Covenant, active inftruments in oppreffing our countrie, which is hard to digeft 4 If, according to your confcience, yow difcharge yourfelf faithfullie as their foules require who are your hearers, yow draw on yourfelfes greater trouble than yow would efhew. If yow be allwayes filent it is a great finne, fhame, fcandale, change of our way of preaching in all our former tymes. 5. Your example drawes out any of all the land, whofe comeing to preach there, or refufeing, may undoe them, and this be a lafting and univerfall ground of work to the beft paftors in the land 6 It will be a difplayed banner to call all our people, with our countenance, to joyne with Sectaries of all forts, though excommunicate, which will be a hodge-podge of all religions under our miniftrie, a farr worfe evill than wicked toleration. 7. Who can recount the mifchieves of that hellifh invention? The Protector to this day hath never aflayed any fuch thing, but yow will learn him the way: prevention will be the beft, and a private earneft dealing with the Prefident that he would be content with one or two conftant chaplaines, be who they will; but I could wifh they were only Englifh, and thefe Prefbyterians The Lord direct yow. I feare the croffe we wold efhew will not be long keeped off I know the fpirit of the Remonftrators is reftlefs, and cannot ceafe from inventing one mifchief after another without end We are too little in prayer for a delyverance from our oppreffion: With verie much adoe I got yow followed in abftaining, etc; bot come of it what will, I will not get yow followed if yow go to this purpofe.

Yours

January 21ft 1656

FOR HIS REVEREND AND WELL-BELOVED BROTHER MR CRANFORD, MINISTER AT LONDON, NEAR THE OLD EXCHANGE

REVEREND AND DEAR BROTHER,

The remembrance of my fweet fellowfhip with yow, and others there, is oft refrefhfull to my heart, though the Lord juftlie has overturned, by the hands of unjuft men, all our once fair bloffoming hopes and labours. The occafion of my calling to yow at this tyme, is my defyre to know the condition of that excellent book, the beft to me that ever was printed, Dr Walton's Polyglott Bible; we have fo much here of three copies as is printed. What is this Dr Walton for a man? where bred? and of what condition? When I was there, there was no fuch name heard of. I am much in love with the man's labour, and almoft would venture to feek acquaintance of him by letters, unlefs I had conceaved it fitter to underftand firft by yow the man's qualities. That which I would defyre of him is the printing of an Arabick and Samaritan Praxis The Samaritan he promifes, by that man who overfees the Samaritan Pentateuch, and I pray yow what man is that?[1] Yow

---

[1] Dr Edmund Castell, who undertook and completed, in 1669, his *Lexicon Heptaglotton*, comprising all the Oriental Languages in Walton's Polyglott,—a work of immense labour and

would doe me a pleafure if yow would give me account of that whole work, and of the men who are employed about it.[8] I have fent yow a copie of a letter of mine to Voetius at Utrecht, and his anfwer to me the laft yeare: I have no hope to obtaine my defyre in thefe paits over-fea; if yow there do it not, it will not be done. I think, if yow or any of our friends would deale in earneft with Dr. Walton,[9] he could eafily give us a Letter grammar of the Arabick, and a full Praxis; alfo of the Samaritane: for Chaldee and Syriack we want not helps. This were a good fervice to the publict, and a help to many who, by his Bible, are ftirred up to the ftudy of all thefe languages. But the great thing we have need of is a Courfe of philofophie. I pray call at fome of your ftationers for my Hebrew Praxis; confider the preface of it, and compare it with thefe two letters, I doubt not but yow and all reall fchollers will be in my mind. If by Dr. Tuckney, our good friend, late Vice-Chancellor of Cambridge, or any of your acquaintance at Oxford, or in the citie, yow could finde out two or three for to goe about this excellent good work, for the great advancement of learning, and great fervice and honour, not only of this Ifle, bot the whole Reformed Churches, which lye under a great difgrace and grievous hurt, that to this day they are fo negligent and bafe as to take the moft of all their philofophy from the worft of the Popifh divines, Friers, and Jefuites. I hope love to this ufefull and noble defigne, and old friendfhip, will make yow content, at your leafure, to let me know if any thing may be expected of this kind from among yow. My heartie love and beft wifhes to yow and all yours. I reft,

Your much honouring and loving Brother,

Glafgow, Auguft 27th 1656   R. BAILLIE.

If my *Appendix Practica ad Epitomen Grammaticæ Hebrææ Joannis Buxtorfii*, printed at Edinburgh, 1653, be not eafily found there, I fhall at the firft occafion fend yow up one.

expense, but for which he was so inadequately recompensed that he had occasion to complain having "spent twenty years in time to the publick service, above £12,000 of his own estate, and for a reward was left, in the close of the work, above £1,800 in debt."

[8] The best account of Walton's Polyglott Bible, and of his assistants in carrying on that great and laborious undertaking, will be found in Archdeacon Todds Memoirs of the Bishop's Life and Writings. Lond 1821, 2 vols. 8vo

[9] As in a former letter Baillie writes Waltons name, "Waltham"

For Mr. Spang at Middelburgh. September 1st 1656.

Reverend and Dear Cousin,

I must intreat that yow would be pleased to write ofter than of late yow have done. Your occasions to Rotterdame, and from thence hither, can no be but frequent. I defyred yow to try if yow can get a courfe of the French Currents of Antwerp or Bruffells, let me try the laft moneth of them. yow remember yow fent me, for three or four years punctually, the French Gazet from Amfterdam, fee if the like can be done from Bruffells or Antwerp, to which yow are now nearer. I long exceedingly for Dr. Strang's book. what yow have for the Colledge fend it with the firft occafion. I hope your bygone count is payed, and more money will be fent yow fhortly. I pray yow, in your firft to Voetius, remember my heartie fervice to him for his kind and prolix anfuer to my letter. Try if he hes any returne, either from Buxtorf or Golius, about my motion to them. we all long for a new enlarged edition of his Bibliotheck, and a third volumne of his Thefes. I am informed that there is no man fitter to draw a Philofophick Curfus than his own fon : will yow try if he can be perfuaded to it, who now is in ley for any fervice. What is Heidanus for a man? What is become of Morus and Blondell? Is there no man who, after Spanheim, does mind the contioverfie with Amiraud? As long fince I defired yow to gather the adverfarie pieces of Voetius and Marefius, and fend them to us, doe it yet. What is my good friend Apollonius doing? Is there no more of Bochartus, or Henricus Philippus, come out? That the more willingly yow may give me ane account of all this, behold I am at the labour to let yow know how all our affaires ftand here.

To myfelf the Lord is ftill very good, continuing my health, wealth, credit, welfare of all my fix children, affiftance in every part of my calling, bleffed be his name! I live peaceably with all men; I go to no Church meeting, prefbyterie, or fynod, on the ground I fhew yow before. Mr. James Durhame is independent with me, (which contributes to my peace,) but his grounds are diverfe. When Mr David Dickfon went to Edinburgh, with very violence he forced us to give Mr James a call to his profeffion of the Colledge; before he entred to it, the Generall Affemblie appointed him minifter for the King. We then called Mr. Robert Ramfay to that profeffion. When Mr. James was wearie of the Court, his partie here was earneft for his retuine to the Colledge. The man then, and before, and to this day, was to me very precious and deare, for however I have (as oft I told him,) been very difatiffied with many of his wayes, yet I counted him one of the moft gracious, wife, and able preachers now in this Ifle. I could have been gladly content he had come to Mr. Ramfay's place in the miniftrie, or to Dr. Strang's place of Principall; but to his former place of profeffion, whereto we called Mr Ramfay, I was not content he fhould returne, and did oppofe it what I could, fo much the more, that I found, from himfelfe, that he was to endeavoui Mr. Patrick Gillefpie to be our Principall, which then to me feemed very inconvenient. When Mr. Ramfay died, then would I gladly have Mr Durhame to any thing he lyked; but all fell croffe to my defyre, my friend Mr Zacharie [Boyd], and others, fell paffionat to have Mr John Young to the profeffion, and caried it, fore againft my mind. Mr P G[illefpie], by the Englifh, fet himfelf doune in Dr. Strang's place. The feffion drew up fo unorderlie a call for Mr. R. Ramfay's place of the miniftrie, that the moft of the towne drew up a proteftation againft it: Mr Durhame counted his proper place to be that of the Colledge which Mr John Young had poffeffed, and not caring to tak [talk?] of the proteftation, did ferve in Mr. R. R[amfay's] place of miniftrie, (no man contradicting him,) from time to time, but in a loufe way; and when our great jarrs in Prefbyterie and Synod arofe, did abftaine as weell as I from all meetings. On this his carriage as malcontent he hes had fundry invitations to other places; but that that I fear may carrie, is an earneft defire of Sir John Clotworthy to have him to Antrim, as he fayes, to further the work of God in all Ireland, and to be Proveift of a Colledge which he hopes to get erected in that place. Sir John hes made the Prefident Broghill deall with him for that effect, and put the Protectour alfo upon it. My heart truely would be forrie if he fhould remove: he is the minifter of my familie, and almoft the only minifter in this place of whom my foull getts good, and whom I refpect in fome things above all men I know: he hes a very fatiffactorie treatife on the Revelation, which I encourage him to print. If the gravell and melancholie cut not his dayes, he may be for much good fervice. I did oft repent my oppofition of his re-entrie to the

College, though I remain in the mind I did no wrong, and as things then were, I could not have weell done otherwayes than I did.

The matters of our Colledge this yeare were peaceable; our gallant building going on vigoroufly; above twenty-fix thoufand pound are already fpent upon it: Mr Patrick Gillefpie with a very great care, induftrie, and dexteritie, manageing it himfelf as good as alone. But our inward and moft neceffar materialls are too much neglected. The Bacheller Regent, Mr George Sinclair, almoft the whole year, was dangeroufly fick, to the great hurt of the claffe. Mr. P. Young, Magiftrand Regent, was exceeding negligent in his attendance, to the great hurt of that claffe. Mr J. Veitch, the Bajon Regent, partly through ficknefs, and partly by tryells and call to the miniftrie, neglected much that claffe Mr. A. Burnet waited, according to his parts, much better on the Semies. Our divinitie ftudents were but few, and however they had leffons enough from Mr. J. Young and me, yet they minded ftudie but little; for when they fee their weak companions, the fecond or third yeare after their laureation, put in the beft places, with exceeding poor fufficiencie, it makes the reft the more to neglect all ftudie, but only to preach in their popular kind of way, which requires little learning

I am glad my hand is free of their plantations totallie. Mr. James Ramfay, a very able and fufficient youth as we have of his age, planted by us in Leinzie, to the great fatiffaction of all, except a very few who choifed ane Englifh fectarie, to whom they promifed the ftipend, when, after two years trouble, the Englifhman removed, our brethren Mr. P. Gillefpie, Mr. James Durhame, Mr. John Carftares, all much obliged to Mr. R. Ramfay for their own places, would not for any intreatie be pleafed to let his fon live in peace: fo we let him go to Lithgow, where he is much better than he could have been where he was, but in his place they have put one evidently of farre meaner parts, Mr Harrie Forfyth, lately a baxter boy, laureat within thefe two years, a little, very fecklefs-lyke thing in his perfon, and mean in his gifts, but the fon of a Gillefpy to him, the parifh weary of ftrife, wherein by the Englifh power they were allwayes oppreffed, yeilded in filence without oppofition. In Campfie likewife, in [place of] Mr. Archibald Denneftone, depofed by them without any confiderable caufe, much to my grief, and againft the heart of his parifh who loved him, they have planted

Mr. John Law, within thir three years brought from a pottinger to be laureat. In Rugland,[1] againſt the people's heart, they have planted a litle maniken of ſmall parts, whom I never faw, and forced old Mr. Robert Young, albeit as able yet as ever, to give over his miniſtrie. In Cathcart, where they had planted an Engliſhman againſt my mind, haveing, after two or three years tryell enough of him, they ſhuffled him over to Ireland, and are to plant another young thing, lately laureat, with ſmall contentment to the people.

In Glaſgow, Mr. Andrew Gray being dead of a purple fever, of a few dayes roveing, the Magiſtrates would have been at the calling of Mr. J. Fergufone, one of the moſt excellent young men of our land. But to this Mr James Durhame and the reſt were ſo averſe, that they were ready, publickly, to have oppoſed it So the Magiſtrates knowing their unabilitie to carry any call contrarie to their mind, yielded to let them call whom they pleaſed. Mr. James Durhame would have been at Mr. J. Law before they put him on Campſie; but Mr. Patrick caried it to Mr. Robert Macquare, who lately, for inabilitie of body, had left his charge in the Colledge, and evidently was unable for ſuch a charge as Glaſgow: yet they put him in *nemine contradicente*, and that without all the ordinarie tryalls, being unable, for his health, to have undergone them: appearandly the burthen ſhortly will cruſh him, except he go on to doe as he hes done yet, frequently to let his place vaike. Through the violence of that partie our Church, in theſe parts, is in a hard condition, and for the tyme remediless. They got a little ſtop lately from whence it was not expected At Blantyre, Mr. John Heriot, of ſeventy-eight years, haveing admitted Mr. James Hamilton helper, with two parts of his ſtipend, becauſe he would not thereafter give over the whole, the Preſbyterie of Hamilton intended a proceſs againſt him, for ſmall unconſiderable cauſes, and depoſed him; when he is charged to remove from his houſe, and all he hes there, his ſon, by the friendſhip of Swinton, gets the Engliſh to take notice of the violent oppreſſion; who, after a full hearing, decerne the old miniſter to enjoy all, even what before he had been content to quite. This preparative is dangerous for our whole Church; but the unhappy violence of theſe unadvyſed men draws on theſe evills on themſelfes and others.

[1] Or Rutherglen The perſon here rather diſreſpectfully mentioned, was John Dickson, one of the Covenanters He was ejected after the Restoration, and for many years was confined upon the Baſs, but at the Revolution, he was reſtored to his pariſh, and died in the year 1700

This is lyke now to be the refuge of all they opprefs; but a miferable one it puts all our Church caufes in the hands of the Englifh, who defyre to be judges of them according to their Eraftian principle, though ordinarily our brethren have the ear of the Englifh to doe with them what they pleafe With much adoe your old friend, a right honeft and able man, more than the moft of his neighbours, Mr Allan Fergufon of Drummen, efcaped their hands The laft Synod had put a committee to the Prefbyterie of Dumbartan to try a number of flanders noyfed upon him: when, befide all his elders, four-fcore and fourteen witneffes are fworne and tryed, nothing at all is found againft him. This procefs, and another of his neighbour Mr. David Adamfone of Fintrie, where alfo, after much noyfe, nothing was found, hes made their fervour of purgeing in our bounds much to relent; for, as oft I told them, they will find on tryell, that the men to be purged out are on their fide, not on ours, if there were any juftice. At that fame Synod the depofition of Mr. R. Hume was ratified, as I was informed, very unjufthe.

In the other parts of the land we fee no relenting of our brethren's fervour Mr Liviftoun, notwithftanding of all the trouble about the planting of Eccles, hes gone on to the lyke enormous practice at Sprouftoun, coming in on the Prefbyterie of Dunfe, with two or three of the neighbour prefbyteries, and planting Mr. S[amuel] Row, one of their partie, contrare to the mind of all the Prefbyterie; how farr againft the fundamental laws of all our difcipline yow will fee in the Prefbyterie's declaration, (A.). Mr James Guthrie is ftill in conteft with the people of Stirling, but in more vexation than formerly, for his colleague, Mr Matthias Simfone, is as headie and bold a man as himfelf, and hes good hearing with the Englifh, fo that he is like to get the ftipend; and [Mr] Rule to live perquue. Mr. James and Wariftoune are on their old defigne ftill, to fet up their Commiffion for tyrannizing over the Kirk; but it's like the Englifh will not countenance them, the thing is fo extreamlie and evidentlie unjuft; alfo fome of us are fallen in with the Englifh farre enough

The Prefident Broghill is reported by all to be a man exceeding wife and moderat, and by profeffion a Prefbyterian: he hes gained more on the affections of the people than all the Englifh that ever were among us. He hes been very civill to Mr. Dowglafs and Mr Dickfon, and is very intime with Mr. James Sharp; by this means we have ane equall hearing in all we have adoe with the Councell; yet their way is exceeding longfome, and all muft be done firft at London It's but the other week that Mr. P G[illefpie's] abfurd order for ftipends was gotten away he puts us in hopes of more favours.

That much talked-of refpect to Mr Wood, (though yet I have not inquired it of himfelfe,) as I hear, was this: Mr. Rutherfoord's daily bitter contentions with him made him wearie of his place exceedingly, the Old Colledge being long vaiking, and he the eldeft mafter of it, and for fundrie years employed to overfee it, almoft as Principall, was wifhed by fundrie who loved it and him, to be placed there; and there is no doubt he was the fitteft man living for that charge: but here was the infuperable difficultie, a fair call could not be gotten The fyve mafters who had power to call were divided, one Campbell, a Remonftrator, minded the place, and, by his party, was no unlyke to have carried it from the Englifh, one Martine, the eldeft mafter then in charge, alledging it to be his right to fucceed, with the confent of other two mafters, went to the Englifh to fute their favour. The Prefident, I think, on Mr. James Sharp's information, moved the Councell, without Mr. Wood's knowledge, to make choice of him for the place They write a peremptor letter to the minifters and mafters of St. Andrewes to admitt Mr. James Wood Principall to the Old Colledge without delay. When the Univerfitie is conveened, and the letter read, Mr. Campbell protefted. the other three were moved to invite Mr James, in obedience to the Englifh command, but not to call him. Mr. James accepted the charge I am glad he is in it, or any other where he is contented; for indeed he is the moft ferviceable man our Church now hes. but I am not yet fatiffied of his accepting of that place on the Englifh command; for if, in Divine Providence, they who had right to call, for their own bafe and hurtfull defignes refufed to call him, I think it was hard for him, upon whatever caufes, to medle with it. I love not that we fhould juftifie or harden the Englifh in their ufurpations in our Univerfities rights: but thefe things I will debate with himfelf at meeting

Ane other paffage of ours I was not fatiffied with: Swinton was excommunicat for his early complying with the Englifh Sundrie of his friends were earneft to have him relaxed, that in their neceffar affaires they might have the more libertie to imploy his help, he was either fo proud, or fo feared to offend his mafters, that he would neither acknowledge a fault, nor petition for favour. When his friends dealt with the Prefbyterie of Edinburgh, they fent two to conferr with him: all that they reported from him was, that he was very willing to live and die in the communion of our Church; and that the reafon of his not-appearance, when cited to the Commiffion of Perth, was not contempt, but juft fear of his life Upon this report, without any fupplication, he is relaxed the next Sabbath by Mr James Hamiltone. This I did not lyke at all as a meere fcorne of our difcipline. Our brethren would not long be behind with us: for at once the Prefbyterie of Air did relaxe good William Govane, who was at leaft on the fcaffold, at the King's execution, if no more, excommunicat on the lyke occafion; yea, the Synod of Glafgow at Aire took the cenfure off Mr P Gillefpie and Mr James Naefmith, without any acknowledgement of a fault, or defyre to be relaxed. To this ftrange enormitie, all formallie voted; only Mr James Fergufone, Mr Thomas Kircaldie, Mr. George Young, were abfent; Mr. John Bell and Mr. Alexander Nifbet removed themfelves; but no diffent wes entered.

Our State is in a very filent condition. ftrong garrifons over all the land, and a great armie, both of horfe and foot, for which there is no fervice at all Our Nobles lying up in prifons, and under forfaultries, or debts, private or publict, are for the moft part either broken or breaking No more word of delyvering Crawford, Lauderdaill, Eglintone, Montgomerie, Ogilvie, Merfhall, and many more, than was the firft houre Glencairne lyes ftill in the Caftle of Edinburgh; Colonel Borthwick betrayed him: the letter he brought to him from the King, he delyvered to Monk before it came to Glencairne's hands, and his anfwer of it alfo before it came to the King; and yet, under the moft fearfull imprecations can be devifed, the villaine wrote, unrequired, that he had done no fuch things. Some fays, it would have ftood hard with Glencairne's life, had it not been the Prefident's favour, procured by Mr. James Sharp. The dyvour act, of lands for creditors at twenty years purchafe, has made much clamour, albeit none who has any credit has made ufe of it. All the Advocats are returned to the barre. Balcolmie and Ker makes fome more difpatch in caufes than was [before] The Great Seall of Scotland, (with Cromwell's large ftatue on horfeback, *Olivarius Dei Gratia Reip. Anglæ Scotiæ et Hiberniæ Protector*, under the arms of Scotland *Pax*

Quæritur Bello,) is given to Defborough, the Signet, with the great fees of the Secretar's place, to Colonell Lockhart; the Regifter's, to Judge Smith; and the reft of the places of State to others. The expences, delays, and oppreffions in law-futes, are fpoken of to be as great as was ever.

The Spanifh warre has wracked many of our merchands; albeit, in God's mercie, as little lofs be fallen on our neighbours of this toune, as on any of the Ifle; for except one little fhip taken by the Bifkainers, near Burdeaux, and James Bar's fhip, which, with himfelf, by a pitifull mifguiding, was blowne up almoft in the harberie, we had no more lofle this year, whileas a world of others has been wracked; many more in a few moneths than was all the time of your warre. It is much talked, that it is both your men and fhips that ferves the Spanifh in all thefe fpoils Our fleet, waiting in vaine on the coaft of Spaine, does little good to the merchands in thefe coafts, and yet the taxes with us are great; the maintainance was towards ten thoufand pound fterling a month They fay the excife will be double; fo that the revenue will be above three hundred thoufand pounds a-year, the halfe whereof is never together among us The trueth is, money was never fo fcarce here, and groweth daihe fcarcer, and yet it s thought this Parliament in September is indicted mainlie for new taxations What England may bear, to whom the Protectour remitted the halfe of their monethlie maintainance of one hundred and twenty thoufand pound fterling, I know not; but Scotland, whofe burthen has been triple, befide the fynes, forfaulters, debts, and other miferies, feems unable to bear what lyes on already. Wife men think the Protector wifer than to defire the emptie title of a King, when he has much more already than the King. No man looks for any good of this Parliament, but fears evill, yet all who are wife thinks that our evills would grow yet more if Cromwell were removed They think his government, as it is, will be farr better than a Parliament, or any thing elfe they expect; only all think this warre with Spain needlefs and hurtfull, and hopes by the Parliament it will be taken away

There was never fo great folicitation for votes to be chofen Commiffioners as now among us It's like there fhall be none of the whole number more cordiall for all the Proteftor's defyres, be what they may, than thefe that come from Scotland. It's faid Mr. James Guthrie and my Lord Wariftoun, with their friends, have been fitting more than this fourtnight in Edinburgh, drawing their papers, to be sent by some of their number to the Protectour or Parliament. They were so absurd, that Mr. P. Gillespie, who was expected to have been sent up to agent them, turned his back, and left them; yet they will not want agents. We think my Lord Broghill, commissioner for the Toune of Edinburgh, will crosse their injustice and irrationall violence. However, our minds will be in no peace till we see what this Parliament will bring forth. No man I know expects any good from it, and that is our condition for the present, that we can be hardlie worse.

Through God's mercie our Toune, in its proportion, thryves above all the land. The word of God is weell loved and regarded, albeit not as it ought and we desyre; yet in no toune of our land better. Our people has much more trade in comparison than any other: their buildings encrease strangelie both for number and fairness. it's more than doubled in our tyme.[2] I pray God to encrease his blessing on this place of our birth, albeit I am feared for it; for on Sunday was eight dayes at four houres in the morning, August 17th, there was a sensible earthquake in all the parts of the toune, though I felt it not. Five or six yeares agoe there was ane other, in the afternoone, which I felt, and was followed with that fearfull burning, and all the other shakings has been among us since. The Lord preserve us from his too well deserved judgements!

For the posture of forraigne affaires, they are thus represented to us: that the frequent tumults of Constantinople, killing Visier after Visier, and threatening the young Sultan himself, does weaken much that Empire, so that Venice the alone has been able to keep up warre with them, these dozen of years, with yearlie advantage, but we think it strange that this Republick this last year has buried no lesse than three Dukes. The French continue their fate of unhappiness beyond the Montes; beside their disaster the other year in Naples, and their calamitie at Pavy, their siege at Valentia at this tyme, for all the help Savoy and Modena make to them, looks very ill-favoured, when the Spaniard lyes round about their trenches.

This Pope seemes as dissimulat a companion as any of his predecessors. His self-denyed Holiness would for a whole yeare have none of his kindred

[2] The population of Glasgow which at different periods presents a striking instance of encrease, in 1610 amounted to 7644, in 1660, to 14,678, in 1755, to 23,546, in 1801, to 77,385, in 1821, to 147,043, and by the late census, in 1841, to 257,592.

come near him; but at laft his old mafter and lord of Siena, the Duke of Florence's importunat prayer muft overcome his obftinacie to permitt his brother and nephews come near; and fo foon as they came, the good of the Church required the chief places of command, both by fea and land, in the whole ecclefiaftick dominions, to be put in their hands. That infamous woman, the Queen of [Sweden], having enough of Rome, and Rome more than enough of her, is landed in France: what will be the end of her wandering, who can conjecture? This terrible plague, which from Naples is flown to Rome, notwithftanding all their extraordinary guards, and affrights, it feems, not only all Italie, but all the neighbouring nations. We are glad that the fearfull civill waries of the Switzers is like to end fo foone in peace. We hope their peace will be a guard to the Proteftants in Piedmont.

We marvell that the Cardinall of France fhould have had fo hard contefts with the Parliament of Paris, and fo many in that popular fubject of money: when the Pope, and the clergy fitting in a Generall Affemblie fo long at Paris, are not very weell content, when Orleans is from Court, and Condée in the head of a Spanifh armie; at fuch a feafon to provoke the Parliament and people of Paris in the tender matter of moneys, feems to favour more of the Cardinall's Roman courage than his Italian wifdom. Turenne, to us afarr off, feems not to have been more unhappie in this fiege of Valencien than unadvifed. A half-eyed man might have forefeen the remedilefs danger of his armie's cutting in two, fo that the only meane of communication was a dam or bridge or what elfe, which the encreafe of waters could eafily break, and make the one half of his armie ufelefs to the other, in whatever danger: this feems an improvidence unanfwerable in a leffe renouned generall than Turenne That Condée did not fall on his halfe of the armie, as he did on Sencterres, it was the great mercy of God to him and our religion in France, that in his ruine might have gott a great wound; and as it is, the wicked Papifts may count it a complot betwixt him and his old friend Condée, that he was not lighted on. If thefe difafters force the Cardinall unto a peace with Spain, I fear it prove much hurtfull to the Proteftants every where. As Orleans is at Court aheadie, fo if a generall peace bring Condée alfo, the Cardinall is undone, and whatever this may worke for our King, yet I fear the hurt of Proteftants every where, if Spain, Auftria, and the Pope, be not hindered by France to execute their wicked defignes.

If Sueden and Brandenburg, immediately on the junction, have defeat Cafimire and his great armie, we look for fome good in thefe lands, for whatever be the originals of the warre, yet to me it's evident, that the ruine of the King of Sueden is the hazard of all the Proteftants round about. I marvell of Dantzick's wifdome, that fo long has been fo great an impediment to his progrefs, and more of your States, that will faill fo farr to provoke that Prince in fo unfeafonable a nick of tyme. It's the Auftrian's great happinefs that gives him, in all the corners of Germany, fo deep a peace, when his deadly infirmities, and tender age of his fon, and weaknefs alfo of his brother Leopold, does fo much require it: I muft excufe him for his help to the Polifh King, and the Spaniard, albeit France and Sueden cannot bot deeply refent it, if they had leafure to mend it. We will ftand on our watch-tower, and look on with ane earneft defyre of any thing may come out of all thefe dangerous commotions, which may look towards the performance of the Lord's great promifes, Antichrift's ruine, the bringing in of the Jews, the breaking or Chriftianing the Turks, and other Pagans: alfo, if any thing may come forth for the putting off our fhame, and repairing of our ruines in thir lands

The King is fo farr forgot here, that not one man, fo farr as I know, keeps any correfpondence with him; nor doe we hear at all what he does or intends: yet I think diverfe pray to God for him, and wifh his reftitution. But if men of my Lord Broghill's parts and temper be long among us,[3] they will make the prefent government more beloved than fome men wifh. From our publict praying for the King, Broghill's courtefies, more than his threats, brought off our leading men My averfenefs from that omiffion, yow fee in my anfwer to Mr Dickfon anent that point, (B): what was faid by Mr. Wood for leaving of it, yow have here alfo, (C). About the time of abftaining I was a more earneft fupplicant for him than ever; whereupon fome of my good neighbours did deferre me to the Councell as an earneft preacher for the King. This was falfe, for in doctrine I ftrack not on that ftring, only, fo long as I might doe it, without fcandall, or reflecting on my wifer and better brethren's omitting of it, I did never paffe it by in prayer.

When in that we had yielded, we were like to be put farder to it our unhappy Remonftrators did ftill occafion trouble Mr Liviftoun made no bones

[3] *I ide infra* page 343

to preach and pray publictly with the English, and perfuaded Mr. Patrick Gillefpie to begin before him; fo that Mr. Patrick, when he came to Edinburgh, made no fcruple to preach in the English church to their Councell and Judges, and goe home in coach with the Prefident, and fay his grace at his table; yea, in Glafgow to preach to their circular court, and feaſt the Judges in his houfe. This made the Councell endeavour to have fo many of our beſt preachers appointed by turne to come to Edinburgh to preach to them. When my opinion was craved in this unhappie motion, I gave it the anfwer yow may fee at (D), and, by God's bleffing, got it cruſhed for the time; but how long, I know no; for Mr. Liviftoun being folifted to go to Ireland, was fent over there by his Remonſtrator brethren to make a vifite and returne. It hes been their defigne this long time to fill Ireland with their partie; and they have come too good fpeed. I did what I could to help that evill, albeit not with that fuccefs I would. Mr. John, fo foon as he went over, he goes immediately to Dublin, and there is content to be employed to preach to the ſtate. What evill this may work we know no: Efpecially Warriftone and Mr. Guthrie's impatience to be out of work, and keeped downe, inclyning them, as fome fay, to come nearer the Englifh than they did. yet their defigne being evident to play the tyrants in the whole Church, and to put the Magiſtracie of the land in their partie's hand, which they call the Godly, fo many will be againſt them as it's hoped they will not prevaill. Mr. P. Gillefpie fand their defigne fo unfeafonable, and fo irrationall, that he left their meeting difpleafed this laſt week: yet Sir George Maxwell, who with him is all one, thought the week before to have caried, by a number of blew caps of that partie, the commiffion of the Sheriffdome of Aire and Baranthrow to himfelf, on purpofe, as they fay, to have been that partie's agent with the Protector in all their defires. But my Lord Cochran's diligence and wifdome bracke Sir George's defigne. Time will let us know more of men's fecret contrivances, which are yet covered.

We remember the other moneth a fingular judgment of God on Mr. Thomas Charteris, a prime one of that partie. When firſt he had declared for Independencie, I preffed in two diverfe fynods to excommunicat him; but I could not be heard, for Mr. P. Gillefpie, Mr. John Carftares, and Mr. Francis Aird, all in face of fynod, avowed he was a godly man and might not be fo ufed. Hereafter, when not only he deferted his poor charge of Stanhoufe, but fet himfelf by the Englifh in the kirk of Kilbryde, the beft ftipend in the weft, taking the manfe and glebe, kirk, and all to himfelf, and his congregation of Independents, gathered from the parifhes about, of twenty perfons, or within thirty, leaving the parifh of about two thoufand to build a houfe, and contribute a ftipend of their owne; this fearfull oppreffion, and of moft pernicious example, made him appear not to be fo good as his faction had counted him, efpecially when he was found to be exceeding greedy and worldly, as Mr. Patrick Gillefpie oft thereafter faid of him; for when he had gotten, befide twelve chalder of victuall, a hundred pound fterling a-year, from the Englifh, out of the ftipends of other kirks, all contented him not; but he made almoft a trade of couping horfes. When no bodie could get order of him, God put to his hand, and eafily killed him. After fundry of his Independent congregation, and among the reft his owne man, had left him and turned quaker, clapping a horfe in the kirk-yard on Saturday at night, the horfe ftrake him on the breaft; of which being tormented all night, he dyed in the morning, without repentance, fo farr as I heard, for any of his publict offences.

This fect of Quakers is like to prove troublefome: they increafe much among the Englifh both in England and Ireland They in a furious way cry doune both miniftrie and magiftracie; fome of them feem actuallie poffeft with a devill, their fury, their irrationall paffions, and bodilie convulfions are fo great. Lieutenant Ofburne, one of our firft apoftates to the Englifh, and betrayers to his power of our armie, for which he had great favour and rewards from Cromwell himfelf, is ane open leader to them in the ftreet of Edinburgh, without any punifhment. Sundry in Clydefdale, of the moft zealous Remonftrant yeomen, hes turned fo; and their increafe is feared, which is the juft recompenfe of admitting the beginnings of error They are patient as yet of ftrokes; but if the Fifth Monarchie men of the late Parliament had prevailed, or if their partie goe on in its grouth, their fury is lyke to goe to unmercifull killing (with their predeceffors) of all their oppofers.

When I had written this farr, your letters, with the boy Maxwell, came to me. I fhall endeavour to fee the boy ufed as yow defire. I have defired that your twenty-two gilders, fix ftivers, which is, as I remember, the reft of my count with yow, may be employed, by John your nephew, for his ufe. I think the Colledge will, in their counts with yow, from time to time exhauſt more than his expenſe. I have not yet ſeen what books yow have ſent, but the Antwerp Gazet I wiſh we had for the two laſt months, to ſee the way of it. I know from them that ſaw and read it, there was a French one printed weekly there, within this twelvemonth; try if it yet be continued. I am glad Dr Strang's book is ſo far advanced; endeavour to get from ſome man there, if yow can, ſome commendation in the frontiſpiece ſo ſoon as it is done, ſend me ſo many copies as yow barganed for gratis, or to be paid as yow have agreed. I am ſorie if he have the leaſt of Amiraldiſme; had I perceived it, I would have ſcraped it out. If that vent weell, the reſt of his treatiſes ſhall follow, wherein will be no matter of offence, I hope, to any. Whatever is to be got of the queſtions of Amiraud *pro* or *contra*, or of the Janſeniſts *pro* or *contra*, let us have it with the firſt. Yow know what we have already; if we fall to have what yow ſend, it is but the ſending of it back, as *Voſſius de Hiſtoricis Græcis et Latinis*, which I hear now yow ſent, we had from London before. I conceive no man ſo fitt to deall with Amiraud and his partie, as Voetius. It were much to be wiſhed he were dealt with to undertake this great and neceſſar ſervice; might not Apollonius be moved to mind that matter? Baxter is lyke to fire England; and ſo be tymous with theſe errours: See what yow can get done againſt that evill.

Our Church ſtrifes are no lyke to agree; the Remonſtrants make it their endeavour to put themſelffes, as the Commiſſion 1650, or under ſome ſuch notion, in a committee to purge and plant all Scotland, with the Engliſh allowance to them as the Godly partie; one of the vileſt, moſt ſhamefull, and tyrannick tricks that ever was heard of in any church in any tyme. To prevent this, our brethren there-Eaſt hes ſent up, with Broghill our profeſſed friend, Mr. J. Sharp to Cromwell; with what inſtructions I know not; but I hear very fair and honeſt. The Remonſtrants cry out on this meſſage, though alone to guard againſt and prevent their miſchievous deſignes; they will not be long a-ſending one after him, to defyre openly, what long, by their letters and ſecret agents, they have been dealing for. This ſtrife at this tyme is ſhamefull and dangerous; I love it not: my advyce was never ſought to it, but on our part, it ſeems neceſſar: I wiſh it may end better than I feare

I bleſs God for that victorie of Venice at the Dardanels, but more for that of Sueden and Brandenburgh at Warſou: The Lord bleſſe and preſerve theſe Princes for the good of the Proteſtant intereſt. Your States, as they ſtand, are not loved here ; they have given to Sueden a great, needlefs, and untymous provocation, which though diffembled, is not lyke will be forgot. My love and fervice to your kind wife, oft remembered by Harie, and all your three daughters, whom I pray God to blefs.

Your Coufin,

1ft September 1656   R B

For the Right Honourable Mr. Francis Rous

Sir,

Understanding by a letter from Miftrefs Lammy, that you were yet to the fore, and helpfull to fupplicants, and mindfull of me, notwithftanding of all the changes paft, yea, for my caufe that poor gentlewoman's good friend, I did rejoyce. I pray God yet to preferve you fome time, for I know, fo long as yow are able to come to the Councell, or fpeak in Parliament, or come near the Protector, yow will, to your power, after your wonted manner, be doing good both to the publict and fo many private perfones as you are able : among others this gentlewoman I ftill recommend. Yow were a fpeciall inftrument to fave the Churches of Brittaine from the mad folies of thefe Fifth Monarchifts of the laft Parliament. I am glad yow are a member of this Parliament ; for I doe affure myfelf you will be a fpeciall watchman in the Houfe, and a continuall remembrancer to the Protector that the Church of God in thefe dominions, (for which I have oft been witnefs of your fpeciall zeall and care,) fhall fuffer no new detriment. We here had been much hurt by the ignorance and error, if no the difdainfull neglect, of Eraftian men, had it not been for the very great wifdome, equitie, and moderation of that excellent man my Lord Broghill ; the moft gaining perfone to the intereft of thefe who imployed him, of any that ever yet came from thence hither. Shall the Prefbyterians in England and Ireland never winn to the exercife of their Difcipline ? Shall that libertie be denyed us in England, which the Kings of France, and Pole, or whoever fo much as tolerate our religion, hes ever granted ? Shall all the labours of the Affemblie at Weftminfter, and fo many Ordinances of both Houfes, turne all to fmoke ? It is worthie your laft fervice to God and his Church, in your extreame old age, to endeavour to obtain of the Protector fome reafon to the fervants of God in this point. Shall fuch men as my Lord Lauderdaill and Crawfurd languifh from year to year in fo hard a condition? While there is tyme, and you are not gone, doe fervice to God and good men Mr. Tate, Mr. Marfhall, Mr Whitaker, Mr Vynes, Mr Henderfon, Mr. Gillefpie, and many more of our late dear friends are gone: at once the reft of us will follow, and ftand before our Mafter Shall there be no more word of our Solemn Oath and Covenant? Is it turned to Martin's Almanack? Is it pulled down from the walls of all your churches? Will the Lord be filent for ever? Can he alter with our changes? We here live as filently and peaceablie as any there could wifh us, but for myfelfe, while I live, by God's grace, I fhall never hold my peace to God in fecret for Sion's fake, nor ceafe to pour out my complaint to you, whom I know hes the lyke intereft in God and Sion as I have. Why is not your Pfalter in England practifed as it is here, and no other? Will you there never come to any Order? Is it poffible to keep the neglected confufions of the houfe of God from ending in a greater confufion of the State than yet we have feen? Will armies of men or humane policie be able to hold off the hand of God? Bot I need not fpeak of thefe things to yow who knows them better, and minds them more than myfelfe The Lord blefs and be with yow to your end.

Your much honouring friend and Servant,
Glafgow, September 6th 1656. R. BAILLIE.

FOR HIS REVEREND AND WEELL-BELOVED BROTHER MR. JAMES WOOD, MINISTER AT ST. ANDREWES

DEAR JAMES,

THESE are thanks for your kind and honeft anfwer, November 28th Your name fhall not be mentioned, nor more ufe made of your information than for myfelfe, for the flagrant fcandall is notour, and a teftimoniall is neceffare by all law and cuftom; yet Mr. R. M[acward]'s high commendation will poffiblie ferve for all; it hath purchafed already too good a pedagogie to him. Thefe people minds nought but faction, to plant all places in church, ftate, fchooles, families, with men of their own ftamp, and no other, fay and fwear what they will to the contrare. See to your Colledges as you may: they are fully masters of Glasgow, Aberdeen, and almost of Edinburgh. This commission of Warnstone's, Greenhead, Mr. P. Gillespie, and Mr. James Guthrie, will draw our affaires to a quick crisis; be this be weell at yow, it's like all the four will be on their way to London I thought it had not yet been time for some men to seek openly their due rewards for their great service. I doubt nothing but one of their chief business will be to get, what Mr. P. Gillespie had obtained, the whole Magistracies in the land put in their partie's hand. If they had this, Glasgow alone, befyde other services, could give them sundry thousand pounds a-year, as they wont to doe, to be disposed on without all count, as they thought fitteft. If the burroughes and shyres see not to it, they will quicklie be their hard taskmasters. This equall committee, to purge and plant without any account, is the totall destruction of our government. Will not Mr Blair give ane honest testimony against it to Cromwell, and all the world, before he die? If he neglect this office to the Church of Scotland, it will reflect much on his reputation. It seems Mr. James Sharp must procure a message for two or three of our mind to decipher these men to the whole world, without more circumloquution. For myself, I like no the baire, nor minds ever, but by violence, to stand before it. If God be not mercifull, I think these men's malapart novations, and seeking shelter to their proud tyrannie from the sword that lyes on our necks, will end in an Erastian slaverie, pulled on us by those that were wont to be most zealous for our discipline. Will Mr. Livistoun bring, from Aberdeen's nest, a professed Independent to succeed to Mr. A[ndrew] Rutherfoord's misorder, and Mr. Blair not upbraid him for it to his face! I pity your pressouis: the Lord help, sustaine, and direct yow. Blessed be God, that continues yow, or any man in those tymes, orthodoxe and honest.

Your's,

December 8th 1656 R. B.

It will be needfull yow write a narrative of your translation from the New Colledge to the Old, for your friends, to stop the mouth of our ill-willers. Send me a copy, to make use of it for your advantage in thir bounds, where there is most need. It would be one of Mr. J. Sharp's chief cares to gett a settled order for our Universities, that Independent *ignari's* may no more, by English orders be planted in them, for the corrupting of our youth.

For his Reverend and dear Brother, Mr. Simeon Ashe,
Minister at London; or Mr. Calamy.

Reverend and Dear Brother,

The kind expreffions of tender affection, not only towards our Church, but myfelf alfo, and diverfe of my brethren, which yow, with your brother Mr. Calamy, have been pleafed now and then to write to me, give me confidence to acquaint yow and him, at this time, with the prefent condition of our Church, which now is fad enough, but is very like quicklie to be much fadder, if the Lord be not pleafed to avert the imminent danger.

Our Brethren, who, thefe diverfe years, have troubled us fore with their very bitter though moft needlefs divifions, are now openly before the world come to exercife their threats upon us, and avowedly to doe at laft what long we feared from them: They have fent up to the Protector their three grand leaders to fupplicate for a libertie to oppreffe our poor Church, contrare to all reafon, confcience, and law. I gave yow an account how farr we went, upon our paffionate defyre of any tollerable peace, to give them all fatiffaction in our conference, November [16]55, weell near a whole moneth; wherein how farr fundry of them declared themfelfes fatiffied, themfelfes and others alfo can weell remember. Our firft and fundamentall quarrell was, that the Commiffion of the Church had anfwered a Querie or two from the Parliament and Committee of Eftates, anent the lawfullnefs of their making ufe of fuch men in their armie, for the defence of the land againft forraign invaders, as were fully reconciled to Church and State for any tranfgreffion fometimes they had fallen into. Their plea here was, that we had Anfwered thefe Queries fo as we were perfuaded in confcience was according to God's word, the law of nature and nations, the conftant and never-controverted practice of our land, or of any land, and the conftant practice of thefe who now are in power, as much as any. This then was all their quarrell

When they feared the Generall Affemblie of St Andrewes would approve of thefe our Anfwers, and would not be gotten to countenance their new moft dangerous and unnaturall both tenets and practices; before that ever any queftion came to be debated, they gave in their Proteftation and declinature againſt that Aſſemblie, and the two other we had ſince, as Null, upon reaſons which make null all Generall Aſſemblies with us for ever, till they be maſters of them, and have them of their own framing. We were content, for our paſſion to peace, to burie all theſe high inſolencies, and never more to mention thoſe controverſies, if ſo they would live peaceablie with us in time to come. This, in a publict write, they flatlie refuſed, except two points farder were granted to them, which were not before in queſtion. Firſt, That all the Preſbyteries and Synods in Scotland ſhould, for the time, be deprived of their power of ordination and juriſdiction in all caſes that any man ſhould controvert; and that ſtanding committees of ane equall number of them and us, they nameing their owne, and we ours, ſhould be appointed for finall determination in all things controverted In many of our Preſbyteries they have none of their mind, and in ſome Synods none; in moſt of the Preſbyteries and Synods where they have any, their number is very few. The grant of this demand to us was impoſſible· We had no power to deprive all the Preſbyteries and Synods in Scotland of that power which Chriſt, and the laws both of our Church and State, did inveſt them with; nor thought we it reaſonable to give our brethren a negative voice in all the eccleſiaſtick juriſdiction of Scotland. This was too rich a reward for the diviſions they had raiſed, and ſo long needleſſlie keeped up, and it was evident this conceſſion had not at all been for peace, but for the continuing and encreaſing of our differences. Yet all this would not content them; but they preſſed on us another conceſſion, that ſince the pluralitie in Preſbyteries were men corrupt, we ſhould agree to them a freedome and exemption from all ſubordination to thoſe judicatories in their preſent condition. This to us was a deſperate demand, to make us content to cut the ſinews of all Preſbyteriall government in our land till the Preſbyteries were fully conformed to their mind; nor could we inflict ſo fore a puniſhment on all the Kirk Judicatories before they were heard to clear themſelfes of ſo baſe an imputation. The preſbyteries and ſynods, to which ſubordination was denyed, was none of the worſt temper, but thoſe chieflie of the very beſt: Lothian and Fife, Edinburgh and St. Andrewes, more nor Argyle or Caithneſs. Beſide that, we in our hearts were perſuaded the challenge was exceeding unjuſt; for notwithſtanding of much infirmitie in many of our preſbyteries, yet we dare ſay the Preſbyteries were never in Scotland generallie ſo good, and ſo free of ſeen faults as they are this day, nor are church judicatories in any Reformed Church generally fo good as ours, our Brethren themfelves being judges; nor to any indifferent beholder are thefe prefbyteries which our Brethren have gotten made up fullie to their mind, in any thing better than others who are all oppofite to them Nor count we this challenge from our Brethren ingenuous, fince we fee it evidentlie, that fo foone as they become mafters of any prefbyterie or fynod, as by their over-diligence they have made themfelfes of fome, there is no more dinn in thefe places of purgeing the infufficiencie or fcandals of their friends is no more heard of When union could not be obtained but on thefe and the like ablurd conditions, with fad hearts we committed our caufe to God; but our Brethren prefentlie did make their addrefs to the Englifh Councell, petitioning to be erected in a Committee to vifite, to purge, and plant all the churches in the land. We did fupplicat alfo to avert fo terrible and fo unexampled oppreffion, and, by the juftice of that court, got it for the time declined: Ever fince, in their own wayes, both clandeftine and open, they have been about the obtaining of that exceeding irregular power. We knowing their refolution to deale with the Protector himfelf for it, when our brother Mr Sharp, on his friends occafions, went up with my Lord Prefident Broghill, fome at Edinburgh gave him inftructions to guard, by right information, againft their attempts Our Brethren, finding that Mr. Sharp's reprefentations had marred all they thought to have obtained by letters and by their Independent agents, they have openlie fent up the chief of their partie to defire, by the great favour they have themfelves every one of them with the Protector, and diverfe about him, a Commiffion to doe by force what we could not yield to them with our confent Their great plea will be, that the government of our corrupt Church fhould be put in the hands of them who are the Godly partie till the Church be well purged. We would have taken this plea the better at our Brethren's hand, if they had not feen, and confeffed with us, the great iniquitie, hypocrifie, and falfehood of this fame alleadgeance among yow to this day by the whole circle of the Sectaries; albeit never one of all the fects among yow did arife to this enormitie of defire to have jurifdiction over their oppofites: they were glad of a toleration for themfelfes, but a domineering power over thofe who loved not to joyne with them, they never fought.

When the other year our Brethren had obtained ane ordinance for putting all the Magiftrates of the fhyres and burroughs in the Godly, that is, their partie's hands, the clamour was fo great againft this injuftice, that quicklie the Councell got that order recalled. When, about that fame tyme, thofe who are now commiffioners had drawn a new large Covenant, farr different from the Solemn League, to be fworn and fubfcryved by all whom they fhould admit to their Godly partie, it was fo hatefull to the Englifh Councell, and fo grievous to many of their own fide, that they were forced to lay it afide; but this their laft defigne which now they come to reprefent to the Protector, (however, we doubt not, in low, foft, ambiguous words, yet, in effect, importing the ruine of our Church goveinment,) will be found worfe than any thing which lately they have defigned

This much I thought fitt to fignifie to yow, and a few which yow and Mr. Calamy think meet to acquaint with it. Mr. Sharp can fully, and will faithfully report the truth of every particular. Sometimes yow have written fad letters to us for our help, by our prayers to God, and induftrie with men, againft the Malignant and Epifcopall partie: you know we were never inlaking to you to the uttermoft of our power, our diftrefs now is great, we defyre your compaffion, your prayers to God for us, and your countenance to our caufe, when yow know it may profit us, and not hurt yourfelfes. We are not fo much feared that the moft unreafonable defyres of our Brethren can be granted, by any of farre leffe underftanding and juftice than thefe who now have audience with the Protector, as that, by our Brethren's fuggeftions and importunitie, both they and we, to the ruine of our dearcoft Ecclefiaftick liberties, be put under a new Eraftian government, which fhall end in perfecution of thofe who are truly godly among us. If by your countenance and counfell to Mr Sharp, or by your dealing with your friends about the Protector, (if fo be yow have any,) yow can help to keep this very dangerous ftorme from us, yow fhall doe an acceptable fervice to God, and a great good deed to our groaning Church, and a feafonable favour to all of us here who defyre, in this hard tyme, to be faithfull to God, and the truft he hath committed to our keeping Expecting herein a comfortable anfwer, I reft

Your loving Brother in the Lord,

January 12th 1657. R B.

(D.) For the Right Worshipfull his assured Friend,
Mr. Francis Rous.

Right Worshipfull,

The conftancie of your kindnefs towards me, which from tyme to tyme yow are pleafed to fignifie, in this feafon, when old friendfhip by the moft is buried in oblivion, makes me ftill confident to ufe with yow my wonted libertie I hope what I wrote fome five moneths agoe with Miftrefs Lammie, yow did receave. The purpofe of my prefent wriiting is to acquaint yow with the imminent danger of the Church of Scotland, (which I know yow have fincerely loved and highly prized,) to be pitifullie oppreft and enflaved to a few of our brethren, who long have vexed us with their moft caufelefs divifions, and when we have been willing for peace caufe to have paft by all their former (as we efteemed) high mifdemeanours, yet flatly they refufed peace, unlefs on new conditions, which we never heard of, nor expected to have heard of: 1. That they behoved to be freed from all fubordination to our Prefbyteries and Synods till they were new conftitute and purged. 2 That, for the interim, the whole jurifdiction of the Church, in every thing controverted, fhould be put in the hand of a committee, confifting of an equall number of them, to be named by themfelfes, and of us, to be named by ourfelfes, who fhould finallie determine in all queftions anent purgeing and planting of Churches, and every thing elfe that concerned the whole Church. The firft is the totall fubverfion of our Prefbyteriall government, on a very injurious and falfe pretence, that fubordination muft be denyed, not to the worft or weakeft of our Prefbyteries and Synods, bot the veiy beft, from which they are moft averfe, as thofe of Lothian and Fyfe. That our brethren would have broken all in pieces our Church government by weaker and worfe pretences than profeffed Independents we would never have expected, but that they would have attempted, as they doe in their fecond demand, the ufurpation of all Ecclefiaftick jurifdiction to themfelfes, a farr fmaller and more inconfiderable faction among us than the Independents are among yow, we did never dreame till themfelfes did openly profefs it ; and when we did refufe it, they fupplicat the Counfell here to be invefted in it ; and now when the juftice of that court hes rejected their ftrange defire, they have affumed the boldnefs to prefent in effect, albeit in more low, foft, and ambiguous words, the fame defires to the Protector himfelf If any of your fects there would not only petition for a toleration to themfelfes, but alfo the priviledge to have the full Ecclefiaftick jurifdiction over the land, I doubt not their defire would be rejected with fcorn, though it were fweetened with a claufe to have an equall number of others joyned with them, whom yet they know affuredly would never affociat with them in any fuch work. Such an enormous phanfie was never yet propond by any of your heteroclites; yet the prefent defyre of our brethren feems to be very like, certainly to the body of this land, even to thefe who are efteemed juftly, as we conceave, the moft godly in it, it would be one of the heavieft church-grievances that ever yet befell them, nothing lighter than that of prelates tyranny, the fountain of all our late troubles We are no wayes feared that the Protector's juftice and wifdome can give ear to any fuch motion, if he were rightly informed; but we are feared indeed, that our brethren, by the great favour they have with fundrie there, and their great diligence and boldnefs to mifinforme, may obtaine, as the refult of their unhappy, rafh, unadvyfed, and caufelefs contentions with us, fome one thing or other that may be very dolorous to our nation, and vexatious to the moft of the truely godlie in our land. There is a brother of ours there, Mr. James Sharp, who can give full and true information of all things which concerne our prefent condition: I wifh yow had fome time with him When you have heard him, I put no queftion but the love yow have to God and his truth, and the refpect yow have to the peace of the Church of Scotland, and the quiet of the nation, (which for the tyme is fo quiet as any could wifh, if thefe men could but reft, and go about their own ftation,) yow will be willing, in this tyme of our diftrefs and danger from our owne, (whom leaft it became, of all men, to have put us to this vexation,) to fpeak a word for us to the Protector, that at leaft we may be fecured from the incroachments of thefe reftlefs men, who, fo long as they expect countenance and affiftance from him, will never ceafe to put their quiet neighbours to new troubles. I would be loath to marre them in any favour they could defyre in other things, for the men are my good friends in all things perfonall and private; but the crufhing of their forefaid defigne, I count it pietie and juftice, their own good, the Protector's honour, the good and peace of our land, whereto (by all the entres yow have been pleafed to grant unto me in your affection) I humbly befeek yow to contribute what yow may, that with the greater cheerfullnefs I and many more here may continue to pray for your remaining yet fometime upon earth, for the perfecting of all yow have in hand, for the glory of God and the good of his whole Church. So doe I truely pray,

Sir,
Who am your affectionat and moft honoring Friend,

January 16th 1657. R. BAILLIE.

For his Reverend and well-beloved Brother Mr. Robert Douglass, Minister at Edinburgh.

Sir,

As yow defired, fo I have written my fenfe: as it is, if yow miflyke it caft it in the fire; if yow defire any thing eiked, or paired, or changed, I fhall doe it; if yow let it goe up, defire Mr. James [Sharp] to conceall, fo farr as may be, my name, for my name, I know, is unluckie and unfavorie to thofe in power there, nor like I myfelfe any thing the worfe for that God help and guide yow

Your's to power,

January 18th 1657. R B

For his Reverend and well-beloved Brother Mr. James Sharp, Minister at Craill.[4]

James,

Yow fee what I have written in the inclofed, at the defire of our friends here; if they miflyke my writes, I have defired them to fupprefs them; if otherwayes, to fend them to yow. If yow, on the place, think fitt to deliver

---

[4] It seems scarcely necessary to remark that Mr James Sharp, Minister of Crail, who appears so prominently as the agent of the Resolutioners, afterwards became Archbishop of St Andrews

them, either to thofe they are directed to, or to the fire, doe as yow think fitt; only I defyre, fo farr as may be, my name to be fuppreffed; for yow know, befide elder quarells, how oft my name ftands printed in Mr. Love's proceffe,[5] fo intreat thofe to whom yow delyver my letters to keep them to themfelfes, elfe my name may hurt yow, and the caufe yow have in hand I hope yow fhall, by God's help, eafily get the defyres of thofe headie men crufhed; but all my fear is, that the end of your ftrife will be the Protector's determination to fubject our poor Church to fome new Eraftian modell, which fhall be very grievous, albeit farr more tolerable than the tyrannik Turkifh yoke of the Proteftors. If for the averting of this mifchief, yow finde it neceffar to caufe fend up for any more, I think M. R D., and M. J. W, fhall be fufficient: if there were need of more, I think G. H., or J. F., or R K. of H.[6] might doe weell. If yow come fpeed in the maine, I wifh yow laboured to get abolifhed that very unjuft commiffion of vifiting the Univerfities; and that which M. P. G[illefpie] did obtaine, that no Independent fhould violently take the church and ftipend of any parifh, as was done in Kilbryde and Leinzie, and much lefs that fuch fhould take up our Univerfities, as they have done Aberdeene, etc I pray God help yow and guide yow; yow had need of a long fpoone:[7] truft no words nor faces, for all men are liars.

                                Your's,   R. B.

January 18th 1657.

                For Me [Mr Robert Baillie].

Right Reverend Sir,

Because I fear I did it not before, I thought fitt now to fhow yow, that your old friend, my Lord Warriftone, did, in that conference before the Protector, affirme, (while he was fpeaking of the evill effects of the Refolutions,)

---

[5] *Vide supra*, foot-note p. 105

[6] These initials stand for Mr Robert Douglas, Mr James Wood and George Hutcheson, James Fergusson, and Robert Ker of Haddington

[7] " He should have a long-shafted spoon that sups kail with the devil,"—(David Fergusson's Scottish Proverbs Edin. 1641, 4to.) Had Baillie sufficiently known his correspondent, he might have taken this Proverb to himself

that there was one of the Refolutioners, who, in the laft conference for union, faid, That the reafon why he ftucke fo clofe to thefe Refolutions was, that he might keep himfelf in a capacity to act for the King when opportunitie fhould offer ; and when it was anfwered by Mr. James Sharp, That he hoped that would not be made good ; in his reply he did correct it thus, It was true it was not publickly fpoken, but one did fpeak it privately to him. I am fearing, by what I have heard of late, yow may be the man that Warriftone did meane; fo yow may think upon it, and make your own ufe of it If yow have had any thing lately from Edinburgh, or if Mr. Patrick Gillefpie be come home, or coming before the reft, let me know, who am

Your moft affectionat Brother to ferve yow,

Hafilhead, March 5th 1657   Pa. Colvill.

For Mr. James Sharp.

Reverend and Beloved Brother,

This is my third ; I think it no reafon yow fhould be burdened with particular anfuers, only I defyre to know, by a word in your's to the Brethren of Edinburgh, that mine did come to your hands. Yow fee the enclofed If I were with Warriftone I would fay to him for anfwer : 1 That his profeffions to me conftantly, fince he was a child, and my fcholler, were of fo great friendfhip, and that fuch offices of uninterrupted kindnefs had allwayes paft mutually betwixt us, that I could never have thought, that for any caufe whatfoever, he would have fpoken of me to any living, much lefs before the Protector, words which tended fo exceedingly to my hurt, without the leaft fignification ever to myfelf, directly or indirectly, that he harboured any fuch thoughts of me. 2. The thing that I am informed (by this letter of a worthy Brother,) he did fpeak, if truely he meaned it of me, (whereof my old and continuing refpects to him make me doubt,) is exceeding falfe, for I doe utterly deny, that in all that long, and weell near a moneth's conference, there was one word fpoken by me, or any other, that looked any thing like the fpeech here written, to my knowledge ; nor was there any occafion of it, for in my judgment, as he weell knows, his new fingular tenets in the Publict Refolutions were no more prejudiciall to the late King than they are to the prefent Protector, and to all that ever were or are in power in any nation, or are like to be hereafter on this earth. 3. That not only that which he fpoke of our publick conference was utterly falfe, as himfelf granted upon your reply, but alfo, that in any private conference I did ever fay any fuch thing to him, is no leffe untrue, as I am ready to depone upon oath ; and I hope my pofitive negation will be as much believed, where I am known, as fome other men's affirmation without proofe. 4. It hes never been the Protector's pleafure to trouble any man for his fimple judgment or heart's affection in queftions anent the Covenant, efpeciallie where perfons did live peaceably and without all offence : Now, as for my peaceable and inoffenfive living hitherto, if I were put to an inqueft even of thofe who differ from me in judgement of the Publick Refolutions, I hope I would pafs with alfe good a report as others of my neighbours 5. I have had many free private difcourfes with my Lord Warriftone, thefe twenty-nyne yeares, as ufe to be among moft intime and more than ordinarily familiar friends, but that one which I fufpect he meaned in his fpeech, (if it related at all to me,) was long before our laft conference ; and, to my beft remembrance, all that then I faid might have been fpoken in the Protector's owne audience, without all offence, for it was bot to this purpofe, That a noble friend of his and mine had told me of a late diftinction of his, which I defired to underftand from himfelf, to witt, that he was clear, notwithftanding of our League and Covenant, of the lawfullnefs to change our prefent civill government, fo farr as concerned the *terminus a quo*, but that he was not clear of the lawfullnefs to joyne with the prefent *terminus ad quem* Herein I defyred to be cleared by him ; as oft times, in fuch queftions, I was wont to feek and receave light from him While I was declareing to him the grounds of my fcruple only upon the *terminus a quo*, and of my full clearnefs in the *terminus ad quem*, without any fcruple of confcience, if I were loofed from the former, and while he was beginning to fhew me how I might be loofed from it, a gentleman did come in to him, and interrupted us, that we proceeded no farder. Since which time, to my beft remembrance, I had no difcourfe with him, private or publick, concerning any ferious buffinefs, and why he fhould have fpoken before the Protector, of this, my proponeing to him alone, fo innocent and fimple a cafe of confcience only for my own fatiffaction, and why he fhould have fo fearfully metamorphofed it, I cannot conjecture Surely if any other man's rafhnefs, (for malice, I know no man living that profeffes to have it at me,) had brought me to any trouble, either for my words or deeds, I would have addreffed myfelf to none fooner than my Lord Warnftone for his counfell and affiftance ; as he may remember, in his late diftreffes, I had been one of his fafteft friends.

This, and much more to this purpofe, I would fay to him if I were near him ; which, as yow find occafion and expediencie, I wifh yow did communicat unto him, or any other, for my clearing from his unadvyfed fpeech, if fo be he will expone it of me ; whereof yet I doubt. Praying God to help yow in your very hard, dangerous, and vexatious tafk, I reft,

Your's,

Glafgow, March 9th 1657. R. BAILLIE.

(J) FOR THE RIGHT REVEREND MR. ROBERT BAILY, PROFESSOR OF DIVINITY IN GLASGOW.[1]

REVEREND AND MUCH RESPECTIT, London, March 21ft 1657.

YOUR third I receaved yefterday ; and that I fent no returne to your former two, I hope will not be imputed to my neglect of the refpects I owe and bear to yow, when yow confidder that, in my letters to Edinburgh, I give notice of the recept of your's ; and that the imployment I am putt upon doeth fo take up my time, as that I have much a doe to give the full account which is neceffarie of all paffages relating to our publick concernements to the correfpondents at Edinburgh, by whom I truft ther is fuch notice given to thefe of our judgement, and to yourfelve in particular, of the ftate of matters heir, as may plead for my omiffions in making thefe particular returnes to letters fent to me, which are in my defire to doe, could my leafure allowe it. Sir, I delivered your letter to M[afte]rs Calamy and Afh, which was acceptable to them , and have often inquired for Mr. Rows, but by reafon of his infirmitie, which occafioneth his feldom beeng in town, I have not as yett had the opportunity of meeting with him ; which caufed my delay of wreating to yow befor this. As to the matter of your laft, I fhall breifly relate to yow what is frefh upon my memorie of the ground of that report, which your worthie

[1] From the Orig.—(Wodrow MSS Folio, Vol. XLIX No. 4.)

Brother fignifies unto yow. While in our debate befor his Highnefs, I had occafion to bring for the proof of my affertion, that ther was that printed to the world by us which did make it out, and was not anfweared by them to this day: The Lord Warıftoun, among other particulars, in his reply, was pleafit to fay, that they had printed that which we had not anfweared to this day; which was, that we had afferted, that one of the reafons why we could not difclaim the Publick Refolutions was, leaft heirby we might barr the body of the land from ryfing in armes for the affiftance of the King, in cafe of his inwafion. Whyl I was fpeaking in anfwear, I took notice of that inftance, pofing the Lord Wariftoun if he could awerr that ther was any Judicature of our Church which paffed any act or declaration to that purpofe. He anfweared, He did not charge any of the Church Judicatures with it, he had only fayed that one of our judgement had profeffed fo much in privat to him, which they had putt in print, and was not takin notice of by us. I anfweared, That what was fpoken by the fuggeftion of any one in privat to him, I knew not, nether came I hither to make anfwear for it; but if he could alleadge any thing to that purpofe of the Judicatures, I was ready to make my reply according to my knowledge; but I left it to be confideied, how impertinent and bloody fuch an allegation was in fuch an audience, upon the privat fuggeftion of any one perfon. This is the truth of the whole which paffed as to that, which I think will not be denyed by the Protefters heir. If the Lord Wariftoun did mean yow, I think he hath dealte injurioufly with yow upon many accounts; but he did not name yow then, nether have I fince heard, by any in this place, yow wer the man he aimed at. Howbeit, I did this day read your letter to one, who hath promifed the nixt week to acquaint the Lord Wariftoun with it. I hope it fhall not much trouble yow, that through an inconfiderat heat, fuch an expreffion was uttered by the Lord Wariftoun which did ftrike at yow, when yow confidder, that all the arguments hitherto brought by them heir, after a full hearing, have been no other then reproaches and calumnies upon the conftitution, acts, and the minifters of the Judicatures of our Church; though, bliffed be God, they have litle advantaged ther own caufe, or præjudiced yow, and the other honeft men who ftand for the intereft of Chrift, with unbyaffed and rationall men heir. And I may fay it upon ground, that ther are none of the Prefbyterian judgement, in and about London, who doe not difown them, and exprefs ther greif for ther fcandalous way; and that they are owned and befriendit by none but fuch whofe principles lead them to oppofe that intereft, which we are bound to maintain and plead for. Our holy and wife Lord who is the living protector of his Church knoweth how to plead his own caufe, and to overrule the rage they have expreffed, the reproaches they have caft upon our poor Church, and to order the fadd exercifes his fervants are putt to becaufe of thefe, for the beft faythfull is He who hath promifed; and that I may be kept up by his ftrength, under this tafk, which yow truelie terme hard, dangerous, and wexatious, your prayers are expectit by him who commends yow to the grace which can ftablifh and perfect yow; and is,   Sir,

Your werie loving Brother in Chrift,
JA SHARP

The relation of our late paffages I leave to what may be given yow from Edinburgh.

A Parcel of a Letter to Mr. James Hamiltoun

However, for fecuritie hereafter, I pray that no fyllab come to me from yow that yow care all in the Meal-merket did know, fo Mr Sharp will be at eafe, and I and yow will need no excufe for our fluarie and rafh effictiencie, yet I fear our too great and too wife filence is our greateft fin. I fee by the Englifh letters, which doubtlefs yow all muft know, wherein yet my name needs not be heard, that as the moft articles of the City's Remonftrance for kingfhip are paft, *nemine contradicente*, fo efpeciallie that of religion, as weell for us in Scotland as them in England, that the publicklie profeffed fhall be the Chriftian proteftant, according to the Scriptures, whereby all our Confeffions and Covenants, and abfolutely all forms and modells befide the text of Scripture, are abolifhed. Alfo, that who differ from thir fhall be protected, if they worfhip God in Jefus Chrift, and doe no civill injurie to the peace, which I think all the fects profefs, Independents, Anabaptifts, Antinomians, Familifts, Seekers, Arminians, Lutherans, Socinians, moft of the Quakers. The only excepted are Poperie, Prelacie, and Licentioufneffe in the abstract: but seeing popish, prelaticall, and licentious men professe the qualification, and will give securitie for this, their exclusion seems to be but of freewill, which is not durable. That this should be concluded in a Civill judicatorie for Scotland by so many of our Nationall commissioners, *nemine contradicente*, and in presence of our chief Protestors and grand Remonstrators, Argyle, War[istone] J G[uthrie,] P. G[illespie,] with their absolute silence, when they are clamouring the Protector for a number of small and very false accusations of our Church, not long ago would have been counted a wonder, if not simply impossible. Yea, I fear we be not free, that our Commissioner joins fully, so far as we know, in that silence with them. too great declining of persecution has never been the surest way to escape it. Any counsell to yow there, much my wifer and better, I offer not God help and direct yow

Your's,

March 30th 1657 R. B

(K) FOR THE RIGHT REVEREND MR. ROBERT BAILIE, PROFESSOR OF DIVINITY IN GLASGOW [2]

REVEREND SIR,

I HAVE receaved laitly three letters from yow, expressing the great recentment yourselve and others have of the Proviso past heir concerning qualifications, etc. It is known what endeavours I usit to praevent the passing of it; and, if our freinds had been in the House, or, as the House was at that time constituted, had that busines been carried by reason, and not by violence and faction, the motioning of it had been explodit with shame I know not what may be the apprehensions of these with yow of the consequences of it, and though I find that the sticklin of one heir for the passing of it was mainly with an eye to your citie, yet I doe not think that the agitators have reached all ther desyres by it, and am of the mind that it shall tend to ther disadvantage, beeng a demonstrable evidence of ther spirit and way to

[2] From the Orig (Wodrow MSS Fol Vol XLIX No 5.)—The passage at the end, inserted within brackets appears to have been purposely omitted in Baillie's MS In this and the preceding letter of Sharp his own orthography is retained

all fober men heir, who fee clearlie they drive at domination and rule, and can be fatiffied with nothing leffe; and doe conceive, that for all ther being reputed with yow that they have overactit and outwitted fome heir, yet they have not kythed great policy as to this, by making ufe of the advantage they had at that time, fo as at the firft to ftretch matters to the higheft pinn Sir, my opinion is, that your people would doe well to compofe themfelves to filence and patience as to what is paft. The leffe notice they take of it, or noife be made about it, the leffe fear they may have of the præjudices of it Were yow heir at the fource of effaires, yow would fee that the Proteftors and ther abettors have not fuch caufe to boaft and bragg as they doe. It is fitt they doe fo, but good for us to wait on God. Doe not think that the late tranfactions heir will be the meafure and rule of future actings in reference to us. Beleeve it, ther will be a greater change then fome doe imagin, though it is not to be expected that we can have a juft fatiffaction to our defires in refeience to our eftablifhed difciplin; yet doe not think that our necks fhall be put under the yoak of thefe men.

I had of late an large conference with the Secretary of State, and made mention of the cafe of your Citty in particular. He promifed to me that fomewhat would be done fpeedilie for rectifying of matters If yow marre not your own bufines by unfeafonable ftirring, and not keeping clofe what may be fuggefted to yow as a remedie for the prefent, that may be done fhorthe which will give fatiffaction; towards which I fhall not be wanting in my endeavours, fo far as they can reach · I cannot wye [vie] with your grandee Patrick. [What yow did hint of your beeng caution for your Town, I did not take up till 2 or 3 dayes agone, when I was fo preffed by your Bailie heir, that he would thruft into my pockett five peeces, that I might not come from London without a pocket-watch. I was furprifed with the motion, and could not obtain of him to take them back. Yow would doe me a favour to wreat to him that he may take them from me, for I know not upon what account they are given I have not been ufit to the lyke, and without budding, if I could ferve the intereft of honeft men with yow, I am very free to it.]

The Spirit of counfail and courage reft upon yow. I am Your's,

JA SHARP.

London, July 28th 1657.

Yow may have a fresh allarum by the agitators procuring of a committee, of which the most are Independents, and favourers of them, to hear our differences, and certify ther opinion to the Councill: but let it not trouble yow, that engyne, I trust, throw the Lord's mercie, shall be countermindit

(F.) FOR MR. JAMES SHARP.

JAMES,

It seemes yow are a very grosse *ignaro* that can no so much as read Arabick letters; yet it's good yow can guesse at their sense. Your neighbour Patrick Gillespie's disease, is the maine thing has been here talked of these three weeks. For myselfe, I wishe his person in all things weell; however, I have exceedinghe mislyked his way. If the Lord at this time remove him, we are in hazard to have his place quicklie filled with a worse. Wariftoun's restlefs diligence will labour his friends there to put in one of his owne humour. Patrick Gillespie's wife will ply her husband's friends, Dr. Owen, etc. to obtain the Protector's order to our Councell here, to command us to make ane election of ane other; but the faction in our bounds are like, if they can start in time, to use all possible means for a third. The brethren here who correspond with yow, as also your friends in Fife, conceive it a matter of very great concernment to have that Colledge out of the Proteftors hands, if possible: what way yow may guard against the two or three parties moving there, yow best know. It is my wish and others yow did assay to obtaine from Secretary Thurloe, and others there, yea, if yow can in time, from my Lord Broghill in Ireland,[3] such letters to the leaders of the Councell here, that they might be pleased to call for Mr. Dowglafs and Mr. Dickson, and follow their opinion in planting of that place; if so, they shall nominate a man whom they themselves, and all who are for the Presbyterian way in both nations, shall acknowledge to be als fitt for that charge, and alfe

[3] Roger Boyle, third son of the Earl of Cork, was created Baron of Broghill in 1628, before he was seven years of age. After the death of Charles the First, having been gained over by Cromwell, he distinguished himself by his services in Ireland, and was persuaded to come for one year, to Scotland in 1655-1656, as President of the Council. *Vide supra*, pp 315, 321, 325. In 1660, he was created Earl of Orrery, and died in 1679, aged 58.

acceptable to the Protector as any in all this land:' Mr. Dowglafs, Mr Wood, myfelf and others, are of this opinion If yow in this alfo can marre the Proteftors defigne, and further ours, it will be a notable fervice; and we all fhall be much bound to yow for it The way and means to accomplifh it, we leave to yourfelf we know it will be the harder to perform, that we think it expedient to keep up the man's name for the time. I hope yow will be loath to returne before the agitators goe before yow. thereafter come fo foone as yow will, not before. I find already the great diligence of the faction to provide that place; doe your beft to marre them. The Lord help yow to doe out your vexatious fervice with fucceffe, and return yow fafe to us.

Read what I have written at Mr. Dowglafs's defire to Mr. Rous: clofe and delyver it if yow think fitt. Forget not the buffinefs of our Town

For Mr. Rous.

Sir,

I DID expect to have heard from yow with your Grandchild, when yow fent him to us However, upon my many obligations to yow, from his firft coming to this time, I have, (as I hope he will bear me witnefs,) been fo carefull of him in his perfon, ftudies, company, dyet, and all things concerned him, as it lay in my power I purpofe, God willing, to continue my overfight of him, and am glad to have the occafion to doe fervice to one of your fo near relations This is all I have for the time to fignifie to yow. Only one word concerning our brother Mr. Sharp; that fo farr as yow may be pleafed to give credit, not fo much to me, as to the farr moft part of the gracious minifters and people in Scotland, what he has delivered in our printed Reprefentation⁵, and from time to time in write to the Councell, and others, there is to our beft knowledge the very truth, unjuftly contradicted by thefe men who have broken the peace of our Church, and continue, by their obftinate error, and reftlefs purfuing of their oppreffive defignes, to keep our dangerous rents from all poffi-

⁴ Baillie here points at the nomination of Sharp to be Principal of the College of Glasgow

⁵ 'A True Reprefentation of the Rife, Progrefs, and ftate of the prefent Divifions of the Church of Scotland London, printed in the year 1657," 4to, pp 58 This tract, according to L

bilitie of healing. Had not your wifdome and equitie there been pleafed to have opened one ear to our anfuers, we were afrayed they fhould, by your power, before this have brought on a heavy and very caufelefs perfecution on us. As in God's mercy to us yow have not hitherto concurred with their unhappie propofals, however gilded with fpecious pretences, fo our truft is in God, that he will not permitt yow hereafter to afflift them, without all caufe, to put us to farder griefe and trouble. Without your help they have thefe diverfe years vexed us to purpofe.

I will hold you no longer at this time, but heartily falutes yow, praying that the Lord would continue yow yet fome tyme to be inftrumentall, with thefe who here have power, for the good of them in both Nations who, in quietnefs, defire to ferve the Lord Jefus in all fincerity of heart. So prays

Your very loving and much honouring freind and Servant,

September 23d [1657.]   R. BAILLIE.

(O) FOR MR. R. BAILLIE.

SIR,

BEING now fick, I make ufe of the hand of another, and doe thank yow for the letter yow fent me, wherein yow expreffe fo much care towards one in regard of his relation to me. But if yow knew the manner of fending him to Glafgow, yow would not have thought it ftrange that he was not recommended to yow; for, upon fome reafons, I did put him away from mine own care, and delivered him over to one who was heretofore Clerk to the Committee for the Univerfities wherein I had the chair, as perchance yow may remember, who did take the care of providing for him: He, meeting with Mr. Gillefpie here, learned of him the way of the College, and of bringing him into it, not knowing your intereft therein, but only as a Divinitie Profeffor there. But now yow have gone fo farr to take notice of him in refpect of me, I muft acknowledge myfelf ingaged to yow, and fhall defyre yow to continue this charitie to him, he being there upon his good behaviour, without which he is like to be loft both with God and man.

As for your publick bufinefs, I am forie that there are fuch differences between thofe that are fo near in fpirit, and defire heartily that to the unitie of the fpirit there might be added the bond of peace. True it is, there have been fuch differences heretofore between faints, and as great as Barnabas and Paul; but they are rather for lamentation than imitation; yet howfoever, it is to be hoped God will produce a good effect out of them, who turns all things to good for his children. As for my part, I was not particularly ingaged on either fide, neither will I as to taking parties, but only apply myfelf to truth and peace. When the bufinefs had been long in hand, then Mr. Sharp acquainted me concerning the matter of the Commiffioners, and the inequall intereft of them Hereupon I made fuch application, that it was returned to me for an anfwer, that there wes not fuch inequalitie in them; and hereupon I fell prefently into my ficknefs, and fo had not opportunitie to act further in it perfonallie, but am ready, if God fhall give power and opportunitie, to advance fuch a work of truth and peace as this is; and fo recommending yow and your Church to the grace and favour of God, and to his Spirit of unity, peace, and holinefs, and remaines,

Your very faithful Friend to ferve yow,

Whitehall, 10th [October] 1657. F. ROUS.

(L) [FOR MR R. BAILLIE] LONDON, OCTOBER 13TH 1657

REVEREND SIR,

YOUR's from Edinburgh I did receive, but becaufe the fubject to which the purpofe of it did relate, hath been fince in another condition than was fuppofed at the writting of it, I thought yow would the more eafily difpenfe with my delay to give yow a return to it. Your's of September 29th came not to my hand till October 12th in the afternoon, and that cafuallie. I had taken my leave of his Highnefs that day in the morning, and had your letter come fooner, I had an opportunity to have fpoke a word for our friends in that particular, however, upon the receipt of your's, I went ftraight to a fignificant perfon of the Councell, of whofe active friendfhip I have had many proofs; I did acquaint him with the bufinefs: he bade me give to him the full ftate of the matter in writing. Accordingly I did draw [it] in paper, with the defire for a prefent remedie expreffed in your letter: I inclofed the copie of his Highnefs letter yow fent to me. I waited the opportunity of putting it into his hand ; when I faw he was to fpeak to other members of the Councell, and probably to his Highnefs, I befought him to move effectually in it, which he promifed to doe, and give me ane account to-morrow That letter hath been furreptitioufly purchafed, I know by what inftrument ; it could not have paffed here by the knowledge of the Councell ; howbeit the Lord may be pleafed to order that particular (as he hath done other paffages of their ftickling here) for a further difcoverie of the practicating domineering fpirit of thefe men, to render them leffe capable to oppreffe, if the honeft men of your Toune do ftand to the maintaining of their juft rights, and ply the Councell in Scotland. I know by letters from fome of them lately fent to leading perfons here, that they have both friends there and here, and hope that your Metropolitan fhall not be able to bring them under his yoke : It might have been expected, that when that letter was obtained, he was in fuch a condition as might have barred violent, carnall, and revengefull intendments ; and his co-agitators fhould have feen the Lord's rebuke of their injurious wayes He intended to be at home before the day of election, but being under the Lord's arreift, he would interpofe by his agents for this delay.

I have nothing now to doe at London, where my ftay and toill hath been fo long that I may be excufed (when the Lord hath now defeated all the affaults of that faction for Church-power) if I meditate a fpeedy return ; which I fhall delay till the next week, that I may doe what I can for the fervice of your honeft men I was not forgetfull of them when I had occafion to fpeak with Mr Secretary, and others of the Councell, thefe weeks paft ; and believe it, they have a prettie good fenfe of their condition, and I think they will evidence it. I fuppofe yow have ane account from Edinburgh, to what paffes our publick bufinefs is brought, fo that I may fpare anie more writing of it Only I fhall prevent the time of my difcharge of the Protector's order to me, at his very civile dimiffion of me, in one particular, in that he named yow as one of our Brethren to whom he defired twice to be remembered by me at my returne. I fent your letter by a fure hand to Mr Rous, who ftayes in the countrey, and hath not been fince at Whitehall I doe remember my refpects to your R[everend] colleagues, Mr. George Young and Mr Hew Blair. The Spirit of the Lord Jefus reft upon yow. I am, Sir,

Your's,

JA SHARP

I receaved one from your bailhe, James Pollock, and was mindfull of his defire fignified by it, though I could not prevent what was in a clancular way here drawne from the Protector to your Towne's prejudice; which may be in time yet remedied. Thefe who covet to rule among yow, I think doe not expect to have it by your good will I pray yow excufe my not fending a particular returne to him, to whom I defire my fervice to be remembred; his ufage of me while he was here, lyeth yet upon my ftomack. Yow know how it may be talked of. But I fhall forbear till meeting.

(M.) [For Mr R. Baillie.]

REVEREND SIR,

Your's of November 9th, I receaved the 20th. I thought yow had gott notice before this what was done by the Councell here in reference to the Town of Glafgow. Upon my reprefentation of their cafe in paper to fome of the Councell, they dealt fo effectually in the bufinefs, as by the Councell's order here, it is wholhe referred to be determined by the Councell of Scotland, but with this exprefs caveat, that they doe nothing to the infringement of the liberties of that burgh. This was told by one of the Councell two weeks agoe, but after the receipt of your letter I did fpeak this day with Mr. Secretary concerning it, who hath affured, that it is fo as above written; which is the expreffion *in terminis* uttered by him to me this afternoon. If Mr. Gillefpie, upon his return, make any buftling in that matter, your honeft men need not be difcouraged from profecuting their juft rights by all he can doe, either there or here. Let them ufe their moyen with their friends in the Councell, at Edinburgh; and if they apprehend any hazard by the power of fome there, let them labour for a delay of hearing of the bufinefs before the Councell till it pleafe the Lord to bring me home, (which I hope will be within 20 dayes at fartheft), and then I may truft they fhall get no wrong I know not what the faction with yow doe bragg; but believe it, their caufe of bragging is more flender fince Warıftoun's removeing from London, than it was. Mr. Gillefpie, and all of them, are better known here than they fuppofe: the Lord our God is holy and true, and will not allwayes further crooked defigns.

It is not fitt your Towne take any notice at all of me in this bufinefs, I fhall be ready to doe them any fervice upon an juft and honeft account I befeek you, Sir, communicate nothing of this letter to any but fuch as yow truft for fecrecie. The Lord's Spirit and prefence be with yow

I am your's, in Chrift,

JA. SHARP.

London, November 21ft, in hafte, 1657.

(N.) [FOR MR. R. BAILLIE.]

REVEREND SIR,

WHILE I am here in towne I receave yours of February 15th. The concernments of your Toune are more upon my heart than that there needed any requefts to engage me to imploy my poor endeavours for preventing their prejudice. I take the libertie in thefe bufineffes to ufe the way I am accuftomed unto with thefe of the Councell here · I cannot upon all occafions folicite them at times when my being with them may be taken notice of; but I hope the refult of the Councell, in reference to thefe affaires, will evidence that I have not been altogether neglectfull to improve the opportunities I had, with all the members of the Councell, fince my laft coming to toune. I fhall only fay this, that thofe among yow are much miftaken who think that Mr. Patrick Gillefpie can carrie here what he will. Providence tryfted my comming over with the very nick of the determination. In reference to what yow did write, I fpake to all of the Councell feverallie in it, and had affurances from them of what now is made good by their order; and if your honeft men fhall take no notice of Mr. Patrick, but goe on in their ufuall way of election, they need fear no prejudice by all he can doe; but if either by his threats, or infinuations, he prevaill with them to fwerve from their liberties in the leaft, they have themfelves to blame for future inconveniences. One of the Councell told me, he had fatiffied Major Darnie [Dorney] with what was done. This is but a hint in hafte to yourfelf, which I hope yow will not make known as come from me, but believe it, there is no caufe why your honeft men fhould in the leaft recede from their way in owning their juft rights, and though I doe not make much dinn in bufinefs of that nature, yet I have matter to blefs the

Lord I have not been altogether ufelefs in ferving fo juft an intereft I muft lay it upon yow to make my excufe to your Magiftrates and Councell that I have not given them a return to their letter. I pray yow, as yow love me, let not me be taken notice [of] as having any hand in what is now paft.

Yours,

JA SHARP

Edinburgh, 25th February [1658] In hafte.

Remember my refpects to Mr George Young. Goe on in your way of election where no fcandall is made out to incapacitate any by the Act of qualifications

(P) FOR HIS REVEREND BROTHER MR. JAMES SHARP, MINISTER AT CREELL[CRAIL].

JAMES,

How our Towne's bufinefs will goe on Tuefday I know not my neighbour is as high as ever If it goe wrong we muft be on yow again. In Mubbot's letter, the laft week, from London, to the Governour of our towne, I fee the Councell of England are on ane oath of renouncing of Charles Stewart's intereft: This, to me, is point-blank a renouncing of our Covenant and Oath to God; if this be not prevented, it is a ground of fore perfecution only for confcience. If we act any thing againft the prefent power, let them doe to us as they find caufe, but if we refufe ane new oath renouncing an old, whilk the laft Parliament of England drew on us to keep them from ruine, and fo to lay a foundation for Cromwell's prefent power, our fufferings for this may be heavie, but unworthie to come from them who drew us to the firft oath, which we cannot renounce, though they have done it. If your power be any thing worth with Broghill, Thurloe, or any other, I humbly intreat yow to prevent this great mifchief, a moft needlefs ground of trouble only to tender confciences: to others, oaths are nought but cobwebs I have given yow a warning; this courfe will undoe many whom yow love, and me with the firft, for any thing I know do in this what yow may This, taken in tyme by yow, may eafily be remeeded . but if the Protector be once engadged in this perfecution moft needlefs, he will not be fo eafily brought off it as he was from the idle oath of tender. Who cares now for an oath but a few quiet confcientious men, who will never trouble the prefent government, if it trouble not them.

Your's to ferve yow

Glafgow, May 3d [1658]

For the Right Worshipfull Sir George Maxwell of Nether Pollock.[7]

Sir,

As yow defired, I did immediatly draw the inclofed, according to your amendments, as yow may fee; but none calling for it, I would not be officious to obtrude it to any; only, Sir, I fend it to yow, who made the motion of it to me, to be made ufe of as yow think expedient. So refts,

Your's

May 3d [1658.]

For his Reverend and Belovfd Friend Mr. John Young

Sir,

Understanding that fome doubt of my confent to thefe of our Acts wherein indeed we were unanimous, I doe teftifie, that I did confent and fubfcryve not only that Act of the Colledge, allowing to Mr. Gillefpie three thoufand merks for his firft fervice to us at London, but alfo to the Act allowing him, during his lifetime, the half of the profits of the Bifhoprick of Galloway that fhould be by his pains and diligence augmented, and likewife for his procuring of our laft gift, I did moft willingly fubfcryve ane Act for a gratuitie to him of three hundred pound fterling, out of the firft and readieft incumes of that gift: That my confent and hand was to all this, I am very willing yow affure, in my name, any whom yow fhall hear to doubt of it.

May 3d [1658]   [Robert Baillie]

[7] Rector of the College of Glasgow This short note probably enclosed the one that follows it See the postscript to Baillie's subsequent letter to Spang, (*infra*, p 371-373,) respecting Gillespie's disputes with the College and Town of Glasgow.

For Mr. Spang [8]

Cousin,

That which oft I promifed yow, a large account of our affaires this twelve moneth paft, yow have it, but in a confufed way for want of leafure Our Church hes been prettie quiet, our troubling Remonftrants not haveing yet prevailed with the Englifh to get authoritie from them to exercife their tyrannie among us. The great inftrument of God to crofs their evill defignes has been that very worthie, pious, wife, and diligent young man, Mr. James Sharp. The purpofe of the few brethren that were on the advife of his going to London, upon my Lord Broghill's defire, yow may fee in his Inftructions, fubfcryved, and at firft feen almoft only by three, Mr Robert Dowglafs, Mr. David Dick, and Mr. James Wood. The Remonftrants agreed not very weell among themfelves. My Lord Warriftoun, Mr. Gillefpie, and Mr. Guthrie, thefe three reftlefs heads, looked not one way But after the affronts Mr Gillefpie received from the Synod of Lothian; and my Lord Wariftoun's domeftick ftraits had made him content, contrare to his former refolutions, to embrace his prior place of Reg fter from his Highnefs; and Mr Guthrie's continuall vexation by Mr. Simpfone his colleague; and Mr. Simpfone of Airth being provocked by the Synod of Perth's meddling with the great fcandall of the fatherlefs child, reflecting fore on him, they refolved at laft to goe up together, and openly to petition his Highnefs for all their defires.

When the Synod of Glafgow had taken off the cenfure of the Generall Affemblie from Mr. Patrick Gillefpie and Mr. James Naefmith, in the ftrange way I wrote to yow of before, that partie thought it advantageous to them to have that act of Glafgow acknowledged by the other Synods. For this end they refolved to fend Mr. Gillefpie correfpondent from Glafgow to the Synod of Lothian : they thought they would not refufe him for many caufes; and if they admitted him, it was a leading cafe to the other Synods to paffe from the act of the Generall Affemblie in its cenfure without all fatiffaction. That meffage was not much to the mind of Mr. Gillefpie himfelf, but Mr. John

[8] This letter has no date in the MS but it appears to have been written in June 1658.

Carſtares and others would needs have it put upon him. When he came, his commiſſion was ſcrupled at by Mr. John Smith and others, and laid aſide to be cognoſced on, they gladly would have ſhifted the matter, and eſchewed all dinn, being unwilling to enter in conteſt; but Mr. Patrick Gillefpie's high humour would not permitt it, but he muſt needs have their pofitive anſwer to admitt or rejeɛt his commiſſion. They lenified the queſtion, and ſince he would have it put, they made it Admitt or Committ. When the votes almoſt of all wes for referring it to a committee to be cognoſced on, he took it ſo ill, that he broke out in a railing, telling them, "Their ſword was but of wood, and their arme was broken," and much more evill language; to which Mr Dowglafs gave ſtout and ſharp replies. I knew this irritation would not be eaſilie forgott; it was a ſpurr for their voyage to London.

There was a very foule ſcandall of new broken out on Mr. James Simpſon of Airth. A young woman familiar with him, and oft in his houſe, was found with child; ſhe granted the child, but denyed ſhe had known any man. Mr. James, with the advice of his preſbyterie, Mr James Guthrie, and other two or three, (for their number is no greater in the Remonſtrant preſbyterie of Stirling,) takes the woman's confeſſion, in face of the congregation, that ſhe was with child, and withall her purgation by oath that ſhe knew no man. For this Mr James and ſhe are both cited to anſwer to the Synod of Perth. both of them ſend in to the Synod a declinator (both written by Mr. James Simpſon's hand) as of a corrupt judicatorie. While this is in agitation, Mr. James is ſent to London, to wait on till his four fellow-commiſſioners ſhould be ready to come. Their commiſſion I did not ſee; but it was ſuch as ſome of their owne, as Mr John Carſtares, and others, refuſed to ſubſcryve: we may know it by their propoſalls, (B.) which to the very laſt they preſſed to obtaine from the Proteɛtor: to wit; Ane order from him, that within the bounds of every Synod there ſhould be named a committee, of equall number Aſſemblie-men and Remonſtrants, who ſhould have power to determine all differences in planting and purgeing in all the Preſbyteries of the bounds. 2 That there ſhould be a committee of delegates from all the Synods, of equall number of Aſſemblie-men and Remonſtrants, to determine finallie all differences eccleſiaſtick in the whole land. 3. That the Proteɛtor ſhould nominate a committee to plant kirks, and that the power of giving of ſtipends in all vacand churches ſhould be in this committee. 4. That the Parliament should renew the Act of Classes, to the end the places of civill power should be in the hands of their party. The last they obtained, for Lieutenant-Generall Lambert, and the Generall-Majors in the Parliament were much their friends; and others, whom their diligent agents Garthland and Tweddall made for them. At first their motion was rejected; but thereafter, when our friends were out of the house, they got it past in an additional propofition. It was intended chiefly for the changing of our Glafgow magiftrates; whereupon I moved our brethren of Edinburgh to write to Mr. Sharp many reafons to ftop the thing if he could. He wrought it fo that it paft with much difficultie, and however got private affureances it fhould doe no harme; and fo that Act of Parliament lay as good as dormant, till of late they obtained, on a fupplication of procured hands in this toune, a letter from the Protector to fufpend the new election of magiftrates in our burgh till farder order. Our late magiftrates, with the concurrence almoft of all the burghs of Scotland, are dealing with the Protector to get the priviledges of their burgh preferved. What will be the iffue we will fee ere long.

For the other three defyres, Mr. Sharp, in diverfe conferences before the Protector, made them appear fo unreafonable, that after more than half a year's importunat foliftation, they could obtaine nothing at all. One of the caufes of fruftrating their hopes was, that the London minifters was flatly for us againft them. Yow fee what information I writ up to Mr Afhe, a prime citie minifter, to be communicat to all our Prefbyterian friends, (C.); alfo to my ancient friend Mr. Rous, one of the Councell of State,(D.). Mr. Rutherfoord did write to Mr. Afhe an information in the favours of his partie; but after both his and mine were read, and Mr. Sharp with his five oppofites had been heard at length, in diverfe meetings of the Citie minifters, all of them profeffed their diffatiffaction with the way of the Remonftrants, and fatiffaction with our proceedings. Mr. Wood had drawne a Reprefentation of our differences, which Mr. Hutchifon, in his fmoothing, to my fenfe, had fomething enervat, not only in its fharpnefs, but vigour. This Mr. Sharp did print at London, which (fince thefe too readie fcribes have not anfwered,) did us much good with all intelligent men.

The Remonftrants, finding no Prefbyterian friends, plyed hardlie the Sectaries, did pray oft with them both privately and publictly, fo that with all their power thefe befriended them; I mean Dr Owen, Lockier, Caryll, and other Independents. Lieutenant-General Lambert and Fleetwood, with the great officers of the armie, moſt anabaptiſts, were affectionately for them. At laſt the Protector, being wearied, did name a duodenarie committee to hear both, and report their judgment to the Councell. Mr. Sharp refufed to appear as being a mere private man, having no commiſſion to tranfact anything of publict concernment to the Church of Scotland; but being charged at the fecond meeting, he appeared, and gave fuch anfwers to his oppofites challenges, that they could get nothing there for a good tyme. Of the twelve, fix were conceaved to be prefbyterians, and the reſt enemies to our church-difcipline. Of the firſt fort none keeped but one, Mr. Manton; the others keeped weell, and were readie at laſt to report to the Councell their advyce to grant all the defires of the Remonſtrants, as they had reafon, being avowed adverfaries to our church-government. When it was at this nick, Mr. Aſhe, by his letters, procured Mr. Godfrey and Mr Cooper, two prefbyterians, who had been named on the committee, to meet; they, with Mr. Manton, after a new full hearing, were fo well fatiffied with Mr. Sharp's replyes, that they drew up their judgement by way of teſtimonie, (E.) againſt the Remonſtrators defyres. This wrought fo upon the Councell, that they refolved not to interpofe in our debates, only to write a letter to the miniſters of Edinburgh, Mr Dowglafs, Mr. Dickfon, Mr Traill, and Mr. Stirling, to agree at home among ourfelves; yet in this letter, by cannie conveyance of their friend Mr. Scobell, (I think,) clerk to the Councell, they had gotten foiſted in a very hurtfull claufe, that where there was difference about ſtipends, it ſhould be determined by the teſtimonie of four named in Mr. Patrick Gillefpie's ordours, which the Parliament had expreſſly aboliſhed. That claufe was reprefented both to the Protector and Counfellors to be fo unreafonable, that it is like there ſhall no letter at all be fent to us. The ſtorme we were afraid for, by God's mercy, for a tyme is put by; but how foon it will waken again, we doe not know.

Mr James Guthrie left them before they came to their greateſt conteſt, whether for want of moneys, or difference among themfelves, I know not, though they put all the miniſters of their mind in our bounds to pay, at the firſt, forty ſhillings ſterling, for their maintenance, and all of their partie, men and women, to a voluntarie contribution; whence, out of Glafgow, fome fay, there went up one hundred and eighty pounds ſterling; yet their charge was so great, and their friends charity, after the firſt fervor, ſo cold, that all of them were ſtraitned enough for moneys, as I was informed. Alſo, they ſay, they agreed not ſo weell among themſelves: certaine it is that Mr. Guthrie oppoſed my Lord Wariſtoun's reſuming his place of Regiſter. If it had been upon both their profeſſed principle of the unlawfullneſs to take places ſubordinate to an unlawfull power, I could the better have excuſed it; but Mr. Guthrie, (as one, who ſhould have known it with the beſt, informed me) with all his power, did labour ſecretly to get that place to his confident friend Swintoun, with the burden of a yearly penſion of three hundred pound ſterling out of it to Wariſtoun; I know not what to ſay to it However Mr. Guthrie left them in the mids, having obtained nothing but a penſion of a hundred pound ſterling to his colleague Mr. Rule, out of the treaſurie of vacant ſtipends, the ſpoill of other churches, which is now dryed up. My Lord Wariſtoun is now alſo returned, having, with his place, obtained the moſt of the Regiſters which were carried out of the betrayed (as many ſay) Caſtle of Edinburgh to the Tower of London.

Mr. Gilleſpie remaines there ſorely ſick, ſome think in diſpleaſure that his defyres were not granted. However, at his laſt going to Hamptoun Court, he got no ſpeech of the Protector: if this grieved him, I know not; but he went immediately from Hamptoun Court to Wombledoun, Lambert's houſe, being Saturnday at night; and haveing ingadged to preach on Sunday morning, before ſermon, he had five ſtooles, and, after his painfull preaching, fourſcore before he reſted; thereafter, for many dayes, a great flux and feaver, together with the breach of an hulcer in the guts, put him to the very brink of death. Many thought it the evident hand of God upon him, and would not have ſorrowed for his death. For myſelf, I was grieved, foreſeeing the hurt of our Colledge by his removeall. He had obtained from the Protector to us, all the beneſices of the whole Chapter of the dioceſe of Glaſgow, alſo the Abbacy of Corſiegall, and ſundrie other things, which, *jure devoluto*, fell in the Protector's power. This gift he could have made advantagious to us; but, as I ſuſpect, no other man ſhall make any thing of it. beſide, our rents are in a confuſed condition, and we in much debt, which hardlie, for a long tyme we will defray; which he, by his ſingular activitie in theſe things, could have taken courſe with; but my moſt grief was, that I feared we ſhould truely have gotten a worſe in his place, with whom my life ſhould have been more unpleafant; fo that, after fome weeks defperat difcafe, when his flux and feaver began to abate, I was glad, and wifhed him to return quicklie in health. When I fand the faction ftickle for fecuring his place to their fide, I writ to Mr Sharp (F) to guard againft that evill, if he could, bot how all thefe things will goe, a little tyme will inform us If he remove, my defire would be for Mr. Sharp, or failing him, for Mr Ferguffon: for myfelf, God willing, I will medle with no place that comes through civill hands, and for that place as yet I never had the leaft ambition. If the faction fet Mr. Durhame in it, or Mr. Young, that his profeffion may be for Mr. Durhame, I mind not to ftickle at all to the contrare; we may foon be worfe ferved.

While thefe debates at London did continue, the reftlefs humour of that partie at home was fomewhat quiet, waiting for the iffue. Our Synod of Glafgow, whether for want of matter, or being deferted and contemned by many, has paft this year without dinn. Mr Robert Semple of Lifmahegu's foule proceffe has been referred to a committee, and little done in it, the man being one of their fyde. Mr. John Hammiltoun of Innerkip, a prime man among them, of a long tyme under very grofs fcandalls, is not fo much as challenged. Mr Harrie Semple, a bufy agent for them, prevented his proceffe by death. The Synod of Lothian and Perth has been carefull to try accurately the challenges of fundrie

The Quakers make fome trouble among us, and increafe in Leinzie, Dowglafs, and other places, moft where that faction has been troublefome Thus does our Church affairs ftand.

For our State, all is exceeding quiet A great armie, in a multitude of garnifons, bydes above our head, and deep povertie keeps all eftates exceedingly at under; the taxes of all forts are fo great, the trade fo little, that it's marvell if extreame fcarcitie of money end not, ere long, in fome mifchief What came out doors of the Parliament was this: All who came thither were complying and confident men, and none more readie to ferve his Highnefs, in every thing, than all that came from Scotland: if any were doubted, they were hold[en] off till their commiffions were weell examined The malicioufnefs of the faction with us keeped out Commiffar Lockhart, commiffioner for Glafgow, a large moneth yet at laft, by Ambaffador Lockhart's letter from France, he got in. The great work at firft was, to fettle the excife, and maintainance for the army; a vaft foume of money was requifite for the garrisons in England, Scotland, and Ireland, for the navies in Spain, at Dunkirk, and Jamaica; for the armie in France; for the Protector's court When this was agreed to without all contradiction, it was so laid by a few of the Protector's fastest friends, not above five, that the city should petition the Parliament to advyse the Protector to take upon him the title and government of King, after the way which, in a long paper of advyce, was sett doun. To this none did oppose but the officers of the army · to take them off, one of the articles of government was, the erection of a Houfe of Peers, to be nominat by the Protector, who doubtlefs was to make lords the chief of thefe officers; yet the thing was so farr against all that was professed, and so oft printed before, that it could not goe doune at first with them That which made some of them, efpeciallie their head, Lambert, so adverse, was his owne evident interest; for in all men's eyes he was the heir-apparent to the Protector's power; but the Kingfhip cutted him off clearlie from that hope. About this, many sharp debates were in the Houfe and out of the Houfe by the officers; all other were to give the Protector whatever he defired, not fo much for recent accidents, which were thought either invented or directed as opportune for that end : to wit, the feafing of a number of gentlemen in and about the citie, as if Charles Stewart had employed them for a prefent difturbance of the peace, which fear quicklie evanifhed as totallie groundlefs; alfo Sundercomb's plot to kill the Pro tector with a blunder-box; the man's denyall of all, and poyfoning of himfelf for fear of quartering quick, made not this to appear; the feafing of the declaration and ftandard of the Fifth Monarchie fools, the imprifoning of Sir Harie Vaine in Cairbrugh [Carifbrook] caftle, and Generall Major Harifon, did quicklie evanifh But that which inclined the moft to further the Protector's Kingfhip, was their expectation of a regular government thereby, without the perpetuating of a militarie rule by the fword, to which fo vaft and arbitrarie charges would allwayes be neceffary; befide that, all did expect a more moderate and meek ruling from the Protector and his children, than from Lambert, or any of all the armie. Some alfo were glad of a profeffed and open royaltie, hoping, in tyme, it might further the returne of thefe whom they counted the lawfull heirs of the Crowne.

When the Protector, as they faid, was willing to have come, and declared his willingnefs to accept, after much debate, private and publick, of the article of Kingſhip, alſo weell as the reſt of the advyce, that ſame morning his good-ſon Fleetwood came to him, with ſome papers, aſſurcing a ſtrong combination in the armie to oppoſe that motion. Upon the which affrightment, his Highneſs went to the painted chamber, and called the Houſe to ſhew them, that he accepted the government according to the petition and advyce in all the articles, except the title of King, which he could not digeſt. His beſt and moſt intime counſellers, Broghill and Thurloe, thought this a great error; yet it ſeems it was the beſt expedient; for at that time Lambert and the Generall-Majors power was ſo great, both in the Houſe and Armie, that if their obſtinacie had continued, they might have overturned all. To prevent this miſchief, a few days thereafter he adjourned the Parliament from June 27th till October.

In the laſt day of the Parliament, June 27th, he was moſt ſolemnly inſtalled Supreame Magiſtrat in a canopie of ſtate and throne, with a royall purple, furr ittobe, a ſword of ſtate, a ſcepter, and Bible in place of a crown, by the Speaker of the Houſe, Withrington, and was graced, like a coronation, with a ſermon and feaſt. In all the action the French and Dutch Ambaſſadors ſtood on his two hands, congratulating in their maſters name. The hearts of many were forc to ſee in effect all the Kingſhip eſtabliſhed on Cromwell in peace. Yet this did not ſatiſfie; for quickly Lambert was called for to a privie conference, wherein declaring himſelf unwilling to comply in all things, his commiſſion was called for, and he made a man moſt privat the chief of the army, in a ſupplication, excuſed their adhering to his way. Broghill got paſt in Parliament a right of a thouſand pound a year for his good ſervice. All men expected that when ſo eaſily Lambert was quaſhed, the next ſeſſion of Parliament would have quickly made Cromwell King, yet it did not ſooner meet but great miſcontentments were apparent: the Houſe of Lords, according to the petition and advyce, did ſit; Mancheſter and many would not ſitt: Caſſilis diſdained it; there was no more Peers for Scotland but Wariſtoun and Lockhart: yet the chiefe of Cromwell's friends were taken out of the Houſe of Commons to fill the other Houſe, and many then came in to the Houſe of Commons who were excluded before, no great friends to him; Scot, Heſilrig, Lambert, and many more, who quicklie began to move high queſtions about the power of the militia, the name and power of the other Houſe, to whom the Supreame Magiſtrate was to be anſuerable. Upon their fticklino fo high, after a few dayes fitting, they were diffolved ; the Protector calling to God to judge betwixt him and them, and they faying, Amen. In his fpeech, he attefted God he had rather chofen at a wood-fyde to have keeped fheep, than have undertaken the office he had, if the love of the people's peace had not conftrained him : he affured of Charles Stewart's readinefs to come from Flanders with an army, and fundrie lifting men for him in London. A ftorme after this was expected, fome prodigies feeming to foretell it: A little after his inftalment, a magazine of powder blowing up many houfes and perfons ; about the houfe in Fogo-muir, near Duns-Law, in December, an army of pickmen appearing to many ; and fome dayes after, fome thoufands of canon, in a formall fhape, for many days being feen by many, both Englifh and Scots, made of the fnow without the hand of man. For all this, nothing to this day is feen but a deep peace.

It's expected a new Parliament may be called, and fundry fhyres are faid to be forming petitions to his Highnefs to accept of the title of King. Many in the army, both in Scotland and England, are caft out ; but who remaine, writ up their fupplication, incouraging the Protector to proceed ; it's thought, on the councell's act and armie's petition, the Crown fhall be put on, and confirmed by the next Parliament. They fpeak of my Lord Fairfax and Lambert's committing In a late fpeech of the Protector to the Mayor and aldermen of London, it is ftill averred that Charles Stewart is ready to come from Oftend, with fix thoufand men and feven thoufand armes : All marvells how this can be ; for the Englifh navie is readie about that place to fink all that come that way ; and the defigne of raifing men in England is fo poor, that none values it, efpeciallie when it is fo well known by the Protector in every circumftance ; befide that, the moft who profeffe themfelves for the King among us, or over fea are of fo exceeding ill principles and humour, that few do wifh to be under their power.

For our more private affaires, thus they ftand : The Magiftrates of our towne have guided their affaires much better than they wont to be here, or any where this day in Scotland ; by a voluntar ftent on the malt, they have payed near two hundred thoufand merks, or a verie great foume of debt left by the former Remonftrants, by buying the Gorbals, Craig's, Blantyr's teinds, &c. at great rates They have payed the Englifh maintainance, fo that no man, thefe three or four yeares, of greateft burden, hes been ftented to a fhilling. They have made the Laigh-Church as good as new; bigged a fair grammar fchooll, a fair mill, and two wells, in the heart of the towne. For all this, Mr. P. Gillefpie, fo foone as recovered from his deadly difeafe, informes the Protector of them as fo mifhent men, that he obtaines an order to ftop them to proceed at Michaelmafs in their ordinarie election When we heard of it, we writ to Mr. Sharp, who took fuch courfe about it at London that his returne was, we needed [not] care for it, for it could not prejudge us; for, indeed, Mr. Patrick Gillefpie's carriage at London was fo high, vain, and fumptuous, that he became to be miflyked; and his frequent familiar walking with Lambert, and fome idle fpeeches, of the Remonftrants power to raife in Scotland twenty-four thoufand able yeomen for the good caufe, reported to the Protector, added nothing to his credit; yet when he came to Edinburgh in his coatch from London, with his horfe of twenty-five peeces walking after the coatch, he made a great bufinefs to have all our magiftrates and councell caft off Mr. James Sharp had procured a letter from the Councell of England to beware to hurt the priviledges of Glafgow Mr. Douglafs and Mr. Dickfon, on my letters, had dealt with the counfellers againft Mr. Patrick's oppreffing and calumnious accufations. The Proveift and Clerk of Edinburgh, and other friends, dealt in the fame, feeing Glafgow's cafe would be a leading one to all Scotland. So for all that Wariftoun, Swintoun, Argyle, and the reft of the faction could doe, little could be obtained againft us; only our folks, being foolifhlie confident, went too foone home, and in their abfence, Mr. Patrick obtains an commiffion to try and report what could be objected againft the magiftrates and counfellers. On the commiffion were five, Major Dorney, a fectarian preacher, but intime with that partie, the Governour of the Caftle of Dumbartane, an anabaptift, as they fay, Lieutenant-Colonell Simons, Commiffar Lockhart, and young [Hamilton of] Orbiftoun. At their firft meeting, their proceeding was fo illegall, that Orbiftoun and Lockhart protefted againft it, and refuifed to fitt Our Magiftrates appealed to the Councell, and refuifed to anfwer; notwithftanding, Mr. Patrick moved the three Englifh fojours to proceed, as they did, till they had fworne and heard all they pleafed, on proveift, bailhes, and moft of the counfell; againft fome they fwore about fourtie witneffes without any libell, but What know ye of this man? in a way fo irrationall and illegall, that all cryed out on it.

In the meane tyme, I was called to Edinburgh, December 30th, to hear Mr Sharp's report. He gave us a very notable relation of every paſſage, how, by the good hand of God, he had gotten all the defignes of the exceeding buſie and bold Remonſtrants defeat, that the Protector had difmiſſed him with very good words, aſſureing he ſhould be loath to grant any thing to our prejudice. He commended himſelf in his laſt ſpeech to four of us in particular, and by name twyſe, Mr Douglaſs, Mr. Dickſon, Mr. Blair, and me, profeſſing his ſorrow that he was a ſtumbling-block to us. The reaſon of this kindneſs, I take to be, 1. My Lord Broghill and Secretar Thurloe's reports of us; 2. That the Preſbyterian partie in England who adheres to us is exceedingly great and ſtrong, and, after the armie, is the Protector's chiefe ſtrength againſt the Sectaries, who generallie are out of conceit of him; 3 That our adverſaries are found but unconſiderable, and a headie partie, much joyning with the way of his adverſaries. However, we bleſſed God, that by Mr. Sharp's labours, was keeped off us for a tyme a much feared ſtorme At his coming from London, he appointed a correſpondence with one Major Beak, a zealous Preſbyterian, for aſſiſting us in what we might have to doe. We appointed Mr. Wood to draw a ſhort declaration of our willingneſs to have any tollerable peace with the Remonſtrants, if ſo, for tyme to come, they would promiſe to be ſubmiſſive to the eſtabliſhed government · this now is printed, (G.), but they ſcirp at all we can doe or ſay for peace, except we ſubject ourſelves to their good pleaſure. There was ſomething moved in our laſt meeting of a few, to doe a little more for ingaging the Protector: I cruſhed the motion at the beginning, inveighing againſt it; ſo for the time it's dead.

At this tyme, Mr. P[atrick] G[illeſpie] was diligent to get his accuſations cloſed in Glaſgow, [before] the three Sojours with their clerk James Porter, (the factious clerk catholick of ſynod, preſbyterie, common ſeſſion, and the five particular ſeſſions, and of every committee they have,) Mr. Patrick and Mr John Spreul inſtructing every witneſs as they thought fitt. When all was ended, they went to the Councell with the depoſitions; but finding the Councell not ſo ready as they expected to goe their way, Mr. Gillespie takes himſelf to a new way, wherein he was like to have obtained all their deſigne Their crafts-baillie, John Hall, a wavering and volage man, albeit the Proveiſt's nephew, ſuffered his lightneſs to be abuſed, and to tell all the evill tales he could of his colleagues Walter Neilſon, deacon-conveener, Mr G[illeſpie's] speciall enemie, againft whom was more deponed of too much drinking and profanitie than any three of their companie, in his ambition to continue in office, was willing to joyne in a clanculary way with the former to ferve Mr. G[illefpie's] defignes; and above all, W. Anderfone, imployed by the towne in their moft fecret actions, and conceaved to be a moft active agent againft Mr. G. was in fecret drawne over by him to joyne with his partie. Thefe three, by Mr. P. [Gillefpie's] and Mr. John Spreul's directions, had laid it fo cunningly, that it was a marvell their plott mifcaried. However, Mr. G as minding nothing but peace and the Town's good, that which he knew the Councell had refolved contrare to all his defires, that he might feem to have fome hand in that he could not help, puts in a fupplication that all fhould be fent home in peace, and accufations laid by, as hopefull they would make a new election, which fhould be right and acceptable; the Councell, nothing the more for this fupplication, but on Mr. Sharp and other foliftation, and their order from England, fent an order whereby they removed the ftop had been put to their election, and permitted them to go on to choife accoiding to their priviledges The day before the election, and no fooner, they fand out Mr. Patrick's new plott, and fundrie of them went about to prevent it the beft might be. When they came to the election, they carried not only that W. Anderfone fhould not be on the lite to be Proveift, but fhould have no place in Councell, as being neither merchand nor craftfman: they got John Anderfone of Dowhill, proveift, [John] Walkinfhaw and James Barnes, baillies, James Campbell, dean of gild, John Hall put off the councell, and all made clofe contrare to Mr. Patrick's mind; only Walter Neilfone, by the power of his partie, was made baillie, but all his followers they gott off the Councell, fo that Wattie now fignifies little thing. At this difappointment, Mr Gillefpie and his partie are inraged: they fend back new fupplications to the Councell againft an irregular election; they obtained fummonds againft fourteen to anfwer to the former depofitions; and now both parties are in Edinburgh to plead this caufe. the event yet is uncertain, and both are very confident to get their defires. The chief of the Toune-Councell are John Bell and John Walkinfhaw, right wife, diligent, and bold men, who hes had many fhrewd rancounters with Mr. Gillefpie before the Councell to his face they threaten to libell him, fince they can no be quite of his cumber, as one who neglects totallie his own office, and in five or fix yeares fervice, for which he takes up a very great ftipend, hes done nothing at all in his proper duetie, no fo much as once to be prefent at a privat or publick examination. 2. That he invents one bufinefs after another to be from his charge; and fpends up, befide his ftipend, the Colledge rent exceffively. That when he was at London, for a by-bufinefs for the Town, he took off them fiftie pieces; and for fome gift he procured to the Colledge, befyde all the charges beftowed on it, which were great, he took three thoufand merks from the Colledge as a gratuity, and a penfion for his lifetime of the half of that gift; the whole whereof he calls two thoufand merks, which yearly, muft make to him a thoufand. That for the laft journey to London, where, only on the by, he purchafed a new gift to the Colledge which they fay is lyke to make nothing but much plea and expences, he took fix thoufand merks out of the Colledge rent at a time, when not only there was not any thing to pay the Mafters ftipends, but in the mids of the year there was nothing to pay the mafters and burfars boord; and as if this had not been enough, befide near three thoufand merks of depurfements for compts of things needlefs to the Colledge, he took ane other gift from the Colledge, for the fame fervice, of three hundred pound fterling, to be payed out of the firft and readieft of any thing came in of his laft gift, he profeffing, at the receiving of the Act for it, that when all was payed to him, he was ftill a lofer in his laft journey, wherein few doubted bot he fpoke truth in regard of his hudge wafte. His partie, who employed him to London, contribute to him above one hundred and fifty pound fterling, which they fuppofed fhould have fufficed for his charges, and the Protector gave him two hundred pound fterling, which he fuppofed fhould liberallie have defrayed him; yet all did it not. They fay that never Bifhop in Scotland lived at fo high a rate; and the maine caufe why he meddled to have his own faction in the magiftracie, was his affurance, that thefe who now are in place, when they come to audit the Colledge counts, will not allow but complaine of his vaft and unreafonable charge. This, and much more, they threaten himfelf to libell againft him: How all will go we will hear fhortly. However, he hes wakened a very great ftrife among our people, who without him would have been pretty quiet

Aberdeen will never be out of fome fire. Mr. Meinzies being wearied of his Independency, feems content to return to the Prefbyterie and Synod; yet Mr. Cant and he hes continuall fighting from the fame pulpit, till at laft

Mr Cant is removed,[1] in fmall reputation. But before his death, his fon, Mr Andrew [Cant,] publickly had foull flytings with Mr Meinzies, in the fchooles, before all the fchollers; whereof Mr Meinzies hes written to all the other Univerfities, complaining, not fo much of the affront, as the erroneous tenets of Mr Andrew. The queftions were *De Concurfu Dei in Actibus Liberis*, wherein Mr. Meinzies follows Twiffe and Rhetorford κατὰ πόδας; the other oppofes thefe expreffly, and goes too farr the Arminian and Molinifts way: however, that plea has made much dinn

In St. Andrewes there is no more concord. The plea about Mr. Wood's fetling in the Provoftrie of the Old Colledge is fcarce fetled, till a worfe does arife about the planting of his place in the New. While he and Mr. Sharp are too lingering in putting in it Mr. Scougle,[2] a good and noble fcholler, minifter of Lewchers, Mr. Patrick Gillefpie, at Mr. Rutherfurd's defyre, gets fecretly the Protector's hand to one Mr. Alexander Jamifone, a regent of St. Leonard's, a man very unfitt for fuch an imployment. About this there is a great prefent ftrife.

In Edinburgh things are more quiet. There is little more concord in their Colledge Mr Lightoun[3] does nought to count of, but looks about him in his chamber · Mr. Dickfon, for fear of Mr. Guthrie, was active to get him there. His fon Mr. Alexander fucceeded Mr. Lightoun in his miniftrie at Newbottle; where my Lord Lothian, his earneft caller, and many of the people, became quickly fo unkind to him, in his ftipend and other duties, that he was outwearied with them. His father,[4] or rather Mr. Dowglafs, moved my Lord Broghill to defire the Toune-Councell to prefent him to the vacant place

---

[1] In the margin of the MS. Baillie has added, "This was generally reportit, but vit he lives." After the Restoration, in consequence of various proceedings, Mr Andrew Cant, senior, withdrew from his ministerial charge in Aberdeen, and died about the year 1664 His son in 1675, became Principal of the University, and one of the Ministers of Edinburgh

[2] Mr Patrick Scougall, son of Sir John Scougall of Scougall, was minister of Leuchars in Fife He was minister of Darsie in 1636, translated to Leuchars in 1645, from thence to Saltoun in 1658, and consecrated Bishop of Aberdeen in 1664

[3] Mr Robert Leighton, Principal of the University of Edinburgh, and afterwards Bishop of Dunblane, and Archbishop of Glasgow

[4] Mr David Dickson, Professor of Divinity His son was appointed Professor of Hebrew, 3d September 1656

of the Hebrew Tongue; which accordingly was done, and he fettled there in Mr. Lightoun's abfence at his yearly progrefs to London : on his return he ftikled more than is ordinar to him, to have the young man out; but his labour was vaine. In a late voyage to London he obtained, after Mr. Gillefpie's example, fome two hundred pound fterling to the Colledge out of fome Church lands, which, in my mind, will be als-foone obtained as the flim-flams of Mr Gillefpie's gifts. However Mr. Sharp obtained, at London, that one of thefe hundred pounds, when gotten, fhould be Mr. Alexander Dickfon's ftipend. This angers Mr. Lightoun not a little; but all is quiet, for the miniftrie there of our mind, carie all things quietly and wifely, without much noife In the Toune Councell there is too much, and feen divifion, the young Proveift carying all over the Clerk and others with a proud high hand, to the Toune's hurt, as I hear.

We grieve for fundry unhappy accidents and fudden deaths among us. My Lord Killmars,[5] a moft gallant youth of nineteen years, among the talleft men of the Ifle, in a few dayes ficknefs of a purple feaver, died. My nephew, my beft friend in Glafgow, the ftrongeft man in the town, fuddenly taken away with the fame So Sir John Grear of Lag, when coming to Edinburgh to marrie the Earl of Athole's fifter. Young Dughall,[6] a very fyne youth of twenty yeares, taken away with the pokes. John Bell, the only child remaining to Mr John Bell our friend, died of a purple feaver. My Lord Rofs, a good young youth, as was fuppofed, fallen in adulterie with his child's nurfe. The Earl of Eglintoun's heir, the Mafter Montgomrie,[7] convoying his father to London, runns away without any advyce, and maries a daughter of my Lord Dumfreis, who is a broken man, when he was fure of my Lady Balclough's marriage, the greateft match in Brittain this unexpected pranck is worfe to all his kinn than his death would have been. The Earl of Murray did little better, for at London, without any advice, he ran and maried Sir William Balfour's fecond daughter ; as my Lord Paflay,[8] the other year, loft himfelf, in marrying, at London, a daughter of

[5] William Lord Kilmaurs, eldest son of Wilham, ninth Earl of Glencairn

[6] Porterfield of Duchal

[7] Alexander, eldest son of Hugh Lord Montgomery, after whose death he succeeded to the title of Earl of Eglintoun.

[8] James, eldest son of James, second Earl of Abercorn

Sir John Lenthal, who had born to Sir William Fleming fome children ; and my Lord Kenmure caft himfelf away, in that fame place, on a foolifh marriage whilk will accomplifh the ruine of his famihe.

The Earle of Rothes is put in the caftle on a moft fhameful occafion · My Lord Howard's fifter matched with my Lord Balgony, Rothes's fifter's fon, Generall Leflie's oye,[1] this Howard's wife, a very light woman, came to make a vifit to Fife, where her carriage every where was exceeding wanton ; Rothes openly bure her too much company, to the offence of many. However, about that tyme fhe is gotten with child, which fhe bears at London her hufband, finding that he had not been near her for three or four moneths from her conception, falls in an outragious jealoufie with her ; fufpects my Lord Bellaffis, whom his brother fights in that quarrell. but fufpects Rothes more, and in a rage pofts towards Scotland to fight Rothes The Protector hearing of it, caufes follow and apprehend Howard, and fends an order in hafte to fecure Rothes in the Caftle of Edinburgh, where yet he lyes in great infamie.

My Lord Fofter [Forrefter,][2] on a great fufpicion of inceft with his wife's fifter, his brother's wife, with grief of that and other mifdemeanours, hes brought his wife to her grave. My Lord Lorne,[3] a moft excellent and honeft-minded youth, prifoner in the Caftle of Edinburgh, walking about while the Lieutenant of the caftle with others are playing with hand-bullets, one of them, rebounding off the wall, ftricks him on the head, whereon he fell down dead and fpeechlefs for a long tyme : his death fundry dayes was expected, but bleffed be God, I hear this day he was better. My Lord Toftes,[4] being weell at night, died ere the morrow. My Lord Clerkinton, Sir William Scot,[5] going up weell his own

---

[1] Alexander Lord Balgony having predeceafed his father, (vide vol. 1 p 203,) his son Alexander Lord Balgony, who is here mentioned on the death of his grandfather, the diftinguifhed General in 1662, became second Earl of Leven

[2] James Baillie of Torwoodhead, eldest son of General Baillie of Letham, by virtue of his marriage with Joanna, daughter of George Lord Forrester, succeeded to the title on his Lordship's death The General's second son, William, was married to another daughter See note in the Appendix of this volume, No. LXXIII

[3] Archibald Lord Lorne, afterwards Earl of Argyle, eldest son of the Marquis of Argyle

[4] Sir Alexander Belches of Toftes, a Lord of Session, died in 1656

[5] Sir William Scott of Clerkington, a Lord of Session, died 23d December 1656

ftair in Edinburgh, before he fat doune, fell dead in lefs than a quarter of ane hour. My Lord Balcolmy,[6] the beft Judge we had, going in weell to the Tolbooth, before he fat doune on the bench, fell dead immediatelie. Sundry other fudden deaths, both of men and women, have been among us this year · the other night Mr William Forreft, an old fchoolmafter, lay down weell at eight o'clock, and before ten was found dead James Tran got not fo much tyme as to make his teftament.

Our friends in town are all weell. Only good Mr. Durhame has keeped his chamber above thefe four monetlis, and his bed more than this moneth, of a lent feaver and defluction, that puts his life in great hazard . in the abfence of Mr. Patrick Gillefpie more than a year, and Mr. Robert M'Quare [M'Ward] feeking his health at London, a great burden of continuall preaching lay on him, and the perfecting of his work on the Revelation[7] for the preffe was very heavie . It were a great pity of the man , albeit I have my own differences with him, and fharp reckonings fometimes, yet I love him dearly, and counts him one of the beft and ableft men in Brittaine. Our good friend, Mr. William Wilkie, unhappilie, by a wrong ftep on the ftreet, fell and broke his leg, which yet, after fome monetlis, is not whole

I blefs God for his kindnefs to myfelf, my health and chearfullnefs continues. Being married October 1ft [1656], it pleafed God, the 15th of July thereafter, to give me a fair daughter, Margaret, who yet is weell. I married my daughter Lilias to a very good young man, Mr. William Eccles, the heir of Kildonald,[8] who now is delivered of a fine child : as a little before my marriage, my wife married her eldeft daughter[9] to Mr. Hew Blair's fon, minifter near Lithgow I took all thefe for favours from God ; only my fon Mr. Robert's long ficknefs troubles me ; he has a fore paine in his belly after a flux, that as yet we cannot get cured, but I hope God fhall be mercifull to me in his delivery. Harie is a hard ftudent befide myfelf, and profits weell. The reft of my children thryve, and are weell, and thefe are fpurrs in my fide to

[6] Sir James Learmonth of Balcolmie, a Lord of Session, died 26th June 1658

[7] Durham s Commentary on the Book of Revelation was publshed at London 1658, folio, but it was posthumous Baillie prefixed to it a commendatory letter, which will be inserted in the Appendix.

[8] Mr. William Eccles of Kildonan, soon after this became Minister of Ayr, but was ejected for non-conformity in 1662. See the account of Bailhe's Life, prefixed to this work.

[9] By her firft hufband, Mr. R b rt Wilkie, one of the Ministers of Glasgow

mind God's fervice I hope to get my Chronologick Queftions to fomething in tyme Thereafter I purpofe to deale in the queftions of Grace, &c. againft Baxter and Amirot, but I would have the ice better broken before I goe in that vaft deep: Voetius I wifh heartilie were on that fubject Thefe three years of abfence from Prefbyterie and Synod, has given me great peace be I wont to have. I know no how long I fhall get this quietnefs enjoyed.

The publick affaires, as reprefented to us by your letters and other papers, fometimes give us matter of griefe, and fometime of joy. That the troubles of the Churches of Savoy are quieted, and the great threats of a fad war in Switzerland are turned to a fettled peace, we thank God. We are fometymes in fear for your States, their unkindnefs to the Britifh familie, and that of Orange, their needlefs provocations oft of Sueden, by open favouring all his enemies, and drawing to their power Brandenburg from him; alfo their too ftrait allyance with Spaine, and neglect of France, portends no good, though their fucceffe againft the Portugall fhips, in the very bay of Lifbone, and their boafting of the Bifhop of Munfter unto a peace with the City, were very pleafant to us They are a very noble member of the Refoimed Church, which we pray God to help and blefs; albeit their State feems to ftand but on tottering props, and they have loft much of the love and reputation fometymes they had, both at home and abroad

We oft thank God that inables the Venetians fo long to hold up with the great Turk, and are forry for their loffe this year, both of Tenedos and Lemnos, and what elfe they had conquered in the Archipelago It's God that bridles and weakens that furious beaft of Conftantinople. If Ragotfi, that noble, wife, and good prince, fhould be put from his eftates, either by the Turks or Auftrians, I fhould be very forry. They made us once believe that the Mufcoviter had been ftobed by his father-in-law; but it feems it was but a fable We are glad that all his affayes againft Sweden are proven fruitlefs

It feems all the great warres of France and Spaine are but the playes of children at the baires, for no fruit at all. Their great armies in Flanders, all the laft year thirty thoufand a peice, what did they but courfed about? Montmedy, Bourburgh, and Mardick, are but three fecklefs bicocks; the getting of Heldin recompences weell the lofs of all the three What has Conty, Savoy, and Modena, with all their noife in Millain this whole year, gotten? And in Catalonia their conqueſt is nothing at all. We were ſorry that the Portugall loſt Olivenza, yet glad that all the Spaniſh power could obtain no more. It ſeems the Spaniſh patience has ſent home the Engliſh navy without all fruit of their three or four yeares ſumptuous attendance, but the loſſe of Blake their generall. As for the burning of ſome veſſels in the Canaries, it was no great buſineſs, ſince now all the plate ſeems to be come home without impediment. Mr Patrick Gilleſpie preached before the Protector, in his velvet rarelie cut caſſick, a very flattering thankſgiving for that ſignall ſervice, thanking God for the great reformation of the Church.

That young prince which Spaine has begotten on his ſiſter's daughter in his old age, ſeemes not to portend great good. But he whom all men begins to look moſt on, is Charles of Sweden. In his quarrell with Pole many were not ſatiſfied, and generallie all here, for his league with the Protector, did maligne him. For myſelf, ſince the battell of Lipſick, I have loved the houſe of Sweden to this day above all foreigners, and by the ſtrange ſucceſſes God gives to their valour, I expect more good to the Church from them than from any others; however that unhappie Chriſtina's apoſtacie, and after miſcarriages, has grieved my heart. I was very glad that the inceſtuous Cardinall Caſimir's crown, which his fooliſh and weak head could not bear, firſt, by a generall conſent of the Poloniſh nation, and then by many ſignall victories over them, who retracted their ſworne conſent, was lyke to be ſettled on Charles, ſo active, wiſe, and ſucceſſfull a prince; when the ſtrong confæderacie of Auſtria, Pole, Moſco, and others, raiſed that hideous ſtorme on him, I was grieved and feared. But moſt of all, my diſdaine was againſt the Dane, whoſe friendſhip the Swede had ſought by his marriage with his couſin, and all other honeſt means lay in his power, that the Dane would needs, againſt all could be offered him honeſtlie, draw Charles from Caſimir upon himſelf. Who can pitie him in all his preſent ſufferings? This his madneſs ſeems to make good that, which many doubted, his father's league with the Emperour, Pole, and others againſt the Swedes, as they alleadged, when Banier came doune and took from his father ſo much of his territorie. That Frederick in his late declaration for his breach with Charles, alleadges nothing of that loſſe, I marvelled, ſince all elſe he propones ſeems lighter than what Charles objected to Caſimir at his breach with him. It ſeems ſtrange, that Charles, with a handfull of men, has ſo eaſily poſſeſſed himſelf of all almoſt that Frederick had on the fouth fide of the fea ; that the Danes every where proved fleeing cowards, efpecially in that laft attempt againft Funnen, where their advantages were fo fenfible Strange that neither the Auftrians, nor Poles, nor Mufcoviters, nor Hollanders, who drew that foolifh weak Prince in their league, had either the courage or honefty to help him, in his greateft need, with the fmalleft fupport, either of men or money It's mercy and wifdome in Charles that he left Frederick any thing, when eafilie it feems, in a moneth or two, it was in his power to have taken all from him that remained. I am glad that by a peace, however extorted, the Swedes are free to take courfe with other enemies I wifh Brandeburgh may returne to his old poftour, and not draw on himfelf next the Swedifh armies, which the Lord forbid; for after Sweden, we love Brandeburgh next beft We wifh Pole in good terms were agreed with Charles, and that the Mufcoviter will agree with him we hope, finding nothing to be gotten from him but ftrokes ; and the Poles has promifed their croune to the Auftrian for his prejudice. Our wifh is that the Mufcoviter, for reforming of his churches, civilifeing of his people, and doing fome good upon the Turks and Tartars, were more ftraitly allyed with Sweden, Brandeburgh, the Tranfyllvanian, and other Proteftant Princes.

We fhould rejoyce if, on this too good a quarrell againft the Auftrians, in ftirring up the Dane to invade Breme, which the peace of Munfter gave to the Swede, he would turn his victorious army upon them and their affociats with the affiftance of France and a good Dutch league. It feems no hard matter to get the Imperiall croune, and turne the Ecclefiaftick Princes into fecular Proteftants.

A long tract of dreames I have on the fuccefs of Charles, if God help him to begin where his heroick uncle Guftave left, but all thefe I put in God's hands, who knoweth his own appointments I expect out of the commotions which the Lord lets be now on the earth, his Majeftie will be pleafed to work out what he has promifed of inlargeing his Son's kingdome, of the bringing in the Jews, of abolifhing Poperie and Mahometifme. And alfo, I pray and hope for the reftitution of our fweet Princes to their owne, by the means himfelf knowes, though invifible yet to men.

Postscript.

While thefe lye long befide me on the occafion I write to yow, I add now this furder. Mr. Gillefpie and our Toune's-folk had fundry hearings before the Councell, the end was, he got nothing at all of his will againſt them; yea they put in a libell againſt him of unfufficiency for his place, and maladminiſtration of the rents of the Colledge. This put him in a very high rage, for he imagined, that whatever libells he gave in againſt other, no man durſt have been fo bold as to have libelled him. So foone as he came to Glafgow, it was his firſt care to call a Facultie, and fhew us the libell, defyring we would joyne in a teſtimonie to clear him of it. All the reſt were moſt willing to give him fuperlative commendations. I told them, I regrated thefe needlefs conteſts betwixt him and the toune, which he had drawn on himſelf by his perfeuing of them both at home and abroad with great eagernefs, that they did not concerne us; for myfelf, at his entrie, I had proteſted of his unfitnefs for the Principall's charge, which under my hand did ſtand in the records of the Councell, which I could not contradict; for the other articles I ſhould be willing to teſtifie any thing was true; however, I defyred they might draw a paper and fhew it me, and if I could I ſhould fubfcryve it. Our Rector[1] brought a draught to me, fo fimple as he could devife, for my fatiffaction, as he faid; but I fhew him a number of clear untruths in it, which I could not atteſt. So excufing myfelf, the Facultie, without me, did write their teſtimonie, and appointed Mr. John Young and Mr. A. Burnett to prefent it to the Councell, together with a teſtimonie from diverfe of the ſtudents of divinitie; the common Seſſion of the Toune did fend George Porterfield with ane other, but verie impertinently drawne; the town infiſted in their petition to be heard, to prove their lybell; the Councell fent all home, advifeing to agree among themfelves againſt fuch a day, otherwayes all ſhould have a hearing. Mr. Gillefpie's fpirit permitted him not to fpeak of agreeance, while he lay under the infamie and fcorne of their lybell, and fo neglected to make an overture to that end. When the day came, the Commiffioners from the towne were earneſt to have their lybell put to probation; the firſt draught of it had been but extemporall, by John Bell's hand; but then, more advifedlie, Mr. Robert Govean had put it in a farr better frame. Mr. Gillefpie and his partie imputed this to me and Mr George Young. He denyes his part in it; I avowed my affiſting to my power, by my letters to my friends of our towne, in their juſt defence; but in their libells I truely medled not; I

[1] Sir George Maxwell, vile supra, p 351.

thought it was no leſſe than behoved to be expected, when ſo long and ſo violently Mr. Gillefpie had been libelling them without caufe ; but for myſelf, their firſt paper I never ſaw till Mr. Gillefpie brought it to our Facultie meeting ; and the other paper, which amended the firſt, came only to my ſight yeſterday. I never libelled man but the Biſhop of Canterbury, and at this time I was farr from defireing the Engliſh to medle with libells againſt any in our houfe, knowing in how dangerous tearmes I ſtood for the tyme with their government. If my open avowing difference from Mr. Patrick in the moſt points of the libell would make him take me for the author of it, I behoved to take in patience that miſtake, as I did many others: for any thing in the libell, they needed no my information, for all was notour to many, as well as to me. However, Mr John Young, the Colledge commiſſioner, was very earneſt in Edinburgh, with our town's-folk not to preſſe it furder ; their friends alſo of the Councell preſſed them to the ſame ; ſo they were content to let it hing over his head for a tyme, till they fee if he move any thing farder againſt them, which he threatens he will doe, but they doe not now regard his utmoſt endeavours

Mr. Durhame yet continues extreamly ſick, much regrated by all : no man looks for his life.² My ſweet boy Rab, on Tueſday May 25th, was removed to my very fore and juſt grief³ All who knew him bore witneſs of his pietie,

² Mr James Durhame, died at Glasgow, on the 25th of June 1658

³ Baillie being alarmed for the state of his eldest ſon Roberts health, applied to Dr Robert Cunningham, an eminent Phyſician in Edinburgh, for his advice stating the case, and enclosing a letter on the subject from Dr Sylvester Rattray of Glasgow Cunningham's reply is still preserved, (Wodr. MSS Fol Vol. xlix, No 8) from which we learn, that in consequence of his absence from Edinburgh, Baillie's letter mu t have reached him after his son's death. The letter, " Datum Edinburgi, 29th Maij 1658," is addressed " For the Right Reverend Mr Robt. Baillie, Professor of Divinitie at Glasgow This." It begins,—

" Right Reverend.—Immediatelie after my returne from Winton legi et relegi epistolam tuam perbrevem quidem, sed ratione morbi diuturni et periculoſi quo corripi audio dilectum tuum Filium, longiorem quam vellem Morbum indigitant præsentes medici hydropem, in quorum sententiam pedibus manibusque eo ." &c —The rest of the letter (in Latin) is quite technical and too long to be printed. The writer expresses but slender hopes of his recovery, from the difficulty of expelling a disease that has baffled all the medical skill exerted to repel its approach ; he regrets the proſtration of strength ; could that be recruited among other things, he suggests a liberal use of water brought from Moffat Well, as it had proved beneficial in a somewhat similar case which he mentions.

wifdom, and learning, above many his fellows. He had two or three year a flux, and when it went away, there remained for other two year a great rumbling of wind in his bellie; which within thefe two moneths did weaken him fore, and made him keep in. Both he and I did ftill expect a recoverie till the laft fourtnight, when his bellie and leggs began to fwell to an hydropick tympanie; then my feares were great, and the doctors who had fpent all their art in vaine became defperate All his feare was for a longfome difeafe and infupportable paine, which the Lord mercifully prevented, far fooner nor I or himfelf or any did expect, for till the laft day he ftill walked with his cloathes on. In that morning, after a potion which he faid to me, in my ear, he thought occafioned his greateft paine, he took fome fhotts of wind in his bellie which tormented him fearfully, to a great crying of as great paine as ever woman had at her laft fhoure: they were indeed the paffions of death: one of thefe, was in the morning at nine, lafted above an hour, another, at fix at night, greater and longer; in both, allwayes crying to God in great devotion and patience, befeeking a haftening of removeall When the height of thefe fitts were over, he craved all pardon for clamour, refted on God, bleffed him, exhorted all to the love and fear of God, recommended to me the care of his brother and fifters, exhorted me to a fpirituall walk and diligence to make ufe of my gift; and then, about ten a'clock, compofed himfelf for reft: He moft quietly, without paine or motion, breathed out his fpirit. Oft he told me, that many years before the Lord had fettled on very good grounds his affureance of election and falvation; this in all his paines wes never brangled. He oft alfo profeffed, that one of the grounds of his comfort was, that from his childhood, God had helped him to endeavour a keeping of a good confcience; that in the world he never had pleafure, but the Scriptures of God had oft been his delight and great refrefhment. I can write no more, this fad fubject, as ever I felt, makes me to clofe. The Lord be with yow and all yours.

         Your forrowfull Coufin,

[Glafgow, June 1658.]   R. BAILLY.

Keep all thefe things to yourfelf: they are the infide of all our affaires, which I defyre none to know from me but yourfelf alone.

[For Mr. Robert Douglass.]¹

Sir,

Being defired by yow to give my opinion of Mr R. his Preface to his Survey of Mr. Hooker's Survey,² with all reverence to my much honoured and beloved Brother, I profeffe my greef and fcandale with fome pages of it, wherein I conceive, moft needlefly, he is pleafed, in the preffes of London, among the midft of all the Sectaries, without any occafion, to fpit in the face of our Mother Church, and to give her fo fore wounds without all caufe, that I doe not wonder of that Reverend man,³ (whom Mr. R. wont to reverence, and, as I think, yet does as much as any elfe living,) who, to diverfe of yow in your High-ftreets avowed, that before he had written any fuch things, he could have rather choiced to have had his right-hand ftricken off at the Croffe of Edinburgh by the axe of the hangman.

Mr. R. avowes,—That the Remonftrants among us are troubled on every fide, in the ftreets, pulpits, in diverfe Synods, and Prefbyteries, more than under Prelacy, and are made to cry to God, under their helplefs affliction, that the prefent power and all men neglect their miferie. This, to my beft knowledge, is utterly falfe. I know fundrie whom they have perfecuted, and, by their favour with the prefent power, have keeped from

---

¹ This letter contains Animadverfions on the preface of a work by Samuel Rutherfurd. The original is preserved in Wodrow MSS Folio Vol xxvi No 11 Except the signature, and one or two verbal corrections, it is not in Baillie's own hand Neither copy has any addrefs, but it appears (*infra* p 387) to have been written to Douglas

² In 1644, Mr Samuel Rutherfurd publifhed at London his large work " The Due Right of Prefbyteries or a Peaceable Plea for the Government of the Church of Scotland " To this an elaborate answer was written by Mr. Thomas Hooker, in New England, but printed after his death, as " A Survey of the Summe of Church-Difcipline, &c " London, 1648, 4to It was this work that drew forth Rutherfurd's volume, " A Survey of the Survey of that Summe of Church-Difcipline penned by Mr Thomas Hooker, late paftor of the church at Hartford upon Connecticut in New England," &c. London, 1658, 4to, pp 521. The publication having been delayed (*supra* pp. 303, 306,) the author took occasion to prefix to it an Addrefs to the Chriftian Reader, containing very severe remarks on the Refolutioners, being the only portion of the work on which Baillie animadverts in this letter.

³ This evidently refers to Mr. Robert Blair

all poffibilitie of remeed; but I remember not any of them that has been put to the leaft fuffering. Sundrie of them, whom whole Synods hes declared unlawfullie admitted, are, to this day, keeped in their ufurped places, by their greatnefs with the civill power. I have feen it too true what the fore-mentioned Brother, reverenced by them as by us, wrote of them in his letter, October 20th 1651,[1] That he ever feared that they would ufurp, and rather put others to fuffer than fuffer themfelves; and I have heard of a moft precious and excellent man,[2] who, with his colleague's continuall vexations and contentions, was fo worn out, that he was put at laft to leave his ftation, and accept of ane other, for to gaine fome quietnefs.

Thereafter we are challenged, in the ftreets of London, before all the Sectaries, and from thence to the world, of Six particular crimes: Firft, That we have framed an Engagement for the prefent power which we allow every intrant to the miniftrie to fubfcribe, or elfe to want his maintenance; to wit, their refolution "to live peaceably under the prefent government." That any man, let be meeting of our mind, did ever frame any fuch write, is more than I know, or ever before heard of, the lawfulnefs and expediencie of the refolution itfelf, Mr R. avows now, that the fubfcribeing of what is lawfull and expedient fhould become unlawfull, when thefe in power requires it, we muft be better taught before we take it on truft. Why fhould the like of this be objected to us, when the whole Ifle knows that their partie procured, and to their uttermoft did keep up, an order from the prefent power, That no intrant to the miniftrie fhould have any maintenance, but they alone to whom they did give a teftimonie under their hand. With how great difficulty this monument of their tyrannous injuftice was gotten overthrowne, the world knows; for this work was done before the fun

The Second challenge. That our Synods make prelaticall acts to debarre godly and able intrants from the miniftrie, becaufe they will not be fatiffied with the Publick Refolutions. Surely unfatiffaction to thefe, to my knowledge, was never cenfured among us. When, after much toile and debate, all on both fides did profeffe their willingnefs to lay afide publick agitation of need-

[1] Baillie here refers to a letter that was addressed by Robert Blair to James Durhame
[2] Mr James Wood, Professor of Ecclesiastical History in St Mary's College, (of which Rutherford was Principal,) was translated in 1657 to be Principal of St Salvador's or the Old College, St Andrews. *Vide supra,* pp 316, 365

lefs queftions, if one Synod (for of more I have not heard it alleadged,) did appoint their intrants to profeffe this much peaceablenefs of mind, whatever was their judgement, was this any great crime? I have knowne diverfe very gracious and able intrants, without any Synodicall acts, by the fecret actings of the faction, keeped out of places for no other caufe but their diffatiffaction with the way of the Remonftrants. That any one man can be produced, who even for his publict preaching againft the Refolutions of the Kirk and State was actuallie keeped out, is more than I think can be fhowne: I am fure it never was in the Synod where I live.

The Third challenge: That we make fuch a fubordination effentiall to Prefbyteriall government as imports a neceffitie of Obedience to knowne unjuft acts, even a tyrannicall and popifh, an abfolute and illimitat obedience. Why fhould fuch an untruth be faftened upon us, which is point-blank contrare to thefe our papers on which it is fathered, where we fpeak exprefly of that, and no other fubordination, which, fince our late Reformation, from 1638 to the 1648, was in ordinarie practife among us without all queftion; which is the doctrine and practice of all Prefbyterians beyond fea; yea, of all Proteftants who maintaine the jurifdiction of Affemblies. Why fhould the fword of fuch a calumnie be put in the hands of Sectaries againft us, that we crave obedience to any of our judicatories, even when they command, not in the Lord, but contrary to the law. Such a queftion to us is moved very impertinently; for the world knowes, that we make no doubt but the acts of our Affemblies pointed at, concerning the Publick Refolutions, are, fo farre, according to fcripture, reafon, and the fenfe of all churches, of all nations, both friends and adverfaries, that the oppofers of them will be diffallowed by all unbyaffed men, to the world's end. Mr. R. might have remembered that the queftion betwixt us and the faction, in the paper cited, was come to this, Whether, when we had fully agreed with them in all things elfe, and granted all their defyres, they would be willing thereafter, without more debate, to be obedient to the ordinarie Judicatories of the Kirk, as they and all were wont, before the rife of the late queftions. This they flatly denyed, and gave us a formall anfwer that they could promife neither to prefbyteries nor fynods, as now conftitute, any fubjection at all, in regard that the body of our prefbyteries and fynods was made up of perfons fo faultie, as no fubjection was due to them; and that their purgeing of all the judicatories behoved to precede their acknowledgement of any duetie to them as they now ftand. This to be the true Scots of their papers, both their formall words, and conftant practife fince that time, puts it out of all doubt.

That new ftarted queftion by them, we alleadge, it did abolifh the very foundation of Prefbyteriall Government in our Church; for grant what fubordination they pleafed to a prefbyterie in generall, or to a prefbyterie in Utopia, or any where elfe, yet denying it to the Prefbyteries of Scotland, as now they ftand, the Independents by this gets all their defire, by the overthrow of the whole government of our Church for the time, and ever till it be framed over again according to the Remonftrants modell.

Farder, what here is added to that new Queftion, feems to overturne not only the prefbyterie among us, but all government, civill and ecclefiaftick, in all places for ever, and brings in every where a neceffitie of anarchie and confufion, that every particular perfon may and muft follow the judgment of his own braine, without controll of any judge or judicatorie upon earth, whether civill or ecclefiaftick. No Chriftian doth queftion but it is better to obey God than men, and when it is known that God commands, the countermand of men is not to be followed, but the queftion is fuppofed alone in a matter of controverfie betwixt the judicatories and a particular perfon. Let all the judicatories proceed as confcientiouflie as can be required: let the Seffion, Prefbyterie, Synod, Generall Affemblie, yea, Œcumenick Councell, unanmouflie determine this to be the will of God. let a particular perfon pronounce them all to erre;—If fuch a perfon, not upon any truth, but his own falfe apprehenfion that an error is truth, fhall be permitted to preach and act at pleafure, contrare to all judicatories, when they avow the truth and righteoufnefs of their proceedings, and proves it fufficientlie, though they cannot convince and fatiffie the obftinatelie erroneous perfon; if fuch a practice be maintained, fhall there be any order remaining under the fun? What poffible remeed fhall there be for the ending of any controverfie great or fmall, till every Quaker, every Anabaptift, every Papift, be not only convinced within, but brought to profeffe without, the juftice of the fentence pronounced by the Judicatories againft them? This extravagancie cuts the finews of all government ever was, is, or can be imagined: It makes every erroneous perfon the fupreme judge on earth to himfelf of all queftions, without any fubjection to any power; were its judgement never fo right, if fo the errant man think it wrong, and adhere to his own fancie, though contrare to fcripture and reafon. It concerns our brethren, and all men on earth who are for any government, as much as us, to fee to the iffue of fuch conclufions. The Judicatories believe their acts to be the will of God, the particular perfon beleeves his contradiction to be according to the will of God: the Judicatories, all of them, higher and lower, propone their fcriptures and reafons, wherewith the whole Church is fatiffied; the erroneous perfon continues refolute in his oppofition and rebellion to all directions of all judicatories on earth, unwilling to be filent for an hour. What fhall the end be? When our Generall Affemblies, Synods, Prefbyteries, Seffions, are all caft off, and when oppofers has joyned themfelves in new focieties of their owne minde, what will they doe when that befalls them, which ever to this day has been the ordinarie cafe of all thefe who has oppofed and divided themfelves from the orthodox Church? One or more of their company difagree from their conclufions, contradict them, and counteract them; when for this they are reproved and cenfured, they deny fubordination in that cafe, avowing themfelves to be right and their cenfurers wrong. What here fhall be the remeed? Muft all order give place to confufion for ever?

The Fourth challenge is a fearfull railling againft the body of our minifterie, and, as their papers for union fpeak, the pluralitie of our prefbyteries and fynods; alfo againft the bodie of our people in all our congregations. The Quakers may weell equall this language, but in any Independent that yet has written I have not read the like. Experience might have taught our Brother at laft to have written more modeftlie of others. He knowes how that exceeding falfe Teftimonie againft the King and our laft Armie, moft unfeafonablie fent before them in their laft marche into Lancafhyre, was receaved by the judicious brethren there; and the no leffe falfe witnefs for the Remonftrators againft our Church fent thereafter to London, was receaved by the gracious brethren there. He knows likewife, I fuppofe, how the moft, if not all, the fained fables which are the great grounds of this verie comprehenfive flander, were convicted of evident falfehood in very publict audiences latelie at London, where by the agents of the faction they were very boldlie fpread. I am fure in the Synod where I live, where thefe invectives againft the crying weaknefs and fcandalls of foul-murdering minifters, wont to be moft frequent and vehement; fo foone as that partie, through their oppofites wearinefs to contend, became mafters of the prefbyterie and fynod, we have heard no more to count of concerning that fubject The few upon whom they tryed their inquifition, after near ane hundred witneffes, befide all the elders, were fworne upon their proceffe, were found honeft men ; and although I have heard fay oftei than once openlie in the face of the fynod, that the true weaknefs and reall fcandalls of minifters would be found on their fide of the houfe, yet, to this day, not any of their faction with us has been put to the leaft tryall . fo doe they purge the Church where they have no impediment!

The Fifth challenge is our receiving to the Covenant and Church-fellow-fhip men who, again and again, had broken their ingagement. This needed not to have been objected, for the taking of men's publict repentance, even when they are hypocrites, fo long as their hypocrifie does not appear, will not be counted a fault except by Novatians and Donatifts. The unjuft feveritie which fome men would have ufed in our land's extreme diftreffe was the leffe regarded, when their defigne became evident by this feveritie to put the King and the armie, yea, the whole land, Church and State, in the abfolute power of their owne faction, in the mean tyme, when their prime leaders intime familiaritie with thefe who had forfaken their Covenant, and was excommunicat for it, did appear vifible. And what doe they fpeak of Covenants who openlie has torne our Solemne League and Covenant in peices, and at their own hand has cutted off divers prime articles from it ? frameing to us a new one of their own mould ; which, had no the prefent power impeded, behooved to have been fubfcribed by all who would not have chofen to have been excluded from the focietie and advantages of their godlie and thryving partie.

The Sixth challenge is but a repetition of the Fourth, that fo many unfuffi-cient minifters are admitted by us. Our order of admiffion is as ftrict as in any Reformed church , nor has there for practice greater accuracie been ufed by our Church in any bygane time than fince thefe late differences. If either the way of tryall, or qualities of men admitted by us and our brethren, were weell examined, it will be found that they needed not to have made any challenge of this nature. They can difpatch, when their intereft requires it, all the tryalls, which ufe to coft us prefbyteriall meetings for a whole quarter or half a-year, in one morning. Sundry are grieved with the great weaknefs of many whom they have admitted moft upon the great qualification of a profeſſed zeale toward their faction. The challenging of us for admitting ſo many ſcandalous and ignorant to the Lord's table, is but the ſtrengthening the arme of calumniating Sectaries, whoſe profeſſed aime long has been the diſſolution of all the ſtanding congregations in the Reformed churches, that a new gathering of churches in their way may be ſet a foot Doubtleſs more ſtrictneſs is now generallie uſed among us than ever was before in admitting to the Lord's table, and much more than is uſed in any church over ſea; and whatever farder ſtrictneſs either ſcripture or reaſon ſhall require, will not be refuiſed by us.

It is in vaine to mention the Miniſters of London, for they all weell know how little their judgements in our preſent debates is valued by the Remonſtrants. When, after their full hearing of them and us, we were approven, and the Remonſtrants diſlyked, did this hinder their agents, by the help of their better friends the Independents, Anabaptiſts, and Eraſtians, their only intime familiars and confidents, with whom they keeped frequent faſtings and prayers in their conventicles, to ſeek from the civill power a tyrannick juriſdiction over us, for the ruine of all the preſent government of our Church? Was not this their paſſionat perſute weell near for a whole year at London? which the Lord, cheefly by the wiſe and gracious endeavours of our Preſbyterian brethren there, did break, or at leaſt delay till this long. How much, firſt and laſt, they have made themſelves the Godlie partie in Scotland, though in the ſtreatching of their charitie they will admitt ſome of us to ſtand with them in that catalogue, even this Preface will evidence. But that either in the year 1648, or any year before or ſince, the chief leaders of their partie were counted by any but themſelves to ſtand in the firſt rank of the Godlie in our land, it is a great miſtake; and they will not doe weell to put to the inqueiſt of their neighbours, the true pietie, let be the degree of it, of ſundrie no the meaneſt of their faction.

So farre for the time I have told yow my mind of a few pages in that Preface I bleſſe the Lord that keeps yet yow and others there at the helme of our Church, when from time to time new ſtormes ariſe, from whom leaſt they ſhould. The Lord continue yow ſtill till better times come, when yow may be better ſpared than now yow can.

Your's to be commanded,

Glaſgow, Julie 31ſt 1658. R. BAILLIE.

[For Mr. William Spang.]　　Glasgow, November 11th 1658.

Cousine,

All yow fent with Robert Smith, with James Maxwell, and the box directed to George Sutie, your gear alfo, and all I think yow fent hither, I receaved; to yourfelf I ufe to fend no thanks, but to your kind wife, my wife fends many. I am glad all your children are weell; I pray God blefs them all Your count with Robert Smith fhall quickly be payed to your nephew John: your one hundred and fifty gilders fhall be payed likewife, with the firft of that legacie I receive of Dr. Strang's: the Colledge and yow will reckon. I fhall, God willing, have fome eye on James Maxwell, and on all yow fend hither. Your nephew Mr. William's heart ferved him moft for Ireland; and I alfo did long much to have him in the miniftrie, without the reach of our good faction. his profperous fucceffe yow will fee in the inclofed. My boy Harie, bleffed be God, growes in pietie, learning and wifdom; at his own defire I permitted him to goe to Sir James Dundas of Arniftoun, near Edinburgh, to be his chaiplane for fome tyme, to fee fome more of the world, and to fitt him to fpeak in publict: he always refents your kindnefs and your kind wife's. I have thought fit to fend to yow the fecond part of Dr. Strang's writ [6] The Latine that is printed either here or at London, is fo exceedingly ill done, that I will be very loath, if I can otherwayes doe, ever to employ them either for myfelf or others. I fent in Summer, with one of our boyes, the memorandum yow have here, yow fie the Elfevir's anfwer. When yow get a fure bearer, fend the book to them, with fo much incouragement from yourfelf and your friends as yow can, for them to print it. If yow cannot get it done, fend it back to me with a fure hand, but doe your beft to have it printed there; for here it will be but fpoiled, for all the Englifh fair promifes to the contrare. Give me an account of Elfevir's returne to yow, fo foone as yow can.

Though fince my laft large one, there is not much I can writ, yet to

---

[6] Probably Dr Strang's work, "De Interpretatione et Perfectione Scripturæ," the publication of which, however, was completed at Rotterdam, but not before the year 1663.

shew yow my diligence, have our affairs since. Our Towne now is prettie quiet, haveing at Michaelmes chofen not only fuch a proveift and bailies, bot alfo a councell as hes not one man in hazard of Mr. Gillefpie's accufations; yet ftill he is pyking fome one pettie quarrell or another, to hold them waking. The chief difference is now about planting their churches. Mr. Durhame, a little before his death, advifed for peace caufe to put in his place one of three, Mr. Francis Aird, Mr. Ralph Rodger, Mr. George Campbell; not only fince his death, June 25th,[7] bot fome moneths before, Mr. Carftares, his brother-in-law, out of his exceffive affection, did continuallie preach and pray of him, in a very extraordinary way, the nomination of his fucceffour, he took it weell near for ane oracle of God. My owne judgement was that two of the three were very unfitt, and the third but of very ordinarie fufficiencie. Mr. George Campbell, a boy of twenty yeares, laureat two years ago with my Harie, who was in the circle with him, and in all things thought his match but in his extreame flattering of Mr. Gillefpie: this boy, when named, had never fo much as fpoken in any publict exercife. Mr. Francis Aird, of ordinary parts, but fo exceeding fickly, that halfe a year's fervice of our towne was like to have buried him; but he was good enough, fince a prime Remonftrant. Mr James Ferguffon, my fucceffor in Kilwinning, was earneftly defired by the towne · my entres in Kilwinning hindred me to joyne in his removeall thence, but I could not deny, that evidently he was much fitter for us than any named. Mr. Patrick Gillefpie led all our feffions whither he pleafed. Mr. George Young's power with the Councell was no leffe. The feffion went on firft with the unfitteft, Mr. George Campbell, though none of them ever had heard him preach; the towne protefting againft his election, till he were heard, he refufed the call. The feffion fell next on Mr Francis Aird. The towne fell on a very good overture, that they fhould joyne with the feffion in the call of any whom they pleafed, if fo they would joyn with the Councell in a call to Mr James Ferguffon, for whom they fhould provide both a new church and a new ftipend, as good as any other, which would have been above fourtie thoufand merks charge to them, this was fo fair, that the moft of the feffion was readie to have accepted it, but Mr. Patrick caufed it to be fhifted; fo the

---

[7] In the MS the date has been altered, apparently from June to July, but Durham's death took place in the former month

towne refuifed to joyn in Mr. Francis Aird's call, and on this difference he could not hearken to it. Therefore, laft, the feffion called Mr. Ralph Rodger, who is as unliklie to accept as the reft. The end of it, I think, fhall be that the feffion, being refuifed by all the three, will turn themfelves to fome headie one of the faction, who will like their call the better that the Magiftrats oppofe it; and the body of the towne finding themfelves fo mifshantlie abufed, and continuallie tyrannized over, without hope of remeed, will endeavour, as it is in Stirling and Lithgow, the erecting of a new Seffion, with the mifregard of the old. This had been done ere now, if I had not both openly and by my owne private wayes oppofed it. Strange, what a few yeares will produce! Some foure yeares agoe, when our Prefbyterie and Synod both divided, I was the laft who confented to that divifion, and when thereafter, Mr. George Young and Mr. James Ferguffon, on very ill termes, had made the reunion, I was the only man who then and to this day refuifed it; and now no man repents more that union than the contryvers of it, for had our divifion but a little continued having the fafhion of a Prefbyterie and Synod, we might legally and orderly have planted new feffions in Glafgow, and gotten a legall call and tranfportation to Mr. James Ferguffon, or any we had lyked: that this now can no be gotten, the authors of that evill union now grieves, and I laugh at their too late repentance.

For the Colledge, we have no redreffe of our difcipline and teaching. Mr. Gillefpie's work is building, and pleas; with the dinn of mafons, wrights, carters, fmiths, we are vexed every day. Mr. Gillefpie, alone for vanitie to make a new quarter in the Colledge, hes caft downe my houfe to build up ane other of greater fhow, but fari worfe accommodation; in the meane[while,] for one full year, I will be, and am exceedingly incommodat, which I bear becaufe I cannot help it. And alfo becaufe Mr Gillefpie hes ftrange wayes of getting money for it, by his own induftry alone; an order he got from the Protector of five hundred pound fterling, (but for an ill-office to the countrie, his delation of fo much concealed rent yearly of the Crown;) alfo the vacancy of all churches, wherein the Colledge had entres: this breeds clamour as the unjuft fpoill of churches and incumbents. Upon thefe foundations are our palaces builded; but withall our debts grow, and our ftipends are not payed, for by his continuall toying our rent is mouldered away. When our magiftrates reprefented this, and much more, in a libell againft him, his good friend, Swintoun, obtained to him a fair abfolution from all without any cognition of the matter; but to pleafe the Toune, his accufations againft them were alfo as good as waved

Ever fince Dr. Strang's dimiffion our œconomie hes been in an ill condition; the mafters wont to have the beft table in the country, and payed no more than fifty merks in the quarter; but thereafter, for the bettering of the table, four pound fterling was allowed in the quarter; a very high rate. Yet when I was laft in Edinburgh, Mr. Gillefpie had agreed with a new *Œconomus* for five pound fterling a quarter, and to bring all the Divinitie-burfars to a fecond table at fiftie merks a quarter, and the Philofophie-burfars at a third table for twenty four pounds a quarter. With this I was not content, for it burdened our rent with above five hundred merks of needlefs charges yearly. For the Principall and four Regents twenty pounds fterling, for the fix Divinitie-burfars of the towne we behoved to add one hundred pound, becaufe Struthers's two and Wilfon's two had but eighty pounds a piece; and when Mr. Zacharie's three were turned to two they would be bot ninety pound a piece. So, among thefe fix, a hundred pound was needfull to make them fifty merks in the quarter a-piece the fix of the new donation for Divinitie, and as many for Philofophie, had to doe their own turne. I thought alfo, that the towne boyes would be hurt who would get nought but their boord, which they had freely from their parents or friends, and employed their penfion on books and cloathes; alfo, fundry moft hopefull young men would refufe, for fhame, to come to a Burfars-table. Againft this was alleadged, the comelie order of all other Colledges, and the grudge of the fchollars when fome were put to the table, and fome not; for the charge, that the fourth vacation quarter of the twelve burfars of the new donation would doe much to fupply it hereupon I was content they fhould try it for one year

At our counts we did not well agree, yet had no dinn The Magiftrates were not called to them, which was againft both right and cuftome. I refufed to fubfcryve without an exprefs exception of the article of fix thoufand merks for Mr. Gillefpie's journey to London. The other year, when I was in Edinburgh, Mr. Gillefpie had obtained from the Facultie twenty fhillings fterling a day, for the eleven moneths he had been in England, befide three or four thoufand merks of other charges in particular accompts This, to me, was unfupportable; for his vaft expenfes before, and the lownefs of the prices of victuall, had put us that we were hardly able to defray our ordinary charge. But this donative I forefaw would make us unable, for fome years to come, to win to our very ftipends. Upon this we had a found reckoning in the nixt Facultie; Mr. Gillefpie afferting his loffe in that journey, and his great fervice to the Colledge in the great gifts he had obtained To the firft I faid little, for I knew indeed he had fpent large fumms that year, and I doubt if twenty thoufand merks, one way and another, did not paffe through his fingers: But I faid his expence concerned not the Colledge, for that journey was not at all for us, but for the fervice of his partie, to trouble the Church · that the commiffion he had from fome of us, (from myfelf he had none,) it was but on the by, in his fpare time, to deale for the profits of the Colledge; what he had done in this kind I was very willing he fhould be liberallie acknowledged, but out of the profits of what he acquired, not out of our other rent, which could not bear it: Withall I told him, that we were not in ufe to give money to the purchafers of our gifts, much above all his; that the purchafers of the parfonage of Govane, of Kilbride, of Renfrew, of the Bifhoprick of Galloway, had not receaved of the Colledge a groat The end was, I diffented; the reft went on, as his own filly creatures, ready to doe whatever he defired. The clamours of his utter infufficiency, for any thing of a fchollar, made him, at the laft Laureation, make long prayers, and orations, and difputations, in Latin; which he faid in a jolly way He found that Mr. Thurloe, Secretar of State, had been very inftrumentall to doe Mr Sharps bufinefs at London againft all his defignes To draw that man off us towards himfelf and partie, he invents this trick. In a Facultie meeting he preffes the expediencie of having a courtier Chancellor of our Univerfitie, and that Thurloe was fitteft I was againft all Englifh flefh; but he carried it, and fent up to him a fcaled parchment of that honour But before that came, we got Mr. Thurloe informed of the defigne, who therefore civillie refufed it. But the beft was, to choice a Vice Chancellor; I could not dream of the purpofe while it was done; himfelf, by all but me, was voted *Pro-Cancellarius*, fo I laugh when I fee this noveltie alfo in his fubfcription, " Pat Gillefpius Pro-Cancellarius et Præfectus:" A poor glory!

Our Church lyes as it did the Reprefentation printed by Mr Sharp at London, they durft never affay to anfwer; but our late Declaration of new defires of peace, they anfwered a peece of it with a very bitter pamphlet; to which Mr. Rutherfoord printed a preamble in his Preface to a late anfwer to Hooker. Being defired, I fent my obfervations on that preamble[8] to Mr. Douglafs; but on that and their whole pamphlet, Mr. Hutchefon hes written a very accurate and folide Review,[9] with fome additions of Mr. Wood's, all which I think are now on the preffe. It is very like the end of this obftinate difference will be a formall feparation: the fooner the better for the Kirk; for they abide among us only to encreafe their partie; and if they were formally feparate, they could doe us the leffe harme.

The Countrey lyes very quiet, it is exceeding poor; trade is nought; the Englifh hes all the moneyes. Our Noble families are almoft gone. Lennox hes little in Scotland unfold; Hamilton's eftate, except Arran and the Baronrie of Hamilton, is fold; Argyle can pay little annuelrent for feven or eight hundred thoufand merks; and he is no more drowned in debt than publict hatred, almoft of all, both Scottifh and Englifh; the Gordons are gone; the Douglaffes little better; Eghntoun and Glencairn on the brink of breaking; many of our chief families [e]ftates are cracking; nor is there any appearance of any human relief for the tyme. What is become of the King and his family we doe not know. fome talks that he fhould be in the Hague. many takes his unkindnefs to Balcarras very ill; efpecially that he fhould oppofe his Ladie's provifion to the overfight of the little Prince of Orange: His obftinate obfervance of Hyde offends all, bot what he minds, no man here knows, and few cares.

The Protector's death was unexpected; the way of it we doe not learn; men fpeak as they lift. What fome fpeak, of troubles of bodie and mind, and, after a fuarfe, the crying out of the Devill and an Northerne armie, muft be but a fable. We were feared for trouble after his death, but all is fettled in peace. We doubted what might become of the Officers of the armie their petition for the Generalitie to Fleetwood; if they infift in it, it cannot but breed evill blood, but they are wifer than to differ when fome would be glad of it.

[8] In a letter which is printed *supra*, p 375

[9] " A Review and Examination of a Pamphlet lately publifhed, bearing the title of Protesters no Subverters, &c.— By some Lovers of the Interests of Chrift in the Church of Scotland Edinburgh, printed Ann Dom 1659," 4to pp 139

For things abroad, this is the common fenfe; that fince all this year the French hes ravaged in Flanders at their pleafure; hes taken in Dunkirk, Graveling, Hirer, Oudenard, and many moe townes; fince the Spaniard hes not been able to keep the field, fince his fortune in Millan and Cataloma hes been little better, and all he makes in the end of the year, to relieve Badajos in Caftill, fo near Madrid, from the long fiege of the Portugals, be within twenty thoufand men; it's thought his condition every where is very low, and the Frenches very high, fo that the former danger from the Monarchy of Spaine may quickly become as great from the Monarchy of France, and that all neighbours, for their own fafetie, may be forced to guard as much againft the one, as they wont to doe againft the other What the great caufes have been to draw back the Swedes from Pomer to Copenhagen, we are expecting to know by that peece lately printed, at London, for that end All marvell that the Danes, after all their cowardice, have been able fo long to defend Copenhagen from the victorious Swedes Brandeburg's armie, and his confæderate Auftrian and Poler, is great in Holften; but the countrey, by thefe pretended friends, is plundered to the bones. I fear Brandeburgh fhall pay dear for that rode. We hear that Opdam, in the Sound, hes done yet naught againft the Swedes; and that the fear of the French and Englifh will keep your States from all action there, for all the fhew they have made Upon this men's eyes are fixed more than on any thing elfe for if they fhould yoke in earneft againft the Swedes, all doe think the French and Englifh will fall on them, both by fea and land, and neither the Spaniards nor High Dutch will be able to maintain them. The Lord himfelf guide thefe great affaires We blefs God that the Turkifh threats hes this year produced no more harme, neither to Ragotfi nor the Venetians. It feems the articles of Munfter are totallie tread under foot; yet it will be a hard pull to caft the Swedes out of Breme, Pomer, and Pruis, and the French out of Alfatia and Lorain It's much that Torn has ftood out all this year What is the caufe that Douglafs is the man employed in Lifland, and not Lagard?

Here I muft end, wifhing all welfare to your wife and children My wife fends to your's a half-barrell of herring, the beft my friend could get

Your Coufin,
R B.

Postscript.

In Edinburgh, at their election, there fell out a paſſage much againſt the mind of many Sir Andrew Ramſay,[1] a right ſharp young man, but very proud, had carried himſelf for two yeares in the place of Proveiſt, very haughtilie; and in his abode at London had been at vaſt charges to the Towne for no profit; yet was ſtill in hope to have gotten from the Protector what might have done the Towne good in their exceeding low condition. Mr. Thomſon, the Clerk, who had brought him to his place, became very ungracious to him, by the ſuggeſtion moſt of Baillie Jauſie, who deſireing to have his ſon conjunct clerk with W. Thomſon, was refuſed, on fear that ſuch a conjunct ſhould put himſelf to the door. Upon this differing, the Provoſt and that Bailhe, did what they could to bear down the Clerk, and were readie, when able, to have ſhuffled him from his place. The Clerk, and all the Towne, would moſt gladlie had Archibald Sincerf for Proveiſt, the farr fitteſt for the charge: bot Ramſay keeped Sincerf[2] from the lites, according to the late act of the Engliſh Parliament, for his guilt of the Ingadgement; and got on the lites himſelf, Baillie Jauſie,[3] and (being perſuaded that none would give him a vote,) Sir James Stewart.[4] Thomſon finding it ſo, he wrought underhand, that any living might be choſen rather than his enemies Ramſay or Jauſie: thus Sir James caried it. This offended many, and feared them, leiſt (the man being very wiſe and active, and an open favourer of the Remonſtrants,) it might make a great change in Edinburgh and all the land for that parties advancement. When I met with Thomſon, my good friend, I railed on him, that for revenge of his private ſpite and ſpleen againſt Ramſay, he had betrayed the public intereſt into the hand of a Proteſtor. I was impatient of all apologies; yet I hear Sir James has given aſſurances enough to Mr. Robert Douglaſs, and others, and denyes his Remonſtrantiſm. For myſelf, I do not

---

[1] Lord Fountainhall, in his MS Decisions, has preserved an account of the litigation between Sir Andrew Ramsay of Abbotshall and certain inhabitants of the Town, for his having, at a subsequent period, continued to hold the office of Provost of Edinburgh for the space of no less than twelve successive years, during part of which time he was also a Lord of Session

[2] Archibald Sydeſerf was First Bailhe in 1656

[3] John Jossie was First Baillie in 1655 and 1657, and again in 1660

[4] The father of Sir James Stewart of Goodtrees He was Lord Provost in 1648 and 1649

weell believe, nor much truft him; but feares the great evill of this pranck of the clerk Sir James once caft him out of his place, if he doe it again, no man will pitie him.

Being wearied, I have now laid afide my Chronologie. I have drawn the ftorie, facred and profane, fhortlie from the fountains through the whole Old Teftament, in feven epochas, to every one of which I have fubjoyned the moft of the ordinarie queftions of chronologie; and, after a prettie free debate with all forts of men, determines them after myne owne mind I have alfo fett downe the ftorie of the New Teftament, the firft epocha of it to the death of John the Evangelift, and at the back of it, feventeen of the chiefeft queftions Being tyred, I fubfift: It may be I revife it and adde more queftions, efpeciallie from the Apocalypfe; therefore what yow find of new books that may further me in this defigne, let the Colledge have them · I think we want few of the old. This year's ftudie I caft it on the noble head of Juftification, moft to meet with Bifhop Forbes, printed latelie at London by Mr. Thomas Sinceif, Bifhop of Galloway, T. G.[5] and our moderat midmen, whom I have efteemed, ever fince I knew them, reall Papifts in the moft and maine; alfo to meet with Baxter, whom albeit I highly efteem for pietie and learning, yet I think a very unhappie bruiller, a full avowed Amiraldift, and a great confounder of the head of Juftification. I pray yow in your firft to Voetius, remember my heartie fervice to him, and tell him from me, that many his lovers here long for a third volume of his Difputations; alfo, that they exceedingly defyre fome Exercitations from him on the way of Amirald, and that the head of Juftification were vindicat by him from Baxter and Forbes, and all other adverfars. We love here very well Marefius's writts, all but his bitter flittings with Voetius We long to hear, that thefe two very eminent and ufefull men were better friends. What yow fent us of Jefuit Sempill is but a preface[z] to his *Dictionarium Mathematicum*, which we pray yow fearch for

---

[5] The initials, T G (Thomas Gallovidiensis) stand at the Editor's preface of the pofthumous work of Bishop Forbes referred to, "Confiderationes Modeftæ et Pacificæ Contraverfiarum de Juftificatione, Purgatorio, Invocatione Sanctorum, &c. London, 1658, small 8vo. pp 466 The Editor, Thomas Sydeserff, was the only one of the Scotish Prelates deposed in 1638 who survived till the Restoration of Charles II

[6] Hugo Sempilius Craigbateus Scotus, De Mathematicis Difciplinis Antwerpiæ, 1635, folio

For his Reverend and Dear Brother, Mr. Simeon Ashe.

Reverend and Dear Brother,

These are to let yow know my defyre to underftand your welfare, and if it be well with gracious Mr. Calamie, Dr Reinolds and others our dear Brethren there. Bleffed be God, your acquaintance here are all as before, except that our unhappy Remonftrants continue in their obftinacie My maine purpofe to yow at this time is, to let yow know that Mr. Baxter does us more harme than all your Sectaries. The man's pietie and parts make us ftill honour, pitie, and fpare him; but his intollerable boldnefs, after his avowed Amiraldifme, to follow and goe beyond miferable John Goodwin, in confounding the great head of Juftification with fuch a flood of new and unfound notions, does vex us: fince, this fame year he has written fo largely in this point againft Mr. Burgeffe, we earneftlie defyre that he would ferioullie reply; yea, that Dr. Reinolds, or if ye have any abler pen, would take him to tafk in all his errors, which truely he has a way to infinuate more than any heterodox I know in this fide of the fea. I entreat that fome of yow would advife how to gett this dangerous evill remeded, at leift ftopped Your addreffe by Dr. Reinolds to his Highnefs, before the Independents by Dr. Goodwin, I doe not weell underftand how it was not a very folemne and public buriall of the Solemn League and Covenant; but here we are exceeding fpareing to put any cenfure upon any of your proceedings, the grounds and reafons whereof, at fuch a diftance, we do not underftand. Our prayer to God for yow is, that yow may be all faithfull to your Mafter to death, that yow may receive the crown of life; fo prays

Your much honouring and loving Brother,

Glafgow, November 29th 1658.   R Bailye

[For Sir James Dundas of Arniston.]

Right Worshipfull,

Your kindnefs to my boy has been fo great, that I know no how ever I shall be even with yow for it. When I had thought fitt to send him to some familie for one year, to serve [as] a chaplane,[7] for to help his breeding, yow were not only willing to receive him, but to use him all the while as a child, not as a servant; and now, Sir, by your great favour having obtained in some meafure my defigne upon him, and finding myfelf fallen more tender than before, my purpofe is to have him at home after the terme, but fo that he ftay till yow gett another. Surely your patience and difpenfing with all his infirmities, and taking all his mean endeavours in fo good a part, has putt upon me a greater obligation than I will be able to difcharge, and whatever, Sir, I could doe with yourfelf, yet what to doe with my Lady, your Mother, I know not, who has been fo kind and tender towards my boy. My purpofe is to pray God for her Ladyfhip's welfare, and the profperitie of your whole familie, and, when I come to Edinburgh, to come out and acknowledge in prefence what now I write. Praying the Lord to blefs your Worfhip, and all yours, I reft

Your Worfhip's moft obliged friend and fervant,
Glafgow, 11th April 1659.   R. BAILIE.

FOR HIS REVEREND BROTHER MR ROBERT DOUGLASS, MINISTER AT EDINBURGH. APRIL 11TH 1659.

SIR,

I HAVE thought fitt to fend yow this account of our Synod and our other affaires. Underftanding a defigne of the Remonftrants, fome weeks before the Synod, to have a petition fent up to the Protector and Parliament againft Toleration, from the Synod of Glafgow, and their three correfpondent Synods of Galloway, Dumfries and Argyle, I did defire fome who came to falute me to beware of that motion, for thefe and the like Reafons. 1. This petition will be a formall addreffe to the prefent power as the Supream Magiftrate, which no Church Judicatorie in Scotland had ever yet attempted, and Glafgow Synod fhould not begin without the advyce at leaft of the Synod of Lothian and Fife, equallie concerned in that motion. 2. The petition to pre-

---

[7] Baillie's only surviving son, Henry, had gone to be chaplain in the Arnifton family, near Edinburgh (vide supra p. 382) and it appears he had been treated with great kindness.

ferve that part of our Covenant which toleration deſtroys, with ſilence of all other articles of our Covenant which now are openly laid aſide and deſtroyed, does avow our contentment with or neglect of the violation of all the other articles againſt which we doe not petition. So much the more as many of the petitioners are known to have framed a new Covenant wherein many articles of the former are deſtroyed and ſcraped out. 3 The Toleration we petition againſt is that which now is in practiſe, according to the petition and advyſe eſtabliſhed in the late Parliament, for the fundamentall Government of the three Nations, while we except only againſt one article of that act of Government, we doe add our ſeal to that not excepted againſt. 4. The Toleration we petition againſt is like ſhall not be full, as in our uncontroverted Aſſemblies our deſires againſt toleration doe ſtand: We muſt be ſilent of Independents, Anabaptiſts, and Eraſtians, theſe being the chief ſtateſmen who muſt agent our petition, or elſe it is like it will never be read 5 What ſecuritie ſhall we have that our commiſſioner againſt Toleration, when he comes to London, ſhall not as much endeavour advantages to the Remonſtrant partie as any thing elſe contrarie to the late articles of union of this Synod; yea, is it not like that the petitioning againſt toleration, which none hes hope will be granted, is but a mere pretence for putting on their deſignes. 6 If the pluralitie of the Synod conclude any ſuch commiſſion, can the diſſenters be guarded againſt a charge of horning for payment of their proportion of what ever expence a committee ſhall modifie for carying on that petition

When Judge Ker and Sir John Cheiſly appeared as elders in the Synod, their deſignes were ſuſpected the more, yet no ſuch motion was made till towards the end of the Aſſembly, at the back of an other triviall act it was like to have been paſt without obſervation, yet Mr W. Eccles and Mr R. Wallace topped it ſo that it was ſent to a committee to be debated; there, after much debate, it was reſolved to acquaint the Synod of Lothian with the motion, and unleſs they gave them ſatiſfactorie reaſons to the contrare at the next diet of the adjourned Synod in the end of May, to proceed with the petition, and to ſend (for the opponents ſatiſfaction,) Mr. P Colvill up with it Mr P. Gilleſpie told them, that ſo ſoon as his health and affaires would permitt him, he would goe to London, but for no man's pleaſure would medle with that petition, nor any thing controverted betwixt any parties In this he had the ill-luck to be believed but by few Sir John told, that he had oft been ſent for to come up to London upon advantagious tearms, but ftill had refufed, and would not go. I was glad that unhappie petition was to come fo flatly to your door: I doubt no but you will deal well enough with it.

I can obferve no relenting at all in that good faction. Their cruelty againft poor Mr R. Hume is ftrange. The parifhioners of Badernock, Montrofe, Keir, and all the heritors, with almoft all the prefbyterie, people, and feffion, would gladly have Mr. John Anderfon there placed, but Mr R Law hes ftirred up a few headie fellows of Bamor to preffe for Mr. Nicol Black, a domeftick of Mr. James Guthrie's For the furthering of that defigne the Synod has joyned a committee, of their fharpeft hooks, with that Prefbyterie for planting that kirk . without hoft, contrary to the Act of the Prefbyterie of Irvine, and all the diffents and proteftations of our towne, they appoint Mr Ralph Rodger, before the firft of June, to come hither

Many were greeved, when the Judges were here, that one Foyer was not hanged; a moft wicked hypocrite, [who,] under the colour of pietie and prayer, hes acted fundry adulteries; but by fome of our faction (to whom he was too dear,) their dealing with the Judges, no more was put in his libell than one adulterie, for which he was but fcourged great appearance of his witchrie alfo, if he had been put to a reall tryell. Yet that which greeves us moft for the time is the very heavie oppreffion of our towne in all their plantations. Our feffion, by an Act of the laft General Affemblie, claimes a divine right to elect the minifter, albeit our feffion for the time is nought bot the good pleafure of Mr. Patrick Gillefpie, who abfolutely rules it; the Prefbyterie is no leffe obfequious The whole parifh, almoft all the houfholders of Mr George Young's congregation did unanimoufly draw a petition to the feffion for a call to Mr. James Ferguffon, wherefore the feffion this day made read out of all pulpits ane admonition againft the miforderly fubfcriving of papers, and that the feffion, according to their right, would provide them of a minifter. The other Sabbath, Mr. James Blair, minifter of Cathcart, the firft whom the Prefbyterie had ordained to fupply Mr. G. Young's place, did preach to the Magiftrates in their faces that their oppofition to the feffion in plantation of their churches (which was only by a petition to the Prefbyterie and Seffion, now the third time, for Mr. James Ferguffon) would draw on them the punifhment of Core, Dathan and Abiram; and much more evills were threatened paffionatly by that weak young man againft them, for their rebellion againſt Jeſus Chriſt. We are exceedingly grieved that there is no viſible remead againſt theſe violent unreaſonable uſurpations of proud men. I humbly pray yow to let me know your mind, if ye know any remedie poſſible againſt this hardly tolerable tyrannie. That which many here would be at, if they cannot have Mr. James Ferguſſon, [is] to deall with ſome ſtout honeſt man, Scots or Engliſh, who on the Magiſtrates, Councell, and Peoples call, will be induced to come under the protection of the Engliſh, with a defiance to Seſſion, Preſbyterie, and Synod, all which, they ſay, is nought but their adverſarie, Mr. Gilleſpie. This I underſtand not. My owne remedie is a Generall Aſſembly, if ſo yow in your wiſdomes there find not that cure worſe than all our diſeaſe. I think Mr Sharp might eaſily obtaine to us a Generall Aſſembly; and that he might get it cautioned againſt the moſt, if not all our feares, but this is a Spagyrick cure in a deſperate caſe, which I muſt leave to your wiſdomes. Indeed, we languiſh and daily decay; and if yow there have no other remead for us but this third, I ſhall acquieſce to it, though I think ere long it will come nearer to yow when we are gone: I meane, that ſtill we ſhall be patient ſufferers, when they in their high pride thruſt in on us whomever they pleaſe. However, my intreſt in the familie of Eglintone and pariſh of Kilwinning hinders me to move for Mr James Ferguſſon's removall from them; yet without all doubt, he were the meeteſt man in Britaine for this place, for many evident good ends, and therefore theſe good men are ſo peremptorie againſt him.

Your very loving and much honouring Friend,
R. BAILLIE.

FOR HIS REVEREND BROTHER MR R. DOUGLASS, MINISTER OF EDINBURGH.

SIR,

We have ſent unto yow this expreſſe. By what the town and I writ to Mr. Sharp, yow will ſee our condition: yow will read and cloſe them. I doe conceive our Church and Land was never in ſo great hazard to be hurt by the Sectaries and Remonſtrators as this hour. And however I ſee no appearance of any friends to us with this preſent power, yet I conceave it exceeding neceffare that Mr. Sharp fhould ftay ftill a little while longer. M. P G[illefpie] is thought here to have taken journey this day, with the Lady Swinton, towards London. He expects no lefs than afk and have; yet I truft the Lord will marr him nothing the lefs that he has no vifible impediment. Having little more adoe in the Weft, I think they will begin the execution of their new orders on Lothian and Fife. The Lord help yow, who, under Chrift, are at the helme of our poor toffed Church in this high danger Your's,

May 18th 1659 R. BAILLY.

Will Mr Blair ever be filent, and never neither fpeak nor write one word for us?

FOR HIS REVEREND AND WEEL-BELOVED BROTHER, MR. JA SHARP, MINISTER AT CREEL.[8]

DEAR BROTHER, Glafgow, May 18th 1659

I WISH this may overtake yow before your coming from London; however, let me know if it comes to your hands. My neighbour, P. G., albeit he have as much to ty him at home as any man I know, having involved himfelf and us in great buildings, in a bargaine alfo of a thoufand pound fterling for tithes, and many law pleas; yet yefterday morning going to loup on, as we thought, for Edinburgh, he told us he was goeing ftraight to London for urgent bufineffes of his owne. I know he expects the quick grant of any thing he can defire from thofe that now are in power, and many here fear he will renew all his former irrationall defires for the prejudice of our Church, of our Towne, of our Colledge, nor know we who will oppofe him, but that, without all hearing and debate, by my Lord Fleetwood, Lord Lambert, and Dr Owen, his familiar friends, he fhall obtaine whatever he lykes: His former committees, for ftipends, yea, for tryall and cenfure, of his owne nomination, yea, whatever new forme he and Warrifton fhall invent for our

[8] The original (Wodr MSS Folio, vol. xxvi No. 17) is addressed on the back, as above, in Baillie's hand, but without any signature or mention of the year In his 4to MS of Letters, the year 1659 is given, but the letter itself would have fixed that date

whole Church; lykwife, the renewing of that late act of Parliament for qualifications of magiftrates in burgh and land, with fuch additions that their partie, to the great hurt and difquiet of the land, may be put prefentlie in place; and though Glafgow have conformed themfelves to that act, yet by new calumnious inventions he will endeavour to have them difplaced. One James Forfyd [Forfyth], not to be Laureat before Lammes, his wife's fifter's fon or oye, muft be, without tryall, put in a Regent's place at Michaelmes that a place may vaik, he deals with Mr. Patrick Young to dimit; on his refufeall he boafts him with a proceffe. When he finds that will not doe except he can cane more votes in our Facultie than in that caufe he is confident of, he refolves to bring in more members to vote with us. Alwayes before it was his care that no Towne minifter fhould be a member of our Facultie, and put them off who were on, and to this day keeped them off; but now, on a meer defire to ftrengthen us, he propones to bring in Mr. R. M'Quard to be our Vice-Chancellor, and Mr. Alexander Jamefone to be Deane of Facultie. The moft part of the Facultie knowing perfectlie the defigne, though too folemnlie denyed, did refufe the motion. To make Mr. Thurloe a friend to himfelf and his party, he fent him up for a bud, a patent from the Colledge of the Chancellorfhip, which I doubt Mr Thurloe never accepted, being informed of the defign, yet in thankfullnefs he got Mr G. the Protector's hand to a charter, and command to us, to add to Mr. Gillefpie's ftipend of a hunder and fourtie pound, out of our rents, whether new or old, a hunder pound more yearlie dureing life, with a narrative altogether untrue and unjuft. When he named Mr Thurloe, Chancellor he took to himfelf the Vice-Chancellorfhip, and fince has ever fubfcribed Principall and Vice Chancellor, but yefterday morning he peremptorlie layes doune his Vice-Chancellorfhip that it might be put on Mr. R. M'Quard, to be fure of a new vote. This we caried over him, that the Chancellor fhould name the Vice-Chancellor His purpofe and profeffion both is to move Mr. Thurloe to put his Vice on his confident Mr. M'Quard. I am fure if you prevent Mr. Thurloe with a right information he would not doe it, for I believe that Mr Thurloe never accepted that vaine-glorious place, or if he did, that at this time he will be loath to medle with it; and however, if he knew that our Chancellor never named a vicar, but by the advyce, confent, yea, defire of the whole Facultie, would not in this oppreffive defigne, hurtfull to our houfe, ferve Mr. G[illefpie's] humor. James, doe your beft in this, and, by whom God will be pleafed to help yow, lay a ftray in Mr. G's gate, though I know no faint now yow or we have there but the Wife's of Kilmarnock, Jefus Chrift alone, when the Reformers had pulled from her all images fhe wont to pray to: Weell is us that Chrift cannot be pulled off his throne. By all means ftay there awhile, were it but to be a witnefs of our countreymen's great infolencies. The Lord be with yow, and give yow courage and direction

Your's to ferve yow on occafion heartilie,

R. B

FOR HIS REVEREND AND WEEL-BELOVED BROTHER, MR JAMES SHARP, MINISTER AT CREEL.

JAMES,

I AM glad yow are there, and fo weell accepted. Yow have alwayes favoured our Towne, and all what concerned any of them. The bearer of this, Robert Cummin and James Ker, are fent up by their partners for a particular of great loffe and oppreffion, for which our Proveft wrote earneftlie to the Generall, and received a very kind and promifing anfwer. Thefe are to intreat yow to hear the matter and information, and help my neighbours by your beft directions and affiftance.

The enclofed is a double of one I fent to yow by Mr Douglafs, before yow came laft from London, I fand after it never came to yow, whereof I was not very weell content. I hope, if things go right there, (whereof yet I am in doubt, fince in their approbation of our Confeffion of Faith, they except the thirtieth and thirty-firft chapter, to which no Sectarie gave in a diffent, but only two Eraftians, that the world may know, within their jurifdiction, Chrift may be allowed no fpirituall government of his Church; this is weell begun): I hope yow will get us Vifitations for all our Univerfities, who hes great need of them, if we can get weell-fitting fheriffs, elfe better to want them, and that we continue under our prefent preffours till a better tyme. Only, in the mean while, I wifh yow advert to Mr. Gillefpie's dihgence for our houfe. He hes written to the Generall to get all our former gifts confirmed in Parliament; and to William Thomfon to be his agent herein. I refused my hand to this, though I wish he got the thing, only with the exception of one gift, moſt unjuſt, a hundred pound ſterling a-year, out of our rents, to himſelf yearly, beſide his ſtipend. Mr. Thurloe, whom I am glad to ſee again Secretary of State, got to him this order from the Protector, Richard, on three very falſe narratives. 1. That he was not ſufficiently provided, while he has ane hundred and fourty pound, much more than ever any Principall here had, and, as I think, more than any Principall in Scotland hes to this day. 2. That his labours were extraordinary, more than any other before him; while his labours hes been as good as none at all in any part of his proper duetie, except in toyes and folies, which concerned us little or nothing. 3. That our rents might weell bear that his augmentation, while it appears they doe not diſcharge our ordinary burdens. Our *Œconomus* for the maſters and burſars table hes not received a tippens this year, but hes laid out of his own money two thouſand merks, and is at the point of laying doun his charge, which none will take up; no man hes gotten a ſixpence of ſtipend this year, nor is like to get This is not only for want of law, but alſo throw his needleſs waſtrie, that hes caſt us in much debt, who, at his coming had many thouſand pounds to the fore. Mr. Thurloe is our good friend, but hes been abuſed by Mr. Gilleſpie to paſs ſuch a unjuſt gift; alſo, he got an order from him, (who, I ſuppoſe, never accepted of our Chancellor's oath,) to nominat Mr. Robert M'Quard our Vice-Chancellor, alone to ſerve Mr. Gilleſpie in his evill deſignes. I know yow could eaſilie have prevented all this, if yow had got my letter in tyme here incloſed Only, now I deſyre yow marre, if yow can, the paſſing of his gift I wiſh the reſt were confirmed, but with a clauſe of excluding any perſonall gifts ſince the year 1650, or ſome ſuch thing Alſo, I think, Mr. Thurloe would doe weell, as a ſtranger to our nation and affairs, and, at ſuch a diſtance, unable to be duelie informed of many things paſſes among us, in a letter to us, to ſignifie his unwillingneſs to continue longer under that title of our Chancellor, which Mr Gilleſpie did put on him, alone for a trick, to ſerve his own deſignes. James, [I] craves yow many pardons for this long libell. Doe in all this as yow think fitt: only by a line, let me know if theſe be come to your hands.

Be carefull none ſee theſe, eſpecially William Thomſon, my old very good and familiar friend, with whom, at the Croſſe of Edinburgh, the laſt tyme I faw him, I bitterlie difcorded for his putting Sir James Stewart in the Proveftrie. Now and then I am praying to God for yow, and purpofes to continue.

Your's,

March 10th 1660.   R. B.

For Mr. James Sharp.

JAMES,

THESE are only to let yow know that myfelf, and, I hope many my betters commends yow, and your employments, now and then heartily to God. If it pleafe God to work out this wonder, his own onlie work, marvellous in our eyes, and more in the eyes of the pofteritie, to bring home our fweet Prince in peace, I think, in this cafe, the greateft pull will be about Epifcopacy. Concerning this great difficultie I fuggeft unto yow this my advyce, to caufe fett with all poffible fpeed fome ferious and judicious pen, (I think Dr Reinold's were the fitteft,) in a few fheets of paper, to print the tenets, and point out the writes of the prefent leaders of the Epifcopall party, Dr Tailor, Mr Pierce, Dr Hamond, Mr Thorndyk, Dr. Heilin, Bifhop Wran, Bifhop Bramble, and others Their humour is exceedingly bitter, and high even, in their late writes, not only againft the Covenant and all Prefbyterians, but the Reformers abroad : they are moft expreffe and bitter for all Arminianifme, for the farre moft of Poperie, as much as Grotius maintains. If fhortly and plainly, their prefent tenets, befide Books and Bifhops, were put in the text, and the proofes in the margins, in their own words, (as I did in my Ladenfium,) I think it might prove a notable meane, by God's bleffing, either totally to withdraw the heart of the King from them, and the heart of a potent party they have, I doubt no, in England ftill, or at leaft to allay and cooll all honeft Proteftants towards their defignes No bodie can undertake this for purpofe and in tyme, but fome there. I think, if half-a-dozen were fet about the reading of the books, and pointing or drawing out the paffages, Dr. Reinolds, or Mr Prin [Prynne], or fundry others, in a fourtnight, might get it readie for the preffe and the view of the King and Parliament, for the crufhing of that high, proud, malicious, and now very active and dangerous party, as I fee fpeciallie by Pierce's lateft peeces. Baxter is unhappy;

he would be requefted either to be filent, or fimplie regulat in his writting, by thefe brethren who are wifer than himfelf.

Tell my Lord Lauderdaill that I am the old man towards him, and readily may dedicat my Chronologick Queftions to him, if he continue honeft, and better tymes make him no worfe. If yow have leafure, let me know your receipt of this and my former.

Your's,

Aprile 16th [1660.] R. B.

POSTSCRIPT.

Dr WALTOUN, albeit bitterlie Epifcopall, yet, for his great work[1], I wifh he were cherifhed, though it were with the Proveftrie of Eaton Colledge. that affe Lockier[2] being caft out, it might be a means either to win or filence that highly deferving man. Our reftlefs Remonftrators, as I hear, are ftill on plotts for new divifions, their firft defigne is, to divide Lauderdaill and Glencairne, two moft eminent men that now are left to our nation. The world knows the Remonftrants love neither, bot would break the one by the other, and fo, once more, us all in them. There is work enough, and reward alfo, for them both, if they agree. The afhes of our former ruine are yet fmoaking, we are fcarce begun to peip out from under that rubbifh, whether the coal of our former remeadilefs divifions, and it alone, lately did bring us if fo foon thefe begin again to befturr it, we are worfe than mad. No man I know fitter than yow to keep thefe two men together, in fpite of the devill; fee to it, as God fhall be pleafed to help yow. I hear the great projectors are my Lord Lie[3] and Sir John Cheiflie, and that their maine end is to bring in Colonell Lockhart in employment for Scotland, a man exceedingly fincere, who, all this while, hes been very zealous for our King, Kirk, and Countrie, no wayes felf-feeking, as all the world knows

[1] His edition of the Polyglott Bible. *Vide supra*, pp. 304, 309, 310

[2] Nicholas Lockyer, an Independent minister, in great favour with Cromwell, by whom he was promoted, on the death of Francis Rous, to be Provost of Eton, 14th January 1658. He did not long enjoy this office, as he was deprived at the Restoration and the place was conferred on Nicholas Monk

[3] Sir James Lockhart of Lee (See Brunton and Haig's Senators of the College of Justice p. 319. Edinb. 1832. 8vo.)

For his Reverend Brother Mr. William Douglass, Professor of
Divinity at Aberdeen.

Reverend and Beloved Brother,

Yow have here inclofed an account of my diligence about that knave · it's lyke he will flee from us to Ireland ; if he abide here, be affured of any reafon of him which yow defire. For famous men of our Univerfity and City, I can fay but little ; yet thefe following come in my minde for the prefent: Guil Elphiftoun, B. of Aberdeine,[1] builder of your Old Colledge, borne in Glafgow, a merchand's fon, but a landed gentleman, near coufin to the Lord Elphiftoun :—Mr. Peter Blackburne, Bifhop of Aberdeine, whofe hand was chief to order your Marifhall Colledge,[2] juft after our orders of Glafgow, borne and bred in Glafgow, an honeft merchand's fon, a Regent of our Colledge, when tranflated by King James to Aberdeine —George Buchannan, borne in Strablaine, feven myles from Glafgow, bred in our grammar-fchool, much converfing in our Colledge, the chief inftrument to purchafe our rents from Queen Mary and King James ; he left our library a parcell of good Greek books, noted with his hand :—Mr. Cameron, borne in our Salt-Mercat, a few doores from the place of my birth, a Regent of our Colledge, and then Principall of it :—Trochrig, borne with us, and our Principall ; fee what I write of his life before his book[3] ·—Dr. Strang, borne in Irvine, but long our Principall, where he write all his books ·—Mr. William Struthers, borne in our towne, minifter of it, very pious and learned ; long chief minifter of Edinburgh, I dare fay the moft eloquent and gracious preacher that ever yet lived in Scotland :—Mr. Dickfon, borne in Glafgow, Regent and Profeffor in our Colledge:—Mr Blair, borne near our towne, bred in our Colledge, long a Regent in it.—Mr. Andrew Melville, long our Principall before he went to St Andrews:—Mr. Thomas Smeaton died our Principall, one of the learnedeft men of the

[1] William Elphinstone, Bishop of Aberdeen, and founder of King's College there, in the year 1494 He was an eminent patron of literature, and died at Edinburgh 25th Oct. 1514

[2] Marischall College, Aberdeen, was founded by George Earl Marischal, 2d April 1593

[3] The posthumous Latin Commentary on the Epistle to the Ephesians, by Boyd of Trochrig, published in 1652

nation, as his book againſt Jeſuit Hamiltone[4] doeth ſhew:—B[iſhop] Spotſwood, as the Superintendent his father, and the Preſident his ſone, were all bred in our Colledge.—Blaſius Laurentius, Mr. R. Laurie's[5] grandfather, born with us, and long a Regent in our houſe, one of the braveſt philoſophs and humaniſts in his tyme.—Marcus Alexander Bodius, that excellent poet, as I knew it of his brother and nephewes, was, I ſuppoſe, borne near to us, and bred with us; Joannes Roſa, Mr. Jo. Roſſe, borne and bred with us, a brave poet, (as Robertus Magnus,[6] borne here, a Regent here, and our Profeſſor of Phyſick;) their verſe yow may ſee in *Delicus Poetarum Scotorum:*—Guil. Hegatus, Principall of the Colledge of Bordeaux, a good philoſopher and poet, borne with us:—Tho. Jakeus, long Maſter of our grammar-ſchool, ane able poet, as his Onomaſticon[7] ſhews; alſo Guil. Wallace, our late ſchoolmaſter, a fine poet:—Mr. Spang, miniſter at Campheir, famous abroad, borne and bred with us. I ſhall hold here for the time, only add Mr. Durhame, laureat with us, and ever after, till his death, with us. Doubtleſs there are many moe that I know no, or do not for the tyme remember.

As for your Sermon,[8] I ſend yow no cenſure upon it, for I was ſo much offended with your former book,[9] before which the glorious name of your Principall, Mr. Row, did ſo magnificently ſtand, and your very idle and falſe gloriation of whole two hundreth year and above antiquitie before St. Andrewes and us, that I have not read any of your writs in patience ſince, nor I think ever will, till, for theſe two lourd eſcapes, yow give great ſatiſfaction. The Lord be with yow. Our Remonſtrators remaine what they were, men for their owne faction alone.

Your's to ſerve yow,

Glaſgow, May 23d 1660. R. B.

[4] Smeton's work, dedicated to James the Sixth, is entitled ' Ad virulentum Archibaldi Hamiltonii apoſtatæ Dialogum,' &c. Edinburgi, 1579, 4to.

[5] Mr. Robert Laurie, who was afterwards Dean of Edinburgh, and Biſhop of Brechin.

[6] Dr. Robert Mayne. See his funeral inſcription in M Ure's Hiſt. of Glasgow, p. 258.

[7] The ' Onomaſticon Poeticum etc.' by Thomas Jack, was printed at Edinburgh 1592, 4to.

[8] "The Stable Truths of the Kirk require a ſutable behaviour. Holden forth by way of Sermon, &c. before the Provinciall Synod of Aberdeen, April 18 1659. Aberdene printed by J. B. in March, Ann 1660." 4to.

[9] " Academiarum Vindiciæ, in quibus Novantium prejudicia contra Academias etiam Reformatas averruncantur, earundemque Inſtitutio recta proponitur." Aberdoniæ, 1659, 4to.

For his Reverend Brother, Mr David Dickson.

Reverend Brother,

I received your's with Mr. Spang's packet; yow fee what he writes to me: fend it back to me with thefe Thefes. What was written the 1ft February, was too long in coming to yow and me. The end of May, I think, our Colledges muft fend their feverall anfwers. Advife me if I fhall communicat this to Mr. P G. According to my proteftations, I never acknowledged him Principall, nor any lawfull member of our focietie; yet, if it be not communicat, he will raife tragedies upon it, as if I did take upon me to depofe him before the time: advife me what to doe Since he came from Edinburgh laft, I find our factions in a new flame of fpirit; it's like fome thing hes been refolved among them there-eaft, they are all mifcontent with fome thing in this change. I have heard fome of them preach thefe three laft Sundays, bot not a word tending to any thanks, or any joy, for the Kings returne, albeit they have fome prayers for him. Then ftudie is to fill the people with fears of Bifhops, Books, deftroying of the Covenant, fetting up of profanitie; and heirupon preffes privie meetings, as in a tyme moft neceffar The fermon this day was fpent on that purpofe Thefe fett meetings, to my fenfe, are exceeding dangerous, caveat them as they will My heart is very grieved, that when myfelf and many others were content to have paffed all their bygone mifdemeanours, not few nor fmall, and made byganes byganes, yet I can fee no hope of any fair play in tyme to come, but a refolution, to keep up a fchifme and a partie of the godly, as they will have them called, for themfelves, that fhall obey no Church Judicatorie farder than they pleafe: This fpirit s now aloft more than ever, ftirred up lately in their Edinburgh meeting, from Wariftoun, Mr Guthrie, Mr Gillefpie, and Mr. Rutherfurd's commiffion, by Mr. M'Quard advert to it, left it goe to a new mifchief Argyle and Mr Gillefpie are this day at the communion at Pafley, with a world at their back: what to do with them I know no; neither fair or other means are like to do with them, if God himfelf put not the evill fpirit of caufelefs divifion from among us, both in Kirk and State, which now againe is burning. I think we fhall yet be a matter of ſcandall to the world for our imminent farder ruptures God help yow who there are at the helme. My ſervice to Margaret and Alexander. I reſt, Your's,

May 27th [1660.] R B

Yow let us know nothing, neither what Mr J. Sharp nor what yow there are doeing. We are wearied with complaints of this and will ſay no more of it.

For my Lord Lauderdaill

My Lord,

I would have been loath to have broken of my long ſilence towards your Lordſhip at this tyme of your ſo many and great affaires, if exceeding grief of minde had not for the preſent put me to it. I was one of thoſe who, in my heart, and all needfull expreſſions, adhered to the King in all his diſtreſſes He had my continuall prayers to God for his reſtitution, any way God pleaſed, even the moſt hard: diverſe know my frequent expreſ- ſions of readineſs to further his returne to his throne, by laying downe mine head on the block for it, and the utter ruin of all my worldly fortoun Alſo yow, and your neighbour Crawfurd, were oft in my prayers. When the Lord lately, at a very cheap rate, had brought all my prayers, and much more than I could have thought upon, to paſs, both for the matter and man- ner, there were few that had a more hearty joy for it than I, and was more offended (even in my pulpit) with thoſe who were not ſo joyfull as I thought became them. While I am going on in my daily renewed joy, behold your unhappy Diurnals and letters from London hes wounded me to the heart. Is the Service-Book read in the King's Chappell? Hes the Biſhop of Elie (I fear Dr Wran), the worſt Biſhop of our age after Dr. Laud, preach- ed there? Hes the Houſe of Lords paſt an order for the Service-Book? Oh! where are we ſoe ſoon? The granting to us in Scotland the confirmation of what we have, brings us juſt back to J[ames] Graham's tymes Is our Covenant with England turned to Harie Martin's Almanack? Is the ſolemne oath of the Lords and Commons, aſſembled in Parliament, ſubſcrybed ſo oft by their hands to eradicat Bifhops, turned all to wind? Why did the Parliament, a few months fince, appoint the Covenant to be hung up in every Church of England, and every year to be publickly read? Is Cromwell, the great enemie of our Covenant, fo foon arifen out of his grave? Can our gracious Prince ever forget his folemne Oath and Subfcription? He is a better man than to do it, if thefe about him be not very unfaithfull fervants. For myfelf, fuch are my rooted refpects, both to his perfon and place, that do what he will, and tolleiat what he will, I purpofe while I live to be his moft loving and loyall fubject. But, beheve me, if I were befide him I would tell him fadly, and with tears, oaths to the Almightie are not to be broken, and leaft of all by him for whom the Lord has wrought at this very tyme a more marvelous mercy than he has done for any or all the princes in Europe thefe hundred years. Bifhops were the very fountain of all our mifchiefs: Will they ever change their nature? Will God ever bleffe that plant which himfelf never planted? It's a fcorne to tell us of moderat Epifcopacy, a moderat Papacy! the world knows that Bifhops and Popes could never keep caveats. The Epifcopall faction there were never more immoderat than this day. You know how farr Pierce, Hamond, Heylen, Taylor, have in their late writs juftified all the challenges in my Ladenfium, and gone beyond them to all the Tridentine poperie of Grotius. T. G, Thomas Gallovidianus[1], for his printing Dr. Forbes, B[ifhop] of Edinburgh's wicked dictats, is now on his way to London, fent for by the Englifh Bifhops, who fcoffe at our Church's excommunication. Yow were the man who procured and brought downe to us the ordinance for abolition of Epifcopacie. I doubt not but yow and Mr. Sharp has done your endeavour, but could I ever have dreamed that Bifhops and Books, fhould have been fo foon reftored, with fo great eafe and filence of the Prefbyterian Covenanters in the two Houfes, the Citie and Affemblie of London, of Lancafhyre, and other fhyres? Be affured, whatever furprife be for the time, this fo hideous a breach to God and man can no faill to produce the wrath of God in the end. Shall all our blood and labour for that Covenant be fo eafilie buried? Though all flefh, Englifh and Scots, for their own defigns were filent at fo needfull a tyme, I doubt not bot the Lord himfelf will hear our cryes againft that beaft, which has gotten fo deadlie wounds as all the kings and parliaments of the earth will never be able to

[1] Thomas Sydeferf, Bifhop of Galloway. *V de supra*, note p 390

cure. I, and many more, who have, and will ever rejoyce for the Reftitution of our King, refolve to complaine to God and man, while we live, for the returne of Books and Bifhops.

Thus farr I have poured out my heart to yow at this tyme, who, I believe, will be loath for any caufe to apoftatife from your well-tryed conftancie This is from your L[ordfhip's] old friend and fervant,

R. B.

June 16th 1660.

[For the Earl of Lauderdaill.]

My Lord,

I receaved on the 30th of June, what long before yow fent to me by Mr. Jo. Wilkie, two copies of the French letters, vindicating the King's conftancie in his religion. The one, as yow directed, I fent immediatelie to our noble friend L. M. Kennedy?; for this favour I thank your Lordfhip. I write the 18th [16th] of June, by Mr. Jo. Wilkie's packet, a very fad regrate, which I hope your Lordfhip hath receaved. This is on a particular. Miftrifs Gillefpie has gone to her friends at London to folicite her hufband's pardon and confirmation in his place of Principall in our Univerfitie I would no be ftrait-laced in pardon almoft to any penitent man; but truelie if his Majeftie fhould be that farr abufed by any there, as to confirm him in that place whereto he had never any call, but the Englifh intrufion, nor any parts to difcharge it as all the nation knows, I would be forced to fubfcribe what his partie preaches in my eares, though not in their fenfe, that we are fallen out of the thornes into the briers. The Generall Affembly is that man's judge; the King knows him not, nor his ways: Whoever will plead for him, may as well plead for Nye, Goodwin, Peters, or for Owen to keep him in Chrift Colledge of Oxford, and Lockier in Eaton. My Lord, the word goes that his chief confidence is in your Lordfhip for the good offices he did to yow with Lambert in your prifon. But by all the intereft I have in yow, I con-

? Lady Margaret Kennedy, eldest daughter of John Earl of Cassillis At a later period, (in 1670 or 1671,) she became the wife of Dr. Gilbert Burnet then Profeffor of Divinity at Glasgow, and afterwards Bishop of Salisbury

jure yow not to medle with him. It would draw infamie upon yow, and the offence of our whole Church, and all who truelie loves the King and hates the Remonſtrance. Ye would wrong our Univerſitie, oppreſt by his evill talent, and myſelf in particular, who deſerves no injurie at your Lordſhip's hands Yow are too wife to be enchanted by that firen's fongs: for her venturous boldneſs ſhe ought to be ſent home, if not with ane affront, yet with a fevere frowne

This is from your Lordſhip's old friend and fervant,

R. B.

Glafgow, July 2d 1660.

For Mr Hutchesonf.

GEORGE,

I GOT your laſt, and all my papers back on Saturday. I am obliidged to yow, and yow only, for a ſerious care to reviſe them. Moſt of your corrections, both literall and reall, are right, whereof I will make uſe Your difference from me in ſome points I take very weell, and ſhall conſider of it The Scripturall hiatus in the ſeventy weeks is my great grief, and I would count him a happie man who could help it. The third edition of my Ladenſium, at London, had additions · I ſhall endeavour to ſend yow one of them. In your notion here of pointing out the Epiſcopall faction I agree with yow: Yow have here a double what I write about it to Mr Sharp, April 16th, whereof he gave me no account, nor of any thing I write to him, this twelve moneth: Would God my opinion had been followed in tyme. I am not pleaſed with what is ſo oft inculcat to yow from London, that the more we medle with the Kirk of England, it will fare the worſe both with us and them What is the Scotts of this, but that we ſhall fitt dumb and never open our mouth, neither to the King nor Parliament, nor our brethren the miniſters of England, to requeſt them to adhere to their Covenant and Petition againſt Books and Biſhops · I fear we cannot anſwer for our miferable ſlackneſs herein alreadie. It is more than time that all the gracious miniſters in the citie and countrie ſhould doe then beſt to procure ſo many and ſo ſtrong petitions as poſſible, to the King and Parliament, to hold out Biſhops and Books. We who had by our Covenant but too great intereſt, and knew their temper to be but dead and cold till quickened and warmed, fhould not have fo long neglected them I was fore afflicted when it was told me, by my neighbour, that Lauderdaill went to the chapell to hear Bifhops preach, and fay Amen to all the fervice, as much as any about Court, and defended his practice by confcience. I hope this muft be falfe; as alfo what I heard, of four and twenty hunder of gracious minifters violently put from their places by the old Service-book men. If it be fo, we are in a hard taking. I pray yow let me know what yow hear of thefe things They are, if true, deeds openly done, which eafily yow will get tryed by daily comers from London We have loft a fair game by meer mifguiding. A pitie but Hyde and fome others had been removed from Court long before this. That Middletone, a fojour, is to be Commiffioner of our Parliament and Affemblie, I fear it import fome unpleafant fervice to be in hand. The Remonftrance, the Act of the Weft Church, the Proteftation, I abhorre, as very bafe and intollerable pranks; but God forbid that any would be put to fuffer for them, who will play fair in time to come. I doe inclyne, as yow advyfe, to deall with Hamond and Jefuit Petavius, and King Charles's Reafons for Epifcopacie; but I cannot determine when, till I have feen Hamond, (I expect him fhortly from London,) and I have gotten my Chronologie to the preffe: in this advyfe me. It is not framed fo that any part of it can goe alone. If Thomas Catherwood, on your recommendation, or your printer at London, would undertake it, I fhould require nothing but fome bound copies, to be diftribute to friends Affift me in this, elfe I muft let it lye ftill, I know no how long. Let me hear from yow fo foon as yow can. Adieu.

Yours,

Auguft 13th 1660 R. B.

[For Mr Robert Baillie.]

REVEREND AND DEAR SIR,

The Lord having returned me to this place in fafetie and health, I have taken the opportunitie of this gentleman, Sir Adam Blair, to give yow an account thereof. I have need begin with a large apologie for my filence to yow all the tyme I was at London, even after twice provocation from yow, but at prefent neither tyme nor expediencie will allow me to write that which may acquitt me from that charge of neglect yow may commence againft me, and therefore fhall entreat your patience, and exercife of your charitie towards me, till I have the opportunitie of fatiffying yow. The King at my firft addreffe in Breda, was pleafed to afk me very kindly about yow; and at my taking leave at Whithall, commanded me to remember him to yow by name, with others; and I can affure yow, he hath a particular kindnefs for yow, and will give a demonftration of it. His Majeftie hath been pleafed to fend by me a gracious Letter to the Prefbytrie of Edinburgh to be communicated to all the Prefbytries in Scotland, which I am confident will fatiffie all who are fatiffiable; it will be printed, and within a day or two, a copie tranfmitted to yow.[3] However the affaires of the Church of England may be difpofed, which I fee are tending to Epifcopacie there, the blame whereof ought not to be laid upon the King; yet we need fear no violation of our fetlement here, if the Lord give us to prize our own mercie, and know our dutie. I have brought a letter from fome citie minifters, bearing an account of their late procedure to an accommodation, for moderated Epifcopacie, and the Church contefts there are fwallowed up by thefe who are for Prelacie in the former way, and thefe who are for a regulated Epifcopacie. The King by his declaration, which will be fpeedilie publifhed, will endeavour a compofeing of thefe differences untill a Synod be called. Your noble friend who hath fent yow the inclofed, (however he is reprefented by fome with yow,) is a fixed friend to the intereft of the Church of Scotland, and to that caufe we have owned · we have caufe to bleffe God that he is putt into fuch a ftation by his Majeftie, wherein he is capacitated to doe good offices to our Church, and honeft men in it, for which I am perfuaded he will lay himfelf forth to the utmoft[4]. I hear of ftories vented by fome with yow to the prejudice of that Noble perfon: they are calumnies, and I hope will not have belief with yow, and other honeft men. I think it were not amiffe yow did make a ftep hither

[3] The King's letter to the Presbytery of Edinburgh, dated the 10th August, and received 3d September, with the answers from the Prefbytery, to Charles the Second, and to the Earl of Lauderdale, on the 20th September, are contained in Bailhe's MS; but they may be found in Wodrow's History, and in other works

[4] It appears unqueftionable that Lord Lauderdale, up till this period at least, was averse to any change of the Presbyterian form of worship in Scotland. How far Sharp himself was sincere in his professions, might best appear were his own correspondence fully published.

to Edinburgh, how foon yow could; there are matters fitt for yow to know, and give advyce, which cannot in this way be communicated. The expectation I have of your coming doth put a ftop to my further writting. I commend yow to the Lord's grace.

Your's to ferve yow,

Edinburgh, September 5th 1660.   JA. SHARP.

I fhall entreat yow to prefent my fervice to Proveift John Bell. I beg his pardon for my incivilitie in fending no return to what he wrote to me at London. I truft the reafon upon which I fell into that omiffion will plead for my excufe when communicated to him, which I purpofe to doe at meeting.

[FOR MR. ROBERT BAILLIE.]

SIR,

YOUR letter of complaints was long of coming, or rather never came, (for I have only got a copie of it,) and I am not unfatiffied with it, for I defire not to know the complaints of my friends, when I cannot help them. Your letters of fears and jealoufies of me came too foon; for, let me tell yow, charity and old acquaintance ought to have made yow not to have been fo credulous as to have hearkened fo much to clatters. My crime, I thought, fhould have been feveritie, and not too much acting for Remonftrants. But we will, I hope, agree when we meet. All the account I can now give yow is, that inftead of pleading for Mr. Gillefpie, I have obtained a grant for another to be Principall of Glafgow, and waits but for a formall prefentation for his Majeftie's hand; he was prefented by the Ufurper, and therefore the King makes no bones of the difpofeing of that place, and, I affure yow, I did not plead for his continuance. This yow may believe better than thefe who told yow I was pleading for Remonftrators, this honeft bearer, Mr. Sharp, will tell yow all that yow would know from this place. I fhall only add, that whatever ye hear, I am where I was, and by confequence,

Your affectionat friend to ferve yow,
LAUDERDAILL.

Whitehall, the 22d of Auguft 1660.

[For the Earl of Lauderdaill.]

My Lord,

I receaved what yow wrote to me with Mr. Sharp. His Majeftie's remembrance of me, I thank yow for it, for it was your Lordfhip's information that, firft and laft, made him take any notice of me. I can fay (I think truely) that yow did not deceave, neither his Majeftie nor yourfelf, in affureing him of my hearty affection, both to his place and perfon, fince my firft acquaintance, and of my readinefs, with all the little pith I had, to doe him willing and fincere fervice; nor did yow deceave yourfelf in believing my true refpect towards yow now of a long tyme, above any in our land of your qualitie. As for my late grievances, I am content to fufpend their debate till we meet. For the prefentation yow write of, I fhall advyfe it, when it comes to my hand, with the brethren of Edinburgh. I was never defireous of any place but one, the regencie of the Bajouns. The Principall's charge of our Colledge twelve years agoe, I have been oft intreated to accept by all who had intereft to call to it, but ever I did peremptorilie refufe it, Dr Strang, to whom it did truely belong, being then alive. Age and weaknefs make me now more unfitt for it than I was then. Befide that, Mr Gillefpie, by his good adminiftration, has put that place for the time in a very mifeiable condition, as at oui fiift Vifitation will be apparent. Befide other grievous burdens, he has left upon us, by his vain-glorious buildings, the debt of above ten thoufand merks, and ten thoufand pound will not perfite, what fore againft my heait he has laid a neceffitie on us to perfite, or be accounted poor feckleis fnifties, who has no witt nor action to end what he has fo magnificentlie begun and advanced. It is true, *viis et modis*, he got to fpend on it above five and forty thoufand pound, whereof from the Englifh he had above twenty thoufand merks, and was confident of other twenty, if Lambert had ftood to this day. But eternal praife to the Lord for that bleffed change that God himfelf had wrought, become of us and our building what God pleafes. The Chancellor affures me, that the King and State will help us to perfite that work, (which indeed is the prettieft building in all our land,) and will not be outftripped by Cromwell in kindnefs to our Univerfitie, but of the time and wayes we muſt advyſe with your Lordſhip at meeting. Only there is one favour for the time we muſt intreat your Lordſhip for: His Majeſtie's Royall Father, when in Scotland 1633, in the firſt page of our Contribution book for our building and library, ſubſcrived to Dr Strang, two hunder pound. This our good Theſaurer Traquair ſhifted ever to pay till our troubles began. The world now knows his Majeſtie's care to ſee his Royall Father's debt payed, ſo far as he can, with increaſe. The Chancellor and others aſſure me of their endeavours, notwithſtanding all their povertie to get that payed to us, if we can have the King's order for it to the Theſaurer. I hope your Lordſhip, who getts his Majeſtie's hand to ſo many things will get it alſo to this little particular,[5] were it but for your kindneſs to me. And what, if in the precept his Majeſty would, of his royall bounty, double it, as oft he hes done to others who can doe him leſſe ſervice? Surely if we get it, or if we get it not, I ſhall, God willing, be carefull to ſett on the frontiſpiece of our work, his Majeſtie's name and armes, (which the Engliſh defaced,) in a more ſtately forme than yet they are in Scotland. And for your Lordſhip's procuration we will advyſe of ſome bud that may be moſt fitting your temper. So ſoon as yow may, let me know what to expect, or rather let me receive from Mr. Sharp, who will ſend it ſafely to me, his Majeſtie's warrand to the Theſaurer for the reall and ready payment, of which his Majeſtie and your Lordſhip ſhall think fitt. I purpoſe never to ſeek, nor to have any thing for myſelf; for, bleſſed be God! I have enough for myſelf, and all my ſix children, but I would fain ſee our College out of that debt [in] which the vanitie and prodigalitie of that man has almoſt drowned us. The Lord bleſſe and help your Lordſhip in that high and ticklifh ſtation wherein now yow ſtand.

Your Lordſhip's, after the old faſhion,

October 12th 1660.   R B.

[5] It is singular that Baillie, in this urgent appeal should have overlooked or concealed the fact of this subscription having actually been paid by Cromwell. This appears from the entry in the Subscription-book to which he refers, viz —" CHARLES R —It is our gracious pleasure to grant, for the advancement of the Librarie and fabrick of the Colledge of Glasgow, the sum of Two Hundred Pounds Sterling." Above this is written, " His Majestie's Contribution was gratiouslie granted at Seton, the 14 of Julie 1633 ,' and beneath it, in a different hand, ' This soume was payed by the Lord Protector, An 1654." Baillie indeed talks of Cromwell's " kindness," which he must have esteemed as in no way cancelling the original obligation.

[For Mr. George Hutcheson, Edinburgh.]

George,

Since I saw yow, reflecting on what I heard and saw there, and somewhat hes come to me since, I am fallen in jealousies and feares, I hope causeless and vaine, yet for the tyme they vex me, and I communicate them to yow alone For the time yow may doe some good, as I conceave, but I know no how long If the wrack of the Remonstrators, with our help, be but a state designe to make us instrumentall to weaken the Kirk, to oppose their fardei designes we are egregiously abused. I fear this Parliament, if they will abolish not only the Act of Patronages, but that whole Parliament, yea will medle with our Solemne League and Covenant, with our connivence and silence, it will be Mr W. Ruflel's prayers, "Lord ! thou knowes, we are false knaves together." I think the matter of English Episcopacie, and Hyde's Chancellorship has been guided with a great deal either of imprudence oi worse. I think my Lord Cassillis will inform yow of more than I know. God knows all, and time will discover a part. Exhortations to yow are needless, yet yow can no be the worse of a little advyse, yow have more power than any man with Mr Dickson and Mr. Dowglafs: yow three hold fast together When Mr. Wood and Mr. Shaip comes over, advyse of our best way to keep the King and Parliament from medleing with our Covenant, else be assured all honest men will exoner their hearts to testifie against mainsworn villanie, and to cry to God against it. We needed not to have been brought to this point, if these at London had not been befooled and bewitched However, look about yow, and let us not be cheated nor forced from our dear Covenant, without a witness to purpose. That business of Robertson, in Kirkaldy, which flowed from your Turner and Wood,[6] try the bottome of it, and be not complemented out of that search. Make much of our correspondent foi he is worthie. These to you alone.

        Yours,   R. B.

Glasgow, November 5th [1660.]

[6] This refers to a letter intended to have been sent to the King on his Restoration, signed by Smith, Wood, Thomson, Turner, Hume, and Robertson Wodrow, (MSS. Fol. Vol xxviii, No. 26,) describes it as being " in an odd style for Presbyterian Ministers"

Let me know if yow have gotten this. I incline to write to Mr. Aſhe and Mr. Clerk, to doe their beſt for a ſtrong petition from the Preſbyterian miniſters and Citie againſt Epiſcopacie and Liturgie who hes marred it till now, they have been fools or knaves. Yow there ſhould have done it, but ere it be not done I will try it, if yow alone approve. I am fore grieved. ſimple men are impatient of cheating

For Mr. Dickson.

Reverend and Loving Brother,

Yow have here what, on your deſire, I promiſed to ſend; diſpoſe on it as yow, Mr. Douglaſs, and Mr. Hutcheſon ſhall find expedient. If yow find meet to ſend it abroad, let it be nameleſs, and well correčted at the preſſe by Mr. Archbald Cameron.[7] But by no means let it come out before the Parliament have ended with all they purpoſe towards the Proteſters; for I would be ſorie that any write of mine ſhould bring trouble to any man: I would rather choice to burne it.[8] But yow three are wiſe enough. I fear for the ill of this Parliament. God help us. My ſervice to Margaret and Alexander.

Yours,

December 3d [1660.]   R. Baillie.

[For Mr. Robert Baillie.]

Reverend Sir,   Edinburgh, 13th December 1660

Your former letter came to my hand at Craill, ſeventeen dayes after the date of it; and I put off the ſending yow a returne, till my coming to Edinburgh, where I apprehended yow might be at the meeting of Parliament. this is the cauſe of the delay of the account, which now I ſhall give yow concerning the matter of that letter   I ſent your letter to Lauderdaill, which came

---

[7] A brother of the celebrated divine John Cameron *vide* vol 1 p 482

[8] This " write " against the Protesters, (to which Baillie again alludes in his subsequent letters,) was probably never published, in consequence of the unexpected change that soon afterwards took place in regard to the Church.

to his hands the feventh day after I fent it to Edinburgh My Brother was with his Lordfhip in the time when he receaved [it] : the King's haftening to meet his Mother the Queene, did divert my Lord from fending to yow an anfwer, which he promifed to my brother, at his parting from him, to fend by the poaft. Since which tyme I have receaved no letter, fave one the other day by my Lord Crawfurd, and all my Lord Lauderdaill writes in his letter of 2d December to me touching that matter is, that "The King's commands keep me here, fo that I fhall not fee yow till the Spring. In the mean tyme, I long for your advyce as to what I wrote of Glafgow, with a draught of the prefentation" Thefe are the words. In that letter I fent to his Lordfhip with your's, I was pofitive in my defire that the prefentation might be fent downe for yourfelf; and fure my Lord, through multiplicitie of bufinefs, hes forgott what then I wrote ; but I fhall this night, by my letter to his Lordfhip, renew my defire ; and I think it will be fitt that a draught of a prefentation, conform to Dr. Strang's, be fent up, if that can be had with yow, or any other which will be valide. Upon fending it hither to my Brother, (if I be not in towne,) I will engage for his fecrecie and fidelitie in tranfmitting it to my Lord Lauderdaill, who, I am confident, will take care of it. Courtiers, they are fo taken up with other bufinefs, that they have neither leafure nor mind for framing draughts, and the readieft way will be to fend a draught to them. I doe not think but he hes either alreadie written to yourfelf, or will writ to yow by his brother Charles Maitland of Halton, who is now coming down.

Mr. Young did his bufinefs, before my coming to towne, with the Committee of States, fo that I had no opportunitie to ferve him, which I would have done upon your accompt. He can acquaint yow with proceedings here I fhall only tell yow this, that I am confident at this Parliament there will be no medling with the matters of our Church. I believe reports and apprehenfions with yow, may lead into fears of the contrare; but I fee no caufe for them. I wifh from my heart the peace yow ftand ingaged to complete were fent hither. I fhall be in this towne again within a fortnight. Let me know wherein I can ferve yow, who am in finceritie,

Sir, Your's,

JA SHARP.

[For Mr James Sharp]

James,

Yours of the 13th I receaved the 15th; whereby I fee your great kindnefs to me continues, for the which I remaine oblidged. That pamphlet (as I write to yow before, which yet I fee is no come to your hands), I made ready for the preffe, and fent a good while agoe to Mr. Dickfon, according to my promife, and had done fooner, had no Mr. Andrew Kerr made me write once, twice, thrice, for fome papers I thought fitt to add. Yow will fee the frame I have put it in, and my additions, and doe with all what yow and the brethren in Edinburgh think fitt I think indeed it will help to difcredit that faction for ever, and, in reafon, make them filent, whatever courfe either Church or State take with any of them; but far be it from me to creat any trouble to any flefh by any of my writs; therefore I write to Mr. Dickfon that it fhould not goe to the preffe till the Parliament (and I wifh the Church alfo) had ended all they have to fay to any of them. However, I have performed what I have ingadged to yow

Lauderdaill fhould no play the courtier with me fince he hes forgot, (as I believe it weell,) both what yow and I write to him, I fend yow herewith the double of mine, that if yow think fitt, he may look on it with one of yours to fecond it Mr Gillefpie indeed hes left us in fuch a condition, that (as I hear he boafts, on too good grounds, few fhall defire it in hafte,) I will be loath to medle with it, if his Majeftie, by Lauderdaill's means, will not help us out of our ftraits My firft motion for a præcept to the Thefaurer I thought would have had no difficultie. For a præfentation yow have here Dr. Strang's laft[7]: he had a larger

---

[7] The following is a copy of the Warrant for Dr Strang's presentation to the Principality of the College of Glasgow as inserted in this place in Baillie's Manuscript:—

Charles R —Right Reverend Father in God, right trusty and welbeloved counsellor, we greet yow weell Whereas we are credible informed that since the departure of Mr John Cameron out of that our Kingdom, the College of Glasgow hath been without a Principall, and being likewise informed of the sufficiencie and learning of Mr John Strang, Doctor in Divinitie, and of his fitness to discharge that place, we have made speciall choise of him,

the year before from King James, which I cannot get, but I think yow muſt draw the forme blank, to be changed by my Lord as he likes. The direction, I think, would be to the Moderators of the Univerſitie, and the narrative, the vacancie of that place ſince the death of Dr. Strang, with a line of his Majeſtie's diſallowance of Mr. Gilleſpie's intruſion. When ſuch a præſentation, with a kind letter from the King and Lauderdaill, comes to me, it's tyme, and not before, for me to advyſe what to doe For the preſent my name is toſſed more than needed, by all here about, and our Houſe ſuffers many wayes by this vacancy : put it to ſome point, the ſooner the better

I have many things to ſay to yow which I cannot write. Cannot our peace be ſecured without Argyle's head? See they go no farder with Mr. Rutherfoord, whatever be his deſerving let him have his ſtipend for his ſhort tyme. If the Parliament medle with our Covenants they will grieve many, and me with the firſt For the tyme yow can help many things [as much] as any man I know, but be aſſured no man's court laſts long be doeing good while yow have tyme. My ſervice to James Wood, if his Archi-Epiſcopall pride will permitt him to accept it; but I let him weell to wit, that the Archbiſhops of Glaſgow were large as proud as ever St. Andrewes could be. James, God help yow!   Your's,

December 17th 1660.   R. BAILLIE.

For MR JAMES SHARP.

REVEREND AND DEAR BROTHER,

My anſwer of the 17th of the laſt to your verie kind one of the 13th, came to your brother, and I hope before this is received by yow. The reaſon of my preſſing yow with this ſecond is a little impatience by the ſcarce good carriage of ſome of my neighbours. I think, indeed, that ſince Dr. Strang's death, the firſt place in our Houſe is no leſſe than my due and juſt deſerving, and whoever medles with it, without my conſent, is injurious ; but the

and preſented him thereunto. And therefore, by theſe preſents, have thought good to require yow to give him collation, and induct him in the foreſaid place according to the order. Wherein, nothing doubting of your ready obedience, we bid you Farewell.—Given at our Court at Sariſburie, the 10th of October 1625

whole tract of my life, as many know, and of my heart, as I think, has been so farre averse from changes and advancement, that I have ever embraced, most contentedly, my present condition, with a true loathnefs to leave it. This difpofition hes keeped me from moveing hand or foot, directly or indirectly, to feek that which I count my due otherwayes. Only when yow advertifed me, and Lauderdaill by his letter alfo was pleafed to fignifie unto me, that it was his Majeftie's pleafure to appoint me for that place, I returned to yow and Lauderdaill, the procurers of this without any defire from me, (as yow know better than any man,) my thanks, fhewing, when that prefentation came to me, I would advyfe about it with my friends. While too long a time goes before any conclufion herein, I find, at leift from many airths I hear, that my neighbour, Mr John Young, by the diligence of his brother-in-law, Proveift Bell, whofe credit with the Chancellor, Regifter, Advocat, Clerk of Edinburgh, and diverfe of the State, is very great, not only is procureing that place for himfelf, but laying thefe things on me with our Statefmen, which are either falfe or no faults. of this I am not content, and, as I wrote to yow in my laft, I repeat, to entreat yow, who I think can doe it, to put that matter to a quick iffue and hafte, at leift to bring me fairly off it, that it may be fettled on fome honeft man who may be for it, but not, if my opinion be followed, on my neighbour, for many reafons I could tell yow. I could ever have lived rather with Mr. Gillefpie than with him; and if he fhould be the man, I think I would leave the Houfe, and go to a country church From time to time I have had ingratitudes and difpleafures from him that hardlie I can bear long. I hoped for a remead of many thing by a Vifitation of our Colledge, but I fee, by his and Proveift Bell's cunning and activitie, that hope is turned into fear, for if our vifitors fhall be the perfons which they will choice, and moft eafily, by canny convoyance of the Regifter, or Advocat, or Chancellor, on the Proveift's fuggeftion, will be paft in Parliament, we may get no good, but much harme of fuch a Vifitation; and I fee now clearly that they are confident, doe what I can to the contrare, to have fuch a Vifitation as they fhall name. I have no way to help this but by yow I think yow, Mr. Wood, Mr Dickfon, etc, would refolve upon a way to vifite all our Univerfities, for fome good purpofe I think poftiblie it were good that the Parliament fhould give that power, for this tyme, to the Generall Affemblie; or if this can no be, that the men chofen for us might be impartiall: for Noblemen, the Chancellor and yow would advyfe of fome who might keep with us, fuch as Montgomerie, Fleeming, not Cochrane at this time, nor Montrofe · [for] Gentlemen, Commiffioners for the Lennox, Luffe, Kilmahew, for Baranthrow, young Houfton, Craigends, alfo Kilfyth, Heiflet, Cunninghamhead, Bedlay, Commiffar Fleeming for Burroughs, the Proveft, and Bailzies, Dean of Gild, and Deacon Conveener of Glafgow, (at leaft two of them, Walkingfhaw and Baillie Barnes,) the Proveft of Aire, Irvin, Dumbartane: for Minifters, Mr. James Ferguffon, Mr. Alexander Nifbet, Mr P Colvill, Mr. Gabriel Cunninghame elder, Mr R Wallace, Mr. Hew Eccles, Mr R. Birnie, Mr James Hamilton of Camnathen: Nine a quorum, four minifters and five others. This, if yow pleafe, yow can manage well, or fomething like this; and becaufe there may be fome Sederunts at Edinburgh, the Thefaurer and Caffills might be put in, Mr. R. Douglafs, Mr Dickfon, Mr Hutchefon, yow, and Mr. Wood, Mr Smith, etc

James, I pray yow let me know if this and my former have come to your hand, and what I may expect from yow; for it is on yow only, under God, that I lay thefe affaires The Lord affift yow; the felfinefs and ill defigns of my neighbours diverts me from the publict and better thoughts. I expect yow will eafe my prefent difcontent

Your's to ferve yow,

January 1ft 1661   R BAILLIE.

FOR THE RYGHT REVEREND MR. ROBERT BAYLY, PROFESSOR OF DIVINITY IN GLASGOW.[1]

REVEREND SIR,

I RECEAVED two of your letters laitly, the one whyl I was at home, two dayes befor I was fent for to attend the Commiffioner; the other by the bearar, who feems to be a difcreet perfon, and can give yow fuch ane account of matters relating to your letters, as will make it unneceffary for me to fend yow a large returne I would not have imagined that fuch an abufe and grofs injurie could have been defigned againft yow. I fhall doe my beft, by the Lord's help, to give them check-meat Any court I may be fuppofed

[1] From the original, addreffed as above, (Wodrow MSS Folio Vol xlix. No 6)

to have, (upon the continuance of which I doe not build,) shall be with all readines and good will, layed out to doe Mr. Baily service. My Lord Commissioner² is a wery judicious and moderat person, and, by his carriage in the publick councills, hath gained wery great esteem. I have layed the way for engaging him to be your freind. Yow will not, I hope, doubt of my Lord Chancellor,³ nor the Thesaurer⁴ my Lord Lawderdaill will not play the courtier with yow. I have now in readines the draught of a presentation for yow, which I will without faile send up by to-morroue's poast, and I doubt not of a speedie and good account therof, though I wish ther be nothing spoken of it to any befor it come doun. I am sure, befor my coming from London, yow had the King's word for it, which I trust he will not alter. It is necessarie yow come, within eight or ten dayes, to this place, to pay your respects from your Universitie to his Majestie's Commissionar, then we shall have opportunity to commune about your visitation. The late Act of your Synod, to my apprehension, and of the brethren heer, was unseasonable, and will doe more harm then good, it scapes not the construction of imprudencie and unhandsomenes putt upon it, at the least. I have not yet seen your peece yow sent to Mr. Dickson. I was pressed to preach the last Lord's day⁵ to the Parliament, of which I hear variety of reports are spread, which will be increased by the foolishnes of the diurnall maker; but I know yow will allow me charity till yow speak with me. Yow see how I scrible; I make no doubt of your coming hither, and therfor shall adde no more, but commending yow to the grace of Chrift, I am,

Your's,

JA SHARP

[FOR MR. ROBERT BAILLIE.⁶]

REVEREND AND WORTHIE FREIND,

To convince yow once more that yow was too credulous in beleeving that I was dealing for Mr. Gilespie, receave the inclosed paper, which indeed

---

² John Earl of Middleton.   ³ William Earl of Glencairne.
⁴ John Earl of Craufurd and Lindsay
⁵ On the 6th January 1661, which serves to fix the date of this letter
⁶ From the original (Wodrow MSS Folio Vol xlix. No 7) the address is not preserved.

is all that I have done in favors of Mr. Patrick. But such reports are now no ftrangers to me Every week I finde, by letters from Edinburgh, that I am reported there to be the great agent for my Lord Argyll, a calumnie as fals as the former; but I am fo hardend with twentie forts of lyes, which I heare are vented of me there, that they make little impreffion on me. By God's grace, I fhall ftudy to fery my gratious Mafter and my Countrey faithfully, let idle men talke, and others beleev what they pleafe; it fhall little trouble me This paper fhould have comd long agoe, if I had fooner gotten a copie of a prefentation. His Majeftie gratioufly promifed it at his firft coming, and readily figned it the other day. So to him yow owe all the thankes. I can onely fay for my felf, that I fhall ever be ready to witnes to yow that I forget not old freindfhip, and that I am, in the old manner,

SIR,

Your moft affectionate freind to ferv yow,

Whitehall, 24th January 1661. LAUDERDAILL.

[WARRANT OF THE KING'S PRESENTATION TO MR. ROBERT BAILLIE AS PRINCIPAL OF THE UNIVERSITY OF GLASGOW.]

CHARLES R

OUR Sovereign Lord taking into confideration that, fince the death of Dr. John Strang, late Principall of the Colledge of Glafgow, the faid Colledge hath been without a Principall, and that the intrufion of Mr. Patrick Gilleſpie into that place, in thefe late tymes of Ufurpation, hath been no fmall prejudice and detriment thereunto, and being very fenfible how neceffarie it is for the good education of youth, and the flourifhing of pietie and learning therein, that this place be filled with a man able and well qualified for difcharging thereof, and knowing well that MR ROBERT BAILLIE, Profeffor of Divinitie there, is a fitt and well-qualified perfon for this employment · Therefore his Majeftie ordains a Letter to be made, paft, and expede, under his Highnefs Privie Seall of his Kingdome of Scotland, nominating, prefenting, and appointing, likeas by thefe his Majeftie nominates, prefents, and appoints the faid Mr ROBERT BAILLIE, during all the dayes of his naturall lifetime, to be Principall of the College of Glafgow, giving, granting, and difponing, likeas his Majeftie by thefe, gives, grants, and difpones to the faid Mr. Robert the ftipend, fees, profites, emoluments, cafualties, with the priviledges, liberties, and immunities belonging, knowen, and accuftomed thereunto formerly to belong; with full power to him to afk, crave, uplift, receive, intromet with, brook, joife, ufe and difpone thereupon at his pleafure, all and every the famen, ficklike as freely and fully in all refpects as any other Princıpall of the faid Colledge has, might, or ought to have done heretofore Heirby requiring the Moderators of the Univerfitie of Glafgow, with all convenient diligence after fight hereof, to enter, admitt, and receive to this imployment the faid Mr. ROBERT BAILLIE, and that the faid Letter be further extended in the beft, due, and ample forme, with all claufes needfull and in fuch cafes accuftomed.

Given at our Court at Whitehall the 23d day of Januar, in the year of our Lord one thoufand fix hundred fixty and one, and of our reigne the twelfth year

MAY IT PLEASE YOUR MAJESTY,

This contains your Majeftie's nomination and prefentation of MR. ROBERT BAILLIE to the place of Principall of the Colledge of Glafgow for all the dayes of his life, with the ftipend, priviledges, profits, and cafualities belonging to the fame.

LAUDERDAILL.

[FOR MR. WILLIAM SPANG.]

COUSIN,

I LONG much now to hear how it goes with yow and your familie, and what is become of Dr. Stiang's book, for it is long fince I have heard from yow. As yow defired, and as my cuftome is, I give yow here ane account of our affaires fince my laft long letter; though yow readilie know all, yet it's not unfitt yow fhould know our fenfe and conception of them alfo We expected this year for great quietnefs at home, and for troubles abroad; but God, who governs all, has much difappointed both our hopes and fears, making farre more confufion at home, and quietnefs abroad, than was expected.

When the Portugalls had defeat the Spanish army at Elvas, and Turein had possessed so many places in the midst of Flanders; the English being master of Dunkirk, and, with their navie on the coast of Spaine, scarring the plate-fleet from comeing home; the Suede being ready to swallow up Denmark, and thereafter, with his French and Dutch friends, to fall on the Emperour, a child, the prosperous fight of Ragotsi, of the Venetians, and the Bassa of Aleppo, increasing the tumults in Constantinople. These things made us expect great changes abroad; but before we were aware the scales turned; France in the midst of his victories stopped, on what true motive we cannot dreame; his allyance with his cousin of Spaine seemed not so desireable, the Lady being so farr in years beyond the King, and no great matter for tocher offered, as we can hear. How Piementillie, who cheated the poor Queen of Sueden out of her religion, her kingdome, and reputation, should have gotten the Cardinal of France so farre inchanted as to lay down armes, when they most prospered, we marvell, and wait for the end. In the meantyme, Spaine has gotten tyme to breath, the riches of his safe-landed fleet; the death of Modena; the discontent of Savoy for the French refuse of his sister, after the interview at Lions, Archduke Sigismund [in] readiness to march to Flanders with the Imperiall army; the changes in England drawing our thoughts home for the time; the Pope's obstinate adherence still to the Spanish against the Portugall; the Queen of Spain's two sons has put that old languishing King once again on his feet, your States beating of the Suedish navie, the King's repulses from his too furious and unreasonable assaults of Copenhagen; the Imperiall, Brandeburgish, and Polish armie, falling on Pomer; the Dutch league of Colen, Mentz, and others, making no diversion; France lying off, the English navie's goeing home, makes the valour of Sueden to be overpowred, and all doubtfull of the event; for we doe not expect any agreement of Denmark without all his confederates, and that they never will put Denmark in the poor terms of Roskill's capitulation. However, the fearfull ruining of all Denmark's countrie, and the stopping of Sweden in all his designes through the strong armies leagued against him, seems to be the work chiefly of your States, on some reasons of their own, more than yet are visible to the world. We bless God, that lesse blood is shed in these bounds than we feared: we are sorie for the ruining of the Prince of Holsten and Courland; the Turks also seem to be in a much better condition; the Perfian invafion of Babylon being a mere fable; the Baffa of Aleppo and all his partie ruined; Ragotfi put to depend on the Emperor for a fubfiftence; the Vizier, by fea, putting in Candy what men he will, the Mufcoviters victories againft the Tartars and Cofaks being of no confequence: So, where we expected a quick overturning of ftates and impires in a fhort time, affaires are fo turned about, that what was fhakeing is more firmly eftablifhed.

But with us all contrare our very firm-like foundations in a moment overturned. The Protector Oliver indeavouring to fettle all in his familie, was prevented by death before he could make a teftament. He had not fupplied the blank with his fon Richard's name by his hand, and fcarce with his mouth could he declare that much of his will; there was no more witneffes of it but Secretary Thurloe and Thomas Goodwin Some did fearfully flatter him as much dead as living. Thomas Goodwin, at the faft before his death, in his prayer, is faid to have fpoken fuch words: " Lord, we pray no for thy fervant's life, for we know that is granted, but to hafte his health, for that thy people cannot want." And Mr. Sterne, in the chapell after his death,—" O Lord, thy late fervant here is now at thy right hand, making interceffion for the fins of England " Both thefe are now out of favour at court as courtparafites. But the moft fpoke, and yet doe fpeak, very evill of him; and, as I think, much worfe than he deferved of them. His buriall was large as magnifick as any King of England Richard immediately fate downe on his chyre, and, after a moft folemn inftalment, got addreffes almoft from all the fhyres, cities, regiments of the armies in England, Scotland, Ireland, Dunkirk, from the navy, from the miniftrie, Prefbyterian, Independent, and Anabaptiftick, all ftriveing who fhould be firft and moft promifeing All neighbour-ftates of France, Holland, Sweden, Denmark, Brandeburgh, Hamburgh, Portugall, congratulating his fucceffion. No appearance of the fmalleft air of oppofition, till the officers of the armie did begin to petition for a Generall, and payment of their arrears. For their fatiffaction a Parliament was fummoned againft the 27th of January. This did meet frequently. fome fay it was prettie well chofen, of men who for the moft had good defignes for the publict, and aimed at a folid fettlement both of Church and State; but among them were many for contrare defignes The firft fencing was about the Act of recognition for albeit, at the entry in the Houfes, every one took the oath in the humble Petition and Advyce; yet when it came to an Act of recognition, many and sharp debates arose. It was carried to acknowledge Richard for Protector; but withall, that the Bill could not passe till the limitations of his power, the full securitie of the priviledges of Parliaments, and libertie of the subjects, should passe in the same Act. A committee was appointed for that work, and Sir Harie Vaine sett in the chaire The House of Lords also did passe; but in a poor and slighting way of ane other House.

In the meantime, Opdam, with the Holland fleet, passed to the Sound. All was alarmed with this; and in a very short time the Protector, with the consent of all, sent Montagu with as great a fleet, to wait upon them All did expect a present breach betwixt us and yow; but since your fleet did nothing but supplie Copenhagen with some men and victuals, and did not transport any of the confederate army to raise the siege; it seems the English and Holland instructions have been, not to fight, and so to do but little service to either partie all this long summer. Whether yow will do so still, when the English are returned, we will shortly see.

The Parliament's nixt work was about pay to the Armie This was a business, and yet is, almost inextricable. The land-armies in Scotland, England, Ireland, Flanders, and Jamaica, with the navie, reckoning every frigot of fourtie guns to a regiment of foote, could not be within a hunder thousand men of daily pay, the revenue, all being exactly counted, did not amount to nyneteen hunder thousand pound sterling; the necessare charge of the Armie and State was above twenty-two hunder thousand; it was no marvell then that the arrears of the armie should exceed twenty-five hunder thousand, and the Protector's debt many hunder thousand pounds also. How all this should be payed without the countrie's ruine, was the Parliament's great care. While they are about this, the officers of the army have their daily meetings, in Fleetwood's lodging or Wallingfurd-house. The Anabaptistick and Republican partie had, by many papers, which now are printed, been secretly, for a long tyme, plying Fleetwood and the officers in conscience, to returne to their first principles, to overthrow Oliver's selfie innovations, to abolish the other House, and all government by one, under whatsomever name. The Parliament finding these popular addresses take much with the officers, and that such meetings on such high consultations could not stand with their authoritie, refolved an Act for diffolving the meeting of Wallingfurd-houfe, and to command all officers to attend their feverall charges in the three Kingdomes, and to take an oath of obedience to the prefent Parliament While the other Houfe is advyfing on that vote, the Protector joyns with it, and accordingly commands the officers to be gone to their charges. He and the Houfe fuppofed that they had fo great a partie of the armie and citie for them, that there was no hazard of any force : but they fand themfelves quicklie miftaken ; for the officers, with all fpeed, making a randivous at the back of St. James's Park, in the Pell Mell, at eleven a'clock at night, before the Protector had provided any thing for oppofition, they came immediately to Whithall, and made the Protector confent, under the Great Seall, not to the adjourning, (which at firft would have fatiffied,) but the diffolution of the Parliament To this moft hardly he did confent, but his uncle Difbrough, and brother Fleetwood, drew him to it with firme promifes of the armie's readinefs ftill to ferve him When the officers faw the Parliament fo eafily diffolved they fand themfelves unfecure, till, contrare to Fleetwood and Difbrough's mind, they made the Protector lay downe his place, and took, for a tyme, the government of all into their own hand. To this alfo the Protector did quietly fubmitt, and, from a very great Prince, did defcend to a very private and quiet gentleman. The officers immediately put down the Councell of State ; removed out of the armie all the Protector's confidents ; the regiments of the Protector, Ingolfby, Whalley, Goff, Falconbridge, Howard, and others, were given to Lambert, Overtoun, Okey, and fuch whom Oliver had outed The Tower was taken from Barkfted, the Great Seall from Nat. Fynes, and a ftrange change made. But the officers were quickly wearie of the burden of the government After much advyfement, they fell on a very unexpected overture, to fet down with a Parliamentary power, fo many of the Long Parliament that remained uncaft out, when the Protector, in the year 1652, had diffolved them Of thefe they fand in the citie and about it, about fourtie ; whom, with Lenthall, their fpeaker, they moved to fit downe in the houfe, the fixth of May ; who fince that time hes ruled as a Parliament At the very firft all the Armie's propofalls paft in Acts of parliament : A Councell of State of threttie-one was conftitute All this was done without any dinne, except what Mr. Prin and fome other fharp pamphleteers made ; which they mifregarded For the citie of London, the moft of all the regiments in the three nations, did fend them congratulatorie addreffes, fo full of good words as ever were made to either of the Cromwells; whofe names by many were then teared in the worft language, pictures, and pamphlets, that could be. Some fturr was expected from Henry [Cromwell] in Ireland, Monck in Scotland, and fome other of the Protector's friends, but all came to juft nothing.

The new old Parliament's firft and chief work was to conftitute the armie. A committee of nomination was to nominate everie officer in every regiment, the crouner, lieutenant, major, every captain, enfigne, etc. All thefe were appointed to come to the barre of the Houfe, to receave their new commiffions, and make their oath there to the Parliament. This was a long and fafhious work, and is not yet ended. Many officers were left out without any accufation Nothing in this was the work of the Generall, which many took for a flighting of him. The armie indured all this as coming from the hands of their trufty friends; but an other work of the Parliament ftartled them more, the eftablifhing of the militia of the counties in fuch hands as the Parliament nominat: thefe went, if complete, to the number of twenty thoufand horfe, and four-fcore thoufand foot, to be paid by the counties when they were in fervice. This was a vifible curb to the Armie's power, and a hazard to their pay. for the countrie was unable to pay both But it feems this countrie-militia was but for a tyme

While thefe things are in doeing, there arife a generall mifcontent among the people every where in England, which bred a confpiracie in many fhyres, to take armes at feverall rendevoufes, the 18th of Auguft. But before the 1ft of Auguft, all was revealed · Maffey, Titus, and others, from the King, were faid to have been for diverfe moneths at work in the citie and countrie to make a pairtie. The chief ftickling was where leaft expected, in Cheffhyre and Lancafhyre. Sir George Booth had drawn the moft of the people after him The report of this thing flew every where, and increafed the number and ftrength of the confpirators hugelie above truth, for when it came to the proof, they were found unconfiderable. Fleetwood and the militia of London, keeped down the citie, the rifeing whereof was moft feared. A few old troupes and the new militia of the fhyres did preveene, and eafilie fupprefle, the rendevoufes in Kent, Hartfordfhire, Glocefterfhire, Notinghame, Derby, Leicefter, Shropfhire, and other places Lambert, with four or five thoufand horfe and foot, making a quick march northward, did meet with Sir George Booth at a bridge fome myles from Chefter· his ten thoufand horfe were become towards two thoufand horfe and foot; the difpute was nought fcarce half an houre, Sir George had not threttie killed, and Lambert hardly one. Chefter, Manchefter, Prefton, Liverpool, randred on the firft fummons; Sir George fleeing towards London, in women's apparell, was taken at Newport-Pennell [Pagnel], the Earl of Derby in Shrewfburry. in a very few dayes all wes compefcit without blood Sir George Booth's confeffions, they fay, are fo liberall, that manie talks he hes been but ane emiffarie of purpofe to difcover who were difaffected to the Parliament, to have them crufhed; but others, who know the gravitie of the gentleman, and confiders his declaration, doe not believe neither this, nor his rumoured confeffions. At the firft, many of the Prefbyterian minifters in the city and country, was faid to be on this plot, but this lykewayes appears now to be a vaine report. Ere long, doubtlefs, we will hear of all the bottome of the bufinefs; for the tyme we know no more but what the Diurnall tells us.

So foone as this was over, the armie was carefull to caufe the Parliament diffolve, and pay off the countrey-militia, that it might not ftand when there was no more ufe of it than to be a vifible curb to them Yet the people's generall mifcontentment remains. for though the decay of trade hes increafed the povertie of the countrie, yet the neceffities of the armie and navie increafes the taxations very much, nor is yet any government eftablifhed. The Parliament and army agree againft all monarchie, whether of Kings or Protectors, and againft the Houfe of Lords; but what forme of Republick to fettle, this they differ on. Some are for the perfeverance, if not perpetuitie, of this part of the old Parliament that now fitts; others for a new Parliament of Commons, chofen according to the qualifications which this Parliament fhall agree upon; others for a Parliament of two or three thoufand of the people, with a coordinat power of a Senate, to be a check on the peoples extravagancie: what of thefe fhall be determined we expect to hear. Some think that difference in the Parliament, not like to be agreed Prevalencie of the Quakers and Fifth-monarchy men fo farr, that they have obtained James Naylor, that monftrous blafphemer, out of prifon; and have moved fome wife Prefbyterians, Independents, and more fober Anabaptifts, to fyncretifme againft their danger, will force the armie once more to raife the Parliament, and fupplicat

Lambert, a very wife, ftout, active, fober, gentleman, to take the government upon him: but what will be the end of all, we refeir it to God

Scotland's condition for the tyme is not good. exhauft in money; dead in trade; the taxes near doubled, fince the fixth of May without all law, nor appearance of any in hafte. My Lord Wariftoun was called to the Houfe of Peers by the laft Protector: when the Parliament was diffolved, his old friend, Sir Henry Vaine, got him in the Councell of State, and the moft ordinare chairman thereof all the weight of Scots affairs lyes on him alone. Argyle, though he went thither a Commiffioner for Aberdeenfhyre, and fat in the Houfe of Commons, complying with the Protector fo long as he ftood, and with the new Parliament fo much as any defired, yet was mifregarded; and for fear of arreiftment for debt, flipped away home with fmall credit or contentment. The reft of the Scots commiffioners, Swinton, Garfland [Garthland], Major Barclay, Earle of Lithgow, Earle of Tweddale, etc, comply as they pleafed, did fignifie little thing; but Wariftoun was all. He was made to believe that our union would be a fhort bufinefs; and that it was better to want law than for to have it before the union: but that conceit lies made us want the Summer Seffion, and may be the Winter too; for the debates of the union grew fo long, that they fay it's laid afide till they have agreed once on the government of England, to which we are to be united. No man pays any debt but of his own accord That which much retarded our union, was a petition from many hands in our countrie, put on by Garfland, young Dundas, our Quakers, and many others, for a full tolleration to be infert in the act of our union. This was fo well backed by fome of the officers of the armie, that till it be fatiffied, nothing can be gotten done, though Warrifton doe his uttermoft againft it.

Upon fufpicion that fome in Scotland might be on the Englifh plot, the Generall called all who had been in armes, and were under bands, to take a new oath, of renouncing the Stewarts, and adhereing to the prefent government· Who refufed were laid up in prifons; Montrofe, Calendar, Lorne, Selkirk, Kenmure, Didup, Loudoun, David Lefley, Sir James Lumfden, and others. Some took it, as Glencarne, and, as they fay, Rothes, Montgomerie, etc.: but it's thought there was no Scots flefh on this defigne, whether becaufe not trufted, or not defired by the Englifh, who would doe it all their alone, is not known; but, however, it's thought none of our nation were upon it.

What was talked of Kinnoul and General Major Montgomerie, landing in our Hielands wes found a mere fable. Our people are so ill bitten, and so exceedingly low, that though there were no garrisons to hold them downe, they have neither a mind nor abilitie to make any noife.

Our Church lyes as it was, full of grief, for inward divifions, and outward hazard. As yet the Englifh troubles us not : and truly they have no caule ; for, whatever be our thoughts, yet in all expreffions we are fo quiet and peaceable as they could wifh Being afrayed for Wariftoun's unceffant defignes, the brethren of Edinburgh moved Mr. Sharp to goe up again to attend his motions. The Protector Richard took very weell with him and fundry members of Parliament ; but when thefe were put down, Warrifton deferred him to the Councell, as correfponding with Maffey and Titus. Being upon this called to the Councell, Sir Harie Vaine and Mr. Scot were fent out to conferr with him, to whom he gave abundant fatiffaction, and a little after was fent home in peace

The paffages of our laft Synod of Glafgow, you may read in my letter to Mr. Dowglafs ; and of our Colledge, in my letter to Mr. Sharp. Mr. Gillefpie, by Secretary Thurloe, had procured from the Protector Richard a patent, commanding us, out of our rents, old and new, to adde yearly to Mr Gillefpie's former ftipend, a hundred pound fterling yearly, upon three very untrue narratives. 1. That he was not fufficiently provided, while he had a hundred and threttie pound, which is more than any Principall hes in Scotland. 2. That the Colledge rent could weell bear it ; while as now, it does not pay our ftipends and table till the year after. 3. That the labour of his charge was extraordinar, while he does as good as nothing in his proper charge, but goes about buildings, pleas, and journeyes, all the year over We thought neither law nor reafon would bear throw that procured patent, and all were difpleafed with it ; yet fince I was to plead nothing before the Englifh, and knew no other would, I was content he fhould have the thing, [1] Upon condition, he held out the narratives ; 2 That it fhould be out only of our new rents of his procurement ; 3. That he fhould paffe from his former gift of the half of the augmentations of Galloway ; 4 That this his gift fhould not be for his fucceffor. On this a write was drawn, and all fubfcryved ; but herein I was offended, that when he defired the by-runs of the augmentations of Galloway paffing from them in time to come, and we granted his defire; in the very firft article, he put in the teinds of Staplegortoun, which came to two thoufand eight hundred pound, which wes to him one thoufand four hundred pound, at this I ftormed, that compofition being obtained in Dr. Strang's tyme, though formallie clofed after his coming, and long agoe fpent. From this he paffed; yet, by debts and compofitions made, thefe bygone augumentations amounts to above two thoufand merks, the half whereof he took. We would have been glad he had refted here; but his nixt motion was, to pull down the whole forework of the Colledge, the high Hall, and Arthurlie, very good houfes, all newly dreffed at a great charge I was very grieved at this not only totallie needlefs but hurtfull motion, and got the moft of our number to be in my mind, though he offered to get it builded without any coft to the Colledge, out of the remainder of Mr Zacharie Boyd's mortification, eight thoufand merks in my Lord Loudoun's hands, the vacancies of kirks, and other means he would procure. All this fatiffied no diverfe of us, yet warring us by Mr John Young's vote, we behooved to let it goe. I reafoned much for a delay, till in the next fpring we had gotten fome money, and faw how the world would goe; but all in vain: prefentlie the Hall was pulled down. All fince, I think, repent their rafhnefs, and all beholders cry out on us. This year and the next our Colledge will lye open; want of law makes us void of money, yet now we muft goe on by our private borrowings, and any other way he can invent. I am now more ready to further it than any who voted to it, for we cannot now let it lye. Another of his notions has alfo fafhed us · we expected great things of the Deanrie and Subdeannie of Hamilton, all came to four or fyve chalder of victual, but he took a conceit of the great advantage to buy the benefice, and beftow on it eighteen thoufand merks. We had fourteen thoufand merks of burfar-money, there would be two or three thoufand of by-run dueties, and we behoved to borrow the reft; to this alfo we confented, but not very willinglie, for fear of clampers in the end The bargain yet flicks unperfected He appointed a new factor to take up the bygones, of the readieft, his wife following him to London, a thoufand merks, as he had done another when he went. Our order is, that our ftipends fhould be payed to all men proportionablie; but when he had that two thoufand merks, there was not a groat to give any man of that year's ftipend, the half whereof was due at January 1ft, and the other at July 1ft.

We were afraid he would do much harme to our Church and Town when he came to London; yet we hear not what he has performed Finding the weight of living there on his own charges, he wrote to our Rector to fee if we would defyre him to ftay on our affaires. We underftood that this did import twenty fhillings fterling a day to him from the Colledge, from what day to what day he pleafed; alfo, we conceived that all our gifts, which concerned none of us but himfelf, which then were fallen, would eafily be gotten renewed by his miffives to his great friends; all of us, therefore, did refufe to fend him any defyre to ftay. This he took very ill, profeffing great content that he was free of the burden of attending our bufinefs, but grieved that we mifregarded our bufinefs fo far as not to have fent up fome other of our number to wait on it. He went up and came down with my Lady Swinton in her coatch. What will be his next defigne we know not, but I think we will not be long a-hearing it.

Our Toune has been in more peace than formerly. Mr Gillefpie's four months abfence, want of publick judicatories has helped to it; but no good will in fome is inlacking to keep in the fire. The laft trick they have fallen on, to ufurp the Magiftracie, is, by the diligence of their feffioners to make factions in every craft, to get the deacons and deacon-convener created of their fide, and herein they have much prevailed. but with fuch ftrife as fometimes it has come to ftrokes: but this lent-way does no fatiffie. It's feared, by Wariftoun's diligence, fome orders fhall be procured by Mr. Gillefpie, to have all the Magiftrates and Counfell chofen as he will. Thefe in place has guided the toune fo moderately and wifely, that none are expected to doe it better: notwithftanding of their hudge charge to defend themfelves againft Mr. Gillefpie's pleas, they have ftill keeped the towne free of all taxes, when all our other burghs are wracked with them They have builded a fair meal-market, which has been near three thoufand merks; a fair bridge at Colin's port, whilk will be above one thoufand merks; a very fair merchant-hofpitall, near the bridge, which will be a great foume, and is moft done by contribution. Their loffe of Mr. George Young[1] was very fad to them; he was wife and active, and very watchful for their good, keeped them at peace among themfelf, prevented and crufhed many defignes of their oppofites, fet them

[1] Mr George Young was brought from Mauchline, in 1644 to be one of the ministers of Glasgow

upon many things for their own good. He preached on March 20th with his ordinar health, only he had a cold, which encreafed upon him, and made him take his bed with fome fever, which grew ftill with a great defluxion, wherewith he was chocked, being hale in all his noble parts, and in vigour enough, he fpoke but little, but very well and gracioufie, and expired without paine on the Saturday March 26th, the fixty-firft of his age, with the great regrate of all, except the faction to whom he ever profeffed oppofition. He was one of the beft and kindeft friends I had. For the provideing of his place there has been much dinn, and like to be more. The Magiftrates, Town Councell, and all the parifh, who are confiderable, did choice Mr. James Ferguffon, but the feffion choice Mr. John Liviftoune as one moft active for their partie, wife and powerfull with the Englifh. Mr John Carftares's fuperlative praifes of him, in his preaching and prayers, were according to his manner exceffive. At the intimation of his call the parifh and magiftrates protefted, but they went on, and fent to invite him from prefbyterie and feffion; but the town and parifh fent to intreat him not to come, on the reafons of their proteftation. His anfwers to both were but coldife; yet the great diligence that is ufed with him, by the chief of the party, may make him to come. If his Synod loufe him, which readilie they will, for any oppofition of magiftrat or people he will not regard it, who diverfe times has admitted others contrare to the mind of feffion, prefbyterie, fynod, and all. We will fhortlie fee the end.

Mr Ralph Rodger, for all his averfnefs, his Prefbyterie's determining him to ftay, and our Town's proteftation, yet on the Synod's act is come; and if he goe on as he has begun, will be as fober and profitable minifter here as any they have. Mr Francis Aird, whom they would have had, is dead fhortlie of a feaver in five or fix dayes. Mr David Veitch, one of the ableft of our prefbyterie, minifter of Govan, having preached on the Sunday, was buried before the next; fo unhappie is it to fucceed depofed men. In Decerfe [Dalferf] poor Mr. John Hamilton was put out, I know no for what: his two fucceffors, good men, Mr John Weir and Mr. Francis Aird, did both die unexpectedlie. Mr Wilham Wilkie, I thought, was unjuftlie put out of Govan, albeit his very evill carriage fince has declared more of his fins, yet both his fucceffors, Mr. Hew Binny [Binning], and Mr David Veitch, died in their youth. Mr. John Crichtoun was too juftlie depofed from Paflay, yet his fucceffor, Mr. Colvert, was fuddenlie overtaken with a palfie and died; and Mr. Alexander Dunlop is fo gone with the fcrubie, that he is not like to live long. I have a long catalogue of fuch fad examples I believe guiltie men, of crimes deferving depofition, ought not to be fpared, but the violence of fundrie perfuing their brethren without reafon, I never did approve

Sundrie heavie accidents have latelie fallen out amongft us Baillie Walkinfhaw's moft prettie boy of four or five years old, on a Sunday afternoon, fell down his ftair, and fpoke no more, but died Thomas Brown, late baillie, having fupped, lay down and died before midnight Thomas Main, our factor, at his breakfaft weel, while he ftretcht out his hand to the cup, is fuddenlie overtaken with a palfie; fpoke no more, but in a day or two dies. Thomas Robifon, in Salcots, fitting at his own fire-fide, is ftobbed to death by a highlandman, put upon him by Pennimor to get his goods to his fon who had married Robifon's daughter. A daughter of Mr Archbald M'Lauchlane, minifter at Luffe, a widow, a very weell-favoured woman, being found in the act of bafe adulterie with William Watfon, and William Hume, was put in the tolbooth where fhe hanged herfelf Janet Hiegat in Falkirk, of a lewd life, vexed with a naughtie hufband, did the like.

My Lord Belhaven, without any example I ever heard of in Scotland, with his Ladie a very wittie woman's advyce, did faine death, and for feven yeares was taken by all for dead, yet now appears againe fafe and found in his own houfe. He was much ingadged for Duke Hamilton: fearing the creditors might fall on his perfon and eftate, and knowing, if he were reputed dead, his wife, by conjunct-fie and otherwayes, would keep his eftate; he went, with his brother and two fervants, towards England Thefe returned, affirming, that in Solway Sands my Lord was caried downe by the river, and they could no refcue him. His horfe and his hatt they got, but when all fearch was made, his bodie could not be found. His Ladie and friends made great dool for him, and none controverts his death [2] In the mean time he goes beyond London and farmes a piece of ground, and lives very privatelie there. He had but one boy, a verie hopefull youth,

[2] Sir John Hamilton of Broomhill, raifed to the peerage by the title of Lord Belheven and Stenton, 15th December 1647. The above incident is alfo narrated with fome additional particulars, by John Nicol, who states that Lord Belhaven was abfent for six years, and returned to Scotland

and prettie fcholler; God ftrikes him with a fever, as his Mother faid, but, as others, with a fall from a horfe, whereof in a few dayes he dies. In this reall death, by God's hand, who will no be mocked, the hope of that houfe perifhed So foon as the Duke's debt was fatiffied by felling his own lands, the fecret journies of my Lord to his own houfe were efpied, and fo much talked of, that he now at laft appears in publict, for his great difrepute; and though he difpofes of his eftate to his good-fon Sillertoun[3] after his death, yet many think both their eftates will goe.

There has been a great plague amongft the horfe in all Britain, to the death of many thoufands of the beft What yow inquire of the apparition in Galloway is notourlie known. In Glenlufs parifh, in John Campbell a webfter's houfe, for two or three yeares a fpirit did whiles caft ftones, oft fire the houfe, and cut the webs in the looms, yet did never any confiderable harme. The man was a good, pious, refolut man, and never left his houfe for all; fundrie minifters of the Prefbyterie did keep fafting and praying in the houfe without moleftation, fometyme it fpoke, and the minifter, Mr. John Scot, was fo wife as to intertain large difcourfes with it. It were long to write all the paffages: this twelvemoneth it has been filent. A fturdie beggar who had been a moft wicked and avowed atheift, for which he was hanged at Dumfreis, did oft lodge in that houfe; about his death it became more quiet, yet thereafter it became troublefome enough, but for the time is filent There is much witcherie up and downe our land; though the Englifh be but too fpareing to try it, yet fome they execute.

For myfelf, bleffed be God, I am weell My laft yeare's fitting in a riven chamber, gave a fwelling and tinging in my bellie which yet remains. I have no pain, yet it makes me lumpifh, and unwilling to travell Harie is well and ftudies. My daughter Lilias lives weell in Aire, and hes heired Kildonel [Kildonan] with a fine boy I maried my ftep-daughter the other moneth to Mr Robert Watfon, minifter at Cardroffe, a young man of verie good reputation. My daughter Helen is almoft a woman: Elizabeth and Mary are growing faft up in grace and ftature. My youngeft, Margaret, Dr Strang's oye. is a very prettie quick child of two years old. I blefs the Lord in thefe evill dayes I get leave to lurk within our precinct; except on the Sabbath to church, goeing very rarely any where abroad.

[3] Sir Robert Hamilton of Silvertonhill.

My defire is that it may be weell with yow, your kind wife, and all your children. Our coufin, good Nanie Gibfon, had a felt gravel ending in a hulcer; it created her great pain, till in a moneth or two it took her away. A daughter of Ja. Tran, of a great ftone, but after a yeare's great pain, of late expired her hufband and his parents were doggitly unkind to the young woman, though a good one, of a good portion. Caftelmilk, a good meek gentleman, near fourfcore, healthy all his dayes, fitting down weell to breakfaft, prefently fell downe in a found, and died in a few houres. John Gibfon of Clayflop, a vigorous old man of eighty yeares, going home from Glafgow on foot, fteps in to Matthew Colquhoun's for a mutchkin of wine, while he is drinking it at table, falls down and dies immediately. John Herbertfon long weak in his chamber, yet on the bonefire-night fupped, drank the King's health, and within an hour died unexpectedly. Mr Gavin Hamilton, late minifter of Cader, was abroad on the Thurfday, on Fryday all day up, but died ere midnight.

This farr had I written with my former long letter much of a year agoe, but it lay befide me, that I might fee fome fettling of thefe extraordinar and happie changes, which the hand of God, above all humane hope or reafon, hes wrought its alone. After Sir George Booth's defeat, all did almoft defpaire of human help for our evills. I heard fweet Balcarras at the Hague did die of grief for that calamitie;[1] his bodie his lady brought home, and caufed burie honourablie at his parifh-church: without doubt that was one of the moft brave and able gentlemen of our nation, if not the moft able. I am not yet fatiffied with Chancellor Hydes very unjuft breaking of his neck · God will fee to it. · It was the Parliament's work, efpecially Vane, Hafilrig, and Scot, to fearch out all the complices of Sir George Booth; and doubtlefs, if God had not, in anfwer to the prayers of the choice minifters and people of Lancafhyre, given them fomewhat elfe to doe, they had made much execution of many good and honeft men. But behold, when they are running to fuck this blood and fpoile, the Lord cafts ane other bone in their teeth. The officers which had defeat Sir George, lifted up with that deferving, expected from the Parliament all they could defyre. With this confidence they approach the citie. Many of them fubfcryve a petition, to get all the generall officers eftablifhed, and when this did not weel relifh in the Houfe, (for Hafilrig and

[1] Alexander Second Earl of Balcarras died at Breda 30th Auguft 1659.

Vane were very jealous of Lambert,) they preft it harder: whereupon the Houfe, trufting to the late oaths of obedience from all the officers, makes bold to cafheir Lambert, Afhfield, Cobbet, and diverfe others. Upon this affront, the officers went to the Houfe, and with threats diffolved them In this new confufion, all was put to a ftand, not knowing what to doe. a judiciall blindnefs fell among them: all were malcontent, and raifed in mind to expect and defire a change; but none durft venture on any more action

Our Noblemen, very fecretly, moft by the mediation of the Lady Weims, a wittie active woman, whofe daughter Buccleugh[5] was in Monck's cuftodie, at Dalkeith, did oft folicit him to attempt for the King; but doubts and feares ftill keeped him off. yet when Hafilrig and others had importuned him from England to affift the Parliament againft the violence of Lambert and his partie, he called the moft of the armie to draw near to Edinburgh He fent for Commiffioners from every one of our fhyres, and defired them to advance fix moneths maintenance. Though this in our deep povertie was almoft to us unfeafible, yet on good hopes, it was cheerfully and quickly done He had of his owne above fiftie thoufand pound fterling, which helped him to give good fatiffaction to his fojors, while the armie in England was put to live on free quarter, all the fhyres refufeing to pay any more money till a free Parliament did command it. There went a ftrong Remonftrance amongft the moft fhyres, againft an arbitrary fword-government and all taxes, till a free Parliament; but to fugar it, there were two claufes put in, one againft the Stewarts and all Monarchie, ane other for full libertie of confcience to all Sectaries. This encouraged Monck to declare to the officers of the armie at London, his defires of a free Parliament. This did much ftartle them; and when many papers had paft among them, and Monck continued refolute to march into England for that end, Fleetwood fent down to him Mr. Caryll, Colonell Whalley, Goff, and his brother-in-law Dr. Clargis. Thefe wrought him to a treatie, for which he fent three of his officers to London, Cloberry, Wilks, and Knight: thefe were fo laboured on by their friends, that they made an accord, and fubfcryved it. But Monck being more and more encouraged both from Scotland and England, and having purged his army from Cobbett, Young,

---

[5] Mary Countess of Buccleugh in her own right, the greatest heiress then in Scotland, married, in the 11th year of her age, Walter Scot of Highchester, who was created Earl of Tarras in 1660 She died without issue in 1661

Sorrie, Holmes, and many Anabaptifts, filling their places with a number of Scottifh old fojors, he refufed that accord as done contrare to his inftructions. Finding him grow in refolution and ftrength, they fent to the north Lambert with five thoufand of their beft horfe, and fome three or four thoufand foot, with which he came to Newcaftle on free quarter. Monck came to Berwick in the mids of December, and lay on the fields in a very cold winter, near Caldftreim, with fix or feven thoufand good foot, and within two thoufand horfe. Many of our Noblemen came to him at Berwick, and offered to raife quickly for his fervice all the power of Scotland; but the moft of his officers refuifed it, fearing the ftumbling of their armie and friends in England; for as yet all of them, in their right-weell penned papers, did declare as pofitively as ever, with divine atteftations, againft all Kings and Monarchie, and for a free Parliament, and all former principles. Lambert was the farr ftrongeft, and eafily might have cutted in pieces all Monck's partie, and made havock in our poor land, as they fay it was their purpofe, defigning the chief of our nobles and minifters for the fcaffold, and many minifters for Jamaica, whereof I heard myfelf was one; but bleffed be the Lord who keeped us from their bloody teeth Monck refolved to keep his ground at Caldftreim, and if he were beaten, to retire to Stirling, and take our help Our nobles, by his allowance, but without all ingagement, fent Major Buntein to Breda, where the King was, with his Sifter, in a very hard condition He had gone to Bayonne, conferred with the Cardinall and Du Haro, to gett his intereft confidered in the treatie He got from both courteous words; but, in effect, was by both neglected. Coming back with a perplexed heart, with his brother York, through France and Flanders, to his Sifter at Breda, fcarce tollerat by the States Generall's connivance, to abide in the Prince of Orange's bounds, he is much refrefhed by what he heard from Scotland. About the fame time Broghill and Sir Charles Couts fends Sir Arthure Forbeffe to him from Ireland, and fome from England makes him hopefull of Lambert. This puts him in an uncertaintie to what partie firft he fhould apply himfelf Hyde inclined moft to Lambert; Lauderdaill's letters, and thefe from Scotland advifed to truft Monck or Scotland; however, Ormont inclyned to accept the Irifh offers. All the meffengers he difmiffed kindly, with good anfwers. But in the meane time, Colonell Wotham invited Hafilrig, and fome of the militia of the late Parliament, to Portfmouth, where he commanded. Here, incontinent, forces are gathered, fome four or fyve thoufand men, who march directly to London. The people favoured them rather than their oppofites. But Fleetwood with his forces in the citie, and Defborough with his canon from the Tower, held the citie at under. Yet fo foon as Hafilrig came near with his forces, repoited to be far above the truth, both Fleetwood and Defborough retired, and Hafilrig entered, and incontinent fat downe in the laft Parliament, fent letters to Monck to hafte up, and emitted an act of indemnitie to all who did fubmit. Lambert was not able any longer to keep his people in order, fo retired fpeedilie towards London, and, with Fleetwood and the reft, accepted the act of indemnitie, and retired to their houfes.

On the 1ft January 1660, Monck did march orderly, and at leafure, to London. wherever he came he was received as an angell, bells and bonfires welcomed him. All declared their earneft defires of a free Parliament, and gave him great encouragement to procure it: he was civill to all, but referved himfelf to fee farder. Mr. Dowglafs and Mr. Sharp had been free with him in Scotland; on his letter, Mr. Sharp followed him and overtook him. So foon as he reached London, he was to him the moft wife, faithfull, and happy counfellor he had; and if it had not been for God's affiftance to Mr. Sharp, Monck was diverfe times on the point of being circumveened, or of himfelf to have yielded to deftructive counfells. The Parliament fent two, and the citie three, to meet him at Nottinghame, with many fair words and great honours; but did joyn three with him in commiffion, to curb his power. They had put Vain, Whitelock, and others, out of the Houfe; they were fecure of Fleetwood, Lambert, and the reft of the army; their only fear was Monck. They defired he fhould not bring his army to the citie: he quartered about it, but himfelf came to the Houfe, and got many good words, and gave als many. Sundry fhyres did petition for a new free Parliament. Sundry of the petitioners were laid up for this. Monck at all was filent and ambiguous. There had fitten long in the citie, very fecretly, a committee of two from every fhyre, and four of the citie, advifeing how to caft off the yoke of flaverie. When they fand the rump of the Long Parliament of forty-four to reject the petition of manie fhyres for a new free Parliament, alfo the petition of two hundred and fifty members, unjuftlie by Cromwell caft out, to be readmitted; and all that could be obtained from Hafilrig, who then ruled all, was to fupply the Houfe againft fuch a day with members of many qualifications, which they made, and whereof they would be judges, chiefly that all fhould fwear againft the Stewarts, and all government by one ; the people, almoft defperat, mett in common councell, and voted no more addreffes, nor more payments, till a new free Parliament did fitt. Herewith the Houfe is inradged, and votes the uncitying of London, a cafting down of all their gates, pofts, and chains ; for walls they had none fince Cromwell pulled down their lanes of communication ; the common counfell was abolifhed, and a new one appointed to be chofen. Monck was commanded to fee thefe votes execut, and fo to become moft odious to the people, that the more eafily they might deftroy both. Monck was in a very hard taking, yet did obey ; and the people permitted him patiently to doe all he pleafed : The gates and pofts are pulled down, the common counfell is changed, but behold a prefent change. The fool Hafilrig had wyped the Citie's and Monck's nofe to the blood Monck, by conference with the fecluded members, prefbyterian minifters, and chief citizens, is encouraged to write a fharp letter to the Parliament, of his refentment of their feveritie to the Citie, and dallying with Fleetwood, Lambert, Vaine, Ludlow, and others, though declared againft ; farder, of his owne ingagement to the Citie, that within five dayes they fhould iffue letters for calling a new free Parliament againft the 25th of Aprile.

In the meane tyme, Hafilrig, Scot, and others, did fend many meffages to him; and near had gained him to come out of the Citie, and lye at Whitehall: but Mr. Sharp's night labours here were happy On the 20th of Februar Monck went to the Houfe, and fett down the fecluded members At this the citie and countrie's joy was unexpreffible ; bells and bonefyres every where ; Monck made Captain-General of all forces by fea and land of the three kingdomes, and General-Major of the citie-militia ; Hafilrig, Secretarie Scot, and others of the rump, fneakit away to the countrie ; Lambert and Overtoun were put in the Tower ; a Councell of State of thirty-one, Lewis, Holice, Crewe, Knightton, Peirpoint, and fuch, the Covenant appointed to be hung up in the Houfe, alfo in every church, and to be read folemnly once every year ; Sir George Booth and all his partie were let free ; alfo Lauderdaill, Crawfurd, and all of ours, were freed of their long prifons. Commiffioners from our fhyres, Glencairne, Durie, Carden, William Thomfon, with Monck's good allowance, came to London. Frequent private meffengers went to the King He, from Breda, fent over Sir John Greenville and Dr. Morley, with a very gracious meffage,

VOL. III 3 K

to both Houfes, to the Citie, to the General, which fatiffied all. An order of Parliament given to proclaime the King, May 8th; which was done over all England moft folemnlie. A Committee of fix Lords, twelve Commoners, three Aldermen, nine Common-Councellors, with fundry citie-minifters, Calamy, Manton, Reinolds, etc. fent to Breda to hafte the King home; fifty thoufand pound [fterling] fent him in money, ten thoufand in gold; to his brother [York], ten thoufand in money, one in gold; to Gloucefter, five in money, one in gold. Landing at Dover, he ftayed Sunday in Canterburie, Monday in Rochefter, Tuefday, May 29th, his birth-day, came to the Citie, with the moft folemn fhew and heartieft joy that, I think, was ever in England At Whitehall, Manchefter and Grimftone, the Speakers of the two Houfes did welcome him in more cordiall than eloquent fpeeches. He had from Breda given full fecuritie, on his word, to men of all profeffions, to live in peace; for fatiffaction to the fojours of their arriers; for keeping them in poffeffion of the Crown and Church lands, till they were fatiffied; for pardoning of all by ganes, except a few, whom the Parliament might except, for their eminent hand in his Father's murder The firft morning he came to Whitehall, he iffued a proclamation againft profanitie, fwearing, and healths. Thankfgivings to God for this his own work, with bells and bonefires, went quickly through all the three Kingdomes. Monck was made Baron, Earle, and Duke of Albemarle, mafter of the horfe, one of the Privie Councell, Generall of all the forces under the King; Ormond, ftewart of the houfe; Manchefter, chamerlaine, Lauderdaill, a gentleman of the Bed-chamber, Hyde, Chancellor; Nicolas and Culpeper, Secretars; Reinolds, Calamy, Manton, Baxter, chaplaines; the countrey militia put in hands confident; the King, Duke of York, Gloucefter, Ormont, the moft of the courtiers, made Colonells of the ftanding regiments, the Colonels willingly ceding to be Lieutenants. But quickly the Parliament fell on a better way, with all poffible fpeed to difband all forces by fea and land. For this end, befyde the maintenance and excyfe, a pole-money was appointed to defray arriers; great foumes came in, and a cheerful eneugh difbanding was made; fo that before this, except a few garifons, and a very few horfe and foot, are all peaceably difbanded in the three Kingdomes: a mightie, unexpected work.

The King, in wifdome, moderation, pietie, and grave carriage, giving hudge fatiffaction to all; the Parliament reftored him the power of the militia, his negative voice, the determination of all ecclefiaſtick differences, and whatever he could have wiſhed; took a courſe for buying back his revenues, and much augmenting them. He endeavoured carefully to relieve all that had been ſufferers for him or his Father. He preſſed the Houſes to haſte the bill of indemnitie. They excepted a very few from it, ſcarce a dozen execute: in which the people had much more ſatiſfaction than he; for he could have been induced to have pardoned all; but it was the juſtice of God that brought Peters, Harriſon, and others to a ſhamefull death; to hing up the bones of Oliver, Bradſhaw, Ireton, Pride, on the gibbet at Tiburne; to diſgrace the two Goodwins, blind Milton, Owen, Sterrie, Lockier, and others of that maleficent crew.

The moſt of our Nobles, with very many of our Gentrie, run up to Whitehall: all were made welcome. Old places were reſtored to Crawfurd, Caffillis, and others. No wonder the Chancellor's and Secretar's place were taken from Loudoun and Lothian, and given to Glencairne and Lauderdaill; yet with recompence enough to them both, whom ſome thought deſerved little. Loudoun had his penſion of a thouſand pound[5], and gift of annuities continued; Lothian got his ſecond fon Director of the Chancelrie, which Sir John Scot[6] was thought not to deſerve. Montroſe's Marquiſat was confirmed; the cuſtomes of Glaſgow given to him till he was payed of a great ſoume; Argyle ordained to refound him a great ſoume. Selkirk made Duke Hamilton, and out of the cuſtomes of Leith twenty thouſand pound ſterling aſſigned. Marſhall got ten thouſand pound ſterling of the cuſtomes of Aberdeen. Dudup, Earle of Dundee, a ſoume out of the cuſtomes of Dundee. The King gave among them all he had in Scotland, and much more For Judicatories, he appointed the Committee of Eſtates of the year 16[50] to ſitt down, and the Parliament, December 12th. For a Commiſſioner, by our Nobles confent, leaſt ſtrife ſhould be for it, the Lord Middletone, Earle of Fettercairne, was nominat; who was not very acceptable to many; eſpeciallie not keeping the day of the Parliament, but cauſeing it to be adjourned to Januar, yet when he is come doune, his wiſdome, ſobrietie, and moderation,

---

[5] In the MS it is "10,000 p " but see vol. i. p 390. In Scotiſh money it would be £12,000

[6] Sir John Scott of Scotſtarvet, Director of the Chancery, pathetically laments that, " albeit he was poſſeſſor of the ſaid place of Chancery above forty years, and doer of great services to the King and Country, yet by the power and malice of his enemies, he has been at laſt thrust out of the ſaid places in his old age, and likeways fined in £500 ſterling, and one [Sir William Ker] altogether unſkilled placed to be Director." (Staggering State of Scots Statesmen, p 163.)

hes been fuch as makes him better beloved, and reputed as fitt for that great charge as any other we could have gotten. So farr it went every where weel, to the great joy of all.

But as nothing is perfectly bleffed on earth, fome water was quickly poured in the wine of many; I am fure in mine, as I expreffed it in a fharp and free letter to Lauderdaill. Bifhops and Liturgies were every where fett up in England and Ireland without contradiction: our League and Covenant, by a number of printed pamphlets, was torn to peeces This was the more grievous, that at the beginning it appeared moft eafie to have been remeeded his Gracious Majeftie was ready to have been abfolutely advyfed by his Parliament, the leading men there were avowed Covenanters and Prefbyterians Lauderdaill and Mr. Sharp, both at Breda and London, had very much of the King's ear, Monck was for us in that at the beginning firm enough; the Queen and her partie was on our fyde: the Epifcopall men were fundrie of them as evill as before; Bramble,[7] Wran, Helein, Thorndik, Coofins, Sincerfe, Hammond, Peirce, none of the beft or moft orthodox; Jukfon and Duppa, fmalhe learned; Sheldon, Morley, able indeed, and very wife men, but the overturning of all the Reformation of England, without a contrare petition, to me was ftrange, and very grievous, and I fufpect we know not yet the bottom of that myfterie I wifh all our friends, Scots and Englifh, have been honeft and faithfull: fure they have not been fo prudent and induftrious as, I think, they fhould have been However, as this was the original of all our late trouble, I think it will not faill in time to procure new commotions, if petitions and remonftrancies doe not prevent them.

It's like the generall joy for the King's happy returne, and the generall abhorrence of our late confufions and miferies, together with fear leaft any juftling, even by petitions, might give occafion to thefe who were watching for it to make fome new commotions, made our friends eafie to be prevailed with not to oppofe the King's defires; efpeciallie the King promifing, by conferrence with the chief Prefbyterians and Epifcopalls, to doe his endeavour for their agreeance; as indeed he laboured much in this, and, by his declaration, did draw both fome nearer than they were; but for little fatiffaction to either of the parties: the Epifcopall, not having all they wont, were difcon-

---

[7] The names of the English Bishops are here somewhat incorrectly written by Baillie's amanuensis, for Bramhall, Wren, Heylin, Cosins, Sydserf, Hammond, Pearce, Juxon, &c

tent; the Prefbyterians fand the other had gotten too much, and more than in confcience they could ever affent to, yet, for love to the King, they were filent, when all the Bifhops were folemnly inftalled, and the Liturgie every where reftored, clear contrare to our Covenant, and Acts of the Englifh Parliament fince 1641. Chancellor Hyde was thought the great actor in all this Epifcopall bufinefs, while a few hour's treaty, or but a petition from the Houfes, Generall, and Citie, fent with the Commiffioners to Breda, might eafilie have freed us, for the great good of the land, of all thefe vexations

It was a hudge grief alfo to us, and more to the King, that the Lord was pleafed to remove that moft excellent and exceedingly hopefull Prince the Duke of Gloucefter, in a few dayes ficknefs of the maifles or fmall poxes; and what came on the back of it, the noife of the Duke of York's clandeftine marriage with the Chancellor's daughter,[8] was to the King and all his loving people a very great grief; efpeciallie that third heavieft ftroke following, the death of that moft excellent Princeffe,[9] and exceedinglie beloved both of the King and all his fubjects. I wifh what fome fpeak of her [Mother's] clandeftine marriage with Harie German's [Jermyn's] brother's fon may be found to be a moft falfe lie. However, thefe moft fad accidents did temper our exceeding great and juft joy. Alfo there were fome feares of the fectarian paitie's plots; but, bleffed be God, they are come to nought: that bloodie mad fpirit of Munfter lodges in many of them The Chancellor's fpeech, clofeing the Parliament, fhew their defigne, on the 25th of December, to have fired the citie, feafed on Whitehall, the King, York, Albemarle, and others. Overtoun, Ludlow, White, and many are taken for this: yet many did not beheve it But fomething of it did actuallie appear fince; for while the King is convoying his Mother to Portfmouth, fome of thefe fanaticks did rife two diverfe times in the night; but were eafily, by the mayor of the citie alone, compefcit, without any confiderable blood, bleffed be God; for fure it is, that partie is yet too ftrong; but likelie then own madnefs will fhortly annihilate them.

The Bifhop of London did baptize Charles the Duke of Cambridge at Worfter houfe; the Lady Ormont was godmother The Queen entertained that night the Dutchefs of York, at her table; and to-morrow the King

[8] Anne, daughter of Sir Edward Hyde, Lord Chancellor of England, better known by his title as Earl of Clarendon

[9] Mary, Princess of Orange, sister of Charles the Second, died 24th December 1660.

entertained her and her hufband, his brother, at his table. The Queen went immediately with her daughter towards France, to agent her marriage with Monfieur Duke of Anjou; albeit fome thinks difcontent at her fon's marriage did further her journey.

For us in Scotland, thus things have went among us. After Monck's march, fome flickling there was in the weft to have had meetings in fhyres for new Commiflioners. They lyked not Glencairne's imployment; they fpoke of Lauderdaill and Crawfurd; but their defigne was, Lockart and the Remonftrators intereft. My Lord Lie, Sir John Cheiflie, Sir George Maxwell, my Lord Stairs, Mr. Gillefpie, and others, were faid to be the contrivers. They laboured to have had Selkirk and Caffihs with them, but this was foon crufhed by Monck and Morgan; for they were informed of their inclination to Lambert more than to them. When the Committee of our Eftates, to our great joy, had fit downe in our Parliament Houfe, to prepare matters for our Parliament, Mr James Guthrie having mett before at Edinburgh, and elfewhere, with diverfe of his partie, did tryft it fo, as he and they met in Robert Simpfon's houfe, the next door almoft to the meeting of Eftates, and did draw up a petition to the King[1], making many profeffions of their joy for his returne, but withall remembering him of his Covenant to fuppreffe Bifhops and Ceremonies in England, and to beware to put the government of Scotland into the hands of Malignants. They alfo writt letters to Mr. P. Gillefpie, and the chief of their partie in the weft, to meet them at Glafgow the next week, with fo many as they could bring with them. The Committee hearing of this, immediately fent fome of their number to them, feafed on their papers, brought them before their court. They were forie, at their firft doune-fitting, to have to doe with minifters, but Mr. Guthrie's reftlefs and proud infolence did irritat, efpeciallie when all their number, Mafters R. Traill, John Stirling, Alex. Moncreif, John Semple, Mr. John Murray, Mr. Gilbert Hall, and fundry others, did abfolutely refufe to acknowledge any fault. Surely they had no warrand to meet, being no Kirk judicatorie, and their ill band of Remonftrance could give them no priviledge in a bodie to admonifh the King, how to govern England, and tax him for making malignants members of judicatories. Upon their obftinacie, all were fent to the Caftle. At once Mr. Thomas

---

[1] This intended Supplication is printed by Wodrow, (App. vol i. no 2) Guthrie and the rest of the subscribers were apprehended on the 23d August 1660.

Ramfay went ftark mad : he was allwayes but a weak foolifh thing. Sundry of them fell fick, and were fent to their own houfes, as at laft all were fent to their lodgings in Edinburgh Mr James Guthrie was confined to the tolbooth of Dundee, and Mr G[illefpie] to the caftle of Stirling; Mr. James Simpfon to the tolbooth of Edinburgh, as alfo Mr John Dickfon, minifter at Rutherglen, for many odious fpeeches in pulpit againft the ftatefmen. Mr. James Nafmith alfo, for fpeeches in pulpit, was confined to his chamber in Edinburgh. But above all, Mr Rutherfoord was difgraced ; his book, *Lex Rex*,[2] burnt by the hand of the hangman at the croffe of Edinburgh and St Andrews ; himfelf confined to his chamber, his ftipend fequeftrat, and himfelf cited before the Parliament Mr Andrew Cant, preaching againft Mr Rutherfoord's hard ufage, was accufed before the magiftrates of treafon He dimitted his miniftrie, and came to his fon at Libberton, where both live very quietlie : The Commiffioner ufed the old man very courteouflie, and likelie will protect him from trouble Sir James Stewart and Sir John Cheiflie were fent prifoners to the Caftle, where yet they abide. Wariftoun fled, whereupon he was declared fugitive, and all his places void : his poor Ladie could not obtain to him a paffe from the King to live in banifhment ; fo he lurks daylie in fear of his life. Argyle, by his fon Lorne's letter, being advertifed that the King took kindlie with all men, ventured to goe to London ; but in the chamber of prefence, before he faw the King, a warrand under the King's hand meets him to be caried to the Tower clofe prifoner: yet when his Ladie came up fhe got free acceffe to him; but could not obtaine to him a hearing before the King Swinton, who, either by a ftrange hypocrifie or tentation, had turned Quaker, was taken at London, and fent to Newgate. Argyle and he were fent to the Parliament by fea in one fhip. By a great guard of citizens both were caried on foot, and Swinton difcovered, through all the ftreets of Edinburgh, Argyle to the Caftle, and Swinton to the tolbooth clofe prifoners. Captaine Govan was caft in the tolbooth for a long tyme in irons ; Jafray of Aberdeen, Ofburne the Quaker, were likewife put in the tolbooth ; the chief of the Remonftrators were cited, and made to fubfcribe their renunceing of the Remonftrance, and appearance before the Parliament, and fomething elfe whereat

[2] " *Lex, Rex:* the Law and the Prince ; a Difpute for the juft Prerogative of King and People, &c " Lond 1644 4to

they stumbled at the beginning; but at once Greinheid, Sir G. Maxwell, Mr. John Harper, and others, subscryved all. Our folks, John Graham and Mr John Spreule, lay long in the tolbooth of Edinburgh for refusing; but at last they, John Johnston, and Thomas Paterson, subscryved it. James Porter, our catholick clerk, was confined to his house, and referred to our magistrates, to be disposed on as they pleased That whole partie was clean run downe to the contentment of the most, for they have been ill instruments of irreconcileable division for twelve years, both in Kirk and Kingdome. For myself, I rejoyced not at the hurt of any of them ; but wished all of them might have been spared, on their good behaviour in time to come, which now it's lyke will be easilie obtained, though before it was desperate. The pitie and favour of many is turning towards them, by the insolent behaviour of some, who are suspected may make a new party among us. Our State is very averse to hear of our League and Covenant. Many of our people are hankering after Bishops, having forgot the evill they have done, and the nature of their office An exceeding great profanitie, and contempt both of the ministrie and religion itself, is every where prevalent : a young fry of ministers in Lothian, and Fife, and elsewhere, looks as if they intended some change, without any fear or reverence to the elder ministers, who latelie put them in their places The wisest and best are yet quiet till they see whether these things will goe The goodness of the King himself is the only hope we have to get any thing going right.

For our private matters in the Colledge, this twelvemoneth we have been at peace, our wanrest[3] being quieted. He sent his wife to London, to offer all service to the King, as Sinclair[4] laid to Glencairne, and he to Mr. Sharp, who writ it to Mr Douglass, he offered to doe his endeavours for Episcopacie, (though this he denyes.) However, she got no accesse nor countenance, only occasioned the King to remember me, and name me to his place Lauderdaill writ to me, that it stuck only at a forme of presentation, which he desired Mr. James Sharp, when he came home to send up to him. The interveening of other things maks it stick yet there, for myself, I never moved in it, directly nor indirectly, nor purposes to doe. Ten yeares agoe I might have had it with the likeing of all who had interest ; but I setled it on good Mr. Robert Ramsay,

---

[3] *Wanrest*, or cause of inquietude, alluding to Mr Patrick Gillespie

[4] John sixth Lord Sinclair He was related, I believe, to Gillespie by marriage.

by an Act of the Generall Affembly Since his death, Mr. G[illefpie] intruded himfelf by the Englifh power At his coming we were large one thoufand pound fterling to the fore; this day we will be as much in debt, and a number of confufed buflineffes in our hands, which few who know will be very willing to undertake; yet, on the report of my refufall, fundry are bufie feeking it by their friends, far and near. Many of my friends deale with me to take it: I have promifed, when the prefentation comes, to advyfe; before, I can neither accept nor refufe.

Your Sifter, I waited on her to her death, which was very peaceable and gracious as yow could have wifhed. Your Nephew is well, as yow may fee in his laft two to me for the time there is no occafion of calling him hither, nor doe I think he defires it For that which Voetius wrote to me concerning Mr W. Bowie's widow, there was nothing poffible to be done, nor will be yet for fome tyme, till there be law among us; which, to the great prejudice of many, is not yet to be in hafte. Mr Patrick Bell's letter to herfelf will tell her and him the true caufe of it. His diligence, indeed, hes fecured the thing, whilk elfe would have perifhed; for Kilpatrick is but a tricker and bankrupt As for his Queftions, I ufed all diligence to have had a quick and full anfwer to them, and was once fair to have gotten it from St. Andrewes, Aberdeene, and Edinburgh; yet fince, they have changed, and thinks fit no to medle in that matter, though to my conception all of them be in his mind. For myfelf, I honour him[5] above any divine now living, and thinks him the moft orthodox, profitable, and deferving man we have, and would be glad to doe whatever is in my power for his pleafure. My own anfwer I quickly drew it, and fent it to Edinburgh, to be communicat to St. Andrewes and Aberdeen, who I think did like it, but were to draw an anfwer in common for us all, by Mr Wood's hand, whereof I was well content; but fince that now is refufed, I have fent my own here as yow fee it. Clofe my letter and fend it to Utrecht.

I have now my piece[6] ready for the preffe: becaufe it's in Latine, and long, I will not get it printed here. I debate fundry queftions modeftly, but roundly, with Doctor Waltoun, and fundrie of the chief Epifcopall men; fo I defpair to get it printed at London. Moft of my matter is new and pleafant. I have fent you the *Summa*, to be communicat to whom ye

---

[5] Gisbertus Voetius [6] Rob. Baillii Opus Historicum et Chronologicum

will: I hope yow may get it printed there freely If yow advyfe, I fhall fend the book with the next. keep thir fheets clean, for they muft be put in the book, either at the beginning or end. John now tells me, that the herring he undertook to me to fend to your kind wife are not fent, on this and that excufe, whereof I am not content. I have no forgot your debt, but want of law puts moft men here to a ftand. My heartie fervice to your good and kind wife, and all your fweet children.

Our information of forraigne affairs is this, which yow who dwell nearer the fun and the world can correct. My heart was very fad for the King of Sueden's death, though moft here were glad of it I hoped fuch a victorious valiant Prince was like to be fitted for putting the world in a new better mould, but God hath otherwayes appointed That generall confpiracie againft him, procured by your State, with the French and Englifh deferting of him, hes broken his heart; though his ficknefs feems to have come from his too fore labours at the fiege of Copenhagen. It was his happinefs to die at Gottenburie, February 15th, in his Parliament, before he had loft any of his reputation, and to have his fon crouned, under the tutorie of his mother and fome ftatefmen, whereof I think neither his brother Adolph, nor La Gard his good brother, are any It is good that peace is made there, which during Charles's ftanding was not probable I thought the Kingdom of Denmark long before had been hereditarie, as weell as Sweden. It feems the peace hes taken more from Denmark than any other; however, it puts all that north countrey to quietnefs, bleffed be God for it What means the foolifh Mufcoviters, after fo manie difafters, to trouble Pole? Shall that inceftuous unhappie Queen ftill be fcorning the world with the offers of the Crown of Pole to whom fhe pleafes? Her laft dealing in France, that Anguen might marry her fifter, Edward of Palatine's wife's daughter, is like a trick of Mazarin to get Condé and his fon out of France, at leift to divert their fanfies for the time, with that peak, from plotting againft him Chriftina grows in follie, in demanding of the Parliament at Stokholm the reftitution of her crowne, her good behaviour hes fo weell deferved. I fear a prifon fhall be her hinder end; whether in Sweden, or fome monafterie in Italie, time will try: it feems none takes notice of her now wherever fhe goes. Ragotfi's calamitie hes grieved us fore; that gallant brave Prince fhould not have been left to the Turkifh furie: I fear his ftates fhall turne Turkifh or Auftrian. Still we marvell what Mazarin can mean by his Spanish peace, when West Flanders, Catalonia, and Millain, were liklier to have been conquerfed by the French than thefe many yeares. Condé is brought home to France. Portugall is totallie deferted: What can the end of this be? The people are nothing eafed of their taxes, the clergie complains as much of their oppreffion The Prince of Orange, too weell deferving of the houfe of France, fpoiled in his minoritie, by treafon, of his patrimonie. The Venetians not affifted either by France or Spaine, with any confiderable help, more in their peace than warre, but the Venetians put in a worfe cafe after their help than before. However, guide as they will, bleffed be God for the peace of the Kirks abroad, and the happy reftauration of our King, when all the world abroad abfoluthe, and at home alfo, weell near, had deferted him. At laft I break off.

Your Coufin,

January 31ft 1661. R. B.

[REVERENDISSIMO CLARISSIMOQUE VIRO D. GISBERTO VOETIO]

REVERENDISSIME FRATER,

Tuas ad me dudum accepi, etfi aliquot menfibus poftquam a te fcriptæ fuerunt; alteras in gratiam viduæ concivis mei Walteri Bowie, alteras de duabus quæftionibus a Facultate veftra Theologica nobis propofitis. Quod præter meum morem refponfum tamdiu dilatum eft, culpa faltem primaria mea non fuit. In viduæ caufa nihil fere a triennio potuit peragi; nam leges apud nos a longo jam tempore filuerunt, et adhuc filent, adeo ut cum nullo debitore ob quodvis æs alienum alicujus momenti lege potuerit aut adhuc poffit agi; præterquam quod viduæ debitor lapfus fit bonis, nec, fi leges aperirentur, folvendo fuiffet, nifi Patricii Beli, de quo fcribis, hominis honeftiffimi, et fingulari D Bowio tam vivo quam mortuo amici, charitate ac diligentia remedium, fpero efficax et tempeftivum, fuiffet adhibitum, de quo ipfe epiftola hac inclufa viduæ rationem reddit. Aufim fpondere veram, tam a meipfo quam D Belo, amicitiam viduæ in quocunque noftra opera poterit illi effe utilis.

Quod ad alteras de quæftionibus, ut primum venerunt in manus meas, in paucis diebus refponfum, quod jam mitto, exaravi, et ad Edinburgenfes tranfmifi, ut cum Andreapolitanis et Abredonenfibus communicaretur, omnefque ad maturum, amicum, et plenum refponfum hortatus fum. Ipfis inftitutum fuit commune noftrum omnium nomine fcriptum concinnaffe, quod cum aliquot menfibus expectaffem, tandem comperi, ex quorundam tam apud vos quam nos cafuum interventu, confilium eos mutaffe. Ne autem ego etiam tibi deeffem, quem profiteor poft breve illud quod tecum habui Ultrajecti colloquium, et perlecta tua varia fcripta (omitto multa amiciffima tua erga me officia) tuliffe me femper et ferre in oculis animoque, ut theologorum qui hodie in ecclefia Reformata vivunt vere primarium pietate, eruditione, diligentia, zelo, et omni quæ theologum ornat virtute; ne, inquam, ego pro mea parte diutius tibi deeffem, et fi fero, tandem tamen, communico fententiam meam quam puto doctrinæ et praxi ecclefiæ Scoticanæ conformem, tuæque ac collegarum tuorum menti confonam. Rerum noftrarum ftatum, imprimis a feliciffimo Regis reditu, et diu defiderata fectariorum ufurpantium ruina, fcripfi, ut foleo, fufe D. Spangio. In præfentia multa nobis funt γ῅ ὑπόπικρα, quæ fperamus mirabiliter nobis benignum Deum fuo tempore commutaturum in dulciora, prout infinita ipfius fapientia videbit fuum honorem noftrumque commodum requirere. Ipfe te tuofque collegas, omnefque reformatarum ecclefiarum veros doctores confervet a malo, et afpiret omnibus omnium alboribus. Sic precatur tui ftudioffimus et honorantiffimus Frater,

R. BALÆUS.

Glafguæ, Cal. Feb. 1661.

To the Right Honourable and Noble Lord the Earle of Glencairne, Lord High Chancellor of Scotland.

MY LORD,

I know it's unfit to divert your Lordfhip by long letters. Your Lordfhip is now, by your goodnefs and all our defires, become the head of our Houfe [7] When I was with your Lordfhip I fhew our extraordinarie neceffitie, your Lordfhip was alfe willing as we could defire to help us to your power. We were, by the good Englifh powers, (who, bleffed be God, are now annihilat,)

[7] William, Earl of Glencairn, Lord Chancellor of Scotland, was elected Chancellor of the University of Glasgow, 25th October 1660.

poffefled in the vacant ftipends about us. This was the chief ground whereupon Mr Gillefpie ventured to caft us in fo great debt The Parliament, we hear, hes for feven yeares decerned all vacant ftipends to belong to the King, to be diftribut unto the minifters who hes fuffered for their loyaltie to him and his Royall Father. I am fure our Houfe hes fuffered more by the adminiftration of one intrudit upon us by the Englifh violence, than all the minifters I know in thir bounds have done If your Lordfhip can obtain to us a part of thefe vacancies, to wit, thefe we had before of the Chapter of Glafgow, and thefe of Galloway we have enteres in, of what is bygane undifpofed of, and for the feven yeares to come, it were a work of great charitie, and, I hope, prejudiciall to no man. Alfo, when Mr. Gillefpie comes before you, it feemes reafonable that he fhould be ordained to find caution to make count with the Colledge; and what he hes taken to himfelf more than was due, at the vifitors of Parliament's fight, he fhould be obliedged to refound it · that Vifitation we referre it wholly to your Lordfhip's difcretion. Bedlay and Mr. Sharp will conferre with your Lordfhip about it at your leafure The Lord blefle your Lordfhip and your whole familie.

Your Lordfhip's fervant,

Glafgow, February 4th 1661 R. Bailie

Had I been weell I would have come alongs to have agented thefe things with your Lordfhip myfelf.

For his Reverend Brother Mr. James Sharp, Minister at Craill.

James,

I hope yow got my laft of thanks for your very kind and refrefhfull one to me; Mr. Hamiltone writes he fent it over to yow. I would not have fafhed yow at this tyme, had it not been the occafion yow will read in the inclofed; yow will be pleafed to read, clofe, and deliver it, yea, for my caufe, yow muft agent it I writ to yow I had no face to come abroad till yow got the returne yow promifed from Lauderdaill; that which I moft defire is a returne of mine, which yow fent him, for his Majeftie's hand to pay his Father's debt with fome increafe: two hundred pound in [16]33, now in [16]61, will excrefce to a great foume. we have great need of it; for we are turned the verieft divers [dyvours] I know. Mr. Gillefpie fand us in twenty thoufand merks to the fore, he leaves us large in twenty thoufand merks behind; as the Vifitors will fee in our counts. he hes left us work now neceffarly to be perfited, which ten thoufand pound will not doe. James, if we get yow no a joynt beggar with us, we are undone. Good James, what fhall I doe with the worme, it hes imprifoned me, and put me from all fervice this while: when I grow better, yow will have me to be the old man.

Your very loving Brother and fervant,

February 1661. R. B.

James, have yow no fo much power as to ftay the railing on us of that very malicious Diurnaller? If the Parliament would put on him the penaltie of my worme, I think it would quickly temper his very uncivill pen.

UNTO THE HONOURABLE THE ESTATES OF PARLIAMENT, WE THE UNIVERSITIE OF GLASGOW HUMBLIE MEAN AND SHOW,

THAT whereas, through the occafion of Dr Strang, a moft loyall divine, his removeall from his place, and Mr Gillefpie s intrufion therein by the Englifh Ufurpers, we are brought to great povertie and debt, fo that this year we have been neceffitate thus to give over our table, and no Mafter within the houfe hes gotten any part of their ftipends; yea, the large half of our laft year s table and ftipend lyes yet unpayed; befide a neceffitie is laid upon us to perfect our farr advanced building, which ten thoufand pound will not accomplifh. We doe humbly fupplicat your Lordfhips that our fuffering condition may be confidered, and recommended to the Honourable Lords of Councell, to be redreffed out of fome part of the vacant ftipends in our bounds, or what other way their Lordfhips fhall find expedient. So fhall your humble Supplicants and Servants allways pray for your Lordfhips profperitie and happinefs.

In name of the Univerfitie of Glafgow, their Commiffioner,

R BAILLIE.

Address by Principal Baillie to the Commissioner.[s]

My Lord,

I am sent to your Grace from our Univerfitie, in all humble dutie, to congratulate your Grace's high employment, and to declare their very heartie wifhes that, as yow have begun and hitherto continued, fo yow may go on to the end, to manage this great truft, with that your wifdom, moderation, and goodnefs, which has given good fatiffaction to all who have with any confideration and judgment looked upon it. As for us of that Seminarie, it is our fixed purpofe, by the grace of God, not only to remaine moft loyall towards his Royall Majeftie, but alfo to be readihe obedient to all your Grace's commandments, hoping that, by your Grace's favour and mediation, we fhall enjoy thefe priviledges which, from our firft erection to this day, his Majeftie and his bleffed progenitors has of their Royall bountie been pleafed to confer upon us, and from time to time to confirm and encreafe. I fhall fay no more for the time, but pray God to bleffe your Grace with the continuance of his Spirit upon yow, for the refrefhing of our languifhing countrey after many fore diftreffes; for fully quieting of our Church from the trembling fears of diverfe, (I hope moft needlefs,) fince we have the word of the beft, and, without all peradventure, moft honeft Prince in the world, for fecureing our Church from all innovation; alfo for the cherifhing and advancement of pietie, vertue, and learning, the fountains of loyaltie in all our feminaries, efpecially that of Glafgow, on which, fince its firft being, all our Soveraigns and their reprefentatives have looked with as becoming an afpect, and beftowed as fenfible marks of their favour, as upon any other Univerfitie in the whole Kingdome.

For Mr. James Robertoun [of Bedlay.]

Sir,

As I told you, I found my Lord Chancellor very kind and courteous to

[s] John Earl of Middleton, Lord High Commiffioner to the Parliament of Scotland

me in all things. For our Vifitation, I left it wholly on his Lordfhip,[9] with your advyfe. I heard of a lift, I think drawn by Provoſt Bell and Mr. John Young's advyce; the perfons were all honourable, and above exception · Duke Hamilton, Marquis of Montrofe, Earl of Eglinton, Earl of Wigton; but what needs my Lord Cochrane? Gentlemen, Kilfyth, Luffe, Kilmahew, young Houfton; but what have we to do with Kier and Carden, who are at odds with us, and lately, as the Chancellor knows, before the Committee of Eftates have fpoken their pleafure of us? What have we to doe with the Provoſt of Lithgow and Stirling, mere ftrangers? with Mr James Ramfay, and Mr. Matthias Simpfon, and Mr. Edward Wright? Thefe are put on us for a trick, I know, and fhall tell you at meeting. Why fhould the Provoſt and Baillie of Glafgow, and John Bell, the auditors of our compts, and for the time interefted in our pleys, be fet over us? May no the Provofts of Aire, Irvine, Dumbartane, ferve for burgeffes? Mr. Gabriel Cunninghame of Miniabrock, Mr. Matthew Ramfay, Mr. James Fergufhill, Mr. William Eccles, are good; but why fhould Mr. Robert Wallace, Mr. Patrick Colvill, Mr William Fullertoun, Mr. David Elphinfton be omitted? Why fhould Craigends, Haiflet, Cunninghamhead, and fuch be forgot? Thir things to yourfelf alone. It is by your advyce mainly I have embraced this place; the Vifitation may doe us great harm, and me difcouragement, if no weell managed. Albeit the condition of the fooles of Aberdeen has procured one, yet both St. Andrewes and Edinburgh has declined it, and I wifh we had none at this time; it will caft out men for fmall faults, and put far worfe in their place; it will be fo compofed as to pafs over the moft guilty. I know, if we muft have it, yow will doe your beft by the Chancellor to have it fo right as may be. I fhall fay no more for the time. The Lord be with yow.

                                Your Coufin,

Monday, Mart.   R. BAILLIE.

So far as I can learne by Patrick Hamilton, your fone, and his wife, and all in Bedlay, are weell.

If we needs muft have a Vifitation, fee it containe no power to plant places but according to the fettled order of our Houfe.

[9] The Earl of Glencairn, as Chancellor of the Univerfity. *Vide supra*, p 452

For my Lord Lauderdaill.

My Lord,

That prefentation ye fent me, with a kind letter, came to my hands long agoe, by the care and kindneffe of Mr. Sharp, as I write to your friend Mr. Drummond. What in his letter I promifed, now when I have by my friends advyce, after fome reluctation, accepted of it, I fend up to your Lordfhip very heartie thanks for this addition to all your former favours, and withall an earneft and humble defire that your Lordfhip would be pleafed, at your conveniencie, to offer in my poor name to his Majeftie (whom the Lord ever preferve and bleffe) my moft humble duetie for his kind remembrance of me in that particular. It does not indeed add any thing to my heart's affection towards his Majeftie, which ever I have found in my breaft fince my fecond meeting with him, by your addreffe, in the Hague. But it is, and fhall be one of my remembrancers, to walk in that place in my great weaknefs according to his Majeftie's expectation, as one minding duetie to God, to his Majeftie, and thofe over whom, how unworthie foever, he has been pleafed to fet me an overfeer. And for your Lordfhip I have no words to change with yow; yow know me weell enough It's my heart's defire ofttimes to God to preferve yow from many, many fnares are dailie near yow. I will write nothing of that I have to fay, if God ever grant me a meeting with yow. Only what I wrote once or twice to yow before of the great neceffitie and debt which Mr. Gillefpie's gloriofitie and vaft fpending has put our poor Houfe into, and our expectation of fome remead of it by his Majeftie's warrand to the Thefaurer to pay us that two hundred pound which his bleffed Father fubfcribed to Dr. Strang in the year 1633 To this yow think not fit to anfwer one word. I fhall fay no more to this; but I know much more of his Majeftie's goods has gone, and will goe fari worfe wayes. If I may by a line from your Lordfhip know of the receipt heirof, it will be a fuperaddition to your old kindnefs However, I reft what long I have been,

Your Lordfhip's affectionat friend and fervant,

Glafgow, Aprile 10th 1661. R. B.

For Mr James Sharp

JAMES,

What I promifed to Mr. Drummond I now performe. Yow fee what I write to the Secretar,[6] I pray yow let it go under your cover. Yow will clofe it, and I hope affift me in my petition. That I beg more quietlie than I have caufe, I have defired Mr John Young, the bearer, to let yow read (and hear him verifie it all,) what havock he [Gillefpie] has made of our goods, and yet has the modeftie to petition the Parliament for more off us whom he has wracked. I hope fuch impudence will not be heard.

The mater of our changes lye near my heart: I think they will haften my death; yet I make no noyfe about them. The Lord blefs yow and direct yow in your eminent ftation.

Your much oblidged friend to ferve yow,

Aprile 13th 1661.   R. B

For my Lord Lauderdaill

MY LORD,

Having the occafion of this bearer, who promifes to me affuredlie to deliver to yow in hand or burn it, I tell yow that my heart is broken with grief, and that the burden of the publict I find it weightie and haftening me to my grave. My prayers daihe, when my heart is loofed, are for the King and yow, for his blefling on yow both. I have no private defires nor fears; but I think we are very ill-guided, and very needleflie fo. What needed yow doe that difservice to the King, which all of yow cannot recompence, to grieve the hearts of all your gracious friends in Scotland to whom the King was, is, and will be, I hope, after God, moft dear, with pulling downe all our Laws at once which concerned our Church fince 1633?[7]

---

[6] The Earl of Lauderdale, Secretary of State for Scotland

[7] The Rescissory Act, on the 28th March 1661, entitled, "Act rescinding and annulling the pretendit Parliaments in the years 1640 1641, &c" viz to 1648 inclusive (Acta Parl vol vii. p 86.) There was no Parliament held between 1633 and 1640; and the Acts of Parliament and (... ...February (ib. p 30.)

Was this good advyce, or will this thryve? Is it wifdome to bring back upon us the Canterburian tymes? The fame defignes, the fame practifes, will they not at laft bring on the fame horrible effects, whatever fools dreame? That old maxime of the State of England is wife and good, that the King can doe no fault, but the higheft minifters of State ought, in all reafon to anfwer on their higheft pain for all mifcarriages. It was one of King James's wifeft practifes to permitt his greateft favourites to fink, before that, by protecting them, the grief of his people fhould fall on his back: ye have feen the contrare principle deftructive, and it will ftill be fo.

My Lord, ye are the Nobleman of the world I efteem moft and love beft I think I may fay and write to yow what I like If yow have gone with your heart to forfake your Covenant, to countenance the introduction of Bifhops and Books, and ftrengthening the King by your advyce in thefe things, I thinke yow a prime tranfgreffor, and lyable among the firft to anfwer to God for that great fin, and opening a door, which in hafte will not be clofed, for perfecution of a multitude of the beft perfons and moft loyall fubjects that are in all the three dominions. And if otherwayes your heart be where it was, as I hope indeed it is, and that in your own way yow are doing what yow can for the truth of God, (yet dailie I have my great feares for yow,) I think yow ftand in a ticklifh place, and fome of thefe yow doe converfe with to be but men. Remember your coufin Hamilton s poifoning before King James's eyes without fearch: my heart whiles trembles for yow I will continue to pray for yow doe what yow will Mr. Guthrie, I ever oppofed his way, but fee that none get the King perfuaded to take minifters heads: banifhment will be worfe for them than death how fhall they get bread if put without the bounds of the Englifh language? Send them to Orkney, or any other place where they may preach and live. yow may obtain this, I think, if ye will

For myfelf ye have buried me: yow have put me in a place which Mr. Gillefpie got in wealth, but, through his waftrie, hes left in twenty thoufand pund of debt, and in a neceffitie of expending twenty thoufand pund in perfecting his glorious buildings. The Englifh furnifhed him liberally. For us we have nothing but what we expect by your Lordfhip from his Majeftie's benignitie. I am an ill beggar, yet I muft ftill craike to your Lordfhip while I live; which I think fhall not be long, for your Prefbyterians at London, their mifguiding hes flaine me I hear there are fome of my twenty year old pamphlets lately reprinted at London, this is totallie without my knowledge, though indeed I remaine fully in the mind I wes then in, and which I write to yow and ye received, though the firft copie perifhed. If yow or Mr Sharp, whom we trufted as our own foules, have fwerved towards Chancellor Hyde's principles, as now we fee many doe, yow have much to anfwer for. This poffible may be my laft to yow, therefore I crave no pardon for its length or impertinencie

Your Lordfhip's old friend,

Glafgow, April 18th 1661. R. B.

[FOR MR ROBERT BAILLIE, PROFESSOR OF DIVINITY AT GLASGOW.[8]]

REVEREND AND DEAR SIR,

YOUR'S to my Lord Lawderdaill, I have kept, till I prefent it from my own hand I am commandit to take a new toyle, but I tell yow it is not in order to a change of the Church. I eafily forfee what occafion of jealoufies and falfe furmifes this my journey[9] will give; but whenever the Lord fhall returne me, I truft my carriage, through the Lord's help, fhall be fuch as my dear freind Mr Baily will not condemne me The reafons of my journey cannot be communicated in this way, but yow may think they are preffing, elfe I may be charged with exceeding folly at this time to enter upon the ftage Your [praye]rs I hope for me will not be wanting I fhall be your [Chancello]r's monitor in reference to the papers concerning your [College, fent] to me by Mr. John Young. All peace and mercy [be with you. I] am,

Your's,

[Edinburgh, end of April] 1661. JA. SHARP.

[8] From the original Wodrow MSS Fol. Vol xlix, No 3 It is not contained in Baillie's own MS The left hand corner with the date, is torn away, but it was no doubt written from Edinburgh before the end of April

[9] Sharp on the 23d April, preached before the Parliament of Scotland, being the day of the Kings Coronation, and on Monday the 29th of that month along with the Earls of Glencairne and Rothes, he set out from Edinburgh on the journey to London here mentioned

For Mr. Hutcheson

George,

Your's came hither when I was out of towne. What ye defire me to write to L[auderdaill] I have done it already, as my Teftament to him, fully and fharply enough. There was no inlaik in that kind. It was to obviat the C[hancellor], R[othes], and Sh[arp], at their laft going up. I think verily if that wicked change come it will haften me to my grave. For the Oath, as I told fome of yow when I was laft there, I doubt your way is not right: yow give occafion to them, that feek no better, to caft the chief of yow out of Edinburgh, that they may plant in your roome the chief of the Epifcopalls. Remember prayer for the King, whereupon fome of us were refolved to fuffer, but were drawne off by your example moft, In this ye will have fome, but, I fear, ere long very few followers. Yow are all fatiffied if the word "Civill" were expreffe added. In my own judgement, ftriving for this addition is but wrangling, which none of the anti-Epifcopall divines in England ever offered, nor our folks did, fo farr as I knew, ever move before. The Courfe of Conformitie fticks not on the oath of Supremacie. Not only the articles of the Confeffion of England, and Uffer with King James's printed thanks, expone that oath only of a Civill Supream power *circa facra*, but all, both Popifh and Epifcopall divines, that are for Divine right of Epifcopacie, contradict the Eraftians who will give the King any ecclefiaftick fupremacie. Did any prince ever plead that he was any more than the civill magiftrate, though ἐπίσκοπος *ad omnia, τὰ ἔξω in ecclefia?* They have declared in face of Parliament, above twenty tymes, that they underftand no ecclefiaftick jurifdiction, that they will not, or dare not, regifter any fuch declaration, and for our fatiffaction they will not alter a letter of what is come down to them. This is their wilfulnefs, and poffible fomething worfe, but is not ground eneugh for our refufeall of the Oath without that word. If they fhould build upon it a power to the King to bring in bifhops and all ceremonies he lyked, and call us perjured if we did not on that Oath take all, to myfelf it is an evidently wrong conclufion and foolifh. Thirty-fix years agoe, when I entered Regent in our Colledge, I took both oaths of

Supremacie and Alleadgeance, but was not hindred thereby to oppofe both books and bifhops to my pith. Though yow get your word "Civill," they would no lefſe conclude all power they intend from it, than they doe without it. I pray God direct yow there in this particular; it may be an occafion of fore trouble to many quickly.

Your's,

June 24th [1661.] R. B.

To the Right Reverend and Right Worshipfull the Brethren of the Presbyterie of Kirkcudbright, and Gentlemen of the Parish of Tungland.[1]

Right Reverend and Right Worshipfull,

Your's of the 10th of Julie I received. That Mr. James Scot I know no[t]; he was not at ws· be affured I fhall never countenance any fuch man as ye defcrive. Aggree among yourfelf[es]: Let the Prefbyterie and people ther, with the fatiffaction of my Lord Kenmure, aggree on a gracious able man; and for our part, we fhall further his plantation in any thing lyes in our power. Wifhing the Lord to be with you, I reft

Your friend and fervant,

Glafgow, the 15th Julie 1661. R. Bailly.

We fhall entreat yow to caufe deliver the tuo enclofed, by a fure hand, with your firft conveniencie.

For Mr. Spang.

Cousin,

I hope ere now yow have receaved my book, and that ere long I fhall have your fenfe of the printing of it. Since my laft long letter, thus our affaires went, fo farr as I underftand and remember. The Commiſ-

[1] From the original, Wodrow MSS 4to vol. xxix No. 95. It relates to supplying a vacancy in the parish of Tungland.

fioner was met at Muffilburgh with a thoufand horfe. The Parliament fat downe the beginning of January, on the Tuefday; it rode[z] in a very magnifick way: few of the nobles were away. The Chancellor had fo guided it, that the fhyres and burroughs fhould choice none but thefe that were abfolutely for the King. Diverfe were cited to the Parliament, that they might not be members. The Parliament's pulfe wes quickly felt; for when Caffillis moved, that the election of a Prefident fhould be by vote of P[arliament], the Commiffioner obtained, that the Chancellor fhould prefide by virtue of his office, as before it wont to be. The Oath of Alleadgeance was next appointed to be taken by all the members: there was infert in mids of it, the maine claufe of the Oath of Supremacie: "That the King was Supreme Governour over all perfons in all caufes." About this fundry did fcruple; yet when the Commiffioner and Chancellor declared, that they intended thereby no Ecclefiaftick power to the King in word, facraments, or difcipline, but a fupreme civill power to put churchmen in all things to their duetie: all were fatiffied, and took it in that fenfe; only Caffillis and Kilburnie refufed, becaufe they could not obtaine that fenfe to be exprefled in write. Thereafter it was appointed, that all Members of Parliament, all Officers of State, Lords of Seffion, and others in fhyres and burroughs, fhould take it. The Minifters of Edinburgh defired a word to be added, which would have fatiffied all, "Civill Supream Governour," and without that word, "Civill," they feemed peremptor to refufe it. At this I was very fore; for I feared it fhould occafion trouble, and a new fchifme, without great caufe, as I wrote to them when the Act of Parliament came out, of putting all intrants in the miniftrie to it; and, as I hear, they will put all Mafters of Colledges to it. For my felf, I took the oath of Alleadgeance and Supremacie thirty-four years agoe, when I entered Regent, and yet never fcrupled it. My Lord Caffillis, without doubt the truely beft man of our nobilitie, and as loyall as any, for this fcruple is as good as removed from Parliament: and though he be fince at London, and hes favour and countenance enough of the King, as weell he deferves; yet it is like to put him from the exercife of all his places, of Juftice-Generall, Lord of Counfell,

---

[z] At the opening of Parliament there ufually was a grand cavalcade, confisting of the Officers of State, the Members of Parliament, and other perfons of distinction, styled "The Riding of the Parliament." An account of the proceffion on this occasion, Tuesday 1st January 1661 is given in the earlieft number of the 'Mercurius Caledonius.'

Seffion, and Exchequer The Sheriffdome of Air had elected Sir James Dalrymple of Stairs, with the laird of Blair, the Chancellor's brother in-law ; but their fcrupulofitie being feared, a new election was made of Kilburnie and Haiflead [Hazlehead]. Kilburnie, following Caffillis's vote, did no more appear in Parliament.

Their next work was about the Prerogative · with very little or no difficultie, all was given to the King he defired ; fole power of peace and warr, of militia by fea and land, of calling and raifing of Parliaments, and all things elfe was in queftion, which lately were called the liberties of the nation. and priviledges of Parliament At firft it was only fpoken to annull the Parliament 1649, which had annulled that of 1648, and had fent for the King on an unreafonable Treatie. This paffed eafilie ; but at once the defigne appeared of annulling all the former Parliaments fince 1633, which had given any civill fanction to the Generall Affemblie of Glafgow 1638, or any after Affemblie which ratified our Solemne League and Covenant or Church Government, and all we had been doing the years bygone This caufed a great noife and all grief over the whole land ; fo that for a while the motion was retired, and fuch intention denyed , but when things were better prepared, it was openly preft, and caried, fcarce fourtie appearing in the contrare. While the Prefbyterie of Edinburgh, Synods of Lothian, Fyfe, Glafgow, and others, were preparing petitions againft this, they were fore threatened, and that of Fyfe raifed by Rothes, that of Lothian by Callander, Dumfries by Annandale, etc When, by our own privie wayes, we had gotten the King informed of all this, we were once in good hopes of a remeed ; but yet that appears no Lauderdaill, in whom we trufted, being overpowered and diverted by the greater court of Hyde. and the great zeall that fundry here hes to his fervice. However, we are filled with grief and fear of troubling both the inward and outward peace of our Church His Majeftie's letter to the Prefbyterie of Edinburgh, confirmed our hopes that no change fhould be made in our Church; but feeing what is paft fince, we know not now what to fay, who defire moft gladly to get any true ground of apologizeing for all the King's and State's actions Some fpeak of a dangerous improvidence in thefe Acts, as if all poffibilitie of any folide agreeance betwixt the King and his fubjects were thereby taken away, if any difcord, which God forbid, fhould ever again fall out: for what fecuritie is left to the King to give to his people, when treaties confirmed by King and Parliament, in all due forms, are not binding, but fo eafily ranverfed, on the alleadgeances of fears, tentations, inconveniences and the like, which will never be wanting

The moſt of the Parliament's work was on delinquents proceſſes The great one was Argyle; many hearings had he on his long lybell; his defences were very pregnant; the Advocat was fome tymes uncivilie tart to him; the Commiſſioner alfo ſharp enough; Sir John Gilmore in many things reafoned for him: there was no inlack of full hearing and debates to the uttermoſt. His act of indemnitie keeped him from all that was libelled before the year 1651; fo all the odious clamors of his crueltie againſt the Lamonds, M'Donalds, and others, were cut off; albeit in all thefe he gave fair anfwers. Much of that guilt lay on his deputie George Campbell; and on his friends Ardkinglafs, Maconochie, and others: thefe appeared not when cited, and therefore were forfault; George appeared, and was made clofe prifoner: yet a pardon came from the King to him, procured, as was thought, by his purfe; for many are poor, and he was very rich. His maſter's chief indytement was, complyance with the Englifh, his fitting in the Parliament at London, his affiſting Monck againſt Glencairne and Middleton on the hills.

When his libelled crimes appeared not unpardonable, and his fon Lord Neill, went up to fee his brother Lorne at London, and fpoke fomewhat liberalhe of his father's fatiffactorie anfwers; Monck was moved to fend downe four or five of his letters to himfelf and others, proving his full complyance with them; that the King fhould not reprieve him. The Chancellor and Rothes went to Court[3] to fhew the hazard of his efcape. The man was very wife, and queſtionlefs the greateſt fubject the King had; fometime much known and beloved in all the three dominions: it was not thought fafe he fhould live. The condemnatorie fentence he took weell; fupped the night after cheerfulhe; parted with his gracious lady that Saturday at night chriſtianly. Mr. Douglafs and Mr. Hutchefon preached to him in the Tolbooth on the Sunday; Mr. Dickfon prayed with him all Sunday-night, except a little tyme of his fleep. On the Monday, he breakfaſted and dyned; about two o'clock he went through the ftreets, with his hat on, with his friends, very cheerfully; did mount the fcaffold, at the Croſſe, fpoke well at the corners of the fcaffold; prayed twyce: Mr. Hamilton and Mr. Hutchefon waited on him. He

[3] Along with Sharp, on the 20th April *Vide supra* p 460

bleffed the King and his family ; attefted God of his freedome from all defignes againft the King or his Father; gave fome pieces to the executioner ; laid down his head on the block very couragioufly ; at the ftretching out of his hand, (the figne agreed on,) the Maiden[4] quickly ftroke off his head However he had been much hated by the people, yet in death he was much regrated by many, and by none infulted over. His friends in the night, in Marifhall's fix-horfe coatch, did cary him through Falkirk and Glafgow, and thence to Kilpatrick, where they put him in a boat for Dunnun [Dunoon], and buried him with his fathers in the Kirk of Kilmun. His head was fet up in the weft-end of the Tolbooth, where Montrofe's head had ftood.

In the beginning of the Parliament, Montrofe's head, and bodie buried in the Borrow-Muir, was appointed to be carried honorably to the Abbay-Church ; whence, on the King's charges, he was carried to St. Geiles to be intombed there, with a greater folemnitie[5] than any of our King's ever had at their buriall in Scotland His fon is a good modeft gentleman, hes given no offence to any, neither at London nor in the Parliament. The King's liberalitie, with his Ladie's portion and vertue, are like to put him in a better condition than was any of his predeceffors.

Argyle long to me was the beft and moft excellent man our State of a long tyme had enjoyed ; but his complyance with the Englifh and Remonftrators, took my heart off him thefe eight years; yet I mourned for his death, and ftill prayes to God for his family. His two fons are good youths, and were ever loyall The ruine of the family may prove hurtfull to King and Kingdome. Without the King's favour debt will undoe it : when Huntlie's lands are randered, and Montrofe payed near a hunder thoufand pund ; his old debts of four or fyve hunder thoufand merks will not be gotten payed. Many wonder of his debt, and think he muft have money, for he got much, and was allwayes fober and fpareing. My goodfon, Mr. R[obert] Watfon, was with his Lady in Rofeneth the night the King landed in England : he told me, all the dogs that day did take a ftrange yowling, and glowring up to my

---

[4] " The Maiden," or inftrument used for beheading State-criminals, is preserved in the Museum of the Society of Antiquaries of Scotland

[5] There was published at the time, probably by Sydserff, " A Relation of the True Funerals of the great Lord Marquesse of Montrose, his Majesties Lord High Commissioner, and Captain General of his Forces in Scotland, &c [Edinburgh] Printed in the year 1661 " 4to, pp 24

L[ord's] chamber windows for fome houres together. Mr Alexander Colvin, juftice-deput, an old fervant of the houfe, told me, that my Lady Kenmure, a gracious lady, my Lord's fifter, from fome little fkill of phyfiognomie, which Mr. Alexander had taught her, had told him fome years agoe, her brother would die in blood.

After Argyle's proceffe, thefe of the minifters took up moft of the Parliament's time. Mr. James Guthrie's hbell was tartlie drawn, and wittihe anfwered; yet he defended all he had done, juftified the matter of the Remonftrance, Proteftation, Caufes of God's wrath, and fathered all on the difcipline of the Church and Acts of Affemblies, even his declinator of King and Parliament at Perth when cited for treafonable preaching. After many dayes hearing, perfifting obftinately, he was condemned to be hanged, and his head to be fett on the Nether-Bow Though few approved his way, yet many were grieved to fee a minifter fo feverely ufed. Mr Rutherfoord, had not death prevented, was in the fame hazard. Mr. Gillefpie had gone the fame gate, had not his friends perfuaded him to recant his Remonftrance, Proteftation, complyance with the Englifh, and to petition the King and Parliament for mercy; all did agree to fupplicat the King for him; and now he hes obtained libertie to abide at Ormiftoun, and fix miles about it, till the firft of March. Mr. James Nafmith, and Mr John Dickfon of Rutherglen, Mr. John Stirling, and Mr. Traill, did follow his way But Mr. Robert Mackward, Mr. Rutherfoord's fervant at London four years, made minifter of Glafgow the way I wrote to yow before, in a fett fermon of purpofe, declared his grief for the Parliament's hard ufage of the Covenant, wherein all honeft men did concurr with him; but in fo high language, as entering a proteftation in heaven againft the Parliament's deed, whereof he took all his hearers for witneffes; fuch termes none did approve, yet for all that either one or other could fay, he did obftinately ftand to all; which provocked them to paffe a fentence of banifhment upon him.[6]

All the reft of the imprifoned minifters are fet free, fome upon one fatiffaction, and fome upon another How long their or our libertie fhall laft, we know no; for the Parliament feems to have fmall regard of any of us.

[6] Mackward was found guilty by Parliament, on the 7th June, but his fentence was delayed till either the 12th or 14th of July Instead of banifhment, he expected to have met the same fate as James Guthrie, and had prepared (for the scaffold) his Last Speech, which is still preserved among the W d w Mss

They took a way to nominat to themfelves preachers; Mr. Douglafs indeed began, but was no more employed; Mr. Dickfon, Mr. Hamiltoun, and others of the minifters of Edinburgh, were paft by; as all we of the weft, except Mr. James Hamiltoun of Camnethan, and Mr. Hew Blair: but in all the nuiks of Scotland men were picked out who were thought inclinable to change our Church-government, and according to their invectives, againft what we were lately doing, were printed good, or fecklefs divines, at the pleafure of a very rafcall, Tom Sincerfe[7] the diurnaller, a profane atheifticall papift, as fome count him. Mr. Blair, Mr. Dickfon, and Mr. Hutchefon, were, without all caufe, mifchantly abufed by his pen, without the refentment of our State, till his Majeftie himfelf commanded to filence him[8] To myfelf I fand the Commiffioner very courteous: with much adoe I got myfelf fhifted of preaching. Mr. Wood and Mr. Colvin did their duetie very honeftly. Diverfe of the northern minifters, and fome others, play'd the fycophants; diverfe are ftaggering. but what his Majeftie was informed, that the moft part of the Miniftrie, efpecially the moft grave, wife, and learned, were for Epifcopacie, is utterly falfe; for the moft and far beft part are lying in the duft before God, for what they fee, and for which they fear, the great plague of God, even for the encreafing abominations of burgh and land.

Many blames Mr. Sharp, as the great court-minifter, by whofe fole advyce the King and Statefmen, both Scots and Englifh, are put on and directed in thefe medlings with our Church; but I have alwayes found him fo kind a friend to myfelf, that I will be loath to admitt fuch thoughts of him. Indeed the Chancellor and Prefident of the Councill, when the Parliament fent them to the King for removeing the garifons, took him up with them, as fome thought, to be an agent betwixt them and Lauderdaill, who was faid to be colder in purfuing Chancellor Hyde's defignes in Scotland than fome others, yet we hear no but Lauderdaill and they agree weell eneugh, and that he keeps fully his court.

The Parliament laid on no taxation, for the land is exhaufted, and very

---

[7] Thomas St. Serfe, or Sydferff, son of the old Bishop of Galloway He afterwards opened a theatre in the Canongate, with a company of Comedians, and was the author of a play " Tarugo's Wiles," printed at London 1668, 4to

[8] The diurnal or newspaper, published weekly under the title of " Mercurius Caledonius," to which Baillie refers, and of which Sydserff was the Editor, appears to have terminated with No 19 [12] on the 28th March 1661

poor; yet they laid on a greater burden than many Parliaments before them thefe many yeares, fourty thoufand pund fterling a-yeare during the King's life; but to be lifted in a way not very burdenfome, a moderat excife on drink alone When all this alfo is diftribute among weell-deferving men, the neceffities of many, and greed of fundrie, will not be gotten fatiffied.

At the beginning of the Parliament there were many brave defigns for Fifhing, and more ufe of Trade; but after much toome-talk, all feems to be vanifhed, the burroughs fticking abfolutely to their old job-trot for their own hurt. The charge of the Parliament was great: it had fitten long for no very pleafant purpofes. The moft defired it to rife without adjournment, and choiced rather to be governed fimply by the King's good pleafure, who was an equitable and wife Prince. While it's adjourned from July 12th to March 12th [1662], it was not very acceptable: they feared the intervall was but for the ripening the defignes of bringing in books and bifhops, either in whole or in part, as præparatorie to all was in England; alfo to fyne many for fmall faults, to fupply the waftrie of undeferving men. The Act of debitor and creditor wes very heavy to thefe had to doe with it. It was a pitie, when the King intended nothing but to eafe his people, and make the hearts of all that loved him rejoyce, it fhould fall out, through the improvidence at leaft of fome, to the contrare. Our good Towne was particularly greived that the nineteinth part of the Excyfe fhould be laid on them alone, notwith-ftanding of all their very diligent commiffioner John Bell could doe to the contrare. The Towne of Edinburgh got a part of their Excyfe to defray their prefent burdens: but get what they will, it does little good; for their debtyit is above nyne hunder thoufand merks, though ftill they be ftenting their Towne for their needlefs prodigahtie They fay, the dinner they gave to the Commiffioner, in the Colledge-hall,[9] did coft them large fyve hunder pound fterling

In England and Ireland thus affairs are: After the King had diffolved the Parliament at London, December 29th, all things being done abundanthe to

[9] On the 29th May 1661, the Lord High Commiffioner was conducted, by the Provost and Magistrates of Edinburgh, to the great hall of the College, where " he was welcomed by Mr Lighton, Principal of the place, with a Latine Speech, which with other pieces of poetry are printed by themfelves. Here was prepared by the City of Edinburgh a most sumptuous and magnificent Feast, that it was thought by many, and these witty travellers, that all Eur..... could... ...ut-d.... "&.. ... T'.. Work g... B......... .r.' Ed..b 1661, 4to.)

the King's contentment, the day of Coronation was appointed to be April 23d, St. George's day. The ceremonie was very folemne, as ever any coronation before our only grief was, that the Bifhops, in anointing, crowning, and all, had fo deep a hand. It was thought the former Parliament, how bountifull to the King foever, had one defect in the legalitie, that it was not fummoned by the King, but called by the former Parliament; to remead this, another was called to meet May 8th Great care was had to get, in all the fhyres, men commiffionat according to the heart of the court: the Prefbyterians alfo made fome ftickleing for this, but to no purpofe; for the Chancellor was fo active, as the moft affectionat of the old Cavileer partie was generallie chofen. When they mett, the Chancellor's fpeech advertifed them to beware of the Prefbyterian minifters, as peftiferous incendiaries: this grieved us fore. But when the Houfe of Commons did not only vote the Bifhops into the Houfe of Lords, but the Solemne League and Covenant to be burnt with the hand of the hangman, all our hopes were turned in defpaire.

The Parliament of Ireland, which fatt downe the fame 8th of May, was not behind, but put Bifhops in the Houfe of Lords; yea, choiced Bifhop Bramble to be fpeaker in the Houfe of Peers, though Mr. Davis of Derrie was readie to challenge him of many adulteries, and other odious crimes. The perfecution of Prefbyterian minifters began to be very hot: almoft all of them, both in England and Ireland, were put from their charges. The King, before the Parliament, after fundry conferences with the chief of the Epifcopall and Prefbyterian partie, had emitted a Declaration, albeit full eneugh for Books and Bifhops, yet it had fundry limitations for the eafe of Prefbyterians; but all was neglected. The Bifhops and Books were fully eftablifhed, as of old, without If's or And's: this caufes a very great mifcontment in many What the end will be, the Lord knows; only for the time, thoufands, who heartilie pray for all good to the King, doe cry to heaven for help againft the Epifcopall oppreffors, who little regard their prayers, knowing that they have neither any will, nor any power, to ufe any force againft them. Pamphlets on both fides flee thick abroad

The King declared to all his three Parliaments the unanimous advyce he had gotten from all his counfellors, to marrie the Infanta of Portugall; and all his Parliaments gave their heartie confent to it, though it was vifible it brought with it a prefent warr with Spaine This was little regarded, efpeciallie fince Holland adhered to our King, and fubmitted to him all their differences with Portugall. The great conditions, which yet are fecret, and the great hopes of the Princeffe readinefs to be of the King's religion, makes all to lyke the match weell, and to pray for a bleffing to it. The Parliament at London would gladlie [have] been (as they fay) at changeing the Act of Indemnity; but the King's peremptor adhereing to it made them let it alone; only fome more executions, and forfaultries of them in the Tower are expected It was much, that Sir Henry Mylmie [Mildmay] and Robert Wallop efcaped with drawing to Tiburne with ropes about their necks on hurdles. They fpeak of Sir Harie Vaine and Lambert as to be tryed for their life: they are two of the moft dangerous men in England Their execution will be weel eneugh taken by all generallie; yea, though Solicitor Saintjons [St. John] fhould be added to them. The King defires the Parliament to adjourne till winter, that he may goe to his progreffe towards Worcefter, and the places of his deadlie dangers, to vifit all who had been there friends unto him.

After the adjourning of our Parliament, fundry of our nobles pofted to court, the Commiffioner, Duke Hamiltoun, Montrofe, the Thefaurer, Athole, Aboyne, and others. There was there before, the Chancellor, Rothes, Lorne, and more. It's thought their agreeance will be fcarce good upon their private interefts, and efpeciallie about Lorne, whether he fhall be reftored or not; but I fear they fhall agree too weell to trouble our poor Church. The King's late declaration is no wayes fatiffactorie; it continues our Church-difcipline only dureing pleafure, and difcharges any preaching, petitioning, or medling with the Church-government. Mr Sharp is the only man with whom the King advyfes; and many fay he is corrupted by Hyde; which I wifh [may] be falfe; otherwayes we are in an exceeding hard taking: yet the Lord ever lives.

For our Towne and Colledge all has been quiet this year. When my prefentation came downe at laft, I was moved to accept of it, with the good will of all. No joy at all had I in it, for the burden is great, efpeciallie of debt and pleas; but importunitie of friends moved me to take it, left in thefe reeling times fome unhappie man fhould be fet over our heads. I moved the Facultie to call to my profeffion Mr. James Ferguffon, a moft wife, gracious, and able man: I was lyke to have gotten him; but when the Synod was ready to have voted his tranflation, Mr. John [Young], my colleague, with an unhappie overture, put them to a delay; and fince, we were difcharged by proclamation to meet, fo I fear I fhall lofe him, which makes my burden the heavier. The Toune now is abfolutelie guided by the Bells and Campbells alone They guide indeed weell, but keeping the government among themfelf almoft alone: I fear ere long it caufe new trouble among us. The act of prefentations to patrons puts the planting of all vacancies in their hands, and I am afraid they make not a good choice. My boy Harie is now a preacher. God has given him a good and a fweet gift; I hope he fhall doe weell I was carefull to get the Chanceller,[1] my fcholler, made Chanceller of our Univerfitie, and Bedlay[2] Vice-Chanceller.

I have gotten fundry of your's latelie, two yefterday together, May 3d and July 4th, for which I thank you. I think before this you have gotten fundry of mine alfo. I long to hear if you receaved my book, and your fenfe of it My Speech at my entry to my place, you have herewith: If you think fitt, I would put it at the end of my book, as a publict teftimonie of my loyaltie; alfo my prayer and exhortation at the laureation.

I expected from yow, before this, the French Gazet of Amfterdam, whiles it is a refrefhment to us to look abroad. It's to me a marvell that the French can fit fo long quiet I know not if this hunder year they were out of fome motion four year together. Who can be the chief Minifter of State in place of the Cardinall? We hear no more of their affairs than if they were all dead. That great earthquake in the fouth of France, what it may portend we expect in tyme. Our Queen's retireing out of England, with her daughter Henriet, fome thought was more on mifcontent for Chancellor Hyde's too great power, than for any realitie of a match with the Duke of Anjou. The match of the Prince of Florence with the fecond daughter of Orleans, might weell have ferved the eldeft God be thanked your State is in fo good tearmes with all their neighbours. We hope Spain, in his old age, and infancie of his fon, will be loath to venture on a warr with England. If the warr of the Turk were reall with the Emperour, it feems Germanie and Italie would not be fo flow drawen to it. Our heart is fore for the condition of Tranfylvania. Is that brave familie of Ragotfi clean rooted out? But what we hear of cafting all out of Pole, by act of Parliament, who will not declare themfelves Papifts, grieves us fore. Though that fool Chriftina of Sueden be contemned

---

[1] William Earl of Glencairn, Lord High Chancellor. [2] James Roberton of Bedlay.

of all, we think it juft with God and man Bleffed be God! who yet defends the Venetians againft the height of the Turk's rage.

When the King was goeing to his progreffe, and the Parliament of England to adjourne, July 20th, they changed, as we hear, their refolution. the Parliament fat ftill, the King gave over his progreffe for this year; he is not for to fend for his Queen in hafte What may be the reafon of this change, we yet doe not know. I am glad to find yow continue juft in my fenfe of our publict affaires.

For Mr. James Sharp at London August 29th 1661.

Dear James,

What yow are doing there now I can learn from no man I am forry that none of our old friends keep correfpondence with yow, at this fo neceffare a tyme. For myfelf I reft on what yow wrote to me, when yow went from this, that your journey was not for any change in our Church Diverfe times fince the King came home, by your letters, yow made us confident there was no change intended for us: Bleffed be God! hitherto there hes been none offered. What now there among yow may be in agitation, yow on the place know. Yow were the moft wife, honeft, diligent, and fucceffful agent of the nation in the late dangers of our Church in Cromwell's tyme: your experience and power now is greater. In this very great danger, apprehended by many, of other changes and forer troubles from the Epifcopall partie, both here and there, I hope God fhall make yow as happy inftrument to prevent all our feares, and to allay all our prefent forrowfull perplexities, as yow have oft been before. Let others think and fpeak of yow as they pleafe, and in their follie give yow matter of provocation, if yow were not wife, grave, and fearing of God, yet yow fhall deceave us notablie, and doe us a very evident evill turne before I believe it. Since firft acquaintance yow have ever been very faithfull and loving to myfelf in all occafions.

For the tyme, there be two favours I intreat from yow. Firft, that you would help our Colledge in its very great neceffitie. This year we keeped no table; not one mafter of us hes gotten a fix pence of ftipend, nor will get in hafte. for our laft year's table a thoufand pound is yet aughtand and the prodigall waftrie of Mr Gillefpie hes put us in above twenty-five thoufand merks of debt. Mr. John Young, as yow know, gave to the Chancellor, our noble Chancellor, fome memorandums for our help, whereof yow promifed to hold his Lordfhip in mind. I wrote to the Secretary once and again, as ye know likewife, in that matter, but without any fruit as yet; except yow join with thofe our two Noble friends, I think we but threfh the water. Had I not expected by yow and them fome relief of that kind, I had never put my head in that comfortlefs yoke, wherein now it fticks. Dear James, help your old friends out of beggarie and dyvorie if yow can : I am fure his Gracious Majefty hes, this twelvemoneth bygone, given many thoufand pounds to them that hes farr lefs deferved, and can doe him farr lefs fervice for it

The other courtefie I defire to be in your debt for is, That if his Majefty be pleafed to fend for any from this to fpeak with anent our Church, as he hes twyce declared he purpofes, yow would fee effectually that I be none of them, for neither am I able, in this my fixtieth yeare, and frequent infirmities, for any fuch journey, whether be fea or land; nor does my mind ferve me to give advyce for the leaft change in our Church, as yow well know, but with all my ftrength I behoved to diffuade it, which would but offend his Majefty ; whom I will be loather in the leaft to offend than any mortall creature, for the particular refpect I have, and ever have had, fince my firft acquaintance in the Hague

Yow fee, James, how ftill I make bold to put yow to fafhrie for me, which ftill I purpofe to doe, fo long as ye like to continue the old man towards me. The Lord be with yow, and help yow, at this moft dangerous nick of tyme, to doe our poor Mother Church your wonted and faithfull great fervice

Your Brother, to love, honour, and ferve yow,

R. B.

FOR THE RIGHT HONOURABLE AND NOBLE LORD, MY LORD CHANCELLOR OF SCOTLAND.

MY LORD,

THERE are many that long for your home coming ; but few more than I Without your Lordfhip's prefence we can get nothing done in our Colledge affaire I wifh your Lordfhip, from my heart, a profperous returne, fo foone as the publick and your Lordfhip's own affaires may permit These papers Mr John Young delivered to your Lordfhip, I hope are remembred. If we get no help from the King, by your Lordfhip's mediation, we are undone. I fent by Mr. John Young, to be fhewed to your Lordfhip, a lift of above twenty-fix thoufand merks of debt, in which Mr. Gillefpie hes left us, befide the ordinarie burden of the Colledge; and ten thoufand pund more will not perfite his too magnificent buildings. He got from the Ufurpers to this work, moft out of the excife of Glafgow, above twenty thoufand merks, and yearly two thoufand four hundred merks for twelve burfars,[3] payed quarterly, out of the cuftoms of Glafgow. I hope I am in no error, to think that your Lordfhip and I fhould be no leffe fibb to the King and his bountie than Mr Gillefpie and his Chancellar Thurloe was to Oliver. My good Lord, be intreated to do for us what ye can, to help us out of our beggarie and dyvorie, whernn we lye, by no fault of mine.

I have but one word more, as your Lordfhip's care and kindnefs did fave all the miniftrie and gentry, be-weft Glafgow, from the fore trouble otherwayes would have come on many of them. fo, if ye would win and weir, while ye live, the bleffing of us all, defert not our poor Church at this tyme of her greateft need. Permitt not our gracious Soveraigne to be deceived, by any whomfoever, that it will be fo eafy a matter, with his people's contentment, to make any change in our Church. It's true, if ye will make moft humble and loyall fupplications a crime and difloyaltie, (which yet hes been a naturall and neceffar libertie for all fubjects in all places and all tymes,) yow may doe what yow will, and none fpeak againft yow fo much as in a fupplication: but I am fure our Prince will egregioufly be abufed, if truth be not told him, that putting of Bifhops upon us

---

[3] As Baillie so often reiterates his charge against Patrick Gillespie for gross extravagance, the following passage from the 'Mercurius Caledonius' may be quoted, in reference to Gillespie's appearance before Parliament, March 6th 1661 — "Mr Gillespie was brought to the Barr he had a handsome discourse, by way of Information, relating to a Vindication" It is a great pitty, that this man should ever have been ensnared in mistakes *for he is a generous and publick spirit'd Soul, witness his great emprovement of the University of Glasgow, both by the enlargement of the fabrick, and encreasing of the burser-ships,* which is the grand nursery of our Clergy, and the first degree of their advancement. *And if there be merit in the Fanaticks of either kinde this man hath the largest share'* p. 102.)

at this tyme will caufe a more generall grief and mifcontent in Scotland, than any action of any of our Princes hes done thefe hundred years. And fince God hes put your Lordfhip for the prefent in the chief place of authoritie in our land, and credit with his Majefty, be not content to lye by, but as ye would be faithfull to your Prince, Countrey, and Mother-Church, to which three after God ye are moft obliged, lend us now a lift; that, in the true account I may readilie give to the world and pofteritie of what is paft among us thefe thirty-fix years, your Lordfhip's juft character may be with the faireft of all, as I wifh and hope it fhall. The confcience of my loving and honouring of your Lordfhip from a child, emboldens me to all this freedome   The Lord blefs your Lordfhip, fo prays

Your humble and much oblidged fervant,
R B

For my Lord Lauderdaill.

My Lord,

THAT I get no anfwer of any I wrote to your Lordfhip, I take it weell, knowing what elfe yow have to doe. It fatiffies me when I know ye receive mine, to be made ufe of as ye think fit   I was a while in perplexitie for yow, hearing ftories of combination againft yow ; but as I took them for fables at firft, fo I am glad they have proven fuch in the end   At this tyme I have but two things to fay : The one concerns our Colledge ; the other our Church ; concerning the firft I have written, I think thryce alreadie.

Mr Gillefpie hes left us both in a debt of above twenty-fyve thoufand merks, and in a neceffity to perfyte his buildings, whilk ten thoufand pound more will not doe. No Mafter of our houfe hes gotten this year a tuppance of ftipend ; yea for our laft year's table we are in debt yet above one thoufand pounds.   Had I not furely expected, by your Lordfhip's mediation, to have obtained fome help from his Majefty, when fo many of no greater deferving have obtained fo liberallie, I had never put my head in that yoke, under the which already I groane. Shall Mr. Gillefpie for his vanities gett between twenty and threttie thoufand merks of the Ufurpers, and we for our neceffities get nothing from the King, no not his Father's debt fubfcryved to us in the year 1633, the Acts whereof, as yet, I hope are no revocked? My Lord Chancellor and Mr Sharp know our condition, and I believe would be willing to affift your Lordfhip for our help, but I hope yow need no affiftance for any fuch matter.

Concerning our Church, we are informed our dangers are daily encreafing. Yow lately fubfcribed a Proclamation difcharging all fupplications anent Church-Government. Were fupplications difcharged to any fubjects in any tyme or place in the world, when modeft and loyall? and for fuch alone, were ever the chief judicatories of the Church diffolved by authoritie? What will the end of fuch work be? If I were able to travell, as truely through age and infirmity I am not, I would venture to come up and doe, at leaft as Willie Hill did to King James, the 17th of December, to greet to him for mere love and favour, and fhew him how he was mifinformed of the ftate of our countrie, that Bifhops would become fo lovelie creatures to us as we were ready to receive them, without fo much as a fupplication to the contrare. I think I could make good that, by his Majefty's permiffion, in twenty dayes tyme, I fhould get the hands to a moft earneft fupplication againft all novations in our Church, of all the minifters of our Synod without exception of one man, and there will be of us above fix fcore in Kyle, Carrick, Cunninghame, Clydfdaill, Barranthrow, and the Lennox. Alfo, in the Synods of Galloway, Dumfries, Argyle, and the Ifles, I hear not of one man that would not joyn on their knees with us. The qualities of thefe light men about Aberdeen, who have been ever for all changes, are weell enough known. It is all the pities in the world, that when his Majefty has no other intention but to give contentment to all his good people, that by the falfe information of fome, none of the beft men, he fhould doe that which infallible would bring the greateft grief and mifcontentment, generally, on all here, that for fome hunder years any action of any of our Princes ever brought on this land. I am fure, though we be debarred from fupplicating either King or Parliament, yet many thoufands of the truely beft of this land would cry loud to the heaven, and never be filent, till that God did deliver them from all thefe novations and their inevitable confequences. If the moft gracious and juft Prince in the world be not fully informed of all thefe things in tyme, before he be ingadged, tye on yow all who are about him. Let the King doe what he will, he will ever get the bleffings of us all; but believe it, that the too juft grieves of the people will light at laft, fickerlie, on fome of your heads.

I have fent my Chronologie to Holland for the preffe. I hope it fhall give offence to no man, though I fall in debates with many. The dedication will not goe this three moneth, and before it goe your Lordfhip fhall fee it, that there may be no word into it which may be difpleafing. The Lord bleffe your Lordfhip to be doing good while ye have tyme. Remember your two coufins, the Father of the laft two Dukes [of Hamilton], and eminent Balcarras. Your Lordfhip's fervant, as ye fhall deferve.

R. B.

If our Kirk were out of danger, and our Colledge out of debt, I would give little for the kindnefs of all the courtiers in Chriftendome.

For my Lord Lauderdaill.

My Lord,

As the world goes now, I fear I will be forced to importune your Lordfhip ofter farr than I purpofed. My Lord Chancellor told me, that his Majeftie had fpoken to him and yow of me, that fome there had given him an evill information of me for reprinting lately my Parallel. I told my Lord Chancellor the fimple truth, wherewith he was prefently fatiffied, and promifed to write up for my clearing. Yet I thought fitt to informe your Lordfhip alfo, that at your conveniencie yow would clear my innocencie to his Majeftie. Thefe obfervations on the Scottifh Service-book I writ twenty-four years ago, and delivered for the moft part in the Generall Affembly of Glafgow; by the advyce of the chief of our Church and State, were printed at London 1640; fince that time I never looked after them, till within thefe few weeks I faw a copie of them as reprinted at London 1661. This is a very falfe lye; for there is not a word of them reprinted but the title-page alone,[4] by fome cheating printer there, to make fome old copies of the firft and only impreffion fell. However, believe me, I knew no more of that cheater's deed than the child unborn; nor know I at all who is the man. Your Lordfhip knows I have

---

[4] This is a miftake as the edition of his "Parallel of the Liturgie and Mass Book," printed in 1661, is unqueftionably not the same as that of 1641. See the account of Baillie's publications in the firft volume.

written half-a-dozen of little tractats againft Books and Bifhops, and near as many againft Sectaries; but I would be loath now to reprint any of them. Yet if any there fhould reprint them utterly without my knowledge, it were not my fault. I expect your Lordfhip, in this particular, will right me with his Majeftie.

Your Lordfhip's Servant,

September 9th [1661]   R. BAILLIE.

For my Lord Lauderdaill

MY LORD,

I HAVE written fundrie to yow of late, with greater freedome poffiblie than the tymes doe admitt, but I fhall endeavour to trouble your Lordfhip with little more of that kind, refolving fo great filence as I may towards all men; but mourning to God, while I live, for thefe things I never thought to have feen. I hope your Lordfhip hes righted me with his Majeftie for the miftake of my reprinted Parallel, according to my information fent up September 9th.

At this tyme I flee to your Lordfhip, as my laft anchor on earth, for help in fome things concerning our Houfe, wherein if ye fhould neglect me, I will be exceedingly afflicted, and ignorant what to doe nixt. Mr Gillefpie, befide the great debt he left us in, having found us in none, continues to vex us yet farder. By his numerous and powerfull friends, in the laft day of the Parliament, got through an Act, whereby he claimes of us fifteen moneths ftipend fince October laft, (twelve whereof are exprefly in my prefentation); and, by other cavills, great fumms of money farther. He hes begun to vex us already before the Councill; and if he get not his will there, (as he is too like to doe,) he is ready to keep us in plea before the Seffion all this winter: there was never more affronted impudence feen. I humbly befeech your Lordfhip, if ye may think it convenient, to get a line from his Majeftie to the Chancellor, to command Mr. Gillefpie to defift from fuch fycophantick perfuits of us, whom he hes peeled to the bones alreadie. His Majeftie, in my prefentation, hes under his hand declared, That Mr Gillefpie *ab initio* was an intruder, and had never any right to his ordinarie ftipend as

Principall, which, on that declaration, feems, might in law be repeated from him, but wifhing him no harme, we only defire that his Majeftie would declare to the Chancellor his pleafure, that he might be difcharged to crave any more money from us, efpecially fince the firft of October 1660, the tyme when he was removed from us to prifon for his crimes againft the State ; and to command him to be comptable for the foumes of money he hes taken from the Colledge, over and above his ordinarie ftipend   fuch an order from his Majeftie, and nothing elfe, I know would eafe us from great trouble and expenfe, which otherwife his reftleffnefs will quickly put upon us.

In a fecond [thing], alfo, I befeech your Lordfhip to pitie our condition. My Lord Chancellor, when laft there, obtained, under the King's hand, a recommendation of our hard cafe to the Councill, to be helped out of the vacant ftipends, and other wayes they could think upon ; but notwithftanding of all our Noble friend could doe, our petition was laid afide, to our no fmall grief. There remains now to us nothing but to renew our fute to your Lordfhip, to prefent a line to his Majeftie for his hand, not to the Exchequer, but the Collector of the Excyfe of Glafgow, to pay us at laft that two hundred pound fterling which his bleffed Father, in the year 1633, gave us a præcept for to the Exchequer, and for which the officers of the Exchequer gave us fundry tymes an order, as the doubles here enclofed do fhew, but never a penny of it could we obtaine to this day. Indeed Mr Gillefpie got from Oliver, weell payed, a gift for our building of fyve hundred pound fterling, alfo for twelve new burfars out of the cuftoms of Glafgow, which puts us in the greater hope of his Majeftie's fatherly bounty in augmenting the two hundred pound we crave.

There is a third thing I have to fupplicat your Lordfhip for, above all the reft ; the Bifhoprick of Galloway, a great part of our fubfiftence, is now taken from us   His Majeftie, I hear, does gracioufly promife to all the Univerfities liberall recompenfes for all is taken from them ; in that we fhall humbly wait with the reft for his Majeftie's conveniency, hoping your Lordfhip will not be forgetfull of us when other Univerfities are provided for   But for the Subdeanrie of Cader and Monkland, which we latelie did purchafe from the Dutcheffe of Hamiltone, with all the mortified money we had, as my Lord or my Ladie, I hope, will teftify to your Lordfhip ; our lawyers advyfed us to feek from the King a fignature of *novodamus* for that our intereft : We did prepare it; but our great friends, my Lord Chancellor and Mr. Sharp thought it unexpedient to fend it up at this tyme. Only we hope your Lordſhip will be carefull that no other gett a prefentation to that Subdeanrie, which we have bought at a dear rate, without the which we are not able to fubfift, and if your Lordſhip could think it expedient to get a line from his Majeftie, fignifying his pleafure to ratifie to us what the Dutcheffe and her Father were fecured in by his Majeftie's bleſſed Father, and all the law which then was in Scotland, it would be a fingular benefit to us, for without this we are in hazard of a prefent ftop of all our rent there, whereof for fome years we have been in peaceable poffeffion.

My Lord, I ſhall be loath in hafte to faſh your Lordſhip with fo long epiftles; but you know I am one of your old fervants, and it is for an Univerfitie which in the tyme of my Prefidencie is like to ruine, if yow my old patron put not to your hand quicklie to help it. What you can get done, or fees yow cannot get done, I intreat with all poffible fpeed I may be advertifed. What yow direct your fervant, John Don, to write to me with, if it come to Mr Hamilton, minifter of Edinburgh, he will fend it me with a fure hand. I preffe hafte becaufe our action with Mr. Gillefpie, before the Councell, begins 19th of this inftant, and ye know he drives furiouflie. I hope old kindnefs will not yet permitt yow to defert me in this very evill world. I remain a fupplicant to God for your Lordſhip's profperitie; and this is all I can doe in the recompence of your Lordſhip's favours

Your Lordſhip's humble fervant,

R. BAILLIE

What I write of Monkland and Mr Gillefpie, let fo few know it as may be for caufes.

Glafgow, October 1ft 1661.

For Mr. JAMES SHARP

JAMES,

I was glad when I looked on the double of my laft to yow, to find your miftake to be the clean contrarie way. Whatever grief my heart has from our changes, and is like to have till I die, I hope it fhall ftand with tearms of great refpect to yow, from whom I have receaved fo many favours, and ftill expect to receive more. As we left, I have now fent to yow a double of the King's grant to us, 1633, with the Exchequer's order thereupon: as yow promifed, I expect yow will prefent a line for us to his Majeftie about it. I have written to Lauderdaill to concurr with yow If yow two in this new world defert me, I muft take me to my books and my beeds, and leave this ftation wherein yow two moved the King to fettle me. Our fignature for Monkland, as yow advyfed, I have delayed till the thick of your bufinefs be over. In our recompence for Galloway I expect yow will deal for us as for St Andrewes.

Are ye not able to conjure for us this new ftorme that comes on us, by a new claime of Mr. Gillefpie of ten thoufand merks, that found us much to the fore, and leaves us in twenty thoufand merks of debt, as he muft confeffe, but, as I count, thretie-fix thoufand? Should he be heard to plead for more money from us, even fince the firft of October, when by the States order he was removed from us, for his crimes, and declared by the King never to have any right among us? Should this impudent injuftice be tolerat? If it goe on, I will be forced to entreat yow to complaine of it to the King; and if no redreffe can be had of it, earneftlie to defyre yow to procure for me fo honeft a regreffe as may be to my former ftation; for truelie, almoft dailie anxious perplexities for his heavie debts, does oft take my meat and fleep from me, and may bereave me of my life, if I be not fome way freed of them James, I doubt not of your kindnefs, and if I did, I would not thus trouble yow with my letters.

Your twenty-year old friend and fervant,

R. BAILLIE.

Glafgow, October 1ft 1661

For my Lady Dutches of Hamiltoun.

MADAM,

YOUR Ladyfhip is my old friend; and, before yow were borne, your Father and Uncle were oft very kind to me. That bargaine good Mr. Gillefpie made for us with your Ladyfhip, our laft payment of it to Preftoun of two thoufand merks, with annualrent, we purpofe God willing, to performe faithfullie at the terme of Martinmas. In our confultation with our lawyers, we find, they think us very unfecure by this new world in our bargaine, except by your Ladyfhip's and my Lord's help we get a new fignature of it from the King. For the time we requeift your Ladyfhip, or my Lord, may be pleafed to declare to my Lord Lauderdaill the truth of our bargaine, and your willingnefs that the King's hand fhould be put to a fignature for us, fo foone as we can gett it readie to prefent   Expecting this juftice and favour from your Ladyfhip, I remain,

    Your Grace's humble and much obliged fervant,

                  R. BAILLIE.

Glafgow, October 1ft [1661]

[FOR MR WILLIAM SPANG.]

DEAR COUSIN,

My laft was by the hand of my lad Harrie. I have keeped my chamber thefe fix weeks, and yet does keep it through a iofe in my legge; but, bleffed be God, I now walk up and downe my chamber and yaird   The Doctor thinks I have a fcrubie: I find an univerfall weaknefs, efpecialhe of my ftomack. It were a favour to me to be gone, yet I am willing to abide my appointed time, and take my part with others in thefe very hard tymes. It was one of my fpeciall defyres to have my Book printed, which yow, of your fingular kindnefs, have procured fullie to my mind. I will not be able to return yow this fpeciall favour. It is in fyne paper, a brave letter and volume; I could not have wifhed it better; only I would intreat yow would haften it fo much as may be, that it be not *opus pofthumum*. As yow have fent me the two firft fheets, I wifh yow fent me likewife what fince are caft off. The corrector had need, for the credit of the preffe, to be more carefull: in thefe two fheets yow fee what groffe faults are efcaped, which makes folæcifms and nonfenfes. Do your beft to caufe help this

Your new peice of Voffius is but a bagg of clatters, blown up with infolent pride, unbefeeming a fchollar, or any modeft man; whom I mind never to know. The reft yow fent us were without catalogue or price, but it is good yow keep befide yow an account of all fuch things. Send me with your next an account of all the Colledge is due, but be intreated to be only in Englifh money which we underftand. I have delyvered to Mary Hamiltone, as yow defyred, one hundred and one pound, fiftein fhilling : yow have herewith her difcharge to yow of it, and fuch teftimonialls from our Toune as yow defired. Let me know your receipt heirof with the fame bearer.

The ftuffe for my Wife's gown, which came not to her till the other day, was very good, but in the meafure there is fome miftake as it feems. Yow write it is elevin Dutch ell and a quarter : it hes gone through many hands ; what came to her is but nine Dutch ell and three quarters ; fo that it is a Dutch ell and a halfe leffe than what yow fent, when Adam Ritchie with a Dutch ell-wand hes meafured it fharplie. This cannot be helped. I have fent yow here a patterne of the ftuffe, that yow may fend me two Dutch ell and ane halfe of the fame ftuffe, for my wife's gowne does require it, and cannot be made up without it.

The publict affaires yow know them as well and better than I. Our Kirk, all the Englifh tymes, had been very faithfull to our King, and fo inftrumentall as we could for his reftitution. We had loft much blood at Dunbar, Worcefter, and elfewhere, and at laft our libertie, in his caufe. We did firmly expect, at his Reftitution, a comfortable fubfiftence to ourfelves, and all our Prefbyterian brethren, in all the dominions ; and believe the King's intention was no other ; but, by divine permiffion, other counfells thereafter prævailed, and now carry all. When the King was at Breda, it was faid he was not averfe, from eftablifhing the Prefbytery ; nor was the contrare peremptorily refolved till the Saturday at night, in the cabbin-councell at Canterbury. At the beginning it went on foftly : Calamy, Baxter, Manton, Reynold, were made chaplains : but at once it altered. This did come from our fupine negligence and unadvertence , for the Parliament, then confifting of the fecluded members, the Citie, Monck alfo, and the Armie, were for us : Had we but petitioned for Prefbytrie at Breda, it had been, as was thought, granted ; but fearing what the leaft delay of the King's coming over might have produced, and trufting fully to the King's goodnefs, we haftened him over, without any provifion for our fafetie. At that time it was, that Dr. Sheldon, now Bifhop of London, and Dr. Morley, did poyfon Mr. Sharp, our agent, whom we trufted ; who, peice and peice, in fo cunning a way, hes trepanned us, as we have never win fo much as to petition either King, Parliament, or Councell. My Lord Hyde [is] the great Minifter of State who guided all, and to whom, at his lodging in Worcefter-houfe, the King weekly, and ofter, ufes to refort and keep counfell with him alone fome hours, and fo, with the King, Mr. Sharp became more intimate then any man almoft of our nation. It feemes he hes undertaken to doe in our Church that which now he has performed eafily, and is ftill in acting.

He had for co-operators the Commiflioner, Chancellor, and Rothes Lauderdaill, and Craufurd, were a while contrare, but feeing the King peremptor, they gave over. His Majeftie's letter to us at firft, penned by Mr Sharp, promifed to keep up our Church government eftablifhed by law; and to fend for Mr. Douglafs and others to conferre about our affaires. The laft Mr. Sharp hindred; for with him alone it pleafed his Majeftie to conferr. and the fenfe of the firft, few of us dreamed till it came out thereafter. We were amazed at the Proclamation, difcharging all petitioning againft Epifcopall government eftablifhed by law, as it was in the year 1633; of putting downe our Synods, and Prefbyteries, and Seffions, of calling up Mr Sharp, Mr Fairfoull, and Mr James Hamilton of Camnethan; alfo Mr. Lighton, then at London, to be confecrate by the Englifh Bifhops; which, after fome tyme, they were by the Bifhops of London and Worcefter, and others, with many Englifh guifes. Their feaft to all the Scots, and many of the Englifh nobilitie, was great. They ftayed there fome moneths longer than was expected, that they might be fufficiently inftructed in the Englifh way. When they came downe, they were receaved by a number of Noblemen, Gentlemen, and the Magiftrates of Edinburgh, magnifieklie. the Commiffioner's Lady feafted them and the Nobilitie that night, as the Chancellor did the morrow thereafter. Mr Sharp had bought a fair new coach at London, at the fides whereof two lakqueys in purple does run.

The Parliament of England did all things for the King he pleafed: augmented much his revenue beyond what any King in England ever had. After fome conferences at Worcefter-houfe, betwixt the Bifhops and a few of the Prefbyterians, where it was hoped his Majeftie would bring the Bifhops to a great condefcenfion, at laft it was found they would yield in as good as nothing. fo the Houfe of Commons formed a Bill of Uniformity, that all fhould be put from their charges who did not conforme to the Bifhops orders On this the Houfe of Lords did make fome demurre, and yet does; but we doubt not of their agreeance to it at laft; and from thenceforth a fearfull perfecution is expected, for the prevalent part of the Epifcopall faction are imbittered, and, both in doctrine and practice, it feems, fully of the old Canterburian ftamp. God be mercifull to our brethren, who hes no help of man, nor any refuge but in God alone: We fear our cafe fhall be little better.

Our Parliament was adjourned from the 10th of March to the 8th of May. The Commiffioner and our Nobles defyred not to leave London till they had feen the Queen. Alfo much talk was of difcord betwixt the Commiffioner and Thefaurer, about the collection of the new revenue of fourty thoufand pound fterling The Thefaurer pleaded it might come in to the Exchequer, and the other had obtained a gift of collecting it to his goodbrother Lord Lyon: the Secretar partied the one, and my Lord Hyde the other; the ftrife was more long and loud than was fitt; the King agreed them at laft as it might be. The Commiffioner came from London on the Wednefday, and came hither on the Sunday morning; the Archbifhops did confecrate other five on the Wednefday at the Abbay church, Mr. Haliburton to Dunkell, Mr. Paterfone to Roffe, Mr. Murdoch M'Kenzie to Murray, Mr. Forbes to Caithnefs, Mr. Robert Wallace to the Ifles; Dr. Wifhart defigned for Edinburgh, and Mr. David Mitchell for Aberdeene, are not yet come out of England; nor old Sincerfe appointed for Orkney. Mr. David Fleafher [Fletcher], whofe patent was for Argyle, refufed it, the rent being naught. The Commiffioner gave the feaft after the confecration, as his Majeftie had defrayed liberallie all their charges in England.

Our Bifhop,[5] the other week, took a ftart to come to Glafgow. The Chancellor convoyed him, with Montrofe, Lithgow, Calender, and fundry more noblemen and gentlemen, with a number of our town's folks, both horfe and foot, with all our bells ringing, brought them to the Tolbooth to a great collation. He preached on the Sunday, foberly and weell; but Mr Hew Blair, in the afternoon, ridiculoufly worfe than his ordinarie. Some of my neighbours were earneft that the Chancellor and he fhould have a collation in the Colledge on Monday morning Againft this I reafoned much; but was over-voted, to our great and needleffe charge: two hundred pound

[5] Andrew Fairfoull Archbifhop of Glasgow

payed not our charge. Mr. John Young made to the Bifhop a fpeech of welcome, befide my knowledge. The Chancellor, my noble kind fchollar, brought all in to fee me in my chamber, where I gave them feck and ale the beft of the towne. The Bifhop was very courteous to me. I excufed my not ufeing of his ftyles, and profeffed my utter difference from his way; yet behoved to enticat his favour for our affaires of the Colledge; wherein he promifed liberalhe. What he will performe tyme will try.

The Councell did call for Mr. Robert Blair fome moneths agoe, but never yet made him appear; we think they have no particular to lay to his charge, but the common quarrell of Epifcopacy, only will not have him abide in St. Andrewes to be a dayly eye-fore to his Grace.[6] Alfo they called Mr. John Carftares, that he fhould not fitt in Glafgow, to preach after his manner againft the tymes, to bear him company. Mr James Nafmith is likewife written for, as is thought, that the Deanrie of Hamiltone may vaike for Mr. James Ramfay; and with him Mr. William Adair of Air, the two minifters of Kilmarnock, Mr James Veitch of Maehlin, and Mr. Alexander Blair of Galftoun The guife now is, the Bifhops will trouble no man, but the State will punifh feditious minifters. We are in the moft hard taking we have feen at any tyme. It's the matter of my daily griefe, and I think it hes brought all my bodily trouble on me, and I feare it fhall doe me more harme.

I pray yow haften my book. I intend no other preface than it hes. I purpofed a dedication for Lauderdaill; but it feems it now will not be welcome to him. I writ to him of it, but he did not anfwer: however that will be the laft fheet. For verfes here, I intend none I care no for vanities. Let me have my count with yow, that I may know what Englifh moneys to fend yow My hearty fervice to your dear kind Wife, and all your fweet children I reft, after the old fafhion,

Your Coufin to ferve yow,

Glafgow, May 12th 1662. R. BAILLIE

[6] James Sharp Archbifhop of St Andrews

APPENDIX

TO

VOLUME THIRD

OF

BAILLIE'S LETTERS AND JOURNALS.

APPENDIX No. I.

LIST OF PAPERS INSERTED IN VOLUME THIRD OF THE MANUSCRIPT COLLECTION OF BAILLIE'S LETTERS AND JOURNALS

M.DC XLVIII.—M.DC LXI

1648.

Fol. 9 b. My Sudden Thoughts, on Saturday 12th February 1648, of the Motion of Warre then in all men's mouths. See page 37

12. The humble Petition of the Prefbytery of Glafgow, unto the Honourable Eftates of Parliament. This paper was drawn up by Baillie, who adds, in the margin of the MS., that " P G. [Patrick Gillefpie] changit much of this to the worfe " . . . 47

25 Baillie's " Extemporall Notions," in anfwer to the Queries, If men who have been active in the Engagement fhould be fufpended from the Lord's Table ? and, If the monthly maintainance may lawfully be payed, before the firft Queftion be determined? . 58

26 b. Inftructions to the Commiffioner of the Univerfity of Glafgow, for the Correfpondence of the Univerfities, 56

23. An Oath of Affociation, in purfuance of the ends of the Solemne League and Covenant · Baillie adds, "by War[riftoun] and Gil[lefpie,]" . . . 37

1649.

69. Collection of Letters and Papers from the Commiffioners fent by the Generall Affembly and the Eftates of Scot-

March 1649 These papers are either printed in the Appendix to the present volume, (Nos LXXIV.—LXXXIII.) pp. 458 (498) to 521, or in Mr Thomson's edition of the Acts of Parliament, vol. vi. pp. 451-459.

1650.

70. Reafons why his Majeftie's owning the League and Covenant for Scotland, cannot be fatiffactorie, 17th April.
71 b. Reafons prefented to the Generall Affembly, by the Commiffioner of the Univerfity of Glafgow, againft the Act of their late Vifitors concerning the Election of Regents.
72 b The Humble Remonftrance and Petition of the Commiffion of the Generall Affembly to the King and Parliament, 29th November.
74. The King's Speech to the Committee of Eftates, after "the Start," [11th October] .   .   .
    Sir James Balfour's Works, vol. iv p 118.
74. A few Animadverfions on the Weftern Remonftrance, by Baillie, addreffed to Mr. Robert Ramfay, but left unfinifhed, December 1650.   .   .   .
77. The fenfe of the Committee of Eftates upon the Weftern Remonftrance, Perth, Friday 20th November.
77 b The fenfe of the Commiffion of the Generall Affembly upon the Weftern Remonftrance, 26th November.
77 b. An Anfwer from the Commiffion of the Generall Affembly to the Quærie of the Parliament, [concerning the admiffion of Engagers to the Army,] 14th December.
78. Act [of the Commiffion] againft thofe that joyne in counfell or armes, or that complie with the Sectarian Army, 14th December.

1651.

79. Reafons of Diffent by Baillie and others, from the vote of the Prefbytery in behalf of Guthrie and Bennet, minifters of Stirling, 11th or 12th March.

85 b. The Commiffion's Confolatorie Letter to Edinburgh. (Baillie adds in the MS. " by my hand.")

89 b. The Humble Petition of the Commiffion to the King's Majeftie, and to Parliament againft the promifcuous admiffion of Malignants to the Army, 18th March,

96 Reafons of Diffent (by Baillie, and others?) in the Synod of Glafgow, againft a vote of diffatiffaction with the proceedings of the Commiffion, 4th April.

101. My Anfwer to Mr Robert Ramfay's Quærie, Whether Ingadging Officers who have fatified the Church, may lawfullie be employed in our prefent Armie?

102 b Two Acts of Affembly, in reference to oppofers of the Publick Refolutions, 31ft July.

103 Lancafhyre's Quæries Anfwered, by L Colonell, (the name is left blank in the MS.)

104. A true Information of the Affaires of Scotland, by one who truelie feareth to lie In Baillie's MS. this paper is faid to have been " Drawen by Mr Rutherfoord, and fent in by Mr. Murecraft to Mr. Gee, in Lancafhire, immediatlie before the Kingis March to Worcefter, June 1651."—There muft, however, be a miftake in this, for the paper itfelf comes down to May 1652, with a Poftfcript evidently written in July or Auguft that year. . . 379

105 Letter from Mr. Robert Blair to Mr. David Dickfon, 20th October . . . 376

Baillie, vol iii p 559

106. The Provinciall Synod of Lothian's Act againft the Protefters Commiffion, 5th November 1651; and " Their [the Protefters] faucie Anfwer," 14th November.

1652.

106 b. The Commiffion's Letter to Mr. John Robertfon, minifter of Dundee: (Baillie adds, " by my hand.") 7th March.

107 A Breiff Information to Minifters, concerning a prefent neceffarie Warning againft the Tender (By Baillie, and intended to have been enlarged by Mr. Robert Blair) 174

112 b. Proteftation againft the Provinciall Affemblie of Glafgow, 8th October [1651]
    Baillie, vol. iii. p. 561
113 b Memorandum for Caution in Conference about Union with Remonftrators
116. Advices and Anfwers from [Mr Robert Douglas, and others, in] the Tower of London, to my Queftions, 29th June. 177-184
    Baillie, vol. iii p 562
119 b. Proteftation againft the Prefbytery of Glafgow for not choofing Commiffioners to the Affembly, 7th July.
121 b. Reafons of a Faft appointed by the Generall Affembly to be keeped in all the Congregations of the land, on the 2d and 3d Lord's days of September.

1653

128 b The Synod of Louthian's Proteftation againft the Ufurpation of the Englifh, in April, after Mr Douglas's returne.

1654

155. C The Proteftation and Declaration of the Synod of [the Refolutioners, at] Glafgow, at their parting from the Anti-Synod, 4th April.
155 b D The Summe of thefe Endeavours ufed for preventing or healing the breach of the Synod of Glafgow, 4th, 5th, and 6th April.
159. E. The Act of Conftitution, 4th April.
159 b. F. An Act for a Synodical Faft, 6th April.
160. G Letter from the Synod [of the Refolutioners], to the abfent brethren of the Prefbytery of Air, &c. 6th April
164. K Mr. James Ferguffon's Letter to the Anti-Synod, prefented by Baillie, 12th June. . . . 254
168. L Mr James Ferguffon's Overtures to the Anti-Synod · or Overtures breiflie proponed . . 254
169. M 1. The fame Overtures enlarged, and the Equitie of them Afferted. 254

176.	M. 2. My Overtures, entitled, " Overtures for Union in the Synod of Glafgow and Air, proponed in a Conference by the Brethren adhearing to the late Generall Affemblies, to the Brethren Protefters againft the famin, 1ft Auguft 1654."	254
177 b	N. Scruples againft the Conftitution of the Synod Anfwered.	259
178 b	O. Overtures agreed upon by the Committee to be proponed to the Anti-Synod. 1. Overtures of Reunion proponed in conference by the Committee of the Synod of Glafgow and Air, to their brethren Protefters againft the late General Affemblie. 2. Overtures for ordering of Planting 3. Overtures for ordering of Purging,	259

1655

208. JJ	Exhortation from the Prefbytery of Edinburgh againft the Protefters Commiffion, 5th December,	301–305

1656.

236 A.	Inftructions to Mr. James Sharp, for London, 23d Auguft. Baillie, vol iii p 568.	330
238. B	Propofalls to be fought by the Protefters from the Lord Protector, Baillie, vol iii p 573	353
243. Q.	Paper given in by the Protefters at London to the Lord Protector and fome Members of Parliament, [for excluding Engagers, &c from places of truft.]	354
243 b. R.	Articles exhibited againft Mr Patrick Gillefpie, wherefore he ought not to be Principall of the College of Glafgow, Baillie, vol iii p 574	363, 364, 372

1657.

245	Information and Reprefentation to the Lord Protector's Council, by three of the Referees, againft the Propofalls referred to them, 14th July: figned, Lambert Godfrey, William Cooper, Thomas Manton	355

1658.

249 b. Approbation by the Prefbytery of Edinburgh of "the Declaration [printed in May 1658,] for healling the woefull differences of this Church,"

256 b. The Declaration [Sir George Booth's in name] of the Lords, Gentlemen, and Freeholders of the once happie Nation of England . . . 428, 437

265   Overtures for Union or promoving of peace in the Church, prefented to the Synod of Fife, &c. 4th November.

1660.

267   Letter from King Charles the Second to the Prefbytery of Edinburgh, 10th Auguft . . . 410
     Wodrow's History, vol i, p 13.

268   Letters from the Prefbytery of Edinburgh to Charles the Second (in anfwer to his Majefty's Letter,) and to the Earl of Lauderdaill, 20th September. . . . 410
     Wodrow's History, vol i. p 14

1661.

274.   Form of the Oath taken in Parliament, 1ft January.   463
     Act. Parl. vol vii. p. 7.

285.   Baillie's Anfwer to two Queftions propofed by the Profeffors of Divinity in the Univerfity of Utrecht, (in Latin.)   451

APPENDIX No. II.

ORIGINAL LETTERS AND PAPERS CHIEFLY RELATING TO ECCLESIASTICAL AFFAIRS IN SCOTLAND
M DC.XLVII.—M DC LXII

CONTINUED FROM VOL II PAGE 516

LXXII.

Mr GEORGE GILLESPIE'S SPEECH IN THE GENERAL ASSEMBLY AT EDINBURGH, 6th AUGUST 1647

[Wodrow MSS 4to Vol xxvi No 12.—In the Appendix to the previous volume, pp 499-512, are inserted various original Letters of Gillespie, while attending the Assembly of Divines at Westminster, in the year 1644 to 1647 That other Letters written by him during that period are still extant, is probable from what Wodrow states to his friend James Frazer, Esq London, in a letter dated 22d July 1722 "As to Mr G Gillespy, (he says) beside what writs are in his printed papers, I have 20 or 30 of his Originall Letters when at the Westminster Assembly; his Speech, giving account of his procedure at London to our Generall Assembly on his return, and I know his Notes which he took of what passed in the Westminster Assembly, in 12 or 14 volumes, are yet remaining in his Grandchild's hands, a minister here of my acquaintance" It is not improbable, that Wodrow, writing from recollection, may have mistaken the precise number of such Letters and Note-books, for it does not appear, from the Catalogue of his Manuscripts, that he possessed more than the twelve Letters which are printed in this work. But it would be desireable that further inquiry should be made in other quarters respecting such MSS The publication of Gillespie's Notes of the Proceedings of the Westminster Assembly, from two copies in Wodrow's collection, although these apparently contain only a portion of the 12 or 14 volumes he mentions, would form a most suitable companion to Dr Lightfoot's Notes, or " Journal of the Assembly of Divines"

Gillespie returned from London, along with Baillie, to attend the General Assembly at Edinburgh, August 1647, and on the 6th of that month, as our author informs us,—

· He and I made our report to the great satisfaction of all" Baillie's own Speech on that occasion is already given at p. 10 of this volume; and Gillespie's, hitherto unpublished, is now subjoined from a contemporary MS., but not being in his own hand the peculiar orthography has not been retained

George Gillespie was chosen Moderator of the General Assembly in July 1648, while he was in a declining state of health. Having gone for change of air to his native place, Kirkaldy he died there 17th December 1648, in the thirty-fifth year of his age, to the great loss of the Church of which he was so distinguished an ornament. He left under his hand, subscribed on the 15th December, a " Testimony against Association and Complyance with Malignant Enemies of the Truth and Godlinesse" Written two days before his death This along with a Letter to the same effect addressed to the Commission of the General Assembly, on the 8th September, are subjoined to his posthumous Tract. " An Usefull Case of Conscience Discussed and Resolved, concerning Associations and Confederacies with Idolaters, Infidels, Hereticks, or any other known Enemies of Truth and Godlinesse"—Edinburgh, 1649, 4to]

[MODERATOR] SIR,—I have been long desyrous to return here, that I might as waitt upon my particular charge so alfo give a farther account to this Honorable and learned Assembly of our employments with the Assembly of Divines at London

I speak ingenuously, the Lord knows that I was altogether unsufficient for so great a work and such an imployment My Colleagues indeed, have been both painfull and succefffull. Only this I would defire to profess, that with some uprightness of heart I have studied to lay hold on occasions of promoving the work of God there, and the service of his Church in this land. Neither have our labours been altogether without success which we ascrive wholly to the blessing of God, and therefore desyre, that as prayers have been made to God in behalf of our Commissioners and that Assembly of Divines, so thanks may be given in behalf of both for their good success, and peaceable setting about the work wherein the Lord hath employed them

Ye know we have acted in a double capacity according to our Commission: We have gone on in a way of treating with the Committee of Parliaments and Divines jointly and have given in many Papers, as concerning the Officers of the Kirk excluding scandalous persons from the Kirk Sacrament, the growth of Heresies, and such things, as in your judgment and ours, was defective among them We have acted in another capacity, debating with and affisting the Assembly of Divines their debates much of their time hath been taken up with the triall of Ministers, for Presbyteries not being established in that land, Ministers to be admitted in several places behoved to be tryed by them, yet the heads of our Commission have been carryed on to no small measure of perfection

The Confession of Faith is framed so as it is of great use againft the floods of heresies and errors that overflow that land; nay, their intention of framing of it was to meet with all the confiderable Errors of the prefent tyme, the Socinian, Arminian Popifh, Antinomian, Anabaptiftian, Independent errors, &c. The Confeffion of Faith fets them out, and refutes them, fo far as belongs to a Confeffion. This Confeffion of Faith hath been, to my knowledge, very much commended of them that had occafion to fee it, even by fome of the Prelatical party too. It is not yet fully approven by the Houfes of Parliament. The Houfe of Lords have approved it; the Houfe of Commons have approved the firft chapter of it, and was going on in confideration of the reft of it, at that tyme when they were taken off by the late commotion there, and emergent differences.

For the next Head of our Commiffion, ye know the Directory for Worfhip is fettled long ago by the Parliaments of both Kingdoms. I confefs it is not yet obferved by all there fo as it ought, yet it is obferved by many, to the great good of that land. We fhall only add to that head, the matter of the Pfalms, all grant that there is a neceffitie of the change of the old Paraphrafe. This new Paraphrafe was done by a Gentleman verie able for the purpofe, but afterward it was revifed by a Committee of the Affembly of Divines, according to the originall, and was approven by the whole Affembly. The Houfe of Commons hath given it a full approbation. The Houfe of Lords hath not as yet, many defyring and preffing other Paraphrafes alfo to be made ufe of in congregations, if they pleafe. All the Animadverfions fent by you were taken in due confideration. There are alfo here fome new amendments made by the Gentleman himfelf. Here is the book, the perfect copy and *ultima cura* of it.

The Third Head was Church Government, which, as it was the moft contraverted of the reft, fo it hath fuffered manifeft obftructions. There was a practicall Directory for Church Government drawn furth without Scriptural Propofitions, bot becaufe fome thought a Model of Church Government could not be framed, which were *Jure Divino*, there was another Directory for Government drawn up in Propofitions, with Scriptural truths, proving the fame. Here they are both.

Now in relation to this head of Church Government, there was a Committee of the Affembly and Parliament appoynted to fee if the Diffenting Brethren might been drawn to agree upon a common rule, according to the word of God, peace of the Kirk, and the Covenant. There was fome hopes of ane Accommodation, but becaufe of fome difficulties, efpecially for that they would have had a liberty of gathering their feperate churches out of others already conftitute; upon this it brake up. Only a new motion was made of it for eftablifhing that Committee of Accommodation before I came away, and their differences are yet lafting, and their ways, as I conceave, inconfiftent.

Now, the erecting of Prefbyteriall Government hath been oppofed by diverfe parties. Firft, By thefe that deny all Governments: Thefe are Eraftians. 2dly, By thefe that would have another form of Government than the Prefbyteriall, of thofe fome have ftudied to get in a moderate Prelacy, and a model of that fort hath been put in the hands of fome Parliament men, as I have feen. others labours mightily for Independency 3 It hath been obftructed, and receaved many wounds, by thefe that would have a Church Government framed in a prudentiall way by the wifdom of the State, and limited as they fhall think meet, as the Parliament hath ftudied to do in the poynt of fufpenfion from the Sacrament. They have made a great deal of reftrictions in that buifinefs, which the Affembly and godly miniftry there dare not condefcend to in confcience, wherenpon the Affembly, fticking to that that they conceive agreeable to the truth, they prefented a Petition accordingly The Petition was caften, being conceived a breach of priviledge Among other incongruities, they urged a double number of Ruling Elders at leaft to that of minifters, and if they pleafe, four tymes more, fo that all what minifters do fay, may be made null by the major part of Ruling Elders To this we gave in our Reafons to the contrarie It wes upon the occafion of this prudential modell, that the Nine Queries were fent to the Affembly by the Houfe of Commons, that the Affembly might be put to it for a particnlar model of Church Government, which was expected by many, they could never doe it, and fo this might be ane ground to go on in their intended prudentiall way Thefe Nine Queries, as I am very confident they may have a full and fatiffactory anfwer from Scripture, fo I believe they [would] have gotten ere now, were it not the Affembly had been neceffarily diverted by other things, put in their hands by the Parliament There is a fourth impediment that did hinder much the Prefbyterial Government, becaufe there be many that would be content of it, fo being it were with Liberty of Confcience that, if they pleafed, they might come under it, otherways not This is become a common plea, not only to Sectaries, but alfo to the Prelatical party: Doctor Taylor, the King's chaplain, hes written a large book for the defence of Liberty of Confcience

The laft Head of our Commiffion was the Catechifm The framing of this the Affembly have been very laborious in, and have found great difficulty how to make it full, fuch as might be expected from an Affembly, and, upon the other part, how to condefcend to the capacity of the common and unlearned. Therefore they are a-making two diftinct Catechifms, a Short and plaine one for thefe, and a Larger one for thofe of underftanding They have had no time yet to do any thing in the latter, bot here is the copy of the Greater, which is almoft compleat

Now, to add to thefe particulars the Dangers threatening religion, as affairs now ftands, which are very great; and though the wifdome of this Affembly can very well judge of them, without great information, yet, fince ye are pleafed to defyre ane accompt of affairs there, I fhall fhortly exprefs what we conceave to be the greateft dangers hindering the advancement of the defyred Reformation in that land, and thefe we conceive are growing greater, when we were in expectation they were growing lefs than before The difeafe was in the body, now it is broken furth in the fpirits,

before the groffe humors were purged away, and fo the danger is double. There is a
conjunction of interefts among thofe that have been averfe from the Covenant, and
thofe that have been ayming [at] a Reformation of religion hitherto, the Prelatical party
and Independent. There is a great deal of indeavour ufed to unite them, although, I
believe, that by this tyme they fee that their interefts and principles are inconfiftible.

2. A fecond danger there is, which needs muft be great, becaufe there is a refidua-
tion which is worfe than the firft difeafe, that which hath been built up is now a-caft-
ing down, and that which hath been a cafting down is a-building up. The Service-
Book, which we thought had been buried, is now allowed at Court, and the fiqueftrat
Minifters are by this means animated to intrude themfelves in their former places, and
fundry are receaved.

3. Before, our difference was with the Prelates and Sectaries, fo much as we knew,
only concerning Church-Government, fcarce imagining other differences, but now they
are grown to that, that there is not an article of the Chriftian Faith but it is contraverted,
and fome have drunk in that principle, The more fundamentall the poynt denyed or contraverted, the more it ought to be tollerated, becaufe being the more remote from fence
and reafon, and fo the denyers or affirmers of it ought the lefs to be controlled.

4. As the Solemn League and Covenant was juftly conceaved to be a fovereign
remedy againft the former evills, fo when that is caft afide, it muft make the dangers
the more and greater. many refufe to fubfcrive that League and Covenant, and it is
no wonder, feeing it hath not a civill fanction urging it upon the people. The King
hath not agreed to it. The Parliament, though it hath enjoyned the fubfcription of it
in all the Kingdom, yet there is no penalty charged upon the not-fubfcrivers of it, and
fo by many is not only flighted, but alfo it is written againft, of late, by the whole Univerfity of Oxford, which hath not as yet gotten an anfwer, but I hope it fhall fhortly.

5. The prefent commotions there makes the caufe to be in a great hazard. Now there
is a divifion between them that have taken the Covenant, as there was formerly between them that took it and them that took it not. As for the Army, it is true they do
profefs, in their publick papers, that it is not their intention to oppofe Prefbyterial
Government. They take God to witnefs their intention is not againft the Covenant.
What is the *intentio mentis* we know not, or the *intentio operantis*, but *intentio
operis* looks far otherways. Neverthelefs of the forementioned dangers, yet, on the other
part, there is hope in Ifraell concerning this thing. We want not our grounds of encouragement for hoping better things.

1. The hand of God that hath done verie great things for us already, gives us ftrong
hope to believe that He will do great things ftill, and I have heard many godly both
minifters and people there fay, That if the Kirk of Scotland which hath had fo many great
proofs of ane Almighty hand working for them, fhould diftruft the thorow bearing of this
work, their fin were greater than of any others. Now, as God's honour is engaged in

it, so hath he given many hearts to pray for the carrying on of the work, and, to my certain knowledge, assuredly to believe, the full satisfaction of their prayers, and a happy closure of the work

2 Next, we have grounds of confidence from the petitions of many, especially of London: Ye may understand very well the hearts of many by the petitions that have been occasionally from tyme to tyme published

3 There is hope from that that is put in execution already You know there is no government owned by the Parliament but the Presbyterial, although they have not come up so far as the Assembly of Divines have holden forth to them, yet that is the only government owned by them, and is put in execution in sundry places in England They have Classical Congregations, Presbyteries, and Synods, in London, and elsewhere there are beginnings There is a parochial eldership in Yarmouth and other some in Suffolk; they have receaved appeals from parochial elderships, as the superior judicatory from the inferior There is so much done as is more than a day of small things, so much as we would have greatly accounted of, if we might have hoped for it ten years ago, when we were a-coming out of Egypt

4 There is encouragement to us, from the great discovery of the ways of Sectaries Many who by their being very plausible gained ground before, are now down in the opinions of many, and their army, though now they prosper very much, yet have lost very many of their friends by their carriage of late, being fully persuaded their ways are not of God

5 From the Assembly of Divines God hath blessed that Assemblie very much and they do resolve, that whatsoever others shall do or whatever dangers or fears shall arise, that they shall not suffer themselves to be led away from the prosecution of that solemn Covenant, and the ends of it; that they will adhere to that Confession of Faith, Directory of Government and Worship which, according to the written word, they have resolved upon.

And truly, Sir they have desyred me to assure this Assembly of their solid resolution of adhering to Presbyteriall Government, and the other ends of our Commission from this Church. I speak with warrant from the Prolocutor of the Assembly, as is clear in this paper, which, for my memory's sake in the premises, I have here, being subscribed by the Prolocutor and the Clerk, And withall, their desire was to make their excuse for their not giving answer to diverse Letters from the Parliament and Assembly of Scotland; for that they being only Assembled for giving advice by the Parliament not being a National Assembly as you are, they were loath to interrupt the Parliament, whose warrant they behoved to procure, the Parliament being now otherways most seriously imployed. I shall only add, friends in England do blesse God for this Assembly's writting at such a seasonable tyme, and expects so much shall come furth from yow as shall refresh their saddened hearts, and advance the opposed work of Reformation

LXXIII.

ATTESTATION IN FAVOUR OF LIEUTENANT-GENERAL BAILLIE
22d AUGUST 1648.

[The following paper forms a sequel to General Baillie's Vindication of his conduct at Kilsyth, and Preston, (Volume 2d, pages 417-425) which he addressed by special request to "his cousin" Mr. Robert Baillie.—In addition to the few notices there given, it may be mentioned, that Lieut.-General WILLIAM BAILLIE of Letham, was the son of Sir William Baillie of Lamington, by Mrs Home, but born during the life of his father's first wife, Margaret Maxwell, Countess of Angus. In order to legitimate his son, Sir William, after the death of the Countess, married Mrs Home; but this proved ineffectual, his son having failed in an attempt made in 1641, to have the settlement of the estate of Lamington reversed and himself declared to be "the righteous air." (See Lamington family, Nisbet's Heraldry, vol. ii. App p. 131. General Baillie, in early life went to Sweden, and served under Gustavus Adolphus. In 1632, in a "List of the Scottish Officers that served his Majesty of Sweden," we find him styled "William Baily, Colonell to a Regiment of foote of Dutch." He returned to Scotland in 1638, and was employed by the Covenanters on many important occasions. In the unfortunate "Engagement," or secret treaty between the Royalists in Scotland and England, Baillie was appointed Lieutenant-General of foot in the army under the command of James Duke of Hamilton. The fatal result of the expedition into England, towards the end of July 1648, is well known. From the accounts collected by Bishop Burnet, (Dukes of Hamilton, p. 357, &c.) we may infer, that the defeat of the Scotish forces by Cromwell at Preston, on the 17th August, was in a great measure owing to the contradictory orders issued by the Duke as General, and the Earl of Callander, as second in command, and that no portion at least of the blame could be thrown upon Baillie. The capitulation entered into is thus mentioned by Oliver Cromwell in his letter to the English Parliament, 20th August 1648 —

" The next morning the enemy marched towards Warrington, made a stand at a Pass near Winaick. We held them in some dispute until our army was come up, they maintaining the Pass with great resolution for many hours, but our men, by the blessing of God, charged very hard upon them, beat them from their standing, where we killed about a thousand of them, and took (as we believe) about two thousand prisoners, and prosecuted them home to Warrington Town, where they possessed the Bridge. As soon as we came thither, I received a message from Lieut.-General Bailey, desiring some Capitulation, to which I yielded, and gave him these terms

That he should surrender himself and all his officers and soldiers prisoners of war, with all his arms, ammunition, and horses, upon quarter for life; which accordingly is done Here are took about four thousand compleat arms, and as many prisoners; and thus you have their Infantry ruined ' (Rushworth, vol. vii p 1238)

This Capitulation may be considered as presenting the termination of General Baillie's military career How long he survived is uncertain; but a few words may be added as to his family His eldest son James Baillie was born 29th October 1629. He married Joanna Forrester, daughter of George first Lord Forrester, on whose death, in 1654, without male issue, he succeeded to the title and property, as Lord Forrester His affairs, however, became much involved, his Lady, as Baillie reports, (*supra* p 367) died of a broken heart, about the year 1657, and he himself closed a profligate life in a tragical manner, being murdered in his garden at Corstorphin, 26th August 1679, by Christian Hamilton, wife of James Nimmo, and a grand-daughter of the first Lord Forrester (See Fountainhall's Hist Notices, p 233 Mr Sharpe's Note in Kirkton's Hist p 182, and New Statist Account, Edinburghshire, p 212) General Baillie's second son, William, born 12th December 1632, married another daughter of Lord Forrester, and on his brother's death in 1679, he succeeded as third Lord Forrester, but did not assume the title He died in May 1681, and his son William, after an interval of 17 years, claimed his right of patent, in 1698, and became fourth Lord Forrester (See Douglas's Peerage, by Wood, vol. i p. 602)]

At Warrington, 22d August 1648

We Under Subscrybers doe hereby declare upon our faith and honour, that We, with the rest of the Officers and Souldiers then present, did advyfe LIEUT-GEN BAYLIE to accept of the under-written Capitulation, and consented to the samyn, before ever it was signed

At Warrington-Bridge, 19th August 1648

IT is aggreit betwixt LIEUT-GEN. CROMWELL and LIEUT-GEN. BAYLIE, that all armes, ammunition, collours, and other furniture and provision of warre, be delyvered without imbattellment to Lieut-Gen Cromwell, or to whom he shall appoint That Lieut-Gen Baylie, with all Officers and Souldiers with him, shall be prisoners of warre, and that with the consent of all the said Officers and Souldiers

That they who shall soe rander themselffes, the said Lieut.-General Cromwell shall assure them all of saiff lyves, goods, and what else belongs to them, except horses, to be delyvered after they are disposed of, for their better accomodation, and in the meantyme to be furnished with horses for their journeys

              O CROMWELL
              W BAYLIE.

We doe lykewayes declair upon our faith and honour, that thefe Reafons following, were the motives of this appointment —

1 We were abandoned by all our Horfemen
2 The number of our Foot then with us did not exceed 26 or 2700
3 Scarce the halfe of them had keeped their armes
4 Since the 13th of Auguft they had received bot 2 pound of victuals a-peice
5 There wes no ammunition at all amongft them
6 When by Lieut-Gen Baylie's ordour they were brought from the open field nearer the Bridge of Waringtone, for the defence of the fame, into ane inclofure, the whole collours were not accompanied with fcarce 250 foldiours; the reft left their armes and ran to the Muir, from whence no perfuafion of Officers could bring them untill the Capitulation wes clofed
7 Before Lieut-Gen Baylie had brought up the reare of all that were uncutt off, my Lord Callander had given ordour to diverfe officers, to witt, to Lieut-Col. Kerr, Major Knox, and Capt Rutherfoord, as Kerr deponeth, to prepare for a baricade to the Bridge, and ftopping of all the ftraggleing foot at the Bridge, till they could fee what beft appointment they could make for themfelffes Likewayes Lieut-Gen Middletone did advyfe Col Dowglas, by Collingtoun, and by mouth, Col Turner, to caufe barricad the Bridge-end and guard it weell, and to tell Lieut-Gen Baylie, when he fhould come up, to make the beft appoyntment he could for himfelff and the reft of the foot The lyke commiffion he gave to Major Wm Dowglas, and defyred that the reft of his horfemen might be fent him up from our reere (*Sic subscribitur*)

  Col Dowglas. Lieut-Col Airny Houme Lieut-Col Johnstone Lieut-Col Andrew Kerr Major W Dowglas Col Wm Buntin (and the reft of the Officers in the field, who rode not away with the horfemen)

INFORMATION WOULD BE HAD OF THE REASONS

1 Why the Horfe quartered, ever after we went from Kendale, fo farr from the Foot?
2. Why the Horfe drew not nearer the Foot after their parties were beat in unto Blackburne? This being made known to the Generall Officers there, on Tuyfday in the night
3 Why we left Prefton-Muir, and our provifion there?
4 Why we left our quarter above Waltone, and our whole ammunition, and did not rather make our Horfemen come up?
5 Why the refolution at Standifh Muir to fight wes altered?
6 Why in the march from Wiggen, there wes not left fuch a reare-guard of Horfe as wes requifite for the retreat of the Foot? for want whereof the moft of them were ruyned.
7 Why at Waringtone the Horfemen did abandon the remnant of the Foot?

LXXIV.

LETTER FROM THE COMMISSIONERS OF THE GENERAL ASSEMBLY TO KING CHARLES THE SECOND. 7th February 1649.

[This and the next eight articles of the Appendix, are given from Baillie's MS.]
[Charles the First was executed on the 30th January 1649. The Parliament of Scotland, immediately upon receiving intelligence of this event, proclaimed Charles the Second King, on Monday the 5th February; and, as Baillie writes to Spang, (*supra* p. 66,) " We have sent the bearer, a worthy gentleman, to signify so much to his Majestie at the Hague We purpose speedily to send a Honourable Commission from all Estates" The following is the letter of which Sir Joseph Douglas was the bearer, and which may serve to introduce some of the subsequent articles. Baillie himself was one of the Commissioners who were sent on the part of the Church; and his private letters, written while in Holland, have already been inserted in this volume, pp. 84-90. See also the preliminary note to No. LXXXIII.]

May it please your Majestie,

As we did allwayes acknowledge your Royall Father his juft power and greatnefs, and powred forth our fupplications and prayers to God on his behalf, and doe abhorre thefe unparaleiled proceedings of Sectaries againft his Majeftie's perfone and life, fo we doe willingly and cheerfullie acknowledge your Majeftie's moft juft right of fucceffion to reigne as King over thefe Kingdomes, and doe refolve, in the power of the Lord's ftrength, to continue in prayer and fupplication for your Majeftie, that yow may feare the great and dreadfull name of the Lord your God, and reigne in righteoufnefs and equitie, and the Lord's people under yow live a quiet and peaceable life in all godlineffe and honeftie

Thefe Kingdomes now for many years paft have been involved in many calamities and confufions, by which the Lord's work hath been obftructed and retarded, and the blood of his people fhed, as water fpilt upon the ground, and we cannot but look upon the counfells of the ungodly as a maine caufe of all thefe evills It hath been the cunning of the Popifh Prælaticall and Malignant partie to traduce Prefbyteriall Government, and the Solemn League and Covenant as deftructive to monarchie, and with fo much witt and induftrie they manage thefe calumnies, that your Royall Father, to our exceeding griefe, was keept at a diftance in his judgement from thefe things, that doe much concerne the kingdome of Jefus Chrift, the peace and fafetie of thefe Kingdomes, and the eſtabliſhing of the King's throne, and was eſtranged in his affection from them who moſt tendered his perſon and authoritie

And ſeeing the Lord now calls your Majeſtie to ſucceed to ane of the greateſt and moſt important imployments upon the earth, which is much heightened by the preſent condition, it is our earneſt deſire unto your Majeſtie, in the name of the Lord Jeſus, whoſe ſervants we are, that ye would not only ſhut your ears againſt calumnies, but avoid the companie, and ſhun the counſells of the ungodlie, who ſtudie to involve your Majeſtie's publick intereſt, and that which concerns the preſervation of your royall perſon, and the eſtabliſhing of your throne, with their private intereſt and ends and to make your loyall ſubjects odious, that they only may be gracious And that your Majeſtie would avoid all the temptations and ſnares that accompanie youth, and humble yourſelfe under the mighty hand of God, and ſeek him early, and labour to have your ſenſes exerciſed in his word, and that your Majeſtie would eſtabliſh Preſbyteriall government, and allow and enjoyne the Solemn League and Covenant, and imploy your Royall power for promoveing and advanceing the work of uniformitie in religion, in all your Majeſtie's dominions. It is by the Lord who bears rule in all the kingdomes of the ſons of men, that kings do reign, and whatever carnall policie ſuggeſt to the contrarie, there is nothing can contribute ſo much for ſecureing the kingdom in their hand, as being for his honour, and ſtudying to doe his will in all things Therefore we know not ſo ſpeedie and ſure a way for ſecureing of Government in your Majeſtie's perſon and poſteritie, and diſappointing all the deſignes of enemies both on the right hand and on the left

We truſt it ſhall yet afterwards be no griefe of heart to your Majeſtie to hearken unto us in theſe things, (we have hithertill obtained mercy of God to be conſtant to our principles, and not to declyne to extreams, to own the way either of Malignants or Sectaries, and we were faithfull and free with your Royall Father, would God he had hearkened to our humble advyce) The Lord grant unto your Majeſtie wiſdome to diſcerne the tymes, and to make uſe of the opportunitie of doeing acceptable ſervice to God, and engageing the hearts and affections of your people in the beginning of your Majeſtie's reigne, by condeſcending to theſe neceſſarie things, ſo ſhall the Lord bleſſe your Majeſtie's perſone, eſtabliſh your throne, and our ſpirits, and the ſpirits of all his people in theſe lands ſhall, after ſo many yeares of affliction, be refreſhed and revived, and incouraged not only to pray for your Majeſtie, and to praiſe God in your behalfe, but in their places and ſtations, by all other ſuiteable means, to endeavour your honour and happineſs, that your Majeſtie may reigne, in proſperitie and peace, over theſe Kingdomes, which is the earneſt deſyre and prayer of

Your Majeſtie's loyall ſubjects and humble Servants,

THE COMMISSIONERS OF THE GENERALL ASSEMBLIE

Edinburgh, 7th February 1649

LXXV.

INSTRUCTIONS FOR THE COMMISSIONERS OF THE CHURCH SENT TO THE KING'S MAJESTIE. March 1649

1 You fhall be carefull to try, fo far as yow can, what is the King's inclination and difpofition, what are his principles, who are his Counfellors in whom he moft confides, and whofe counfells he moft followes, efpeciallie, how he is grounded in Religion, what countenance he gives, or what affection he bears to Prelacie, the Service Book, and the government, worfhip and ceremonies that were in the Kirk of England; and what forme of worfhip he ufes in his familie, what minifters he hath with him, whether he feeks God in private or not.

2. Yow fhall expreffe our deep fenfe and deteftation of the proceedings of the Sectaries againft religion and government, and of their proceedings againft the perfone and life of his Majeftie's Father

3 Yow fhall reprefent unto him the affection of the Kirk of Scotland unto Monarchie, and the continuance of the fame, as in the perfone of his Father, fo in his perfone and pofteritie

4 Yow fhall fhow him how Prefbyteriall government is not only confiftent with, bot helpfull to Monarchie, and to take off calumnies to the contrarie.

5 Yow fhall reprefent unto him our faithfull dealling with his Father, and our continueing conftant in our principles in reference to religion and government, without declyning unto the extreams either of Malignants or Sectaries.

6. Yow fhall in a difcreet way, at fitt opportunities, reprefent unto him the finnes of his houfe, becaufe of oppreffion to the work and people of God, and perfuade him thereupon to humble himfelf under the Lord's hand, that the guilt thereof may be taken away.

7 Yow fhall labour to informe him of things contained in the Nationall Covenant, and League and Covenant, and the true grounds of ours and England's entering thereunto, and perfuade him to fubfcribe thefe Covenants, and to enjoyne the fame, and to advance the work of Uniformitie, and eftablifh Prefbyteriall government, the Directorie of worfhip, and Confeffion of Faith, and Catechifme, in all his Majeftie's dominions And yow fhall fhow him how that this only and effectuall way for fecureing Religion, eftablifhing his throne, and fettleing and fecureing the union and peace of thefe Kingdomes

8 Yow fhall take occafion to fhow him that Prelacie was a mere ufurpation in Scotland, and never eftablifhed by a law. That he is as yet under no oath nor obligation, as his Father was, for Prelacie in England.

9 Yow shall labour to perswade him to lay afide the Service Book, if he ufe it in his familie, and to conforme himfelf to the practife of the Kirk of Scotland

10 Yow shall effectuallie and ferioufhe reprefent to him the evills of the counfells and defignes of the Popifh, Prelaticall, and Malignant partie, and labor to perfuade him to forfake their counfells and courfes, and to cleave to thofe that are ftraight for Religion and Government, and will be faithfull both to God and him

11. Yow shall shew him that we look upon the former idolatrie of his Mother as a maine caufe of the evills, both of finn and of punifhment, that have afflicted thefe Kingdomes And thereupon ferioufhe to reprefent unto him the evill and danger of Popifh marriage, and labour to difwade him from marrying any that is not of the Reformed religion

12 Yow shall labour to perfwade him to hearken to the defyre both of Church and State, as that which will fecure Religion, eftablifh his Throne, fatiffie his People, and fettle Peace

LXXVI

LETTER FROM THE COMMISSION OF THE GENERAL ASSEMBLY TO Dr. FREDERICK SPANHEIM

[This letter, as well as the next, was the compofition of Baillie. He introduces them both as being of his *draught*. Spanheim was Profeffor of Divinity at Leyden.]

REVERENDE VIR,

Humanitas tua vere fingularis, quam expertes abunde fe funt profeffi fratres a nobis ad Synodum Weftmonafterienfem deputati in fuo ad Hollandos diverticulo, efficit ut noftros jam ad Regiam Majeftatem in Hollandia delegatos tuæ curæ fidenter audeamus commendare In magnis cum Rex tum res tota Britannica in præfentiarum hærent anguftiis Attollimus oculos ad Dominum, in quo noftrum auxilium et unica fpes fixa remanent Expectamus a fratribus tranfmarinis perfeverantiam in fuis ad Deum pro nobis precibus, omnibusque qua fe dat occafio charitatis officiis et mutuis operis, ut Chrifti Regnum, quod mancipia Satanæ cunctis infernis machinis labefactari ftudent, fartum tectum confervetur, et incrementum capiat Non laborabimus, fcienti, ut putamus, commonftrare quæ fit rerum noftrarum hodie conditio Si quæ, hac in parte, dominum lateant, docebunt quam voles prolixe coram quos mittimus fratres. Abs te, Reverende Vir, obnixe petimus, ut pro magna tua prudentia, et auctoritate qua in Aula Araufionenfi ac Reginæ Bohemiæ polles, velis pro virili promovenda curare quæ Sereniffimo Regi per deputatos fratres humillima poftulata et faluberrima confilia deferenda commifimus

Quam hic navaveris Deo, Regi, Ecclefiæ, et nobis operam, faufta fit et fœlix, remunerabitur certe cœlitus Jehova ; et nos gratiffima mente repofitam confervabimus.

Tui in Domino Fratres amantiffimi a Nationali
Synodo Deputati, ac, omnium nomine,

Dabantur Edinburgi, pridie Kal.   R Douglassius. *Conventus Moderator.*
Martii 1649

LXXVII

LETTER FROM THE SAME TO Dr ANDREW RIVET

CLARISSIMO VIRO AC FRATRI IN CHRISTO DILECTISSIMO, DOMINO ANDREÆ RIVETO, IN ACADEMIA LUGDUNENSI SACRÆ THEOLOGIÆ PROFESSORI.

REVERENDISSIME, DILECTISSIME FRATER,

EXPLORATUS a multis jam annis tuus in domum Dei zelus, compertumque de reformatis omnibus eccleis ftudium efficit, ut quis fit rerum apud nos in præfentia ftatus per fratres noftros dilectiffimos tuæ prudentiæ confidenter aperire, et a tua pietate fraternum auxilium expectare non dubitemus Probe novifti, fat fcimus, quam atrocia, quam diuturna mala, Regna hæc et Ecclefias jamdudum vexent Maximum femper bonorum hic omnium defiderium fuit per profperam pacem imponendi tandem aliquando finem duriffimis calamitatibus, quibufcum integro jam decennio, et quod excurrit, conflictati fumus, fed ecce nova femper tempeftas, prioribus fævior incumbens, rejecit in novum malorum mare. Dederant noftri quantam maximam valebant operam, ut æquis conditionibus thronus, priftinufque fplendor, et quæcunque defiderari ullo jure poterant, Regi reftituerentur, fed male feriati fufurrones, calamitatum noftrarum vel primi auctores, vel affidui fautores, nunquam definebant peffime confultum principem fuis artibus perdere Status Regni, ut primum infauftum de Patris nece (quod facimus toto pectore execramur) nuncium accepere, quam fieri potuit maxima folennitate abfentem ftatim Filium edicto publico Regem declararunt, et Literas egregiæ fuæ voluntatis plenas tam terra quam mari perfcripferunt, Legatos fuos Londino veftram Hagam proficifci jufferunt, et alios iftius Legationis focios hinc amandarunt, qui humillima fua poftulata, et faluberrima confilia novo Regi communicarent. Id quod ante alia in præfentiarum folicitos habet, tenella eft Regis adolefcentis indoles, licet optimæ fpei, quem circumfederunt jam multi piorum in utroque regno confiliis vel aperti femper hoftes, vel non fatis conftantes amici · hoc eft, Reverende Vir, in quo tuam operam induftriamque nobis neceffariam arbitramur Scimus quo zelo flagres erga Dei veritatem, et quo tenearis defiderio videndi noftram Britanniam in puritate religionis, et jufta legum libertate, firmaque pace ftabilitam fcimus quantopere abhorreat tua æquanimitas ab eorum hominum perverfitate, qui vel fuis erroribus pervicaciter adhærentes, vel fuis privatim compendiis promovendis, aut reparandis difpendiis inhiantes, incautum regem in præcipitia fecum abducere, totaque regna, ac integras nationales Ecclefias novarum ruinarum laxis illidere flocci non faciunt. Hic eft ubi magnum Legatis noftris a Diabolo certamen metuimus, et ubi tuam pietatem exoratam cupimus, ut velis non gravate confilio et auctoritate tua, quibus plurimum iftic locorum vales, adefle fratribus quos illuc delegavimus ad res omnino maximas procurandas, quam non noftram tantum tam Regni quam Ecclefiæ, fed et totius infulæ, regis infuper regiæque familiæ falutem, imo vero reformatarum omnium Ecclefiarum emolumentum, unice fpectare certiffimum habemus Exiftimamus Auralıæ Principem, et regiam ipfius conjugem, Reginamque Bohemiæ, flectendi tenellum Regis animum ad fana confilia non mediocri facultate pollere. Scimus quanta meritiffime gratia apud iftorum omnium Serenitates valeas quantumcunque tuæ prudentiæ vifum fuerit piiffimo huic operi incumbere fperamus Dominum in fuo die remuneraturum, nos certe gratiffima femper mente recognituros pollicemur.

Tui in Domino fratres amantiffimi, a Nationali
Synodo Deputati, et, omnium nomine,
ROBERTUS DOUGLASSIUS, *Conventus Moderator.*

Dabantur Edinburgi, pridie Kal.
Martii 1649.

LXXVIII

BAILLIE'S LETTER TO RIVET.

[A BLANK IS LEFT IN THE MS FOR THIS LETTER, BUT NO COPY OF IT HAS BEEN DISCOVERED]

RIVET'S ANSWER TO BAILLIE

REVERENDO, CLARISSIMO, ET DOCTISSIMO VIRO D ROBERTO BALÆO, S THEOL D ET PROFESSORI, ET VERBI DIVINI FIDELI ADMINISTRO, NUNC INTER NATIONALIS, DELE-GATOS DEGENTI HAGÆ COMITIS, S. P.

REVERENDE VIR, ET MIHI OBSERVANDE IN CHRISTO FRATER,

MEMINI probe quantum debuerim ab octennio, et ultra, humanitati et benevolentiæ omnium veftrum, quorum Londini confortio et communicatione fum ufus, tua imprimis, qua etiam Hagæ Comitis, fed, vobis feftinantibus, ad breve tempus fum fruitus Filius meus, qui inter Principis domefticos Hagæ vivit, monuerat quidem veniffe ex veftra Scotia delegatos, qui agnitum Regem falutarent, et cum eo agerent de juftis conditionibus ei proponendis, ut Regnum apud fe inchoaret, et inter eos effe quofdam eximios Dei fervos, fed eorum nomina non mihi indicaverat, alioquin ego te faltem præveniffem, et veterem inter nos confuetudinem renovaffem; quod nunc facio, tuis literis, et noftri Spangii fratris & amici conjunctiffimi, admonitus Ego certe, fi ab initio accepiffem literas, quas a celeberrima Synodo ad me mififtis, et credidiffem me aliquid poffe, ut aliqua ratione negotium veftrum promoverem, nihil me retinuiffet quo minus ad vos excurriffem, præfertim hac anni fatis favente et non incommoda tempeftate Sed cum mihi fuiffet nunciatum Celfiffimum Principem meum pronum fatis ex feipfo effe ad res veftras promovendas, et Regi Sereniffimo confilia omnia fuggerenda quibus flecteretur ut fe fidei fuorum apud vos fubditorum committeret, quod etiam D Spangii nomine fuerat confirmatum, atque ita apud eum neceffarium non effe meum interventum, fubftiti hic, meque ad preces converti, ut Deus veftræ negotiationis eventum ad optatum finem dirigeret Non fine angore animi intelligo alia prævaluiffe confilia, et Regem effe in procinctu, ut ex Gallia in Hiberniam fe conferat, et per nos etiam hic brevi iter fuum inftituat; quæ via mihi videtur ad perniciem Regis et regnorum, reformatæ in illis ecclefiæ, tendere, et indicium effe iram Dei nondum deferbuiffe, qui hæc confilia finat prevalere. Vices etiam veftras doleo, et laboriofæ peregrinationis parum felicem fucceffum, nifi quod perceperitis bonorum omnium in his regionibus benevolentiam veftris rebus faventium, fed efficaciam deeffe, cum folius Dei fit animos regum inflectere ad meliora confilia Scribo ad Reverendiffimos Synodi veftræ Paftores, eis gratias maximas ago pro fuo de me judicio, et omnia defero quæ a me expectari poffunt in communi Ecclefiarum caufa, quod apud te, Vir Reverende, iterum profiteor, tibique, et D D. Collegis, felicem et fauftum ad veftros reditum, et meliorem eventum rerum veftrarum voveo, quam qui expectari debeat a confiliis eorum, qui non folum a carne et fanguine pendent, fed qui, affectibus etiam fuis indulgentes, animos gerunt adverfus Dei caufam exacerbatos, quos vel flectat Deus, vel reprimat Interim me precibus tuis commendo, et mearum viciffim fubfidum vobis promitto, tibique omnia profpera voveo Vale

Tuus omni officio et affectu in Chrifto,

ANDREAS RIVETUS

Brædæ Brabantorum, 5 Kal Junias CIƆ IƆC XLIX

LXXIX

MEMORANDUM FROM A FRIEND TO REPRESENT TO THE QUEEN

[" This I intended (says Baillie) to have fent with my Lord Percie, but did not being offended with the untowardnes of his difcours."]

1. That the King's refuseing to take the Covenant, and to give assurance for his consent to Acts of Parliament, injoining it in England and Ireland, seems destructive to his affaires, for it alienats from him his greatest strength, the hearts of Scotland and the Presbyterians of England, more than from his Father, who had more impediments within his owne breast to take the Covenant than the King can now have.

2. The Scots and English Covenanters will never forsake that Covenant, nor joyne armes with any of the Anti-Covenanting partie, for any persuasion, for any terror, as they love God and their soul, and will not be perjured, to this they are fixed

3. The King's joyning in that Covenant, joines together, for his service, not only the whole Covenanting party in the three Kingdomes, but also the most of the Malignant, who have no scruple of conscience to enter in that Covenant, and will have no scruple of honour if the King were into it

4. The uniting of all his subjects of the three Kingdomes for the King against the Sectaries, is necessary, the only visible meanes for it is his cordiall joyning in that Covenant; his refuseing of that meanes is clearly to keep all his friends devyded amongst themselves, and to force the most of them to sitt still and doe nothing for him

5. Upon this dissatisfaction, the Scots and the English Covenanters sitting still, the King must putt himselfe upon strangers and his Father's broken party, whose first service must be to overthrow the Presbyterians in the three kingdomes, who gladly would have been serviceable friends, but when once their blood is shedd by the hands of strangers, and their former enemies the Malignant party, they may turne desperate In the meane tyme, the Sectaries gett time to settle their new Republick

6. It is believed, generally, that the King's obstinacy comes not from himselfe, bot his Counsellours, and that they durst not hold him on so apparently destructive wayes, if they had not warrant, and encouragement from some other elsewhere.

7. That it is marvelled what can be the true ground of the stick The Popish party are no more at all hurt by the Covenant, than by these Acts of Parliament against them, to which the King's Father allwayes promised his full consent. The Covenant cannot come near any Papist, bot by particulare Acts of Parliament; and such Acts can bring all the trouble on them they feare, as much without as with the Covenant

8. As for the Prælats, the King's father offered Acts of Parliament to abolishe their vote in Parliament, to divest them totally of all civill imployments, to sett up Presbytries with them, to put the power of Ordination and Jurisdiction in the Presbytrie, as much as in the Bishop, their Moderator These concessions destroy whatever argument either his Majestie or the Prelats can bring for keeping up any roote of Episcopacie, either of honour from former lawes and customes, or of conscience from scripture For the legall and alledged scripturall Bishope is offered to be abolished, and a new one essentially different from the former, a meer stranger to England and the world abroad, altogether also unsatisfactory to the Covenanters, is urged to be put in his place

9 See if they be happy and wife Counfellours who will have the King and all his people deftroyed for fuch a neceffity as this, and if fatiffaction in this poynt may be obtained, confider if his Majeftie's affaires doe not require that with all fpeed, cheerfullnefs, and fullnefs, it be offered; how often hes gracious conceffions by parcells, and out of time, been for no purpofe?

1. But it is Objected, The King, by granting this defyre of the Scotts, will lofe the fervice of many more than he gaines.

Ans This is a groundlefs alleadgeance No Scottfman at all will fall off him for the Covenant All the late ingagers profeffit ever for it James Graham's friends alfo doe boaft of zeall againft Bifhops and Ceremonies None of the Englifhe or Irifh Proteftant nobilitie or gentrie, and very few of the Cleargie by their owne principles, believes Bifhops and Ceremonies to be fo neceffare, bot the Church of England may want them as the reft of the Reformed doe, and that the King and Parliament may lawfullie lay them afyde on the preffour of fmaller inconveniences than now doe compafs the King and his kingdomes. If any of the Clergie be in ane other judgement, their number and power is fo inconfiderable, that their obftinacie in this needs not be ftuck upon As for the Papifts in Ireland, they need be no more offended with the King's joyning in the Covenant, than with his affenting, as his Father did, to Acts of Parliament as fevere againft them as the Covenant Their offence here is not much to be valued, the King will not employ them, being idolaters, and the moft of them guiltie of much innocent blood Howfoever thefe things may be, let it be confidered whether, by taking the Covenant, his Majeftie's gaining to his fervice of Scotland entire, of all the Covenanters in England and Ireland. and fo many other, as by his Majeftie's example and authoritie, will be added to them, be a more fenfible advantage then by refufing of the Covenant, his keeping thefe of the Popifh, Prelaticall, and Malignant party, who will in no tearms joyne in the Covenant, with the certain lofs of all the true Covenanters in the three Kingdomes, who are tyed in confcience not to affociat in armes or counfells with Anti-Covenanters remaining in that condition

2 *Object* His Majeftie's confcience is contrare to the matter of the Covenant.

Ans How can it be fo? Shall the King enjoyn in Scotland what is againft his confcience? But what in the Covenant is againft his confcience? The abolition of Poperie cannot, for in this he is no more tyed to perfue the perfons of Papifts than his Father and Grandfather, and Queen Elizabeth, were by many Acts of Parliament, neither, any farther than the Oath of Coronation bindeth Kings of England to doe, though there were no Covenant for it Is it the abolition of Prelacy? I hope the King's confcience may be gotten clear from Holy Scripture, that there is no more a neceffitie for a Bifhop in England than in Holland, or any other of the Reformed Churches, who all have laid them afide, his Majeftie's Father offered to deveft Bifhops of all civill employment, and to joyn with them for ordination and jurifdiction a prefbyterie. This is to abolifh the legall and alleadged fcripturall Bifhop, and to put up in his place a new Bifhop effentially differing fiom the former, whofe abolition, not being the fcripturall Bifhop, cannot be againft a righthe informed confcience, nor againft the honour of the King of England, not being the Bifhop which either the law or cuftomes of England did ever know

LXXX

A NOTE INTENDED FOR MYN HEERE WILLEMS

I EARNESTLIE defyre, fince his Majeftie in his third paper to the States Generall does plainlie declare his refolution to go for Ireland, that the Prince, Princefs Douager, and fome of the States Generall, were dealt with to indeevour, that the States Generall in their anfwers to his Majeftie's defyres, might be pleafed in a friendlie earneftnefs to advyfe his Majeftie much rather to goe to Scotland than Ireland, for fuch reafons as their own wifdomes will eafilie fuggeft; for the prefent thefe come in my minde

1. His goeing to Ireland now joynes him with the worft part of his fubjects, and declares that his chiefe confidence is in them who, befyde their avowed Poperie, are fo defiled with innocent blood, that ane affociation with them cannot bot be curfed of God, and detefted by all the reft of his good fubjects

2. This cannot faile to blaft his Majeftie's defignes at the very beginning

LXXXI

THE COMMISSION FROM THE ESTATES OF PARLIAMENT

[Only the Title of this Commission and of the Instructions that follow are contained in Mr Thomson's Edition of the Acts of Parliament *Vide* Vol VI, pp 400, 435]

THE Eftates of Parliament being moft defyreous that his Majeftie by his authoritie would joyne and give his Royal affent and concurrence in all things for the good of Religion, his own honour and happinefs, and the welfare of his Kingdomes, and confidering how neceffarie it is that this Kingdome make their fpeedy addreffes, and render to His Majeftie their faithfull advice in thefe things which are neceffarie and effectuall for thefe ends, doe hereby therefore nominate, appoint, and authorize, and give power to the Right Honourable the Earl of Caffills, Earle of Lothian, Laird of Brodie, Laird Libbertone, Sir John Cheefly, Alexander Jaffrey, and William Glendinning, all feven being prefent together, or to anie two of them in cafe of the abfence of the reft, to repaire to the King's Majeftie, for doeing, acting, and profecuting every thing which may tend moſt to the good of Religion, ſettling of the Government, and peace of his Kingdomes, according to the Solemn League and Covenant, and the inſtructiones given, or to be given to them, in purſuance of theſe ends, firm and ſtable holding whatſoever ſhall be done by them

A. JOHNSTON, *Clericus Registri*

LXXXII

INSTRUCTIONS FOR THE COMMISSIONERS OF PARLIAMENT SENT TO THE KING'S MAJESTIE. MARCH 1649

Yow ſhall, with all poſſible diligence, repaire to the King's Majeſtie, deliver our letter, ſhow your commiſſion, and tell the true reaſones and excuſes of your not comeing ſooner to his Majeſtie

Yow ſhall ſhew his Majeſtie, that as this Kingdome was not wanting in their faithfull counſells to his Royal Father, for preventing the dangers which were then feared, and have ſince, to our great grief, fallen out; ſo did they, with all care and faithfullneſs, contribute their utmoſt endeavors for the preſervation of their late Soveraigne, as their letters, inſtructions, declarations, and their Commiſſioners papers witneſs

Yow ſhall ſhew his Majeſtie with what unanimitie, alacritie, diligence, and ſolemnitie, the Parliament did acknowledge him King of Great Brittane, France, and Ireland.

Yow ſhall ſhew his Majeſtie that his Father's oppoſition to the Covenant and work of Reformation was the chiefe cauſe of his and theſe Kingdomes troubles

Yow ſhall ſhew his Majeſtie how unacceptable the enemies and oppoſers of the Covenant and Reformation are to his Kingdome

Yow ſhall communicate to his Majeſtie the Act of the date of the 7th of February inſtant, as that which contains the neceſſarie ſatiſfaction which is defyred and expected from his Majeſtie by this Kirk and Kingdome, for ſecureing religion and the peace of the kingdome, and for gaining, not only the outward obedience, bot alſo the inward affection of all his good people to his Royall perſon, authoritie, and government, after ſo great diſtractions and troubles, and notwithſtanding the appearance and apprehenſion of new ſturrs and dangers; lykewiſe yow ſhall, by all the good reaſones which yow can thinke upon, endeavour to perſuade his Majeſtie to give the ſatiſfaction defyred heartilie and ſpeedilie

If his Majeſtie ſhall ſhew his willingneſs and reſolution to give the ſatiſfaction defyred in the ſaid Act, and to make the ſame known to the Parliament here, and to the Commiſſioners of the Kirk, yow ſhall in our name invite his Majeſtie to come to his kingdome of Scotland, and aſſure his Majeſtie, that he ſhall be received and entertained with all ſafetie, freedome, and honour, duety and reſpect, which can be demanded or expected by a gracious King from contented subjects, who are tied to him by so many bonds and oathes

If his Majestie upon these grounds resolve to come hither, his Majestie would be pleased to leave all these persones who were excluded by the Propositions of both Kingdomes, or against [whom] this Kingdome hath just cause of exception, and declare, that he will in matters civill, follow the counsells of his Parliament, and such as are or shall be authorized by them, and in matters ecclesiastick, the counsell of the Generall Assemblie, and of such as are or shall be authorized by them

You shall delyver our letters to the Queen of Bohem, to the Prince of Orange, and to the Princess Royal, and yow shall desyre them to interpose, and make use of their assistance to move the King to give satisfaction as is above specified

You shall lykewise delyver our letter to the Estates of Holland, and shew how sensible we are of their kinde respects to our King, and our desyres to entertaine all friendship and amitie with them; and you shall deal both with the Prince of Orange and them for a safe and honourable convoy to his Majestie to this Kingdome

You shall shew his Majestie the great dangers, and irreparable losses which most inevitably ensue upon his delay or refusal of the foresaid desyres, for by delay his enemies will be encouraged and strengthened, and the people be forced to couch under the burdens, and submit to their yoke, despareing of any meanes of reliefe or delyverance, and then the redresse will be more difficult, and opportunities once lost cannot be recovered. The neglect of opportunities which were frequently offered, and not taken hold on by his Royall Father, (as may be evidently instanced,) was the chiefe cause of his and the kingdomes troubles, and proved sad and fatall at last

And the sooner his Majestie begins to move that way which may be acceptable to God and good men, and offer to settle religion and peace, and upon these grounds claime the right of his Government, before Democracy, or any new modell of Government under the name of ane agreement of the people, or any other name or devyce be settled or take root, it will be more easie to maintaine Monarchicall Government, than to repeall and cast out any new forme of Government, after it is once establshed, and the people habituated thereto And if now, when by the power and prevalencie of sectaries, and the armie in England, that Kingdome is subdued and almost lost, and Ireland in very great distraction, his Majestie shall delay or refuse to satisfie the desyres of the Kingdome of Scotland, especiallie concerning Religion and the Covenant, which is the strongest bond to tye subjects to their King, it will weaken all who love Religion and Government in England and Ireland, and will wholly discharge [discourage] and disable Scotland to doe for him, and constraine them in such ane extreamitie to resolve upon some effectuall course by the Parliament to preserve Religion and the Kingdome from ruine and distraction

And his Majestie's granting of the foresaid Desyres, will so farr indeare him to this

Nation, and aſſure their affection and duties to him, as they will not only receave him with all thankfullneſs, and moſt willinglie render to him that ſubjection and dutiefull obedience which can be expected from loyal ſubjects to their King, bot lykewiſe to contribute their utmoſt endeavors by all neceſſarie and lawfull meanes according to the Covenant, and the dutie of loyall and faithfull ſubjects, that his Majeſtie may be reſtored to the peaceable poſſeſſion of the Government of his other Kingdomes, according to his undoubted right of ſucceſſion; and as his Majeſtie's coming in the Covenant with God and his people for ſettling religion, is the ſureſt foundation of a weell-grounded peace, ſo it will certainly be the beſt and the moſt effectuall way to eſtabliſhe his Throne in righteouſneſſe

Yow ſhall concurre with, and be aſſiſting to the Commiſſioners of the Church, in purſueance of their Inſtructiones, taking their advyce alſo in manageing of your's, eſpeciallie in theſe things relating to Religion

If the King's Majeſtie be willing to give ſatiſfaction to this Kingdome, yow ſhall deſyre him to recall all Commiſſions iſſued forth for acting any thing by ſea or land, to the prejudice of the Covenant or this Kingdome, or the prejudice of any who doe or ſhall adhere to the Solemne League and Covenant, and Monarchicall Government in any of his other Kingdomes

LXXXIII

THE REPORT OF THE COMMISSIONERS OF THE CHURCH, OF THEIR PROCEEDINGS WITH HIS MAJESTY AT THE HAGUE, MADE IN THE GENERAL ASSEMBLY, JULY 10th 1649

[The Commiſſioners, on their return from the Hague in July 1649, preſented a Report to the Parliament, and alſo to the General Aſſembly, containing copies of the ſeveral Papers interchanged with Charles the Second in the courſe of their negotiations. Moſt of theſe papers and letters are included in Baillie's Manuſcript; but they were publiſhed officially at the time under the following title.—

"The Proceedings of the Commiſſioners of the Church and Kingdom of Scotland with his Majeſtie at the Hague, and the Papers interchanged betwixt his Majeſtie and them, as they were Reported in Parliament and the General Aſſembly Appointed by Authority to be publiſhed Edinburgh, printed by Evan Tyler, Printer to the King's moſt Excellent Majeſtie, 1649" 4to, pp. 30 There is alſo an edition reprinted the ſame year at London, 4to, pp. 27. The firſt portion, or the Report to Parliament, may be found in Mr Thomſon's edition of the Acts of Parliament of Scotland, Vol VI pp 451–459. The other portion containing the Report of the Church Commiſſioners, in which Baillie was more immediately concerned, is here ſubjoined]

REPORT, &c

As We were commanded by the Commiffion of the Church, we made ready with all the fpeed we could for our voyage to Holland. According to your prayers, the good hand of our God brought us fafe through the fea. On Tuefday March 27, we made our firft addreffes to his Majefty, we delivered our Letters and Commiffion, expreffing in our fpeech, according to our Inftructions, the deep fenfe and grief of this Church for his Majefties afflictions, their deteftation of the principles and proceedings of the Sectaries in England, their conftant affection to Monarchie, and moft hearty defires for the bleffing of God upon his Majefties perfon and government. All this was well taken from us, and we were courteoufly difmiffed, to return when we thought fit with our Propofitions.

The Commiffion's Letter was as foloweth —

May it please your Majesty,

While the Parliament of this Kingdom are making their [humble] addreffes to your Majefty by their Commiffioners, We thought it our duty to fend fome of our number alfo inftructed with Commiffion from us, by whom your Majefty may underftand the integrity of our intentions towards Monarchicall Government, and the continuance thereof in your Majefties perfon and pofterity, and our utter deteftation of thefe abominable and unparalleld practifes of fome againft the Perfon of your Majeftie's Father, and their fubverting the ancient and fundamentall Lawes and Government of thefe Kingdomes. Our humble and earneft petition to your Majeftie is, That you would be pleafed to grant the defires of your loyall fubjects, who fincerely feek the eftablifhment of your throne in righteoufnefs, and as you love the glory of God, the good of religion, your own honour and happinefs and the peace and welfare of thefe kingdoms, you would not hearken to the counfells, nor countenance, or own the courfes of them who have been, and are ufurpers upon the priviledges, and difturbers of the peace of this Kirk and Kingdom. Our Commiffioners will acquaint your Majeftie more fully with our minde, unto whom we humbly defire your Majeftie may give credit, and interpret our freedom and plain dealing by them, as a reall teftimony of our unfained affection to your Majeftie's perfon and government. We have hitherto laboured to approve our felves in all fidelity to our Lord and Mafter Jefus Chrift, and in all loyalty to Kingly authority, and we are refolved to walk ftill after the fame rule, in our feveral ftations and vocations, amidft all the difficulties and oppofitions wherewith we are affaulted on either hand. Praying for your Majeftie, that the Lord of the whole earth would multiply all forts of mercies upon your Royall perfon, and gratioufly incline your young and tender heart unto the fpeedy embracing and following of the counfels of truth and righteoufnesse, and grant unto your Majestie a long and happy reign, that we may live under you, a peaceable and quiet life in all Godlinesse and honestie, who are

        Your Majesties loyall and loving Subjects, and humble Servants
          in the Lord, the Commissioners of the General Assembly
       [And in our name, and at our command.
                     Mr R DOUGLASS, Moderator.]

Edinburgh, March 1, 1649

Before we offered any of our desires, we thought it convenient to assay the putting away of that which we feared might prove obstructive to all our intentions. Before our comming that unhappy and cursed man James Graham had been sent for, and too well intertained by these of the English Counsell, who left affected our Covenant, and all the late proceedings of our Nation: Our first Paper therefore on Fryday, March 30, was for the removall of this evill man from his Majestie's presence and Court. The Commissioners of Parliament had desired the same before, the first answer they got was but dilatory, we conceived it the more necessary for us to joyne with the same their desire again, our Petition was in these terms —

MAY IT PLEASE YOUR MAJESTY

According to our Commission, we do represent in the name of the Kirk of Scotland their earnest desire, that such as lie under the censure of Excommunication may be discountenanced by your Majesty, and removed from your Court; especially James Graham late Earle of Montrosse, being a man most justly, if ever any, cast out of the Church of God. It hath been the custom of Christian Princes in all places and times, to maintain so far the discipline of all Churches which themselves did protect by their laws, as (according to the order of Christ) to decline the familiar conversing with every one whom the highest censure of excommunication made as Ethnicks and Publicans. Your Majestie's walking in any other way would be contrary to the rules of Scripture, to the practise of these Princes whose gracious examples will be your Majestie's most wholsome paterns, and would certainly give a great stroak to all the discipline of the Kirk of Scotland, which your Majestie's Royall Grandfather by many of his laws, and your Royall Father in his Parliament of Scotland 1640, hath expresly ratified, and we trust your Majestie will never intend to alter: least of all at this time, in the hopefull beginning of your reign, for gratifying of a person, upon whose head lies more innocent blood, then for many yeers hath done on the head of any one, the most bloody murtherer in our Nation.

We hope for so much mercie from our God, that his gracious Spirit shall incline your Majestie's heart to give us just satisfaction in all our necessary desires, that the cordiall union of your Majestie with your people, so much longed for on all hands, may with all speed be fully accomplished: And that this cursed man, whose scandelous carriage, pernitious counsell, and contagious company, cannot fail (so long as he remains in his obstinate impenitencie) to dishonour, and pollute all companies, and provoke the anger of the most high God against all places of his familiar accesse, shall not be permitted by your Majestie to stand any longer in the entry of our hopes, to our great discouragement and fear, left by his guilt, example, and acting, all the humble desires and wholsom counsels which we are intrusted with, should be obstructed and frustrate.

Friday March 30, 1649

CASSILS   ROBERT BAILLIE
GEORGE WYNRAM.   JAMES WOOD.

His Majestie's Return to us both was in this Paper

I DO insist upon my former Answer, and do desire and expect that you do deliver all the Propositions or Desires you or any of you are entrusted to present to me, before I make an answer to any particular one, being resolved to consider of the whole, before I declare my resolution upon any part

April 10. N Stil 1649   C. R

We took it for no good presage, that notwithstanding all we could doe by ourselves, or by others, this man remained still in our way, as an open enemy to all our designes, also that his Majestie's answer to us was put in one paper, and was altogether the same with his answer to the Commissioners of Parliament, without any direction either to them or us, expressing his acknowledgement of our capacity as Commissioners; yet having obtained the King's promise of a satisfactory answer in reason, to that our first Petition, so soon as the rest of our propositions were given in; and judging his Majestie's receiving of our message, and answering of all our papers without any quarrelling of our Commission, whereof in every paper we made expresse mention, to be a reall acknowledgement of us as Commissioners from the Church, and not being instructed to break off all treaty at the beginning, upon dissatisfaction in such things, as the Commissioners of Parliament, so we also thought fit to proceed

The main things we were instructed to propone to his Majestie, were the Nationall Covenant of Scotland, the Solemne League and Covenant of the three Kingdomes, the Directory of Worship, the Confession of Faith, the Propositions for Presbyteriall Government, the two Catechismes, as they were agreed unto by the Generall Assembly and Parliament of Scotland These six peeces we did bind together in a book, and delivered them to his Majesty, speaking somewhat to the matter of every one of them, and entreating that his Majesty would be pleased to read and peruse them all, what ever scruple might arise in his mind from any of them, we offered our best endeavours to fatiffie him therein, But our pofitive defires concerning thefe particulars, we gave in on Thurfday, April $\frac{5}{16}$, in this Paper.

MAY IT PLEASE YOUR MAJESTY,

WEE the Commiffioners of the Church of Scotland, hoping for an anfwer fatiffactory in reafon to our firft paper, according to your Majeftie's gracious promife, do go on according to our Commiffion, to fignifie, in the name of that Church, that after their hearty prayer to God, for his bleffing on your royall perfon and government, It is their moft earneft defire that it may be your Majeftie's pleafure to give them affurance, under your hand and feale, of your approbation of the Nationall Covenant of Scotland, fubfcribed by your Royall Grandfather, approven and enjoyned by your Royall Father in the Parliament of Scotland, 1640 And of the Solemn League and Covenant, which now, for divers years, the Parliaments, and Generall Affemblies of Scotland, the two Houfes of the Parliament of England, and the Affembly of [Dyvines at] Weftminfter, after long and ferious deliberation, have unanimoufly found to be the beft and neceffary means of fetling Religion, of eftablifhing the Throne, and bringing back profperity to your Majefty, and all your three now lamentably diftreffed Kingdomes alfo of the Directory of Worfhip, Confeffion of Faith, Catechifme, and Prefbyteriall Government of the Church, agreed upon, according to the Word of God, by the Affembly of Divines at Weftminfter, and the Generall Affemblies of the Church of Scotland the copies of all which we did, the other day, deliver to your Majefty. Likewife that your Majefty would be pleafed to fubfcribe the Nationall Covenant, with the Solemn League and Covenant, and give your royall affent to fuch Acts of the Parliament of Scotland as fhal be offered to your Majefty, for the eftablifhing and enjoyning of the premifes in Scotland, and to fuch Acts of Parliament as fhall be offered by the two Houfes of the Parliament of England, for the eftablifhing and enjoyning the fame in England and Ireland; and in the mean time, that your Majefty would be pleafed to lay afide the ufe of the Service Book, and conform the worfhip of God in your Royall Family to the Directory. We are fully perfwaded that your Majeftie's cordiall joyning with your loving fubjects in thefe means of advancing the honour of God and true religion, fhall procure from heaven the Lord's powerful affiftance, to bring your Majefty and your people out of the great tribulations and dangers wherein both for the prefent are plunged We are alfo confident that your Majeftie's granting thefe moft humble and earneft defires fhall be a chief and effectuall mean to knit to your Majefty, in all duty, the hearts of all your good fubjects, not in Scotland alone, but every where elfe, and fhall loefe to your Majefty none at all, who either loves the truth of God, or minds your Majefties happineffe above their own particular unjuft interefts

| | CASSILS | ROBERT BAILLIE |
| April $\frac{5}{16}$. | LIBBERION | JAMES WOOD. |

Upon Friday the day following we received from his Majefty this fhort Return

C. R. April 16

I DESIRE, for the reafons mentioned in my former papers, to know whether the laft papers I received from you contain the full demands and propofitions you or any of you have to make in reference to Church or State, and if not, that then you deliver what remains, that I may confider of the whole, and proceed accordingly

April 16, 1649

To this on the Satterday we made this Reply

UNTO the paper delivered to us by your Majefty this day, we doe make this humble return, that the laft your Majefty received from us the Commiffioners of the Kirk of Scotland, doth contain the fubftance of all we have to demand of your Majefty, the grant whereof will make any other humble advice we are to propone moft eafie What the Commiffioners of Parliament have to deliver in reference to the State, we leave it wholly to themfelves, they being in a commiffion and capacity altogether diftinct from that which we have from the Church alone.

April $\frac{7}{17}$, 1649

CASSILS   R. BAILLIE.
LIBBERTON. JAMES WOOD.

The dayes thereafter, his Majefty and the Commiffioners of Parliament interchanged divers papers about points of State, wherein we had no place to meddle, in the mean while we were not idle, but went about our inftructions, both by conferences with his Majefty, and by frequent dealing with divers perfons of quality whom we conceived to have ability or any opportunity to promove with his Majefty the grant of our defires; Alfo by anfwering fometimes even in print, a multitude of calumnies wherewith our malignant enemies, with much artifice and malice, did labour to poifon the eares of his Majefty and all about him againft our Church and Kingdome

But finding time to drive over, and no anfwer according to our mind appearing, we gave in on May $\frac{18}{28}$, the following Writ

UPON the $\frac{5}{15}$th of April, We, the Commiffioners of the Kirk of Scotland, did in their name prefent their humble and earneft defires of thefe things, which they conceived neceffary for the fecurity of religion, for the eftablifhment of your Majeftie's throne, and for putting of them in a confident expectation of the Lord's bleffing upon your Majeftie's Government, fince that time we have been alwayes wayting, and often humbly moving for an anfwer, but as yet none at all is given, we cannot conceal, but fo long a delay hath affected us with griefe, fo much the more as your Majefty hath declared your resolution to be gone from this on Thursday next, which makes the time we have to consider what your Majesty shall be pleased to offer very short Wherefore with all humility and earnestnesse we doe supplicate that without the losse of more time, now at last we may have so gracious and satisfactory a return to our former papers, as may make us leave your Majesty with joy, and carry home to them who have sent us, matter of praise to God for inclining your heart towards these their counsels: which are most likely to procure to your Majesty and all your dominions, an happy deliverance from all their present distresses

May $\frac{18}{28}$, 1649

CASSILLS.   RO BAILIIE.
LIBBERTON   JA WOOD

Hereby we obtained from his Majesty, May $\frac{19}{29}$, this Answer.

I HAVE considered the severall Papers and Propositions, delivered to me by you, and do assure you, that I desire nothing more, then that I may entirelie unite the hearts and affections of all my good subjects of Scotland to me, and amongst themselves als well for the honor, peace, and prosperitie of that Kingdom, as that they may joyntly and unanimously assist me, in the revenge of that horrid and impious murther of my Father, and the recoverie of my just rights in my other Dominions. (to which they are equally ingaged by the laws of God and of that Kingdom,) and to the obtaining of such an Union, I will consent to all that in conscience and honour I may, without imposing on my other Kingdoms   As first I will maintain, confirm, and defend the Government, Ecclesiastical and Civill, of Scotland, as is settled by law, and the ancient known laws of that Kingdom, as likeways all such Acts of Parliament as have been actually consented unto by the King my Father, being personally present in Parliament, or by his Commissioners lawfully authorized by him ; and particularlie, the laws concerning the National Covenant, the Confession of Faith, and Presbyteriall Government of that Church ; touching that part of the League and Covenant which concerneth my other Kingdoms of England and Ireland, it is not in my power justly to take any resolution therein, without the advice of my respective Parliaments of these Kingdoms, by whose advice and consent onely, lawes are there to be made and altered, neither can I consent to any thing which shall oppose or disturb the Peace lately concluded in Ireland, but I am very willing to refer the full consideration of the said League and Covenant, and of all the other particulars you mention (as to England) to a free Parliament to be conveened there by my writ, as soon as the condition of that Kingdom will permit me so to do, by whose advice I am resolved to govern myself therein, in the mean time, as I am very ready to do all that is in my power to the safe and quiet protection of my people in Scotland, under the benefit of the laws of that Kingdom, as likeways further to gratifie them in all that may really tend to their welfare, fo I fhall expect that obedience and duty from them in the exercife of my Royall power, as is due to me by their allegiance, to which they fubmitting, and for the burying all bitterneffe and animofities which the former diftractions and divifions may have produced, and the better effecting the happy union before mentioned, I am very willing and defirous to confent to any Act of Oblivion and Indemnity to all perfons of what condition foever of that Kingdom of Scotland, excepting oncly fuch perfons, (if any fuch there be, in or of that Kingdom,) that fhall hereafter, upon fufficient and due evidence in a lawfull tryal, be found actually and exprefly guilty of that late, unparaleld, horrid act, of the murther of their late Sovereign. And if it fhall appear unto me, that the League and Covenant containeth any thing in it not comprifed in thefe Acts concerning the Nationall Covenant, and Prefbyteriall Government of the Church of Scotland, and neceffarily to the welfare of the faid Church and Kingdom, without refeience to England or Ireland, I fhall, upon the firft fetling of fuch an Union, and the paffing of fuch an Act of Oblivion as is before mentioned, apply myfelf to give ful fatiffaction therein. Paffionately defiring to remove all occafions of mifunderftanding between myfelf and all my good fubjects of that my Kingdom of Scotland; and what is not particularly anfwered at this time, fhall be fupplied by an exprefs, whom I will difpatch into Scotland as foon as convenientlie I can.

May $\frac{19}{29}$ 1649   CHARLES REX

Our grief for this Paper was great, it was much worfe then any thing we expected, not only the hand of the worft of the Englifh counfell, but of James Graham alfo, and others of our evil Countrymen, was vifible therein; we refolved to give unto it this plain Reply.

MAY IT PLEASE YOUR MAJESTIE,

We the Commiffioners of the Kirk of Scotland, having confidered your Majeftie's Paper of May $\frac{19}{29}$, given to us in anfwer of all our former, muft in confcience of our duty with all humility make known to your Majefty, that to our great grief, we find it in many the chiefeft points of our defires very unfatiffactory. Unto our firft paper, for difcountenancing excommunicate perfons, to which a fatiffactory anfwer in reafon was promifed, nothing at all is faid. To our other defires no proper return is made unto us, but we are fent to gather it here and there out of your Majeftie's Anfwer to the Commiffioners of Parliament, wherein, though we find fome things returned to their defires which they had common with us, yet the moft part thereof runneth upon matters of State, wherewith our condition permits us not to meddle; but rather then to goe away without all further conference, we are willing, in obedience to your Majeftie's defire, to confider what in that writing we conceive may have any reference to our Propofitions.

We bleffe God that your Majefty affures us you will maintain, confirm, and defend the Ecclefiaſtick Government of Scotland as it is ſetled by law; and particularly, theſe laws which concern the Nationall Covenant, Confeſſion of Faith, and Preſbyteriall Government of our Church, their blame muſt be the greater, who have been authors to your Majeſty, to give ſo frequent, open, and familiar acceſſe to James Graham, moſt ſolemnly and juſtly excommunicate by that Church, which thing cannot but be thought, as it is indeed a great violation of the Ecclefiaſtick Government. To our defire in the matter of our Nationall Covenant; that as your Grandfather by his own hand, and your Father by the hand of his Commiſſioner, had ſubſcribed it, ſo your Majeſty would be pleafed to ſubſcribe the ſame, no anſwer at all is given. But our prime diſſatiſfaction is, that what we petitioned concerning the Directory, Confeſſion of Faith agreed upon by the Aſſembly of Divines at Weſtminſter and approven by the General Aſſembly and Parliament of Scotland, Catechiſmes and Propoſitions for Government is clearly denied; and our greateſt defire about the Solemn League and Covenants fully fruſtrate. The Covenant itſelf is broken in pieces, ſome parts are avowedly laid aſide, the other parts are refuſed to be taken unto confideration till they be proven, firſt not to be compriſed in the Acts concerning the Nationall Covenant, and Preſbyterial Government of the Church of Scotland, next that they are neceſſary to the welfare both of the Church and Kingdom, and thirdly, that they have no reference either to England or Ireland. When all this is made to appear, an Act of Oblivion of all that James Graham and his complices, or any other have done during all the time of theſe ſad diſtractions, muſt be paſt, and a union with all theſe men muſt be fully ſetled, before your Majeſtie do ſo much as apply yourſelf to give any ſatiſfaction in theſe things.

Such an Anſwer we know cannot fail to grieve the whole Church of Scotland, and all their Covenanted Brethren in England and Ireland; who under the pain of moſt ſolemn perjury, ſtand bound to God and one to another, to live and die in that ſolemn League and Covenant, as the chief and neceſſary ſecurity of their religion and liberties: which the popiſh, prelaticall, and malignant faction, by their pernicious counſels and actions, now of a long time have been overturning, and to this day continue diligent in promoving to their power that their deſtructive defigne. We marvail how any can object conſcience or honour againſt your Majeſties granting to us what we defire in the Covenant for ſecuring the Proteſtant Religion who have themſelves been counſellers and perſwaders that your Majeſtie, without all ſcruple either of conſcience or honour, ſhould conclude, ſubſcribe, and ſeal, antecedently to, and without any Parliament, yea contrary to all the Parliaments of England theſe hundred years, a libertie of the Popiſh Religion to the bloody rebels of Ireland.

Your Majeſtie would be pleaſed to confider, that any relation theſe things we defire may have to England, hindereth them not to be lawful Acts of the Generall Aſſembly of Scotland, legally ratified by the Parliaments of that Kingdom; which, when your Majeſtie does approve, nothing is impoſed upon England, ſince their own Houſes of Parliament and Affembly of Divines did not only act the fame things, but in all their treaties with the King and with Scotland, for divers years together did earneftly preffe them. Your Majeftie's Father, in his laft meffage to the Commiffion of our Church, did offer to ratifie the Solemn League and Covenant for all that had taken it, or fhould take it in any of the three Kingdoms, and in his laft treaty with the Englifh Commiffioners in the Ifle of Wight did, as we are informed, offer to confirm the Directory, Prefbyteriall Government, and what elfe was required for Religion in England and Ireland, ever till he and his Parliament fhould agree upon a fetled order for the Church. We do not conceive what in this Covenant can ftumble your Majeftie. The abolition of Epifcopacy and of the Service-Book your Majeftie maintains, confirms, and defends in Scotland : the duty done with a good confcience and allowance of God in Scotland cannot be againft confcience, nor offend God in England. no Reformed Church, no Proteftant Divine out of England, did ever efteem Epifcopacie or Liturgie neceffary. All Scotland, the moft of England, the beft part of Ireland, do judge the abolition of Popery of Prelacie, of Liturgie, and joyning in a Covenant for that end, a neceffary duty. Your Majeftie, and all the world may fee, to the very great grief of our foul, the wrath of the Lord burning like a flame, no better mean know we to quench it, then for your Majeftie to be humbled under his mighty hand, to feek and relie on his favour, to be zealous for advancing his affairs, to eftablifh the Solemn League and Covenant, to provoke him no more by holding up in his Houfe, againft the hearts of all the orthodox abroad, and of the godly at home, humane inventions borrowed from Rome, moft unhappy to Britain. No mean in our judgement is comparable to this, for opening the armes and hearts of your beft people to imbrace your Majeftie's perfon, to fecond, with their lives and eftates, all your juft defires, to imploy, with chearfulneffe, their whole ftrength to fettle you upon all your thrones. The refufing thereof, we are perfwaded, will be difpleafing to God, will difcourage and difcontent extreamly all your Covenanted Subjects, who otherwife are moft cordially affected to your Majeftie's fervice, may tempt you to allyances with idolaters, to a dependence upon ftrangers, to a courfe of cruell perfecution againft your beft fubjects, will be pleafant to none but to fuch as are your Majeftie's mortall enemies, who cannot but accompt it the joyfulleft news that can come to them; or to fuch as, whatfoever be their pretences or true intentions, yet by their counfells and actions, more then any other men living, do ferve the defignes and advance the work of the Sectaries at Weftminfter and Derby-houfe for ruining your Majeftie and us all.

Our defire to be faithful to our Mafter in Heaven, and to be anfwerable to the truft we have from the Church that has fent us, the tendernes of our hearts towards the more and more diftreffed condition of your Majeftie and your Kingdoms, have made us bold to lay out thefe our free, loving, and loyall thoughts at your Majeftie's feet, expecting your Majeftie will be pleafed to review our former Papers, and yet grant us fuch a fatiffactory return as may fend us home rejoycing, and make us be received for our glad tydings with praife to God, with bleffings upon your Majeftie, and confident expectation of a fpeedy change in the face of affairs in all your Dominions

May 23 } 1649　　　　　CASSILLS　　　　R BAILLIE
June 2 }　　　　　　　LIDBERTON.　　　JA WOOD.

Hereunto we received from his Majeftie this laft Anfwer

I AM much unfatiffied with your Papers of the firft and fecond of this month, in anfwer to mine of the 29 of May, finding by them that my reall endeavour to give all juft fatiffaction to my good fubjects of Scotland are undervalued, and mifinterpreted, and obferving in them feveral inferences, oppofing the natural fenfe and true intent of what I have propofed, with moft intire intentions for the good of that Church and Kingdom, and unfeafonably ftirring ufeleffe queftions, neither properly arifing out of any thing contained in any of the former Papers, nor conducing to the common peace But neither thefe nor any difcouragements fhall prevail with me to omit any thing that may tend to the peace and happinefs of all my good fubjects of Scotland, to which I fhall moft affectionately, to my utmoft power, (upon all occafions,) apply myfelf, according to the duty which I owe to the Almighty God, in the exercife of my Royall power for the good of my people, in order whereunto I fhall, with convenient fpeed, fend you by the Exprefs mentioned in my laft Paper, the more particular anfwer I then promifed I fhall likewayes more fully exprefs myfelf concerning the new matter contained in thefe Papers, and fhall particularize, what I now complain of in them. In the mean time, I expect and require from all my fubjects of Scotland, fuch obedience as is due to me their King, by the laws of God, of Nature, and of that Kingdom

C. R

To this we thought fit to make no Return in writ

We did indeed expect, by the affiftance of the Prince of Orange, whofe conftant friendfhip we felt all the time of our abode there, and by the induftry of fome Noblemen of our Nation, to whom, for their affectionate fervice to us in our negotiation, we counted ourfelves not a little obliged. by the Lord's bleffing we fay on their labours, we expected towards the time of our return a better and more fatiffactory Anfwer; but his Majeftie, as we heard, being refolved before he made any conclufion to fpeak with the Queen his Mother, and to fend an exprefs hither with more of his minde; we kiffed his hands, and took our leave in difcomfort and grief, yet not without fome hope, certainly with moft earneft defires, that the promifed Exprefs may bring to us much more matter of fatiffaction and joy, then for the time we have any warrant to fpeak of

We have but one thing further to give an account of: The Commiffion did write with us to the Reverend Divines Doctor Rivet and Dr Spanheim Dr Spanheim received his letter, but before he did anfwer, the Lord, to our grief and the very great regrate of all the Churches abroad, did end the pilgrimage of that truely eminent, and now much defiderat divine Doctor Rivet's abode was not at the Hague as we expected, but in Breda we thought it a pitty, in his extream old age to put him to the pains of fo long a journey as from Breda to the Hague, but we had his beft affections and prayers going along with us in all our defires, as he fignified to us in his private letters, and as, we fuppofe, he doth exprefs in this to the Affembly, which here we prefent

CASSILLS   ROBERT BAYLIE
GEO WYNRAME.   JAMES WOOD

Edinburgh, 10 July 1649   Ante meridiem, Seff VI

THE Generall Affembly, having taken in ferious confideration the Report of the Travells and Proceedings of the Commiffioners fent to his Majefty, prefented by them this day, together with the Commiffion and Inftructions which were given unto them, doe find by the Report, that they have been very diligent and faithfull in the difcharge of the Truft committed to them, and therefore, do unanimoufly Approve of their carriage, and return them hearty thanks for their great pains and travells in that Employment

A KER

LXXXIV

LETTERS FROM GEORGE WYNRAME OF LIBBERTON.

[Orig Wodrow MSS Fol Vol xxv Nos 61, 62, 74 —Wynrame was admitted Advocate 20th December 1620 In public life, he first distinguished himself by undertaking to convey to London the Supplication of the General Assembly in 1638, justifying to the King their proceedings in having abolished Episcopacy; (vol i p 187.) During the following years he was confidentially employed by the Covenanters in various important affairs In February 1649, he was appointed Colonel of one of the regiments raised in the County of Edinburgh, and in March that year he was one of the Commissioners from the Estates of Scotland sent to Charles the Second at the Hague. On his return, 22d June, he was admitted a Lord of Session, under the title of Lord Libberton Wynrame again visited Holland towards the close of 1649, as the bearer of letters from the Estates to Charles, urging him to comply with their requests. In March 1650, he was a third time deputed by Parliament, in conjunction with the Earl of Cassillis and other Commissioners, to conclude the Treaty with the King at Breda Lord Libberton was present at the battle of Dunbar

VOL

in September 1650, and was there so severely wounded, as to occasion his death within eight days after that disastrous event. (Balfour's Hist. Works. vol. iv p. 98 Brunton and Haig's Senators of the College of Justice. p 341)]

No I
Rotterdam, wltimo Octob 1649

RIGHT REUEREND,

ALTHO I had not the happines to fe yow at my pairtng I know ye will neither forgett the worke nor the unworthy inſtrument that is [in] imployment : and I beg it of yow. I know ye will fie all. and theirfor I fall only tell yow how much the Aſſembleis Declaratione iacks with the Engadgers. that they fay, (with all humble fubmiſſione to the Kirk of Scotland.) they can not fubferyue that. wnles they will proclame themſelues perjured traitours . and wnles fomething be done in relatione to them. it will be impoſſible to exſpect ane accommodatione with the King Sʳ. think wpone it I can not conceall frome yow alſo, that the Prince of Orange faves he is informed, in Scotland the young miniſters are putting out the old. And believe it, Mr. Will. Colwill's comming hither will doe much hurte, tho I hear, the man is very moderate. hunes the company of Engadgers, and will doe nothing to firengthen their hands. He preaches heir. and if he will embrace it can not want a call longe. I hear he fpeaks with a great deall of fubmiſſioune of, and prayes earneftly for the Kirk of Scotland.

Sʳ. their is hopes that the King will acknoledge the Parl. and defyre a treaty , which, if he doe, I am perfuaded it will be your care to ſtudy foe much moderatione as ye ar able. with faity to Religioun and the Couenant wnleſs his Maˑ get fatiſfachone in ſome things, they will fuffer him to die in mifery. and we will haue no fettled peace. The Engadgers fay it is hard that more is craued of them then all Jas. Grahame s complices God willing, ye fall hear more nixt week frome your affectionat feruand,

GEO WINRAME.

For the Right Reuerend Maiſter ROBERT DOUGLAS.
 Miniſter at Edʳ

No 2

RIGHT REUEREND,

IF I fould follou myne owne inclinationes I wold troble yow more at every ocafione then were fitting in regaird of your imployment. I know ye ar not a loner of repetitiones. therefore I muſt refer yow to my Lo Chanᵏ and Regiſter's letters. The bearer will acquaint yow with all particulars paſſages. Sʳ. now is the tyme to pray that the Lord wold prevent the King with his tender merceis. for indeed he is broght very low : when he hes not bread both for himfelfe and his feruands. and betuixt him and his brother not ane Inglifh fhilling, and worfe yet, if I durft wryte it. I am confident no ingenous fpirite will tak advantage of his neceffiteis, but for all this, (as I haue heard yow aduyfe them to deall with [his] Father,) wfe him princely. France is neither able nor willing to helpe him: The Prince of Orange hes fuffered not a little for his Father and himfelfe, till he is forced to alienate the moft confiderable thing of his ancient patrimony. Scotland is neir exhaufted, foe that his cafe is very deplorable, being in prifone where he is liuing in penurie, forounded be his enemeis, not able to liue any where ells in the world, wnles he would come to Scotland, by giuing them fatiffactione to their juft demandis, yet his pernitious and deuillifh Counfell will fuffer him to ftarue before they will fuffer him to take the League & Covenant. I am perfuaded no rationall man can thinke he will come y^t length at firft; but if he could once be extricate frome his wicked Counfell, their might be hope. If a treaty be effectuat, much will depend wpone the perfons; and I know yow, S^r, fo well, as I am perfuaded it will be your ftudy to pointe at thees who will not make the buffines defperate. But I perfuade myfelfe it will be the wifdome and piety of the Commiffione to fend fuch as may gaine the King by the fpirit of meiknes, and not fuch as fay their is no helpe for him in God. But I fear I haue gone to farr, and that my affectione haue made me ftretch myfelfe beyond my lyne. I fall only intreat the continuance of your prayers and good opinione, which are highly efteemed be

          Your affectionat feruand,

Campveer, 9ber, 18-8, 1649   Geo Wynrame

Sir, I fall entreat that thees may remember my loue and feruice to all friendis, and to Mr Baillie, with whome, (as I hear,) the King is very angry for fome paffages in his booke, efpecially one concerning himfelfe; and if I can doe yow any feruice in the pairts where I goe to, I hope ye will ufe freidome with me

  For the Right Reuerend Mr Robert Douglas,
    Minifter at Ed^r

No 3

Right Reverend,

I know ye ar particularly informed of all that hes paft from other hands, yet I can not lett this bearer goe without a lyne. Ye will parceave be the papers fent yow what length the King is come in his conceffiones, and his Ma^{ty} hes faithfully promifed to perfyte them at their fight who reprefent Church and State, in tyme and place convenient. All of ws ar fully perfuaded of his ingenuity and fueit difpofitione. he can not be perfuaded to diffemble, tho no fmall induftrie haue bein ufit to perfuad him to it. And when ye confider his educatione, and what counfellers ar about him, both for his confcience and affaires, and what doctrine is taught to his face, that if he fubfcryue the Covenant, he is not only guyltie of his Father's murther, but can not efchew damnatione, efpecially be our countrieman Crichtoun, whome old Ruthen did chyde bitterly, faying, it was a ftrange thing that he could not preach and hold his tongue

Canterftein is come from Suedland to attend this Treaty, and promifeth, in his Mafter's name, all affiftance for a happy agriement; which ye will perceaue more fully be the letter to the Parl‍t

S‍r, I will not troble yow with neidles repetitiones, but refer yow to my other letters, which I know will be communicate wnto yow This much I dar pofitively affirme, that when the Lord fall bring the King to Scotland, (which he paffionatly defyres,) it fall be no greiff of hearte wnto yow, that ye was inftrumentall in this addreffe, and I hope ye will then fay that ye haue not been deceaued be

Your affectionat feruant.

Breda, Aprill $\frac{30}{20}$ 1650.   G WYNRAME.

For the Right Reuerend Mr ROBERT DOUGLAS,
 Moderator of the Commiffion of the
 Generall Affembly

LXXXV

LETTER FROM KING CHARLES THE SECOND.

[Orig.—Wodr MSS Fol. Vol XXV, No 48. This letter to Mr Robert Douglas, may be confidered as containing the firft overture to the Treaty of Breda It is entirely in the King's hand, and is dated Jersey, 15-5 February 1649, (that is 1649-50) As Baillie was not personally concerned in the Negotiations with Charles the Second at Breda in March, and terminating in June 1650, no other letters of this period are here inserted It may, however, be noticed, that Peck's Desiderata Curiosa, Vol. 2 p 425-429, contains, (1) The Letter from the Commiffioners of the Affembly, figned by Douglas, 21st February 1650, in reply to the following letter from Charles (2) The Commiffion from the Estates of Parliament, 8th March. (3) Letters to the King from the Earl of Loudoun, Lord Chancellor of Scotland, and the Marquess of Argyle, 9th March, both of them exhorting him moft earneftly to fatisfy the defires of the Kirk and Kingdom of Scotland Many Original Papers relating to the Treaty at Breda, confifting of Inftructions, Letters, Demands, &c may alfo be found in the Clarendon State Papers, Vol 2 App p. 51-65 Oxford, 1773, folio]

MR ROBERT DOWGLAS,

I AM confident that you truly defire to promote the agreement betweene me and my fubjects of Scotland, afwell for God's glory as for the peace and happines of that Nation, and truely I am foe defirous of it, that I fhall be very much oblig'd by all thofe that shall be induſtriouſly inſtrumentall to it I intreate you therefore to vſe your creditt amongſt the Miniſters, to perſwade them to reaſonable moderation, and to that confidence in me, and kindnes to me, as may produce the like affections in me towards them, and be the ground of a right vnderſtanding betweene vs, for the laſting happines of that nation I hope you ſhall neuer haue cauſe to repent what you ſhall doe herein, and I aſſure you it ſhall be effectually acknowledged by

Your affectionate friend,

Jerſey, the 15-5 of Febru. 1649   CHARLES R

For Mr. ROBERT DOWGLAS, Moderator of the
    Generall Aſſembly.

LXXXVI

NOTICES REGARDING THE METRICAL VERSIONS OF THE PSALMS RECEIVED BY THE CHURCH OF SCOTLAND

THE Metrical Version of the Psalms still in general use in Scotland was completed and received by the authority both of Church and State, in May 1650. It was the labour of many years, and from the numerous occasions on which Baillie alludes to its progress, it is evident he had taken a peculiar interest in furthering the work. It may therefore not be deemed out of place to present the reader with some further particulars respecting the origin and progress of this Version, and the more so, as our Ecclesiastical Historians afford little or no information on the subject.

I.—THE OLD VERSION. 1565

Without entering upon any minute details respecting the older Version of the Psalms, it may briefly be noticed, that the Scotish Reformers at an early period resolved to follow the example of some of the Churches abroad, in making Congregational Psalmody a stated portion of public worship. For this purpose the metrical Version of the Psalms commenced in the reign of Edward the Sixth by Thomas Sternholde, and enlarged by the English exiles at Geneva in the following reign, was adopted. The edition printed at Geneva in 1556, along with "The Form of Prayers," &c. contained only 51 Psalms, but this number was encreased in subsequent editions, that of 1561 having "Fourscore and seven Psalmes." It does not appear, however, that the entire Psalter was translated previous to the edition revised by John Hopkins, and first printed at London (according to Warton) in 1562, or more probably in 1563, under this title

"THE WHOLE BOKE OF PSALMES, collected into English Metre, by Thomas Starnho   o synge them withall faithfully perused and alowed according to the order appoynted in the Queenes Maiesties Iniunctions, &c Imprinted at London by John Day dwelling ouer Aldersgate, be nethe Saint Martins Cum gratia et priuilegio Regie Maiestatis per septennium An 1563." 4to The same year. (and again in 1565.) Day published the Psalms with the Music in Parts, viz " The whole Psalmes in fourt partes, (Tenor, Contra Tenor, Medius, and Bassus.) which may be song to al musical instruments, set forth for the encrease of vertue and abolyshing of other vayne and triflyng ballades" 4 vol 4to. According to Hopkins's revised text this version, received by publick authority, has since continued to be republished for the Church of England

Had the original Acts and Proceedings of the General Assembly been preserved, we might perhaps have obtained some more accurate information on this subject But at whatever date this English version was adopted, we may infer, that the Assembly appointed some of their number to revise and prepare it for the press, as we find it stated, that in December 1561, ' The Kirk lent Robert Lekprevick, printer, twa hundreth pounds [Scotish money] to help to buy irons, ink, and paper, and to fee craftismen for printing of the Psalmes" And the Assembly, on the 26th December 1564, further ordained, " That every Minister, Exhorter, and Reader, sall have ane of the Psalme Bookes latelie printed in Edinburgh, and use the Order contained therein in Prayers, Marriage, and Ministration of the Sacraments The edition that was referred to, has no separate title-page to the Psalms but forms a portion of the volume bearing this title —

" THE FORME OF PRAYERS AND MINISTRATION OF THE SACRAMENTS &c vsed in the English Church at Geneua, approued and receiued by the Churche of Scotland. whereunto besydes that was in the former bokes [of 1561 and 1562], are also added sondrie other prayers, with the whole Psalmes of Danid in English meter PRINTED AT EDINBVRGH BY ROBERT LEKPREVIK, M D LXV ' small 8vo On comparing this, or subsequent editions reprinted in this country, with those in England, there will be found considerable variations, consisting chiefly in the substitution of different versions of forty-one Psalms in the place of those in use by the English Church

Of the Psalms in this version common to both collections, there are, by the following authors, 1st 40 translated by THOMAS STERNEHOLD, Groom of the Robes to King Henry the Eighth and to Edward the Sixth, and who died in 1549; 2d 37 by JOHN HOPKINS, a Minister in Suffolk, (the 45th Psalm, in the Edinburgh editions, being erroneously marked W. K). 3d. 10 by WILLIAM KETHE, of whom some farther notice will be given: 4th, 11 by WILLIAM WHITTYNGHAM, who became Knox's successor as Minister of the English congregation at Geneva, and was afterwards promoted to the Deanery of Durham and died in 1570, 5th, 8 by THOMAS NORTON, an English Barrister, and best known as the joint author with Sackville, Lord Buckhurst, of the tragedy of Gordabuc, also 2 marked M supposed to be an error for N or Norton, and

6th, 1 by JOHN PULLEYN, an English divine, who becames Archdeacon of Colchester, and died in 1565. These Psalms amount to 109. Of the other 41 Psalms, peculiar to the copies published in Scotland, there are 15 by Kethe, 4 (67, 71, 115, 129,) by Whittyngham, and 1 (149) by Pulleyn, which appear to have been previously printed in the 1561 edition of " Fourscore and Seven Psalms", and there were added, for the first time, 6 by Robert Pont, and 15 bearing the initials of " I. C." as the translator.

Of these Translators, the initials " I C " are supposed to denote JOHN CRAIG, who had been a monk of the order of St Dominic at Bologna, but having embraced the Protestant faith, he escaped from Italy, and returning to his native country, after an absence of 24 years, he became minister of Holyrood-house, and of the King's Household, and died 4th December 1600, aged 88. His Psalms are 24, 56, 75, 102, 105, 108, 110, 117, 118, 132, 136, 140, 141, 143, and 145.

WILLIAM KETHE is described, by Strype and other writers, as a native of Scotland. He was an exile during the reign of Queen Mary, and one of the translators of the Geneva Bible. He wrote some popular religious ballads, the most noted of which was " A Ballad on the Whore of Babylon, called *Tye thy mare Tom boye*." He became minister at Child-Ocktord, in Dorsetshire. In the dedication of a sermon to the Earl of Warwick, in 1571, he states, that he had been with his Lordship in Newhaven [in 1563], as minister and preacher, and had also accompanied him the previous year [1570] to the North parts, as one of the preachers " of the Queen's Majesties armie". The versions by Kethe, included in the Scotish copies, are Psalms 27, 36, 47, 54, 58, 62, 70, 85, 88, 90, 91, 94, 101, 138, and 142.

ROBERT PONT was successively Commissioner for the diocese of Moray, Provost of Trinity College, and Minister of St Cuthberts, Edinburgh. He also filled for several years the place of a Senator of the College of Justice, but was deprived of his seat on the bench, in consequence of an act, prohibiting " all persons exercising functions of ministrie within the Kirk of God to bear or exercise any office of civil jurisdiction." His Psalms are 57, 59, 76, 80, 81, and 83. In some copies 149 is marked R P. by mistake for I. P or Pulleyn. In May 1601, the General Assembly appointed him " to revise the Psalms, and that his labours sould be revised the next Assemblie," but no further notice occurs of any such revisal. He died 8th May 1608, in the 81st year of his age.

A short specimen of these three chief contributors to our Old Version may be given. The verses selected will show that some use was made of it in preparing our present Version, and indeed the second copy of the 100th Psalm, in long metre, *All people that on earth do dwell*, and of the 124th Psalm, in peculiar metre, *Now Israel may say*, were retained, with only a few slight changes on account of the style. The translator of the 100th Psalm was William Kethe, and of the 124th, William Whittyngham, already mentioned as Dean of Durham.

PSALME LVII. v 1—3, and 5   By ROBERT PONT
From the Edition printed at Edinburgh by Robert Lekprevik, 1565

1 Be mercifull to me, ô God,
  be merciful to me
 For why? my soule n all assaultes
  shall euer trust in thee
 And till these wicked stormes be past,
  which ryse on euerie syde
 Vnder the shaddowe of thy wings,
  my hope shall alwayes hyde

2 I will therefore call to the Lord,
  who is moste high alone
 To God who will his worke in me,
  bring to perfection

3 He will sende down from heauen aboue,
  to saue me, and restore
 From the rebukes of wicked men,
  that fayne wolde me denoure
 God wil his mercie surely send,
  and constant trueth also
 To comforte me, and to defend
  against my cruel foe

5 Exalt thy selfe, ô God, therefore
  aboue the heauens hight
 And ouer all the earth declare
  thy glorie and thy might

PSALM XC Ver 1—7 and 12   By WILLIAM KETHE

1 O Lord thou hast bene our refuge,
  and kept vs safe and sounde.
 From age to age, as witnesse can
  all we, which true it founde
2 Before the mountaines were foorth brought,
  yer thou the earth didst frame
 Thou wast our great eternal God,
  and stil shalt be the same.

3 Thou dost vaine man strike downe to dust,
  though he be in his floure,
 Againe thou saist, Ye Adams sonnes,
  returne, to shewe your power
4 For what is it a thousand yeares
  to count them in thy sight
 But as a day which last is past,
  or as a watche by night?

5 They are, so sone as thou dost storme,
  euen lyke a slepe or shade,
 Or like the grasse, which as we knowe,
  betymes away doth fade
6 With pleasant dewes, in breake of day,
  it groweth vp full grene.
 By night cut downe, it withreth, as
  no beautie can be sene

7 O Lord, how sore do we consume
  in this thy wrath so hote?
 We feare thy furie be so fierce,
  that death shall be our lote

12 Teache vs therefore to count our dayes,
  that we our heartes may bend
 To learne thy wisedome and thy trueth
  for that shulde be our end

PSALM 145, v 1—6, 11—15, and 19—21   By L C

1 O Lord that art my God and King,
  Vndoubtedly, I wil thee praise
 I will extoll and blessings sing,
  Vnto thyne holy Name alwayes
2 From day to day I wil thee blesse,
  And laude thy Name worlde without end,
3 For great is God, most worthy praise,
  Whose greatnes none may comprehend.

4 Race shal thy workes praise vnto race
  And so declare thy power, ô Lord.
5 The glorious beautie of thy grace,
  And wondrous workes, wil I record
6 And all men shall the power (ô God,)
  Of all thy feareful Actes declare
 And I to publishe all abrode,
  Thy greatnes, at no tyme will spair

11 The glorie of thy Kingdome, they
    Do shewe, and of thy power do tell
12 That so mens sonnes his might knowe may,
    And Kingdome great, that doth excell

13 Thy Kingdome hath no end at all
    Thy Lordship euer doth remaine
14 The Lord vpholdeth all that fall,
    And doth the feble folke sustaine
15 The eyes of all things, Lord, attend
    And on thee waite, that here do liue
    And thou in season due dost send
    Sufficient foode them to relieue

19 The Lord wil the desire fulfil,
    Of such as do him feare and dread
    And he also their crye hear wil,
    And saue them in the tyme of nead
20 He doth preserue them more and lesse,
    That beare to him a louing heart.
    But workers al of wickednes
    Destroye wil he, and clean subuert

21 My mouth therefore my speache shal frame
    To speake the praises of the Lord,
    All fleshe to blesse his holy Name,
    For euermore, eke shal accord.

Some proposals for revising this Old Version of the Psalms, and at least one attempt to supersede it, were made, at different intervals, but without success, and it continued to be reprinted in a variety of forms, usually with musical notes, until, in Scotland, it was wholly superseded in the year 1650. There are several editions of this Old Version printed at Middleburgh and Dort, from 1594 to 1610 or later, and it was used by the Scotish congregations in Holland for some years after the present Version had been received in this country.

It may be noticed, that in the edition of the Psalms, "Printed at Edinburgh be Henrie Charteris, 1595," (if not also in some previous ones,) there appeared a kind of Doxology in different measures, added as "The Conclusion, or *Gloria Patri* eftir the Psalme;" the use of which seems at a subsequent period to have been disallowed as a prelatic innovation. After the Restoration of Charles the Second, (but previous to any change in regard to the Church,) notice is taken in the Mercurius Caledonius, of a minister, who, preaching before Parliament on the 27th January 1661, "restored us to *Glory to the Father*, to be sung at the end of the Psalmes," and this, it is said "has been a great stranger to our Kirk these many years."

11. KING JAMES'S VERSION, 1631

KING JAMES the First, after his accession to the English Throne, endeavoured to assimilate the forms of worship in Scotland and England, and having entrusted "the most learned Divines of the Church," with revising the English translations of the Bible, which was happily completed in the year 1611, he himself undertook to perfect a new version of the Psalms in metre, for general use. "The revising of the Psalms (says Spottiswood) he made his own labour; and, at such hours as he might spare from the public cares, went through a number of them, commending the rest to a faithful and learned servant, who hath therein answered his Maiestie's expectation." (Hist. p. 460.

Williams, Bishop of Lincoln, we are further told, his Majesty " was in hand" with this new Version of the Psalms, " which he intended to have finished, and dedicated withall to the onely saint of his devotion, the Church of Great Britaine, and that of Ireland, when God called him to sing Psalmes with the Angels "

The " faithful and learned Servant' here spoken of, was the Earl of Stirling, (then Sir William Alexander of Menstrie,) a poet of great distinction in his time, who has a much better title to be considered the true author of the version, than King James under whose name it was published. The attention of his son and successor, Charles the First, having been early drawn to the perfecting of this work, as connected with his proposed changes in the Church, he seems never to have lost sight of it, so long as there was any prospect of carrying through those measures to which he was unfortunately but too much attached The following letter respecting it was addressed by him to the Archbishop of St Andrews :—

" Whereas it pleafed our late dear Father of famous and eternall memorie, confidering how imperfect the Pfalmes in Meeter prefentlie vfed ar, out of his zeal to the glorie of God, and for the good of all the Churches within his dominions, to tranflate them of new, Therfor, as We have gevin commandement to our truftie and weilbeloved Sr William Alexander knycht, to confider and revew the meeter and poefie thairof, So our pleafour is, that zow and fome of the moft learned Divynes in that our kingdome confer them with the originall text, and with the moft exact tranflations, and thairefter certifie back zour opinions vnto ws concerning the fame, whether it be fitting that they be publifhed and fung in Churches, inftead of the old tranflation, or not , To the intent that we may neglect nothing fo much importing the memorie of our faid late Father; and far less if zow find that it may tend to the advancement of the glorie of God , and fo recommending the famyne to your earneft care, We bid, &c Windfore, 25th Auguft 1626 "

This Version was at length published, bearing on the engraved title—" THE PSALMES of KING DAVID, TRANSLATED by KING IAMES   Cum Privilegio Regiæ Maiestatis ' Another engraved leaf has the royal arms, and the King's authority, allowing these Psalmes " to be sung in all the Churches of oure Dominions ;" and this imprint is at the end of this volume,—" Oxford, Printed by William Turner, Printer to the famous Univerfity, M DC.XXXI " 12mo, pp. 329 A patent of exclusive privilege for the space of thirty-one years print this version, had been granted to Sir William Alexander, on the 28th December 1627, in consideration " of the great paynes already taken, and to be taken, in collating and revising the same, and in seeing the first impression thairof to be carefullie and well done." When the copies of this edition had got into circulation, some zealous Presbyterian, probably David Calderwood the Historian, drew up at considerable length, " Reasons against the Reception of King James's Metaphrase of the Psalmes" This paper is inserted in the Bannatyne Miscellany, vol. · pp. 227—256, Edinb 1827 4to. with some further notices respecting the version itself. But in this place it may be sufficient to mention, that Charles the First, in December 1634, " being fully convinced of the exactnesse" of the translation, enjoined the Privy Council of Scotland " that no other Psalmes of any edition whatsoever, be either printed heiretter within that our Kingdome, or imported thither, either bound by themselff or otherways, from any forrayne parts" The Version was accordingly republished in 1636, and attached to the Service Book of 1637; but on collation it proves to have been so much altered, in consequence, as it would appear, of the objections urged against its reception in 1631, that many of the Psalms may be considered as entirely re-written, although still bearing the same title " THE PSALMES of King DAVID: Translated by King JAMES London, printed by Thomas Harper, 1636, folio, pp. 147. It contains music notes, and is printed in long lines, in black letter, but no notice is taken of its revisal, or of any assistance having been rendered by the actual translator Two specimens from these editions may suffice to shew such variations

PSALME 1	PSALME I.
(Edit Oxford, 1631, 12mo)	(Edit London, 1636, folio)
The man is blest that doth not walke where wicked Councells guide Nor in the way of Sinners stands, nor Scorners sits beside	The man is blest, who to walke in th' ungodlies counsell hates, and stands not in the sinners way, nor sits in scorners seats.
2 But of the Lord he on the law doth ground his whole delight, And on his law doth meditate devootly day and night.	2 But in the Lords most holy law, he hath his whole delight, and in his law doth meditate devoutly day and night
3 Hee shall be like a planted tree, The streames of waters neare, Whose pleasant boughs bring timely fruit, in season of the yeare.	3 He shall be like a tree that grow'th the streames of waters neare, whose pleasant boughs bring timely fruit in season of the yeare
4 His leafe it never wither shall as winters blasted prey And whatsoever he designes, shall prosper every way	4 His leafe shall never withered be, as winters blasted prey, and whatsoever thing he doth, shall prosper every way
5 But wicked men are nothing so, for they as chaffe shall proue; Which whirling windes doe driue away, and from the earth remoue.	5 They who are wickedly dispos'd, no such assurance finde but like unto contemned chaffe, are tossed with the winde.
6. And therefore they who wicked are, In judgement shall not stand Nor shall the sinners suffred be amongst the righteous band	6. And therefore they who wicked are, in indgement shall not stand, nor shall the sinners suffred be amongst the righteous band
7. For well the Lord doth know what way the righteous follow all But	7. For well the Lord doth know what way the righteous follow all

PSALME XXIII.	PSALM XXIII.
(Edit Oxford, 1631.)	(Edit. London, 1636.)
The Lord of all my shepheard is,	The Lord of all, my Shepheard is
I shall from want be free :	I shall from want be free
2 He makes me in greene pastures lie	2. He makes me in green pastures lye,
and neare calme streames to be.	and neare calm streames to be
3 He doth restore my weary soule,	3 He doth restore my soul, and leads
that it new strength may take	the way that I should take
And in the pathes of righteousnesse	Into the paths of righteousnesse,
mee leads, for his names sake.	even for his own names sake
4 Yea though I through deaths shadow walke,	4 Though through the vale of deaths black shade
yet feare I in no sort,	I walk, I'le fear no il
Thou art with me, thy rod and staffe	Thou art with me, thy rod and staffe
with comfort me support.	afford me comfort still
5 Thou for my food before me foes,	5 Thou for my food, before my foes
a table dost bestow	a table dost bestow
And dost with oyle annoynt my head,	And do st with oyle annoynt my head,
and makes my cup o're flow	and mak'st my cup o'reflow
6 Thy goodnesse and thy mercy sure,	6 With mercy, goodnesse, all my daies
shall whilst I live blesse me	shall surely follow me
And of the Lord I in the house	And in the Lords own house, I will
a dweller still will be	a dweller ever be

The unexpected and irresistible opposition to the Liturgy in July 1637, having extended also to the Psalms. Sir William Alexander, (who had been created Earl of Stirling) was probably no less disappointed in realizing any pecuniary advantage from his exclusive monopoly, than his Royal Master must have been in the accomplishment of the still greater object he had in view when that privilege was granted.

III Francis Rous's Version, 1643

In tracing the origin of our present Version of the Psalms, it may be noticed as a singular circumstance that this Country should have been indebted, in the first instance, for the translation that was adopted to a resolution of the House of Commons It is well known that a similar design with that contemplated by Charles the First, of bringing about a Uniformity in the doctrine, discipline, and form of church-government and worship in both Kingdoms, was very nearly accomplished by the Presbyterians in England The labours of the Westminster Assembly in England were chiefly directed to promote this object; and a New Version of the Psalms was specially recommended to their notice. Several metrical versions had been previously published in England in the view of superseding Sternholde s, and although considerable exertions were made, chiefly in the House of Lords, to adopt a translation by Mr William Barton, the preference was awarded by the English Parliament to that by Mr Francis Rous, one of He himself states, in the preface to his Psalms, printed in 1643, that many passages in the old version " seemed to call aloud for amendment," of which he selected " some patternes," but " apprehending many years past (which experience hath showed to be a true conjecture) that a forme wholly new would not please many, who are fastned to things usual and accustomed, I assaied only to change some pieces of the usual version, even such as seemed to call aloud, and, as it were, undeniably for a change These being seen, it was desired that they should be increased, which being done, they are here subjoyned" In Wood's Athenæ Oxonienses, (edit by Dr Bliss, vol iii p 468,) Rous's version is supposed to have been first printed in 1641. There is no reason to believe that it appeared earlier than 1643; in a diminutive volume, neatly printed, in 24to or 48vo, with this title —

"THE PSALMES OF DAVID in English Meeter, set forth by FRANCIS ROUS Psal 47, Ver 7 ומרו משכיל   Aprill 17, 1643. It is this day ordered by the Committee of the House of Commons in Parliament for printing, that this Book, entitled, *The Psalmes of David*, &c. (according to the desires of many reverend Ministers) be published for the generall use: And for the true correcting of it, be printed by these the Author shall appoint   *John White*

I do appoint *Philip Nevill* and *Peter Whaley* to print these Psalmes

Francis Rous

London, Printed by James Young, for Philip Nevill, at the signe of the Gun in Ivie-lane, 1643 ' This volume contains in all pp [xii] 312, and 12 leaves not paged of " Psalmes of harder and lesse usuall Tunes corrected, and the Tunes not altered," along with " A Table of the Psalmes "

The translator, FRANCIS ROUS, a younger son of Sir Anthony Rous, Knight, was born at Halton in Cornwall Some account of his life and writings will be found in Wood's Athenæ Oxonienses, by Dr Bliss, (vol iii p 466) He was several times returned a Member of Parliament; and was chosen one of the lay commissioners to the Assembly of Divines On the 29th January 1643–44, it was " Ordered, That Mr Prideaux do bring in an ordinance for the settling of Mr. Rows in the place of Provost of Eaton College, and to receive and enjoy all profits, privileges, and emoluments, thereunto belonging." This lucrative appointment he held till his death, on the 7th January 1658

The following are specimens of this rare edition, from a copy in the possession of Lea Wilson, Esq, Norwood-Hill, Surrey, (a gentleman who possesses an unrivalled collection of editions in English of the Holy Scriptures). The volume probably had only a very limited circulation

PSALM I
(By FRANCIS ROUS   London, 1643)

The man is blessed, that to walk in wicked waies doth feare,	2 But in the perfect Law of God he greatly doth delight,

3 He shall be like a tree by streames
of waters planted neare,
Which in his season doth not faile
his pleasant fruit to beare
Whose leaf shall never fade nor fall,
but flourish still and stand
Even so all things shall prosper well
that this man takes in hand

4 So shall not the ungodly men,
they shall be nothing so,
But as the dust, which from the earth
the wind drives to and fro
5 Therefore shall not the wicked men
in judgement stand approv'd,
But sinners from the just shall be
divided, and remov'd

6 Because the way of righteous men
God doth with favour know,
Whereas the way of wicked men
ends in their overthrow

PSALM XXIII.

My shepheard is the living Lord,
and he that doth me feed,
How can I then lack any thing
whereof I stand in need?
2 In pastures green and flourishing
he makes me downe to lye
And after drives me to the streames
which run most pleasantly

3 And when I feele my selfe neere lost,
then home he me doth take,
Conducting me in his right paths,
even for his owne Names sake

4 And though I were even at death's doore,
yet would I feare none ill;
Thy rod, thy staffe do comfort me,
and thou art with me still

5. Thou hast my table richly stor'd
in presence of my foe,
My head with oile thou dost anoint,
my cup doth overflow

6 Thy grace and mercy all my daies
shall surely follow me,
And ever in the house of God,
my dwelling place shall be

PSALM LVII v 1—4.

Be mercifull to me, O Lord,
be mercifull to me,
Because according to thy word
my soule doth trust in thee
2 Yea, she unto the shadow flies
of thy wings, her to cover,
Untill these sad calamities
be wholly passed over

3 To God most High my earnest cry
in praier sent shall be,
Even to that God, who graciously
performeth all for me
4 From heaven shall his power descend,
to save me from their spight
That would devoure me, God shall send
his mercy, truth, and might

PSALM XCIII

The Lord doth raign, and cloth'd is he
with majesty and light,
His works do shew him cloth'd to be,
and girt about with might
2 For this round world by his great strength
established hath he
Yea, he so surely hath it set
that mov'd it cannot be.

3 Of old most firmly stablisht is
thy Throne of majestie,
And thou without beginning art
from all eternitie.
4 The flouds, O Lord, have lifted up,
they lifted up their voice
The flouds have lifted up their waves,
and made a mighty noise.

5 The Lord this noise of many flouds	6 Thy testimonies are most sure,
so might exceedeth farre,	and surely lead to blisse
The Highest overcomes the sea,	And holinesse for ever, Lord,
when his waves mighty are	in thine house comely is

IV.—VERSIONS BY SIR W. MURE AND MR ZACHARY BOYD.

Before proceeding to notice the revised copy of Rous's version 1646, it may be mentioned, that Baillie, although a personal friend of Rous, expresses on more than one occasion the very favourable opinion he entertained of an unpublished version by Sir William Mure of Rowallane. On the other hand, some of his countrymen were inclined to give a preference to the translation by Zachary Boyd, one of the ministers of Glasgow. A couple of specimens of each may be here given. Those by Boyd are from "THE PSALMES OF DAVID IN MEETER. By Mr. ZACHARY BOYD, Preacher of Gods Word. The third edition. Printed at Glasgow by George Anderson, *Anno* 1646," 12mo. Mure's are from a MS. in the possession of James Dennistoun of Dennistoun, Esq. The author appears to have prepared them for the press, (no doubt at the instigation of some of his friends, such as Baillie), under this title,—" Some Psalmes Translated and presented for a proof to publick view, wherby to discerne of the whole being conformed to this Essay. By a Weilwiller to the work of Reformatioun, who makes humble offer of his weak endeavours." But they are not known ever to have been printed. One or two other specimens from a more perfect MS. are given in the Appendix to "The Historie and Descent of the House of Rowallane. By Sir William Mure knight, of Rowallane. Written in, or prior to 1657." Glasgow, 1825, 8vo.

PSALM I.
BY SIR WILLIAM MURE.

The man is blessed verilie,
  who walketh not astray,
In Counsell of ungodlie men,
  nor stands in sinners way
2. Nor sitts in scorners seat But setts
  on God's law his delight,
And stedfasthe his law doth mynd
  and muse on, day and night

3 Hee shall be like unto the Tree,
  sett by the river syde,
In seasoun due, which fruit brings foorth,
  whose leaves ay blooming byde,
4 His works shall prosper all Not so
  ungodlie men, for they

PSALM I.
BY ZACHARY BOYD.

Blest is the man that walks not in
  th' ungodlies counsel ill,
Nor stands in ways of sinners, nor
  in scorners seats sits still.
2 But in the law of God the Lord,
  is chiefly his delight,
And also he doth meditate
  in his law day and night

3. He shall be like a planted tree,
  rivers of waters by,
That in his season bringeth foorth
  his fruit most plenteously.
His leaf also at any time
  not wither shall at all,
And whatsoever thing he doth
  it prosper surely shall

Shall be like chaffe, which stormie wynds
sweep suddenlie away

5 In judgement therefore shall not stand,
men wicked and profane,
Nor sinners, where the righteous flock
assembled doe remaine.
6 For, who so righteous paths persue,
the Lord doth know their way,
But perrish shall the way of sin,
wherein the wicked stray

4 The men ungodly are not so,
but in their wicked way
Are like the chaffe, which stormy wind
doth quickly drive away
5 Therefore the ungodly shall not stand
in judgement stedfastly,
Nor sinners in th' assembly of
all such as righteous be

6 For the Lord knoweth well the way
ev'n of the righteous all
But the way of ungodly men
most surely perish shall.

PSALM 23
By Sir William More

The Lord my sheepheard is, of want
I never shall complaine,
2 For me to rest on, hee doth grant
greene pastures of the plaine
3 Hee leads me smoothest brookes beside,
and doth my soul reclame,
Yea me by righteous paths doth guyd
for glorie of his name

4 The valley dark of deaths aboade
to passe, I'le fear none ill,
For thow art with me, Lord, thy rodd
and staffe me comfort still
5. For me a table thow dost spread
in presence of my foes,
With oyle thow dost anoint mine head,
by thee cup o'rflowes

6 Mercie and goodnes all my dayes
with me shall surelie stay,
And in thy house, to dwell alwayes
O Lord, my count I le lay

PSALME 23
By Mr Zachary Boyd

The Lord's my shephoard, I'le not want
2 He makes me by good will
Ly in green pastures, he me leads
beside the waters still
3 My soul likewise he doth restore,
and me to lead doth take
Into the paths of righteousnesse,
and that for his Names sake.

4 Yea, though through valley of deaths shade
I walk, I'le fear no ill,
For thou art with me, thy rod and
thy staffe me comfort still.
5. Thou set'st in presence of my foes
a table me before,
Mine head with oyl thou dost anoint,
my cup it runneth o're.

6 Goodnesse and mercy all the dayes
of my life surely shall
Me follow, and in the Lord's house
for ever I will dwell

V.—Rous's Revised Version, 1646

After the publication of Rous's volume in 1643, the version appears to have undergone repeated revisals, and the following notices may be compared with what Bailhe has stated in his Letters, Vol 2, at pages 120, 121, 259, 280, 286, 293, 321, 326, and 329 to 332.

In Dr Lightfoot's Journal of the Westminster Assembly of Divines, this notice occurs on the 22d November 1643 —" The first thing done this morning was, that Sir

Benjamin Rudyard brought an order from the House of Commons, wherein they require our advice, whether Mr Rous's Psalms may not be sung in churches, and this being debated, it was at last referred to the three Committees, to take every one fifty Psalms

The notices in the Journals of the House of Commons are as follows —

20° Novembris 1643 —Ordered, That the Affembly of Divines be defired to give their advice whether it may not be ufeful and profitable to the Church, that the Pfalms fet forth by Mr Rous, be permitted to be publickly fung, the fame being read before finging, until the Books be more generally difperfed (vol iii p. 315)

December 16th 1644 —The Houfe being informed, that divers Divines of the Affembly were at the door, they were called in; and Doctor Burgeffe prefented the advice of the Affembly of Divines, now by Ordinance of Parliament fitting at Weftminfter, concerning Vifitation of the Sick He further informed the Houfe, that touching the Directory for all parts of publick Worfhip, in ordinary, they have brought up all the Parts to the Houfe, fave only fome Propofitions touching the Singing of Pfalms

(ib vol iii p. 724)

December 27th 1644 —The Houfe being informed, that fome of the Divines of the Affembly were at the door, they were called in Dr Burgeffe prefented the remaining Parts of the Directory for Publick Worfhip concerning the keeping Days of Publick Fafts, of Publick Thanksgiving, and fome Propofitions touching the Singing of Pfalms

(ib vol iv p. 3)

The Version by Rous having been carefully revised by the Author, who availed himself of the corrections and amendments recommended by various Committees, it was republished, under this title,—

"THE PSALMS OF DAVID IN ENGLISH MEETER (Pfal 47, v 7 וזמרו משכול. Sing ye praises with understanding) London, printed by Miles Flesher, for the Company of Stationers, 1646" 12mo, pp [viii] and 255 A leaf facing the title contains the following extract, and serves to identify the work,—" Die Veneris, 4 [14th] Novemb 1645 —It is this day ordered by the Commons assembled in Parliament, That this Book of Psalms set forth by Mr Rous, and perufed by the Affembly of Divines, be forthwith printed And that it be referred to Mr Rous to take care for the printing thereof· and that none do prefume to print it, but such as shall be authorized by him H Elsinge, Cler Parl. Dom. Com '

In the Journals of the House of Commons, this resolution is introduced with this notice, " The House being informed, That some of the Affembly of Divines were at the door, they were called in And Mr Wilson acquainted the Houfe That according to a former Order of this House, they had perused the Psalms set out by Mr Rouse, and, as they are now altered and amended, do conceive they may be useful to the Church Resolved," &c as above [ib. p 342] This is likewise noticed in one of the newspapers of the day —" Friday, Novemb 14. 1645 —A message from the Assembly of Divines to both Houses of Parliament, acquainting them, that according to the order of Nov 20, 1643. they had perused the Psalmes translated into English out of the Originall, by Mr Rouse, conceiving them fit to be publickly made use of throughout the Kingdome. That they had likewise perused the Psalmes translated by Mr Bartue [Barton], who deserved much commendation for his great care and pains in them. but conceived the other most fit for publike use.'—(*The Kingdomes Intelligencer*, No 126)

Oct 7, 1645 —Upon the humble petition of Wm Barton, Master of Arts, read this day in the House It is ordered, &c. That two Books of David's Psalms, composed in English metre by the Petitioner, and presented to their Lordships, are hereby referred to the Assembly of Divines, to be read over, and judged by them, and the result of their judgments thereupon returned to this House, that such farther direction may be given touching the same, as shall be meet —(Lords Journals, vol vii p 627.)

Nov. 14, 1645.—Message from the Assembly concerning Mr Roufe's and Mr Barton's Verfions of the Pfalms

TO THE RIGHT HONOURABLE THE HOUSE OF LORDS ASSEMBLED IN PARLIAMENT

The Assembly of Divines having received from this Honourable House an order, bearing date October 7 1645, to read over and judge of two Books of David's Psalms, composed in English metre, by Mr William Barton, and thereupon to return their judgment to this Honourable House, do humbly certify, That they had long before received an order from the Honourable House of Commons, bearing date Novembr 20, 1643, to give their judgment touching the Psalms composed in metre by Mr Roufe, a Member of that House, and that thereupon there was a Committee appointed by this Assembly to consider of these Psalms, and that the same Committee had with much care perused, and with great diligence concurred with the same Learned Gentleman, to amend and perfect his copy, and had fully finished that Work, before they received the said order from the Honourable House of Lords, and withall that the greatest part of this version was sent to the General Assembly of the Church of Scotland, and there put into the hands of a Committee, and by that Committee, so far as they have examined it, very well approved; yet, in obedience to the order of this Honourable House, they appointed a Committee to consider thereof, and, upon the whole matter, do find reason to certify this Honourable House, That albeit the said Mr Barton hath taken very good and commendable pains in his Metaphrafe, yet the other verfion, so exactly perufed and amended by the said Mr Roufe and the Committee of the Assembly with long and great labour is so closely framed according to the Original Text, as that we humbly conceive it will be useful for the edification of the Church

       Cornelius Burges, *Prolocutor pro tempore.*
       Henry Robrough, *Scriba*
       Adoniram Byfield, *Scriba.*
        (Lords Journals, vol vii p 704.)

March 26, 1646.—Upon reading the Petition of Mr Wm Barton, concerning his Translation of his Book of the Psalms, it is ordered to recommend the same to the Assembly of Divines, to certify to this House why these Psalms may not be sung in Churches as well as other Translations, by such as are willing to use them

               (ib vol viii, p. 236.)

April 15, 1646.—Ordered, That the Book of Psalms, set forth by Mr Rous, and perused by the Assembly of Divines, be forthwith printed in sundry volumes. And that the said Psalms, and none other, shall, after the first day of January next, be sung in all Churches and Chapels within the Kingdom of England, Dominion of Wales, and Town of Berwick-upon-Tweede, and that it be referred to Mr. Rous, to take care for the true printing thereof.—The Lords concurrence to be desired herein.

         ' (Commons Journals, vol. v p 509.)

April 16, 1646.—Mr Knightley carried to the Lords for their concurrence, &c. The order for singing of Mr. Rous his Psalms through the Kingdom of England, Dominion of Wales, and Town of Berwick   (ib vol v p 511.)

April 18, 1646.—A message was brought from the House of Commons by Mr Knightly, &c. to desire their Lordships concurrence in divers particulars, &c. An order for the using of the Book of Psalms, set forth by Mr. Rous, and appointed by the Assembly of Divines

The order concerning the Book of Psalms translated by Mr Rous, was read twice and committed to the consideration of these Lords following, who are to report their opinions thereof to this House. Comes Essex, Comes Sarum, L Viscount Say and Seale, Comes Lyncolne, Comes Suffolke, Comes Midd D² North, D⁵ Willoughby, D² Bruce, D⁵ Wharton, any three to meet. The answer returned was, That to the order for using the Book of Psalms translated by Mr Rous, their Lordships will send an answer by messengers of their own   (Lords Journals, vol viii p 277.)

April 25, 1646.—A message was brought from the Assembly of Divines, by Mr Walker, &c as follows,—

To the Right Honourable the House of Lords Assembled in Parliament.

The Assembly of Divines received April 9th from this Honourable House, an order bearing date March 26th 1646, to certify this Honourable Houſe why the Translation of the Pſalms made by Mr Barton, may not be uſed and ſung in Churches, by ſuch as ſhall deſire it, as well as any other Tranſlation, do humbly return this anſwer, That whereas, on the 14th of November 1645, in obedience to an order of this Honourable Houſe concerning the ſaid Mr Barton's Pſalms, we have already commended to this Honourable Houſe one Tranſlation of the Pſalms in Verſe, made by Mr Rous, and peruſed and amended by the ſame learned Gentleman and the Committee of the Aſſembly, as conceiving it would be very uſeful for the Edification of the Church, in regard it is ſo exactly framed according to the Original Text, and whereas there are ſeveral other Tranſlations of the Pſalms already extant, we humbly conceive that, if liberty ſhould be given to people to ſing in Churches every one that Tranſlation which they deſire, by that means ſeveral Tranſlations might come to be uſed, yea in one and the ſame congregation at the ſame time, which would be a great diſtraction and hinderance to edification CORNELIUS BURGES, *Prolocutor pro Tempore*

(ib vol viii, p 283-4)

(Extract from a paper presented by the Commiſſioners at London to the Grand Committee there, in December 1646, and laid before the Commiſſion of the General Assembly at Edinburgh, by Mr Robert Baillie, 21st January 1647)

And becauſ the ſinging of Pſalmes in Churches is a part of the publike worſhip of God, We deſire that the Paraphraſe of the Pſalms in metre, as it is now examined, corrected, and approved by the Aſſembly of Divines here, and by the Commiſſioners of the Gen Aſſembly in Scotland, may be lykwiſe authorized and eſtabliſhed by Ordinance of Parliament

(Minutes of the Commiſſion of the General Aſſembly, p. 150)

(Extract of a Letter from the Commiſſioners at London, 2d February 1647)
The new Pſalme book, reprinted with the laſt amendements ſent us from your Committee there, is not yet come from the preſſe, but it is promiſed to ws the next week, and we ſhall then, God willing, ſend it to yow   (ib p 156)

11th February 1647

The Commiſſion appoynts a letter of encouragement to be writtin to Mr Zechariah Boyd, for his paines in his Paraphraſe of the Pſalmes, ſhewing that they have ſent them to their Commiſſioners at London to be conſidered and made uſe of there by theſe that ar upon the ſame work

(ib p 157)

(Extract of a Letter from the Commissioners at London, 9th February 1647.)

The new Pfalme book cannot be ready till the next week. So commending your labours to the bleffing of God, we reft,

                     Your affectionat Brethren to ferve yow,

Worcefter-Houfe, the   SAMUEL RUTHERFURD
  9th of Febr 1647/8.   GEO GILLESPIE

Direct, For the Right Reverend the Commiffioners
  of the Gen. Affembly of the Kirk of Scotland   (ib p 165)

(Extract of a Letter from the Commissioners at London, presented to the Commission, 23d February 1647.)

WEE now fend yow the new Edition of the Paraphrafe of the Pfalmes as it wes approved by the Affembly heir, and by yourfelves, the Animadverfions wch you fent us being taken in their propper places, as the worthy Gentleman, who hath taken moft paines in the worke, affureth us. If yow be now fatifhed with it as it is, wee fhall defire to know fo much. One Pfalme-book in the three Kingdomes will be a confiderable part of Uniformity, if it can be fullie agreed upon both there and here · And we believe it is generally acknowledged, there is a neceffitie of fome change, there being fo many juft exceptions againft the old and ufuall Paraphrafe. And we humblie conceive there will be as little controverfy that this which we now fend yow, as it hath come through the hands of more examiners, fo it will be found as neir the originall as any Paraphrafe in meeter can readily be, and much neerer then other works of that kynd, which is a good compenfation to mak up the want of that Poeticall liberty and fweet pleafant running, which fome defire. However, wee expect to know your pleafure in this, and in any other thing contained in our former letters, which yourfelves fhall judge to need an anfwere ; and fo wee reft,

                   Your moft affectionat Brethren to ferve yow,

Worcefter houfe, the 16th   G WYNRAME.
  of Febr 1647/8.   SAMUEL RUTHERFURD
                                         GEO GILLESPIE

Direct for the Right Reverend the Commiffioners
  of the Gen Affembly, mett at Edr

The Commiffion of Affembly thinks it verie neceffar that a number of the new Paraphrafe of the Pfalmes be writtin for, and appoynts the clerk to fend them to Prefbyteries, and returne to the letter from the Commiffioners at London, this following anfwer

REVEREND AND LOVING BRETHREN,

  Yours of the 16th of this inftant moneth we have received this day, together with the new Edition of the Paraphrafe of the Pfalmes, whereof we cannot give opinion by this occafion, efpecially feing fo few copies have been fent. We do acknowledge that one Pfalme-book in the three Kingdomes wer a confiderable part of Uniformity, but it can hardly be fullie agreed upon, if Prefbyteries gave a previous confideration of it before the meeting of the Affembly, which may give them great fatiffaction, and facilitat the approbation of it in the Affembly. Therfor, yow will be pleafed to fend down a number of copies of this late Edition to our Clerk, whom we have appoynted to caufe difpatch them to Prefbyteries with diligence, to be confidered by them; which we think the beft and fureft way to obtaine a full approbation of the work heir, wherof we make litle queftion if yow fend a competent number of copies in tyme.

We remain, Your loving Brethren,

The COMMISSIONERS OF THE GENERAL ASSEMBLY

Edinb 23d Febry. 1647

Direct for their Reverend and Loving
Brethren, the Commiffioners of the
Kirk of Scotland at London

(Minutes, p. 171-4.)

Edinb. 18th Martij 1647, Poft meridiem.

This day two letters from the Commiffioners at London were read with the papers there inclofed. Tenor of the letters followes —

REVEREND AND BELOVED BRETHREN,

WEE received yefterday your's of Feb' 23d, and fhall take care to provyde (according to your defire) as many copies as can be had of the new Paraphrafe of the Pfalms in metre. Wee have already fpoken for 70 copies, which we fhall, God willing, fend with the firft occafion . .

We reft, Your moft loving Brethren,

G WYNRAME
SAMUEL RUTHERFURD.
GEO GILLESPIE

Worcefter-houfe, the 2d
of Marche 1647
Direct for the Right Reverend the Commiffioners of the Gen Affembly, mett at Edr

REVEREND AND LOVING BRETHREN,

WEE have, according to your defire, provided a number of copies of the new Paraphrafe of the Pfalmes in Metre, as it is approved by the Affembly of Divines, and fince corrected in feverall places according to the Animadverfions which ye fent us. Wee have now fourfcore copies in readines to be fent by the firft fhip to your Clerk, that by him

they may be directed to the feverall Prefbyteries
direct and bleffe yow in all your affairs, we reft,

So befeeching the Lord to

Your loving Brethren to ferve you,

G. WYNRAME.
SAMUEL RUTHERFURD
GEO GILLESPIE.

Worcefter-houfe, the 9th
of March 164¾
Direct for the Right Reverend the Com[rs] of
the Generall Affembly of the Kirk of Scotland, mett at Edinburgh

(Minutes, pp 184-185.)

Edinb. 8th Julij 1647, Ante meridiem.

Recommends to Mr. Johne Adamfone to revife Rowes Paraphrafe of the Pfalmes, and Mr Johne Rowe's obfervationes thereupon, and to have his opinion thereof ready for the next Affembly. (ib p 231)

Sefs XXV—Edinburgh, 28th Auguft 1647, Ante meridiem

ACT FOR REVISING THE PARAPHRASE OF THE PSALMES BROUGHT FROM ENGLAND WITH A RECOMMENDATION FOR TRANSLATING THE OTHER SCRIPTURALL SONGS IN MEETER.

The Generall Affembly having confidered the report of the Committee concerning the Paraphrafe of the Pfalmes fent from England, and finding that it is very neceffary that the faid Paraphrafe be yet revifed Therefore doth appoint Mafter John Adamfon to examine the firft fourty Pfalmes, Mafter Thomas Cranfurd the fecond fourty, Mafter John Row the third fourty, and Mafter John Nevey the laft thirty Pfalms of that Para- phrafe, and in their examination they fhall not only obferve what they think needs to bee amended, but alfo to fet downe their own effay for correcting thereof; and for this purpofe recommends to them to make ufe of the travels of Rowallen, Mafter Zachary Boyd, or of any other on that fubject, but efpecially of our own Paraphrafe, that what they finde better in any of thefe works may be chofen, and likewife they fhall make ufe of the animadverfions fent from Prefbyteries, who for this caufe are hereby defired to haften their obfervations unto them, and they are to make report of their labours herein to the Commiffion of the Affembly for Publike Affaires, againft their firft meeting in February next And the Commiffion, after revifing thereof, fhall fend the fame to Provinciall Affemblies to bee tranfmitted to Prefbyteries, that by their further confidera- tion, the matter may be fully prepared to the next Affemblie And becaufe fome Pfalmes in that Paraphrafe fent from England are compofed in verfes which do not agree with the common tunes, therefore it is alfo recommended that thefe Pfalmes be likewife turned in other verfes which may agree to the common tunes, that is, having the first line of eight syllabs, and the second line of six that so both versions being together, use may bee made of either of them in congregations as shall bee found convenient. And the Assembly doth further recommend that Mr Zachary Boyd be at the paines to translate the other Scripturall Songs in meeter, and to report his travels also to the Commission of Assembly, that after their examination thereof, they may send the same to Presbyteries to be there considered until the next Generall Assemblie.

(Printed Acts of the General Assembly.)

(Extract of a Letter to the Assembly of Divynes at Westminster.)

The other things communicated from thence unto this Church, namely, a Directory of Church Government, Catechisme, and new Paraphrase of the Psalmes in metre, are printed and published here, to be considered and examined against the next Generall Assemblie, to be held in July 1648.

Subscribed in name of the Commission of the Generall Assembly of the Kirk of Scotland, by

Edinburgh, 26th November 1647. Mr Robert Douglass, Moderator

Direct. To their Reverend and welbeloved bretnren,
the Assembly of Divines at Westminster, the
Ministers of London, and all other well-affected
Brethren of the Ministrie of England. (Minutes, p 278.)

Edinb 14 Aprilis 1648. Ante meridiem.

The Commission appoynts the Ministers of this town, or any three of them, to be a committee to examine the corrections of the Brethren appoynted to revise Rous's Psalms, and to confer with those brethren therupon, and to report their opinions to this Commission. The first dyet upon Mononday at 10 houres in this place.

(ib p 375.)

Edinb 20 Aprilis 1648. Post meridiem.

The Commission appoynts Mr John Adamson, Doctor Colvill, James Hamiltoun, John Smith, John Neve, and Patrick Gillaspie, James Gutterie, to revise Rous's Psalmes, and the amendements sent in from these that wer appoynted by the Assembly to revise them, and to report their opinions. Their meeting to be the morne at 7 houres in the Colledge.

(ib. p. 886.)

Edinb 1 May 1648. Post meridiem —Sederunt.

Ministers:		Elders
Mr Rot. Douglas, Mod	Mr. Zacharie Boyd.	Libbertoun
Mr James Hamiltoun	Mr. George Leslie	Findawrie.
Mr Evan Cameron	Mr. Rot. Blair.	Sir James Stewart

Mr Samuell Ruyrfurd   Mr John Bell.   George Porterfield
Mr Heugh Mackall   Mr James Guthrie   Lawrence Henderson
Mr John Nevi.   Mr Mungo Law.   John Semple

The Commiſſion appoynts Mr Roᵗ Douglaſs, George Gillaſpie, William Colvill, James Hamiltoun, John Smith, with Mr John Adamſon, to reviſe Rouſe's Paraphraſe of the Pſalmes in meeter, the Animadverſiones thereupon, and to Report their opinions.

(Minutes, p 433)

Edinburgh, 10th Auguſt 1648—Seſs XXXVIII.
ACT FOR EXAMINING THE PARAPHRASE OF THE PSALMS AND OTHER SCRIPTURALL SONGS

The Generall Aſſemblie appoints Rouſe['s] Paraphraſe of the Pſalms, with the corrections thereof, now given in by the perſons appointed by the laſt Aſſembly for that purpoſe, to be ſent to Preſbyteries that they may carefully reviſe and examine the ſame, and thereafter ſend them with their corrections to the Commiſſion of this Aſſembly to be appointed for publick affairs, who are to have a care to cauſe re-examine the Animadverſions of Preſbyteries, and prepare a report to the next Generall Aſſembly, intimating hereby, that if Preſbyteries be negligent hereof, the next Generall Aſſembly is to go on and take the ſame Paraphraſe to their conſideration without more delay. And the Aſſembly recommends to Maſter John Adamſon and Mr Thomas Craufurd to reviſe the labours of Mr. Zachary Boyd upon the other Scripturall Songs, and to prepare a report thereof to the ſaid Commiſſion for publick affairs, that after their examination the ſame may be alſo reported to the next Generall Aſſembly

(Printed Acts of the General Assembly)

Edinburgh, 5 January 1649, Ante meridiem

The Commiſſion of the Generall Aſſembly having this day received a printed copie of Rows Paraphraſe of the Pſalmes, corrected according to theſe Animadverſions given in to the late Aſſembly · Therefore, doth appoint a competent number of theſe corrected copies, now printed, to be ſent to Preſbyteries, that according to the Act of Aſſembly, they may reviſe and examine the ſame, and thereafter return the Animadverſions and corrections thereof to this Commiſſion, otherwiſe the ſaid next Aſſembly is to goe on and take this Paraphraſe to their conſideration without delay.

(Minutes, p 115)

(Extract from a Letter directed to Preſbyteries)

RIGHT REVEREND,

Yee ſhall receive   copies of the new Paraphraſe of the Pſalmes, at a merk the peece, which yow will be pleaſed to peruſe carefully, and that yow would amend any fault yow finde in them, and fend in your corrections to us with diligence, for it is not enough to finde out faults except yee alfo fet downe your owne effay correcting the fame.

Your loving Brethren,
The COMMISSIONERS of the GENERAL ASSEMBLY

Ed^r 30th January 1649   (Minutes, p. 147)

Edinb 7 Junij 1649.—The Commiffion appoints the Reports of the corrections of Roufe's Paraphrafe of the Pfalmes to be delyvered into the Clerk, that he may lend them out to Mr Johne Adamfone, to be confidered againft the next Affembly.

(ib p. 226)

Edinburgh, 6th Auguft 1649.—Ante meridiem   Sess ult

REFERENCE TO THE COMMISSION FOR PUBLIC AFFAIRES FOR RE-EXAMINING THE PARAPHRASE OF THE PSALMES, AND EMITTING THE SAME FOR PUBLICKE USE.

The Generall Affembly having taken fome view of the new Paraphrafe of the Pfalmes in Meeter, with the corrections and animadverfions thereupon, fent from feveral perfons and Prefbyteries, and finding that they cannot overtake the review and examination of the whole in this Affembly; therefore, now after fo much time, and fo great paines about the correcting and examining thereof, from time to time, fome yeares bygone, that the worke may come now to fome conclufion, they do ordain the Brethren appointed for perufing the fame during the meeting of this Affembly, viz Mafters James Hamiltoun, John Smith, Hew Mackail, Robert Traill, George Hutchefon, and Robert Lowrie, after the diffolving of this Affembly, to goe on in that worke carefully, and to report their travels to the Commiffion of the Generall Affembly for publick affaires, at their meeting at Edinburgh in November. And the faid Commiffion, after perufall and re-examination thereof, is hereby authorized, with full power, to conclude and eftablifh the Paraphrafe, and to publifh and emit the fame for publick ufe

A. KER.
(Printed Acts of the General Assembly)

Edinb 7. Auguft 1649.—The Commiffion recommends to the Brethren appointed by the Generall Affembly for correcting the Pfalmes, to haften their corrections, and fo foone as they have done, that the Moderator conveen the Commiffion, or a quorum of thefe that are neareft, to confider their travells, and præpare the matter againft the Quarterly meeting

(fame date)—The Commiffion of Affembly confidering the power they have from the late Affembly to give a competent and honeft acknowledgment and reward to the young man that hes been employed in wrytting of the feveral copies of the Paraphrafe of the Pfalmes corrected from time to time, Doe therefore appoint the Brethren appointed to revise that Paraphrase, who can best know his paines, to consider what shall be given unto him, and to report their opinions therein to the nixt Quarterly meeting

(Minutes, p 234.)

Edinb 20 Novemb. 1649, Post meridiem.—Sederunt

Ministers		Elders
Mr. Ro{t} Douglas, Mod{r}	Mr Sam{ll.} Rutherfuird	Quhytbank
Mr Gavein Young	Mr. Thomas Lundie	
Mr. George Hutcheson	Mr. James Hamiltoun	
Mr Jo{n} Moncreiff	Mr James Gutterie.	
Mr W{m} Oliphant.	Mr Hew Mackaell.	
Mr. George Bennet	Mr George Leslie	
Mr John Livingstoun	Mr Pa{t} Gillaspie	
Mr John Scott	Mr John Hamiltoun	
Mr John Douglas	Mr. Ephraim Melvill	
Mr Jo{n} Dalzell	Mr Arthur Forbes	
Mr David Layng	Mr. Jo{n} Neive.	
Mr. Mungo Law.	Mr James Ro{t}sone	
Mr W{m} Row	Mr. Jo{n} Currie	
Mr Ro{t.} Home.	Mr Thomas Donaldson	

This sessione spent only in the reading and examining the Paraphrase of the Psalmes.— The nixt meeting the morne at 8 houres (Minutes, p 244.)

Edinb. 21 Novemb 1649 Post meridiem.—A number of the Psalmes of the new Paraphrase this day surveyed (ib p 245.)

Edinb 22 Novemb 1649.—A number of the Psalmes this session surveyed
(ib p 246.)

Eodem die, post meridiem.—A number of the Psalmes this day surveyed and examined
(ib p. 247.)

Edinb 23 Novemb 1649.—The rest of this Session spent in reading of the Psalmes
(ib p. 248.)

Eodem die, post meridiem.—Sederunt

Ministers		Elders
Mr Ro{t} Douglas, Mode{r}.	Mr John Livingston	Lord Register
Mr George Hutchesone	Mr James Hamilton	L Craighall.
Mr. James Gutterie	Mr George Leslie	L Brodie
Mr. Ro{t} Row	Mr Jo{n.} Neave	L Ther-Depute
Mr Pa{t} Gillaspie.	Mr W{m} Row	Quhytbank
Mr John Murray	Mr George Bennet	S{r} John Cheislie

Mr. Hew Mackaell.   Mr Jon Douglas
Mr David Laing   Mr Thomas Lundie
Mr Mungo Law

Act for Establishing and Authorizing the new Psalmes

The Commiffion of the Generall Affembly having with great diligence confidered the Paraphrafe of the Pfalmes in Meter, fent from the Affembly of Divines in England by our Commiffioners, whilft they were there, as it is corrected by former Generall Affemblies, Committees trom them, and now at laft by the Brethren deputed by the late Affembly for that purpofe· And having exactly examined the fame, doe approve the faid Paraphrafe, as it is now compiled And therefore, according to the power given them by the faid Affembly, doe appoint it to be printed and publifhed for publik ufe· Hereby authorizing the fame to be the only Paraphrafe, of the Pfalmes of David to be fung in the Kirk of Scotland, and difcharging the old Paraphrafe and any other than this new Paraphrafe, to be made ufe of in any congregation or family after the firft day of Maij in the year 1650; And for Vniformity in this parte of the Worfhip of God, doe ferioufly recommend to Prefbyteries to caufe make publick intimation of this Act, and take fpeciall care that the fame be tymeoufly put to execution, and ducly obferved

Commission to the Ministers of Edinburgh for Ordering the Printing the New Psalmes, and for Satisfieing the Transcribers.

The Commiffion of the Generall Affembly, for the better ordering of the printing of the new Paraphrafe of the Pfalmes, that they may be correctly printed, and that the people be not extortioned by Printers or Stationers in the prices, doe hereby give power to the Moderator and Miniſters of Edinburgh, or any three of them, with the Clerk, to order the printing of the faid new Paraphrafe, and to fett doune pryces thereof, and to take fuch courfe with Printers and Stationers as they may neither wrong the people, nor any of them another Recommending efpecially to them to have a care that copies be correctly tranfcribed for the preffe and that the printed copies be well corrected Giving them alfo power to determine and modifie what they think reafonable to give to the tranfcriber of the copies for all his paines he hes or fhall be at

                                        (Minutes, pp 248 and 253.)

                Edinburgh, 8th January 1650

The Committee of Eftates having confidered the Englifh Paraphrafe of the Pfalms of David in Meeter, prefented this day unto them by the Commifs. of the General Affembly together with their Act and the Act of the late Affembly, approving the faid

Paraphrafe, and appointing the fame to be fung through this Kirk. Therefore, the Committee doth alfo approve the faid Paraphrafe, and interpone their authority for the publifhing and practifing thereof; hereby ordaining the fame, and no other to be made ufe of throughout this Kingdom, according to the tenour of the faid Acts of the General Affembly and their Commiffioners

T. HENDERSON

VI.—THE PRESENT VERSION, 1650

The preceding notices, chiefly extracted from the Journals of the Lords and Commons, and from the Original Minutes of the Commission of the General Assembly, will shew the very great care bestowed in revising Rous's translation of the Psalms Along with these extracts, the reader might compare the additional passages contained in Baillie's correspondence respecting this Version (Vol II pages 379 and 401, and Vol. III. pages 3, 12, 21, 60, and 97.) It would seem from some of these notices that one or more intermediate editions between 1646 and 1650, must have been printed, for the use of Committees in revising the text, but no such copies are known to be preserved At length, after all hope of its being adopted in England as part of the proposed Uniformity had been frustrated, the new Version, being duly sanctioned for use in this country, was published under this title;—

THE PSALMS OF DAVID in Meeter· Newly translated, and diligently compared with the Original Text and former Translations More plain, smooth, and agreeable to the Text than any heretofore Allowed by the authority of the General Affembly of the Kirk of Scotland, and appointed to be fung in Congregations and Families Edinburgh · Printed by Evan Tyler, Printer to the King's Moft Excellent Majefty, 1650 Small 8vo, pp 15 and 308 Prefixed are the Acts of the General Assembly, 6th August, of the Assembly's Commission 23d November 1649, and of the Committee of Estates, 8th January 1650, (as already quoted,) authorizing this Version to be used from and after the 1st May 1650

This was the first authorized edition of our present Version, and other editions by Tyler were printed in the same year Since then it has continued to be republished in countless numbers, and having now remained unaltered for the space of nearly two centuries, (unless some slight variations in orthography,) it would be unnecessary to insert any specimens of it, except for the convenience of comparison with the text of 1646. That this Version of the Psalms should have remained so long in use must be mainly attributed to the great care that was bestowed by many learned divines to render it at once a simple and faithful paraphrase of the original text To a modern critic it will no doubt appear destitute of poetical sentiment or felicity of expression Fidelity, however, was the great object aimed at, and mere elegance was sacrificed to a close adherence t   former translations, by substituting verses or lines, instead of such as had appeared in Rous's version. And while every thing like superfluous ornament and redundacy of language was very scrupulously avoided, in order to render it the more acceptable to persons of all ranks, the common measure was adopted throughout. The changes that have taken place in accent and pronounciation, makes it frequently liable to the charge of want of common prosody. Still with all its poverty of style, and manifest imperfections, it must be admitted, that long familiar use has given it a firm hold on the affections of the people of Scotland, and much as it might be improved if carefully revised (for the sake of metre) by some skilful and judicious hand, and enlarged by adding particular Psalms, in different measures, to lessen its present monotonous character, the Version itself to all appearance will not speedily be superseded. Such in effect was the opinion of Dr Beattie, who was not likely to entertain any strong partiality in its favour. His words, as contained in his letter to Dr Blair "On the Improvement of the Psalmody in Scotland," in 1778, may be quoted. After referring to Sternhold's and King James's versions, he says, "The next English version of the Psalms in metre, is that which is now used by all the Presbyterian congregations in Scotland. And this, notwithstanding its many imperfections, I cannot help thinking the best. The numbers it is true, are often harsh and incorrect; there are frequent obscurities and some ambiguities in the style; the Scotch idiom occurs in several places; and the old Scotch pronounciation is sometimes necessary to make out the rhime. Yet in this Version there is a manly, though severe, simplicity, without any affected refinement, and there are many passages so beautiful as to stand in need of no emendation."

PSALM I

(By F. Rous, from the Edition 1646.)

The man is blest that in th' advice
  of those that wicked are
Walks not, nor stands in sinners path,
  nor sits in scorners chaire
2 But in God's law delights, on's law
  both day and night doth think,
3. He shall be like unto a tree,
  set by the river's brink,

Whose fruit's in season, leaf fades not,
  all that he doth shall thrive:
4 Not so the wicked; but like chaffe
  which winde away doth drive

PSALM I

(From Evan Tyler's Edition 1650.)

That man hath perfect blessednesse,
  who walketh not astray,
In counsell of ungodly men,
  nor stands in sinners way,
Nor sitteth in the scorners chaire,
  2 But placeth his delight
Upon God's law, and meditates
  on his law, day and night

3 He shall be like a tree that growes
  near planted by a river,
Which in his season yeilds his fruit,
  and his leaf fadeth never,
And all he doth shall prosper well
  4 The wicked are not so,
But like they are unto the chaff
  which wind drives to and fro

5 In judgement therefore wicked men
   shall not stand justify'd,
Nor in th' assembly of the just,
   the sinners shall abide
6 Because the way of righteous men
   the Lord with favour knowes,
Whereas the way of wicked men
   unto destruction goes

PSALM XXIII
(From the Edition, 1646.)

The Lord my shephard is, I shall
   not want, he makes me ly
2. In pastures green, me leads by streams
   that do run quietly
3 My soul he doth restore again,
   and me to walk doth make
On in the paths of righteousnesse,
   ev'n for his own name's sake

4 Yea, though I walk in death's dark vale,
   I'le fear no evil thing,
Thou art with me, thy rod, thy staffe,
   to me do comfort bring.
5 Before me thou a table fit'st
   in presence of my foes
My head thou dost with oile anoint,
   My cup it overflowes

6 Goodnesse and mercy all my life
   shall surely follow me,
And in God's house for evermore
   my dwelling place shall be

PSALM LVII v 1—3
(From the Edition, 1646.)

Be mercifull to me, O God,
   thy mercy unto me
Do thou extend, because my soul
   doth put her trust in thee
Yea in the shadow of thy wings
   my refuge I will place,
Untill that these calamities
   do wholly overpasse

2 My cry I will cause to ascend
   unto the Lord most hy,

---

5 In judgment therefore shall not stand
   such as ungodly are,
Nor in th' Assembly of the just
   shall wicked men appear
6. For why? the way of godly men
   unto the Lord is known
Whereas the way of wicked men
   shall quite be overthrown.

PSALM XXIII
(From the Edition, 1650.)

The Lord's my shepherd, I'le not want
   2 He makes me down to ly
In pastures green, He leadeth me
   the quiet waters by
3. My soul he doth restore again,
   and me to walk doth make,
In to the paths of righteousness,
   ev'n for his own Names sake

4 Yea, though I walk in death's dark vale,
   yet will I fear none ill,
For thou art with me, and thy rod
   and staff me comfort still
5. My table thou hast furnished
   in presence of my foes,
My head thou dost with oyl anoint,
   and my cup overflowes

6. Goodnesse and mercy all my life,
   shall surely follow me,
And in God's house for evermore
   my dwelling place shall be

PSALM LVII v 1–3
(From the Edition, 1650.)

Be mercifull to me, O God,
   thy mercy unto me
Do thou extend, because my soul
   doth put her trust in thee
Yea, in the shadow of thy wings
   my refuge I will place,
Untill these sad calamities
   do wholly overpasse

2 My cry I will cause to ascend
   Unto the Lord most hie,

Even unto God who all things doth
for me work perfectly
3 He shall from heaven send, and me
from his reproach defend
That would devour me, God his truth
and mercy forth shall send

PSALM XCIII

(From the Edition, 1646.)

1 God reigns, God's cloth'd with majesty,
God is with strength array'd,
He girds himself therewith, the world
moves not, it is so stay'd
2 Thy throne is fixt of old, and thou
art from eternity
3 The flouds, Lord raise, flouds raise their
voice,
flouds raise their waves on hy

4 But yet the Lord that is on high
is more of might by farre,
Than noise of many waters is,
or great sea-billows are
5 Thy testimonies every one,
in faithfulnesse excell,
And holinesse for ever, Lord,
thine house becommeth well

To God, who doth all things for me
perform most perfectly
3 From heav'n he shall send down, and me
from his reproach defend
That would devour me God his truth
and mercy forth shall send.

PSALM XCIII

(From the Edition, 1650.)

The Lord doth reign, and cloth'd is He
with majesty most bright.
His works do shew him clothed to be
and gird about with might.
The world is also stablished,
that it cannot depart
2 Thy throne is fixt of old, and thou
from everlasting art

3 The flouds, O Lord, have lifted up,
they lifted up their voice,
The floods have lifted up their waves,
and made a mighty noise
4 But yet the Lord, that is on high,
is more of might by far,
Than noise of many waters is,
or great sea billows are

5 Thy testimonies, every one,
in faithfulnesse excell
And holinesse, for ever, Lord,
thine house becometh well

In England, some attempts still continued to be made in favour of Barton's Version, (first printed in 1644,) as appears from the following entry in the Journals of the House of Commons —

Sept 27, 1650 —The humble Petition of Wm. Barton, Preacher of God's Word, was this day read, Ordered, That it be referred to Mr. Carill, Mr Nye, Mr Bond, Mr Stronge, Mr Sedgewick, and Mr. Byfield, or any three of them, to peruse and consider of the Translation of the Psalms set out by Mr Rous, and since reviewed by the said Wm. Barton; and, if they shall approve of the same, then to license the printing thereof —(Vol. vi p 474)

" The Book of Psalms in Metre. close and proper to the Hebrew smooth and pleasant for the Metre To be sung in usuall and known Tunes. By WILLIAM BARTON, Mr of Arts," appeared at London, printed by Roger Daniel, 1654, 12mo. Prefixed is this authority for printing it "Wedneſday January 11th 1653[-4] At the Councill at White-hall Ordered by his Highnes the Lord Protector, and the Councill, That Mr William Barton have the ſole printing of his tranſlation of the Pſalms," &c This edition differs materially both from the firſt publication of Barton's Pſalms (licenſed by the Committee of the Houſe of Commons concerning Printing, April 2nd 1644,) " London, printed by Matthew Simmons for the Companie of Stationers, 1644," 18mo, and from another edition, " London, printed by G M 1645," 12mo, with ' the approbation of more than forty eminent Divines" The later editions contain '- Amendments, and addition of many freſh Metres ' In the copies ſubſequent to 1654, the Author (who takes credit to himſelf for having, ' compiled the whole Book, as near as may be, in the ſame order of words with the original, *and for the most part in as perfect Prose as Verse,*") has introduced this ſentence into the middle of his preface to the Reader: " The Scots of late (he ſays) have put forth a Pſalm-Book, moſtwhat compoſed out of mine and Mr Rouſe his, but it did not give full ſatiſfaction, for ſomebody hath been at charge to put forth a new edition of mine, and printed ſome thouſands of mine in Holland, as it is reported, But whether they were printed there or no, I am in doubt, for I am ſure that 1500 of my Books were heretofore printed by ſtealth in England, and carried over to Ireland "

Several eminent Non contormiſt Divines in London and the neighbourhood having adopted our preſent metrical verſion of the Pſalms, in the editions printed at London, 1673. 1683, &c they prefixed an addreſs " to the Reader," which concludes thus — " The Tranſlation which is now put into thy hands, cometh neareſt to the Original of any that we have ſeen, and runneth with ſuch a fluent ſweetneſs that we thought fit to recommend it to thy Chriſtian acceptance, Some of us having uſed it already, with great comfort and ſatiſfaction " Signed —

THO MANTON, D D	THO DOOELITTLE
HENR LANGLEY, D D	THOMAS VINCENT.
JOHN OWEN, D D	NATHANAEL VINCENT.
WILLIAM JENKYN	JOHN RYTHER
JA INNES	WILL. TOMSON.
THO WATSON	NICO BLAKIE
THO. LYE	CHARLES MORTON
MAT POOLE	EDM CALAMY.
JO MILWARD	WILL CARSLAKE
JOHN CHESTER	JAMES JANEWAY
GEO. COCKAYN	JOHN HICKES
MATTHEW MEADE	JOHN BAKER
ROBERT FRANKLIN	RI. MAYO

WILLIAM BARTON took his degree as B A at Oxford, 23d October 1633 In 1656 he was appointed Minister of St Martin's, Leicester, and had the rectory of Cadeby given him by Cromwell, but he was ejected in 1662 He died sometime between 1672, when he published "Two Centuries of select Hymns and Spiritual Songs," and 1682, when an edition was printed of his "Book of Pfalms," bearing on the title to be "as he left it finished in his lifetime" In this amended state his version continued to be reprinted till 1705

VII—SCRIPTURAL SONGS AND PARAPHRASES.

As a suitable sequel to these notices, the following extracts respecting certain proposed additions to the Psalmody may be given.—

Edinb 25 Februarij 1648 —The Commiffion defires Mr. Johne Adamson to revife Mr David Leitch s papers of Poecie, and give his opinion to the Commiffion thereof
(Minutes of the Commission, p 306)

Edinb 5 April. 1648 —Concerning Mr David Leitch, The Commiffion appoynts the letter following to be written to the Presbytery of Allau, [in the margin, Ellon]—

RIGHT REVEREND AND WELBELOVED BRETHREN,

THESE are to fhow yow, that our brother Mr. David Leich, being employed in Paraphrafing the Songs of the Old and New Teftament, hes been in this town fome tyme, and for als much as he yet is appointed to continue in that employment, our earneft defyre is, that yow endevour your felfes joyntly, for his further encouragment in that work, provyding that it be no hinderance to him in his prefent charge. So recomending yow and your labours to the bliffing of God, Wee reft,

Your louing Brethren, etc.

Edinb 5 Apryll 1648
Direct to their Reverend Brethren of the Prefbytery of Ellon (ib p 362)

Edinb 1° Januarij 1650, Ante meridiem.

The Commiffion of the Affembly underftanding the paines of Mr. Jo Adamfon, Mr Zacharie Boyd, and Mr. Ro^t Lowrie have been at in the tranflation of the Pfalmes and other Scripturall Songs in Meeter, and how ufefull their travells have been in the correcting of the Old Paraphrafe of the Pfalmes, and in compileing the New, Doe therefore returne them heartie thanks for thefe their labours, and that the Moderator fhew this to Mr Jo Adamfone, Mr. Robert Lowrie, and wrytte to Mr Zacharie Boyd to this purpofe
(Minutes, p. 260.)

Edinb 22d Feb^{ry} 1650
The Commiffion underftanding that Mr Ro^t Lowrie has taken fome paines in put-

ting the Scripturall Songs in Meter, They therefore defire him to prefent his labours therein to the Commiffion at their nixt meeting. (ib. p. 286.)

It may be added, that in the Minutes of the Commission, no further notice is taken either of these Scriptural Songs by Leitch, or Lowrie, which do not appear ever to have been printed. Of the persons commended for "their travells and pains," in this pious work, a few particulars may be mentioned 1. MR. JOHN ADAMSON held the office of Principal of the University of Edinburgh from 1623, till his death in November 1653, and was the author of various works 2 MR. ZACHARY BOYD, one of the Ministers of Glasgow, has obtained a much greater degree of notoriety. To a work (in verse) called "The Garden of Zion," printed at Glasgow 1644, he annexed, and afterwards republished, with his Psalms, in a revised form, "The Songs of the Old and New Testament" He died at Glasgow in the beginning of 1654 but his fond expectations, if not positive injunctions, for having his works published after his death were wholly disregarded. 3 MR DAVID LEITCH, (in Latin Leochæus,) was minister of Ellon in Aberdeenshire He was previously a Professor in King's College, Aberdeen, and pronounced, 9th April 1635, a Latin funeral oration on the death of Patrick Forbes of Corse, Bishop of Aberdeen, which is included, along with a Latin poem by him, in the volume of the Bishop's Funerals, printed that year in Aberdeen; and in 1637, he also published an academical oration, "Philosophia Illachrymans," &c In an account of the "Learned men and writers of Aberdeen," it is said, Leitch "wrote several learned poems, and was one of the chaplains to King Charles II and also of the army that went into England." A volume of Latin poetry by him was printed at London 1657, 12mo 4 MR ROBERT LOWRIE was one of the Ministers of Edinburgh Having conformed at the Restoration, he was appointed Dean of Edinburgh; and in 1671 he was advanced to be Bishop of Brechin He died in 1677

The proposal of enlarging the Psalmody by joining Paraphrases of other passages of Scripture, was afterwards brought under the deliberation of the Assembly, at various intervals. See the printed Acts of Assembly, 1706, act 4 Ass 1707, act 16· and Ass. 1708, act 15 In 1745 a collection of such Paraphrases was published, and being remitted by the Assembly to the several Presbyteries, it came to be used in churches in public worship. The Assembly in 1775 appointed a Committee to revise that collection, and it was again published, with considerable alterations and additions, and retransmitted for the consideration of Presbyteries, 1st June 1781; and meanwhile it was allowed " to be used in public worship, in congregations where the Minister finds it for edification." This collection of Translations and Paraphrases in verse, although only partially adopted at the time, is now in general use throughout the country; and it has been contemplated to have the collection further enlarged

Before dismissing the subject of the Psalmody of our Church, it is worthy of notice, that the editions of the Old Version, previous to 1650 are almost all accompanied with the tunes set to music. This would imply a much more general knowledge of sacred music than now prevails; but instructions in singing then formed an ordinary part of education and music-schools were supported, at least, in the chief borough towns. A striking incident is recorded in relation to one of these tunes. In 1582, John Durie, one of the Ministers of Edinburgh, after a temporary suspension and banishment, (in consequence of having incurred the displeasure of some of King James's favourites,) on his return was met at the Netherbow Port, or one of the gates of the City, " by the haill Toun," and the whole assembled multitude marching up the High Street, with their heads uncovered, and with loud voices joined in singing the old version of the 124th Psalm,—

> Now Israel may say, and that truly,
> If that the Lord had not our cause maintained, &c.

In the edition of the Psalms, printed at Edinburgh, by the heirs of Andrew Hart, 1635. 8vo, the Editor, (only known by his initials. ' E M " but who appears to have been a devoted enthusiast,) has given the tunes in four Parts, from a careful examination of the best copies. while he acknowledges · the whole composition of the Parts to belong to the primest Musicians that ever this Kingdom had, as Dean John Angus, Blackhall. Smith. Peebles. Sharp. Black, Buchan, and others, famous for their skill in this kind." (See Introduction to Johnson's Scots Musical Museum, edit 1839. vol i pp xxvi-xxxiv.) Some of these airs are foreign, either German or French, others are English, while several of them. such as ' Dundee,' ' New London, ' Martyrs,' and St. David's,' are still to be heard in our Churches, and these fine old simple airs will always be admired for their · grave sweet melody."

LXXXVII

LETTERS OF MR ROBERT BLAIR, MINISTER OF ST ANDREWS

[The first four Letters addressed to Douglas are printed from the Originals, in Wodr MSS Fol. Vol xxv Nos 99 100, 112, 113. and that to Dickson. from Baillie's MS The last is that of which Baillie makes special mention, *supra*, p 376]

No 1

REVEREND & BELOVED BROTHER,

I HAVE conferred with some of our Brethren from the West, of whom ye did wryt to me, and albeat they be very unsatisfied with publick proceedings, yet I fand them more desyrous of conjunction then I expected I wiss the rather a dyet be appointed for the delayed conference, and the mean tyme tendernes to be used toward them & other diffenting brethren As for the Act of Claffes, ye know my mind, that though I was not fatisfied with fundrie things in it, yet I think it very unexpedient it be cancelled in anie pairt at this tyme Ye know well how all the anfwers given to ther Quæries have bein abufed, to the farder renting both of Kirk & Eftate, wherof they would be gravelie remembred and admonerfhed at this tyme Yea, farder, I have often heard, and from a good hand this daye, that they whom the Act moft concerns, ai moft filent about it, and they that defyies it leaft, & yet will yeald to it for the ftrenthening of ther fachon, mak moft din about it, and yet will be readie to fcoff at a yealding anfwer, and traduce you therefter. As alfo, it is better to keep this Act over the heads of them that now are admitted to imployment, to mak them bettir bairnes when favours ar granted to them by degries Confider alfo how, in yealding, we pafs from our late anfwer to the firft Quærie, wherin we defyred that power fould not be put in ther hand: to recall that fo quicklie, I think it both fin and fhame, till they deferve it bettir And yet farder, wer not this the waye to unite us with our Brethren the lefs hopefull and faider out of fight, when needlefhe we goe farder from them And albeat, evin this confideration is not to be flighted, as I know yow will not, yet that which we ought mainlie to look to is the Lord's intereft, the Act being made to keap judicatories and places of truft clear, (the rigour, ye know, and felfynes vented therin, I never lyked,) it would be well advyfed what to putt in the roome therof They that have been ill affected doe too much lift up ther creft every wher, which we have nead to look to in tyme, if it be not alreadie almoft out of tyme My opinion and earneft requeaft is, that this matter be left intear to the Gen[eral] Afs[embly] for fo ye and others that lye under the burdein of bufines will be beft exonered Grace be with you

Your loving Brother,

M. ROBERT BLAIR.

For his Reverend and beloved Brother, Mr Robert Douglas,
  Minifter of the Gofpell

No 2

S^t A^{rs} [St Andrews,] 16th March 1651

REVEREND AND BELOVED BROTHER,

I STILL continow craffie [infirm], and am not like to recover health or ftrength I like not the prefent repealing of the Act of Claffes, it was ill made, and now it were as ill refcinded, for thereby would be ftrengthened mightily the oppofition that is made to Publick Refolutions We have rather need to fee how to curb the too great inclination thereaway I hear, that if Mr. James Guthrie and his colleague be fairly defyred by the Commiffion, and a place affigned to him for the interim, that he may be induced to hearken to that defyre I earneftly wifh that courte be tollowed, and so can to firft the expected advantage of our wicked invaders therein will be difappointed, as alfo the expectation of wicked men among ourfelves will be fruftrated, as alfo the jealoufy of fome more forward than wife will be abated, and the moderate fort of honeft profeffors will be moft fatiffied But I have no will Mr William Livingftoun's bufinefs be flighted, I complained to the King when he was here, and wifhed him to fhow his diflike of all fuch flatterie. I defyre ye would think of a publick humiliation, and private in families, contriving the Caufes fo as may be leaft offenfive to any, and yet comprehenfive enough The Lord himfelf fteer the helm in this tempeft, and direct yow by his Spirit in all things, which fhall be the prayer of

Your loving Brother,

M ROBERT BLAIR

For his Reverend and Beloved Brother Mr. ROBERT DOWGLAS,
 Minifter of the Gofpell of Chrift, Thefe

No 3

REVEREND AND BELOVED BROTHER,

IN this troublefome tyme ye ar putt to great travell, and hath but fmall incuradgements, when all things ar fo far out of frame The fetling of difcipline in the airmie is a thing very neceffarie, and Oh that the Lord may be pleafed to blefs his owne ordinance Our unfatiffied Brethren, I fear, will ftill be unfatiffied for anie thing can be done that waye, but I hope the Lord will be pleafed, in Chryft, with endeavoures of that kynd The firft daye I came out to the Prefbiterie, which was Wedinfday laft, I was furpryfed with the reading of ane Exhortation and Warning, indirectlie applying the characters of Malignants to diffenters, and requyring Prefbiteries to cenfure them I had heard fuch a thing muttered, but did not beleive it, albeat letters from Glafgow compleaned of it In my judgement it is unfeafonable and not healing, nor fitt to be made ufe of. It is lyke to make the rent wyder, and doe no good, but to crye Bellum The Spirit of counfell and couradge reft upon yow.

Your loving Brother,

27th Apr 1651 M ROBERT BLAIR

For his Reverend and Beloved Brother, Mr. ROBERT DOWGLAS,
 Minifter of the Gofpell of Chryft.

No 4.

REVEREND AND BELOVED BROTHER,

THOUGH the enimie be w thin few mylles, yet my infirmitie puts me from thoughts of going anie wher. We ar under a terrible ftorme of Divein difpleafure. The folie of the Protefters, I think it very prefumptuous, yet I think it not wifdome to goe to the height of deferved cenfures, confidering the extremitie of the tyme, and former deferving of the perfones Forget not Mr. Ja Durrham: it was againft my opinion he was loufed from his charge. Mr. Baylie told me they had a mynd to call him to it again Though they fould be flack in it, hald hand to it I pray yow, it will help fomewhat to mitigat the alienated mynds of good people Mr Ja Fergufon is a wyfs and grave man. I wifs he wer joyned in attendance upon the King This fame ftribling ftreffes my bodie. Counfell from heavin fhyne in upon your heart

Your loving Brother,

[Between the 20th and 31ft July 1651]   M ROBERT BLAIR

For his Reverend and beloved Brother, Mr ROBERT DOWGLAS,
Moderator of the G Affemblie at Dundie.

No 5

REVEREND & DEAR BROTHER,

WE fcaircehe gott a word one of another, when we were beaten afunder I ever feared, our Brethren would ufurpe, and would raither put others to fuffering than to fuffer themfelves. They invited me to come to their meeting at Edinburgh, by ane letter dated from Glafgow; but befide the inabilitie of my bodie, I had fundrie reaffons why I went not to them I wrot to fome of their number, that they fhould content themfelves with conference, and not ufurpe power to which they had no calling from God or man Notwithftanding they have begune their ufurping wayes, and fitts, as haveing Commiffion from the Affembly 1650, whilk is expyred And though they fitt peaceablie, they [there] are parties fent out to apprehend minifters in this fhire, fo that our fynodicall meeting was hindered The prefbyteries here are mending the matter, as they beft may, and this day our Prefbyterie hes emitted the inclofed Act, and tranfmitted it to their neighbours, haveing alfo appointed ane Faft, the Lord's day come eight dayes, for the finnes and fufferings of the land God help us, we are compaffed with innumerable evills Lord help our captive Brethren, whofe burthen is made heavier then [throw ?] the proceidings of our ufurping Brethren Grace be with you and your toffed familie

Your, &c

20th October 1651   M. R BLAIR
For Mr DAVID DICKSON.

LXXXVIII

MR. JAMES DURHAME, [TO MR ROBERT DOUGLAS]

[Orig.—Wodr MS. Fol Vol XXV. No 121.—The address of the letter is not preserved, but it was evidently written to Douglas.]

RIGHT REVEREND,

I was once in doubt whither to have staid till the Assembly or not, but being recovered in my health, and not knowing quho may be with the King, I have resolved, upon Mr Blair's advice, to goe immediatly to that charge, untill the Assembly dispose of me and it, as shall be thought best. I doubt not quhen men are to be named, but yee will be carfull to fee them such as that taske requirs, which I ingenouslly confesse does not only requir mor zeall faithfullnes and abilities then I have, but mor then I could have thought of before experience of the snares and discouradgements which accompanie it. I can say litle of the publike being allmost affraid of everie event I can think of; yet, if God wold blesse som overturs I heard from Mr Blaire, of waveing all bypast debats at this tyme by entreing on a new ground. I thinke it the only way of healing, quheras, if things shall conclud by hotenes, after debat it doth not cure y' evill, but will readily bring on acts and censurs on men, quhich will be of greater standall to the Church, in my judgment then the thing debated and may probably draw more favourers, out of desire to suffer, with som, and by others, quhairby manie will be deimed to act by ane other principle in that then the present contraverfie. I was greived to heir of som offence given at Stirling within these few days about preaching quherin though I did never wreat to Mr James Guthrie, and thinks he might have done otherwise yet I see not hou he can justly be charged in that, having undertaken no promise, and stayed so longe a tyme, mor than I thinke wold have beine desired, if a tyme had beine set. Besid, the longest that was expected was only till the armie were up, or wer removed from thence. The days being few till the Assembly, it had beine lesse offence to have forborne. But I know yee see in these things further then I and how farr men may outrune resolutions, for pursueing ther own principles and ends hes beine observed by yow long befor this. Though I grant ther be sundrie things in some men, quherin yee may be offended, yet I doe expect yee wil rather privatl cheke them for it then anie way publikly to seim alienated in your affection from them, quherof I my self have no feare. The Lord direct yow in this strait tyme, quhen the eys of all are on yow, som with feare, and others with expectatione, quho I hope, shall be prevented or disapointed, which is and shall be the prayer of your looving Brother,

July 14. 1651

M J DURHAME.

LXXXIX

PROTESTATION AGAINST THE PROVINCIAL SYNOD AT GLASGOW, 8th October 1651.

[From Baillie's MS Letters, &c. Vol. III fol 112, where the date 1652 is given, but this is unquestionably an error]

Whereas the paper called " Teftimony," etc., voiced in the Provinciall Synod of Glafgow October 8th, doth very injurioufly reflect upon the late Generall Affembly, and was caryed on mainlie by men cenfured by that Affembly, and others preingadged in a Proteftation againft it cenfureable by the Acts of our Kirk: For thefe and other Reafons to be given in, in time and place convenient, We under fubfcribers, in our oune names and in the name of foe many as fhall adheare, doe Diffent and Proteft againft that paper, and all other proceedings of that Synod contrarie to the late Generall Affembly, appealling therefra to the next lawfull Generall Affembly, and defireing this our Proteftation and appeale to be infert in the Synod books

J. Bonar.	Mr R Baillie.	Mr R. Watsone elder
M. H. Blair.	Mr Zach. Boyd	Mr Jo Sterling
Mr. Johne Burne.	Mr R Inglis	Mr J Adamsone.
M R. Wallace	Mr Jo Bell.	Mr. Ro. Watsone younger.
M Allan Fergusone	Mr Jo Vetche	
M J Stewart	Mr Wm Russell	Ja Buchanane.
William Blair	Mr Wm Crookfs	Mr Math Ramsay
[A blank in the MS.]	Mr Wm Castellaw.	Mr Ja. Fergusone
Mr Robert Aird	Mr Ja Taillour	M. Jo Cochrane
D McAlpine	Mr. Jo Hume	Mr Pat. Colvill
M R. Spruile	Mr Tho Kirkaldie	
Mr Hugh Eccles	Mr. Wm. Mortone	
Mr Ja. Inglis	Mr. Geo Young	
Wm. Rodger	Mr Gab Cunynghame	
M R Maxwell	Mr. Ard. Dennfstone	

Reasons of Dissent

1. *First.* That we were content to goe alongft with them, for Union's fake, in all things demanded, fo that ane publict vote of the Synod fhould not pafs difallowing the Publict Refolutions; but this was refufed, as appears be their Inftructions.

2 They divided the Overture, and to make the firft part more taking, they changed the word in the Overture ' Diffatified,' into ' Not being cleare to read prefentlie '

3 The Synod haveing voted only 'That they were not clear to read presenthe,' they voiced the whole Overture in a second vote, they keept the word 'Diffatiffied,' which, for obtaining voice in the other, they had taken away.

4 They not only voted Diffatiffaction with Publict papers, bot did imply, that while [untill] they were fatiffied, they would no wayes jovne for oppofeing the enemie: as appears be compareing the first and third Infruction

5 They did admitt Ruleing Elders to voice who had no commiffion to inftruct their power to the feffion and had no feat in the Prefbyterie fince the laft Synod, as the Prefbyterie books did declare.

6 That while in their Infructions they did challenge the Commiffion in many things of neglect of duty, and it being offered be the Brethren to fhow, that the Commiffion had not been deficient in thefe things, be their fupplication prefented to the Parliament, yet it was refufed to fuffer thefe papers to be read, which could have cleared the Commiffion

7. That while the Countrey was in great danger of the Sectarians as was fhown be diverfe Brethren of the Synod, that fome did keep meetings with them, and fome gone in to them of their number, yet all, for the Teftimonie againft the Sectarians, was delayed for fyve or fex weeks after the Synod, albeit it was proponed in the Synod and Committee be them, yet nothing was done againft them in the Committee, and nothing fpoken againft them till the Synod was to ryfe, and nothing at all was reported againft the Sectarians be the Committee.

8 And while diverfe Infructions were given, wherein every member of the Synod could not fay he had a fcruple, yet they would have the fcruples fent as from the whole Synod, although there was not one member of the Synod would owne them all: but when it was required that the Caufes of the Faft fhould be read, the moft of them being agreed upon be them all, yet the like was refufed though the prefent condition of the Kingdome did neceffarly require the fame.

9. Though the prefent condition of the Kingdome did neceffarlie require the Warnings to be read, and the Caufes of the Faft, as faid is, yet they did delay all till probably their reading will be ufelefs

XC

ADVICES AND ANSWERS FROM DOUGLAS AND OTHERS IN THE TOWER OF LONDON, TO BAILLIE S QUESTIONS, 29TH JUNE 1652

[From the same, fol. 116—See *supra* pages 188 and 189 respecting this paper The following extract from the Presbytery Records of St Andrews, furnishes the names of the Ministers who were surprised at Alyth, and carried prisoners to London

Sept 1, 1651 —" The Prefbyterie mett occafionallie for advyfeing q' is incumbent to be done by y^m in relation to certaine Brethren, latelie taken prifoners at Eliot, as Mr Robert Douglas, Mr. James Hamilton, Mr Mungo Law, Mr Johne Smith, Mr James Sharp, Mr George Pattullo, Mr Johne Ratray, Minifters, and Mr Andro Ker, Clerk to the Generall Affemblie; did appoint a letter to be written to Lieutenant-Generall Moncke for y^r reliefe, and a letter to the Brethren for comforting and encouraging y^m under y^r fuffering, and Mr Alex^r Wedderburne appointed to goe with both"]

It is hoped that care has been taken for the elections in Prefbyteries of qualified and well-affected perfones The next labour is for the conftitution of the enfuing Affembly To which effect it will be neceffarie that fome few meet together on the Mononday or Tuefday before the meeting of the Affembly, to prepare, order, and confult on all things neceffarie, and to informe themfelves of the refults of the meetings of the Declyning pairtie, and to arme themfelves accordingly

If the Commiffion of Affembly have not already taken courfe for preaching and opening the Affembly, the time being fo fhort, it will be neceffarie that the prefent Moderator of the Commiffion fpeak to Mr Robert Blair, and failzieing him, to write to Mr David Dickfone to fhow them it's a duetie lying upon one of them as laft Moderator to open the Affembly, and that both of them prepare to preach, the one before, the other after noone, according to the cuftome, in refpect of the abfence of the Moderator of the late Affembly 1651, and the incapacitie of the Moderator 1650 to moderate in this now enfueing Affembly by his Declining [the Affembly of] 1651, and confequently this which is conveened by the authoritie of that: In cafe of Mr Blair's infirmitie or abfence, one of the minifters of the towne where the Affembly meets, may be written unto to preach with Mr David Dickfone

If Mr Andrew Cant, Moderator of the Affembly 1650 be there, and take the chaire, offering to open the Affembly as laft Moderator, or if it be moved, that he may doe it, (both which may be done upon defigne), it is not our opinion that he can be admitted as a member, much leffe to moderate untill he have paffed from and renunced under his hand-writing the Declinator, which neither he can give, nor the Affembly receive, before they be conftitute; and fo ane other muft moderate and open the Affembly much lefs is it queftioned that he fhould be debarred, if he acknowledge this Affembly under any Proteftation or declaration, That the acknowledgeing of this is not to be underftood as any acknowledgement of the preceeding Affembly, or fuch like

That the Affembly may be conftitute be vertew of the Indiction of the preceeding, Let the Act of Indiction be firft read before receaveing in of any Commiffions, and thereafter, the Act for the order of calling the roll, and fpeciall care would be had that no way b⋯ pretence of peace and union,) for afferting the authority of this Affembly, either directly or indirectly difowneing the preceeding

For the Reasons following.—

1. Any Declaration bearing that the acknowledgement of this Affembly is not to import any acknowledgement of the former, is fo clear, that it needs not to be fpoken to But fmooth Overtures paffing over the queftion, or not takeing notice for the time of the Act of Indiction; or, That the Affembly is to be held legall or lawfull without relation to the Indiction, or any fuch, are all upon the matter reall paffing from the Affembly and burying of it for ever: For what Affembly could owne it, when this indicted by it doeth not owne it, efpecially feeing tyme may and would certainly, in that cafe, make the difference wyder and the Declyners pairtie ftronger. What Synod, or Prefbytries, or Minifter, would or could owne that Affembly or their Acts, if the authoritie of it were fo flighted by this Generall Affembly, no obedience to their Acts could be urged, nor difobedience cenfured

2. It were at the leaft to keep the authoritie of the preceding Affembly under queftion, and fo the Declyners fhall have juft reafon to think that yet *sub judice lis est*, which were a weakening of the authoritie of the Affembly, and a ftregthening of their ufurpatione.

3 If this Affembly either put or leave the authoritie of that under queftion, the Declyners fhould have juft reafon to difacknowledge their cenfures, and notwithftanding thereof to exerce their miniftrie untill it be taken from them by ane unqueftioned authoritie And this were in the Affembly a fearfull proftituteing of the Ordinance of the Miniftrie and Church cenfures to contempt, and to leave the precious Ordinances of Chrift to be efteemed valide or invalide, lawfull or unlawfull, according to the pleafure and humor of men, and their vertue and value to be changeable with times and perfons

4 It's a falvo to all fuch as doe, or can be moved to difclaime the late Affembly, that a ftrong pairtie of fuch may be admitted, under pretence of peace and union, but indeed to trouble the publict peace and order of the Kirk; who, being admitted, will plead (and poffiblie can with fome appearance of reafon, from the fame argument of peace and union,) that other Acts, alfewell as the Act of Indiction, thefe efpecially of cenfures may for a time not be owned, and fo as they have a falvo to difowne the authoritie, the Declyners fhall obtaine a libertie to exerce miniferiall duties with a *non obstante* of the Acts of that Affemblie.

5 As fuch a Declaration will work in favour of the decliners of, fo in prejudice of the adhearers unto the authoritie of that Affembly, as putting or leaving the authoritie of it in queftion, yea it feems to be a plaine admitting of a declaration or proteftation againft it To doe a deed commanded under proteftation or declaration, that it is not by vertue of, or in obedience to the command, is to proteft or declare againft the commander and

his authoritie, and the thing commanded being performed, it can import nothing elfe and if the authoritie commanding accepts of performances with fuch declarations and proteftations, he accepts and admitts of proteftations and declarations againft himfelffe and his owne authoritie: Soe, if the Affembly either themfelves declare, or admitt others to declare, That they doe not hold their meeting to be in relation or by warrand of the preceeding Affemblie, they thereby fignifie no leffe than a denyall or difowning of the authoritie of that Affemblie

6 If the authoritie of the late Affembly be not acknowledged, the authoritie of this muft be queftioned, the meeting of this haveing no other warrand but from that, and foe it muft be a meeting without warrand, and illegall, and fuch a meeting cannot give authoritie to it felfe

7. No Commiffioners can affirme or declare that their meeting is not in relation to the Indiction of the former Affembly, without manifeft and unfaithfull contradicting of their Commiffions, which doe expreflie relate to that Indiction, and bears that as the narrative and caufe And fo fuch declarations being of neceffitie to be regiftred, and the Commiffions alfo to be keept *in retentis*, their unfaithfullnefs shall inevitably be keept in record to all pofteritie.

If any Commiffions from Prefbyteries bear fuch Declarations and Proteftations (which is to be carefully obferved,) or any Commiffioners make fuch verbally, in our opinion the Commiffions may be rejected as limited, and the Commiffioners removed, as limiting themfelves; at the leaft they ought to be laid afide untill the remanent Commiffions be given in, and the Affembly be conftitute of uncontroverted members

None depofed or fufpended can in any tearmes be admitted to this Affembly, nor can thefe who fubfcryved the Declinator given in at St Andrewes, except they paffe from and renunce the Declinator by a declaration under their hands: as for the adhearers unto it fince the Affembly 1651, this Affembly cannot take notice of them untill their adhereing to it be judicially delated and made good. and if it be informed and inftructed, they are then to be removed alfewell as declyners

After the Commiffions are given in, the nixt is to choife the Moderator, for ordering whereof, the Act made thereanent is to be read And we pray the Lord to direct the Affembly upon one of abilities for the imployment, unqueftionable integritie for the caufe of God, and of knowledge and foundnefs in the prefent debates and differences

For want of the Regifters, the Affembly muft be content at this time with the printed Acts, and extracts of fuch Acts, as ufually are called for And the Clerk, in refpect of his reftraint, will appoint one to attend the Affembly with fuch neceffarie papers as he can at prefent think of But it will be neceffarie, after the conftitution, that the Affembly formallie warrand any they pleafe to fupply the Clerk's place in this Affembly, and fubfcribe the Acts of it in his abfence

In our humble opinion it will be fitting, That the Affembly ufe all poffible hafte to a conclufion, ingadgeing themfelffs in alfe little buffinefs either of publict or private concernment as can be. But thefe feem neceffarie --

1 That a full and plaine Declaration be emitted againft all and every encroachment upon the liberties, priviledges, and authoritie of the Kirk, the Judicatories, Miniftrie, and other ordinances of Chrift, and againft Separation, with a reccommendation to Prefbytries and Synods to take effectuall courfe for oppofeing thefe evills, efpeciallie where any Separatifts already appear

2 The Commiffion for publict affaires would be renewed, 1. Of a recommendation, for further cenfure of any depofed or fufpended minifters by the late Affembly at Dundee, or by any others whatfoever judicatorie of this Kirk, or commiffions iffueing from them that have exerced any part of the minifteriall function fince the fentences given againft them 2 Of a particular power to confider the feveral conditions of all cenfured minifters, according to their abilities for the miniftrie, repentance for their offences, and good behaviour fince their cenfures, to put them in a capacitie of readmiffion to the miniftrie, if the Lord fhall offer them a call

3 There would be a generall renovation ard continuation of all the references and commiffions appointed by the preceeding Affembly.

4 It feemes neceffarie alfo that there be a recommendation to Prefbytries and Synods to take notice of minifters that have imployed any depofed or fufpended to preach, or exerce any pairt of the minifteriall calling

We conceave, in our humble opinion, it better that the Affembly indict the nixt to fome day in the nixt year, than that this be continued and prorogated

If the Affembly fhall meet with any Declinator, they know what they ought to doe, yea, if they meet with greater oppofition, we confidently hope that confcience of deutie, and former prefidents, will animate them to fhew faithfullnefs, courage, and refolution againft it; and fhall conftantly pray for the fulfilling of that promife, Ifaiah 4, " That the Lord may create upon every dwelling-place of Mount Zion and her affemblies a cloud and fmoke by day, and the fhineing of flaming fire by night, and upon all the glory a defence," etc.

Thefe are our thoughts, as we can conceave, of your bufinefs, from fenfe of duty, without the leaft prefumption of prefcribeing or limiteing any man's better judgment

XCI

JOHNSTONE OF WARRISTON TO MR JAMES GUTHRIE,
29th March 1654

[From the Original in the Editor's possession The initials 'M S R,' 'M. R D,' 'L B,' 'S J Ch.,' 'M J G,' 'M P G stand respectively for Mr Samuel

Rutherford, Mr Robert Douglas, Lord Broghill, Sir John Cheesley, Mr James Guthrie, and Mr Patrick Gillespie]

LOVING BROTHER,

BLISSED be the Lord that preserved you in your homgoing I shal soone goe throu the booke, and preffe diligence on vthers who ar too floue. For neues, Lieut Gen Monk, wee heare, is nou, or wil be this week, on his journey to command in Scotland, and withal is reported to haive sayd, that he could live with any but the Remonftrators and Protefters in Scotland, and that he hes commiffion to burne and deftroye wherfoever the Highlanders are refetted Ther is fom report as if the M[arques] of Neucaftle. Incbquin & Langdayle, wer com to the North Their is a declaration of the Caufes of a Faft in Ingland, in which their are fom good, fom doubtful, and fom bad things M S R hes feen the ordnance to the thirty minifters and elders about planting Kirks, and fayes, it is lyk the old High Commiffion I haive not yet feen it, but on[e] of the diurnals fayes, the Councel of State is about the fettling a gouver' of the Church as before of the Staite M R D. preached laft Saboth bitterly againft vs as marking humiliations and communions in the countrey only for a nayme to ourfelves, and that people might idolize vs, &c And then in privat he fpake to my L B againft the King and nobles and our native reulers as worfe than the Inglifh, and that he durft not in fecret praye for their reftitution. Midleton, I heare, hes an abfolut commiffion, not only in military and civil affaires, but alfo in ecclefiaftical, with expreffe power to depofe and putt out minifters I think it an obfervable circumftance of tyme by Providence tryfting the 20th of Merch to be the day of the Inglifhes apoynting their Faft, and of our begining our notes of our Teftimonye, and the 24th of Merch to be the daye of their Faft, and of our finifhing our Teftimonye letter, and meeting; which I wifh they would taik for an good aunfwear of their Faft I heare their ordinance about trying of minifters exprefly declares their tryal and approbation to be no facred or foleme fetting a man apart to the minifterye, but the ground and warrant of the magiftrats giving to fuch the ftipend, and fo to fhuffle and fhutt out ordination, &c It pleafed the Lord to affift M. S. R. on Sunday al day to lecture on the 50th Ifay, and preach on the 4, 5. 6, v Their was fuch a throng in the Grayfreers in the foreanoon, and in the Tron Kirk in the afternoon, and fuch a thinnes in the reft of the kirks as we haive not readily feen the lyke fince the 1638. He preached pairt of our Teftimonye. M. R D fayd wee had fent vp three of our number, and fom of vs maid fom oppofition to it only becaus wee was not called vp ourfelves Yee would not foigett to fend in the papers to S J Ch and alfo y\` draught of the Teftimonye to the fynods We haive fent an exprefle to Mr Jh. Levifton with the letter and tuo fubferyved Teftimonyes. I heard that Col Lilburne fayd to on[e], that he was the occafion of fending for thes three minifters, by a letter of his to the General, as a waye to fatiffye the godly in Scotland, and if he had knouen befor what he hard nou, he fhould haive defyred lettres to haive been written alfo to M S R and M J G Som hes maid a report goe throu the countrey as if wee had quyetly agreed with the Inglifhes, and that wee wer ravfing a Whigimyre road vnder Argyle, who, in the meantyme, I heare, hes written baifely flattering and ingaging lettres to the Protector. Alex^r. Jaffray is lying feake, and fo is Mr. Jhon Meinzeis bedfaft and not aible to goe vp I haive written you al the neues I know I fend to you heirwith a copye of the firft paper which was written, to mark the cheifeft paffages of fcripture, to be the matter of meditation and an advifandum befor any incorporation or ingagement, that you may fend it to Mr Jam Simpfon to pervfe, at the leaft the laft pairt of it from the midle of the 8th fheet to the end, which is anent arguments from the Covenants and Ingagements, wherwith he may compare the neu gouver^t in its four articles, and fett doun fhortly the direct antithefes between the tuo Lykas I fend you the firft fix Aunfuers that war written in 1652 to the objection about Daniel ch vlt, about our former principles, that you may fend it to him, becaus the vther paper which he hes relates theirto, and defyre him to fend me back both thes papers, and the former that he got with him, and his fhort draught and his long draught both of his reafons againft taiking places I cannot aunfuer that any of thir copyes ar right, for I haive borroued them from Mr. R Trayle, and hes promifed to re delyver them Anent vther things I wil faye no moi at this occafion, but that I haive found the Lord's temple tryftes and condefcentions as fenfible fince our pairting as ever of befor, bliffed, bliffed be his nayme A fpeaking Chryft will proove a working reigning Chryft in the fight of his freinds and foes The grace of the Lord be with you, and with your wyfe and children

Your loving Brother,

M P G is not yet come heir
29th Merch 1654.
A JHONSTON.

To my loving Brother Mr JAMES GUTHRIE, Minifter of God's Word at Stirling

XCII

INSTRUCTIONS TO MR. JAMES SHARP, FOR LONDON, 23D AUGUST 1656.

[From Baillie's MS Letters, &c, Vol III fol 236 See pages 324 and 330 of this volume, where notice is taken of Sharp having been sent to London, to Cromwell, on the part of the Public Resolutioners]

1 Yow would labour to give a right impreffion of the difpofition of the Minifters in this nation who ftand for the Publict judicatories of the Kirk, to live peaceably and in-

offenfively under the prefent government, by fhewing what teftification they have given heirof 1 By their quiet behaviour hithertill fince they were brought under it, 2 By what was declared by fome of them, underftanding well the mind of the reft, to my Lord Præfident in February laft, and 3. By what many others of them, from the feverall Prefbytries, ar at this prefent tyme voluntarlie declareing in petitions to the Councell of Scotland

2 To clear and make manifeft the groundlefs arrogancy of our Brethren, in affirming to themfelves the name of the Godly Partie of the miniftrie, together with the injuftice and falfhood of their afperfing of the generalitie of the reft of the miniftrie as infufficient, or fcandalous, or both And for this purpofe to fhew:—1. That the greateft part of the minifters who before our late differences were juftly efteemed and looked upon as the moft eminent, honeft, and godly minifters in this Kirk, and were moft inftrumentall in the work of God, doe adhere unto the Publick Judicatures unto this day 2 That (which is undenyable and notour,) a great part, if not the farr greateft part, of our Diffenting Brethren, have been admitted to the miniftrie within thefe very few years, moft part of thefe alfo being bot very young men, and very few of all of them that were minifters when the late work of Reformation did begin 3. That although our Brethren did blaze abroad in publick, and fuggeft to thefe in power fuch afperfions againft the generalitie of the miniftrie; yet, when in their refpective Prefbytries, at the vifitation of Kirks, and in their refpective Synods, at the tryall of the feverall Prefbytries, they are required, upon their confciences, to declare their knowledge and judgement concerning the life and abilities of every one of their Brethren, little or nothing hath been reprefented by them of any challenge concerning the converfation or qualification of any particular minifter in their judicatures, yea, although upon occafion of fuch generall afperfions fpread and publifhed by them, they have often been in judicatures and publick meetings earneftly attefted to condefcend upon particular perfons and challenges, and folemne promifes have been made to them that judicatures fhould forthwith goe faithfullie and impartiallie about the tryell and cenfure thereof, yet never would they be induced to doe this 4 That within thefe three years, as many fcandalous, unable, and unprofitable men, in all the corners of the land, have been removed from the miniftrie, fo, through the Lord's goodnefs, many able and gracious young men have been, in our bounds, placed into their roomes, and we can warrantably affirm it, that within thefe laft three or four yeares, there have been more able and pious men admitted to the miniftrie in the feverall parts of the land than was at any tyme in fo fhort a fpace, or much more, fince our late Reformation 5 We can alfo warrantablie affirm, that as never more frequent nor more accurat vifitations of particular Kirks, for infpection and tryall of the converfation, doctrine, diligence, and faithfulnefs of minifters in their charges, have been than of late within thefe three or four yeares laft bypaft; fo that we have thereby found not only good evidence of the godly converfation, and of the found and edifying doctrine of minifters generallie, but

VOl

also more painfulness in their labours, and more fuccefs thereupon, throw the Lords bleffing, than hath been before   6 Although we will not deny, but it is very probable that in fundrie parts there may be found fome men in the miniftrie unfuitable in converfation to their holy calling and infufficient. (and we wifh from our hearts that our Brethren who afperfe us, had not thefe late years admitted fo many infufficient men, as is notour they have done,) yet we may truelie fay it, that our Brethren's wayes and actings this tyme bypaft, by which they have taught men to vilifie the authoritie of Judicatures, and to contemne the exercife of Difcipline, hath been a great obftruction and hinderance to tryall, finding out, and cenfuring of fuch   And we give affurance that the Judicatures of the Kirk, they not being hindered to go about the work, nor being expofed to have their authoritie in the exercife of ecclefiaftick Difcipline contemned, fhall ufe all diligence, faithfulnefs, and impartiality to try and cenfure fuch where they can be found within their refpective bounds, as fome Synods of late, alfooue as they had libertie to conveene, have given proofe of their fidelitie and zeale in this work, by removeing from the miniftrie fome who were of their own judgement as to the matters of Publict differences   7. In a word, we can fay in truth, the Lord bearing us witnefs, that this afperfion of infufficiencie, fcandaloufnefs, and corruption caft by our Brethren upon the generalitie of the miniftrie of our judgement throughout the land, is moft uncharitable, unjuft, and falfe

In relation to the prefervation of true Religion and Government of the Church eftablifhed among us, it is to be defired.—

1 That effectuall courfe be taken for the fuppreffing of Poperie, fo much increafed and abounding of late in this land, which, if it be not tymouflie obviat, cannot but prove moft dangerous to Religion, and to the peace and fafetie of the State.

2. That the ecclefiaftick government be permitted and allowed to runn in its right channell, and to goe on in its exercife, as it is eftablifhed in this nation, according to the word of God, by Acts of Generall Affemblies, and Acts of Parliament.

3. Yet if on fuggeftion from this, or from themfelves above, any motion be made towards the calling of a Generall Affemblie, yow would moft ferioullie reprefent the inexpediencie thereof for the time, and indifpofednefs of this Kirk for it in regard of the prefent differences and diftempers, which would readily be encreafed and heightened to the great prejudice of religion if there were a meeting in a Generall Affemblie, before there be time to compofe and fettle matters and men s fpirits in inferior judicatories

4 That there be no intrufion allowed of perfons into the miniftrie in congregations, without the lawfull and orderlie confent and election of the congregations, or without orderlie tryall and ordination by prefbyteries, but that the whole calling of perfons to the office of the miniftrie be permitted and allowed to be acted and carried on according to the eftablifhed order of this Church, and particularly that Act of the Generall Affemblie 1649, intituled the Direction for Election of Minifters.

5 That the Ordinance concerning the fettleing of maintainance upon minifters in Scotland, emitted in the year 1651, be made void and taken away, in regard it doth overturne the eftablifhed order and government of this Kirk, efpeciallie as to the plantation and calling of minifters, as hath been evidenced in the confiderations upon the faid Ordinance which were given by us to the Lord Generall.

6 That perfons produceing certificats from their refpective Prefbyteries, bearing teftimonie of their calling and admiffion unto the miniftrie, in congregations within the refpective bounds of the prefbytries certifying conforme to the order abovementioned, and of their blamelefs and godly converfation, and of their abilitie and fitnefs to preach the gofpell, have, by the Civill power, allowed to them the ftipend and whole benefits belonging to the refpective charges whereunto they are called and admitted. And that the ftipend of no congregation be fettled upon any perfon intruded upon a people to be their minifter, contrare to the aforefaid lawfull and eftablifhed order of calling and admitting minifter-

7 That the Ecclefiaftick difcipline be permitted to be exercifed by the Judicatures of the Kirk according to the order therein eftablifhed, and the Ecclefiaftick cenfures that fhall be enacted and pronounced againft any members of this kirk, minifters, or others, for fcandales and offences, be not impeded nor ftoped, nor any perfones fo cenfured difobeying, contemning, or oppofeing the difcipline of this Kirk, be countenanced or incouraged in their difobedience, contempt, or oppofition.

And whereas fome may be buffie to fuggeft, and upon fuch fuggeftion it may haplie be objected that the Judicatures of the Kirk being fuch for the moft part as ftand for the authoritie and conftitution of the two late Generall Affemblies, doe exercife oppreffion over thefe that diffent from them; and that were they permitted to exercife their full power and authoritie, they would crufh the other part, by cafting out many godly minifters, holding out manie godly expectants, and cenfuring all others diffenting from them. This may be made evidently appear to be nothing elfe but a forged, unjuft, flander, by the Act of the Generall Affembly at Edinburgh, 1652, intituled, "an Act and Overture for peace and union of the Kirk," and by the Overtures made by us to our diffenting Brethren in November laft; efpeciallie as they are expreffed in our Reprefentation given to them November [24th], and our carriage in our Judicatures all along the tyme of our differences, wherein we have borne with much and conftant patience many fad, bitter, and unjuft afperfions caft upon us by them, in preaching, write, and print; yet never to this day cenfured or challenged any of their judgement upon the account of our differences, or for any of their injurious afperfions caft upon us, nor ever oppofed we the entrie of any of their judgement into the miniftrie; but was ever willing to admitt him upon an orderlie call, if they would only have declared their refolutions to live peaceably with us, and to abftaine from holding up debates and contentions about the matters of our Publict differences, (which thing we were allwayes reallie willing to declare and performe for our part) leaveing to them the full freedome of their judgement in thefe matters

8 That no companie of Ministers or others be esteemed or acknowledged to be a presbytrie or other kirk judicature, who have not been owned as such a Judicature, and that if any few ministers, or others who are not authorised in manner aforsaid, take upon them the authoritie and jurisdiction of a kirk judicature and doe exercise any acts of government, in calling or depofing of ministers, or inflicting any other cenfures, that they be not countenanced, nor any of their actings ouned as deeds of a laufull Judicature.

9 Becaufe our adverfaries may be buffie to mifreprefent us as having been averfe from Union, the matter of the Overtures of Union which we condefcended unto, would be made known to thofe in power, and to the godly Prefbyterian Minifters there. As alfo the points on which they ftuck and refuifed to unite with us, which were thefe two. 1 That we granted not unto them Committees of equall numbers of both judgments for purgeing 2. That we required fubordination and fubjection of inferiour judicatures to their refpective fuperior judicatures, according to the nature and order of Prefbyteriall Government in this Kirk, and the conftant uncontroverted practice thereof before the time of our unhappie differences The unreafonablenefs and inconfiftency with Prefbyteriall Government, and the eftablifhed order in this Church, of requiring the former and refuifeing the latter, is fully and clearly evidenced in our laft two papers relateing to the Conference

10 If it fhall happen that any new motion be made for union with our diffenting Brethren, it would be fhowen that we cannot poffiblie condefcend any further then we have done alreadie for obtaining Union with them in our above mentioned Overtures in November laft, as they are expreffed in our Reprefentation in the faid moneth of November unlefs we would condemne ourfelves and renunce our judgment in the matters of difference betwixt them and us, which we could not doe without wronging our own confciences quitting truth, provoking God, and rendering our Church and Religion hatefull to all Civill powers, nations, and Churches about us. And if it be moved that an Union be made between them and fome of us whom they are pleafed to favour with the eftimation of honeftie and godlinefs, laying by others, it would be declared that we are moft willing that all fuch perfons in the miniftrie as can be challenged for fcandale or infufficiencie be impartiallie tryed and cenfured in an orderly way by the Judicatures of the Kirk, or committees of unqueftionable judicious and godly men, to be nominated by the faid refpective Judicatures; but that we neither can in confcience, nor will ever hearken to fuch a motion as that whereby a great part of the minifters of this Kirk, (whereof many are pious and able men, whatever our Brethren think of them,) fhall be condemned as infufficient, fcandalous, and corrupt, without hearing, without any tryell or proceffe, and not only a more woefull rent made in this Church but alfo the very conftitution and frame of this Nationall Church overturned and rafed, and all caft doune into a confufion

Mr DAVID DICKSON.   Mr. ROBERT DOWGLASS   Mr JAMES WOOD

XCIII

PROPOSALS OF THE PROTESTERS TO THE LORD PROTECTOR

[From the same, fol 238.—At page 353, Baillie refers to these Proposals of the Protesters which they sought to obtain from Cromwell, by sending some of their number to London, but in this they were defeated by Sharp, who had been sent thither as agent for the other party in the Church]

1 That your Highness will pleafe to give warrand for a Commiffion to be iffued to fuch perfons of abilitie and foundnefs who underftand the affairs of the Kirk, as your Highnefs fhall think fitt, who may have and exercife the power which was heretofore in the Commiffion of the plantation of kirks in that Nation, and that the faid Commiffioners may be authorized and required to difpofe of the publick maintainance, according to the rules and acts of uncontroverted Affemblies of the Church, and lawes of that land before the year 1651

2 That a particular Vifitation may be, confifting of an equall number of both judgments, of approved godlinefs and zeale for the work of reformation, whereof the one half to be agreed upon by thefe who are for the Publick Refolutions, and the other half by the Remonftrators, for planting and purgeing of minifters and elders, and for compofing of prefent and future divifions in Prefbytries and Congregations within the bounds of every Synod; having power and authoritie for that effect from the refpective Synods themfelves

3 That there be alfo a general Committee of delegates from the feveral Synods, of an equal number of both judgements, to be choifen and agreed as aforefaid, authorifed by the Synods, without whofe previous advyce and confent the refpective Synods may not ranverfe any thing done by the forefaid Vifitations, and fuch Vifitations and Committees to continue untill the prefent differences be healed, or the Lord fhall in providence minifter fome better way for the fettleing of peace amongft them

XCIV

LETTER, LORD BROGHILL TO MR. ROBERT DOUGLAS.

[From the Orig. Wod MSS Fol Vol. XXVI No 8]

Worthy Sir

I send this on purpofe to defyre you to favor me with your, Mr Wood, and Mr Sharpe's company, fomewhat early to-morrow morninge, becaufe I heare of fom trends wil be with me all the afternoone, wherby otherwife I may be deprived of that time I intend to fpend amongft yow. Pray favor me with fendinge to Sterlin for Mr. Sympfon, to be with me at Edinbrough, on Tuifday morninge, without fayle, before the Councill does fit, for fom reafons fhalbe communicated to you when you com out

Sir,

Your very aft frend,
and humble fervant,

Pinky. Lord's day in the evening,
10 of Augt [16]56.

BROGHILL.

For my worthy frend Mr Robt Douglas, Minifter of the Gofpell at Edinbrough In his abfence, for Mr James Wood, or Mr James Sharpe, Minifters of the Gofpell, or either of them, at Edinbrough.

XCV

ARTICLES EXHIBITED AGAINST MR. PATRICK GILLESPIE

[From Baillie's MS Letters, &c Vol iii fol 243 This appears to be the libel mentioned by Baillie, at page 372 of this volume, and which he says was imputed to him, but he denies his having seen it till produced by Gillespie at a meeting of the Faculty.]

ARTICLES WHEREFORE MR PATRICK GILLESPIE OUGHT NOT TO BE PRINCIPAL OF THE COLLEDGE OF GLASGOW. BOTH FOR INSUFFICIENCIE, NEGLECT OF DUETIE AND MALADMINISTRATION OF THE REVENUES OF THE SAID COLLEDGE —AND FIRST OF HIS INSUFFICIENCIE AND NEGLECT OF DUTIE.

1. *First*, THE Principall of the Colledge of Glafgow, according to its foundation, and the ordinarie practife ufed in that Houfe, is obliedged to be chief Profeffor of Theologie therein, to have each week publick leffons of Theologie and Philofophie, as thefe who formerly were Principalls did carefully act the fame to the great advantage of the Students of Theology and Philofophie, and credit of the Univerfitie, and that notwithftanding that the burden of the manageing of the public affaires thereof, and the ordering of what related to the building of the edifice lay upon them as now it doth upon Mr Patrick Gillefpie, but fo it is, that the faid Mr Patrick, under pretext all this time of going about the Colledge affairs and buildings, hath neglected that part of his charge, and hath taught as good as none, for his whole dictates of Theology Leffons, for the fpace of five yeares, will be comprehended in two fheet of paper And therefore he is not fufficient for that charge

2. *Secondly*, The Principal of the said Colledge, according to its foundation and ordinary custome of the House, ought to preseed to all publict actes and disputes: To wit, when the Theologues give out Theses before they be licentiat to preach, or those who by publick programmes were invited to dispute for a Regent's place, when any vaiked, the Principall alwayes was Preses in these disputes: But so it is, that to this day Mr. Patrick hath not at all preseeded in any of these disputes, but left them still to be gone about by ane other. And for the private disputes of the Theologues amongst themselves, which used to be weekly, he hath very seldome been present at these, but ordinarily leaves these to be ordained by the other Professors, notwithstanding that by agreement betwixt him and them, he be oblidged to wait upon them course about · And therefore he is no wayes sufficient for the said charge

3. *Thirdly*, The Principal, by his place, is an ordinary examinator of the Students of Philosophy, both at those times when they are to be promoved and called in yearly, and likewise at the solemne examinations that they undergoe when they passe Masters of Arts, which duetie, as a chief part of their charge, all the Principals in the Colledge went about very carefully, and made search how the Students were taught by their Masters, and did profite But so it is, that Mr Patrick, since his taking upon him the office of Principall in the said Colledge, to this day hath not examined, at these solemne times, the Students of Philosophy, neither hath at any other tyme tryed how they are taught by their masters, and how they profite in their studies. And therefore, it being palpably knowne that he is unfitt for going about any of these dueties to any purpose, he is altogether insufficient for the said charge

4. *Fourthly*, Albeit the teaching of the Oriental tongues, by the Visitation of the Colledge, was put upon another Professor, and the Principall was eased of that burthen, yet it is most necessarie that he who is Principall, and so by his place the Prime Professor of Theologie, should have skill in these languages, and should clear and expound to Students the hard places of Scripture: But so it is, that Mr. Patrick is so farr from that, that it is known how little insight he hath in the Latine, and this he evidenced at his first speech in Latine, that he had at a public meeting of the Colledge, at the Laureation of a Classe of Philosophy, when he began his prayer as an imprecation, useing these words —" *Auspicus nostris Domine Deus adesse dedigneris*," that is,—" Deinzie not Lord to be present at this our meeting ," And when in the close of that action he was desired by one of that meeting, to pray and send away the new lie Lawreat schollers with a blessing, after a little pause, when it was expected that he would pray, he rose up, and without prayer dismissed them, saying " *Ite*,"—"Goe away ," Yea, it is his ordinarie custome, (which used not to be done by any Principall before,) to pray in English when he meets with the Theologues at their private disputes, or with the Students of Philosophy in the Common-hall · And therefore, his deficiency and weaknes being known, he is altogether insufficient for the forsaid charge

Articles of Maladministration of the Rents and Revenues of the Forsaid Colledge.

1 *First* Howbeit the said Mr Patrick Gillespie hath a fair and large sallary each year of the first and readiest of the rents of the said College, yet he not being satisfied therwith, hath taken of the revenues of that House to his owne use the summes following, at least he hath obtained right thereunto by the Moderators of that House. As first, when he was called up by his Highness the Lord Protector some three yeares agoe, he obtained of his Highness a gift to that Colledge of the Superiorities of the Bishoprick of Galloway, together with two hundreth merks sterling money for maintenance of some Bursars of Theology, and notwithstanding, his Highness did allow him sufficient maintainance for his journey, and that according to his own account given up by himself of his disburfements, in obtaining of the forsaid gifts to the said Colledge, there was payed to him by the Colledge ane hundreth pund sterling or thereby, yet the said Mr Patrick took of the Colledge rent, at his return, three thousand merks Scots money as a reward for his pains.

2 *Secondly*, At the last time when Mr Patrick went to London he was commissionat by the Remonstrating partie, with others, to negotiat these things which by them were committed to him, and those who were joyned to him in that commission, and by that partie large summes were collected and given to him and others joyned with him, for defraying their expenses in that journey, and further his Highness the Lord Protector did liberallie allow to the said Mr Patrick a larger soume of money, nor might have been sufficient for his maintenance dureing that space. The said Mr Patrick having a particular Commission from the Colledge, (which he took from them after he was engaged to the Remonstrating partie to goe up for them,) to do what he could for obtaining some new gift from his Highnes to them, as if his journey had been only undertaken for the Colledge, and that it was incumbent to them to bear all his charges dureing his long abode at London, (beside all that he gott liberallie from his Highness, and lykewayes from the Remonstrating partie, who were those that sent him up in that journey,) he hath taken of the Colledge 20 sh sterling money for ilk day, from his going from Scotland to his returne back againe, which being the space of eleven monethis, will extend to three hundred pound sterling, and above.

3 *Thirdlie*, As if the samen had not been enough he hath obtained a warrand (some eight or ten dayes after he had gotten warrand for the precedent soume) under the hands of the Masters of the Colledge, for 300 pound sterling further, which bears that the said 300 pounds shall be payed out of the first and readiest that the Colledge shall obtaine by the late gift of the tithes of these benefices, chaplaunries, and others, within the Bishoprick of Glasgow, which his Highness has past in favours of and for the behoof of the said Colledge. And besides both these soumes, which extend to 600 pound sterling, the Colledge, upon his account given up to them of deburfements and expenses he was at

procureing and paffing of that late gift, have allowed the faid Mr. Patrick 120 pound fterling or thereby

4 *Fourthlie,* Howbeit it be incumbent to Mr Patrick, in regard of his place and truft, by all lawfull meanes to better the yearly revenues of that Colledge whereof he is Principall, yet he hath taken a gift, and hath a right paffed to him by the Moderators thereof that what he can finde out for augmenting the old rentall of the Colledge, fpeciallie in the Bifhoprick of Galloway, the equall half thereof fhall be appropriat to himfelf yearly, during all the dayes of his lifetime, and that by and attour his large falary which yearly is provided and payed to him

5 *Fifthlie,* All this is the more to be taken notice of, *First,* Becaufe it is well known that other gracious, learned, and moft able men, who have been Principals in that Colledge thefe many yeares bygane, and faithfullie went about the difcharge of their duetie therein, diverfe of them did obtain, by their diligence and care, from the late King, his Father, and others who were Governours in this nation, a great deal more nor yet hes been in that kinde by Mr. Patrick; as Mr Patrick Sharp obtained the Perfonage of Govane, Principall Boyd the Perfonages of Renfrew and Kilbryde, and Dr Strang the Bifhoprick of Galloway, and other cafualities, yet none of them either did require, or took any thing of the faid Colledge, or of the benefices that were brought in to it by their paines, by way of gratuity or otherwayes *Secondlie,* Becaufe it was well known that unlefs the Principall of the Colledge be willing, and confent, no right can be granted of anie part of the rents of that Houfe to any perfon, which makes it clear that what is granted to Mr Patrick of this kinde, hath made its rife from himfelf, or if it was firft moved by others, that he hath readilie accepted what was offered *Thirdlie,* Becaufe it is certaine that the whole rents of the Colledge is to be imployed in pious and publict ufes, for the behoof and maintenance of poor Students, of the Fabrick, and Bibliotheck, and that the Principall and Mafters are only adminiftrators of the rents of the Houfe, who can not be anfwerable to God nor man, if they fhall appropriat any part thereof to themfelves, except what is allowed to them for their falary; and this they muft make appear in their yearly accounts, which are to be made yearly, whereof the Proveft and Baillies of Glafgow are appointed to be Auditors

No XCVI

LETTER, MR. PATRICK GILLESPIE, TO MR DAVID DICKSON

[Orig —Wodrow MsS. Folio Vol XXVI, No 22]

RIGHT REVEREND, London, July 2d 1657.

I AM heartily forrie that our breach fhould beare fuch characters of judgement, as ar mor then legible in the mifgiving of all endevours which haue been applied for healing, and doe put a difcouragement vpon all men who wifhe our Vnione henceforth to endeuour it. I need not reprefent to yow things which haue been experimented by us on all hands, how much the work of the Gofpell, and the ordinances of Chrift, fuffer through our divifiones; but I defire to put yow in mind how much wee ar at a loffe, by our differences, vpon this account, that the minifters of Scotland being fo much on in judgement, and aggreed in fo many things as that they ar mor on[e] then any fuch number of minifters in any of the Reformed churches, yet cannot walk together becaus of difference about thefe things, which gaue the rife to our breache. This befpeaks us in the judgement of fober men, to be of very vnfober fpirits and of extremlie rigid principles toward all others who differ from us in the leaft things. I am therfor humbly bold with yow, (to whom I acknowledge I owe verie much, and for whom I haue an efteeme becomming my obligations), to befeech yow yet to take into your ferious confideration thefe things which were required by yow from us at the laft Conference for Vnion and were not agreed unto vpon on[e] part, and to fee what abatement may be of your demands, and what farther condefcenfion for peace-fake, as I am alfo willing in like maner to think of thefe things demanded on on[e] part, and fo farr as I can, with a good confcience, to ftretch myfelf, and to befeech others, to all poffible and lawfull condefcenfion. And however I have been reprefented to yow, in my vndertaking this journey, or management of my truft heer, (as I haue mor then probable ground to think I haue been mifreprefented), yet I am confident to make it appear that an honeft peace hath been defigned in the firft place by me and thefe who fent me hither, and that *inculpata tutela* hath but a fecond confideratione with us. If yow judge any thing heer worthie your thoughts, (wherin I profeffe I haue no defigne befide the preferuation of our Churche Government by our own concord, for which I could be exiled if that could procure it). vpon your intertainement of the motione, in any probable way of agreement for careing on the work of Reformation, yow fhall command my cordial fervice, and poor endevours for that end. Your louing Brother to ferue yow,

P. GILLESPIE

For the Reverend Mr David Dickfone, Profeffor of Theologie in the
 Colledge of Ed^r., and Mr Robert Douglas, Minifter at Ed^r.

XCVII

MR JAMES SHARP TO BAILLIE, AND BAILLIES REPLY

[Orig Wodrow MSS Folio Vol XXVI, Nos. 86 and 75 —These letters are not contained in Baillie's own collection. They should have been included in the body of the work, at page 382 of the present volume, but they were overlooked at the time, from the circumstance of the first letter having no address, and the second, being simply indorsed

" Double of ane letter sent to Mr J Sharp,' and having neither the writer's name, address, or date An examination of the letters, leaves no doubt as to the writers or persons who were addressed A few corrections, and the words near the beginning of the last letter, printed within brackets, are in the hand-writing, apparently, of John Bell, who may have been the bearer of the letter itself]

No 1

Reverend S^r   Craill, Auguft 2, 7 aclock in the morning, 1658

The boxe yow fent, with all the papers yow mention, came to my hand yefternight, the 1 of this currant I am fo overcharged with bufines at prefent, beeng to preach tomorrow, and on Weddenfday the exercife befor the Prefbytrie lyeth upon me, that it will not be poffible for me to goe about the difpatches to London, in reference to your Town's bufines. Since the petition from the burghs, and that alfo from your Town, are not fent to London, I know no furer way to gett them prefented to his Highnes then by our friend there, elfe Mr Lockart, or the Provoft of Edinburgh might have offered them, if they had been in time fent to them I am hopefull that our freind will be returned to London befor that our letters can come thither, and I think I may perfwade him to ufe meanes that thefe petitions fhall be delivered to the Protector, that if he find not the opportunity to prefent them by himfelf, the Secretary or one of our freinds of the Councill at Whythall, may doe it; and, for this end, I purpofe to wreat to the Secretary and one of the Councill Some three dayes agone I receaved the refolution of the Printer above, anent the readie deliverie of the books to the Stationar, and that yow may know what it is, I have fent it heirin inclofit for your perufall, that when yow have feen it, and confidered of it, yow may fend it to Edinburgh to my Brother I know the fubfcryver of the letter, Alex^r Blair, to be diligent and punctually faythfull in what I or my Brother will put upon him, and a fitt perfon to manage fuch a bufines, but I think his allowance he craves for change and exchange exorbitant, and if the way he mentions in his letter, which I do not know, or any other yow could fall upon, could make it more eafy, I wifhe it were fpeedily done and therfor I have fent away the bearer to yow, that yow may have time to fend your refolution theranent to Edinburgh again Fridayes night the 6 inftant, again which time I fhall have my letters ready to our friends above, and fhall fend them by an exprefs to Edinburgh, that by the Saturnadayes poaft they may be tranfmitted to London Since yow judge it fitt that books be delivered to the Stationer, I think it will be conducing to the more effectual managing of your Town's bufines, that an effay be made upon him by the Printer at the time of the delivery of my pacquett to him I could wifh that the charge of thefe books might be awoydit: but I am ftill of opinion it is the moft promifing way yow can fall upon for the effectuall profecuting of your bufines I fhall wreat to our freind, upon fuppofition that the ⸻ deliver thef books, and fhall fend the petitions with

your other papers to him   I ſhall wreat alſo to Col Witham to further the buſines by
his letters   I know not if M Patrick hath got the report to be ſent up; but I hope
your papers will come in time   I have not the time now fully to peruſe them, but I
ſhall, upon my ſending of them to Edinburgh, give yow an account of what ſhall be
done with them   The account of the port charge will be given to yow by my Brother
alſo   I would not keep the bearer for loſing of time to yow   I need not mind yow of
the neceſſity of keeping the matter of the books and the Stationar with all cloſenes, and
that your reſolution therin be ſpeedily ſent to Edinburgh   I have not as yet ſeen M.
John Carſtares   I am ſo ſtraitned that I can adde no more; but commending yow,
with the Lord's work in your hand, to mercy and grace, that I am,
                    Your nery loving Brother,
                                        JA SHARP

Preſent my reſpects to M. Baily, as alſo to Mr. Bell, and excuſe I have not ſent a
particular returne to his   My Wife hath yow kindly remembred

                            No. 2.

REVEREND AND DEIR BROTHER,

VPON the recait of yours and the ſicht of the incloſed that was direct to your Brother,
by Alex^r Blair, John Bell was ſent from this to Edinburgh, wha, (as ye defyred in
yours,) delyvered Alex^r. Blairs to your Brother   As for the books mentioned thairin,
your Brother thocht fitt that David Thomſoun ſhould have them, and [Mr. Schaip being
aff town, at his returne, Mr Bell ſpak to him again, and appointed to meit with him the
morrow afore I went of the Toune, bot that morning he uent to ſie my Ld Suintoun, ſo I
miſſed him becaus I behooved that day to uait upon Deſborou, and I left the monie
w^t Wm Mitchell, merchant to be delyvered to him quho hath ſent me the letter,] and
ſince a letter beuing ſo much is cum to this place, directed to John Bell, wha, befoir he
cam bak fra Edinburgh, your Brother ſhew me the box with the letters quhilk cam from
yow to go to London, and geav aſſurance for the port, &c. quhatſomever it ſhould be
How ſum thes letters, with the books, quhilk by the Printer wer to be put in the Stationer's hand, wei ſent away, wee heir have not haid, bot wald be glaid to ken
quhat zee have hard thairanent, for it was not thocht fitt that ame of our wyfe ſecreit
freinds heir ſhould mak inquirie for thes things, leaſt uthirs thairupon micht have
drawne inferences   The Lord Keiper and Swintoun have bein heir this ouk. The
Lord Keiper was at the Newmils, drinking of the waters thair for his helth; and
duiring his abod at Newmils, was waited vpon by ſum ſent fra this, quha caried
with them ſik things as wer fitt for the Lord Keiper, quhilk reddilie that place
quhairin he was could not afford him   He cam to this toun vpon the Wedneſday quhair
nathing was left undon that could evidenc thair reſpects to his Lordſhip, Swintoun

alfo was faluted, and courteflie intertimed The Lord Keiper at his going fra this fpak the Proveft, with Baillie Walkinfhaw, and fum few vthirs anent that debait quhilk had long bein betuixt them and Mr. Gillefpie, and told, that Mr. Gillefpie was willing to fubmitt all to him; quhairvnto they replyed, that if the particular quhairin the difference hes bein, wer a mater of thair fortoun, or fik as wer in thair power, they wald willinglie lay it doun at his feit, to be difpofed vpon at his Lordfhip's pleafour. Bot in regaird that it was the liberties of thair Burgh, quhilk to thair pouer they wer oblidged by oath to mentein, and that the whol Royall Burghs had looked vpon that buffines as a mater concerning them all, and vpon that confideration had petitioned his Highnes, the Lord Protectour for the burgh of Glafgow; upon thir and uther weightie reafouns they wer forced to beg his Lordfhip's favour, and intreat that he wald not tak it ill that in that they could not agre to anie fubmiffion And with all they fhew his Lordfhip that if he or the Councell of Stait in all the nerrow and acurat fearch that had bein taken, fand anie perfoun of thes quha wer in office, or on the Toun-Councell, that deferved to be removed fra truft, or for a tym to be laid afyd, they profeffed that moft willinglie they fhould geiv obedience thairvnto. Quhen the Lord Keiper fand them thus refolved, without anie fignification ather of diffatiffaction or of fatiffaction with thair anfuer, his Lordfhip preffed them no farther, onlie it was thocht that he fhew Mr. Gillefpie that the interpofition quhilk he offered to mak wald not prove effectuall for what Mr Gillefpie defyred Quhat courfe heirafter will be followed by Mr Gillefpie in profecution of that report, (whilk yit is not fent vp to Lundoun) wee can not tell, or how the Lord Defburiow will carie in the buffines, wee heir ken not; onlie, it is apprehendit that one of thrie may now be effayed, ather to get the report with all fpeid fent up and baked with Swintoun's moyen, that upon its being prefented to the Protectour, ordour may be givin to remove the prefent Magiftrats, and put in P G his pairtie; or it may be that the tym of the election being neir at hand, vpon the firft Twyfday of October, they will deall for a new letter fra the Protectour to ftope a new election, as they did the laft zeir or that the whol mater be fent back to the Councell of Scotland that they may determine in that buffines heir, and till that be don, a letter be procured fhortlie fra the Councell of Stait in Scotland, direct to the prefent Magiftrats to ftay anie new election till his Highnes, upon the report fent up to him, declair his pleafour quhat he will have don in that mater for the clofing of it As oft befoir, the Toun, in thair ftraits, fo now alfo they have fent this exprefe, and by my letter to zow, acquants zow with thair buffines how it ftands, intreating that ze wald be pleafed to writ anew to zour freind above, and try at the Prenter's quhat is becum of the books that wer to be put in the Stationer's hand, and how he was fatiffied with them, as alfo quhidder zour freind the Stationer hes gottin the box above fent vp, and quhat is don with the petitions and uthir papers that went up in it As alfo, they wald be glaid that, if zee think fitt, zour freind be informed of quhat now I have acquainted you with, and hee intreated to gaird above, in fo far as may be, againſt anie courſe that can be taken vnderhand or vtherways by P G and his freinds thair to the Toun's prejudice, and becaus C[ol.] Watham will beſt found Deſborrow's mynd anent his ſatiſfaction or diſſatiſfaction with the Toun's anſuer geivin to his Lordſhip heir, they intreat that zee wald writ to him thairanent, in ſo wyſe and cannie a way as zee think will be moſt convenient, and with all deall with the Colonell, that if anie motion be mad[e] be Swintoun, or anie vther to the Councell of Stait heir, that he wald ſie to it, and hinder it ſo far as may be, at leaſt till the Toun be called to plead for themſelf Your ſecreit freinds heir have ſum thoughts of ſending upe a verie active and honeſt young man to wait for ſum tyme on thair affairs thair   They will direct him to Mr John Lockhart, quha is now at Court, (if at all he be ſent,) bot thair purpoſe is that he may by letters weiklie, let them ken if anie thing be in agitation relating to them, and that he may underſtand thes mainlie by the Stationer, no that ather the Toun, or he that ſhall be ſent thair, may ken quha zour fieind is that acts for them abov, at zour intreatie, bot the information may be conveyed to him be the mediation of the Printer or ſum vther handſum way yee will preſeryve   Pot in this they intend to follow zour advyſe, in ſending one vpe or not to wait than as agent for them, to remember than freinds of their buſſines, as ſaid is   The Toun has hithertills holden aff anie nomination of a perſoun for filling Mr Durham's place, and by fair general dealing with our commoun ſeſſion hes keiped them fra thair paremptour way   Bot in end, quhen maters cums to a paremptour, they then intend to follow the advyſe they have gottin fra than freinds thair Eaſt, and withall they have thouchts of ndevouring, (if they ſend vp anie perſoun to attend thair effairs,) to obtain a letter fra the Protectour to the Councill of Stait in Scotland, for ordaning that the Toun of Glaſgow may be warranted to mak choiſe of a miniſter for thair vacant place, and that none, againſt the conſent of the Magiſtrates and Councell and the bodie of the Toun, be thruſt vpon them. If ze think this feaſable, zee will geiv zour beſt advyſe how it ſhall be obtained, and quhat courſe ſhall be followed for that effect   And lykways they conceav it may be eſſayed to obtain fra the Protectour a favorable letter for the Toun of Glaſgow direct to the Councell of Stait heir, vpon the Burrows thair petition preſented to his Highnes for the toun of Glaſgow   Your ſingular reſpects to the publick intereſt and to the good of this place, imboldens me to be thus trubleſum, as to intreat for zour patienc in reading, and wiſdom and wonted reddines to do, in the above mentioned particulars, ſo far as zee conceav may be for thair good, and with all by zour letter with this beirer, to let me ken quhat zee think fitteſt to be don in thair ſending of one vp, and in that whilk relaits to a Miniſter, and to the Burrows thair petition For the teſtifeing of the Toun's reſpects of thankfulnes, to zour ſelf for all the expenſſe and pains zee have bein put to in thair effairs, I ſhall for the tym ſay nothing. Bot if they can be vieſnll to the publick intereſt, or any thing can be don[e] by them to teſtifie thair reſpects thairto, let me know, and I dar ſay in thair nam they will not be inlaiking

XCVIII

BAILLIE'S COMMENDATORY LETTER PREFIXED TO DURHAM'S COMMENTARY ON THE BOOK OF THE REVELATION, 1658

[Baillie incidently mentions (vol iii p 312) his being a hearer of Durham's Lectures, and referring to his last illness (ib. p 368), he says, " the perfecting of his work on the Revelation for the presse was very heavie " It was published at London three or four months after his death —" A Commentarie upon the Book of the Revelation, &c Delivered in several Lectures, by that learned, laborious, and faithfull servant of Jesus Christ, Mr James Durham, late Minister of the Gospel in Glasgow —London, printed for the Company of Stationers, Anno Dom 1658," folio
The particulars of Durham's life—by birth a private gentleman,—his serving in the army,—his call and devotedness in the work of the ministry—his death in July 1658 at the early age of 36—are well known, or may be found in numerous biographies; and his various writings, always highly esteemed, are still deservedly popular in this country]

Reader,—Being desired to speak my knowledge of this subsequent Work, I acknowledge that I was one who frequently encouraged the Author to let it go abroad For, however he had no time to polish it, and what is here almost all was taken from his mouth by the pen of an ordinary hearer : Yet I am assured, the matter of it, as I heard it weekly delivered, is so precious as cannot but be very welcom and acceptable to the world of believers I am confident, that the gracious design which some worthy Brethren amongst us have in hand, and have now far advanced to the good satisfaction of all who have tasted of the first fruits of their labours, of making the body of Holy Scriptures plaine and usefull to vulgar capacities, is not a little furthered by this piece For, albeit with greater length (as the nature of the Book of necessity did require) than these Brethren's design of shortnesse doth admitt, yet it maketh very plain and usefull that without all question hardest of all Scriptures This I can say, that diverse of the most obscure texts of that holy Book, which I understood little at the beginning of his Lecture, before he closed his Exercise, were made to me so clear, that I judged his Exposition might well be acquiesced into without much more debate

That wit were more than ordinary weak, which durst promise from the pen of any man a clear and certain Exposition of all the Revelation before day of performance of these very deep and mysterious Prophesies It was not for nought, that most judicious Calvin and acute Beze, with many other profound Divines, would never be moved to attempt any explication of that Book : Yet I hope I may make bold to affirm, without hazard of any heavie censure, that there is here laid such a bridge over that very deep river, that whoever goeth over it, shall have cause to blesse God for the Author's labour

The Epiftle fpeaketh to the man I fhall adde but this one word, That from the day I was employed by the Prefbyterie to preach and pray and to impofe, with others, hands upon him for the Miniftery at Glafgow, I did live to the very laft with him in great and uninterrupted love, and in an high eftimation of his egregious induements, which made him to me precious among the moft excellent Divines I have been acquainted with in the whole Ifle. O if it were the good pleafure of the Mafter of the Vineyard to plant many fuch noble vines in this land! I hope many more of his labours fhall follow this firft, and that the more quickly, as this doth receive the due and expected acceptance. Thefe in the Lord

ROBERT BAYLIE.

["The Epiftle" to which Baillie refers in this last paragraph, is an address "To the judicious and Christian Reader," by Mr. John Carstares, one of the Ministers of Glasgow, from which the following is an extract:—]

THE Reverend (now triumphing and glorified) Author was fo famous and defervedly in high efteem in our Church, both becaufe of the fingular and extraordinary way of God's calling him forth to the Miniftery of the Gofpel, having left the Univerfity wherein I was at the fame time a ftudent) before he had finifhed his courfe of Philofophie, and without any purpofe to follow his book, at leaft in order to fuch an end, and having lived feverall years a private gentleman, with his wife and children, enjoying a good eftate in the countrie, from which he did, no doubt, to the great diffatiffaction of many of his natural friends and with not a little prejudice to his outward condition, retire, and (being called thereto) humbly offer himfelf to trials, far from his own home, in order to his being licentiated to preach the Gofpel; in the Miniftery whereof he was immediately therafter fettled here at Glafgow, where it hath not wanted a feal in the confciences and hearts of his hearers. And alfo becaufe of his eminent piety, ftedfaftneffe gravity, prudence, moderation, and other great abilities, whereof the venerable General Affembly of this Church had fuch perfwafion that they did, in the year 1650, after mature deliberation, very unanimoufly pitch upon him, though then but about eight and twenty years of age, as amongft the ableft, fickereft, and moft accomplifhed minifters therein, to attend the King's family. in which ftation, though the times were moft difficult, as abounding with tentations and fnares, with jealoufies, heart-burnings, emulations, and animofities, and flowing with high tides of many various and not a few contrary humours, he did fo wifely and fathfully behave and acquit himfelf, that there was a conviction thereof, left upon the confciences of all who obferved him, and fo as he had peace through Jefus Chrift as to that miniftration . . . .

In the whole feries [of thefe Lectures]—thou will difcover—great light in the Scriptures, and very deep reach in the profoundeft and moft intricate things in Theologie, to a publick profeſſion whereof, in this University of Glaſgow, he was ſometime (to wit, a little before his being appointed to attend the King's family) by the Commiſſioners of the General Aſſembly, authorized for viſiting the ſaid Univerſity, moſt unanimouſly and ſolemnly deſigned and called, to the great ſatiſfaction and refreſhment of many, and more particularly, and eſpecially of famous and worthy Mr Dickſon, to whom the precious Author was choſen to ſucceed in that profeſſion (he being called to a profeſſion of the ſame nature in the Univerſity of Edinburgh), as one of the ableſt and beſt furniſhed men, (all things being conſidered) in our Church, that were not already engaged in ſuch employments and moſt likely to fill Mr. Dickſon's room . . . . . .

JOHN CARSTAIRS

Glaſgow, 23d September 1658.

XCIX.

GENERAL MONCK TO MR. ROBERT DOUGLAS. MARCH 1660.

[Orig.—Wodrow MSS. Folio XXVI. No. 50. The words printed in Italics are deleted in the MS.]

SIR,

I RECEIVED your letter of the firſt of March which was very welcome to mee, and muſt acknowledge myſelf much bound to you and the reſt of your Brethren for your prayers and councell, and I hope through grace I ſhall not be found wanting to God and my country in the purſuance of thoſe ends for which I vndertooke this quarrell. I have bin very much ſatiſfied with ſeverall diſcourſes that I had with yow, nott long before my leaving Scotland, wherein yow have expreſſed your care of the Church of God, *and your indifference as to Civil Government*. And truly, Sir, I hope that all wiſe and good Chriſtians will not thinke itt their intereſt to runne into blood for any ſingle or particular Civill forme of Government whatſoever. As for Preſbytery, what I declare to the world, which was both my conſcience and reaſon, ſo I aſſure yow I adjudge itt the beſt expedient to heal the bleeding diviſions of theſe poore Nations, ſoe itt be moderate and tender, otherwiſe itt will but image our diſeaſe and increaſe our wound. And I bleſſe the Lord that I have received your concurrence in this particular. As Scotland hath bin alwayes deare to mee, ſoe much more am I now ingaged for thoſe large expreſſions of their love and affection to mee, which I have ſoe lately experienced. And I doe aſſure yow, Sir, that there is nothing wherein I can ſerve them with ſecurity to the Common Wealth, but they ſhall command mee. The great allurements that drew me from that defired privacy were none others but to endeavour a ſettlement wherin wee might have protection from Tyranny and Anarchy, and the Churches of Jeſus Chriſt their juſt liberty, ſoe that I hope, while wee are going forward to theſe good ends, good men will nott quarrell with vs if wee doe nott proceed in every particular according to their judgements, but will acquiefce in the Providence of God, and in the Refolutions of thofe in authority I know yow have bin a great inftrument of good in that Church, and therfore doe defire yow to vfe your intereft for the prefervation of the peace, and the quieting mens fpirits, which is indeed both the duty and the glory of a Chriftian, and the efpeciall worke of the Miniftrie of the Gofpell. I hope yow will nott mifinterprett thefe expreffions as if I had the leaft jealoufye of my deare freinds in Scotland, but judge they proceed from my tendernes and care, for the prevention of future troubles and divifions I have noe further but to begge the continuance of your prayers I am,

Your very loving freind and fervant,

S James's 14° Mar 1659 [1660] GEORGE MONCK

Mr Robert Douglafs.

For the Reverend Mr ROBERT DOUGLAS at Edinburgh. Thefe

C

THE EARL OF MIDDLETON TO THE LORD CLERK-REGISTER

[Orig.—Wodrow MSS. 8vo XI No. 7.—The Act to which this letter refers was unqueftionably one " of the greateft confequence imaginable," being the Act Rescissory, passed on the following day, the 28th of March, by which all Parliamentary proceedings subsequent to the year 1639, were at once annulled.]

Edinburgh, March 27, 1661

MY LORD,

THE Act that is now before you is of the greateft confequence imaginable, and is like to meet with many difficulties if not fpeedily gone about Petitions are preparing, and if the thing were done, it would dafh all thefe buftling oppofitions. My Lord, your eminent fervices done to his Majefty in this Parliament cannot but be remembered to your honour and advantage I am fo much concerned becaufe of the great help and afhftance I have had from you, that I cannot, without injuftice and ingratitude, be wanting in a juft refentment. Now I am more concerned in this than I was ever in a particular The fpeedy doing is the thing I propofe as the great advantage, if it be poffible to prepare it, to be prefented to-morrow by ten o'clock in the forenoon to the Articles, that it may be brought into the Parliament to-morrow in the afternoon The reafon of this hafte fhall be made known to you at meeting by,

My Lord,

Your moft affectionate Servant,

MIDDLETON.

For [Archibald Primrofe] my Lord Regifter.

GLOSSARY OF OBSOLETE WORDS.

A

Accresse—increase, accession.
Adoe—exertion
Adoes—concerns
Affraye—to terrify
Aflought, inflocht—fluttered, in a flurry
Agreeance, greance—agreement
Airth—direction
Allanerlie, allenarly—only
Allutterly—altogether
Alssoone—as soon.
Always—however, nevertheless
Amirs—embers
Ancessouris—ancestors
And—if
Anent—concerning
Assession—the act of assessors
Athort,—abroad, far and wide
Athort—athwart, through, across
At once—by and by
Attoned—at one, brought to concord
Aught—ought
Aughtand—owing
Avocke—call away, prevent
Ayre (1 133)—first whisper

B

Babies—infants
Back, backs—a body of followers or supporters.
Backing—supporters, followers partizans
Bains—baths
Baird—beard.
Bairns—children
Band—oath, written obligation
Bardish—impertinent.
Baseness—humble terms
Bavard (ii 75)—bankrupt.
Baxters—bakers.
Beddall—sexton
Been—be-en—being.

Bensail—bent-sail, bias, propensity,
Beseek—beseech
Bicker, bikkering—contention, strife
Brocks—a term of reproach.
Blaw—to flatter, to coax
Blenk, blink—to look with a favourable eye
Bleak, blink—slight perusal, a glance
Blephum—mere pretence
Blew bore—fair appearance, an opening in the clouds
Block—to plan to devise
Blocking—framing rough hewing.
Blustered—blotted, disfigured in writing
Blythe—glad
Boast, boasted—threats to threaten
Bocardo—spectre, bugbear
Bonny—elegant, fine, beautiful
Boord-head—head of the table
Boording—boarding
Brae—declivity
Braid and wide (i 16)—far and near
Brangled—to confound, to throw into disorder
Breast a brae—to climb, to surmount a difficulty
Brether—brethren, brothers
Broaching—hatching, opening up
Bruckle—brittle
Bud, budds—a bribe, bribes
Buits—matches for firelocks
Burn-ill—suffered severely.
By—besides
Bygane—in time past
Bygones—denoting what is past

C

Caged—imprisoned.
Call ca'—to drive
Canny, cannie—sly, prudent, cautious
Cannyness—prudence, caution skill
Carder—player at cards
Cass—to annull

GLOSSARY.

Catches—ketches, ships
Cauldrifeness—coolness, want of ardour
Caulms, chalmes—moulds.
Causey—street
Cavell—lot, to cast cavels
Ceeding—ceding, yielding.
Cessing—taxing assessing
Chainzied—chained
Chock chouck—critical moment, or state
Clamm—clog
Clanculary—secret.
Clap—instantaneously, in a moment
Clatters—idle reports
Coft—bought, purchased
Coinzie-house—mint-house.
Coldrife—lukewarm
Comprar—appear
Compearance—presenting one's self
Compesce—to restrain
Compesced—defeated, restrained
Conditions—stipulates.
Concase—to combine
Cotters—cottagers
Coule—cap, night-cap
Coupers—horse-jockies, horse-dealers
Craw—crow
Cracking—credit decreasing
Craig—throat
Creevishes—crayfish
Crise—crisis
Crooke—iron chain by which the vessel is suspended above the fire
Cronner—colonel, commander of troops raised in one county
Crub—curb
Cuffes—blows
Cummer—gossip
Cunninglie—skilfully
Cusing—cousin
Currants, currents—diurnals, journals
Curious—anxious, fond
Cuttedly—hastily, sharply.

D

Dainties—a rare thing
Dear, deir—to hurt, injure, grieve
Deaced—deafened
Deboische (ii 341)—to corrupt, debauch
Deboisching (ii 72)—corrupting
Deboirded (i 148)—*deboirdeit* (ii 384)—swerved, gone beyond bounds.
Decairt (i 303)—discard
Decerned—adjudged, gave judgment.
Decreet—sentence
Dement—to deprive of reason.
Demented—distracted, unsettled in mind
Devorre—devour, swallow.
Dilled down—died away
Dilligat (i 307)—accurate, refined
Dimit—to resign
Dimitted—gave in his resignation.
Ding—beat, drive
Dinn, dinne—noise
Disjune—breakfast, to swallow up at once
Dittay—indictment, accusation
Divott—turf
Doctor—teacher
Doen—doing.
Dool—grief, mourning
Doolfull—doleful
Dorlach (i 212)—dagger, or short sword
Double—a duplicate.
Double—to transcribe, to take a duplicate of
Doun-sitting—session of a court
Dow—to be capable of
Driffling, drisling—small rain
Drumly—muddy, troubled, applied to the state of public matters
Dwanging—oppressing, twisting one about
Dyte—to dictate to an amanuensis
Dyted, dicted—dictated, indyted
Dyvour—bankrupt.
Dyvourie—state of bankruptcy

E

Effirat—to make wild, to madden
Eik, eiks—an addition, additions, to add
Ershu (i, 250)—eschew
Eldership—kirk-session, or vestry of a particular congregation.
Else—already, even now.
Emme (i 241)—aim.
Enaynes (i 97)—abilities
Entresse, enteres—interest.
Erch, to (ii. 76)—to scare, to shrink from
Evited—shunned.
Exeemed—exempted
Expone—to explain, expound
Eyed, not yet much, (i 113)—not yet much examined or looked at
Eylist—eye-list, a flaw, an eye-sore

GLOSSARY.

F

Faill—failure
Fairly (ii 161)—gently, in a civil manner.
Falset—falsehood
Fanged—laid hold of
Farder—farther
Fasch, fasched—to trouble, troubled
Fascherie—trouble of mind as well as body
Faschious—troublesome
Faught—fight, battle
Feck—number, quantity, effect.
Fickless—helpless, useless
Fred—fend
Fill—considerable.
Ferd—force, fervour
Feus—quit-rents
Field-coming—coming abroad
Flim-flams—trifles, whims
Flitt—remove
Flocht, flouet, flought—flame, combustion
Flyting—scolding
Foot (i 191)—system of executive
For against—opposite to
Foranent, foranence—in front of
Forbears—predecessors, ancestors
Frae—since
Francke—frank, forward
Fray, frayes—terror, alarms
Fray—to be afraid
Frequent numbers—great concourse
Frequently—numerously
Fussus (i 197)—fosses
Fyle—to stain, to defile, to bring in a verdict of guilty

G

Galliard, galliard—brisk, lively.
Gatt—got
Gloom, glowming—frown, gloming.
Glowring—staring.
Good-brother—brother-in-law
Good-dame—grandmother
Good-son—son-in-law
Gourd—cross-grained, twisted.
Greance—agreement, accord
Gripp—hold.
Grit—great.
Gutt—gout.
Guyses—fashions, ceremonies
Gyed not—turned not to one side, ajee.
Gyred—reered.

H

Hable—able
Haill—whole
Hair, against the—against the grain
Half quick—half-alive
Halse—throat
Hask (ii 63)—coarse, or ungracious
Haunched haunshed—eagerly catched, snatched at as a dog
Headiness—rashness
Heard—to be heard scolding or wrangling
Hemly—familiar, homely.
Henwile—a lure, stratagem.
Here yesterday—day before yesterday
Hiest—highest
Hinch—reserve
Hinderend—latter end
Hinging—hanging, in suspense
Hings—hangs
Hipped—passed over, omitted
Hoast, host—a cough, a hem, hesitation
Horn, put to the—outlawed, denounced a rebel
Horning—denouncing one a rebel
Hose-nett—a snare
Howbeit—although
Howes—difficulties, the background
Hunder—a hundred.

I

Ignaries—ill-informed persons
Ilk—each
Illighten—enlighten
Impeachit—accused
Impesched—prevented, impeded
Ingeminat—to repeat, reiterate
Inkling—distant hint
Inlaik—deficiency to run short
Interesse—interest
Interloquitor—(a law-term) decision, intermediate decree
Inthorned—entangled, surrounded
Into—often used for *in*

J

Jutors, jutes—tipplers

GLOSSARY.

K
Kist—chest
Kyth, kythed—appear, shew, shewn

L
Ladderit—scaled with ladders.
Laigh—low.
Lambes, Lammess—the term of Lammas
Lashnes—laxness
Latters—hinderers
Law—hill.
Lay to—charge one with.
Leaguer—encampment
Leek—leaky
Lest, lest—list
Lent, upon the, Letit—in nomination to be elected to an office
Legers—resident commissioners
Lent-fire—slow fire
Let be—much less
Libel—indictment
Loft—gallery
Lope (i 6)—passed to their friends
Loppen (ii. 217)—past time of leap.
Lourd—to stoop for concealment, to steal a march
Lourden, Lirdane—a lazy, worthless fellow.
Lunts (ii 422)—matches

M
Maisser messer—macer
Make (to)—to muster, to assemble
Malison—evil wish, curse
Mr—Master of Arts
Mastress—Mrs, wife.
Mins, mole meins—use means
Mell, mell't—to meddle, meddled
Mends—reparation
Mids midss—means
Minded—resolved
Mint—to attempt, to aim at
Mischant—mischievous
Mishappens—misfortunes unfortunates
Misken—to misknow overlook
Miskent—to seem to be ignorant of.
Mister—want, need.
Mo—more (in number)
More matters—greater matters
Morrow—the next day, the day after.
Moyen—influence

Muntoure—piece of mechanism a watch
Mynde, myndit—to mine undermined

N
Neaves—fists
Niggi-naggies—trifles
Nill he will he—whether he will or not.
Nipshot—drawback ' or to give the slip '
Nocht—nought, not
Nomothetick—legislation
Non-fiance—want of confidence.
Nor—than.
Notars—notaries, attorneys
Notour—publicly known.
Novations—innovations
Nuiks—corners.

O
Oblish—oblige.
Opposite—opponents
Outermost—utmost

P
Paiked, pyked—drubbed
Palme—the hand, or index of a watch.
Paised—pensive, thought.
Parte—opponent
Pasche—Easter
Patrocini.—patronage
Peats—turf
Peck of troubles—many, a deal of troubles
Pendicle—appendage, a pendant
Perquire—by heart, distinctly.
Phrase—pretence.
Pickeand—piquant
Picks—pikes
Pley—plea, quarrell.
Pock—bag
Port—carriage
Posed (i 72)—questioned
Posed (i. 169)—imposed
Pouch—pocket
Predomining—predominating
Pretead.—to neglect
Preveen—to anticipate, prevent.
Profession—professorship.
Propone—to propound.
Prospect—a perspective glass
Pudder, pudder—powder
Pudlit—besmeared
Pure—poor.

GLOSSARY.

Pyked—drubbed, thrashed.
Pyking—picking

Q

Quatt—quitted

R

Racked—raked
Raid—rode
Ramage—wild, reckless
Ramadge hawk—a wild untamed hawk
Ratt—a file of soldiers
Readily—possibly, probably.
Recrew—recruit
Reek, reik—smoke.
Refers, referres—matters referred
Rejagges—compunction, self-reproaches?
Rejected—remitted back
Remeid—remedy
Repes (n 369)—presses?
Reponed—replaced
Restringed—restrained, limited
Retreat—retract.
Ridd-hand—taken in the act
Roumes—vacant places.
Rowne round (in the eare)—to whisper
Ruie roove ruif—to clinch settled beyond the chance of alteration
Ryves—teareth.

S

Salebrosities—rugged or ticklish grounds
Sark—shirt
Sawin—sown
Scabrous—rugged, troublesome.
Scailled—to dismiss, to break up
Scairced, (m. 417)—scarcity scanty
Scant—scarce, scarcity
Schoot—shout
Scrip—to carp.
Sconces—fortifications
Scrubie—scurvy.
Scunner at—to loath
Scutching—drubbing
Sea-bank—sea-coast
Secourse—support, succour, help.
Seller—cellar.
Send—sent.
Sess, sessing—cess, assessing
Setter of tacks—letter of leases
Shards—sherds

Shew—the past time of show
Shoare—to threaten
Shored, shorit—threatened
Shreue (shaird)—wicked, unhappy
Shryving—confession.
Sib—nearly related
Sickerlie—surely, smartly
Sicklike—such-like, in the same manner.
Sinle—seldom, few
Skaith—damage, hurt, harm
Skugg—shelter
Slippen—slipped
Smallie learned—an indifferent scholar with a small share of learning
Smoord—smothered
Snid—to lop, to prune
Snell—smart.
Snifties (in 412)—insignificant persons
Sojors, sojours—soldiers
Solist, solisted—to solicit, solicited
Soone or syne—sooner or later
Sopit—to lull asleep
Sopour—slumber
Souple—supple, active.
Soupe—sweep.
Soupit—sweeped.
Spaite, speat—inundation.
Speared spered—asked, inquired
Spied—observed.
Spleen—heat, irritation, umbrage
Spunk—spark.
Staffage staffrige—obdurate unyielding
Staill—numerous.
Staill-post—main-post, in the army
Stark—strong.
Stearing—stirring
Stick—stob, stab
Stick—interfering obstacle
Stoops—supporters, pillars
Strang—strange, strong, bitter.
Stray, straes—straw, straws
Sturr—stir.
Sua—so
Subdolous—cunning, subtle
Sunry—sundry.
Sute—request, supplication.
Sutit—solicited.
Syncretisme—promiscuous union.

T

Tacks—leases

GLOSSARY.

Taill—tale
Takin—taking, being taken
Tapouns (1. 298)—long fibres at the roots
Targe—shield
Tasses—drinking cups
Teddered (1, 355)—tethered stranded
Tender—sickly.
Truchist—toughest.
The morn—to-morrow
Thereanent—concerning it
There-east—in the east, eastward.
There-forth, there-out—opposed to therein
Thir—these
Thought—though
Thraw—to twist, to wrest
Thraward—backward, reluctant, cross
Through—to carry through, to perfect
Throught—throughed, carried through
Thrumbling (1. 123)—pressing into
Thus and sua—so and so
Tig, tag (ii. 113)—to triffle with, or teaze one another
Tinkled upon—to ring chimes about
Tint—lost.
Tirlies—trellis or lattice
To—till
Tocher—dowry
Tod's birds—fox's brood, evil brood
Tolbooth, tolbuith—prison, jail
To-morrow—the day after, the next day
Toome—empty.
Toone—tone
Tope (ii. 88)—to check, to resist, to defeat
Traiked—weakened by fatigue
Trash—refuse lumber.
Travell—labour, pains.
Trewes-men—Highlanders, men wearing trews, or long pantaloons
Trinketting—clandestine correspondence with an opposite party
Tryst—appointment, to meet with.
Tuilzie, tuilyie—contention, affray
Tuitch, twitch—touch
Twa part—two-thirds
Tyne, tine—to lose

U

Uncanny—mischievous, dangerous
Undermyndit—undermined.
Unfriends—enemies
Unkent—unknown
Unlaws—escheat
Unpaunded—unpledged

V

Vacsse (ii. 420)—to evade
Vaike—to be vacant
Vaiking—becoming (or already) vacant
Voice, voyce—to vote.
Volee—volley

W

Wailed—selected
Wait—blame.
Wanrest—one who causes inquietude
War, warr—worse.
Waried, waured—out-stripped
Water-brae—river-bank
Wear—wear
While—till
Whiles, whyles—sometimes, at times
Whilk—which
Whinger—hanger.
Win—to get in, to reach
Wrack—wreck
Writt, wryte—writing
Wyte—blame

Y

Yorking—engaging
Yocked—begun engaged
Yondmost—uttermost.
Yowling—howling

Z

Zuill—Christmas

Twenty-shilling or one pound Scotish money is 20 pence Sterling
One merk is 13½d Sterling
To reduce Scotish money to pounds Sterling divide the pounds by 12, the merks by 18.

INDEX OF NAMES.

ABERCORN, Earl of, 65, 81; ii. 317, iii. 366
Abercromby, Adam, ii 88
Abercromby of Birkenbog, Alexander, 370, ii 91
Aberdeen 70, 93, 94, 205, 221, 222; ii 164, 261, 262, 264, iii. 18, 35, 52, 177, 250, 443 v Assembly, 1640,
Aberdeen, Bishop of, v. Bellenden Forbes. Mitchell
Aberdeen Doctors of, 63, 96, 97, 101, 107, 116, 117, 121, 169
Aberdeen, Ministry, 368–371, iii 477
Aberdeen, Presbytery of, 135.
Aberdeen, University of, 135, 491, iii 242, 244, 282, 365, 456.
Aberfoyle, iii 255
Abernethie, Major Andrew, iii. 128
Abernethie, Thomas, Jesuit, 82, 101, 222
Abernethy, John, Bishop of Caithness, 165, 166, 425.
Aboyne, James, Viscount of, 197, 204, 220, 221, ii. 74, 116, 126, 137, 141, 164, 442, iii. 471.
Accommodation with Independents, ii. 230, 232, 260, 325–328, 343–346
Acheson of Glencairne, Sir Archibald, Secretar, 425.
Act of Classes, iii 72, 80, 88, 92, 125, 160, 557.
Act of Grace, iii 251, 252
Adair of Kinhilt, Sir Robert, 111, 147.
Adair, William, minister of Ayr, ii 69, 71, iii 53, 61, 111, 487
Adamson, David, minister of Fintry, iii 278, 315, J (David), 561.
Adamson, John, Principal of the College of Edinburgh, 52, 121, 129, 133, 136, 146, 147, 212, 363 463: ii 85 330, iii 543-546, 555

Adamson, Patrick, Archbishop of St Andrews, 129, 157, iii 373, 377.
Advocate, Lord, v. Fletcher Hope Johnston
Affleck v Auchinleck
Agnew of Lochnaw, Sir Patrick, 425.
Aikenhead, Thomas, commissary, 426
Ainsworth, Answerth, 12
Aird, Francis, minister in 144, 322, 382, 384, 434
Aird, Robert, minister, iii. 561.
Airds, Viscount of, 337, iii 61, 97, 100
Airly, Earl of, 276, ii. 60, 74
Airth, James, clerk of Pittenweem, 147.
Aithie v Carnegie.
Albemarle, Duke of, v Monck
Alexander, John, parson of Hoddam, 426
Alexander, Sir William, Earl of Sterline, v. Sterline
Alexander, William, Lord, 32, 76, 77 447, 452
Alford, ii 302, 304, 419, 423
Alger, Algiers, iii 291
Allen, Francis, goldsmith, ii 353, 359
Almond, Amont, Lord, Lieutenant-General, 77, 123, 145, 212, 256, 306, 378, 383–393, passim.—v Callander, Earl of
Alhat v Elliot
Alyth, Eliot. iii 176, 563.
Amisfield v. Charteris of
Amsterdam, iii 24; Classis, ii 202
Amyrault, Amiot, Moses, ii 265, 324, 342, iii 101, 311, 324, 369
Anabaptists, ii 117, 121, 140, 157, 169, 185, 191, 215, 218, 224, 228, 327, 342 343, 406, iii 289
Ancrum, Earl of, 115, 425
Anderson, George, printer, ii 404, iii 555
Anderson of Dowhill J. iii 369

INDEX OF NAMES

Anderson, John, preacher, iii. 394
Anderson, John, writer, 108
Anderson, William, iii 363
Andover, Lord iii. 72
Andrews, Dr. L Bishop of Ely, 1, 2
Angus, Archibald, Earl of, 14 50, 123
  379, 389, 440, 458 462 ; ii 67, 85, 89 ,
  iii 54, 136, 248 249
Angus Forfarshire, ii. 417† 419, 442 ; iii
  96, 117, 182. 248
Anjou Duke of, iii. 446
Annan James, minister of Inverness, 369
Annan, William minister of Ayr, 19–21.
  62, 63 89, 167, 221 425
Annandale, Earl of, 386, 424 , ii. 67, 77,
  314 , iii 464.
Anstruther, Sir Robert, ii 195 243.
Anstruther, Sir William, ii. 162
Antinomians, ii 117, 123, 140, 157, 169,
  185, 191, 215 218, 224, 228, 327, 342,
  343, 406
Antrim, Antrum, Earl of. 72 92, 193, 194,
  196, 206 , ii. 73, 74, 80, 105, 116.—
  Marquis, 164 214 217, 377 , iii. 312.
Apollonius, William minister of Middle-
  burgh, ii 180-190, 193, 197, 202 205,
  218, 226, 239, 240, 246, 265, 288, 315,
  322, 324, 327, 365, 371, 387, 398 , iii
  57, 67 101, 324
Apologetick Narration, ii 129–131, 143,
  144, 146 147, 188 343
Apparitions, iii 360, 436
Arbuthnot, Robert, Viscount. iii 35
Archer, John, ii 306,
Ard of Kilmound, 472
Ardincaple v M Aulay.
Ardoch v. Stirling,
Areskine v. Erskine.
Argyle, Bishop of, 6, 425 ; iii 486, v
  Farley. Fletcher.
Argyle, (Archbald, Earl of), 123, 126,
  129–131. 143–147 152, 155, 157, 170,
  171, 175, 192–196, 200, 204, 211, 220,
  238 247, 257–265, 304 306, 356, 358,
  362–368, 376–396, 471, 473, 485, 489 ,
  Marquis, ii 5, 35, 39, 41, 43-47, 53-59,
  64, 68-74, 84, 91-96, 128, 164, 176,
  217, 225–227, 233, 251, 262–264, 281,
  321, 345, 357, 362, 376, 379, 383, 386,
  402, 407, 417†,-424†, 441, 447, 471,
  473, 478, 485, 510, 516 , iii. 6, 18, 33-
  36, 45, 48, 53, 64, 99, 105-109, 114,
  11.

160, 167, 171, 249 250, 256 259, 288,
  361, 387 404, 418, 422, 430, 443, 447,
  465-467, 524 568
Argyle, Marchioness of, ii. 319, 362, iii
  447, 465, 466.
Argyle's Regiment, ii 422.
Argyleshire, ii 427† , iii 97 255.
Argyle, Synod of, iii 81.
Arminius, Dr James, professor at Ley-
  den, 114
Arminianism, 149 , iii. 304
Armour, Alexander, 246, 267.
Armour, minister of St Andrews, 97
Armstrong Archie, ii. 125
Armyne, Sir William, ii 89, 299, 302
Arnot, Sir Charles ii 418†, 422.
Arnot, Mr. iii. 9.
Arnot, Dr 387
Arrowsmith John, ii 123, 148, 184
Arundell, Earl of, 10. 72, 92, 204, 211 ;
  Lord High Steward. 315, 317–319
Ashburnham, John, ii 66, 244, 364, 368,
  370 373, 375
Ashe, Simeon ii 209, 359, 415 , iii. 302
  306, 307, 328, 338, 354, 355, 391, 415.
Ashfield, Colonel, iii 438
Ashley, Astley, Jacob, ii 158
Ashton, Colonel, ii 65, 138
Assembly of Divines at Westminster, ii,
  80, 89, 99, 101, 102, 104, 107–112, 115
  –124, 128–131 136 139, 143–149 158,
  164, 176, 184–187, 245, 255–257, 325
  349 377–379, 390, 393, 397, 400, 478 ,
  iii 2, 3 62, 108 449–454, App., 532.
  536–544 548—Vide Catechism Confession of Faith Church Government.
  Directory. Ordination Psalms Remonstrance
Assemblies, Corrupt, 147, 151.
Assembly. General, 1638, at Glasgow, 92,
  95, 98-109, 111-115 118-175, 184, 219,
  221, 223, 294, 476 , iii. 464.
—1639, at Edinburgh, 221-224,
—1640, at Aberdeen, 231-234, 245-255
—1641, at St Andrews, 358-377 ; translated to Edinburgh, 360
—1642, at St Andrews, ii. 45-54.
—1643, at Edinburgh, ii 83-97
—1644, at Edinburgh, ii 195, 196.
—1645, at Edinburgh, ii 242-250, 255-260
—1646, at Edinburgh, ii. 384, 397, 398
—1647, at Edinburgh, iii 10-15 19-21

INDEX OF NAMES 595

Assembly, General,
—1649, at Edinburgh, iii 91-97, 521
—1650, at Edinburgh, iii. 105, 106, 115.
—1651 at St Andrews and Dundee, iii 176-188, 328, 562-566
—1652, at Edinburgh, iii, 188-194, 562-566.
—1653 at Edinburgh, iii. 225
Atherton, 318.
Athole, Earl of. ii 418-419†, 468, iii. 117, 250, 288, 366, 471.
Auchinbreck *v* Campbell.
Auchinleck, Affleet, Andrew, minister of Largo, 136, 366, 472; ii. of Dundee, 49, 53, iii 34
Auchinleck, James, minister at—153, 172
Auchinmoutie, Auchmouty, of Gosford, Sir John, 425.
Auld, Robert, ii 276
Auldbar *v.* Lyon.
Auldearne, Aldearne, ii 275, 418, 423.
Austin, Samuel, minister of Penpont, iii 279.
Ayr, 173, ii. 399; iii 61, 111, 249, 464
Ayr, Presbytery of, iii 137, 142, 145, 316
Ayr, Provost of, iii 420, 456

B

Badenoch, Badzenoch, ii 418†
Bailie, Lord Forrester, iii, 367, 455 App
Bailie of Lamington, Sir William, 123; ii 417
Bailie of Letham, Lieutenant-General William, 212, 256, 270, 355; ii. 67, 100, 128, 204, 206, 262, 264, 277, 302, 305, 357, 386, 417-425, iii. 95, 367, 455-457 App.
Bailie of Lochend, Sir James, 426
Bailie, Dr. ii 124
Baillie, James, ii 258
Baillie, Robert, minister of Kilwinning, 131, 134 149, 154, 162, 172, 183 215, 242, 245 253-255, 264, 267-272, 295, 299, 339, 359, 362, 371, 472, 480, 465
—Professor of Divinity at Glasgow, ii. 51, 52 55, 76, 86, 88, 93 99, 161, 198, 248, 250, 254, 255, 258, 279-285, 323, 336, 404, 463, 472, 478, 482 487-498, 516, iii. 37-41, 52, 62, 82-88, 91-93, 96, 162, 194, 200-220, 222, 236, 242, 266, 279 287 296, 321 336 362, 369
—Principal of th Universty iii 411 412, 422 462 540, iii 561

Baillie, his Translation to Glasgow, 248, 371, ii 2-33, 443-449—iii 7-33, 37-39, 49, 52.
Baillie, his Family, 246, 268, 269, 278, 299; iii 62, 311, 368, 436, 472, 483 — his Son Harrie, 109, 110, iii 252, 253, 294, 295, 325, 368, 382, 391, 392 — his Son Robert, iii. 286, 287, 368, 373, 374 —his Friends, 162, 172, ii 311, 313, 330, 340, iii 62, 91, 366
Baillie his Works 242, 257, ii 385, 386, iii. 369, 390, 401, 409, 415-417, 421, 449 478
Bainton, ii. 492.
Baird, James, advocate, 381
Baker, John iii 553
Balæus *v.* Baillie
Balcanqual, Robert, minister of Tranent. 90, 426, 477, 478, 490.
Balcanqual, Dr Walter, Dean of Durham, 1 83, 98, 106, 122, 136, 139, 140, 155, 174, 175, 208, 279, 280, 286, 357, 443-7, 467, 475-491, ii. 339, 404, 429-431, 435-438.
Balcarras Alexander Earl of, 211, ii. 45, 85, 382, 419-424, 514, iii 35, 98, 117, 119, 134-139, 147, 154, 166, 170, 172, 212, 250-255, 387, 437, 478
Balcarras, Lady, iii. 212 387
Balcarras's Regiment, ii 419, 419†, 422
Balcleugh *v* Buccleugh.
Balcolmie *v* Learmont.
Balfarg *v* Beton.
Balfour, Alexander, ii 472, 473
Balfour, Sir James, Lord Lyon, ii. 472
Balfour, Michael, ii. 472
Balfour, Sir William, 282, 286, 315, 316, 344, 350, ii 42, 151-153, 155, 156, 158, 227; iii 366.
Balgony, Alexander Lord iii 367.
Ballantyne, Major, 73
Balmerino, John Lord, 35, 38, 39, 43, 48. 123, 125, 136, 147, 159, 169, 190, 355, 375, 381, 384, 386, 390, 429, 430, 465, 472, ii 73, 85, 89, 128, 217, 324, 430, 441, 442, 473, 513; iii. 33, 54
Balmerino, Master of, ii 506
Balmore, Ramor, iii 394
Balvaird, Andrew Lord, ii 91 472, 473
Banfield, Col. iii. 105, 108
Band and Banders, 374, 375, ii 34, 105 141 292
Banff Ogilvy.
Berl Chirt Ju Co 19 as, 292.

Barclay of Towie. 123. 432
Barclay, Major David. iii. 430
Barclay. Colonel Harry. ii. 419+.
Barclay Robert, provost of Irvine. 63 104.
  136. 171 365. 366 388. 473 , ii 42 45
  50. 59. 66 89. 106 217. 241 251. 323.
  357. 487 , iii 136.
Barenfrew. Barranthrow e. Renfrew.
Barksted. Col iii 427
Barnes. James. merchant. 484.
Barnes David. preacher. 363
Barnes. George. iii. 286.
Barnes James. iii. 363
Barnes John. dean of gild. Glasgow.
  229 ; ii. 12 ; iii. 286. 420
Baronius Cardinal. 358.
Barr. James, iii. 318.
Barr. Robert. ii 289. 290.
Barrington. Sir Thomas. 341.
Barron. Dr John. St. Andrews 66. 93
  97 144. 477
Barron, Dr Robert. Aberdeen. 135 163
  221 425.
Barton. William. iii. 532 540. 552-554
Barwick. Dr ii 398.
Bastwick. Bastock. Dr. John. 273. 277.
  283 429 ; ii. 279.
Bathgate. Parish of iii. 245. 248.
Bavaria. Bavier. Duke of ii. 114. 388 ,
  iii 10 32
Baxter, Richard. iii 303. 307. 324. 369
  391. 400. 442 484
Baylie e Bailhe
Beak. Major. iii. 362
Beale. Beele Dr. Vice-Chancellor. Cambridge 225 ii. 148
Bedford. Earl of. 292 304. 305 . ii. 56 99
  126 178.
Bedlay e Roberton.
Beere. Colonel. ii 226.
Belhaven. (Sir R Douglas of Spott) Lord.
  77. 106, 107. 123.
Belhaven. Hamilton. Lord, iii. 435. 436
Bell. James, provost of Glasgow. iii. 236.
Bell. John. provost of Glasgow. iii. 115.
  163, 363. 372, 411. 419. 456 469.
Bell. John. minister of Glasgow. 21 37.
  63. 104. 106. 108 122 124 126. 127.
  170 426. 481 ; ii. 5 448
Bell. John. minister of Stevenston. 13 14.
  94. 104, 232 246. 267. 289. 473 , ii 10.
  161 . iii 136. 182 236. 279 317. 545.
  56

Bell. John. son of the preceding. 237. 238
Bell. John. junior minister of Glasgow
  63 88. 104 133
Bell. John. ii. 219 ; iii 366.
Bell. Patrick. provost of Glasgow. 8. 105.
  106. 108 147, 171. 234. 243 n 3.
Bell. Patrick. merchant. Glasgow. son of
  the preceding. iii. 449 451
Bell. Robert. minister of Dalry. (Ayrshire).
  13 473. 448
Bellasis. Lord. iii 367
Bellievre. Monsieur, iii. 388
Belsches of Tofts Sir Alexander. 367.
Bellenden. Adam. Bishop of Dumblane and
  Aberdeen. 161. 169. 288 421 422. 425
  430-438 , ii. 92. 474
Bennet, David, minister of Stirling iii. 123.
  146. 283.
Bennet. George minister. iii 257. 547.
Bennet. William. parson of Ancrum. 426
Bennet. William. minister of Edinburgh.
  370 491
Berkshire. Earl of. 343.
Berne (an Irishman) 335
Berridale Berridaill. Master of. 492
Berwick. Barwick. ii. 100. 322. 43 9.441.
  463 , iii 37, 38 51. 439.
Best, Paul. ii. 306.
Beton of Balfarg. ii 473.
Beton of Creich. David. iii. 54
Beverlie minister of Leinzie iii 217.
Beverwert. Lord. iii. 73.
Beza, Theodore ii 265 277
Binnie. John. ii. 46
Binning. Binnie. Hugh. minister of Govan.
  iii 124. 195. 200 258. 434
Binning e. Haddington.
Birkenbog e Abercrombie
Birnie Robert, minister of Lanark. iii.
  420
Biron. Byron. Lord. iii 51 88
Bishops. 18. 74. 75. 77. 87. 98. 129-139
  217. 221 274. 288 e Complaint. Declinature. Excommunication.
Bishoptoune e Brisbane.
Black. Blackie. Nicholas. minister of
  Roberton. iii 394. 553.
Blackburn. Peter Bishop of Aberdeen.
  iii. 402
Blackhall. Andrew. minister of Aberlady.
  363. 472 ; ii. 49.
Blackhall e Stewart of

INDEX OF NAMES. 597

Blair of Blair, senior, 14, 63, 171, 195, 382, ii 136, 464
Blair of Bogtown, Adam, iii. 136
Blair, Adam, clerk, ii 474, 475
Blair, Sir Adam, iii. 409
Blair, Alexander, 128, 129, iii 53
Blair, Alexander, minister of Galston, iii. 487.
Blair, Colonel, 256
Blair, Hugh, minister of Eastwood, 368, ii 5 39 158, of Glasgow, 173, iii 142, 150, 164, 206, 243, 347, 368, 468, 486, 561.
Blair, James, brother of Robert, 28
Blair, James, minister of Portpatrick, 87, iii 140.
Blair, James, minister of Cathcart, iii 394
Blair, John, minister of Bothkennar, iii. 257, 284
Blair, Robert, minister 31, 62, of Ayr. 89, 106, 146, 171, 173, of St. Andrews, 250, 269-273, 284, 295, 299, 303, 339, 355, 362, 365-367, 375, 394, ii 11 22. 25-28, 31, 32, 42, 45-50, 70, 76, 83, 106, 159, 163, 185, 208, 270, 303, 382, 385, 389, 406, 414, 516; iii. 8, 20, 33, 39, 52, 55, 57, 62, 91 106, 110-116, 133, 136, 140, 149, 167, 173-184, 188, 189, 197, 199, 201, 212, 231, 238, 241, 248, 253, 262, 279-281, 296, 363, 375, 396, 402 468, 487, 544, 556-563.
Blair, Routmaster, ii 422
Blain, William, minister, iii 561
Blake, Admiral, iii 291, 301, 370.
Blantyre, Lord 152, ii. 4
Bodius v. Boyd
Boigs, Bogs, Laird of, iii 246
Bonar, Boner, Bonner, James, minister of Maybole, 19, 82, 106, 121, 127, 129, 130, 136, 171, 254, 355, 361, 363, 364, ii 45, 46, 52, 84. 95, 505, iii 136, 561.
Bonar, Sir John, 263.
Bond, Master of the Savoy, iii 552
Book of Canons, 4, 28, 119, 120, 147, 152, 428, 430, 436-440, 471
Book of Common Prayer v Service-Book
Book of Ordination, 4, 119, 147, 152
Booth, Sir George, iii 428, 429, 437
Boroubrig, Boroughbridge, 271
Borthwick, Colonel, iii 317
Borthwick, Eleazar, minister of Leuchars, 98, 150, 250 295 339 ii 42 45
Boswell Sir Wilham, at the Hague

Bothwell, Earl of, 37.
Bouillon, Duc de, ii 44
Bovius, Bowie, Walter, iii. 23, 101, 104 449, 451.
Boyd, Lord, 63, 106, 124, 137, 178, 195, 201, 211, 262, 481, ii 363, 468
Boyd of Trochrig, Robert, ii 14, iii 184, 226, 402.
Boyd, Mark Alexander, iii 403
Boyd, Stephen, Stevin. 383, 385
Boyd, Thomas, iii 276
Boyd, Zachary, minister, Glasgow, 83, 104, 106, 426, ii 86, 87, 173, 196 271, 295, 393; iii 3, 42, 119, 142, 194, 212, 238, 239, 241, 285, 312, 432, 535, 540, 543-545, 554, 555, 561.
Boyn v. Aboyne.
Braco v Graham.
Bradshaw, iii 443
Bramhall, Bramble, Bishop of Derry, 206, 318, 319, 339; iii 79, 87, 90, 103 400, 444, 470
Bray, Dr. 347.
Braynes, ii 290
Brechin, Bishop of. v Whiteford
Breda, iii 102, 114, 115, 118, 439, 484 523-5
Brederod, in Dutch Embassy, 208, 294
Brentford, Brainford, ii 56
Brereton. Sir William ii 112, 118, 131, 146, 272, 276
Brian Col iii. 255
Bridge, Bridges, William, ii 110, 111, 145, 199
Brisbane of Bishopton, John 104 472, iii 136.
Brisbane, H minister, ii 513
Brisbane, W minister of Erskine, 104, 426.
Brisbane, Matthew, minister of Killellan, 63, 104, iii 43
Bristol, Earl of, 262, 271 289, 300, 304-307, 313, 329, 341, ii 125, 137, 139
Brodick, Brodwick Castle, 196
Brodie of Brodie, Alexander ii. 418, iii 173, 234, 507-521, 547.
Broghill, Roger Boyle, Lord, iii 276, 295, 296, 298, 309, 312, 315-19, 321 322, 325, 330, 343, 350 352, 359, 362, 365, 439, 567
Brooke, Lord, 199, 275, 351, ii 56, 63
Brooke, Sir Basil, 295, ii 132, 133
Broomhill, Robert Brace Laird iii 136
Brown M P ii 47

INDEX OF NAMES.

Browne, James, 69.
Browne, James, printer at the Hague, iii. 128, 129
Browne, John, regent at Edinburgh, 64, 91, 110.
Browne, Major, ii 201, 226.
Brown, Robert, the sectary, ii. 184, 193.
Brown Robert, minister in Annandale, ii 48, 275
Brown Thomas, baillie of Glasgow, iii 435
Brownism, 54, 76, v. Novations.
Bruce, Lord, iii. 539
Bruce, Doctor Andrew, 97, 425 , iii 6
Bruce, Crowner, 206 , ii 132
Bruce, George, burgess of Culross. 472
Bruce, Sir Harrie, 72
Bruce, James, minister of Kingsbarns, 365, 449 ii 49
Bruce, John, preacher, ii. 49, 50.
Bruce, Thomas, provost of Stirling, 171
Bruce of Stanhouse, Sir William, iii. 248, 257, 258
Bryson, Robert, bookseller, 441.
Buccleugh, Countess of, iii 366 438
Buccleugh, Francis, Earl of, 85.
Buchan, James Earl of, iii 117.
Buchan, Scoutmaster, iii. 110
Buchanan, Captain, 212
Buchanan, David, ii. 179 197, 252, 253, 276, 367 , iii 136
Buchanan, George, iii, 402.
Buchanan, George, minister of Kirkpatrick juxta 426
Buchanan, James, minister, iii 561
Buchanan, Walter, minister of Ceres 146
Buchanans, 482
Buckhurst, Lord, iii, 526
Buckingham, Duchess of 333 , ii. 132
Buckingham, Duke of, ii. 315.
Bunce, Bunch, alderman, 101
Buntein, Major, iii 439—(Colonel William) iii. 457, App.
Burgess, Dr Cornelius, 302, 308 , ii 89, 99, 108, 121, 122, 134 198, 199, 346, 381 382. 411, 415 , iii 304, 307, 391, 537, 539 540
Burleigh, Burghlie, Robert, Lord, 123, 137, 377, 382, 385, 386 , ii 45, 420†, 424 ; iii. 35, 98
Burne, John, minister, iii 561
Burnet of Leys. 492
Burnet, Andrew, regent, at Glasgow, iii. 242 313 372

Burnet, James, minister of Lauder, 426
Burroughs, Jeremiah, 303 , ii 110, 111, 145, 279
Burrows, iii 98, 99
Burton, Henry, 273, 277 , ii 132, 192, 279, 296, 299.
Butter, James, stationer, 305
Buxtorff, Buxtorfie, ii 290.
Byfield, Adoniram, ii 108, 109, iii 539,552.

C

CABELJAVIUS, Cabellarius, ii. 311, 371
Caithness, Bishop of, v Abernethy. Forbes
Calamy, Edmund, ii 148, 415 ; iii. 224, 228, 285, 307, 328, 331, 338, 391, 442. 484, 553
Calderwood, David, minister, 137, 139, 155, 158, 362, 363 369, 372, 486 . ii. 40, 70, 95, 182, 260, 373, 384, 505, 510 ; iii 14 19-21 33, 36, 55, 59, 64, 65, 94, 95, 530—his History, ii. 374, 384 , iii 60
Calderwood, Thomas, iii 409
Caldwell of Caldwell, William, 382
Cales, Cadiz, iii 291
Calais, Calice, iii 19
Calandrin, Callendrin, ii. 186, 226
Callander, Earl of, (Vide Almond, Lord,) ii 67, 68, 100, 176, 181, 185, 188, 191 196, 199, 204, 211. 216, 217, 226, 227, 262, 345, 357, 417†-468 , iii 32 38, 40, 45 48-51, 73 81, 95, 101, 127, 410. 464, 486, (457, App)
Calvert, Giles stationer, ii. 404.
Calvert, Henry, minister of Paisley, iii 425
Cambridge, University of, ii 130, 148, 393
Cambridge, Charles Duke of, iii. 445.
Cameron, Cambron, Archibald, 482 ; iii 415
Cameron, Evan, minister, iii 544
Cameron, (John) Principal of the College of Glasgow, 8, 53, 188 , ii 251 , iii 402, 415
Campbell, Lord Neil, iii 465.
Campbell of Ardkinlas, 425 ; iii 465
Campbell of Auchinbreck, Sir Duncan, 425 , ii. 263
Campbell, John, younger of Caddell, 425.
Campbell of Cessnock, Sir Hew, iii 98.
Campbell of Lawers, Colin 147

INDEX OF NAMES

Campbell, Lieutenant-Colonel, ii. 422
Campbell, (a remonstrator) iii. 316
Campbell, Colin, minister of Dundee, 425
Campbell Dougall, minister of Knapdaill, 426
Campbell, George, afterwards minister of Dumfries, and Edinburgh, iii. 383
Campbell, George sheriff-depute of Argyle, iii. 465
Campbell, James, iii. 141
Campbell John, iii 436
Campbell, Neil, Bishop of the Isles, 164
Campbells, 70, 82, 199, ii. 74
Camphire, Campvere, ii 169; iii 46
Canne, John, minister in Amsterdam, 113.
Cant, Andrew, senior, minister of Alford, Pitsligo, 85, 88, 96, 121, 141, 146 154 —Aberdeen, 172 —Newbottle, 248, 255, 257, 362, 364, 368, 373 472; ii 45, 46, 50 51, 469, 516, iii 39, 52, 53, 61, 62 91, 110, 123, 217, 219, 242, 364, 365, 447, 563
Cant, Andrew, junior, minister of Libberton iii 365, 447
Canterbury, Archbishop of, *v* Laud
Canterstein, a Swede, iii. 524
Capell Lord, ii 112.
Capington *v* Cunningham.
Carden *v* Stirling.
Carmichael, Lord. 198
Carmichael Daniel, ii 372, 381
Carmichael, Sir Daniel Treasurer-Depute, ii. 273; iii 24, 155, 547
Carmichael, Sir James Treasurer-Depute, 39, 201, 390, 396, 425, 452, 458, 462, 484
Carnegie, Lord, *v* Southesk, 126, 132
Carnegie of Aithie, 144.
Carnegie of Lour 375.
Carnegie, D., ii 468.
Carnwath, Earl of, ii. 67, 75 77, 78, 80
Carse, Alexander minister of Polwart, 151, 159, 487.
Carsse, Dr, 77
Carstares, Carstairs, John, minister of Glasgow, 120, 141, 143, 144, 162, 165, 195, 199, 200, 249, 257, 279, 280, 297, 313, 322, 353, 383, 434, 487.
Carter, Thomas, ii 110
Cary, John, ii. 492, 495, 498.
Caryl, Joseph, ii 110, 145, iii 354, 438, 552
Casaubon,
Case, Th

Cassillis, John Earl of. 53, 84, 91, 123, 137, 173, 189, 201, 211, 219, 266, 360, 362, 383, 489; ii 42, 45, 46, 55, 85, 96, 419†, iii 35, 48, 54, 61, 86, 88, 91, 98, 99, 101, 106, 112, 116, 359, 414, 420, 443, 446, 463, 464, 507-521
Cassillis's Regiment, ii 418, 419.
Castell, Dr. Edmund, iii 309
Castellaw, William, minister of Stewarton 19, 94; iii 561
Castlehaven, Earl of, 324; iii 233, 238
Castlemilk *v* Stewart
Catechism, ii 232, 242, 248 266, 272 306, 336, 348, 79-88, 404, iii 2, 165, 9
Cathcart, parish of, iii 193, 215
Cathcart, Hew, 259
Catherwod *v* Calderwood
Cavers *v* Douglas
Cesnock *v* Campbell
Challoner, Thomas, ii. 511.
Chancellor (Lord) of Scotland, *v* Glencairn, Loudoun Spottiswood
Chapell-Royal, 424, 428-438-441, 470.
Charenton, Charrantone iii 174
Charles I. 1-19, 33, 39, 47-51, 117, 174, 215, 245, 264, 301, 385-400, 421, 424 429, 430, 440, 443, 448, 479, ii 3, 7, 9, 56, 132, 289, 360, 370, 396, 472, iii 4, 9, 17, 32, 39, 63, 105, 106, 114, 409 530-532, et passim
Charles II Prince of Wales, ii 138, 297 317, 328, 344, iii. 6, 41, 54 —King, iii 66, 69, 72, 84-90, 100 137, 151, 174, 292, 296, 305, 321, 358, 360 387, 400 406, 410, 439 441, 442, 448, 512-520, 524, et passim.
Charteris, Thomas, minister of Stenhouse, iii. 187, 322, 323
Charteris, Henry, printer iii 529.
Charteris of Amisfield, Sir John, 425, ii. 470.
Cheisly of Kerswell Sir John 472, ii 138, 370, 382, 484, iii 14, 24, 32, 97-100, 111, 114, 118, 173, 186, 187, 296, 298, 393, 401, 446, 507, 547, 567.
Cholmondeley, Chomley, ii 57.
Churches, Foreign, ii 115, 117, 128, 169 174, 179, 180, 184, 186.
Church-Government, 273-275, 280, *v* Episcopacy; ii. 81, 104, 131, 139, 145-148, 245, 248-250, 299, 306, 325, 328, 3, 416,

INDEX OF NAMES.

Church-Registers, 128. 129. 136. 138
147. iii. 137 356.
Clandonald, Clan Ronald. 193 194.
Clapperton. John. minister of Yetholm.
373
Clare. Clair Earl of. 327. 342. 347. ii
99 178.
Clarendon. Earl of. ι Hyde
Clargis. Dr ni. 438.
Classes. r Act of.
Clavering Colonel. ii 215. 216. 224
Clerk. Clarke. Samuel. minister of St. Bennets Fink. London. ii. 359. iii. 226 415
Clerkington. Lord. r Scot.
Cloberry. Colonel. iii 438.
Clotworthy Sir John. 273. 318 334. 337
338 ; ii 141 155. iii 312.
Clotworthy Lady. iii. 205.
Clydesdale. Cliddisdaill. 196. 201: ii 422.
iii. 48. 49 111. 112 255
Clyst, (an Englishman.) 429.
Cobbet. Colonel. iii. 438.
Cobroun r Cockburn
Cochrane of Cowden. Sir William. 84.
ii. 310 ; iii. 35 Lord Cochrane. 84. 95
322. 420. 456.
Cochrane. Colonel John. 190. 260. 383
382. ii 9. 310
Cochrane. John. minister. iii. 561
Cochrane. James. baillie. Edinburgh. 37
44. 46. 123 136. 147
Cockburne of Langton. Sir William. 385.
Cockburn. William. minister of Kirkmichael. ii. 69. iii. 144. 236. 278
Colines John. minister of Campsie. 370.
Colkittoch. (Macdonald). ii. 74. 217. 270
499. iii 10.
Colman. Thomas. minister of Bilton. ii
306. 340
Cologne. Cullen. Elector of ii 9
Colquhoun of Lusse. sir John. iii 136
420. 456.
Colquhoun. Matthew. iii 437
Colvert r Calvert.
Colville. Colvin. Dr Alexander. 360. iii
61. 96. 544
Colville. Alexander Justice Depute. iii.
460
Colville. Patrick. minister of Beith. iii.
136. 143. 181. 200. 210. 219. 236. 336.
393. 420. 456. 561
Colville. Samuel. iii. 244
Colvill

Colville. William. minister of Cramond.
136. 362. of Edinburgh ; ii. 85 463 , iii
19-21. 34. 41. 63. 64. 92. 96. 105. 184.
284. 493. 522. 545
Commissary of Glasgow r Fleming. Lockhart
Commission of Assembly. ii. 54. 58. 59. 69
75, 80. 97. 104. 406. 481. iii 5 47. 57.
64. 65. 81. 95 106. 107. 109 111. 120
122. 126. 131. 134. 141. 163. 174. 458
App. 461 483 511
Commission of Assembly 1650. iii. 297-
300. 305. 324
Commission. The High. 280. 282.
Commission, The High, in Scotland. 16.
147. 153. 424.
Commissioners. Scotish, to England. 262.
269. 305-307. ii 41-43. 60 63-68. et
passim.
Commissioners from the General Assembly
to the Assembly of Divines at Westminster, 41-43. 55. 95.
Commissioners from the English Parliament. ii. 88.
Committee of the Estates in Scotland. iii.
111. 116-163. 120 122. 129. 141. 443
446. et passim.
Committee of both Kingdoms. ii. 141 142.
154. 172. 178. 187. 199 202. 221. 224.
238. 294. 341. 415.
Committee of Lords for religion. 308. 313
Complaint and Declinature against Bishops.
35-37. 39 43-46. 51. 125 126. 129.
137. 147-167.
Comray r Cumbra.
Cone. Monsieur 199. 412
Conference at Worcester House. iii. 485
Confession of Faith. in 1560. 124.
Confession of Faith. r Covenant. (The
National.)
Confession of Faith. The Westminster.
ii. 232. 242. 248. 266. 272. 306. 325.
326. 328. 336 344. 348. 349. 368. 397.
400. 401. 403-6. 411. 415. et passim.
iii 2. 11. 20
Conservators of Peace. ii 57-60. 65. 78.
Constable of Dundee, r. Scrimgeour
Constable of Edinburgh Castle. r. Lindsay. 194. 195.
Constable of Scotland r Errol. Earl of.
Constable of the Threve. 424
Convention of Estates. ii. 68. 80. 104.
104

INDEX OF NAMES.

Convocation, 280, 282, 303.
Conway, Lord, 259, 341, ii 99, 178
Cooper, Mr. minister, iii. 355
Cooper, Colonel, governor of Glasgow, iii 246, 259
Cooke, English secretary, 72
Coote, Couts, Cutts, Sir Charles, iii 100, 439
Cork, Earl of, 318, 322, 323, 324, 331.
Corbet, John, minister, 162, 189, 243.
Corbet, M. P. ii 80, 81, iii 7
Coronation, iii 107, 127, 128.
Cotterill, Lieut.-Col. iii 225.
Cottington, Lord, 286, 332, 333, 342, 343, 345; ii 125, 137, 139, 494, iii. 72, 88.
Cotton, John, ii. 190 240; iii 227, 237, 285, 303
Cousins, Coosins, Dr. 286, 294, ii. 148, iii 444.
Covenant, The National, 52, 62, 84, 88, 96, 97, 111, 143, 206 239-241, 247, 351, 386, ii 44, 53, 454-460, 468, et passim.
Covenant The King's, 105-107, 111, 115, 118-120, 142, 155.
Covenant, The Solemn League and, 273, ii. 90 91, 95, 98-103, 121, 132, 141, 220, 253, 261, 335, 352, 370, 371, 406-411, 436, 438; iii. 17, 25-29, 33-40, 42, 54, 66, 70-78, 83-89, 98, 108 112 113, 116, 118, 174, 196, 225, 302, 306, 308, 326, 336-340, 350, 380, 391-393, 404-408, 414, 441, 444-448, 464, 470, 453 App. 458-460 App 505-523, passim.
Cowper, James Lord. ii. 85.
Cowper, William, Bishop of Galloway, 443
Cragingelt, John, minister of Alloway, 472.
Craig, John, minister of Edinburgh, iii 527
Craig, Thomas, minister of Largs, 13, 245.
Craighall, Lord v Hope, Sir John,
Craigends v. Cunningham
Craigie v. Wallace of
Cranford, James, minister, London ii. 278-285, 303, 310-316, 333 494; iii 309.
Cranston, Lord, iii. 36,
Cranstoun Robert, minister of Scoonie, 472
Crawford and Lindsay, John, Earl of, Treasurer, ii 386, 418-422†, 424†, 443, iii 33-38, 45, 60, 64, 235, 290, 317, 320, 405 413 410 420, 421 441 443, 446, 471 4.. 466. Lindsay
VOL III

Crawford, Ludowick Earl of, 391-393; ii 56 113, 118, 119, 314
Crawford, George, minister of Kilbride, 13
Crawford, Gen.-Major, ii. 151, 195, 200, 218, 226, 229, 230, 232, 235, 501
Crawford of Kilburnie, iii 463
Crawford Thomas, iii. 543, 545.
Creich Creigh, v, Beton
Creichton, Crichton, Lord, 124
Creichton, John, minister of Paisley, 10, 12, 24, 29, 88 94, 97, 98, 104, 172; ii. 340, iii. 434, 524
Crew, Crux, John, 308, ii. 238, 281, 487, 488; iii 441
Cromwell, Colonel, ii 409
Cromwell, Henry, iii 290, 428
Cromwell, Oliver, ii 151, 153.—Major-General, 203, 209 218, 226 229-235, 244-247, 276-280, 286, 287, 294, 317, 359, 365-369, 376, 425, 501, iii 7, 16, 19, 32, 46, 51, 60, 65, 68, 97, 100-107, 112-120 125-129, 137-140, 148 160-168, 172, 178—Lord Protector, 244, 251 253, 256, 281, 289-291, 302, 305, 309, 312, 317, 324, 325, 328, 331, 333, 337, 339, 343, 347, 350, 353-362, 370, 387, 406, 412, 425, 443, 473, 456 App. 553, 567, et passim
Cromwell, Richard, Protector, iii. 397, 399, 425-431.
Crook, Andrew stationer, ii 404, iii. 306.
Crooks, William, minister of Kilmaurs, iii. 561.
Crosbie, Laird of, iii 122.
Crosbie, Sir Pierce, 318, 324.
Cross Petition, ii 59, 63, 69, 76, 78, 427†.
Crux v. Crew, Crooks.
Culen v Cologne, 3
Culpepper, Lord, iii 72, 88, 442.
Culross, Provost of, 44.
Cumberland, Duke of, v Prince Rupert.
Cumbernauld, Leinzie ii 262.
Cuming, Cummin Robert, iii 398
Cunningham of Aitket, 372, 373, 473.
Cunningham of Auchinharvie, Dr. Robert, iii 373.
Cunningham of Capington, Sir William, 14, 425.
Cunningham of Craigends, iii 420, 456.
Cunningham of Cunninghamhend, 13 14, 44 105 24, 267 352 473 iii. 136, 420, 456

INDEX OF NAMES.

Cunningham of Robertland, ii 138
Cunningham, Adam, commissar. 426
Cunningham Alexander, merchant, Craill, ii 472 474.
Cunningham, Alexander, 27, 225-228, ii 219
Cunningham Gabriel, provost of Glasgow, 230, 233, ii 5, iii 420
Cunningham, Gabriel, minister of Kilsyth, iii. 136, 142 194, 202, 456, 561.
Cunningham, James, minister of Cumnock 44, 46, 121, 166; ii 8
Cunningham, James, ii 138
Cunningham, Robert, Kinghorn, 137 144
Cunningham, Thomas, conservator, ii 163, 169, 175, 186, 200, 202, 218, 239, 265, 316, 322 327, 387, iii 71, 73, 83, 91
Cunningham, William, 62 228, ii 28 116, iii 71.
Currie, John, iii 547
Cutts v Coote.

D

Daek, Dawick, 79
Dalgleish, David, minister of Coupar, 136, 139, 154, 166, 361, 363, 371, 472, ii. 46, 47
Dalgleish, Robert, ii 92—Church-treasurer, 301
Dalgleish, William, agent for the Church 175, 387; ii 330
Dalhousie, William, Earl of, 211, ii 85, 226, 443
Dalrymple (of Stair), Sir James, regent in the College of Glasgow, ii 37. iii. 464
Dalzell, John, minister, iii. 547
Dalzell, Lord, 123, 194. 425.
Dane, Mr ii 288
Darley, Mr ii 89
Darney v. Dorney.
Darnton, Darlington, 269
Daniel, Roger, printer, iii 552
Davis of Derry, iii. 470
Davison, Dr W., ii. 392
Dearing, Deering, Edward, ii. 56
Declaration of Assembly, 1647, iii 20, of Commission 34, 37 41.
Declaration of Assembly, 1648, 57, 65 — to be subscribed by Engagers iii. 93, 95, —

Declaration by the Resolutioners, 1658 iii. 362, 386.
Declaration against Cross petition, ii 59. 63, 69, 76.
Declaration, King Charles's Large, (v. Balcanqual, 140, 208; ii 429-431.
Declaration, King James's, (by Adamson), ii. 371, 373
Declinature and Protestation by Bishops, 126, 129, 135-139, &c
Defensive Arms, 53, 81 116 188-190
Denbigh, Earl of, ii 191, 194, 241, 303
Denmark King of, 190, 191.
Denniston, Archibald, minister of Campsie iii, 142, 194, 202, 278, 313
Denwitt Thomas 327
Derby, Earl of, ii. 57, 77; iii 429.
Derry Bishop of, v Bramhall
Desborow, Disbrough, Colonel, iii 318 427. 440.
Deskford Ogilvie, Lord, 447, 448
Devert, Donavert? ii. 82
Devonish ii 137
Devonshire, Earl of, 40
Devonshire Lady, 40, 354
Dick, v. Dickson
Dick William, merchant, provost of Edinburgh, 192, 489
Dickson of Boughtrig, 472
Dickson, Alexander, ii 336, iii 210 365, 366, 405, 415.
Dickson, Dick, David minister of Irvine, Professor of Divinity in Glasgow and Edinburgh, 23, 32, 35, 42, 52, 63, 82, 86, 93, 96, 102, 106, 108, 121, 125, 127 132-136 144, 146, 149, 154, 170, 171 178-180, 200, 239 243 250 255, 359. 362-368, 373, 472, 481, 486; ii. 3-5, 8, 10, 14-18 21-24, 27, 30, 31, 37 40, 46-50, 61, 70, 75, 83-89, 94-98, 116, 155, 161, 171, 176, 179, 189, 195, 211, 229, 270, 276, 288, 295 321, 336 340, 347, 356, 360, 390, 392 397, 400, 404, 414, 415, 440 441, 472, 513, iii 9, 32, 37, 52 55, 59, 71 80, 91, 96, 108, 110, 115, 126-128, 134, 137, 140, 145 154, 168, 173, 178, 184, 188-193, 196, 200 209- 212, 215-220, 225, 248 262, 279-281, 286, 295, 303, 311 315, 321 343, 352 355, 361, 365, 402, 404 414-421, 465 468 556, 559, 563 passim.
Dickson, John, ii 207 212 219, 231,

INDEX OF NAMES.

Dickson John, minister of Rutherglen, in 314, 447 467
Dickson, Margaret, ii 398, iii 405 415.
Digby, Lord, 257 302, 307, 308, 325, 340, ii 42, 125, 132, 133, 137, 139 244, 278-285, 288, 303, 319, 320, 323 487-498
Digby, Sir Kenelm, 295.
Dillon, Lord, 327, 331.
Diodati, John, ii 188, 229, 251, 271.
Directory, ii 117, 148, 162, 187, 195, 204, 213, 224, 232, 240, 242, 244, 248 250, 261, 291, 377, 398, iii. 1, 11
Discipline, Books of, iii. 94
Dishington Sir Thomas, 377, ii 243.
Doctor or Teacher, his office, ii 110
Don, John, iii 481
Donald, David, (Baillie's nephew.) iii 91
Donaldson, Thomas minister of Smailholme iii 547
Doohttle, Thomas, minister London, iii 553.
Dorney, Major, iii 349, 361.
Dorpe, Admiral ii 328, 347
Dorset Earl of, 352, ii. 497
Douglasses 70, iii. 387.
Douglas, Marquis of, 65, 70, 71 194 196, 201, ii 314, iii 248, 249.
Douglas Sir Archibald, 261
Douglas, Sir Joseph, iii. 66, (9), 71 83, 458, App
Douglas Sir Robert, ii. 319
Douglas of Cavers, Sir William, sheriff of Teviotdale, 123 136, 147, 216, 224 269 397, 425
Douglas, Colonel, iii. 457 App
Douglas, Dr John 425
Douglas, John iii 547, 548
Douglas, Robert minister of Kirkaldy 85, 136 172 —of Edinburgh 480, ii 45-55, 69 84, 88, 96, 102, 128 161, 186, 255, 331, 427† 444, 446, 482-487, 500, 512-516, iii. 6, 20, 33, 37 52, 62, 80 82 88-99, 105, 109 115, 118, 120-128, 133 136, 137, 140-147, 153-155, 165-170, 174, 178, 179, 198, 215-227, 248, 253, 262 276, 279, 281, 295, 296, 307, 315, 334, 335, 343 352, 355 361, 365, 375, 387, 389, 392 395, 398, 414, 415, 420, 431, 448, 465, 468 485, 492 App 512, 522 544, 545, 556-560, et passim
Douglas
Douglas,

Douglas William, minister of Forgue, 492, professor in Aberdeen iii 279, 402
Doune Lord, 51, 458, 462
Dowgaire r Dugar
Downie, William, clerk iii 249
Downing, Dr. 286
Drelingcourt Drillingcourt ii 197
Drumlanriek Lord, 124
Drummond, Lord 124, 247, 262, ii 233 468, 469,
Drummond of Riccarton, Sir William 266 269, 384, 397
Drummond, Sir John, ii. 223, 262
Drummond Sir Patrick conservator 71 87, 88, ii. 169, iii. 457, 458.
Duchal, Dughall, i. Porterfield
Dudhope, James Viscount of, ii 47 49 85, iii 117, c Scrimgeour, Dundee
Duffus Lord, ii. 50.
Dugar, John, (a M Grigor) 193 222
Du Haro iii 439
Dumbarton Castle, 194, 195, 258, iii 171, 249 259 361
Dumbarton, provost of, iii. 420 456.
Dumblane, Bishop of, r Bellenden Wedderburne,
Dumfries iii 118-120
Dumfries Earl of, 16, 123 166, 193, 386, 425, 440, 447, ii 164, iii 366
Dun i. Erskin.
Dunbar of Grange 472
Dunbar, George, minister of An, 62
Dunbar, William 465
Dunbar, iii 102, 106, 111 114 117, 132 484, 521
Dundas of Arniston, Sir James, iii. 382, 391
Dundas of Duddingston, George, ii 217 iii. 122, 125, 128
Dundas of Dundas 137, iii. 174 —younger, 430.
Dundee, Constable of i Dudhope
Dundee, James Earl of, iii. 443 r. Dudhope.
Dundee, 70 150, 205, ii 233, 264, 418, iii. 35 117, 248, 250, 280, 443
Dundee, Town-Clerk of, r. Wedderburne
Dunfermline, Charles Earl of, 205, 215 216, 359, 269, 272, 377 380 383 397, ii. 45-54, 67, 68, 85 476, iii 95
Dunglass, 207 258, ii. 440

INDEX OF NAMES

Dunlop of Garnkirk, John, iii 136.
Dunlop, Alexander, minister of Ardrossan, 13, 245, 473.—Paisley, iii. 200, 245, 276, 435.
Duppa, Dr, iii 444
Dunse, Dunce, 214, 239, ii. 438, 440, 442 —Castle, 212, 215, 258.—Hill or Law 175, 210, 211, 216, ii. 438, 460.— Pacification, 222, 223, 263.
Durham, James, minister of Glasgow 334; iii. 97, 110, 114, 123, 126, 143, 145-159, 162, 165-168, 171, 177, 179, 181-185, 189, 197, 201, 203, 222, 236-240, 249, 277-281, 296, 297, 311-314, 357, 363, 373, 376, 383, 403, 559, 560.
Durham, Patrick, dean of Ross, 426
Durham, Bishop of, 263
Durie e. Gibson.
Durie, John, minister Edinburgh, iii. 556
Dury, Durie, John, 9, 117, 358, 364, 376, ii. 166, 342.
Dysart, provost of, 360.

E

EARLE, MR ii 492
Eccles, Hew, minister iii. 420, 561
Eccles, William, of Kildonan, minister of Ayr iii 368, 393, 436, 456
Edinburgh, 18, 37, 46, 155, 170, 220, ii. 275, 314, 345, 399, 435-438; iii. 18, 35, 52, 62, 64, 98, 120, 130, 249, 319, et passim.
—Bishop of, e Forbes, Lindsay, Wisheart.
—Castle, 74-82, 160, 194, 195, 202, 219, 220, 224, 247, 258, 290; ii 435, 443; iii. 125, 128, 356, 367.
—Magistrates and Council, iii 55, 56, 66.
—Ministers, 149, 150; ii. 171; iii. 56, 90, 174, 215, 248, 254, 280, 463 et passim.
—Presbytery, iii. 174, 305, 317, 410.
—University, iii. 96, 244, 365, 456.
Edwards, Thomas, ii 190, 193, 201, 215, 251, 279, 352, 358, 416, iii. 302.
Eglintoun, Alexander, Earl of, 13, 88, 104, 106, 120, 123, 134, 147, 170, 201, 211, 214, 235, 238, 257, 266, 286, 289, 365, 489, ii. 3, 6, 8, 11, 18, 27-30, 37, 45, 49, 72, 85, 93, 174, 204, 209, 219, 299, 369, 445-449; iii. 35, 36, 48, 136, 139, 145 ...

Eghntoun Hew, minister of Dunlop, 13, 244, 473
Eghonby, (Aghonby) Dr, ii 40.
Exxxx Baxxxxx, iii. 87.
Elcho, Alexander Lord, 124, 137, ii 45, 47, 85, 225, 227, 262, 418†, 420†, 421, 472
Elders, 133, 135, 137, ii. 110, 115, 116, 120, 175, 478
Elliot, Robert, minister of Linton, 132
Elliot, Dr James, minister of Edinburgh, 78, 108, 150, 426
Elphinston, Lord, 381, 458, 462
Elphinston Master of, 425
Elphinston, David, minister of Dumbarton, iii. 136, 182, 456.
Elphinstone, Sir George, 107
Elphinstone, Sir W Justice-Generall, 106, 123, 220, 397, 448, 458, 462.
Elphinstone, William, Bishop of Aberdeen, 109; iii. 402.
Embassy Dutch, 288, 294; ii 113, 143, 150, 151, 154, 199; iii. 251, 359.
Embassy French, 484; ii. 113, 114, 143, 149, iii 251, 359.
Embassy Portuguese, iii 251
Embassy Spanish, iii. 251
Emperour L', ii. 265, 277, 311, iii. 24.
Engagement, Engagers, 1648, iii 54, 57, 59, 63, 92, 95.
English, Robert, ii. 158
Ennerteil, Innerteil, Lord, e Erskine
Episcopacie, 155, 158, 247, 273, 280, 285, 292, 302-314, 350, 354, 356.
Erastians, Erastus, ii. 129, 199, 265, 277, 307, 311, 315, 318, 338, 360, iii. 1, 365, 371
Erpenius, Thomas, ii. 387
Erroll, Earl of, Constable, 47, 205, 368, 378, 389
Erskine, John, Lord, 124, 144, 210-212, 379, 425.
Erskine of Dun, 132, 378, 464
Erskine of Scotscraig, Arthur, 51, 570 ii. 53, 54, 473.
Erskine of Innerteil, Sir George, Lord of Session 111.
Erskine, Sir Charles, ii. 217, 241, 325, 503
Essex, Earl of, Generall, 293, 301, 304, 305, 351; ii 56, 65, 81, 99, 103, 112, 118, 126, 130-143, 149, 153, 157, 170-172, 178, 181-200, 206, 211-238, 246, 276, 401, 488, 490, 496, 499, iii. 539

INDEX OF NAMES

F

FAIRBAIRNE, iii. 174
Fairfax, Lord. ii 56, 57, 79, 81, 104, 280.
Fairfax, General, Sir Thomas, ii 139, 141, 163, 167-172, 176, 179, 181, 185, 188, 195, 201, 203, 215, 260, 278 283, 288-300, 305-309, 315-324, 356, 361-369 504, 508, 514, iii 16, 18, 46, 51, 360
Fairfoul, Forfair, Andrew, minister of North Leith, 64, 363, ii. 51, iii 20, 34, Archbishop of Glasgow, 485-487.
Fairley, James, bishop of Argyle, 6, 18, 164, 372, minister of Lasswade, ii 53 93
Falconbridge, Lord, iii. 427
Falkland, Viscount, 302, 307, 322, 323, 329, 332, ii 66
Fast, Public, 71, 78, 92 102, 111, 122, 258, 292, 294; ii. 45, 53, 60. 184, 227, 238, 313, 378, 461, iii 5 107, 127, 134, 143, 169, 190-196
Fenwick, Finnik, Colonel, iii 173
Fergus the Second, ii 314.
Fergushill, John, minister of Ochiltree, 14; ii. 144
Ferguson, Allan, minister of Strathblane, 472
Ferguson, Allan, minister of Drymen, iii 315, 561
Ferguson, David, minister of Dunfermline, iii. 335.
Ferguson, James, minister of Kilwinning, ii 161; iii 15, 56, 120, 134 140-143 168, 175, 181, 184, 199, 210, 217-222, 236, 254, 275-281. 296, 314, 317, 335, 357, 383, 394, 420, 434, 456, 471, 559, 561.
Fiennes, Nathaniel, 302; ii 126, iii. 427
Finch, Lord Keeper, 283, 286, 291, ii. 472, 473
Findaune, Land of, iii. 544
Finlater, Finlature, Earl of, 205
Fintrie *v* Graham
Fisher, minister, London, ii. 333
Fleetwood, General, iii 355, 359, 387, 396, 426-428, 440
Fleming, Lord, 106, 124, 137, 195, 210, 211, 262, 372, 379 486, ii 93, iii. 95, 420
Fleming Archibald, Commissary of Glasgow. 86, 105 ii 87 319 322 339 340 iii 420

Fleming, James, minister of Yester, ii. 46, iii 184
Fleming, Fleeming, Lady, ii. 501.
Fleming, Robert, ii 428†
Fleming, Sir William, 260; ii 322, iii.367
Fletcher, David, minister of Edinburgh, 78, 108, 150, 494.—Bishop of Argyle, iii 486.
Fletcher, James, provost of Dundee, 136 147.
Fletcher, John, advocate, iii 211, 419, 465
Fletcher, Miles, printer, iii. 537
Forbes, Lord, 107, 222
Forbes, Alexander, Master of, 204, 205, 472, 492
Forbes of Boyndlie, Alexander, tutor of Pitsligo, ii 54.
Forbes of Granard, Sir Arthur, iii 439
Forbes, Alexander, minister of Campsie, 133, 245
Forbes, Arthur, minister, iii 547
Forbes of Corse, Dr. John, professor 93, 248, 437, ii. 65, 92, 166, 313, 327
Forbes, John, preacher, 144
Forbes, Dr William, Bishop of Edinburgh, 76, 248, 431 433; iii. 400, 406
Forbes of Corse, Patrick, Bishop of Aberbeen, 425, 437, iii. 555
Forbes, Patrick, minister at Delft, ii 175, 181, 193, 201, 276, 351, 365, 378
Forbes of Craigievar, Sir William, 378
Forbes, William, minister of Fraserburgh, 492
Forbes of Rires, ii. 225.
Forbes, Bishop of Caithness, iii 486.
Forbesses 82, 262.
Foreign, Ecclesiastical matters 3, 9-12, 225-228, 247, 357, ii. 65, 115, 143, 155, 165, 179, 193, 197, 201, 239, 251, 265, 276, 311, 313, 324, 327, 342, 365, 371, 378, 387, 431-433, iii. 22-24 31, 41, 67-70, 82, 101-104, 256, 267-275, 309-311, 324, 390.
Foreign, Literary matters, 35, 224-228, ii 65, 290; iii 24, 41, 56, 69, 101. 309-311, 390
Foreign, State matters, 3, 9, 109, 190, 224, 288, 294, 311-313, 357, ii. 9, 44, 62, 81, 126, 163, 190, 192, 215, 222-228, 269, 287, 293, 308, 310, 322, 338 369 376, 380. 388 391. 405, 409, iii 10 32 50 60 256 291 294, 301, 319-324 369 371 386 424 450, 472

INDEX OF NAMES

Forrest Forret David, minister of Kilconquhar, ii 52, iii 173 178 183 187, 212.
Forrest, William, schoolmaster, iii 368
Forrester Joanna, iii 456 App.
Forrester Foster, Lord, ii, 367 456.
Forrester, Thomas, minister of Melrose 164 165.
Forsyths Forsuiths, 88
Forsyth, David, regent in College of Glasgow, ii 37 87, 289
Forsyth, Gavin, minister of Cathcart 133, ii, 87. 377
Forsyth, Henry, minister of Leinzie, iii 313
Forsyth, James, student, iii 397.
Forsyth, James, minister of Kilpatrick, 89 97 98, 137 162, 484
Forsyth, John, minister of Leinzie 133 ii 377.
Forsyth, Lieutenant-Colonel, iii 251
Forth, Earl of *c* Ruthven
Forther *e*. Pitcairne.
Foulkes alderman, ii 358, iii 17
Foules, Sir David, 321.
Fouhs, Sir William, 472
Foyer a criminal iii 394
Fraser Lord, 107, 204 492
Fraser of Philorth, 123
Fraser of Strichan 369.
Fraser, Thomas, murderer 373
Fraser Dean of the Isles, 426
Fraser, Dr iii 117
Frasers the 82, ii 262
Fuller, Thomas iii 265
Fullertoun, James minister of Beith, 13, 245 473
Fullertoun, William, minister of St. Quivox, ii 69, iii 200, 236 456
Fullertoun Colonel, ii 250
Futhie Harrie, minister ii 92
Fynes *c* Fiennes.

G

GAIRDNER, an Anabaptist, iii. 178
Galbraith John minister of Bothkenner, ii. 69, 428+; iii. 257.
Galbraith, William iii. 257
Galloway, Earl of, 123, 145, 194, 373, 384, 424 ii 468, 469 iii 95
Gallov

Galloway Sir James, 425, ii 317
Garden, Gardyne, Gearnes, ii 54
Gardner Sir Thomas, solicitor-General, 292 348, ii. 133
Garret n. 186, 238, 251.
Garthland Garfland, *c* M Douall
Garraway, Henry alderman, 343
Gask *c*. Oliphant.
Gataker, Thomas, ii 110
Gavre, John, Lord Mayor ii 400.
Gelhbrand, Samuel bookseller 357
Gerard, Sir Gilbert, ii 488
Gerard the tailor, iii. 290
Gerard, knight of the Bedchamber, iii 88
Gemmel, John minister, iii 200
Gibbs iii. 17.
Gibson, of Durie, Sir Alexander Lord of Session, 111 212. 378.
Gibson Alexander, younger of Durie 16, 84, 91, 123 129 137, 161, 256 270, 355 —Clerk of Parliament, 382 385, 396 —Lord Register, ii 68, 93, 94, iii 441
Gibson, General-Major, ii 139.
Gibson, Nancy, iii 436
Gibson of Clayslop, John iii 437.
Gibson of Leith, 62
Gibson, Harie, clerk of Glasgow, 229 246 268; ii. 12
Gilbert, Eleazar, ii. 276
Giles, Captain 338
Gillespie, George, minister of Wemyss, 90 145, 189 269, 295 303 339, 362, 365, 367, 480, ii. 5 —of Edinburgh, 47, 53 70, 76, 85-88 96-98, 100, 111 117 140, 159 161 175, 177, 199, 237 248, 250, 254, 259, 265, 273 295 321, 378, 380 385, 387, 392, 394 397, 404, 406, 414, 482, 485 499-512 516, iii 12, 20 33, 37, 44, 46 52, 68 70 91 94, 231, 326, 449 App 541, 543, 545
Gillespie Patrick minister of Kirkcaldy and Glasgow, ii. 4, 506; iii. 61, 109-112 126 131-137, 140-144, 147 150-156, 162, 167 169-171 173, 181, 186 187 193, 200-203, 213 217, 220, 221, 234 237-244, 249, 253 257, 276-288, 295-301, 312-319, 322, 327, 335 341-345 348, 356, 361-364, 383-386, 393, 396-399, 404, 407, 411, 417-422, 431-433 446-449, 474-476, 479-483, 544 547 567
407 448

INDEX OF NAMES.

Gillon, John, minister of Cavers, iii. 61
Gilmour Sir John, advocate 382, iii 465 477
Gladstanes, Dr Alexander Archdean of St. Andrews 97, 149, 151, 425,
Glamorgan, Earl of. ii 338, 347, 350
Glanderston v Mure
Glasfuird, Parish of. 237, ii. 96, 450.
Glasgow City of, 106 120, 194, 228-235, 398, ii 234, 262 314 317, 321, 323, 339, 345, 399, 405 410 417, 443-449, iii 5, 18, 52, 62, 98, 118, 122-125, 161-168 172, 249 255 319, 443.
—Assembly, 1638, 118-175
—Bishop of, e Lindsay
—College, 63 133, 171, 399, ii 7-33, 37, 39 71, iii 135 139, 146-160, 206-213, 237-244, 282, 285-287, 311-313, 364, 384-386 408 448, 452-457, 471-483.
—Council and Magistrates 106, 228-234, ii 12, 339 428+, 479 480, iii. 18, 47, 161-165, 346-350 354, 360-364 420, 433, 456
—Learned Men, iii. 402
—Ministers, 8; ii 189, 399, iii 61, 215-220 249 258, 280, 314, 383, 394 434.
—Presbytery, 104, 120, 133, iii 202-217, 245
—Synod of, iii 115, 142-144 177-190, 215 236, 245-248, 254, 259 275-278, 297 317, 352, 393, 421 431 501.
Glen, Henry, baillie, Glasgow. 106, 228 234, 246 268; ii 12.
Glen John, ii 240, 242, 285
Glencairn, William Earl of 98, 123, 205, 396, ii 5, 45, 47, 68 83, 419†, iii 35 36, 54, 57, 230, 250-255, 287, 317, 387 401, 412 413 419, 420, 430, 441, 443, 446 448 452, 455 456, 460, 461, 463 465, 468, 471, 472, 474-481 485, 487
Glendoning, William, 472, iii 507.
Glengarie, iii 250, 255
Glenham, Sir Thomas ii 215, 316, 317
Glenurchie, Laird of. iii. 255
Gloucester Duke of, Henry ii 297, iii 442 445
Glyn, serjeant, 328-332, 340, 343-347
Godfrey, Mr minister, iii 355.
Goff, Colonel, iii. 427 438
Gomarus ii 251, 290 327
Goodman 302

Goodwin, John, ii. 111, 180, 192, 279 443, iii 391, 443.
Goodwin, Thomas, ii 110, 111, 118-123 131, 140, 145 175, 190, 198, 218, 228 236, 242, 291, 296, 299, 302, 343 344 iii 391, 407, 425, 443.
Gorcum, Captain iii 90, 91
Gordon v Huntly,
Gordon Lord, 393, 425, ii 45, 234 262 321, 323.
Gordon, Lord, Lewis iii 117.
Gordon of Earlstown, William, 16, 146
Gordon of Gordonston Sir Robert 425, ii 3, 4
Gordon, Mr. ii. 303.
Gordons 70, 82; ii 263, iii. 387.
Goring, General, Lord 291; ii 43, 113, 163, 260 283-286, 291, 295, 298-300, 305, 308 315 317, 322, 328, 489, 494, 501 504.
Gorme, Gorrum, Sir Donald, 193 194 ii 74
Govan, Lieutenant William iii. 113 122 124 243, 317 447.
Govean, Robert, iii 372
Graham, James. See Montrose
Graham of Braco, ii 233
Graham of Duchray John, iii 287
Graham of Fintry, 383, ii 233
Grahame, Archibald, minister, 5, 6
Graham, George Bishop of Orkney 150, 163.
Grahame, James, iii 135
Graham, John, minister of Auchterarder ii 92
Graham, John, merchant provost of Glasgow iii 150-152, 162, 163, 171, 448.
Grallator iii 79
Grandeson, governor of Windsor ii 57
Grants, 82, ii 263.
Grant of Grant, 70, ii 234
Grant, James, 193 222
Gray of Wark, Lord, ii 81, 89
Gray, fiar of Nauchtone, 472
Gray, Colonel, ii 100 105
Gray, Andrew, minister of Glasgow iii. 258, 314
Gray, James, ii. 397
Gray John, assistant-clerk 129
Gray Robert 355
Greenhead v. Ker.
97
441

INDEX OF NAMES.

Grier[son] of Lag, Sir John, iii. 366
Grier[son] of Lag, Sir Robert, 425.
Grimstone, Harbottle, speaker in 442
Guebriant, Marischal, ii. 114.
Guild, Dr. William, minister of Aberdeen, 97, 135, 136, 172, 472, 492
Gurse, Duke of, 23
Gunn, crowner, 221
Gustavus Adolphus, iii. 301, 371.
Guthrie, Henry, minister of Stirling, 249, 254, 358, 359, 361, 369, 371, 426, ii 69, 76, 91, 94, iii. 55.
Guthrie, James, minister of Lauder, of Stirling, iii. 19, 44, 46, 55-61, 96, 111-116, 118, 123, 126, 131-137, 139 141, 143, 146, 173, 193, 213, 234, 240, 245, 253 257, 276, 279, 283, 296, 298, 301, 305, 315, 318, 322, 327. 352-356, 365, 394, 404, 446, 459, 467, !544, 545, 547, 560, 566-568
Guthrie, John, Bishop of Murray, 7, 163, 365, 366, 446.
Guthrie, John, minister. ii. 50.
Guthrie, William, minister of Fenwick, iii 53, 193 246
Guthrie, Town-Clerk of Edinburgh, ii 51.
Gwyn, 318, 319, 324, 325

H

Haak, Theodore, ii. 188, 226, iii 7, 231, 304
Hacket, Halket, Colonel ii. 419, Robert iii 111
Hacket's Regiment, ii. 419
Haddington, Earl of, 47, 64, 70, 74 77, 81, 123, 258, 424, 440, ii. 100.
Hague, Treaty at the, iii. 67-102, 458, App. 521.
Halstead, Heslet, v. Montgomery.
Halden, Major, ii. 421†, 422.
Haliburton, George, minister of Crail, 136, 153 —of Perth, ii. 47, 50,—Bishop of Dunkeld, iii 486
Haliburton, George, junior, ii 47, 50
Hall, Gilbert, minister of Kirkliston, iii. 446.
Hall, Henry, ii 110.
Hall, John, iii 362, 363
Hall, Joseph, Bishop of Norwich. 293, 303, 442
Hambden Hampden. John ii. 79

Hamilton, Marchioness, Dowager of 98
Hamilton, James, Marquis of, 7, 47, 64, 70 —Commissioner, 77, 87, 90-94, 97, 108-116, 118-144, 146, 155, 166, 171, 187, 194, 200, 220, 247, 273, 277, 292, 304, 310, 317, 337. 342, 356, 359, 381, 386, 388, 391-396, 400, 424, 437, 445, 462, 471, 475, 482-489: ii. 39, 46, 58-60, 63, 68, 72, 77, 87, 100, 119.—Duke of 124, 127, 131, 138, 163, 201, 354, 366, 378. 383, 400, 425, 429. 438, 18, 33, 35, 38, 40, 45, 47, 51, 57, 65, 249. 387, 435, 481.
Hamilton, William Duke of v. Lanerick. Earl of —(Secretary,) 98, 115, 260, iii 101, 109, 249, 435, 436, 482
Hamilton, (Selkirk) Duke of. iii 443, 456. 471, 480, 483
Hamilton, Marquis of, iii. 478.
Hamilton, Dutchess of, iii 480-483
Hamilton of Bargeny, Sir John, 425.
Hamilton of Barncleugh, ii 314.
Hamilton of Broomhill, Sir John, v. Belhaven
Hamilton, Alexander, crowner, General of Artillery, 98, 195, 203, ii 100; iii. 40
Hamilton, Alexander, minister of Monigaff, 426.
Hamilton, Archibald, Jesuit, iii 403
Hamilton, Claud, 246, 268, ii 10
Hamilton, Christian, iii 456 App
Hamilton Sir Frederick, 472.
Hamilton, Gavin, minister of Cadder, iii 437.
Hamilton, George, minister of Newburn, 449, ii. 49, iii 173.
Hamilton of Priestfield, Sir James, ii 317.
Hamilton, James, minister of Carnwethan, iii 420, 468, 485.
Hamilton, James, minister of Wigtoun, 426
Hamilton, James, 490
Hamilton, James, minister of Dumfries, 64, 146, 172, 472: ii 48, 52,—of Edinburgh 96, 386, iii 63, 80, 168, 193, 215-222, 275, 307, 308, 340, 453 465, 468, 481. 544-547, 563
Hamilton. James, dean of Glasgow, 425
Hamilton, James, minister of Blantyre, iii 314
Hamilton. John, minister of Innerkip, 104 172, ii. 547; iii 357

INDEX OF NAMES.

Hamilton of Orbiston Sir John, Justice-Clerk, 48, 64, 70, 105, 197, 390, 396, 440, 452, 458, 460-463, 487, ii 68, 437
Hamilton of Silverton Hill, Sir Robert, iii 436.
Hamilton, John, minister of Dalserf Decert iii 434
Hamilton, John ii 124
Hamilton, Mary, iii 484
Hamilton, Patrick minister, iii 60
Hamilton, Patrick, iii. 456.
Hamilton, Dr Robert, minister of Glassford, 129, 151 165, 168, 237
Hamilton, Robert minister of Lismahago 16, 65, 169, 170, 245
Hamilton, Robert, skipper, ii 385.
Hamilton, Thomas, ii. 437
Hamilton William, bailie of Linlithgow 266
Hamilton, clerk, 577
Hamilton, gentleman of the Horse, ii 437
Hamiltons, ii. 59, iii. 250
Hammond, Dr Henry, iii 400, 406, 409, 444
Hanna George, minister of Torphichen 76 425
Hanna, Dr. James, dean of Edinburgh, 6, 18, 22, 76, 78, 89, 91, 137, 150, 425
Hans, (Lauderdaill?) ii 515
Harcourt, Prince de, ii 113 143, 149 293
Harderwick, University of, iii 82
Harper, Sir John, iii. 448.
Harper Thomas, printer, iii 531
Harries v. Herries
Harrison, Major-General, ii. 200, iii 298, 358, 443
Harrison Mr 274.
Hart, Andrew, printer, iii. 556
Hartfield, Earl of, ii. 314
Hartford, Earl of, ii 56
Harvie, John, minister of New Machar, 135
Hatcher, Mr ii 89, 99, 104, 299 302, 483
Hay, Sir Henry, commissary Edinburgh, 426.
Hay, Sir John, Clerk-Register, 8, 22 23, 33, 38, 41, 44, 46, 70 75, 93, 123, 150, 220, 276, 279, 425, 440 446, 448, 452, 458, 462
Hay, John

Hay, Dr Theodore, archdeacon of Glasgow, 425
Hay, William, 384, 427
Hazlehead v Montgomery
Hegatus, Gulielmus, iii 403
Helvetian Divines, ii 431
Henderson Abram, minister of Whithorn, 426
Henderson, Alexander, minister of Leuchars, 19, 23, 35, 42, 52, 84, 85, 93, 96, 121 125, 127-132, 134-168—of Edinburgh, 175, 188, 189, 204, 216 241, 244, 249-253, 257, 269, 271 280, 285, 289, 303-305, 307, 339, 359-379, 385 394-397, 446, 449 480, 485; ii 1, 11 22, 24, 27, 30, 32, 40, 45-51, 55, 59, 66 70, 74, 76, 83-98, 102 104, 106, 110, 117, 120, 123, 128, 146, 159, 161, 172, 177, 182, 184, 198, 212, 220, 237, 253, 258, 261, 276, 279, 295-298, 323-327, 331, 342, 370-373, 378, 382, 384-389, 392, 398, 440, 447, 463, 468, 482-487, iii 3, 12, 83, 93, 227, 326, v Mackay.
Henderson, David, minister of Kilmarnis, 6.
Henderson, Col Sir John, ii 127, 150
Henderson, John, ii 266, 311.
Henderson, Lawrence, iii. 545
Henderson, Robert, minister of Lochmaben, 146
Henderson, Thomas clerk, ii 486, iii. 549
Henrietta Maria, Queen, ii 57, 63, 67, 73 77, 81, 125, 132, 151, 168, 171, 194 211, 213, 228, 244, 277, 310, 347, 350, 363; iii. 41, 416, 444-446
Henrietta, Princess, iii. 446
Hepburn of Humbie, Adam, ii 89, 100, 213, 216, 218, 383
Hepburn of Wauchton 136, 269, 397
Herbert, Lord, 11, 310
Herbert, Attorney-General, 292.
Herbertson, John, ii. 289, iii 213, 241, 437.
Hereford, Marquis. ii 317
Heriot, John, minister of Blantyre, iii 314
Heriot, Lieutenant-Colonel, iii. 251.
Herle, Charles, ii 118, 140, 201, 236, 404, 415
Herries, Lord, 81, 193

INDEX OF NAMES.

Hesse, Landgrave of. 3.
Heylin, Dr. 226 286; iii 400, 406, 444
Hibbets, Lady. 330 331
Hibbets, Thomas, 331
Hickes, John. iii. 553.
Hiegat, Janet. iii. 435.
Highlanders, 196, 211, 212 221; iii 6, 18, 117 — c Clandonald Dugar
Hill. Thomas, ii. 220
Hill. Willie, iii 477.
Hinnyman c Honyman
Hobbes Hopes. Thomas ii. 388 395
Hodancourt, ii 114.
Hodger. Hodzeard. Robert iii 286, 287.
Hog John minister of Larbert. iii. 257.
Holborn Hobourne, General-Major ii. 206, 421 422, iii. 38 40 45.
Holland. Admiral of. 198
Holland. Earl of 204, 210, 306 341; ii 99, 135, 178, 439
Hollis Denzil. ii 63, 141 155 303, 311 489, iii 16, 19, 441.
Holmes. Major. iii. 439.
Home Earl of 50, 123 219, 224; ii. 468, 469
Home of Aytoun, William, 472
Home of Wedderburn, 147
Home, Colonel ii 419 421, 422
Home, Lieutenant-Colonel Alexander iii 457 App
Home Abraham, minister, ii 502
Home, John, minister. ii. 86, iii. 561.
Home, Robert, minister iii 547.
Home, Robert, minister of Crawford-John. iii 187, 247 394.
Home, William, minister, iii 142.
Home, William, baillie, 235, iii 139
Home. William. iii 435
Homes, 392.
Homes Dr ii 111 180
Honorius Reggius c Hornius
Honyman, Hinnyman, Andrew, minister. St. Fillan's, 370, ii. St Andrew's 49 iii 176, 178, 183 187, 201, 212
Hooker, Thomas, ii 239, iii 303 306 375, 387
Hope of Hopton. Sir James iii 114 249
Hope of Craighall, Sir John 111, 378; iii 37, 249 547
Hope. Sir Thomas, Lord Advocate, 11, 40, 50 65 75, 107, 111, 125, 212, 256, 381, 390, ... 473 .

Hope of Kerse. Sir Thomas, 384, 385 397, ii 59.
Hopkins, John, iii 526
Hopton. General Lord, ii 57 113, 118, 126 131 133, 151 154-156, 158, 181, 206, 213 215, 260 283 305, 308, 351, 356, 361.
Horne Gustave Swedish officer, ii 9.
Hornius Georgius (Honorius Reggius) iii. 9.
Hotham, Sir John ii. 43, 56, 79.
Houstoune, James minister of Glassford. ii 96
Houston of Houston, iii 136.
Houston of Houston younger, iii. 420, 456
Howard. Lord, 72, 260, 393; iii. 367, 427
Howard Mr ii 490, 495 498
Howie Dr. Robert provost of the New College, St. Andrews, 97, 361, 425
Hoy, Mr., 331.
Hoyle, Dr. Joshua, minister, ii. 102.
Hudson. ii. 375
Huit (Hewitt) ii. 175
Humbie c. Hepburn,
Hume c. Home
Hunter of Hunterstoun 13
Huntly. Marquis of 63, 70, 81, 97, 107, 188, 192-197, 205, 222, 393, 465 ii. 74, 92, 164, 172, 176, 181, iii. 87, 249, 466
Hurrie, Sir John, Colonel, ii. 56 79 127, 141, 238, 264, 275, 417†-419†.
Hutcheson George, minister of Calmonell afterwards of Edinburgh, ii 69.; iii 56, 61 114 149, 173, 194 210 234, 281 335, 354, 387, 408, 414, 415, 420 461 465 468, 546.
Hutcheson James minister, 133.
Hyde Lord Clarendon. ii. 66, 244 398, iii 72 88, 387 409, 414, 437, 439, 442, 445, 460 464, 468 471, 485, 486.
Hyde, Anne Duchess of York, iii. 445

I

Incheqtin. Earl of. ii. 214 222 233, 347, iii. 567.
Independents. 287 311; ii. 110, 117, 120-123, 128-131, 136-140, 143-149 157, ...

INDEX OF NAMES. 611

Independents, v Accommodation. Apologetical Narration Remonstrance Toleration.
Inglis of Ingliston, Major, ii 422†.
Inglis, Archibald, minister, iii 247
Inglis, Anna, 372.
Inglis, James, minister of Dailly iii 561
Inglis, Robert, minister, iii. 561.
Ingoldsby, Colonel, iii 427
Ingram Sir Arthur, 333
Innerteil, Ennerteil, v Erskine.
Innes, of Balvenie, Sir Robert, 425
Innes of Innes, Robert, 385, 492.
Innes, Major. iii. 36, 95
Innes, ii 141
Innes, James, iii 553.
Inneses, 82.
Ireton, Henry, iii 443
Irvine, James Earl of. 193; ii 52, 281
Irvine. Provost of, iii. 420, 456. v. Barclay.
Irvines Irwynes, 82.
Isles, Bishop of, v. Campbell 425.

J

Jack, Jacheus, Thomas, iii. 403
Jack William, iii. 246
Jackson 8
Jacobus, ii 213.
Jaffray, Alexander, provost of Aberdeen. iii 120 447, 507 568
James VI 2, 42, 129, 298, 322, 328, 443, ii. 371, 373, 515, iii 128 459 529-531, 556
Jamieson, Baillie, ii. 322, 378 ; iii 70, 105-108. 137, 167.
Jamieson v Waugh
Jamieson, Alexander minister of Govan. 365, 397.
Jamieson, John minister of Eccles in 284.
Jamieson, William, minister of Swinton, ii 84 ; iii 182, 279.
Jausie v Joussie
Jenkins, Jonkyn, David, merchant 31
Jermyn, Germane Henry (Earl of Bury,) ii. 125, 139, 494, iii 117 445
Johnston, Lord, 110, 123 147, 166, 472, ii. 322 468, 469
Johnstone, Archibald, afterwards Sir Archd 13 and Lord Warriston 14 34, 48 ... 216, 2.. .

280, 285, 289, 304 356-378 passim. 384 394, 396, 464, 480, 485, 492, ii 11, 22, 26-32 41, 43, 46, 59 65 68 75, 77, 83-97 106, 128, 140, 172, 176, 178, 187, 217, 220, 237, 251, 281, 297, 323, 325, 345 357, 368, 403, 406, 427†, 440, 450-460, 474, 478, 483, 488-498 506, 512 516, iii 6, 18, 33, 35 46, 53-64, 88, 91, 99, 102, 111-120, 129, 136, 173, 164, 194, 213, 234, 240 245 249, 279, 283, 296-301, 305, 315, 318 322, 335-341, 348, 352, 356, 359, 361 396, 404, 430 433, 447, 522, 547, 566
Johnstone, Lady, of Warriston, ii 512, iii 64
Johnston, Lieutenant-Colonel, iii 457 Ap.
Johnston, John, Glasgow. ii 349, iii. 443
Johnston, Dr Robert, historian, ii 9
Johnstons, 392.
Jones Captain ii 235—Col. 382, iii 100.
Jortein, ii 183
Joussie, John baillie, iii. 389.
Joyce, Captain, iii 290
Judge-Advocat, ii. 136, 510.
Judges, English, iii 205 208-212, 238
Juxon, Dr. William, Bishop of London 7, 293, 341, 438, ii. 474, iii. 444

K

Keir Andrew, minister of Linlithgow, 369.
Keir v. Stirling
Keith, William iii. 526, 527
Kelly, Earl of, 77, ii 64
Kelly Edward, 435.
Kenmure, Viscount, 16, 82, iii. 36, 95, 250, 367, 430, 462
Kenmure, Lady, iii. 467.
Kennedy, Lady Margaret, iii 235, 407
Kennedy, Hugh, 269 ; ii 217, 273, 279, 295, 299, 325, 382, 488-498, iii 136.
Kennedy Lord, 90
Kent, Earl of, ii. 133
Ker, Henry Lord 391, ii 64, 435, 436.
Ker Lieutenant-Colonel Andrew, iii 457 App
Ker, Andrew, clerk of Assembly, ii 280, 330, 374, 384, 386, iii 60, 137, 145, 153-157, 167-170, 188, 417 521, 563
Ker Andrew of Kirkton, iii 60, 317, 393

INDEX OF NAMES.

Ker, James, iii. 398
Ker, John minister of Prestonpans 23, 91 127, 472.
Ker, Robert, minister of Haddington, iii 55 136, 182, 188, 210, 214, 218, 277, 296, 335
Ker of Greenhead, Sir William, iii 327, 348
Ker, Sir William Director of Chancery, iii 443
Kerrs, 292
Kerse v. Hope.
Kid, Francis, (Peter) minister of Douglas, iii 247, 248
Kilburnie v Crawford of
Kildonnan, Kildonel v Eccles
Kilmahew, v. Naper
Kilmallock, Lord, 325
Kilmaurs, Lord, iii. 360
Kilpont, Lord. ii 225, 233, 262
Kilsyth. Battle of, ii 420-423; iii 255
Kilsyth v Livingston
Kilwinning, ii 443-449, iii. 9, 120
Kincaid, Kinkaid, George, minister, ii 52
King, General, Lord Ythan. 269, ii 57, 112, 201 203, 204.
King, Sir Robert, 341
Kinghorne, Earl of, 123, 145, 205, 375, 378, 424, 448, 458 462, ii 468
Kingston, Lord ii 178
Kinneir, Alexander, parson of Whitsom, 426
Kinnoul Earl of, 77, 206, 424, ii 67, 71, 141, 233, iii 251, 431
Kirkaldy, Thomas, minister, iii 144, 317, 361.
Kirkcudbright Lord 211 425, ii 468, 469, iii 54
Knave i Nevay
Knight, Col iii 438
Knightley, Mr. iii. 539
Knighton, , iii 441
Knowalls, Francis, 164
Knowes, Christopher, 164
Knox, John, the reformer, iii 12
Knox, Robert, minister of Kelso ii 52, iii. 62 182, 214, 253, 279
Knox, Major, iii 457 App.

L

LAMB, Andrew, Bishop of Galloway, 8
Lamb, Thomas, minister, 367, 383
Lambert General, iii 47, 49, 51, 124, 171, 290, 354-361, 396, 407, 412, 427-30, 438-441, 446, 471.
Lamington v Bailhe of
Lammie. Mrs iii 197, 325, 332
Lamont of Lamont, younger, 425
Lamonts, iii 465
Lane, Mr the Prince's attorney, 348
Lanerick, William Earl of, 260-263, 276, 386, 394, ii 41, 58, 66-69, 72, 76, 83, 124, 132, 138, 234, 353-356, 386, 480 506, iii 15, 17, 33-37, 46, 73, 81 e Hamilton, William, Duke of
Lang, James, minister, 87
Langdale, Sir Marmaduke, ii 260, 323; iii 47, 49, 567
Langham, Alderman, ii 400
Langton v Cockburn
Lathrisk, Laird of, ii. 473.
Laud, Dr William Archbishop of Canterbury, 2, 4, 7, 22 32-34, 44, 48 65, 71, 73, 77, 94, 97, 102, 105, 111, 116, 119, 140 152, 161, 176, 208, 248, 274-280, 283-287, 291, 295 300, 303, 305, 309, 318, 320 345, 422, 428-440, 475, ii 23, 40, 139, 208, 430-435, 472-475
Lauderdall, John first Earl of, 40, 50 123, 126, 129, 425 452, 456, 458, 462, 480, ii 45-47, 85 94, 263, 437, 495.
Lauderdall, John Lord Maitland Earl 379 389, ii 45, 50, 55, 65, 85, 88, 91 95-98, 106, 134, 146, 237, 241, 279 288, 293-298, 302, 330, 352, 396 463 428+, 473, 482, 485, 503, 505 516, iii 22, 33-36, 45, 52, 64, 73, 81 91 93, 95, 101, 105, 117, 136, 138, 147, 154, 166, 170-172, 230, 249, 265, 290, 317, 326, 401, 405, 410-423, 439-448, 453, 457-464, 468, 474, 476 483-486
Laudian, Mr chaplain, 77
Laurence, iii 187
Laurentius, Blazius, regent iii 403
Laurie, James, 355.
Laurie, Joseph, minister of Perth, 148
Laurie, Lowrie, Robert. minister of Edinburgh, iii 34, 95, 179, 181-184, 189, 403 546 554 555

INDEX OF NAMES. 613

Law, John, minister of Campsie, iii 314
Law Mungo minister of Dysart 370—
  of Edinburgh, ii 52, iii. 61, 91 136,
  153 218-220, 545-548 563
Law, Robert, minister of Kilpatrick iii
  186, 304
Lawenburgh, Lovingburgh, General, ii 9,
  44
Lawers e Campbell, 147; ii 226, 264,
Layng David minister, iii 547, 548
Learmont of Balcolmie Lord of Session,
  361 iii 317, 368,
Learmonth, Andrew minister of Liberton,
  76, 97, 430
Leckie of that Ilk 249-254 358, 371,
Lee Mr ii 393
Lee e Lockhart
Legg Mr. ii 392
Legge, Colonel William, ii 317 468, 494
Leicester Earl of, 343,
Leighton, Dr. Alexander 273
Leighton, Robert, (afterwards Bishop,) iii
  244, 258, 305, 483
Leitch David, minister of Dundre man
  426
Leitch David, minister of Ellon, iii 554
Lekpreuik Robert, printer, iii. 526
Lennox, Duke of, (Richmond) 7, 11, 14
  17, 21 33 47 64, 70, 74, 105, 315
  365 387, 393-396 424, 445, 469, ii
  29 244 247, 249, 250 316 383 497,
  iii. 249, 387
Lenthall Sir John iii 367—Speaker, iii.
  427
Leslie Field-Marshall Alexander, Earl of
  Leven, 100 111, 191, 194-197 203 207,
  212-215, 222, 247 256-263, 355 385,
  388, 392; ii 100 155 172 176, 179,
  195, 203, 227, 261, 264, 438 440-443,
  470 471, iii 40 45 367
Leslie General David Lord Newark, ii
  185, 204 209 218, 309, 315 321 423+
  509; iii 6, 10 18, 36, 38 40, 45 90
  111, 118, 120, 132 200 430
Leslie General-Major ii. 422, 422+,
Leslie of Newton, Sir John 123, 168 361,
Leslie Colonel 256,
Leslie George, minister, iii 544, 547,
Lesley Dr Henry, bishop of Down, 89
  243, 332 463
Lesley, Dr John bishop of Raphoe 463
  464 ii
Leslie, Pa
iii 61,

Leslie, Robin, King's page, 215
Leven Earl of, e Leslie,
Levingston e Livingston
Leviston, Mr 77
Leys e Burnet, of 491
Libbertoun e Winram
Lightfoot Dr. John iii 536
Lilburne, Colonel John, ii 333, iii 32 244
  290 567,
Lincoln, Bishop of e Williams
Lindesay Earl of 315, 316, ii 56
Lindores, Lord, 373
Lindores, Lady, ii. 472, 473
Lindsay Lord, 44, 50 70 79, 123 150,
  173, 195 211, 256, 260 306, 395 464,
  472, 491; ii 41, 58, 83 85, 89, 204
  209, 226, 263, 303—Earl of Crawford
  and Lindsay, 386—Thesaurer 418+-
  422+, 424+ 443, iii 33-36, 45, 60, 64
  117 235 249 290, 317 326, 405 413
  416, 420 441 443 446 471 485 466
Lindsay of Belstane, constable of Edinburgh Castle, 203, 383, 385,
Lindsay Sir Jerome, commissary 426
Lindsay Alexander, Bishop of Dunkeld
  153 165, 425
Lindsay, David, Bishop of Edinburgh, 4,
  16, 18 22, 41 78, 87, 160 425, 432,
  442 445, 448, 452 462, 474
Lindsay David minister of Belhelvie, 97,
  135, 146, 148 170, 253 300, 303, 308,
  492, ii 84
Lindsay, George, 426
Lindsay John minister of Carluke, 169,
Lindsay, John minister of Carstairs, 29
  65, 169, 245, 426
Lindsay Patrick, Bishop of Glasgow, 7,
  11, 17-22 108, 156, 168, 288, 424 440
  447 448 462, 481 ii 213
Lindsay, Roger, ii 93
Lindsay, William minister, 473,
Linlithgow, Earl of, 77 123 206 212,
  424, iii. 95 430, 486
Linlithgow, Provost of iii 456
Linton Lord 124 ii 78
Little, secretary to the Earl of Strafford,
  332
Littleton, Lord Keeper, 292 301, 315
Liturgy e Service-book
Liturgy, English, 273, ii 221
Littletour, (Littlejohn?) John, minister of

Livingstone, Mr 250
Livingstone, John minister of Stranraer 64, 146, 250, 252, ii 48, 94, iii 55, 59,—of Ancrum 61, 91-97, 113, 173 194, 243 253 279-284, 298, 301, 315, 321 327, 434, 547, 567
Livingstone, Robert, factor to Lord Montgomery, 246-263, 268: ii 6.
Livingstone, William, iii. 558
Livingstone, William, minister of Lanark. 39, 83-85, 121, 125, 129, 136 169 245
Lochaber, Laird of, ni 255
Lockhart of Lee, Sir James, iii 35, 36 401, 446
Lockhart of Lee younger, 425
Lockhart, Allan, 573.
Lockhart, George, commissary of Glasgow, rector of the College, iii. 148, 150 156, 212, 238-243, 246, 341, 357, 361.
Lockhart, Robert, iii 115
Lockhart Colonel Sir William, iii. 249, 259, 288, 290, 318, 357, 359, 401, 446
Lockyer, Nicholas, iii. 177, 214, 354, 401, 407, 443
Loftus, Lord Chancellor of Ireland 273. 325-327, 337.
Logan, James, minister of Smailham 426
Logie, Andrew, minister of Rayne 376, ii. 92
London, Bishop of, iii. 445, v. Juxon
London, Elders, ii 388, 403.—Ministers, ii 367, 377, 411, iii. 553
London, Petition against Episcopacy, 280, 286, 292, 302 307.—Petition for Presbyteries and Sessions, ii. 327 336, 366 —Petition for Peace, ii. 412, 416 — Remonstrance, ii 370 372.
London, Synod or Province, iii. 1, 307.
Long Mr. iii. 88.
Loraine, Duke of, ii. 301, 388.
Lorne, Archibald Lord, (Marquis of Argile) 16, 40, 44, 50, 64, 69 80, 82, 92, 100 107, 425, 447, 456, 458, 462, 465
Lorne, Archibald Lord, iii. 250, 251, 255, 256 288, 367, 430, 447, 465.
Lothian, Earl of, 115, 123, 220, 248, 257, 374, 378 ; ii 105, 115, 124 163, 262, 417†, iii 35, 54, 98, 99, 106, 119, 365, 443, 507.
Loudoun, John Earl of, 35, 38, 44-46, 52, 79, 80, 86, 91, 95, 103, 106 108 123, 125 127 130, 134 136, 141 143 147 171, 255, 269, 271, 280, 304, 362, 377, 380, 384, 387,—Chancellor, 390, 396, 455 464 473, 480 486, ii 5, 24, 39-43, 46, 55, 57, 59, 65, 69, 71, 85, 102, 217, 227, 237, 287, 292-297, 302, 323-326 357, 368, 370, 386, 402, 407, 414, 419†, 424, 440, 447, 449, 476, 484, 487-498, 515, iii 7, 15, 17, 33-38, 53, 69, 72, 83, 93, 99, 106, 112, 119, 126, 128 136, 139, 167, 249 283, 430, 432, 443, 522, 524.
Loudoun, Countess of, ii 319.
Lour, Lord, ii 468, iii 54, v Carnegie
Lour Master of ii. 468.
Love, Christopher, minister. London iii 105, 108, 335.
Lovelace, Lord, ii 99, 135, 136, 317.
Lowrie v Laurie
Lumsden, Major. ii. 128, 154, 204.
Lumsden, Sir James, ii 386, 514, iii 430.
Lucas, Sir Thomas, 342
Ludlow, Colonel, iii 441, 445
Lundie, John, professor, Aberdeen, 135, 169.
Lundie, Thomas, minister of Rattray, iii 547, 548.
Luss v Colquhoun
Lyle, Lisle, Lord, ii. 347 ; iii 16
Lyon King-at-Arms, iii. 472, 480
Lyon of Auldbar, James 44 53, 123, 137, 147, 159, 360

M

MACALEN, M'Kullamore v. Argyle.
Macalpine, D. minister, iii. 561.
Macaulay of Ardincaple, 195
Macconochie, iii. 465
Maccovius, ii 371.
Macdonald, Alexander, ii 73, 217, 233, 262, 321, 323, 338 499 514, iii 6.
Macdonald, Colkittoch ii 74 217, 499.
Macdonalds 82, iii 465.
Macdonald, of Slait, Sir Donald, 425
Macdougall of Garthland, Sir John 425, iii 354, 430
Macghie of Large, Sir Patrick, 257.
Macgie, Thomas, writer, 373-384
Macgilhnorish, Donald, minister of Inverary 426
M——— M—— —— of Mous-

INDEX OF NAMES

Macintoshes 82.
Mackaill v Mackell.
Mackart, iii 100
Mackay v Reay.
Mackay, Alaster, (Alexander Henderson,) 382
Mackayes, 82
Mackell, preacher. 144
Mackell, Hugh, 104 473, minister of Edinburgh. ii 10, 23, in 56, 173, 184, 194, 210. 232, 279 296, 545-548
Mackenzie of Pluscardine. iii 113
Mackenzie of Tarbet, Sir John 123—135. 147
Mackenzie Murdoch minister of Inverness, 369, iii 486.
Mackenzie Murdoch, parson of Dingwall, 426
Mackenzie, Thomas minister of Tarbet, 135, 168, 426
Mackenzies, 82.
Maclachlan Archibald minister of Luss, iii 435
Macleans, 82, ii 74.
Macleland, John, minister of Kirkcudbright. 146, 250, 252 255, ii 48, 92, 94; iii 55, 97
Macleod of Herries. John, 425
Maclure Dr 387.
Macmath, John, minister. 164
Macward, Macquard, Robert minister of Glasgow, iii. 240 241 285. 314. 326, 368, 397 399, 404 467
Maderty. Lord ii 233.
Magnus. Maine. v Mayne.
Mainwaring. Mannering. Dr. 282 286.
Malach, Alexander. ii 508 512
Malach, John. ii 508
Malcolme, John. ii 472.
Maitland, Charles, of Halton, iii 416
Maitland, John parson of Eddilston, 426
Maitland Captain, ii 422†
Manchester. Earl of. ii 83, 103, 112, 126 130, 133, 139 142, 148, 151-154, 158, 166-172, 176-181, 185, 188, 193 201-204, 209, 216. 224, 227-238, 244 247, 359, 487 501, iii 359 442
Mandeville Lord. 260, 290, 293, 295, 304.
Manton. Dr Thomas, iii 355. 442. 484, 553.
Mar, Earl of. 77, 123. 145 195, 354, 378, ii. 468
Marczu- 311,

Marischall, George Earl (1593), iii 402
Marischall, Earl, 96, 203, 207, 221-224. 260, 378, 384, 424, ii 74, 85, 164 234 261-264, 418†, 442. 468 470, iii 249, 317, 443, 466.
Marshall Marschell, Robert, iii 165, 171
Marshall. Stephen, minister. London, ii 81, 89, 97, 104 110, 118, 121-123 134 140, 145, 148 165, 184, 198, 220, 230 235, 260, 304. 343, 415, iii 17, 302, 306 326.
Martin, regent. iii. 316.
Martin, Dr. George, 97. 425
Martin, James, minister of Peterhead. 146 492
Martin, Robert, minister of Ettrick 472
Mary. Queen of Scots 51
Mason. George, burgess of Ayr, 472
Massie, General, ii 226 291, 300, 308 317, iii 16 101, 107, 134. 137 155 426, 431
Mauchlin, iii. 48 53
Maurice, Prince. ii. 114, 151, 181 193. 206, 213 215, 244, 268 272, 278, 287. 324, 504.
Maxwell of Pollock. Sir George, iii 54 112, 243, 246 276 322, 351, 373 433. 446, 448.
Maxwell of Pollock, Sir John 37, 425
Maxwell Gabriel, minister of Dundonald 97, ii 69, iii 53 112 144, 296
Maxwell, James. 213; iii. 328 382
Maxwell. James, keeper of the black rod 272 286, 296, 316.
Maxwell, John, minister of Glasgow 13 19, 29. 63, 106, 122, 133, 228, 426
Maxwell. John Bishop of Ross 4-8, 16, 22 31 65, 70-78 93, 97 112, 135 138. 148, 150, 156, 161, 208, 241, 294 428-430, 434, 436-440, 447 452 464 ii. 116, 125, 207, 221, 373, 377, 474
Maxwell. Patrick, 162, 288
Maxwell, Robert. 561.
Maxwell, William, minister of Dunbar. 150. 164.
Maxwell William, minister of Stow, 426.
Mayerne, Sir Theodore. M D. ii 213
Maynard, Serjeant, 319-325, 330-335 342-344
Mayne, Magnus. Dr. Robert, iii 603, ii. 8. 14. 72.
M

INDEX OF NAMES.

Meade, Matthew iii 553.
Meath, Bishop of, 332.
Meldrum, Sir John ii 126. 152 156, 158, 167, 191, 224
Meldrum Robert, 150 190 355 398, ii. 81, 90, 99 103, 104 127
Melos General ii 44
Melville, Mr. iii 275
Melville, Andrew, 361, iii 402
Melville, Ephraim, minister of Linlithgow, iii. 487.
Melville, Thomas minister of Cadder iii 195
Menzies Major ii 422
Menzies John professor Aberdeen iii 243, 282. 364, 568
Menzies William, minister of Kenmure, 147, 472.
Meredith, Sir Robert 331
Mernes D (John) minister of Carnbee ii 53
Merrick, ii 227.
Middlesex, Earl of, iii 539
Middleton, Countess of, iii 485
Middleton John, Earl of ii 112 118. 213 222-224, 227 309 345, 363 512 515, iii 40, 45 48, 95, 105 117, 120, 126 251 255, 409, 421 443, 447, 455, 463, 465, 469 471, 485 457 App. 567
Mildmay Sir Harie ii. 492, iii. 471
Milton, John, the poet, 366, ii. 499; iii. 443
Mitchell, David, minister of Edinburgh, 16 78 89 108, 137, 148, 425, 463 473, 474, iii. 488
Mitchell James 13 246 268, 287, ii 219 380, 392.—his Son 219.
Mitchell, Thomas, minister of Turreff. 146 492
Mitchellson, Dr. John minister of Bruntisland 425.
Moffat-well, iii. 373.
Monck, General George iii. 251-255, 259, 276, 281, 295, 305, 317, 398, 428, 430 438-442 —Duke of Albemarle, 444, 446, 465, 563
Monck Nicholas, Provost of Eton, iii 401
Moncreiffof Moncreiff, Sir John, iii 54 567.
Moncreiff, Alexander, minister of Scoony iii. 446
Moncreiff, John, minister, iii 547
Monro David regent in the College of Gla.

Monro Dr David, parson of Kinnuchar, 6 94, 97, 425
Monro George iii. 100, 255
Monro George, (Chancellor of Ross) 426.
Monro, Colonel, 192, 200, 210, 247, 260 383, ii 73, 164 224, 232, 238, 240, 264, 375 470
Montague, Colonel, ii 286, iii 426
Montague, Dr 248 282, 286, 358
Montague, Walter. 295
Monteith, Robert minister.. 164
Montgomery, Lady, 269 284, 286, 306, 353, ii 34, 35, 369, iii 119
Montgomery, Hugh Lord, 13, 28, 33 125 137, 147 178, 200 201, 214, 228, 236 244, 246, 256, 263, 268, 289, 354 379, 389 473 486 ii 3, 6, 11 18, 27, 34-37, 41 43 67, 161, 218 226 234, 322, 369, 446, iii 317, 366, 420, 430
Montgomery Master of, iii 366.
Montgomery of Hazlehead ii. 373, iii 420, 456, 464
Montgomery of Skelmorly Sir Robert 13, 170, 425
Montgomery Sir Alexander, Colonel, ii 49.
Montgomery Sir Henry, ii 219.
Montgomery, Sir James, 281, 332 337
Montgomery, Colonel Robert, ii 204, 210, 360, iii. 117 431
Montgomery, Lieut.-Colonel, ii 204, 210.
Montnorris Lord, 273, 325-333.
Montreuil French Ambassador, ii. 388.
Montrose, James Earl and Marquis of, 44, 70, 86 91, 93, 121, 123 132 136, 145 168, 170 194-197, 205-11, 220-224, 247 256, 262, 266, 374-379, 381-387, 391, 394 472, ii 35 60, 67, 73, 116, 124, 138, 141 150, 164, 172, 176, 181, 188, 196, 215-217, 225, 233, 238 244 261-264, 269, 275, 280, 297, 301 305, 309, 314-316 321-323, 343, 345, 362, 377, 399, 420, 448, 467-469, 501-514 iii 6, 31, 40, 48 72 78, 81, 86, 88, 101, 113, 196, 195, 460, 512.
Montrose, Second Marquis, iii. 394, 420, 430 443, 456, 466, 471 486.
Montrose Marchioness of, 466
Moore, Dr 325, 326
Moray, Morray, v Murray.
Morerins, Mordehus, ii. 115, 153 165, 179 184 188 192

INDEX OF NAMES. 617

Morley, Dr. iii. 441, 444, 484
Morton, Earl of, 7, 64, 70, 74, 77, 219, 263, 340, 386, 390, 397, 424, 452, ii 35, 46, 67, 77, 80
Morton, Andrew, minister of Carmunnock, iii. 195
Morton, Arthur, minister, ii 49.
Morton, William, minister, iii 561
Morus, Alexander, of Geneva, iii. 6, 101, 311
Moulin, in Sedan, ii 180, 197, 239
Mouline, Muline, physician, ii 428†.
Mowat, Matthew, minister of Kilmarnock, ii 69; iii 58, 142, 144, 487.
Mowat, Roger, advocate, 381.
Moysley, Dr. 200, 204, 271.
Moysely, Edward, judge, iii. 206, 209, 217, 220
Moysely, Lieutenant, ii 137
Mubbot, iii 350
Mucklejohn, ii 125.
Munroe, Duncan, iii. 134
Munro v. Monro
Mure of Glanderston, iii 112, 244.
Mure of Rowallan, Sir William, 178, 425, ii 42.
Mure of Rowallan, Sir William, younger, 14, 178, ii 101, 121, 329, iii 535, 543
Mure, Thomas, minister of Cumbra, 170.
Murecraft, William, iii 214, 379, 445 App.
Murray, Earl of, 51, 123, 205, iii 366
Murray of Polmais, 51
Murray, Andrew, minister of Abdie, v Balvaird, Lord.
Murray, Annas, ii. 507
Murray, Frederick, ii 508
Murray, George, ii. 508
Murray, James, Wariston's clerk, ii 54
Murray, John, minister of Methven, ii 507, 508, 511, 512, iii 446, 547
Murray, John, minister of Strathmiglo, 472
Murray, Lieutenant-Colonel 422†
Murray, Mary, ii 508, 512
Murray, Margaret, (Mrs. Geo Gillespie) ii 502-511
Murray Mungo, ii 35
Murray, Robert, Commissary of Stirling 426
Murray, Robert, minister of Methven, 129, 383, 472, ii 51, 84, 447, 502-512.
Murray, William, of the bed-chamber 393, 396, ii 5 35 48 58 66 124 125 278,
394, 401 407-409, 477, 509-512; iii 94, 99.
Murray, Mrs William, ii 265, 275
Murray, Bishop of, v Guthrie, 42
Musicians, Scottish, iii 536.

N

NAIRNE, Nerne, minister of Carmichael, 169
Napier, Neper, Lord, 50 145, 266, 379, 381-383, 440, 448 452 458, 462
Napier, Master of, 379.
Napier of Kilmahew, iii. 420, 456.
Napier, Mr ii. 493
Nasmith, James, minister of Hamilton, iii 56, 143, 296, 317, 352, 447, 467, 487.
Naylor, James, iii 429.
Neill, Dr Archbishop of York, 47, 270, 349
Nevay, Neve, Nevoy, Knave, John, minister of Loudon or Newmills, ii 10, 69, 94, iii 53, 112, 123, 145, 147, 543
Nevill, Philip, iii 533
Newark, Lord, v Leslie
Newburgh Lord, 341
Newcastle, Earl of, 352, ii. 43, 58, 66 100, 104, 112, 108, 155, 163, 167, 170, 176—Marquis, 201, 203, iii 567.
Newcomen, Matthew ii 110 415
Newport, Lord, 72, 351
Newton c. Leslie
Nicolas, Secretary, ii. 66, 113 124; iii 442
Nicoll, John, writer, 128
Nicolson, Robert, commissary of Edinburgh, 426
Nicolson, Sir Thomas, 65, 381
Nicolson, Thomas, Clerk to the General Assembly, 128, 129
Nicolson, Thomas, advocate, 381.
Nisbet, Neisbet, Alexander, minister of Irvine, iii. 134, 135, 236, 281, 317, 420
Nisbet, John, advocate, 382.
Nithsdale, Earl of, 70, 193, 260, ii 74, 116, 124, 138, 164
Niven of Dort, iii. 91.
Niving of Monkridding, 473
Norfolk, Duke of, ii 125
North, Lord iii 539
Norton, Thomas, iii. 526.

VOL. I I

Northumberland Earl of 327 341; ii. 83 99, 107 114 133, 141, 487, iii 19
Norwall, J minister of Baltron. 472
Novations. ii 46 51. 69-71. 76. 94 427, iii 529.
Nye. Philip. ii 81 89. 97 99, 110, 120, 121, 131, 137, 145, 149, 199, 201, 218 236, iii 407, 552

O

Oath, Coronation, 477, iii 128
Oath imposed on Scots in England and Ireland, 279. 337-339.
Oath, Montrose, &c 1644. ii 141, 150
Oath proposed in 1648, iii 34. 37 40
Oath Renouncing Charles II iii 350
Oath of Allegiance and Supremacy. iii 461, 463
Ochiltrie, Lord iii. 40
Ogilvie, Ogilbie of Airly e Airly.
Ogilvie, Lord, ii 60, 67, 124, 141, 164, 314 iii 95 117 317
Ogilvie of Banff, 204, 206 321
Ogilvie of Boyne. ii 60
Ogilvie of Inchmartin, Sir Patrick, ii 225
Ogle Captain, ii. 137.
Orston, William, minister of Collington 76.
Okey Colonel, iii 427
Oliphant of Gask, ii 225.
Oliphant, William, minister of Dunfermline. iii 547
O'Neil, Earl of Tyrone 336
O Neil Colonel, 257.
Orange, William Prince of, 190, 288 294 298 312, 349-353, ii 57, 82 143 150, 199 200, 225 228 293, 308, 322, 338, 437, 472, 501, iii 73-79, 83-90, 256, 387, 439, 451 461 App 507 509 520, 522, 523.
Orange, Mary, Princess of 298, 316, 351, iii. 74 86, 439, 445 509
Orange, Princess Dowager of, iii 86, 90. 507, 509
Orbiston, Lord, v. Hamilton
Ordinance against Blasphemies, ii 396 398, 402 411
Ordinance for the Covenant, ii 409, 411
Ordinance for Planting, iii 282 300, 305, 316
Ordination, ii 139, 148, 159, 168, 196, 213 221, 223 377, iii 284

Orknay. Bishop of, v. Graham. Sydserff.
Orleans, Duke of ii 293 328, 363
Ormond, Lady. iii 445
Ormond, Marquis of, ii. 103 233, 301 374 388, 401, 405 411, iii 100 103. 439 442
Osburne, John. 472
Osburne, Lieutenant, iii 323, 447
Oswald, Osall, minister of Pencaitland 371.—of Aberdeen, ii. 96, iii 184
Owen, Dr John, iii 343. 354 596 407 443 553.
Oxenbridge, Independent minister, iii 178.
Oxford University of, ii 386, 393
Oxford, Parliament at. ii 80, 137. 138 140 244
Overton, Major-General iii 290 427, 441, 445
Overtures of Union, iii 182-185, 254

P

Paget John 12 357, ii 184
Paget, Lord 290, 345
Paine Mr 483
Palatine, Prince Elector, 10, 11 65 89 224, 312, 313 316, 357, 385, 387; ii 62 221, 473
Palmer, Herbert, ii. 111, 118. 140 145. 148, 184, 220 236 313, 404, 415.
Palmer, M P. 334-387
Panmure Earl of. 370, ii. 509
Panter Dr Patrick. Professor, St Andrews, 93, 97, 148, 169 361 425
Park John. minister of Stranraer, iii 140
Parker, Mr. 529, ii. 165
Parlan James. ii. 404
Parliament Long. 261, 272-353, ii 150 190, 360, 378, iii 9, 14, 46, 51 63 244. 427, 437, 440. 446
Parliament. (1653). iii. 289, (1660) iii. 405, 469, 473
Parliament Irish, iii. 470
Parliament. Scottish 95, 103, 202, 223 376-393, ii 352 420-425, iii 5, 35-40, 46 77, 97-99, 107, 115, 121 126, 128, (1661) 454 463-469.
Paræus David ii 464
Parrie, Mr 336.
Pastor, his office, ii 110, 120, 129
Paterson, John, minister of Foveran, 492. —Bishop of Ross, iii. 486

INDEX OF NAMES.

Paterson. Thomas, 123, 472, iii 448
Patronage, 113, 237-241; ii 47, 48, 94 450-460, iii. 414
Patullo, George, minister, iii 563
Peace (1639), Conferences, 216-219
Peace (1640). 259 263, 268, &c
Peace, (1644 &c.), ii 142, 149 151, 154 167, 172, 176 178 187 217, 222, 238 241, 244, 246, 251, 292, 297, 300, 328, 337, 344 348 350, 377 386-395, 401 406-411, 416.
Pearce, Pierce, iii 400, 406, 444
Pearson of Southhall, Alexander advocate. 129, 381,—Judge, iii 249
Peebles, Hugh, minister, iii. 123
Pembroke Earl of, 11, 204, 296, 313 352; ii 155 238, 436
Penn, Admiral William, iii 291
Pennimor, laird of, iii. 435.
Pennington. Admiral 288
Pennyman, Sir William, 321.
Percy, Harie, ii 125, 277, iii.88 464 App
Perne, minister, ii 415.
Perth, Earl of, 123, 452, 458, 462, ii 448
Perth Articles of, 119, 158 176-183.
Pest, ii 275, 314 323, 343 417, iii. 5, 6, 9, 18, 41, 52, 62
Petavius, Jesuit 358.
Peters, Hugh, ii 165 338, 345, iii 407, 443
Petition of 800 Ministers, 286, 292, 299
Petition for Episcopacy 293, 296
Petrie, Alexander minister of Rhind 147, 253, ii. 53, iii. 69, 71, 72, 80
Philorth v. Fraser
Philips, Henry, ii 110
Pickering, Pikering ii 66, 286
Pierce Bishop of Bath, 286, iii. 400, 406
Pierrepoint, ii 487 488; iii 16, 441.
Pitcairne, Andrew, ii 473.
Pitcairne of Forther, ii 473
Pitcairn, Patrick, ii 418.
Pluralities, 373 374.
Pluscardie v Mackenzie
Poinz, Pointz, Colonel iii 316, 317 375
Pollock, Nether,—v Maxwell
Pollock, bailie James, iii 348
Pont, Robert, minister of St Cuthbert's, iii 527 528
Poole, Matthew, minister, iii 553
Poomeese, Poolmais, v Murray

Porter, Charles, 259
Porter, James, iii. 246, 362, 448
Porterfield of Duchal 63, iii 366
Porterfield, Captain George, ii 207
Porterfield Provost George, 107 244, ii 5; iii. 123 272 545
Portland, Lord 333
Potter, Dr 286
Power, Powrie, 378
Power, Gilbert, minister, ii 51-53
Power, James, 367
Prayer for the King, iii 252, 253 276, 281, 295, 305, 321.
Praying meetings, 249-255, 356, 358-363, 369, 371, ii 46
Preachers Itinerant, ii 393.
President of the Session v Spottiswood
Preston, Mr agent to the Duchess of Hamilton, iii 483
Price, William ii 110
Pride Colonel, iii 443
Prideaux Mr, ii 237, iii 538
Prideaux Humphrey 309.
Primrose, Archibald Clerk Register, iii 419
Primrose, James, clerk of the Privy Council, 34, 45, iii 65
Prince, 316, iii 51.
Pringle of Whitebank iii 547
Privy Seal v Roxburgh
Provost of Glasgow, ii 189, iii 150 v Anderson, Bell, Cunningham Graham Porterfield, Stewart, Wallace
Prynne, 273 277, ii. 315, iii 400, 427.
Psalms Metrical Version of iii. 3, 8, 59, 97, 451 App, 525-556
Public Resolutions, iii 107 125 145, 147 169 213 321, 335-339, et passim.
Pulleyn, John, archdeacon, iii 527
Pym, John, 272, 296, 301 317, 319, 324, 331, 335, 338 351, ii 118, 133, 216.

Q

Quakers, iii 323 357 429
Queen of Bohemia, ii 64; iii 41, 86, 461, 463 App, 509
Queen of Sweden, Christina. 398, iii 256, 301, 320 450, 472
Queensberry, Earl of, 123, 194 256, 425, ii 85, 314

INDEX OF NAMES.

R

Raban, Edward, printer, 438
Rae, Lord, v Reay.
Rae, John, 162.
Raes 205, 222.
Rainbow, Rainbone, Dr ii. 148
Rainsborough, Colonel, iii 32
Rait, Rate, William, minister of Brechin, iii. 182, 248, 279.
Raith Reth, Lady, ii 509
Ralston of Ralston, lieut-colonel, iii 125
Ralston, , 328, 329.
Ramsay of Balmain Sir Gilbert, 492
Ramsay, Colonel, 270
Ramsay, Andrew, minister of Edinburgh, 6, 18, 23, 34, 39, 52, 64, 76, 78, 82, 101, 123, 127, 129, 135-139 144, 147, 154-156, 248, 252, 254, 359, 362-365, 386, 425, 463, 472, ii. 45, 85, 260, 389, iii 34, 63, 92, 96, 105
Ramsay, Andrew, provost of Edinburgh, iii 366, 389.
Ramsay, James, minister of Linlithgow, iii 216, 220, 222, 278, 313, 456, 487
Ramsay, Matthew, minister of Old Kilpatrick, iii 456, 561
Ramsay, Robert, minister of Dundonald, 245,—of Glasgow, 248, 368; ii 3-5, 8, 10, 15, 20, 23, 37, 45, 48, 54, 86, 116, 155, 161, 171, 173, 176, 189, 195, 211-213, 231, 270, 295, 321, 333, 392, 415, 427, iii 39, 62, 110, 115, 122, 142-147, 150, 152-156, 165, 168, 207, 216, 238, 312, 448
Ramsay, Thomas, minister of Dumfries, 44, 426.
Ramsay, Thomas, minister of Mordington, iii 447
Rankine, Robert, regent in college of Edinburgh, 64, 91, 110
Ranulagh, Lord, 318, 323, 327, 328
Ratcliffe, Sir George, 273, 281, 282, 318, 325, 337, 341, 342.
Rathband, William, minister, ii. 144
Rattray, John, minister, iii 563
Rattray, Dr. Sylvester, iii 373
Rattray, Thomas,
Read, Colonel, ii 132, 133.
Reading, Redding, Ridding, ii 57, 58, 65, 241.

Reay, Mackay Lord, 70, 465; ii. 138, 141
Register, Lord Clerk, v Gibson Hay Johnston, Primrose.
Registers v Church.
Reid, John, v. Lauderdale. iii. 154.
Reid, William, v. Balcarras, iii. 154
Remonstrance by Assembly of Divines, ii 325-327, 333, 336, 365, 366
Remonstrance of Commission of Assembly (1643) ii. 76, iii 22, 23, 131.
Remonstrance, English, against Episcopacy, 286, 292, 296, 299, 312, 313, 317-319.
Remonstrance (Independent), ii 318, 327 328, 344
Remonstrance, Irish, 273
Remonstrance of Glasgow Synod, iii 108 112-119.
Remonstrance, Seaforth's, ii 354, 362, 363,
Remonstrance, (Western) and Remonstrants iii 108-116, 124, 128-147, 153-171, 176, 214, 238, 244, 250, 299, 408, 446, 447, 567,
Rescissory Act 1661, iii 458, 586
Reynolds, Dr Edward, ii. 155, 236, iii 391, 400, 442, 484
Richardson, Robert, Dumfries, 472.
Richelieu Cardinal, 3, 304, 310, ii. 10, 62
Richmond v Lennox
Rigg of Athernie, William, 253, 361, 381; ii 50 94,
Rippon Treaty of 262, 271, 353
Ritchie, Adam, iii 484
Ritchie John, Assembly Clerk, 129.
Rivet, Dr Andrew, 9, 92, 351, 357, ii 115, 155, 165, 169, 189, 197, 201, 239, 251, 265, 275, 290, 327, 362; iii. 67 72, 462-464 App, 521.
Rivius, , ii. 371
Rizzio, David, 51
Roberton, James, of Bedlay, ii 413, iii 420, 455, 472.
Roberton, Margaret ii 392
Roberts, a soldier, ii. 227
Roberts, Francis, minister, St Dunstans, London, ii. 333 345, 358, 359
Robertson, Mr , 112
Robertson, in Kirkaldy, iii 414.
Robertson, James, iii 547
Robertson, John, minister of Dundee, iii. 248, 279
Robertson, John, minister of Perth, 147, 150, 172, 383.

Robertson Richard, regent, iii 150, 223 239, 240
Robertson, Thomas, in Saltcoats, ii, 435.
Robisone *c* Robertson
Roborough Henry, scribe, ii. 108, iii. 539.
Rodger, Mr., iii 221.—William 561.
Rodger Ralph minister iii 383 384 434
Roe James, merchant 246, 267.
Roe, Sir Thomas, 313
Rolles, Daniel, ii 289, 290 —His father, ii 289
Rollock Andrew, minister of Dunse, 103.
Rollock Henry, minister of Edinburgh, 6 8 16, 23, 52, 64 76–79 108 121 127, 136, 144 146 163 213, 243 255, 355, 359 363 375, 397, 463, ii 30 463.
Ross. Lord, iii. 35, 366.
Ross. Rosa John. iii. 403
Ross, James ii 161.
Ross, Bishop of, *c* Maxwell
Rothes Rothus, Countess of 354
Rothes John Earl of 14, 33 40 44 47, 50, 53 70 79, 86 91, 100, 121-130 135, 141-150 155 168, 211, 216 220 255, 266, 269 279, 285 289 304 353-356, 381, 388, 464, 473, 491; ii. 261 440, 447, 513
Rothes, John Earl, son (afterwards Duke) of iii 367.
Rouse, Francis ii 120 157, 198, 237 280, 293, 312 329-335, 359 379, 388, iii. 197 231, 325, 332 338, 344-347, 354, 532-556
Row, James minister, ii 92, iii 61
Row, John, minister of Aberdeen, ii 329, 502 iii 54 244, 463 543.
Row, John, minister of Carnock, 127, 129, 175.
Row Robert, minister, iii. 547
Row Samuel, minister of Sprouston ii 315
Row, William minister, iii 547
Rowallan *c*. Mure
Rowat James, minister of Kilmarnock iii 487
Roxburgh. Lady, ii 105, 436.
Roxburgh. Earl of, Privy Seal, 25, 37, 40-50 54-61, 64, 69, 74 80 123, 126 386, 390 424, 429, 438, 446, 448, 454, 457-459, 463; ii. 59, 67, 77, 103 436
Rudyerd, Sir Benjamin 307, iii 537

Rule Robert, minister of Stirling, iii 283 315, 356.
Rupert, Prince ii 50, 65 105 —Duke of Cumberland 138 141, 143, 151-158 163, 166 170 172 176 181, 185 191, 193-195 199-206 213, 216, 218 224 226, 240, 241, 244 268 272, 286 308 315, 317, 324, 504, iii 88 100
Russel, William, minister of Kilbirnie 13 104, 473, ii. 10, iii 115, 136, 279 414, 561.
Rutherford, Captain iii 457 App
Rutherford Andrew, minister of Eccles iii 284, 327.
Rutherford, Samuel minister of Anwoth 8, 77, 79, 85 88 134 146, 171—St Andrews 252, 266 364 480, 486, 491 ii 27 45, 49, 55 65, 70 76 85 89, 94 96, 98 104, 106 111, 117 120 123 159, 161, 165, 175, 177, 199, 212, 251 277 290 311 321 380, 385 392, 397 404 406, 444, 446 481, 516, iii. 12 33, 35 82, 94, 96 110, 123 126, 199 214 241, 248 279, 296 303, 306, 316 354 365, 375-381 387, 404, 418 447, 467 541-543 545.
Ruthven, Reuthen, Riven, General Earl of Forth 219, 259; ii. 56, 124 142 151 154-156, 181, 240, 437
Rutland, Earl of, ii 89, 133, 299, 302
Ryley scout-master, ii 132

S

SADAEL, SADELL, ii 115 155, 165, 184 188.
St Andrew's. University of, iii 316 365 456.
St John, Oliver Solicitor-General, 349, ii. 113, 133, iii 471
St Johnston *c* Perth.
Salisbury, Earl of, ii 99 107, 155, iii 539
Salmasius Somais, iii 67, 256
Salmon, Schoolmaster, 337
Saltonstall Robert, iii. 206, 209
Sanders, James, bookseller 24
Sandilands, Mr iii 240.
Sandilands, James, comissary Aberdeen 124 128 426.
Sandilands, Thomas, 124, 128 129
Savill, Mr. 373

INDEX OF NAMES.

Sarum *v.* Salisbury
Saville, Savill, Lord, 304, 305, 327, 335, 348, 349, ii 281 284, 294 303 310-313, 487-496.
Saville, Sir Henry, 227
Savoy, Duke of, iii 292
Schurman, Anna Maria, iii. 104
Scinder, Mr 281
Scobell, Henry clerk of council, iii. 355
Scot, John, minister, iii 547
Scot of Clerkington, Sir William, iii 367.
Scot of Harden, Sir William, 425
Scot of Highchester *v.* Tarras
Scot of Scotstarbet, Sir John, 111, 368, 370, 425; ii. 88, iii. 443.
Scot, James, minister of Tungland, 426, iii. 462
Scot, John, minister of Glenluce, iii 436.
Scot, Thomas, iii 359, 431, 437, 441
Scot, William, minister of Couper, ii 49
Scotseraig *v.* Erskine of.
Scougal, Scougle, Patrick, iii 365
Scrimgeour, Dr Henry, minister of St Fillan's 168, 425
Scrimgeour of Dudhope, Sir John, constable of Dundee, 37 372, *v.* Dudhope.
Scroggie, Dr Alexander, minister of Aberdeen, 248, 373
Seaforth, Earl of, 70, 221, 252, 375, ii. 225, 234, 263, 314, 356, 362, 363, 408, iii 101, 250, 255, 288
Seaman, Lazarus, ii 110, 148, 184, 236, 415, iii 227.
Seatoun, Lord, ii 6
Seaton, Sir John, 72; ii 57, 92, 210, iii. 174
Secretary of State for Scotland, *v.* Acheson Alexander. Lanerick Lauderdale
Sedgwick, Mr. iii 552.
Selden, John, 303, 307, 308, ii 129, 198, 265, 312, 277.
Selkirk, Earl of, iii 430, 443, Duke of Hamilton, 446
Semple, Lord, 65, 238, ii 6.
Semple, Harry, iii 357.
Semple, Hugh, Jesuit, iii 390
Semple, John, provost of Dumbarton, 137, 195, 381, ii 42
Semple, John, minister of Carsphairn, iii 446, 545
Semple, Robert, minister of Lesmahago, iii. 357

Semple, William, regent in the College of Glasgow, ii 37, 87, 290.
Service-Book, 1, 4, 12, 15-23, et passim, 65, 87, 112, 119, 147, 152, 429-432, 436, 438-461, 464, 466, 471, 478; ii 117, 240.
Seuster, Sheuster, Robina, iii. 290
Sey and Seale, Viscount, 199, 270, 275, 293, 301-305, ii 85, 107, 117, 136, 139, 141, 146, 220, 236, 248, 294, 303, 311, 344, 368, 487-489, 492, iii 16, 539
Sharp, James, minister of Crail iii 137, 153, 212, 279, 281, 315-317, 324, 327, 330-357, 361-366, 386, 395, 396, 398 401, 404-411, 414-421, 431, 440, 444, 448 453, 454, 457, 458, 460, 461, 465, 468, 471-474 477, 481-487, 563, 568.
Sharp, James, minister of Govan, 104, 106, 171,—of Paisley, 172, ii 4, 8, 85, 444.
Sharpe, Dr John, principal of the College of Edinburgh, 64
Sharpe, Patrick, minister of East Kilbryde, 237, 238, iii 136
Sharp, William, iii 416, 580
Sheldon, Bishop of London, iii 444, 484
Shepherd, Mr. minister, 168
Sibbald, Dr, Aberdeen 135, 248 365.
Silverton-hill, Sillerton, *v.* Hamilton of
Simmons, Matthew, printer, iii. 553
Simonds, Mr., 311
Simons, Lieutenant-Colonel, iii 361.
Simpson, James, minister, ii 19
Simpson, James, minister of Bathgate 252.
Simpson, James, minister of Airth, iii 177, 257, 352, 353, 447 568
Simpson, Matthias, minister of Stirling, iii 315, 352, 456
Simpson Patrick, minister of Stirling, 161, iii 19.
Simpson, Sydrach, ii 145, Simonds, 311.
Sincerfe *v.* Sydserfe.
Sinclair, Lady, ii 4
Sinclair, Sinklar, Lord, 123, 210, 374, ii 45, 85, 100, 322, 509, iii 36, 101, 448
Sinclair of Roslin, Sir William 425
Sinclair, George, regent in the College of Glasgow iii 285, 313
Sindercomb, iii 358
Skelmorlie *v.* Montgomery of
Skippon, General, ii 126, 227, 235, iii. 16

INDEX OF NAMES

Skular, Edward, convict, 383
Slingsby, 342.
Smeaton Thomas, principal of the College of Glasgow, iii 402.
Smart, Peter, prebend of Durham, 294
Smith, Hew, iii 240
Smith, James, ii 515
Smith of Grothill, Sir John 37, 44, 46, 84, 397 472, ii 89, 217, 345, 385.
Smith, John, minister of Burntisland and Edinburgh 269, 295 339, ii 487 500, 516, iii 21, 52, 53, 55, 57, 60, 94, 136, 137 153 171, 179, 189, 214, 218-220, 231 296, 307, 353, 414, 420, 544-546, 563
Smith, Dr Peter, ii 110
Smith, Robert, iii 382
Smythe, George, judge, iii 206, 209, 210, 318
Soemans, Socinianism, ii. 191
Soliciton-General, 349, ii 117, 133 141, 145, 220 235 236, 280, 368, 487, iii 16, e St. John
Somerdyke, 294, r Embassy, Dutch
Somerville, Alexander minister, Dolphinton, 121, 363.
Somerville, William, iii 246.
Sorrie, iii 439.
Southampton, Earl of, ii 244, 246, 247, 249, 260, 488
Southesk, Earl of 50, 81, 91 100, 123, 129, 394, 425, 452, 458, 462, ii. 46, 68, iii 6, 54.
Southook, Laird of, 473
Spalato, bishop of 248
Spang, William, minister at Campvere, 2, 10, 15, 39, 62, 69 71, 73 88, 96, 109, 112, 118, 184-225, 243, 247 355, 358, 338, ii 2 10, 36, 42 61-65, 72, 75, 81, 87, 101, 107, 127, 128, 143 163, 165, 169, 171, 174, 180, 183, 186, 190, 193, 197 200, 202, 216, 225, 232, 239, 245, 250 258, 275, 287, 290, 310, 313, 321 323, 327, 342 351, 363, 364, 370, 374 380, 386, 398, 415, iii 1, 5 9, 23, 31, 43, 50, 60 —Anderson, 67—84, 93, 110, 237 256, 311, 352 403, 404, 423 449, 462 483, 464 App e Contents—Parents, 10, ii. 65, 100, iii. 32.
Spang's nephews, John and William, iii 382
Spang, Mrs. iii 16

Spanheim, Frederick, ii. 115, 180, 197, 265, 288, 311, 324, 327, 342, 365, 378, iii 67, 104, 461 App 521
Spittal, Thomas, person of Falkirk, 426
Spottiswood, John, Archbishop of St. Andrews, Chancellor of Scotland, 4-9, 10, 17 19, 33, 41, 45, 47, 50, 53, 66, 70 73 75, 78 87, 90, 93, 94, 97, 105, 129, 148, 152, 154, 208, 424 428 429, 437, 438, 440, 442-444 447, 448, 452, 459-466, iii. 403, 529
Spottiswood, Sir Robert, president of the Court of Session, 47, 48, 50 70, 75, 76, 88, 93, 221, 276, 279, 385, 425, 429, ii 125, 322, iii 403.
Spottiswood of Darsie, Sir John, 425
Spottiswood, John, superintendent, iii 403.
Spreule John, town-clerk of Glasgow, iii 162 163, 213, 241, 244, 249, 287, 362, 363, 448
Spreule, Robert, minister of Dalrymple, iii 561
Stamford, Stainford, Lord, 348, 349, ii. 57.
Stapleton 358
Stapleton, Sir Philip, iii 16, 19.
States-General, iii 86, 90.
Star-Chamber, 280, 282
Start, the, iii 109, 116
Sterline v. Stirling
Sterne, Dr ii 148
Sternhold, Thomas iii 325
Sterry, Peter, ii 110; iii 125, 443
Stewart of Blackhall, Sir Archbald 14 145, 381-393, 448
Stewart of Castlemilk, iii. 437
Stewart of Chrystwall, James, 104
Stewart of Goodtrees, Sir James, iii 389.
Stewart of Grandtully, ii 225
Stewart of Minto Sir Walter 425
Stewart, Andrew, ii 50
Stewart, Bailie, ii 515
Stewart, Barnard, ii 316
Stewart, Captain Walter, 194, 381 ii 203 209, 210.
Stewart, Dr ii 175, 202, 216 288, 311 327, 387, iii 7, 79, 82
Stewart, Henry, 337-340
Stewart, James, provost of Glasgow, ii 4
Stewart, Sir James, provost of Edinburgh iii 389, 400, 447, 544
Stewart, John, ii 163

INDEX OF NAMES.

Stewart John, commissary of Dunkeld, 381-383, 391.
Stewart, John, provost of Ayr. 173
Stewart, John, minister, iii. 561
Stewart, Sir Lewis, 11, 65, 125, 126, 263 380, 382.
Stewart, Patrick minister in Bute, 170, 426.
Stewart, Richard, dean of Westminster, ii. 437.
Stewart, Sir Robert, iii 100.
Stewart, Walter, 377, 383, 388.
Stewart Walter, minister of Kilpatrick. 426.
Stewart, William, 234,—provost of Glasgow ii 12.
Stirling Provost of, iii. 456
Stirling William Earl of, 7, 33, 45, 48, 74, 76, 425, 429-431 436, 439, 443-447, 453, 454, 474, iii 530-532 —His family, 76 77
Stirling of Ardoch, ii 91
Stirling of Carden iii 441, 456
Stirling of Keir, Sir George, 44, 63, 123, 136, 144 147, 266, 379, 381-384, ii 475; iii 394, 456
Stirling John, minister of Edinburgh, iii 243, 280 355, 446 467.
Stirling, John minister of Kilbarchan, 561
Stobs, Laird of, iii. 174
Stormont, Viscount. 425 ii 91, 468.
Strachan Colonel Archibald, iii 107, 111-113, 115 118-124, 129 132.
Strachan William minister of Old Aberdeen, iii. 182
Strafford, Earl of, 189 190, 192, 198, 247, 272-275, 279-286 291, 295-305, 309, 311 —his Trial. 313-353 355; ii 40
Strang Dr John principal of the College of Glasgow, 28, 63, 66 105, 133-137, 170, 246, 268, 365 374, 425, 476, 480-483, 490; ii 14, 37 62, 71 72 86, 189, 270, 289, 322, 364, 377 399, 404, 405, 412, 469, iii 5, 32, 70 93, 105, 150, 237, 242, 295, 311 324, 382, 385, 402 412, 416 423, 432, 436, 454, 457
Strang, William, regent in the College of Glasgow, iii 150.
Strichan v. Fraser.
Strickland, Walter, envoy, ii 169 202, 218, 322 327
Stroud, Strode, 309, 330, 339.
Stronge, Mr iii. 554

Struthers, William, minister of Edinburgh, 402
Struthers, Mrs William, 96.
Stuart v. Stewart
Suffolk, Earl of, iii. 539.
Summervaill v. Somerville.
Sundercomb v Sindercomb
Supplication against Service-Book, 13, 19, 21, 33, 54, 85, 174, 204, 215
Sutie George iii 382.
Sutherland, Earl of 21, 82, 224, 492, ii 234
Swaine, Swan, Sweden v Queen of 190
Swinton of Swinton, Sir John, iii 114, 125, 249, 288, 314 316, 361, 385, 430, 447.
Swinton, Lady, iii. 396, 433
Swinton, A 472
Swintons, iii 174
Sydserfe, Sincerf Archibald, ii 36. 389
Sydserfe, George, minister of Cockburnspath 150, 164, 426
Sydserfe, Thomas Bishop of Galloway, 7, 9, 11 16, 37, 38, 51, 70, 72-75, 78, 87, 135 150 153, 276, 425, 448, 452, 464, iii 390, 406 —Bishop of Orkney, 486
Sydserfe, Thomas, iii 468 —Diurnaller 454

T

Tables, The 38, 39, 102
Tanner, Jesuit, ii 290
Tarbet v Mackenzie.
Tarras Earl of. 438
Tate, Mr ii. 237 333, 359, 388, 398, iii 199, 326.
Taillour, James, minister; iii. 561
Taylor, Dr Jeremy, iii, 400 406, 452 App.
Taylor, William, minister, London iii 230
Temple Lady, ii. 303 489
Temple, Dr Thomas, ii. 110 236.
Tennent, John, parson of Calder 425
Terens, Tirens, Mr. ii. 178, 357, 387
Teviotdale, Sheriff of v Douglas
Thesaurer, Treasurer, ii 263 v Lindsay Traquair
Thesaurer Depute, ii 68, v Carmichael, Sir James, Sir Daniel.
Thomasius ii 275
Thomson, — Edinburgh iii. 91.
Thomson, Alexander, minister, Edinburgh, 78, 137, 150

INDEX OF NAMES.

Thomson, Sir Thomas, 44
Thomson, William, Town-Clerk of Edinburgh, iii. 174, 366, 389, 398, 399, 419
Thorndyke, Herbert, iii 400, 444
Thurloe, John, secretary, iii 342, 347, 350, 359, 362, 386, 397, 399, 431, 475, 579
Titus, Captain Silas, iii 101, 428, 431.
Tofts, Belsches Lord ii. 79, iii 367
Toleration, ii 226, 230, 234-237, 241-250, 258, 261; iii 340, 392, 393, 430
Tombes, John, minister, ii. 342; iii. 227, 237, 285
Torphichen John Lord, iii 35, 54
Torstenson, General, ii. 81
Towie v Barclay.
Traill, Mr ii 493
Traill, Robert, minister of Edinburgh, iii 56, 248 258, 276, 279, 280 296, 355, 446, 546, 568.
Tran, James, 234, ii 12, iii 368 437
Traquair, John, Earl of, 4, 6-8, 11, 14, 16-18, 22, 25, 37-51, 54-61, 64-66, 69-72, 74, 75, 79, 81, 84, 97, 120, 123-132, 194, 195, 220 — Commissioner, 224, 247, 261, 263, 277, 279 280, 283 284 290, 317, 340 341, 357, 359, 374, 278, 384, 425, 434, 435, 440, 445-448 452, 456-464, 487, ii. 59, 60, 64, 78 80, 103, 124, 125, 141, 515, iii 7, 32, 35, 413
Treaty v. Breda Hague Uxbridge
Trennant, ii 178
Treves, Trier, Elector of 3
Trewman, 206, 338
Trochrig v. Boyd
Trotter, John, iii 102.
Trump, Martin, admiral, ii 473
Tuckney, Dr. Anthony, ii 198, iii 310
Tulhbardine Earl of, 123, 205, ii 225, 420-422.
Turner, Archibald, iii 414
Turner, Sir James, iii 457, app
Tweeddale, Earl of, iii 354, 430
Twislington, Colonel, iii 259
Twisse, Dr. William, prolocutor of the Westminster Assembly, 303, ii 89 101 107-109, 121, 184-186, 313.
Tyler, Evan, printer, 441, ii. 475 iii 214, 510, 549
Tyrconnell, Earl of, 336

U

UNIFORMI
VC

Uniformity, Act of, iii 485, 486
Union of Protesters and Resolutioners, ii 177, 179-186, 251, 276-280, 296, 297 430
Union of Protestants v Dury John. 9
Universities, (Scotish), 299; ii 46, iii 64, 199, 205 327 402 449, e Aberdeen Edinburgh Glasgow. St. Andrews
Universities Dutch, 9, iii 449, e Foreign Ecclesiastical matters
Universities, English e Cambridge, Oxford
Urquhart of Cromartie, Sir Thomas, 425
Usher, James, Archbishop of Armagh, 287 309, 329, 332, 338, 339, 341
Uxbridge, Treaty of, ii. 249, 261, iii 348

V

VANE, Vaine, Sir Harrie, 72, 204, 263, 286, 302, 317 341 342, 345, ii 89, 104, 117, 133, 135, 136 141 145, 146, 299, 230 231, 235, 237-240, 280 302, 487, 490, iii. 16, 19 178 426, 430 431, 437, 438, 440, 441, 471
Vane, Sir Harrie, senior, ii 121, 299, 302
— Thesaurer, 341, 345, iii 358
Valkemer, Dr iii 82.
Valle, (Walæus?) 9
Vallet (Valois?) Duc de, 316
Vedelius, Nicolas ii 371
Veitch Vetch, James, iii 50, 239, 241, 254, 259-264, 313, — minister of Mauchlin, 487
Vertch, David minister of Govan, iii 434
Vertch, John, minister of Roberton, iii 724 561
Vermeuden, General, ii 276
Verney (Vername), Sir Edmund, 215
Vien Vienna, 117
Villiers, Lady Mary, 11.
Vincent, Nathaniel, iii. 553
Vincent, Thomas, iii. 553
Vines, Richard, ii 110, 145, 148, 184, 198, 236, 415, iii 304, 306, 307, 326
Violet, Thomas, ii 132, 133
Voetius, Gisbertus, 9 92, 357, ii. 72, 115, 165 169, 175 189, 202, 205, 218, 239 240 265, 327, 378, iii 21, 70 82 101 103 267, 275, 281, 310, 311, 324, 369, 449
Vossius Gerard, ii 311, 327, 365, 371

INDEX OF NAMES.

W

WALIS, Charles, Prince of, v. Charles II.
Walden, Mr, ii 77, 100
Walker, George, ii. 110, 111
Walkinshaw of that ilk, iii 246
Walkinshaw, John, 363, 420, 435, 581
Wallace of Achans, younger, James, iii 140
Wallace of Craigie, 37
Wallace, Guhelmus, schoolmaster, iii. 403
Wallace, Michael, minister, Kilmarnock, 14, 15, 63, 94, 104, 178, 426, 473.
Wallace, Robert, ii 502.
Wallace, Robert, minister of Barnweill, ii. 62, iii 134, 236, 279, 393, 420, 456, Bishop, 486, 561
Wallace, Sir William, ii 314
Waller, Sir William, ii 56, 81-83, 99, 104, 107, 112-115, 118, 126, 131, 133, 140, 142, 151-156, 163, 166, 170-172, 178-182, 185-187, 190, 193, 200, 206, 213, 217, 223-231, 237, 484, iii 17.
Wallop, Robert, ii 488, iii. 471
Walton, Waltham, Dr Brian, iii 304, 309, 310, 401, 449
Wandesford, Christopher, depute of Ireland, 281, 282
Ward, John, minister, ii. 415
Ward, Samuel, lecturer, 288, 309
Wardlaw Whartlaw, ii 114.
Wardhouse, Lady, 161
Warristone v Johnstone, Sir Archibald
Warristone, Lady, iii. 64
Warwick, Earl of, admiral. 274; ii 43, 104, 133, 135, 140, 159, 163, 183, 185, 193, 238, 488, iii 46, 527.
Watson, Robert, senior, minister, iii 561
Watson, Robert, minister of Cardross, iii 436, 466, 561.
Watson, William, iii 435
Waugh, John, minister of Borrowstouness, iii 228, 248, 253
Waughton v Hepburn
Wedderburne v Home
Wedderburne, Sir Alexander, iii. 36.
Wedderburne, Alexander, minister of St. Fillans, iii 563.
Wedderburne, Alexander, toune-clerk, Dundee, 63, 129, 269, 397
Wedderburne, James, Bishop of Dumblane, 16, 22, 78, 87, 93, 167, 248, 421, 425, 430, 437, 452.

Weems, v. Wemyss.
Wen, John, minister of Dalserf, iii 434
Wemyss, John Earl of, 123, 147, 157, 359-376, 380, 425; ii 45, 47
Wemyss, Lady, iii 438.
Wemyss, fiar of Bogie, J 472
Wemyss, canon-maker, 72.
Wemyss, James, commissary of St Andrews, 426
Wemyss, Matthew, minister of Canongate, 64, 404
Wemyss, Sir Patrick, iii 103.
Wenman. ii 303
Wentford v Wandesford.
Wentworth, Sir George, 341, 344
Westfield, Thomas, a divine, 309.
Wetham, Colonel, iii 439, 580, 582
Whaley, Peter, iii 533.
Whalley, Colonel, ii. 427, 438.
Wharton, Lord, 290, 344, ii 117, 130, 133, 145, 236, 298, 299, 302, 344, 475, 488, iii 539
Whartlaw v. Wardlaw.
Whitaker, Jeremy, ii 415; iii. 235, 302, 326
Whitaker, Dr William, 358
White, John, assessor in Westminster Assembly, ii. 89, 108
White, John, M P ii 294, iii 445, 533
Whitebank, Quhytbank, v. Pringle.
Whiteford, Dr. Walter, Bishop of Brechin, 7, 41, 65, 70, 72, 74, 78, 93, 97, 105, 135, 151, 154, 288, 425, 437, 447, 448, 454, 458, 460
Whitelock, Bulstrode, 337-342; ii. 303, iii. 440
Whittingham, William, iii 526, 527
Wigton, Earl of, 38, 44, 50, 107, 123, 145, 168, 385, 424, 448, 452, 458, 462, ii 408, 469, iii 212, 220, 456
Wilkie, James, 484, 491.
Wilkie, John, iii. 204, 224, 226, 231, 407
Wilkie, Robert, minister of Glasgow, 13, 19, 27, 37, 63, 104, 105, 133, 170, 426, 484, 491, ii. 5, iii. 368
Wilkie, Thomas, minister, 146
Wilkie, William, minister of Govan 1, 28, 31, 62, 65, 88, 106, 134, 479-491, ii 87, 189, 339, 348, 377, 399, 404, 412, iii. 92, 308
Wilks, Colonel, iii 438
Willems Mynheere, 101, 507.
Williams, John, Bishop of Lincoln, 273, 293; ii 112; iii. 530.

INDEX OF NAMES.

Wilhams, Roger, ii 191, 212, 397.
Willoughby of Parham, Lord, 385, ii 153, iii. 101, 539
Wilmot, General Major, 257, 327, iii 88
Wilson, Adam, iii 163.
Wilson, Matthew, iii 163
Wilson, Mr. iii. 537
Winch, Mr iii. 295
Winchester, Marquis of, 315
Windrebanks, secretary, 247, 275, 278, 282, 286, 291
Winram of Libberton, George, 115, 187 n. 98 418, 431, iii 37, 88, 99-103, 513-524, 541-544
Winram, Robert, depute-clerk of the Assembly, 129
Winter, Sir Thomas, Queen's secretary, 295
Winton, Earl of, 81, 213, 424, 448 452, 458, 462.
Wintoun, (William') G ii 46
Wisheart, Dr. George, minister of St. Andrews, 151, 168, 425, iii. 31, 486
Wisheart, Dr William, minister of Leith, 76, 97, 425
Wiseman, Thomas, 343
Wither, Mr. ii. 371.
Withington, Sir Thomas, iii 359
Wodrow, William, iii 162, 163.
Wood, iii. 414
Wood, James, minister of St. Andrews ii 406, iii. 88, 93-96, 99, 106, 110, 123, 127, 133, 140, 167, 173, 176-183, 186-189, 199 210-214, 241, 246, 262, 277, 279-281, 285, 295-297, 316, 321 326, 335, 344, 352, 354, 362, 376, 387, 414, 418-420 449, 468, 513-521
Wood, Patrick, 79.
Worcester, Earl of, 304, 310.
Wotham v Wetham.
Wren, Matthew, Bishop of Ely, 349, 351; iii. 400 405, 444.
Wright, Edward, minister of Clackmannan, 147, 367,—of Glasgow, 368, ii 3-5, 86, 270, 377, 399, iii. 456
Wale, Mr. ii 136.
Wright James, minister, ii. 52.
Wright, Robert, minister, iii 257

Wyllie, John, iii. 162, 164.
Wylie, Thomas, minister of Borg, ii. 491, —of Mauchlin, iii 53

Y

Yair, Zaire, William, 232
Yester, Lady, ii. 6
Yester, Lord, 123, 211, 384, 472, ii 440, 443
Yester, Master of, ii 45
York, Bishop of, v. Neill.
York, Dutchess of, iii 445
York, Duke of, 294, 315, 351, ii 138, 297, 416, iii. 439, 442, 445
Young, an English officer, iii 438
Young, Eliza, Mrs. George, ii. 190
Young, Gavin, a minister, iii 547
Young, George, minister of Glasgow, 52, 373, 394, ii 39 46 53, 55, 61, 95 160, 171, 173, 179, 189, 196, 212, 231, 270, 295, 318, 335, 392, 402, 406, 410, 412 415, 513, iii 142, 150, 162, 182, 184, 194, 197, 208 212-219, 238-241, 275-278, 317, 347, 350, 372, 383, 394, 433
Young, Dr. James, Dean of Winchester, 443
Young, James, printer, iii. 533
Young John, professor of divinity, Glasgow, ii 190, 290, iii. 150 211, 228-243, 259, 285, 312, 351, 357, 372, 416, 419 432, 456, 458 460, 471, 474.
Young, Patrick, regent, iii. 239, 241.
Young, Robert, printer, 436, 439, 442, ii 475
Young, Robert, minister of Rutherglen iii 142, 194, 296, 314.
Young, Dr. Thomas, 366, ii. 110, 118 140, 148, 336, iii 302, 306

Z

Zaire v. Yair
Zealand, Synod of, ii. 202.
Zester v Yester
Zurich, &c Ministers of. ii. 431-433

ERRATA IN THE INDEX

Adam of Kinhilt read 147, m. 111.
Anderson v Spang in 67-84
Bailhe, Mrs, 353, m 237, 368.
Baillie, Robert, &c. add 578-584
Bell, John, provest, &c add 579, 580
Belsches of Tofts, for 367 read in 367
Blackhall, Andrew, 85.
Blan, Alexander, in 579, 580
Blair, Hugh minister, iii 368
Boyd of Trochrig, add 577
Broghill, Lord, add 573, 574
Bute, Sheriff of, 170
Campbell of Lawers v Lawers.
Carmichael, Sir James, add n 68
Carstaires, John, read iii 120, &c., 580, 584
Charles II, for 54, read 52.
Cromwell, Oliver, &c. add 573, 576, 579-582
Desborow, Lord-Keeper, add 580-582
Dickson, Dick, David, add 572, 577, 578
Douglas, Robert, &c. add 572-574, 578.

Dunham, James, add 582-584
Fletcher, David, for 494 read 491
Gillespy, Patrick, add 574-582
Guthrie, John, Bishop, &c. insert 425.
Kinhilt v Adair.
Lamb, Bishop of Galloway, 367
Lincoln, Earl of, m. 539.
Lindsay of Belstane v Constable
Lockhart, John, m. 579, 582.
Mackay, Alaster, for 382 read n. 382
Mayne, Magnus, read n 8, 14, 72, iii 403
Murray, Bishop of, for 42 read 425.
Ramsay, Andrew, provost, &c add 570
Sharp, James, minister of Crail, add 573, 574, 578-584.
Sharp, Patrick, iii 577
Sharp, William, add 579, 580
Simpson, Mathias, add 574
Strang, Dr. John, add 577
Swinton of Swinton, Sir John, add 580-582.

ERRATA IN THE LETTERS.

Vol. I

		For	Read
35	10	feared and	feared, and
43	18	20th	19th
45	29	22d	21st
84	8	Reafons	Reafons (E)
87	19	nouct	nocht
91	17	thotts	thott
92	33	flouct	flocht
93	26	bygons	bygane
94	20	England	England (S)
108	3	(K)	(R)
128	3	defeafe	difeafe
130	16	that, his witt	that his witt,
140	4,5	delivered	brought
143	34	incraving	in craving
171	22	then	thir
171	28	Tuefday	24 Tuefday
250	8	finother	[finother]
250	32	meetings	meetings (B),
253	12	Act	Act (A),
259	30	out of	non (in MS)
280	4	would	would not
281	17	ordered	willed
285	9	would goe	was likely to goe
293	26	connection	correction

311	17	Simonds	Simpfon
345	13	dangling	jangling?
432	4	little	little more

Vol. II

		For	Read
79	29	Hotham's	Hothams
241 note		Ayrshire	Argyleshire
296	15	Thomas	John
344 note		Godwin	Goodwin

Vol. III

105	24	friends, thir	friends there
109	3	comeing	cuming
131		Thurfday	Tuefday
136 note		Robertfone of Bedlaw	Roberton of Bedlay
179	15	founder	founded
241 note		Scottifh	Scottifh church
286&287		Hodges	Hodger, Hodzeard
297	31	Guthrie hae	Guthrie had
335	14,	Univerfities, and obtaine that	Univerfities, and] obtaine; that
469	25	debtyit	debt yit
527		8th May 1608	8th May 1606
536		by cup	my cup

Lightning Source UK Ltd.
Milton Keynes UK
UKHW050954260521
384312UK00013B/64